1991

The Governmental Process

POLITICAL INTERESTS AND
PUBLIC OPINION

THE

Governmental

Process

POLITICAL INTERESTS AND
PUBLIC OPINION

David B. Truman

**PROFESSOR OF GOVERNMENT
COLUMBIA UNIVERSITY**

GREENWOOD PRESS, PUBLISHERS
WESTPORT, CONNECTICUT

Library of Congress Cataloging-in-Publication Data

Truman, David Bicknell, 1913-
  The governmental process.

  Reprint. Originally published: New York : Knopf, 1951.
  Bibliography: p.
  Includes index.
    1. Lobbying—United States. 2. Public opinion—United
States.   I. Title.
JK1118.T7 1981   322.4′3   81-13162
ISBN 0-313-22912-0 (lib. bdg..)   AACR2

Published 1951.

Reprinted with the permission of Alfred A. Knopf, Inc.

Library of Congress Catalog Card Number: 81-13162
ISBN: 0-313-22912-0

Reprinted in 1981 by Greenwood Press,
88 Post Road West, Westport, CT 06881
An imprint of Greenwood Publishing Group, Inc.

Printed in the United States of America

The paper used in this book complies with the
Permanent Paper Standard issued by the National
Information Standards Organization (Z39.48-1984).

10 9 8 7 6 5 4 3 2

For
Elinor and Edwin

Preface

SIGNIFICANT amounts of power are wielded in American politics by those formations usually known as "pressure groups." Most people recognize, in fact, some dimly and some sharply, that these groups are critically important elements in the political process. The power such groups dispose is involved at every point in the institutions of government, and the efforts of these formations are in various ways aided by, restricted by, and identified with institutionalized government. Partly because the diversity of relationships between groups and government is bewildering, we have had no inclusive working conception of the general political role of "pressure groups" or, as I prefer to call them, interest groups. The treatment of the interest group in most books on American government and politics is like that accorded the party in political writing until about the end of the nineteenth century. Nonparty groups have been dealt with in a manner that has been relatively casual and unsystematic. The interest group by and large is known as anatomy without being adequately understood as physiology.

We have had no dearth of muckraking exposés designed to rouse a presumably ignorant citizenry by revealing the allegedly evil activities of "lobbies" and "special interests." The end of such tracts has not yet been seen and undoubtedly will not soon appear. They perform a political function themselves that is likely to continue indefinitely.

More important for purposes of this book are the academic monographs on particular interest groups, of which there have been a considerable number over the past three decades. These monographs have scrutinized techniques utilized by these groups in connection with the enactment and administration of particular public policies. The relations between interest groups and particular governmental bodies, including legislatures, have been studied. A few investigations —too few—have been made into the relationships prevailing within certain organized groups. Many other kinds of examinations of matters governmental have touched upon the activities of interest groups.

The various treatments, whether journalistic or academic, of non-party groups have one limitation in common. They have not developed—or have not been based upon—a consistent conception of the role of interest groups in the political process. This common limitation can be noted without treating the two types of documents as similar in other respects and without doubting their political or intellectual value. Yet without some working conception of the political role of interest groups, their functions, and the ways in which their powers are exercised, we shall not be able adequately to understand the nature of the political process. Descriptions of that process that treat the nonparty group peripherally and merely anecdotally are not sufficient. The puzzle cannot be solved if some of the pieces are virtually ignored.

The incomplete incorporation of nonparty groups into explanations of the dynamics of democratic politics has many and complicated causes. One of them, however, probably lies in the nineteenth-century heritage, largely English, that the study of politics shares with economics. In crude terms the classical theories in both fields implicitly or explicitly started from the isolated individual. Both economic man and political man, it was assumed, exercised rational choice and acted independently for the maximization of individual advantage. No one man, behaving in this fashion, could affect significantly the general result, whether that was a governmental policy or a price in the market; only the aggregate of individual behaviors was determining. Deviations from these behaviors were increasingly recognized by both economists and political scientists, but for a long time they were treated as pathology rather than as evidence that the underlying theory did not account for the observed facts. The values associated with these theories were heavily loaded with emotion, and modification was therefore both a slow and a painful process. The reconstruction of classic explanations to accommodate group behavior has been common in recent years, however, to both economics and politics, although in the latter field it has proceeded rather slowly.

A second reason why there has been no systematic conception of the role of interest groups in the political process is more immediate and, in a sense, more concrete. In view of the way in which such organizing conceptions usually develop, it was to be expected that a large mass of essentially specialized and monographic case materials would be accumulated before an inclusive theoretical explanation appeared. This has been the way general concepts have developed in most of the social sciences, whether the specialized studies were set in an adequate framework of theory and hypothesis or not.

The accumulation of data on political interest groups, although scarcely complete, has proceeded a long way. Thanks to the analytical work of a number of political scientists, to the insights of several discerning commentators, and to the zeal of a host of vigorous polemicists over the past three decades and more, we have at hand the materials for an attempt at a restatement of the role of groups in the political process. The performance of that task is, in my opinion, a matter of great urgency. It requires an evaluation and a resulting synthesis that will give an explanation of group politics, fully utilizing the established data and suggesting subjects for further investigation. Such is the task of the present study.

A work of this sort must build upon the observations of a great many writers. Although the persons whose published works I have used are too numerous to list here, the footnotes in the text record the extent of my indebtedness. Among these many items there is one book, however, that deserves special mention because it has given the subject much of what systematization it has so far received. That is Arthur F. Bentley's *The Process of Government,* first published in 1908. As the title of the present volume suggests, Bentley's "attempt to fashion a tool" has been the principal bench mark for my thinking. In fact, my plans for this study grew out of my experience in teaching from Bentley's work.

The starting point of this book is the proposition that political interest groups are specialized combinations but are not unique. The origins, structure, and operation of these groups are shared, in their essential features, with nonpolitical patterns of social interaction. At the same time the political interest group derives its peculiar significance from its connections with the more formalized institutions of government. Part I (Chapters 1–4) deals with both these points: the role that interest groups, in common with other such formations, play in the operation of a complex society; and the circumstances of their involvement in the activities of governing.

In this first section I have inevitably drawn heavily upon findings and formulations in social psychology and applied social anthropology.

Many of these are so fully verified as to warrant their use by the political scientist with complete confidence. Others, however, such as those propositions based exclusively upon the observation of relatively small, face-to-face groups, must be employed with some caution in discussing groups of larger compass. Even as hypotheses and analogies, the findings concerning circumscribed groups can be projected upon more inclusive patterns of interaction only tentatively and in a fashion that is necessarily somewhat conjectural. Attempts of this sort in the following pages are offered with some diffidence in the spirit of Graham Wallas's counsel: "We must aim at finding as many relevant and measurable facts about human nature as possible, and we must attempt to make all of them serviceable in political reasoning." [1]

The argument of Part II (Chapters 5–7) stems from the view that the role of groups in the governmental process cannot be adequately understood apart from their internal dynamics. Formal structure and internal politics are treated as interdependent aspects of group life. Particular attention is given to the problems and techniques of leadership that spring from the connection between group cohesion and the conflicting attitudes and affiliations of members. The implications of overlapping group membership, a central element in the book, are introduced and developed at some length.

The longest section of the book is Part III (Chapters 8–15), which deals with the tactics of interest groups in the governmental arena. It opens with a discussion of the nature of group dependence upon public opinion and of propaganda techniques. The whole book in a sense is concerned with the phenomena of public opinion, but this chapter focuses rather explicitly upon the nature of public opinion and the problems involved in group propaganda. After this opening chapter, I have dealt with the activities of interest groups in the various subdivisions of the governmental institution. Although these chapters focus successively upon political parties, elections, the legislature, the executive branch, and the judiciary, this method of organizing the material was adopted primarily because of the convenience of familiar categories. Under these headings the treatment of the material follows observed relationships between groups and public officials wherever they may lead, among as well as within the various segments of the institution. The formalities of legal structure cannot be ignored, but they should not be permitted to obscure the dynamic patterns in the governing process. The data of politics are

[1] Graham Wallas: *Human Nature in Politics* (3d edition, New York: Alfred A. Knopf, Inc., 1921), p. 140.

the behaviors of participants in the government, whether or not such activities fit the specifications of the legal blueprints, and lines of power and influence are not fully recorded in statutes and constitutions. Seen in the context of interest-group operations, the functions of many bits of governmental procedure and the institutional life of various units in the governmental structure take on a new significance.

The single chapter in Part IV (Chapter 16) returns to some of the questions raised in the opening pages: How can we account for the existence of a going and generally accepted polity in a context of diverse interest groups? Under what circumstances can one appropriately view with alarm the growth and activity of political interest groups? The conscious values underlying this chapter and the book as a whole should be made as explicit as possible. They can be stated succinctly as, first, a preference for the essential features of representative democracy and, second, a belief in the virtues of peaceful change. Other and less fundamental personal preferences may have guided the selection of some illustrative materials, although for the most part I have used whatever examples I could extract from the literature. Since, however, I have not intended to pass judgment upon any group or groups, my basic propositions concerning the governmental process need not depend upon the reader's accepting the propriety of my treatment of particular organizations.

My efforts to synthesize the materials of this field have been personally rewarding in part because they have provided an opportunity to identify those areas where the gaps in our knowledge are most troublesome. Inevitably I have had to deal with topics upon which adequate and relevant data were not available. At such points, many of which I have identified in the text, the formulations I have presented are hypotheses or simply conjectures growing out of evidence available in related areas; at this stage they cannot be regarded as validated conclusions. Among the most striking of these insufficiently explored areas are: the incidence and precise effects of conflicting group affiliations; the long-run political effects of the contents of the mass media; the informal processes involved in nominations and related aspects of selection for public office; the group or institutional life of legislatures and other public bodies; and the exact incidence and dynamics of widely held interests that are only in part represented in organized groups but which are potentially organizable. Finally, even where narrative data or heuristic formulations appear fairly adequate there is a great need for further systematic and, where possible, quantitative investigation. If these pages should persuade a few hardy researchers to join in examining these and similar problems, they would have served a useful purpose.

A number of people have given me the benefit of their advice, criticism, and assistance in the preparation of the book. While I absolve them of responsibility for the study's deficiencies, as is customary, I want to express my deep gratitude for their help. Professor V. O. Key, Jr., of Yale University, has read the manuscript and has contributed mightily of his knowledge and critical insight. I owe a very special debt to him. My Williams colleague, Professor James M. Burns, read and criticized the whole study and has permitted me to impose repeatedly upon his time and friendship. Professor Theodore M. Newcomb, of the University of Michigan, examined the early chapters in their original form. His suggestions helped me to avoid numerous errors, and his generous encouragement was invaluable. The opening chapters were also examined by Professor Conrad M. Arensberg, of Columbia University, whose pioneering work in the analysis of social relations was the source of many of the concepts I have employed. Professor C. Herman Pritchett, of the University of Chicago, gave his informed attention to the chapter on the judiciary. I am especially grateful to the President and Trustees of Williams College for a grant of funds to aid in the preparation of the manuscript. Miss Ethel Richmond and other members of the staff of the Williams College Library skillfully and generously facilitated my research. My wife has participated in every phase of the project, has taken on many of the more trying tasks of documentation, and has typed the manuscript. My son has also made sacrifices for the study, after his fashion, and has shown a measure of forbearance beyond that to be expected of one of his years. The dedication of the book to him and to his mother is a token of gratitude as well as a mark of affection.

DAVID B. TRUMAN

Williamstown, Massachusetts

Contents

PART TWO

Group Organization and Problems of Leadership

PART THREE

The Tactics of Influence

PART ONE

Groups in the Political Process

1

The Alleged Mischiefs of Faction

MOST accounts of American legislative sessions—national, state, or local—are full of references to the maneuverings and iniquities of various organized groups. Newspaper stories report that a legislative proposal is being promoted by groups of business men or school teachers or farmers or consumers or labor unions or other aggregations of citizens. Cartoonists picture the legislature as completely under the control of sinister, portly, cigar-smoking individuals labeled "special interests," while a diminutive John Q. Public is pushed aside to sulk in futile anger and pathetic frustration. A member of the legislature rises in righteous anger on the floor of the house or in a press conference to declare that the bill under discussion is being forced through by the "interests," by the most unscrupulous high-pressure "lobby" he has seen in all his years of public life. An investigating committee denounces the activities of a group as deceptive, immoral, and destructive of our constitutional methods and ideals. A chief executive attacks a "lobby" or "pressure group" as the agency responsible for obstructing or emasculating a piece of legislation that he has recommended "in the public interest."

From time to time a conscientious and observant reporter collects a series of such incidents and publishes them, exposing in the best muckraking tradition the machinations of these subversive "interests," and, if he is fortunate, breaking into the best-seller lists. Or a fictionalized treatment of them may be presented as the theme of a popular novel.[1]

Such events are familiar even to the casual student of day-to-day

[1] For early and somewhat quaint treatments of this sort, see the novels of Winston Churchill: *Coniston* (1906) and *Mr. Crewe's Career* (1908).

politics, if only because they make diverting reading and appear to give the citizen the "low-down" on his government. He tends, along with many of his more sophisticated fellow citizens, to take these things more or less for granted, possibly because they merely confirm his conviction that "as everybody knows, politics is a dirty business." Yet at the same time he is likely to regard the activities of organized groups in political life as somehow outside the proper and normal processes of government, as the lapses of his weak contemporaries whose moral fiber is insufficient to prevent their defaulting on the great traditions of the Founding Fathers.[2] These events appear to be a modern pathology.

Group Pressures and the Founding Fathers

Group pressures, whatever we may wish to call them, are not new in America.[3] One of the earliest pieces of testimony to this effect is essay number 10 of *The Federalist*, which contains James Madison's classic statement of the impact of divergent groups upon government and the reasons for their development. He was arguing the virtues of the proposed Union as a means to "break and control the violence of faction," having in mind, no doubt, the groups involved in such actions of the debtor or propertyless segment of the population as Shays's Rebellion. He defined faction in broader terms, however, as "a number of citizens, whether amounting to a majority or minority of the whole, who are united and actuated by some common impulse of passion, or of interest. . . ." His observations on the source and character of such group differences merit quotation at length:

> The latent causes of faction are . . . sown in the nature of man; and we see them everywhere brought into different degrees of activity, according to the different circumstances of civil society. A zeal for different opinions concerning religion, concern-

[2] A learned example of this position is presented by Robert Luce: *Legislative Assemblies* (Boston: Houghton Mifflin Company, 1924), p. 385, quoting the opinion of a New York judge that contracts for lobbying services should not be enforced by the courts: "It is against the genius and policy of our government that her legislative and executive officers shall be surrounded by swarms of hired retainers of the claimants upon public bounty or justice." (Rose and Hawley v. Truax, 21 Barb. 361, 1855.) As Luce indicates, this view was not limited to the courts of New York.

[3] For comments on the concern of ancient historians and of various political philosophers with the role of interest groups, see Robert M. MacIver: "Interests," *Encyclopaedia of the Social Sciences*.

ing government, and many other points, as well of speculation as of practice; an attachment to different leaders ambitiously contending for pre-eminence and power; or to persons of other descriptions whose fortunes have been interesting to the human passions, have, in turn, divided mankind into parties, inflamed them with mutual animosity, and rendered them much more disposed to vex and oppress each other than to co-operate for their common good. . . . But the most common and durable source of factions has been the various and unequal distribution of property. Those who hold and those who are without property have ever formed distinct interests in society. Those who are creditors, and those who are debtors, fall under a like discrimination. A landed interest, a manufacturing interest, a mercantile interest, a moneyed interest, with many lesser interests, grow up of necessity in civilized nations, and divide them into different classes, actuated by different sentiments and views. The regulation of these various and interfering interests forms the principal task of modern legislation, and involves the spirit of party and faction in the necessary and ordinary operations of the government.

It should be noted that this analysis is not just the brilliant generalization of an armchair philosopher or pamphleteer; it represents as well the distillation from Madison's years of acquaintance with contemporary politics as a member of the Virginia Assembly and of Congress. Using the words "party" and "faction" almost interchangeably, since the political party as we know it had not yet developed, he saw the struggles of such groups as the essence of the political process. One need not concur in all his judgments to agree that the process he described had strong similarities to that of our own day.

The entire effort of which *The Federalist* was a part was one of the most skillful and important examples of pressure group activity in American history. The State ratifying conventions were handled by the Federalists with a skill that might well be the envy of a modern lobbyist. It is easy to overlook the fact that "unless the Federalists had been shrewd in manipulation as they were sound in theory, their arguments could not have prevailed."[4]

Since we have not yet come to the point of defining our terms, it

[4] Samuel E. Morrison and Henry S. Commager: *The Growth of the American Republic* (New York: Oxford University Press, 1930), p. 163. See also Charles A. Beard: *An Economic Interpretation of the Constitution of the United States* (New York: The Macmillan Company, 1913), chaps. 6, 8, and 9.

may be asserted that the instances cited carry with them none of the overtones of corruption and selfishness associated with modern political groups. Such characteristics are not the distinguishing feature of group politics, but early cases of the sort are not hard to find. As early as 1720 a nearly successful effort was made to control the New Jersey Assembly, allegedly in the business interests of an outside manipulator.[5] The funding of the State debt in the First Congress provided a colorful record of the pressures used in support of the proposal. Senator William Maclay of Pennsylvania, a bitter partisan and therefore a not altogether objective observer, made the following entry in his diary under the date, March 9, 1790:

> In the Senate chamber this morning Butler said he heard a man say he would give Vining (of Delaware) one thousand guineas for his vote, but added, "I question whether he would do so in fact." So do I, too, for he might get it for a tenth part of that sum. I do not know that pecuniary influence has actually been used, but I am certain that every other kind of management has been practiced and every tool at work that could be thought of. Officers of Government, clergy, citizens, Cincinnati, and every person under the influence of the Treasury. . . .[6]

Jefferson, no less partisan though perhaps somewhat more objective, in February, 1793, made the following note after a conference that he had had with President Washington:

> I confirmed him in the fact of the great discontents to the South, that they were grounded on seeing that their judgments and interests were sacrificed to those of the Eastern States on every occasion, and their belief that it was the effect of a corrupt squadron of voters in Congress at the command of the Treasury, and they see if the votes of those members who had an interest distinct from and contrary to the general interest of their constituents had been withdrawn, as in decency and honesty they should have been, the laws would have been the reverse of what they are in all the great questions.[7]

As a careful student of American legislatures has put it: "No one can read the story of the assumption of the State debts and the location

[5] Cited in Luce: *Legislative Assemblies*, p. 367.
[6] Quoted ibid., p. 409.
[7] Quoted ibid., p. 410.

of the capital without wondering whether the legislative manipulators of our day have really gone much beyond our forefathers in point of questionable practices." [8]

In the lusty years of the Jackson administration Alexis de Tocqueville, perhaps the keenest foreign student ever to write on American institutions, noted as one of the most striking characteristics of the nation the penchant for promoting a bewildering array of projects through organized societies, among them those using political means. "In no country in the world," he observed, "has the principle of association been more successfully used or applied to a greater multitude of objects than in America." [9] De Tocqueville was impressed by the organization of such groups and by their tendency to operate sometimes upon and sometimes parallel to the formal institutions of government. Speaking of the similarity between the representatives of such groups and the members of legislatures, he stated: "It is true that they [delegates of these societies] have not the right, like the others, of making the laws; but they have the power of attacking those which are in force and of drawing up beforehand those which ought to be enacted." [10]

Since the modern political party was, in the Jackson period, just taking the form that we would recognize today, De Tocqueville does not always distinguish sharply between it and other types of political interest groups. In his discussion of "political associations," however, he gives an account of the antitariff convention held in Philadelphia in October of 1831, the form of which might well have come from the proceedings of a group meeting in an American city today:

> Its debates were public, and they at once assumed a legislative character; the extent of the powers of Congress, the theories of free trade, and the different provisions of the tariff were discussed. At the end of ten days the Convention broke up, having drawn up an address to the American people in which it declared: (1) that Congress had not the right of making a tariff, and that the existing tariff was unconstitutional; (2) that the prohibition of free trade was prejudicial to the interests of any nation, and to those of the American people especially.[11]

[8] Ibid., p. 367.
[9] Alexis de Tocqueville: *Democracy in America* (ed. by Phillips Bradley, New York: Alfred A. Knopf, Inc., 1945), Vol. I, p. 191. See also Vol. II, p. 106 and *passim*.
[10] Ibid., Vol. I, p. 193.
[11] Ibid., Vol. I, p. 194.

Additional evidence might be cited from many quarters to illustrate the long history of group politics in this country. Organized pressures supporting or attacking the charter of the Bank of the United States in Jackson's administration, the peculations surrounding Pendleton's "Palace of Fortune" in the pre-Civil War period, the operations of the railroads and other interests in both national and state legislatures in the latter half of the last century, the political activities of farm groups such as the Grange in the same period—these and others indicate that at no time have the activities of organized political interests not been a part of American politics.[12] Whether they indicate pathology or not, they are certainly not new.

Political Groups Abroad

The political activities of organized groups are not, moreover, a peculiarly American phenomenon. As Herring observes: "Small groups have always striven for their particular interests before governmental powers." [13] If we look at the government of Great Britain, for example, we find such groups operating very much as they do in the United States, though with significant differences stemming in part from variations in the institutional milieu.

Organized political groups in Britain cover fully as extensive a segment of the life of the society as do such groups in the United States.[14] Industrial and trade organizations number in the hundreds; agriculture and its related activities are covered by twenty or thirty; welfare societies are "at least as numerous, though they are not so

[12] See, for example, E. Pendleton Herring: *Group Representation Before Congress* (Baltimore: The Johns Hopkins Press, 1929), pp. 30–9; A. M. Schlesinger, Jr.: *The Age of Jackson* (Boston: Little, Brown & Company, 1945), *passim*; G. G. Van Deusen: *Thurlow Weed: Wizard of the Lobby* (Boston: Little, Brown & Company, 1947), chap. 14; P. S. Reinsch: *American Legislatures and Legislative Methods* (New York: The Century Company, 1907), chap. 8; Robert Luce: *Legislative Assemblies*, chaps. 17–19. An especially interesting set of examples, notable for the careful analysis of the social setting of the groups and covering the State of Pennsylvania from 1776 to 1860, will be found in Louis Hartz: *Economic Policy and Democratic Thought: Pennsylvania, 1776–1860* (Cambridge, Mass.: Harvard University Press, 1948).

[13] Herring: *Group Representation Before Congress*, p. 241. Copyright 1929 by and used with the permission of The Brookings Institution.

[14] This section is based on W. Ivor Jennings: *Parliament* (Cambridge: Cambridge University Press, 1939), chaps. 2 and 7.

well organized for joint action" as are the trade groups; the hundreds of professional organizations place a major emphasis upon political activity; citizens who pay large sums in taxes are represented by associations, as are their counterparts in America; the "persistent" pedestrians are organized as well as the automobile owners; and there are the trade unions with their several million members.

Depending on their circumstances, these groups may take an open and active part in party politics in the electioneering sense—in fact, in several cases a far more active part than any such groups in this country. Such activity is not confined to the obvious case of the labor unions. The National Farmers' Union makes no pretense of impartiality between parties. It aids Conservative candidates not only by endorsement, but also by financial support. The National Union of Ratepayers' and Property Owners' Associations is a subsidiary of the Conservative party. The National Union of Teachers, in order to assure adequate representation in Parliament, is willing to give financial support to at least one member of the House of Commons.

An expected *quid pro quo* is quite as likely as in the United States to be involved in such partisan support. Jennings reports a series of demands by the National Farmers' Union after the general election of 1935 that will not sound strange to American ears. Following the election, in which it had given the successful Conservatives its usual support, the Union submitted to the Prime Minister a comprehensive policy for agriculture. A committee interviewed him shortly thereafter, and the President of the Union, who was a Conservative member of the Parliament, visited the Minister of Agriculture. Apparently dissatisfied with the results of these efforts, the Union urged each county branch to set up an "active parliamentary committee" and to engage in "intensive local propaganda so that members of Parliament in agricultural constituencies should be fully informed of the problems which were facing the industry." [15]

Because no private member's bill can pass over the Government's opposition in the House of Commons and because the Government's control of financial matters is complete, the major effort of most groups is focused on the ministers. Jennings says of measures involving financial policy: "Where log-rolling takes place the Chancellor of the Exchequer captains the team. The pork-barrel is kept locked up in 11 Downing Street, and those who want to take part in the distribution must stand on the door-step and prove their credentials." [16] The process is different in detail from that in the Congress of the United

[15] Ibid., p. 214.
[16] Ibid., p. 189.

States, because of differences in institutional practice, but the basic resemblance is unmistakable.

Although most legislation thus has its origins in the executive departments, the "inspiration" is shared with the organized interests. The groups may play an even more open role in the criticism and amendment of a proposed measure. The Government, for all practical purposes, can force the enactment of virtually any bill it chooses to support, but in a system that is fundamentally dependent on free elections the Cabinet will inevitably give satisfaction to any clear expression of public opinion. Less open methods of opposition failing, therefore, a group will attempt to bring an aroused public opinion to its support.

The political devices available under the American and British constitutions are not identical, but in both countries the organized political group is a major element in the political process. Other examples could be given to demonstrate further that the political interest group is not a peculiarly American institution. One might note that in France organized groups of business men, workers, and farmers, to say nothing of the Catholic Church, have been a central element in the governing process both before and since World War II.[17] One might elaborate on the development of such groups in Sweden, where they have become not only a vehicle for political demands but also, to a remarkable degree, administrative agencies of the state. Their activities are visible in every country where freedom of association is an element in the constitutional fabric.[18]

The Problem

It should be apparent from this brief discussion that the political interest group is neither a fleeting, transitory newcomer to the political arena nor a localized phenomenon peculiar to one member of the

[17] On the role of such groups in the Third Republic see David Thomson: *Democracy in France: The Third Republic* (London: Oxford University Press, 1946), pp. 39–74 and *passim*.
[18] J. A. Corry: *Elements of Democratic Government* (New York: Oxford University Press, 1947), chap. 8; Gunnar Heckscher: "Group Organization in Sweden," *Public Opinion Quarterly*, Vol. 3, no. 4 (Winter, 1939), pp. 130–5; interesting data on manufacturers' associations during the 1930's in Germany, Italy, Japan, France, Great Britain, and the United States are given in Robert A. Brady: *Business as a System of Power* (New York: Columbia University Press, 1943), chaps. 1–6, although the broad thesis advanced in the book is of dubious validity.

family of nations. The persistence and the dispersion of such organizations indicate rather that we are dealing with a characteristic aspect of our society. That such groups are receiving an increasing measure of popular and technical attention suggests the hypothesis that they are appreciably more significant in the complex and interdependent society of our own day than they were in the simpler, less highly developed community for which our constitutional arrangements were originally designed.

Many people are quite willing to acknowledge the accuracy of these propositions about political groups, but they are worried nevertheless. They are still concerned over the meaning of what they see and read of the activities of such organizations. They observe, for example, that certain farm groups apparently can induce the Government to spend hundreds of millions of dollars to maintain the price of food and to take "surplus" agricultural produce off the market while many urban residents are encountering painful difficulty in stretching their food budgets to provide adequately for their families. They observe that various labor organizations seem to be able to prevent the introduction of cheaper methods into building codes, although the cost of new housing is already beyond the reach of many. Real estate and contractors' trade associations apparently have the power to obstruct various governmental projects for slum clearance and low-cost housing. Veterans' organizations seem able to secure and protect increases in pensions and other benefits almost at will. A church apparently can prevent the appropriation of Federal funds to public schools unless such funds are also given to the schools it operates in competition with the public systems. The Government has declared that stable and friendly European governments cannot be maintained unless Americans buy more goods and services abroad. Yet American shipowners and seamen's unions can secure a statutory requirement that a large proportion of the goods purchased by European countries under the Marshall Plan must be carried in American ships. Other industries and trade associations can prevent the revision of tariff rates and customs regulations that restrict imports from abroad.

In all these situations the fairly observant citizen sees various groups slugging it out with one another in pursuit of advantages from the Government. Or he sees some of them co-operating with one another to their mutual benefit. He reads of "swarms" of lobbyists "putting pressure on" congressmen and administrators. He has the impression that any group can get what it wants in Washington by deluging officials with mail and telegrams. He may then begin to wonder whether a governmental system like this can survive, whether it can carry its responsibilities in the world and meet the challenges presented by a ruthless dictatorship. He wants to see these external threats effectively met. The sentimental nonsense of the commercial advertisements aside, he values free speech, free elections, representative government, and all that these imply. He fears and resents practices and privileges that seem to place these values in jeopardy.

A common reaction to revelations concerning the more lurid activities of political groups is one of righteous indignation. Such indignation is entirely natural. It is likely, however, to be more comforting than constructive. What we seek are correctives, protections, or controls that will strengthen the practices essential in what we call democracy and that will weaken or eliminate those that really threaten that system. Uncritical anger may do little to achieve that objective, largely because it is likely to be based upon a picture of the governmental process that is a composite of myth and fiction as well as of fact. We shall not begin to achieve control until we have arrived at a conception of politics that adequately accounts for the operations of political groups. We need to know what regular patterns are shown by group politics before we can predict its consequences and prescribe for its lapses. We need to re-examine our notions of how representative government operates in the United States before we can be confident of our statements about the effects of group activities upon it. Just as we should not know how to protect a farm house from lightning unless we knew something of the behavior of electricity, so we cannot hope to protect a governmental system from the results of group organization unless we have an adequate understanding of the political process of which these groups are a part.

Our first step in the development of a workable conception of political groups will have to be away from formal government and politics as such. We shall examine the dynamics of social groups in general, regardless of whether they are or are not involved in politics. What do we mean by the term *group?* What are the social functions of groups? What relation do they have to the behavior of individuals? How do they come into existence? Assuming that the political groups in which we are primarily interested are not basically different from other social groups, what are their distinguishing features? What variations in origin and function can we observe among political groups?

We may then consider certain general features of the relations between political groups and government in the United States. What are the difficulties that confront an attempt to analyze the role of groups in the political process? What are the connections between the increased complexity of governmental operations in the United States and the recent increases in the number of organized groups? Why have particular types of political groups become increasingly numerous and active? Why and under what circumstances do organized groups become involved in the operation of government?

In this general discussion of groups and government we shall note that the character of a group's relationship to the governing process is in part a function of the group's internal structure and of political behavior within its ranks. We shall therefore examine in some detail the variations in group organization, the factors affecting group cohesion, and the nature and techniques of group leadership. In this part of the analysis we shall be concerned with two major questions: How do these factors affect the relations between groups and government? What restraints, if any, do they impose upon the political activity of groups?

Upon these foundations we can begin to develop a meaningful conception of the role of political groups in the governing process. We shall look first at their propaganda activities and generally at their relation to what we call public opinion. We shall then analyze the connections between interest groups and political parties and their relations with the more formalized institutions of government at the various levels of the federal system. It will be convenient to discuss the latter under the conventional headings of the legislature, the executive, and the judiciary, but we shall be careful to focus our analysis upon observable operating relationships among, as well as within, these branches in order that we may avoid the pitfalls of a too literal formalism. Throughout this part of the book the questions with which we shall be primarily concerned will be: What are the factors which determine the power of groups in the various phases of the governmental process? To what extent and under what circumstances is government action the product of organized group activity? What features of the American system tend to maximize the influence of organized groups and what features, if any, operate to confine the activities of such groups within tolerable limits?

A conception of the political process broad enough to account for the development and functioning of political groups is essential to a reliable evaluation of the alleged mischiefs of faction. To work out such a basis of interpretation is the purpose of this book.

2

Groups and Society

————————◆————————

MAN is a social animal. Among other meanings involved in this Aristotelian statement is the observation that with rare exceptions man is always found in association with other men. John Dewey has observed: "Associated activity needs no explanation; things are made that way." [1] This association includes varying degrees of organization; that is, certain of the relationships among a collection of men regularly occur in certain consistent patterns and sequences. But there is another meaning in this classic proposition, closer to the one that Aristotle probably intended, namely, that men must exist in society in order to manifest those capacities and accomplishments that distinguish them from the other animals. These human accomplishments embrace not only the wondrous array of skills and creations that are thought of as civilization but also humbler and more fundamental developments such as primary intellectual growth and language.

We do not have to rely solely on Aristotle's confidence concerning the virtues of life in the city-state for support of the proposition that man is essentially social. The Robinson Crusoe hypothesis that men are best conceived of as isolated units is inadequate psychology as well as unfashionable economics. Accounts, at least partially authenticated, of children who by some chance of fate have been raised among animals, isolated from all contact with human beings, indicate not only that speech is not acquired under such circumstances but also that it is developed only very slowly after the child has been returned to human society. Cases of children who have been kept in solitary con-

---

[1] John Dewey: *The Public and Its Problems* (New York: Henry Holt & Company, Inc., 1927), p. 151. Copyright by and used with the permission of Henry Holt & Company, Inc.

finement during their early years illustrate the same point. An essentially human and social characteristic, speech, is not acquired, and, in fact, the very capacity to learn is apparently stunted or atrophied.[2] Man becomes characteristically human only in association with other men.

A more obvious sort of interdependence also requires man to live in society—purely physical dependence on others of his species. The family, the most primitive social unit, the only one that man shares generally with other mammals, exists in part to provide protection and training for the offspring during their long period of helplessness. Furthermore, the division of labor or specialization, which appears even in the simple family unit on the basis of age and sex differences and on which a high degree of skill and large productivity fundamentally depend, almost by definition involves the mutual dependence of men. A modern urban dweller who has experienced the consequences of an interruption in the milk supply, in the public transportation system, or in the distribution of electric power needs no introduction to the implications of specialization.

In this chapter, as the remarks above suggest, we shall not focus our attention primarily upon "political" behavior. We shall rather examine groups of all kinds and their significance in the social process generally. The point to bear in mind is that the dynamics of groups are not essentially different because the groups are labeled "political." Basically they show the same regularities as do other continuing social patterns. In this connection we shall discuss the meaning of the terms "group" and "interest group" and shall examine some of the characteristics of a peculiarly important type of group, the association.

Group Affiliations and Individual Behavior

In all societies of any degree of complexity the individual is less affected directly by the society as a whole than differentially through various of its subdivisions, or groups. In the first place, even in the simplest society, it is literally impossible for any one individual to function in all the groups of which the society is made. Just as he can become highly skilled in only one or a few techniques, so he can participate in only a limited number of the groups that are formed

[2] See Arnold Gesell: *Wolf Child and Human Child* (New York: Harper and Brothers, 1939) and Kingsley Davis: "Extreme Social Isolation of a Child," *American Journal of Sociology*, Vol. 45, no. 4 (January, 1940), pp. 554–65.

about such specializations. In a society in which locality groupings are important, an individual never "belongs" to more than a few and rarely to more than one. In the second place, the positions occupied by the individual in his society limit the effects upon him of society as a whole. The technical term usually applied to these positions is *statuses*.[3] He may not participate in those groups confined to persons of the opposite sex or of a differing age level. Ordinarily he belongs to only one "extended" family, one church, one economic institution, and one political unit at a given level, such as the nation. At any point in time and frequently over his entire life span he cannot belong to more than one class or caste grouping.

To the extent that the range and type of behavior in these groupings vary from one to another—and even in the simplest societies they inevitably vary to some degree—the patterns of action and attitude among individuals will differ from one another in large measure according to the clusters of group affiliations that the individuals have. In John Dewey's words: "The underlying and generative conditions of concrete behavior are social as well as organic: much more social than organic as far as the manifestation of *differential* wants, purposes and methods of operation is concerned."[4] Because such groups may come into conflict from time to time, various theorists have attempted to account for both the groups and the conflict in terms of "instincts." Gaetano Mosca, for example, asserts that men have an "instinct of herding together and fighting with other herds" that accounts not only for the conflicts between societies but also for "the formation of all the divisions and subdivisions . . . that arise within a given society and occasion moral and, sometimes, physical conflicts."[5] It is quite unnecessary to resort to any such crude *deus ex machina*, for, like the similar devices employed by the social contract philosophers of the seventeenth century to account for the origin of government and society, it implies the temporal priority of the individual over the group. That is, it implicitly assumes that individuals exist first in some degree of isolation and then form into societies or groups, a notion impossible to document.

It is simpler and more realistic to say with James Madison that the

[3] Ralph Linton: *The Cultural Background of Personality* (New York: Appleton-Century-Crofts, Inc., 1945), pp. 75–82.

[4] Dewey: *The Public and Its Problems*, p. 103. Copyright 1927 by and used with the permission of Henry Holt & Company, Inc.

[5] From *The Ruling Class* by Gaetano Mosca, translated from the Italian by Hannah D. Kahn, edited by Arthur Livingston, p. 163. Copyright 1939. Courtesy of McGraw-Hill Book Company, Inc.

tendencies toward such groupings are "sown in the nature of man," meaning by that statement, as he apparently meant, that such tendencies are "sown" by the differing group experiences of individuals. When such groups become active, whether in conflict or not, that stage of development can be accounted for, again in Madison's words, in terms of "the different circumstances of civil society." [6] In slightly different terms: "The human being whom we fasten upon as individual *par excellence* is moved and regulated by his association with others; what he does and what the consequences of his behavior are, what his experience consists of, cannot even be described, much less accounted for, in isolation." [7]

In recent years the social psychologists and the cultural anthropologists have done much to explain the manner and extent of group influences upon our behavior. [8] The most important of these influences from the standpoint of molding the individual's personality and adjusting him to his surroundings are those that operate during infancy and childhood—the family, neighborhood, school, and friendship groups, commonly known as primary groups. In the process of growing up, the child receives from face-to-face groups, especially those that include adults, and from the opportunities that they afford, the means whereby he defines his self in relation to the world about him. He learns what to do and what to avoid and in what terms various objects and behaviors are to be understood if he is to be an accepted and approved member of the unit involved. These terms vary considerably among groups, depending on their circumstances. Such groups almost without design select those aspects of the culture with which the child becomes acquainted and determine the values which he shall attach to them. "The exposure to the attitudes of others and to their definitions of situations through language and emotionally toned gestures takes place almost as gradually as language itself is acquired. . . ." [9] A young person's aspirations and values, even his skills, will be very different depending on the character of this early

[6] *The Federalist*, No. 10.

[7] Dewey: *The Public and Its Problems*, p. 188. Copyright 1927 by and used with the permission of Henry Holt & Company, Inc.

[8] Perhaps the most elaborate attempt of this sort is the "Yankee City" investigation directed by Warner. See W. Lloyd Warner and Paul S. Lunt: *The Social Life of a Modern Community* (New Haven, Conn.: Yale University Press, 1941), esp. chap. 2, and *The Status System of a Modern Community* (New Haven, Conn.: Yale University Press, 1942), *passim*.

[9] William I. Thomas: *Primitive Behavior: An Introduction to the Social Sciences* (New York: McGraw-Hill Book Company, Inc., 1937), p. 36.

group experience. If he has spent the early years of his life on a family farm in the Middle West, some distance from any urban community, in a large family the demands of whose daily existence limit the household's recreational facilities to the radio and the Bible, he will be quite unlike his contemporary whose parents move from one section of the country to another with the changes in the social "season," who has almost endless varieties of amusements and has been educated in the most expensive private schools. Both will differ from the products of a trim but modest suburban community, a sharecropper area of the South, or a section of a large city inhabited almost entirely by a closeknit population of recent immigrants. Although no two human organisms will develop identically in any one of the environments mentioned, the limitations, aspirations, and values that each holds will have developed in relation to the groups with which each has been early associated.[10]

Psychologists distinguish various mechanisms whereby the group places its imprint upon the personality of a participant.[11] It is unnecessary to go into these here. In general terms, every individual, from infancy onward, tries to make himself an accepted participant in a group, or, more properly, a set of groups, that makes up his social environment. Once he finds himself in such groups or, as he matures, aspires to be a member of some group, he in effect discovers more or less unconsciously that he must exhibit the kinds of behavior that will identify him as belonging or else accept a position as an outsider. This adaptation will occur whether the values of the culture as a whole call for a high measure of co-operative behavior, as among the Zuni Indians of the Southwest, or whether they place a premium upon individual aggressiveness, as with the Kwakiutl of the Puget Sound area or the modern Americans.[12] Most individuals in any cultural setting find it intolerably painful not to be accepted by the

[10] See Muzafer Sherif and Hadley Cantril: *The Psychology of Ego-Involvements* (New York: John Wiley & Sons, Inc., 1947), *passim;* Hadley Cantril: *The Psychology of Social Movements* (New York: John Wiley & Sons, Inc., 1941), chap. 1.

[11] Gardner Murphy, Lois B. Murphy, and Theodore M. Newcomb: *Experimental Social Psychology* (New York: Harper and Brothers, 1937), chap. 4; Theodore M. Newcomb: *Social Psychology* (New York: The Dryden Press, 1950), chaps. 8, 14–17. Cf. Max L. Hutt and Daniel R. Miller: "Social Values and Personality Development," *Journal of Social Issues,* Vol. 5, no. 4 (Fall, 1949), pp. 2–43.

[12] See Ruth Benedict: *Patterns of Culture* (Boston: Houghton Mifflin Company, 1934), chaps. 4 and 6.

groups in which they move or in which they hope to move. A measure of conformity is the price of acceptance.[13]

The psychological pressure on the individual from his group affiliations does not decrease in intensity or effectiveness as the individual matures. When the full set of attitudes toward "me," "I," and "mine," which make up what the psychologist calls the ego, are formed—though their exact content is not static—the individual feels even more strongly the need to be accepted in his "own" group and to avoid being left out. Thus, "in a group of good friends whose opinions matter to us, we make a point of showing that we understand a joke, that we catch the drift of a subtle conversation, *whether we actually do or not.*"[14]

These group experiences, particularly those that occur in connection with unfamiliar situations, give the individual, either directly or by sanctioning or censoring attitudes and behaviors stemming from isolated individual experiences, a general outlook, or frame of reference, in terms of which he perceives and evaluates events. Sherif has performed a series of laboratory experiments that bear closely on these influences. He used the autokinetic phenomenon, an effect long known to scientists, in which a single, stable pin-point of light in a pitch-dark and silent space appears to move, often quite erratically. The probable reason for the apparent movement is that there is in the situation no perceived external frame of reference in relation to which it is obvious that the light is not moving. In the social psychologist's terms, the situation is not structured. When an individual is placed in this sort of experimental setting and told to announce how far the light moves, he will establish internally a point of reference and a norm about which his distance judgments in this situation will cluster. This norm tends to persist in subsequent experimental sessions. When a group is placed in this situation, the members of which are told to announce their judgments in random order, they do not produce a welter of widespread judgments, but they develop a group norm. This norm also persists for the individual members when they are later examined alone. Individuals who have established a norm before the group experiment tend to converge toward a group

[13] See Sherif and Cantril: *Psychology of Ego-Involvements,* pp. 5–6. An important variant of this situation, conflicting group demands upon an individual, will be discussed in a later chapter.

[14] Muzafer Sherif and S. Stansfeld Sargent: "Ego-Involvement and the Mass Media," *Journal of Social Issues,* Vol. 3, no. 3 (Summer, 1947), pp. 10–11.

norm less sharply.[15] For present purposes these experiments indicate that in an unstructured situation the interaction of the members of a group produces a group frame of reference in terms of which the situation is experienced. The same psychological principles are involved in the development of other social norms through which groups influence and control the behavior of their participant members.

Newcomb's study of attitude changes in a highly self-contained college community is also significant at this point.[16] The college studied was a small one; although the overwhelming majority of its students came from backgrounds in which a "conservative" position was taken on most public issues, the dominant opinions within the college on these matters were "liberal." Studying virtually the entire student body over a period of four years, he found that student attitudes changed significantly during the four college years in the direction of less "conservatism," these attitudes tending to persist at least through the first two years after graduation. The effects of community norms were more immediate in the cases of those whose personalities tended to cast them in leadership roles: "Within a few weeks of entering college they . . . 'sized up' the dominant community trends, toward which they adapt themselves in proportion to their habits of seeking leadership and prestige." [17] Nonconservative attitudes were developed "primarily by those . . . both capable and desirous of cordial relations with their fellow community members." [18] It was the price of "belonging." Those whose attitudes remained atypically "conservative" were likely to show their slight degree of membership in the community through unawareness of the "liberal" community frame of reference or through their closer identification with and dependence upon outside groups, particularly the family.

Other examples of these group influences could be drawn from a number of sources. Justly famous is the study made in the Hawthorne works of the Western Electric Company. Fourteen men in three related occupations—wiremen, soldermen, and inspectors—were

[15] Muzafer Sherif: *The Psychology of Social Norms* (New York: Harper and Brothers, 1936). See also his paper, "An Experimental Approach to the Study of Attitudes," *Sociometry*, Vol. 1 (1937), pp. 90–8, condensed in Theodore M. Newcomb and Eugene L. Hartley: *Readings in Social Psychology* (New York: Henry Holt & Company, Inc., 1947), pp. 77–90.

[16] Theodore M. Newcomb: *Personality and Social Change* (New York: The Dryden Press, 1943). See also his *Social Psychology*, chap. 6.

[17] Newcomb: *Personality and Social Change*, p. 149.

[18] Ibid., pp. 148–9.

paid on the basis of the group's total output. This arrangement was designed to maximize production, but it was a failure. Productivity was not a function of the desire to obtain as much pay as possible, but was based rather on a group-established norm of what constituted a fair day's work. The observers detected four other norms, called by them "basic sentiments," that supported this one: (1) the individual worker should not turn out too much work or he will become a "rate buster" (will invite a lowering of the piece-work rate); (2) he should not produce too little or he will be a "chiseler"; (3) a worker who casts a reflection on another worker in talking to a supervisor is a "squealer"; (4) a worker functioning as an inspector should not be too officious. The significant aspect of this analysis for present purposes is its conclusion: "To be an accepted member of the group a man had to act in accordance with these social standards." [19]

It appears, then, that the group experiences and affiliations of an individual are the primary, though not the exclusive, means by which the individual knows, interprets, and reacts to the society in which he exists. Their significance here is that they produce in their participants certain uniformities of behavior and attitude that must be achieved by the individual if he is to be a completely accepted member of the group. The process by which the individual reaches these uniformities or conformities is essentially what is meant by the term socialization. These uniformities, moreover, cover, and in a sense regulate, the whole range of man's attitudes toward groups of which he is not a member, his work habits, and his political attitudes and behavior.[20] It is the last item with which we are particularly concerned in an examination of the political process. With variations that we shall develop in later chapters, such "pressure groups" as the C.I.O., the National Association of Manufacturers, and the American Farm Bureau Federation develop as well as reflect uniformities in the attitudes and behavior of their members. These patterns are, or are rapidly becoming, the primary data of the social scientist. To identify and interpret these uniformities—their dynamics, their interconnections, and their relative strength—is the most effective approach to understanding a society, "primitive" or complex, or a segment of it such as its political institutions.

[19] F. J. Roethlisberger: *Management and Morale* (Cambridge, Mass.: Harvard University Press, 1941), pp. 22–3. For other discussions of these experiments see F. J. Roethlisberger and William J. Dickson: *Management and the Worker* (Cambridge, Mass.: Harvard University Press, 1939), Part IV; and Elton Mayo: *The Social Problems of an Industrial Civilization* (Boston· Harvard Graduate School of Business Administration, 1945), *passim*.

[20] Sherif and Cantril: *Psychology of Ego-Involvements*, pp. 10–11.

Because two men belong to the same group or have a number of such memberships in common, they will not, of course, necessarily hold identical attitudes on all issues or exhibit the same behaviors. They will tend to do so on certain matters, however, and the degree of such correspondence is a basic variable to be measured. Such variations, of crucial importance in the interpretation of political interest groups, are not a denial of the thesis that group affiliations significantly affect behavior, but are an essential part of it. In the first place, the thesis recognizes, as it must, that no two human organisms are identical in biological functioning and endowment, though their physiological and psychological processes are the same. Some behavioral differences inevitably stem from this fact. In the second place, even though the group affiliations of two adults are at a given point in time virtually identical, which is unlikely, their group experiences presumably cannot have been identical since birth. Their behavior and attitudes are not simply the product of their current affiliations, but are the result of a genetic process that includes in some measure the whole of their life experience. The child is, in a sense, father to the man. Degrees of behavioral uniformity are nevertheless observed within social groupings. The task of the social scientist who takes these as his basic data is to identify them and explain to what areas of behavior they apply, to measure the extent of such uniformities, and to specify the conditions under which they occur.

An example in the area of political behavior may clarify this point somewhat. When Paul Lazarsfeld and his associates made a study of voters' preferences in Erie County, Ohio, in 1940, they found a significant measure of agreement among the members of certain social groupings on their choices between the two major-party candidates for President.[21] Catholics were more likely than Protestants to be Democratic. Those who lived in the urban sections of the county tended to be Democratic, whereas those in the rural areas tended to be Republican. Those of higher socio-economic status tended to be Republican, whereas at each lower step in the scale people were more likely to prefer the Democratic candidate. The word "tended" does not mean that all in these groupings shared the same preference. It means only that a significantly large majority in each took this position. Sharing the attributes of these social groupings did not necessarily "cause" these voters to have the same political preferences. Other groups, those more properly designated by the term, had a

[21] P. F. Lazarsfeld, B. Berelson, and H. Gaudet: *The People's Choice: How the Voter Makes Up His Mind in a Presidential Campaign* (2nd edition, New York: Columbia University Press, 1948).

more clearly identifiable influence in this direction. There was very infrequent disagreement within immediate families; three fourths of the voters followed the traditional family party preference. Friendship groups were highly influential in achieving conformity, as were formal organizations, including labor unions. These more intimate group influences may well have functioned as surrogates for the broader religious, status, and residential groupings, reinforcing their tendencies toward uniformity, although the evidence on this point is not clear. In general these findings were substantiated by a similar nation-wide study during the election of 1944 and by a study in Elmira, New York, in 1948.[22] Both testify to the significance of group affiliations in regulating attitudes and behavior.

The Group Concept

If the uniformities consequent upon the behavior of men in groups are the key to an understanding of human, including political, behavior, it will be well to specify somewhat more sharply what is involved when the term "group" is used. An excessive preoccupation with matters of definition will only prove a handicap. "Who likes may snip verbal definitions in his old age, when his world has gone crackly and dry."[23] Nevertheless, a few distinctions may be useful.

We find the term "group" applied in two broad senses. Both popularly and in much technical literature it is used to describe any collection of individuals who have some characteristic in common. These are sometimes known as categoric groups. In this sense the word is applied to persons of a given age level, to those of similar income or social status, to people living in a particular area, as Westerners, and to assortments of individuals according to an almost endless variety of similarities—farmers, alcoholics, insurance men, blondes, illiterates, mothers, neurotics, and so on. Although this sense of the word may be useful, it omits one aspect of peculiar importance. The justification for emphasizing groups as basic social units, it will be recalled, is the uniformities of behavior produced through them. Such uniformities do not depend immediately upon such similarities as those mentioned

[22] Sheldon J. Korchin: Psychological Variables in the Behavior of Voters (unpublished Ph.D. dissertation, Harvard University, 1946); Helen Dinerman: "1948 Votes in the Making," *Public Opinion Quarterly*, Vol. 12, no. 4 (Winter, 1948-9), pp. 585-98.

[23] Arthur F. Bentley: *The Process of Government* (Chicago: University of Chicago Press, 1908), p. 199. Copyright by and used with the permission of Arthur F. Bentley.

above, but upon the relationships among the persons involved. The significance of a family group in producing similar attitudes and behaviors among its members lies, not in their physical resemblance or in their proximity, as such, to one another, but in the characteristic relationships among them. These interactions, or relationships, because they have a certain character and frequency, give the group its molding and guiding powers. In fact, they are the group, and it is in this sense that the term will be used.

A minimum frequency of interaction is, of course, necessary before a group in this sense can be said to exist. If a motorist stops along a highway to ask directions of a farmer, the two are interacting, but they can hardly be said to constitute a group except in the most casual sense. If, however, the motorist belongs to an automobile club to the staff of which he and the other members more or less regularly resort for route information, then staff and members can be designated as a group. Similarly, groups in the first sense—collections of people with some common characteristic—may be groups in the proper sense if they interact with some frequency on the basis of their shared characteristics. If a number of mothers interact with one another as they tackle problems of child training, whether through a club or through subscription to a mothers' periodical, they have become a group, though the two forms differ in structure and frequency of interaction. If the members of any aggregation of blondes begin to interact as blondes, alcoholics as alcoholics (or former addicts), people over sixty as aged—they constitute groups. That is, under certain recurring conditions they behave differently with each other than with brunettes, teetotalers, or the young. In fact, the reason why the two senses of the term "group" are so close is that on the basis of experience it is expected that people who have certain attributes in common—neighborhood, consanguinity, occupation—will interact with some frequency. It is the interaction that is crucial, however, not the shared characteristic.[24]

These groups, or patterns of interaction, vary through time in a given society, and they obviously differ sharply in different societies. Why this variation occurs has been only incompletely ascertained, since comparative studies of simple cultures are relatively few and

[24] George A. Lundberg: *Foundations of Sociology* (New York: The Macmillan Company, 1939), pp. 340–1, 360–1. For other definitions from the same general viewpoint, see Sherif and Cantril: *Psychology of Ego-Involvements*, p. 280; William F. Ogburn and Meyer F. Nimkoff: *Sociology* (Boston: Houghton Mifflin Company, 1946), p. 250. Cf. Amos H. Hawley: *Human Ecology: A Theory of Community Structure* (New York: The Ronald Press, 1950), chap. 12.

competent comparative analyses of complex cultures are virtually nonexistent. The most satisfactory hypothesis, however, indicates that the relative complexity of such interactions depends upon the degree of diversity in the everyday business of living. The latter in turn reflects refinement in the techniques by which the society adapts to its environment and the degree of specialization and division of labor that these techniques involve.[25] In a simple society in which all activities—economic, religious, political—are carried on within the family, the division of labor is rudimentary, the techniques are simple, and the patterns of interaction are few and standardized. The latter become more complex as the routine activities of existence alter in conformity with altered techniques for dealing with the environment.

Variations in the division of labor are nowhere more striking than in the activity of house building. An Eskimo igloo is usually constructed by a single family, each man erecting the structure of snow blocks with the aid of his wife and sons. Division of labor is slight, and the interactions among the participants—the patterns of superordination and subordination—are simple. Frequently among a sedentary farming people, however, such as the Riffians of North Africa, relatively elaborate and permanent dwellings are constructed by work parties in which a fairly complex division of labor occurs, based upon more developed techniques and differences in the skill with which particular individuals can perform the various operations:

> Among Riffians, some of the men will bring stones, others will nick them into shape and set them in the walls, while still others puddle clay for the mortar. When the walls are up, two men . . . climb up and set the ridgepole and rafters in place. Meanwhile other men have been cutting young alders and other small saplings near the stream; they peel these and hand them up in bundles. Most of the men have now climbed to the roof, and they tie these sticks to the rafters to form a foundation for the clay.[26]

It is a considerable step from this moderately complex division of labor to the elaborate activities necessary in the construction of an ordinary American house. The collection, preparation, and transporta-

[25] Eliot D. Chapple and Carlton S. Coon: *Principles of Anthropology* (New York: Henry Holt & Company, Inc., 1942), pp. 443–62; Sherif and Cantril: *Psychology of Ego-Involvements*, p. 47.
[26] Chapple and Coon: *Principles of Anthropology*, p. 105. Copyright 1942 by and used with the permission of Henry Holt & Company, Inc.

tion of materials, the elaborate behavior involved in procuring and readying the site, and the welter of specialities that contribute to its erection bespeak a series of complicated interaction patterns.

The complexity and variation of group life among human cultures apparently grow out of the daily activities of their participants and reflect the kinds of techniques that the cultures have developed for dealing with the environment. These techniques, however, are not confined to those directly utilized in providing food, clothing, and shelter. The invention of a written language and its diffusion through a population include techniques of at least equal importance. Similarly, group patterns in a culture in which the priest, or *shaman*, deals with the crises and problems arising from birth, sickness, death, flood, drought, earthquakes, thunderstorms, and eclipses of the sun and moon will be far simpler than the group patterns of a culture where these crises are separately dealt with by various specialists. The activities of the shaman, and those of his functional descendant, the specialized scientist, consist of techniques for adjustment to the environment fully as much as do those of the farmer, the weaver, and the bricklayer. The skills of shaman and scientist are parts of different group patterns and their resulting attitudes and behavioral norms.[27]

The Equilibrium of Institutionalized Groups

In any society certain of these group patterns will be characterized by "a relatively high degree of stability, uniformity, formality, and generality. . . ." These are customarily designated by the term *institution*.[28] The word does not have a meaning sufficiently precise to enable one to state with confidence that one group is an institution whereas another is not.[29] Accepted examples, however, include the courts, legislatures, executives, and other political institutions, families, organized churches, manufacturing establishments, transportation systems, and organized markets. All of these, it will be noted, are rather highly organized (formality); examples of the same type of institution show the same patterns (uniformity); and these patterns are characteristic of, though not necessarily peculiar to, a particular society, such as the American (generality).

[27] Ibid., p. 459.
[28] Lundberg: *Foundations of Sociology*, p. 375.
[29] A more precise, but slightly different usage is employed in Chapple and Coon: *Principles of Anthropology*, p. 287. This usage corresponds to what in the present instance will be called institutionalized groups.

The institutionalized groups that exemplify these behavior patterns, and the patterns themselves, represent almost by definition an equilibrium among the interactions of the participants.[30] In a typical American family, for example, it will be accepted almost unconsciously and without discussion that the male parent will almost always make certain kinds of decisions for the family group, such as what kind of automobile tires to purchase, whether they can afford a new washing machine, and how much money can be spent on the family vacation. He will be expected to take the lead in such actions, and the rest of the family will accept his decisions. The mother will make many more decisions affecting the children than will the father. The husband, moreover, will follow her lead in such things as home decoration, the color of a new car, and the guests to be included at a dinner party. These and the other expected patterns of interaction that make up the institutional group are normally in balance, or in a state of equilibrium. The same situation applies to any institutionalized group, although perhaps in a somewhat more complicated fashion, whether political, economic, or religious.

An equilibrium of this sort must be worked out within an institutionalized group or an institution if it is to survive. That is, the equilibrium must be achieved along standardized lines if the pattern is not to be radically altered or if the particular group is not to be irrevocably disrupted, as, for example, in the case of a family by the separation or divorce of man and wife. It is characteristic of such balanced groups that if the equilibrium is disturbed by some event outside the group, the equilibrium will be restored when the disturbance is over. This tendency to maintain or revert to equilibrium is what is meant by the stability of an institution. The existence of the equilibrium and its stability presumably can be measured by observing the consistency of interaction patterns. Although such observations have been made for simple groups and in a general way for more complicated ones, the possibilities in this area are largely still to be explored. The basic propositions, however, have been sufficiently tested to give them strong presumptive validity.[31]

[30] The following section is based largely upon Chapple and Coon: *Principles of Anthropology*. Some writers use the term "integration" to convey approximately the meaning of the word "equilibrium" intended by Chapple and Coon, although the latter has somewhat more explicit methodological meanings. See Ralph Linton: *The Study of Man* (New York: D. Appleton-Century Company, Inc., 1936), chap. 20.

[31] See E. D. Chapple and C. Arensberg: "Measuring Human Relations," *Genetic Psychology Monographs*, Vol. 32 (August, 1940), pp. 3–147; Chapple and Coon: *Principles of Anthropology, passim*; Warner and Lunt: *The Social*

Although institutionalized groups are characterized by stability, that is, by the tendency to revert to an equilibrium among the interactions of the participants following a disturbance from outside the group, not all disturbances are followed by a return to such a balance. If the disturbance is of great intensity or if it persists over a long period of time, a quite different pattern of interactions is likely to be established in place of the previous one. How serious the interruption must be and how long it must last in order to produce an alteration of the pattern are matters for careful observation, precise or approximate depending upon the use to which the observations are to be put.

An obvious example can be seen in the case of a family that loses one of its members through death. Since the remainder of the group can no longer interact with the deceased, any subsequent stable interaction pattern in the group will differ sharply from the preceding one. The possibilities of establishing a new and stable pattern will depend in part upon the role of the deceased in the previous balance. That is, it will be far more difficult if a parent or an only child has been withdrawn from the group, since relationships with a parent or only child will have constituted a very large segment of the total behavior pattern of the remaining members of the family. The death of one of eight or ten children, however, may be far less disruptive, since almost inevitably a major portion of the total interactions in the group will not have depended upon one of eight or ten children.

If the removal of one member of a family group is not permanent, but temporary, a quite different situation will result. If the male parent is obliged to be away from the rest of the family for a short period of time or if his breadwinning activities temporarily require him to spend less time in the family than has been customary, the equilibrium of the group will be disturbed. The pattern and frequency of interactions will be altered. When the husband-father has returned from his travels, however, or when his duties permit him again to participate in the group with normal frequency, the previous balance probably will be restored.[32]

In the strictly political sphere there are obvious parallel instances of

---

Life of a Modern Community and *The Status System of a Modern Community;* William F. Whyte: *Street Corner Society* (Chicago: University of Chicago Press, 1943); William F. Whyte (ed.): *Industry and Society* (New York: McGraw-Hill Book Company, Inc., 1946).

[32] For a careful critique of the concept *stable equilibrium* and for a discussion of change as a function of a great number of interdependent factors whose effects are cumulative, see Gunnar Myrdal: *An American Dilemma* (New York: Harper and Brothers, 1944), pp. 1065–70.

the effects of disturbances in established patterns of interaction. Thus the death or unexpected resignation of the "boss" of a highly organized political "machine" constitutes a serious disturbance to the group. It will be followed by a more or less prolonged tussle among aspiring successors. Unless some stable new pattern is established under the leadership of one of the previous "boss's" henchmen, the group will disintegrate into competing factions. Similarly, take the case of a trade association whose principal function is the fixing of prices. If it finds its methods outlawed as a result of government action, this disturbance will result in the disappearance of the group unless equilibrium is re-established in one of three ways. First, the group may secure the repeal of the disturbing decision. Second, new methods of performing the function may be developed. Third, an entirely different set of functions may be developed. The first of these results in a restoration of the disturbed pattern, whereas the second and third produce new patterns of interaction.

An important point must be kept in mind in talking of patterns, equilibriums, and the like. These terms do not refer to a mystical entity like a "group mind" that suffers, changes, and dies. A group is "real" in the sense that the interactions that are the group can be observed, and these terms are convenient ways of describing interactions. But one is dealing with the activities of individuals too. To draw any other inference is to become involved in the literally false and disastrously misleading distinction between "the individual" and "society." When men act and interact in consistent patterns, it is reasonable to study these patterns and to designate them by collective terms: *group, institution, nation, legislature, political party, corporation, labor union, family,* and so on. Similarly, it is reasonable for some purposes to study particular individuals, as do the clinical and individual psychologists. But these are merely two approaches to the same thing, not separate entities. Men exist only in society; society is the interactions of men.

It follows, therefore, that when one speaks of a disturbance in an institutional pattern, one refers as well to a disturbance in the individual organisms whose activities have made up the pattern. One of the features of an institutionalized group, as has been noted, is its persistence. It may be thought of as a habit and as being made up of certain habitual activities of a number of individuals. When the pattern is interrupted, there is disturbance or frustration in varying degrees of the habits of the participants, a circumstance that is always unpleasant and may be extremely painful. One may study the consequences for the affected individuals or the changes in the interaction patterns or both, but "the equilibrium of the internal environ- ment [the organism], the equilibrium of the individual in relation to others, and the equilibrium of the group are similar and related phe- nomena." [33]

When the equilibrium of a group (and the equilibriums of its participant individuals) is seriously disturbed, various kinds of be- havior may ensue. If the disturbance is not too great, the group's leaders will make an effort to restore the previous balance. As we shall see in more detail later, this effort may immediately necessitate re- course to the government. Other behaviors may occur if the dis- turbance is serious to the point of disruption. These may be classified in various ways for different purposes. In the present context three broad types of behavior may be distinguished on the basis of their effect upon the existing or potential groups involved.[34] In the first place, the participants may individually engage in various kinds of inappropriate or aberrant or compensatory substitute activities: com- plaining, rumor-mongering, phantasies, alcoholism, drug addiction, in- discriminate aggression, and the like. Thus, in a revolutionary situa- tion where the equilibriums of a wide range of institutions have been disturbed or disrupted, there is a constant possibility that large seg- ments of the populace will engage in undisciplined loafing, irrespon- sible violence, or other activities useless to a successful revolutionary movement. It is the task of revolutionary leadership to limit such be- havior by providing new and "constructive" forms of interaction in the place of those that have been disrupted.[35] Similarly, a sudden change in the relations (interactions) between management and workers in a factory, initiated by the former, may at first result in gossiping, griping, and picking on scapegoats.[36] The adolescent, whose roles are in a highly fluid state alternating between those of an

[33] Chapple and Coon: Principles of Anthropology, p. 47. Copyright 1942 by and used with the permission of Henry Holt & Company, Inc. On this section generally see also Lundberg: Foundations of Sociology, chaps. 1 and 5, esp. pp. 163–73.

[34] A suggestive experiment concerning some of these problems is reported in John Arsenian: A Study of Reactions to Socio-Economic Frustration (un- published Ph.D. dissertation, Harvard University, 1945).

[35] See Harold D. Lasswell: "The Strategy of Revolutionary and War Propaganda," in Public Opinion and World Politics (ed. by Quincy Wright, Chicago: University of Chicago Press, 1933), p. 202; Sherif and Cantril: Psychology of Ego-Involvements, pp. 283–4.

[36] Gordon W. Allport: "The Psychology of Participation," Psychological Review, Vol. 53, no. 3 (May, 1945), p. 122.

adult and those of a dependent child and necessarily involving disequilibrium, will frequently indulge in daydreams and phantasies. These substitutive activities may be harmless or may have neurotic consequences, depending on the situation.

Secondly, the disturbed individuals may increase their activities in other groups in order to restore some sort of personal balance. Thus a state of disequilibrium in the family group may be compensated for by increased interaction in the work group (longer hours at the office) or in a recreational group (increased attendance at meetings of a bowling league, woman's club, and the like).

The third type of behavior that may result from a serious disequilibrium is the formation of new groups that may function to restore the balance. For present purposes this type is the most important of the three, especially if a considerable number of individuals is affected, since these new groups are likely to utilize political means of achieving their objectives. They are likely to become political groups, although they need not do so. Adolescents who cannot establish a stable set of relationships in family groups may join others of the same age level in informal or formal clubs or gangs. This behavior is particularly likely where the adolescent adjustment is made more difficult by special problems such as arise for American-born children of immigrant parents, or for young men and women who are unable to establish stable and satisfactory relationships in an economic group.[37] Among adults new groups are likely to develop or old ones to grow and increase their activity where a serious disequilibrium is produced in family and work groups by a depression or similar economic crisis. Farm movements throughout American history have developed and reached their peaks of strength in times of great economic distress, such as the 1870's and the early 1920's.

When Japanese Americans and Japanese aliens resident on the West Coast were ruthlessly uprooted from their homes in early 1942 and sent to relocation centers, the disruption of established equilibriums was profound. In his distinguished study of the relocation camp at Poston, Arizona, Leighton found ample evidence to this effect: "Although social patterns did exist, some new and some old, more prominent was disarticulation and the *absence of the accustomed habits of human relationship.* People were strangers to each

---

[37] Whyte: *Street Corner Society*; Sherif and Cantril: *Psychology of Ego-Involvements*, chaps. 9 and 10; F. M. Thrasher: *The Gang* (Chicago: University of Chicago Press, 1927); H. W. Zorbaugh: *The Gold Coast and the Slum* (Chicago: University of Chicago Press, 1929).

other in a strange situation and *did not know what to expect.*[38] (Italics added.) This imbalance involved not only the family groups, work groups, and neighborhood groups but more inclusive institutions such as the nation itself. That is, the attitudes and behavior of wide segments of the American people, especially in the West, with whom Niseis in particular had been accustomed to interact peacefully and on a basis of considerable equality, sharply contradicted what most of the victims had been accustomed to expect.[39] The imbalance was not temporary or minor, but persistent and inclusive: "Most aspects of life were lived with acquaintances made since coming to Poston and every individual and every family was trying to adjust to a society that had no framework and no stability. Hardly anyone had a confident expectation as to how anybody with whom he worked or had contact would behave from week to week."[40] Out of this situation a series of new groups emerged, some spontaneously and some under the guidance of the camp's administrators. Among the former were gangs that administered beatings to alleged informers.[41]

Examples of the emergence of new groups in compensation for disturbances in the equilibrium of existing institutionalized groups can be drawn from simpler societies as well as the more complex. When government officials and missionaries arrived in the Papua Territory, New Guinea, in the 1920's, they attempted to alter the ways of the natives and particularly to keep them from holding some of their customary religious ceremonies. The resulting disturbance in the established patterns of interaction was followed by the development of a series of religious movements that spread over New Guinea.[42]

When one views any society as a sort of mosaic of groups, one is confronted with a bewildering array of groups that may be classified in different ways. Thus various characteristic activities seem to be carried on in one group that make it different from another in that particular respect. The examples used in the preceding paragraphs are sufficient illustration. Similarly, although it is an observable fact that all groups involve the same fundamental process, the interaction of individuals, they seem to differ from one another in the form that this

[38] Alexander H. Leighton: *The Governing of Men* (Princeton, N. J.: Princeton University Press, 1945), p. 140. Copyright by and used with the permission of Princeton University Press.

[39] Ibid., pp. 143 ff.

[40] Ibid., p. 158. Copyright 1945 by and used with the permission of Princeton University Press.

[41] Ibid., pp. 149–50, and chaps. 7–9 and 18, generally.

[42] Chapple and Coon: *Principles of Anthropology*, pp. 401–2.

process takes—for example, in the degree of formality. In the pursuit of meaning and understanding, students of society, particularly sociologists, have classified groups on these and other bases, distinguishing and defining classes of groups. These efforts have varied with the purposes, skills, and insights of the classifiers. In addition to the category "institution," which has been examined briefly above, various sub-categories have been designated on the basis of fairly obvious differences of function—the family, economic groups, political groups, and religious groups. On somewhat different bases distinctions are drawn among crowds, publics, assemblies, organizations, mobs, primary groups, secondary groups, in-groups, out-groups, and a host of others.[43]

Interest Groups

Various of these established designations will be useful from time to time, but one identifying term, which was used without definition in the previous chapter, may be discussed at some length, since it involves the central concern of these pages, the term "interest group." Like so many terms associated with the processes of government, it has been used for the purposes of polemics so freely that it has acquired certain emotional connotations which may render it ambiguous when used in analysis. *Political, partisan,* and even the word *politics* itself share with *interest, vested interest, special interest,* and *interest group,* among others, a connotation of impropriety and selfishness that almost denies them the neutral precision requisite to careful discussion.

As used here "interest group" refers to any group that, on the basis of one or more shared attitudes, makes certain claims upon other groups in the society for the establishment, maintenance, or enhancement of forms of behavior that are implied by the shared attitudes. In earlier paragraphs of this chapter it was indicated that from interaction in groups arise certain common habits of response, which may be called norms, or shared attitudes. These afford the participants frames of reference for interpreting and evaluating events and behaviors. In this respect all groups are interest groups because they are shared-attitude groups. In some groups at various points in time, however, a second kind of common response emerges, in addition to the frames of reference. These are shared attitudes toward what is needed or

[43] See, for example, Lundberg: *Foundations of Sociology,* chap. 5; and Ogburn and Nimkoff: *Sociology,* chap. 9 and *passim.*

wanted in a given situation, observable as demands or claims upon other groups in the society. The term "interest group" will be reserved here for those groups that exhibit both aspects of the shared attitudes.

The shared attitudes, moreover, constitute the interests. It has been suggested that a distinction be made between the two terms, reserving the latter to designate "the objects toward which these . . . [attitudes] are directed." [44] Such a distinction may be highly misleading. If, for example, reference were made to oil interests, one would presumably be referring, among other things, to certain elements in the physical environment, petroleum and its by-products. These features, however, have no significance in society apart from the activities of men. There were no oil attitudes prior to the time when the productive behaviors of men led them to do something with petroleum.[45] As a consequence of the use of oil, an array of attitudes with respect to that use has developed—that it should not be wasted, that it should be marketed in a particular way, that it should be produced by many small groups or enterprises, that it should be controlled by an international organization, and so on. Some of these attitudes are represented by interest groups asserting that the behaviors implied by the attitudes should be encouraged, discouraged, or altered. The physical features of oil production have no significance for the student of society apart from the attitudes, or interests, and the behaviors that they suggest.

Definition of the interest group in this fashion has a number of distinct advantages in the task of political analysis. In the first place, it permits the identification of various potential as well as existing interest groups. That is, it invites examination of an interest whether or not it is found at the moment as one of the characteristics of a particular organized group. Although no group that makes claims upon other groups in the society will be found without an interest or interests, it is possible to examine interests that are not at a particular point in time the basis of interactions among individuals, but that may become such. Without the modern techniques for the measurement of attitude and opinion, this position would indeed be risky, since it would invite the error of ascribing an interest to individuals quite apart from any overt behavior that they might display.[46] In the

[44] Robert M. MacIver: "Interests," *Encyclopaedia of the Social Sciences.* Cf. Avery Leiserson: *Administrative Regulation: A Study in Representation of Interests* (Chicago: University of Chicago Press, 1942), pp. 1–10.

[45] Cf Bentley: *The Process of Government,* pp. 193–4.

[46] Ibid., p. 213.

scientific study of society only frustration and defeat are likely to follow an attempt to deal with data that are not directly observable. Even the most insistent defenders of the scientific position, however, admit that, although activity is the basic datum of social science, a "becoming" stage of activity must be recognized as a phase of activity if any segment of a moving social situation is to be understood. There are, in other words, potential activities, or "tendencies of activity." [47] These tendencies are the central feature of the most widely accepted social psychological definition of attitude. Gordon W. Allport, after examining a series of definitions, arrived at his own generally used statement: "An attitude is a mental and neural *state of readiness*, organized through experience, exerting a directive or dynamic influence upon the individual's response to all objects and situations with which it is related." [48] On the basis of widely held attitudes that are not expressed in interaction, therefore, it is possible to talk of potential interest groups.

In the second place, as these statements suggest, this concept of interest group permits attention to what Lundberg calls the "degree of integrative interaction." [49] The frequency, or rate, of interaction will in part determine the primacy of a particular group affiliation in the behavior of an individual and, as will be indicated in more detail later, it will be of major importance in determining the relative effectiveness with which a group asserts its claims upon other groups. [50] This approach affords all the advantages and none of the disadvantages that once accrued to the sociologists' concepts of "primary groups" and "secondary groups," meaning by the former face-to-face interaction as opposed to indirect contacts such as those made through the media of mass communication. Before the enormous expansion and development of the latter techniques, and still in societies where they have not penetrated, it was a verifiable fact that solidarity of group behavior depended largely upon physical proximity. Frequent face-to-face contact in no small measure accounted for the influence of such primary groups as the family, the neighborhood, and the like. As the social functions performed by the family institution in our society have declined, some of these secondary groups, such as labor unions, have achieved a rate of interaction that equals or surpasses

[47] Ibid, pp. 184 ff.
[48] Gordon W. Allport: "Attitudes," in Carl Murchison (ed.): *A Handbook of Social Psychology* (Worcester, Mass.: Clark University Press, 1935), chap. 17.
[49] Lundberg: *Foundations of Sociology*, p. 310.
[50] See below, chaps. 6 and 7.

that of certain of the primary groups. This shift in importance has been facilitated largely by the development of means of communication that permit frequent interaction among individuals not in face-to-face contact or not continuously so.

In this connection note the confidence that James Madison, in seeking restraints upon the "mischiefs of faction" (interest groups), placed in "the greater obstacles opposed to the concert" of such groups by the "extent of the Union."[51] Such faith in physical dispersion had some basis in a period when it took a week to travel a distance of three hundred miles. It would not be true to say that primary groups no longer achieve the integration once ascribed to them. A recent study has indicated, for example, that the prolonged resistance of the German army in the face of repeated defeats in 1944 and 1945 was a result largely of the solidarity and continued structural integrity of such primary groups as the squad.[52] It is primarily from the degree of interaction that the face-to-face group fosters, however, that its influence is derived. A high degree may also be achieved through secondary means.

In the third place, this concept of the interest group permits us to evaluate the significance of formal organization. The existence of neither the group nor the interest is dependent upon formal organization, although that feature has significance, particularly in the context of politics. Organization indicates merely a stage or degree of interaction.[53] The fact that one interest group is highly organized whereas another is not or is merely a potential group—whether the interest involved is that of affording more protection to consumers, greater privileges for brunettes, or more vigorous enforcement of civil rights—is a matter of great significance at any particular moment. It does not mean, however, that the momentarily weaker group, or interest, will inevitably remain so. Events may easily produce an increased rate of interaction among the affected individuals to the point where formal organization or a significant interest group will emerge and greater influence will ensue. The point may be illustrated by noting that this increased rate of interaction is usually

[51] *The Federalist*, No. 10; see also No. 51 for similar arguments.

[52] Edward A. Shils and Morris Janowitz: "Cohesion and Disintegration in the Wehrmacht in World War II," *Public Opinion Quarterly*, Vol. 12, no. 2 (Summer, 1948), pp. 280–315.

[53] For an influential characterization along similar lines of the phenomenon of organization, see John M. Gaus: "A Theory of Organization in Public Administration" in John M. Gaus, Leonard D. White, and Marshall E. Dimock: *The Frontiers of Public Administration* (Chicago: University of Chicago Press, 1936), pp. 66–91.

what is meant when the journalists speak of "an aroused public opinion."

Finally, this use of the concept also gives a proper perspective to the political activities of many interest groups that are the principal concern of this book. Although a characteristic feature of these groups is that they make claims upon other groups in the society, these claims may be asserted or enforced by means of a variety of techniques and through any of the institutions of the society, not merely the government. An interest group concentrating upon replacing the valuable shade trees in a village adjacent to a large gentleman's farm may achieve its objective by prevailing upon the baronial family to purchase the trees and pay for their planting. A group interested in the protection of certain moralities among the younger generation may secure the behaviors they desire in part through inducing motion picture producers to permit its officers to censor films before they are released.[54] Whether a group operates in such fashions as these or attempts to work through governmental institutions, thereby becoming a political interest group, may be a function of circumstances; the government may have primary or exclusive responsibility in the area involved, as in the war-time allocation of scarce materials. Or the choice between political and other modes of operation may be a function of technique; it may be easier or more effective to achieve temperance objectives through the government than by prevailing upon people to sign pledges. The process is essentially the same whether the interest group operates through other institutions or becomes political.

To summarize briefly, an interest group is a shared-attitude group that makes certain claims upon other groups in the society. If and when it makes its claims through or upon any of the institutions of government, it becomes a political interest group. These are the meanings that we shall attach to these terms throughout this book. At times it will be convenient to omit the modifying term "political" in discussing interest group activity in the government. In such instances it will be clear from the context whether we are dealing with political interest groups or with groups that are making claims otherwise than through or upon the institutions of government.

It follows that any group in the society may function as an interest group and that any of them may function as political interest groups, that is, those that make their claims through or upon governmental institutions. An economic group, such as a corporation, that seeks a special tax ruling is in that respect functioning as a political interest

[54] Ruth A. Inglis: *Freedom of the Movies* (Chicago: University of Chicago Press, 1947), chaps. 3–5.

group. Trade associations, labor unions, philatelic societies, world government societies, political parties, professional organizations, and a host of others can and do seek to achieve all or a portion of their objectives by operating through or upon the institutions of government. Even a family group, whose prestige or financial interests approach imperial proportions, may make such claims. It will be useful and significant to identify or classify such groups according to the regularity or the success with which such claims are advanced through these channels. Even the casual observer will give somewhat different places to the philatelic society that prevails upon the Postmaster General to provide special handling for letters bearing a new stamp issue and a trade association that seeks legislation to protect it against its competitors. These may sensibly be placed in separate subcategories, but they both display the fundamental characteristics of such groups.

Seen in these terms, is an interest group inherently "selfish"? In the first place, such judgments have no value for a scientific understanding of government or the operation of society. Schematically, they represent nothing more than the existence of a conflicting interest, possibly, but not necessarily, involving another group or groups.[55] Judgments of this kind are and must be made by all citizens in their everyday life, but they are not properly a part of the systematic analysis of the social process. Secondly, many such political interest groups are from almost any point of view highly altruistic. One need only recall those groups that have consistently risen to defend the basic guarantees of the American constitution, to improve the lot of the underprivileged, or to diffuse the advantages stemming from scientific advance. Evaluations such as these may be made of particular groups, depending on the observer's own attitudes, but, as was indicated in the preceding chapter, they will not facilitate one's understanding of the social system of which the groups are a part.

Where does the term "pressure group" fit into this scheme? This expression, perhaps more than any other, has been absorbed into the language of political abuse. It carries a load of emotional connotations indicating selfish, irresponsible insistence upon special privileges. Any group that regards itself as disinterested and altruistic will usually repudiate with vigor any attempt to attach this label to it, a fact that suggests that the term has little use except to indicate a value judgment concerning those groups of which one disapproves. Some

[55] See, for example, the transparent interest preferences involved in the interesting popular treatment by Kenneth G. Crawford: *The Pressure Boys: The Inside Story of Lobbying in America* (New York: Julius Messner, Inc., 1939).

writers, however, in a courageous effort to reclaim for the term a core of neutral meaning, use it as a synonym for "political interest group." [56] This usage has certain disadvantages aside from the obvious possibility that many readers will be unable to accept the suggestion that "the objectives of the pressure group may be good or bad; the group may be animated by the highest moral purpose or it may be driving for the narrowest kind of class gain." [57] If the word "pressure" has more than a simply figurative meaning, it suggests a method or a category of methods that may be used by an interest group to achieve its objectives.[58] Even if the methods implied can be described precisely, unless we can demonstrate that all political interest groups use them, the term "pressure group" will indicate merely a stage or phase of group activity and will not serve as a satisfactory equivalent for "interest group" or "political interest group," as these have been defined.[59] In view of the improbability of satisfying the conditions specified, it will be avoided in these pages in favor of the more inclusive and more nearly neutral term.

Associations as Interest Groups

Any group, as we have already seen, may function from time to time as an interest group. There is one type of group, which almost invariably operates as an interest group, that has become of such importance in our culture that it deserves special treatment. This type may be called the association. We are using this familiar term in a technical sense. The justification for doing so is that we are here making use of a recent and highly significant body of research in the measurement of human relations in which this concept has been developed to

[56] See, for example, V. O. Key, Jr.: *Politics, Parties, and Pressure Groups* (2nd edition, New York: Thomas Y. Crowell Company, 1947). Key, however, uses the terms somewhat more narrowly, confining them to "private associations formed to influence public policy" (p. 15). A similar use of the term will be found in Ogburn and Nimkoff: *Sociology*, p. 287.

[57] Key: *Politics, Parties, and Pressure Groups*, pp. 16–17.

[58] Robert M. MacIver: "Pressures, Social," *Encyclopaedia of the Social Sciences*.

[59] Mary E. Dillon specifies the method of propaganda as the distinguishing characteristic of the pressure group, a usage that does not make it the equivalent of the political interest group. "Pressure Groups," *American Political Science Review*, Vol. 36, no. 3 (June, 1942), pp. 471–81. The best case for a specific meaning of the term "pressure" can be made in connection with the effect of a group on its own membership rather than on those outside its boundaries.

designate a type of group whose genesis and functions are unique.[60] The association is a type of group that grows out of what have been called tangent relations.[61] In a society of any appreciable complexity we find many institutionalized groups and well-defined subdivisions within them. We also find in these cases that there are individuals who participate in or are common to more than one such group, or subdivision. Such groups or subdivisions are said to be tangent to one another through the individuals who participate in both. Thus, to use a simple example, a family and a school are tangent to one another through a child who interacts in both. The workers in the motor assembly department and those in the body stamping department of the Ford Motor Company are tangent to one another through the managers who direct both. The General Motors Corporation is tangent to the International Harvester Company through the officers of the United Automobile Workers of America, who lead labor unions in both companies. This tangency between groups may exist not only through an individual, but through a third group by which the tangent groups are similarly affected or through a common technique.

When a disturbance occurs within two or more of these tangent groups, or subdivisions, the affected individuals are likely to seek an adjustment through interaction with others in the tangent group, with whom they have "something in common." Thus in a family that is disturbed by a child's poor performance in school, the mother is likely to visit (interact with) the teacher or principal to discuss the problem. This interaction is called a tangent relation. Similar tangent relations may occur between workers in the departments of the Ford Motor Company in consequence of an unusual "speed-up" in the assembly lines. They may occur also between officials of General Motors and International Harvester as a result of extreme demands by the U.A.W. leaders.

An association is said to emerge when a considerable number of people have established tangent relations of the same sort and when they interact with one another regularly on that basis. It is a group, a continuing pattern of interactions, that functions as a "bridge" between persons in two or more institutionalized groups or subdivisions thereof. The word "tangent" is appropriate because it suggests a set of relationships that are in a sense peripheral to those that define the cen-

[60] See Chapple and Coon: *Principles of Anthropology*, chap. 17, from which this section is adapted; the items cited in note 31, above; and note 62, below.

[61] Chapple and Coon: *Principles of Anthropology*, pp. 337 ff.

tral functions of the institutionalized group. Thus, if, out of the family-school tangency mentioned above, a number of mothers and teachers interact fairly regularly with one another in consequence of their tangent relations, an association may be said to exist. Such is the nature of the Parent-Teachers Association that is a familiar feature of a great many American communities. The P.T.A. has its origins in disturbances in the equilibriums of individuals in two or more institutionalized groups. Mothers and teachers may interact in casual tangent relations for an indefinite period of time without an association (group) emerging. At some point a disturbance occurs in these casual relations—owing to a sudden increase in their frequency or to a crisis resulting from the failure of a number of students to be accepted by a university (if the school is a high school) or from an increase in juvenile delinquency, playground accidents or any number of such things—and it is felt that "something must be done." If that "something" involves establishing the teachers and mothers as an habitually interacting group, an association has been formed.

As the above example suggests, the function of an association is to stabilize the relations of individuals in tangent groups. This stability it may create at the expense of disturbing the accustomed behavior of those through whom the participant individuals are tangent. Thus the formation of the P.T.A. may result in restraining some of the disapproved behaviors of the school children, such as studying with the radio on, loafing at a pool room, or engaging in dangerous play. The formation of a labor union may similarly disturb the habitual actions of managers by preventing their paying whatever wages they wish to and by equivalent actions. The processes of the association—which may involve a formal constitution, officers, and meetings governed by Robert's *Rules of Order,* or which may depend upon certain largely informal techniques—facilitate among the participant individuals an adjustment of the equilibriums within the institutions disturbed by the events that gave rise to the association. If the association persists, that is, if it meets satisfactorily the needs of the participants that grow out of their tangent relations, similar and related disturbances in the institutional groups will also be adjusted by the association.

The simple example of the Parent-Teachers Association can be supplemented by hundreds and thousands in our society whose origins and functions are of the same type. A few additional cases will suffice here, since the development of these groups will be discussed in more detail in the following two chapters. The labor union organizes tangent relations among workers that are created by workers' contacts with management (or perhaps an employers' association). Thus, when the character or frequency of the customary interactions between workers and management is disturbed, the workers may increase the frequency of their tangent interactions. This increase may result in the formation of an association (labor union). Its function is that of a "compensatory mechanism" that stabilizes the relations among workers and tends to order those between management and workers through the union hierarchy. It is a "bridge" between workers in different plants or different departments of the same plant. Similarly, the merchants of a community are tangent to one another through their customers and through the town government. Consequently a disturbance in these relations, such as is reflected in a slogan like "patronize home enterprise" or such as might follow upon a drastic increase in taxes on business property, may result in the formation of a merchants association, chamber of commerce, or board of trade. This association would act as a bridge between the mercantile establishments, would stabilize their relationships, and would tend to order their relations with their customers or with the city government. Again, businessmen in a particular line have tangent relations through their customers (or "the market"), the government, the labor unions, and their specialty. Disturbances in the accustomed interactions in these areas are likely to produce a trade association or employers association. College students, also, have tangent relations through the officers of the school. In the 1830's these relations were disturbed by the resistance of college faculties to the introduction of "modern" secular literature and similar materials into the curricula. In part for this reason student associations—fraternities—developed as literary societies. They still constitute a means of stabilizing relations between their members and college authorities, though along somewhat different lines. Other fraternal societies, professional associations, political parties, philanthropic organizations, and a host of others are of the same type.

In all societies the association operates to relate and stabilize the interactions among persons in basic institutionalized groups.[62] The association also has the attitude-forming, behavior-influencing group functions that we discussed earlier in the chapter.

Because of their functions, moreover, associations are peculiarly likely to operate both as interest groups and as political interest groups. The political role constitutes their importance in the present

[62] Ibid., pp. 424–5 and 426–9. See also Eliot D. Chapple: The Theory of Associations as Applied to Primitive and Civilized Communities with Special Emphasis Upon the Functional Approach (unpublished Ph.D. dissertation, Harvard University, 1933).

context. In the process of affording a means of adjustment for the members of various institutionalized groups, they are likely to make claims upon other groups not part of the institutions of government —as the labor union upon management. They are equally likely to assert claims upon or through the government. So common is this tendency that some students choose to limit the concept of the political interest group to groups that qualify as associations.[63] Although a large proportion of the familiar political interest groups are of this type, it is not strictly accurate, for the reasons indicated in an earlier paragraph, to omit from the category other types of groups whose relations with governmental institutions are of the same general character. The Standard Oil Company of New Jersey is not an association. Nevertheless, it may operate as a significant political interest group. In addition, its officers may function through an association, such as the National Association of Manufacturers, that is also a political interest group. Any group in the society may at one time or another operate as a political interest group. The considerable political importance of associations, that is, the groups formed around tangent relations, lies not only in their strong tendency to operate through or upon the institutions of government but in their stabilizing functions, in the larger resources of various kinds that they can command as compared with any of the participant elements, and in their great numbers in our society. These points we shall examine more fully in the following two chapters.

Conclusion

Stating the argument of this chapter in general terms, we find that any society is composed of groups, the habitual interactions of men. Any society, even one employing the simplest and most primitive techniques, is a mosaic of overlapping groups of various specialized sorts. Through these formations a society is experienced by its members, and in this way it must be observed and understood by its students. These group affiliations, with varying degrees of completeness and finality, form and guide the attitudes and therefore the behavior of their participants. How completely and finally a particular group controls the attitudes and behavior of its members is a matter to be determined through observation of the degree to which habitual patterns of interaction persist. The frequency and persistence of interac-

---

[63] See Key: *Politics, Parties, and Pressure Groups.*

tions within a group will determine its strength. The groups that form this mosaic emerge from the particular techniques of the society. Some, especially associations, which constitute a major concern of these pages, develop more immediately out of crises and disturbances within those groups in which the basic techniques of the society are institutionalized. The moving pattern of a complex society such as the one in which we live is one of changes and disturbances in the habitual subpatterns of interaction, followed by a return to the previous state of equilibrium or, if the disturbances are intense or prolonged, by the emergence of new groups whose specialized function it is to facilitate the establishment of a new balance, a new adjustment in the habitual interactions of individuals.

3

Groups and Government:
Introduction

———————

GOVERNMENT, like all other social institutions, grows out of the relationships existing between man and man—their character, their complexity, and the disturbances to which they are subject. Although it would be erroneous to assert that this observation is subject to historical verification, it can be supported by evidence of a different sort, but of equal value. Accounts of the so-called primitive societies report the emergence of differentiated institutions, resembling our governments in their basic functions, that include all family groups within a given territory. These appear as a result of a new kind of interaction among the persons involved or the increased frequency and persistence of a previously familiar but casual relationship. Examples of this sort would include group organization for warfare, whether for defense, pillage, or conquest. Warfare is by no means the exclusive source, however, for similar governmental institutions seem to have developed out of the necessity for ordering such relationships as those consequent upon a new technique of hunting or upon new sources of wealth.[1] The most significant aspect of these data is that even in its nascent stages government functions to establish and maintain a measure of order in the relationships among groups for various purposes. What a particular government is under these circumstances, its "form" and its "methods," depends upon the character of the groups and the purposes it serves.

[1] See Chapple and Coon: *Principles of Anthropology*, chap. 14; and Thomas: *Primitive Behavior*, chap. 14.

Observation of the changes in activity that have occurred within recent years in American government supports the validity of this view, as this and subsequent chapters will attempt to demonstrate. Groups are "a part" of American politics, as was indicated in Chapter 1, and they have always constituted an aspect of politics. In addition, they are so intimately related to the daily functioning of those constitutionalized groups—legislature, chief executives, administrative agencies, and even courts—that make up the institution of government that the latter cannot adequately be described if these relationships are not recognized as the weft of the fabric. Unless one denies, first, that the notion of differentiations in the habitual interactions of men is synonymous with the notion of groups and, second, that government is made up of just such patterns of habitual interaction, acceptance of groups as lying at the heart of the process of government is unavoidable.

It is remarkable that such recognition is so rarely encountered. The "lobby" and the "pressure group" are familiar to many, but they are accepted in the way that the typhoid bacillus is, as an organism that is a feature of civilized existence but that must be eradicated if society is to develop and prosper. The interest group as defined in these pages is far less familiar. Since the publication in 1908 of A. F. Bentley's pioneering book, *The Process of Government*, academicians have given increasing attention to political groups.[2] As often as not, however, the assumptions implicit in such treatments have been close to those popularly held. The so-called pluralist school of political philosophers, which reached the height of its vogue in the first quarter of this century, produced some brilliant insights concerning the group basis of society. Although these writers recognized multiple patterns of group affiliations or loyalties, nevertheless, they did not consistently see in these the functional basis of the institution of

[2] Among the most significant of these studies are the following: Peter H. Odegard: *Pressure Politics: The Story of the Anti-Saloon League* (New York: Columbia University Press, 1928); Herring: *Group Representation Before Congress* (1929); Harwood L. Childs: *Labor and Capital in National Politics* (Columbus, Ohio: Ohio State University Press, 1930); E. E. Schattschneider: *Politics, Pressures and the Tariff* (New York: Prentice-Hall, Inc., 1935); E. Pendleton Herring: *Public Administration and the Public Interest* (New York: McGraw-Hill Book Company, Inc., 1936); Belle Zeller: *Pressure Politics in New York* (New York: Prentice-Hall, Inc., 1937); Dayton D. McKean: *Pressures on the Legislature of New Jersey* (New York: Columbia University Press, 1938); Oliver Garceau: *The Political Life of the American Medical Association* (Cambridge, Mass.: Harvard University Press, 1941).

government; they were so bent upon discrediting prevailing conceptions of the state that they frequently overlooked the central significance of their own point of view.[3]

Difficulties in a Group Interpretation of Politics

Since we are engaged in an effort to develop a conception of the political process in the United States that will account adequately for the role of groups, particularly interest groups, it will be appropriate to take account of some of the factors that have been regarded as obstacles to such a conception and that have caused such groups to be neglected in many explanations of the dynamics of government. Perhaps the most important practical reason for this neglect is that the significance of groups has only fairly recently been forced to the attention of political scientists by the tremendous growth in the number of formally organized groups in the United States within the last few decades. It is difficult and unnecessary to attempt to date the beginning of such attention, but Herring in 1929, in his groundbreaking book, *Group Representation Before Congress*, testified to the novelty of the observations he reported when he stated: "There has developed in this government an extra-legal machinery of as integral and of as influential a nature as the system of party government that has long been an essential part of the government. . . ."[4] Some implications of this development are not wholly compatible with some of the proverbial notions about representative government held by specialists as well as laymen, as we have earlier noted. This apparent incompatibility has obstructed the inclusion of group behaviors in an objective description of the governmental process.

More specifically, it is usually argued that any attempt at the interpretation of politics in terms of group patterns inevitably "leaves something out" or "destroys something essential" about the processes of "our" government. On closer examination, we find this argument suggesting that two "things" are certain to be ignored: the individual,

---

[3] The best single treatment of these writers is Kung Chuan Hsiao: *Political Pluralism* (London: Kegan Paul, Trench, Trubner & Company, Ltd., 1927), especially chap. 6. See also Dewey: *The Public and Its Problems*, pp. 73–4.

[4] Herring: *Group Representation Before Congress*, p. 18. Copyright 1929 by and used with the permission of The Brookings Institution.

and a sort of totally inclusive unity designated by such terms as "society" and "the state."

The argument that the individual is ignored in any interpretation of politics as based upon groups seems to assume a differentiation or conflict between "the individual" and some such collectivity as the group. Those who propose this difficulty often state or imply the view that society is a series of individual persons "each assumed to have definite independent 'existence' and isolation, each in his own *locus* apart from every other." [5] They further assume that when this individual is a part of a group he becomes a different person in some obscure fashion, that his "complex character" experiences "a degeneration or simplification." [6]

Such assumptions need not present any difficulties in the development of a group interpretation of politics, because they are essentially unwarranted. They simply do not square with the kind of evidence concerning group affiliations and individual behavior that we presented in the preceding chapter. We do not, in fact, find individuals otherwise than in groups; complete isolation in space and time is so rare as to be an almost hypothetical situation. It is equally demonstrable that the characteristics of any interest group, including the activities by which we identify it, are governed by the attitudes and the circumstances that gave rise to the interactions of which it consists. These are variable factors, and, although the role played by a particular individual may be quite different in a lynch mob from that of the same individual in a meeting of the church deacons, the attitudes and behaviors involved in both are as much a part of his personality as is his treatment of his family. "The individual" and "the group" are at most merely convenient ways of classifying behavior, two ways of approaching the same phenomena, not different things.

The persistence among nonspecialists of the notion of an inherent conflict between "the individual" and "the group" or "society" is understandable in view of the doctrines of individualism that have underlain various political and economic conflicts over the past three centuries. The notion persists also because it harmonizes with a view of the isolated and independent individual as the "cause" of complicated human events. The personification of events, quite apart from any ethical considerations, is a kind of shorthand convenient in every-

---

[5] Arthur F. Bentley: *Behavior Knowledge Fact* (Bloomington, Indiana: The Principia Press, Inc., 1935), p. 29.

[6] E. F. M. Durbin: *The Politics of Democratic Socialism* (London: George Routledge & Sons, Ltd., 1940), p. 52.

day speech and, like supernatural explanations of natural phenomena, has a comforting simplicity. Explanations that take into account multiple causes, including group affiliations, are difficult. The "explanation" of a national complex like the Soviet Union wholly in terms of a Stalin or the "description" of the intricacies of the American government entirely in terms of a Roosevelt is quick and easy.

We need not reckon with such notions of personal causation except as data on the behavior of certain segments of the society. Similarly, we need not accept at their face value the assertions of an inherent conflict between "the individual" and "society." The latter are merely the terms in which protests against particular social formations, such as the mercantilist system and a limited franchise, gained advantage by being clothed in the language of universals. They are not verified propositions about society in general.

It is not intended, however, that we should reject the general human values asserted in the militant doctrines of individualism. Since we have assumed the task of developing a conception of the political process in the United States that will enable us to determine the bearing of group organization upon the survival of representative democracy, we have in fact assumed the importance of those values. Far from leaving them out of account, we are primarily concerned with their place in the process of group politics.

We do not wish, moreover, to deny that individual differences exist or that there is evidence to support the notion of individuality. This assertion would be nonsense. No conception of society or of the political process would be adequate if it failed to accommodate the hard facts of personality differences. Although we shall have to deal quite explicitly with these, nevertheless, they should offer no insuperable obstacles. We have already admitted the essential facts of individuality when we have noted the infinite variations in biological inheritance and when we have pointed out that the experiences, the group experiences, of no two persons can be identical in all significant respects. It follows that the personality of any reasonably normal individual is not wholly accounted for by any single group affiliation. This proposition not only must be accepted; it must be a central element in any satisfactory explanation of the political process in group terms.

The second major difficulty allegedly inherent in any attempt at a group interpretation of the political process is that such an explanation inevitably must ignore some greater unity designated as society or the state. Thus MacIver sees such sharply different schools of political thought as the *laissez-faire* Spencerians, the Marxists, the pluralists, and group interpretations such as Bentley's, as being alike in one respect: "that they denied or rejected the integrating function of the state." [7]

Many of those who place particular emphasis upon this difficulty assume explicitly or implicitly that there is an interest of the nation as a whole, universally and invariably held and standing apart from and superior to those of the various groups included within it. This assumption is close to the popular dogmas of democratic government based on the familiar notion that if only people are free and have access to "the facts," they will all want the same thing in any political situation. It is no derogation of democratic preferences to state that such an assertion flies in the face of all that we know of the behavior of men in a complex society. Were it in fact true, not only the interest group but even the political party should properly be viewed as an abnormality. The differing experiences and perceptions of men not only encourage individuality but also, as the previous chapter has shown, inevitably result in differing attitudes and conflicting group affiliations.[8] "There are," says Bentley in his discussion of this error of the social whole, "always some parts of the nation to be found arrayed against other parts." [9] Even in war, when a totally inclusive interest should be apparent if it is ever going to be, we always find pacifists, conscientious objectors, spies, and subversives, who reflect interests opposed to those of "the nation as a whole."

There is a political significance in assertions of a totally inclusive interest within a nation. Particularly in times of crisis, such as an international war, such claims are a tremendously useful promotional device by means of which a particularly extensive group or league of groups tries to reduce or eliminate opposing interests. Such is the pain attendant upon not "belonging" to one's "own" group that if a normal person can be convinced that he is the lone dissenter to an otherwise universally accepted agreement, he usually will conform. This pressure accounts at least in part for the number of prewar pacifists who, when the United States entered World War II, accepted the draft or volunteered. Assertion of an inclusive "national" or "public interest" is an effective device in many less critical situations as well. In themselves, these claims are part of the data of politics. However, they do not de-

---

[7] Robert M. MacIver: *The Web of Government* (New York: The Macmillan Company, 1947), p. 56. Copyright by Robert M. MacIver and used with the permission of The Macmillan Company.

[8] For a trenchant criticism of this notion see Walter Lippmann: *Public Opinion* (New York: The Macmillan Company, 1922), chap. 1.

[9] Bentley: *The Process of Government*, p. 220. Copyright 1908 by and used with the permission of Arthur F. Bentley.

scribe any actual or possible political situation within a complex modern nation. In developing a group interpretation of politics, therefore, we do not need to account for a totally inclusive interest, because one does not exist.

Denying the existence of an interest of the nation as a whole does not completely dispose of the difficulty raised by those who insist that a group interpretation must omit "the state." We cannot deny the obvious fact that we are examining a going political system that is supported or at least accepted by a large proportion of the society. We cannot account for such a system by adding up in some fashion the National Association of Manufacturers, the Congress of Industrial Organizations, the American Farm Bureau Federation, the American Legion, and other groups that come to mind when "lobbies" and "pressure groups" are mentioned. Even if the political parties are added to the list, the result could properly be designated as "a view which seems hardly compatible with the relative stability of the political system. . . ." [10] Were such the exclusive ingredients of the political process in the United States, the entire system would have torn itself apart long since.

If these various organized interest groups more or less consistently reconcile their differences, adjust, and accept compromises, we must acknowledge that we are dealing with a system that is not accounted for by the "sum" of the organized interest groups in the society. We must go farther to explain the operation of such ideals or traditions as constitutionalism, civil liberties, representative responsibility, and the like. These are not, however, a sort of disembodied metaphysical influence, like Mr. Justice Holmes's "brooding omnipresence." We know of the existence of such factors only from the behavior and the habitual interactions of men. If they exist in this fashion, they are interests. We can account for their operation and for the system by recognizing such interests as representing what in the preceding chapter we called potential interest groups in the "becoming" stage of activity. "It is certainly true," as Bentley has made clear, "that we must accept a . . . group of this kind as an interest group itself." [11] It makes no difference that we cannot find the home office and the executive secretary of such a group. Organization in this formal sense, as we have seen, represents merely a stage or degree of interaction

[10] Robert M. MacIver: "Pressures, Social," *Encyclopaedia of the Social Sciences.*

[11] Bentley: *The Process of Government*, p. 219. Copyright 1908 by and used with permission of Arthur F. Bentley. On this general point, see pp. 218–20 and 371–2.

that may or may not be significant at any particular point in time. Its absence does not mean that these interests do not exist, that the familiar "pressure groups" do not operate as if such potential groups were organized and active, or that these interests may not move from the potential to the organized stage of activity.

It thus appears that the two major difficulties supposedly obstacles to a group interpretation of the political process are not insuperable. We can employ the fact of individuality and we can account for the existence of the state without doing violence to the evidence available from the observed behaviors of men and groups. The development of this interpretation must wait until we have examined more closely the operation of groups and government. It is important to bear in mind, however, that any complete conception of the political process must incorporate the facts of individual differences and must reckon with the inclusive system of relationships that we call the state.

Group Diversity and Governmental Complexity

For all but those who see in the growth of new groups the evil ways of individual men, it is obvious that the trend toward an increasing diversity of groups functionally attached to the institutions of government is a reflection of the characteristics and needs, to use a somewhat ambiguous term, of a complex society. This conclusion stems necessarily from the functional concept of groups presented in the preceding chapter. Not all institutions of a society necessarily become complex simultaneously or at an even rate, of course. The religious institution may be highly complicated, for example, whereas economic institutions or the family may remain relatively simple. The political institutions of any culture are a peculiarly sensitive barometer of the complexity of the society, however, owing to their special function. Since they operate to order the relationships among various groups in the society, any considerable increase in the types of such groups, or any major change in the nature of their interrelationships, will be reflected subsequently in the operation of the political system. For example, as the Tanala of Madagascar shifted from a dry-land method of rice growing to a method based on irrigation, a series of consequent changes in the culture gradually took place. Village mobility disappeared in favor of settled communities, since the constant search for fertile soil was no longer necessary; individual ownership in land emerged, since the supply of appropriate soil was sharply limited; a system of slavery was developed; and the joint family was broken up into its constituent households. Finally, as a result of these changes in relationships and interests, and with the introduction of conflicts stemming from differences in wealth, the decentralized and almost undifferentiated political institution became a centralized tribal king ship.[12]

Alterations in response to technological or other changes are more rapid and more noticeable in a complex society in which a larger number of institutionalized groups are closely interdependent. Changes in one institution produce compensatory changes in tangent institutions and thus, inevitably, in government. A complex civilization necessarily develops complex political arrangements. Where the patterns of interaction in the society are intricate, the patterns of political behavior must be also. These may take several forms, depending upon the circumstances. In a society like ours, whose traditions sanction the almost unregulated development of a wide variety of associations, the new patterns are likely to involve the emergence of a wide variety of groups peripheral to the formal institutions of government, supplementing and complicating their operations.

This kind of complexity seems to stem in large measure, as was suggested in Chapter 2, from the techniques employed in the culture and especially from the specialization that they involve. This situation is so familiar that it hardly needs explanation, yet its very familiarity easily leads to a neglect of its basic importance. The specialization necessary to supply a single commodity such as gasoline may provide a miniature illustration:

> An oil operator brings oil to the surface of the ground; the local government prevents the theft of oil or destruction of equipment; a railroad corporation transports the oil; State and Federal Governments prevent interference with the transport of oil; a refining company maintains an organization of workers and chemical equipment to convert the oil into more useful forms; a retail distributor parcels out the resulting gasoline in small quantities to individuals requiring it; the Federal Government supplies a dependable medium of exchange which allows the oil operator, the railroad, the refining company, and the retailer to act easily in an organized fashion without being under a single administrative authority, and enforces contracts so that organizing arrangements on specific points can be more safely entered into; finally, government maintains a system of highways and byways

[12] Linton: *The Study of Man,* pp. 348–54.

which allow an ultimate consumer to combine the gasoline with other resources under his control in satisfying his desire for automobile travel.[13]

The intricacies of what are ordinarily thought of as economic behaviors by no means exhaust the picture, of course. One has only to think of the specialities appearing in various kinds of amusement and recreation to realize that these characteristics pervade the society. Professionalized sports such as baseball and an increasing number of others, the motion pictures with their wide range of "experts" of all sorts, not to mention the specialists necessary to the operations of the press—all illustrate the basic fact.

These specializations are created by the various techniques with which we meet the challenges and opportunities of the physical environment, and they are allocated to individuals, at least in such simple forms as in the house-building examples discussed in Chapter 2, roughly on the basis of differences in skill. They produce a congeries of differentiated but highly interdependent groups of men whose time is spent using merely segments of the array of skills developed in the culture.[14] Men are preoccupied by their skills, and these preoccupations in large measure define what the members of such groups know and perceive about the world in which they live. As has been remarked in a slightly different connection: "Machines . . . make specifications, so to speak, about the character of the people who are to operate them."[15] Under favorable circumstances groups form among those who share this "knowledge" and the attitudes it fosters. Both the nature of the techniques utilized in the society and the interdependencies that they imply dictate the amount and kinds of interaction of this sort. Where the techniques are complex, the interactions must be also.[16]

It is unnecessary here to attempt to trace historically the increasing diversity of groups. MacIver sees the "dawn of modern multi-group society" in the splitting of the single church in the sixteenth century, the consequent struggles over religious toleration, and the demands of the middle economic classes.[17] It is obvious that the process has

[13] U. S. National Resources Committee: *The Structure of the American Economy, Part I: Basic Characteristics* (Washington, D.C.: Government Printing Office, 1939), p. 96.

[14] See Linton: *The Study of Man*, pp. 84, 272–3.

[15] U. S. National Resources Committee: *The Problems of a Changing Population* (Washington, D.C.: Government Printing Office, 1938), p. 244.

[16] Chapple and Coon: *Principles of Anthropology*, pp. 140, 250–1, 365.

[17] MacIver: *The Web of Government*, pp. 52, 71.

been greatly accentuated by tremendous technological changes, well meriting the appellation "industrial revolution," which inevitably produced new contacts, new patterns of interaction, and new "foci of opposing interests." [18]

A precondition of the development of a vast multiplicity of groups, itself an instance of technological change of the most dramatic sort, is the revolution in means of communication. The mass newspaper, telephone, telegraph, radio, and motion pictures, not to mention the various drastic changes in the speed of transportation, have facilitated the interactions of men and the development of groups only slightly dependent, if at all, upon face-to-face contact. This factor in the formation of groups was noted by De Tocqueville when the first-named medium had scarcely appeared on the American scene:

> In democratic countries . . . it often happens that a great number of men who wish or want to combine cannot accomplish it because they are very insignificant and lost amid the crowd, they cannot see and do not know where to find one another. . . . These wandering minds, which had long sought each other in darkness, at length meet and unite. The newspaper brought them together, and the newspaper is still necessary to keep them united.[19]

The revolution in communications has indeed largely rendered obsolete, as we have observed in another connection, Madison's confidence in the dispersion of the population as an obstacle to the formation of interest groups.

Among other influences greatly facilitating group formation are such major national efforts as a war mobilization or a collective attack upon the problems of an industrial depression. In recruiting the national resources for such an emergency, the Government stimulates interaction throughout the nation. It is no accident, for example, that the periods of most rapid growth of trade associations in this country have included the years of World War I and the vigorous days of the ill-starred N.R.A.[20] Once the habit of associated activity was established under the stimulus of government encouragement, most such groups tended to persist and to invite imitation.

[18] MacIver: *The Web of Government*, p. 52. Copyright 1947 by Robert M. MacIver and used with the permission of The Macmillan Company.
[19] De Tocqueville: *Democracy in America*, Vol. II, pp. 111–2.
[20] Herring: *Group Representation Before Congress*, pp. 51–2; U. S. Temporary National Economic Committee: *Trade Association Survey* (Monograph No. 18, Washington, D.C.: Government Printing Office, 1941), p. 368.

Associations and Government

One of the inevitable consequences of increasing specialization and division of labor is thus the formation of groups at various stages in the growing chain of interdependent activities; but division of labor alone does not account for the proliferation of groups in our society. Groups indeed develop to carry on each of the specialties involved in a complicated operation, as in the example of the production and marketing of gasoline cited above. These institutionalized groups, furthermore, from time to time may have recourse to the political institutions in facilitating the operation of their specialties. Were this state of affairs the whole story, the complicating effects within government would be bewildering enough. Far more important, however, for their numbers and their complicating effects upon politics are those interest groups designated as associations. These are in a sense dependent groups, since they are peripheral to institutionalized groups and grow out of the tangent relations among individuals interacting in various of the latter. Their significance in the present context, however, is not limited by these characteristics. Associations are rather a major concern in the examination of political interest groups for two reasons: their generic functions and their great number in our society.

The function of the association, it will be recalled, is to stabilize the relations among their members and to order their relations as a group with other groups. Thus a labor union not only will guide the interactions of workers in various departments of a plant or various plants in an industry—involving such matters as seniority, skill levels, and the like—but also will order relations between the union workers and employers in a particular plant or industry. This stabilizing function bears a close relation to the degree of specialization in the society. For institutionalized specialties, as has been suggested above, necessitate interdependence; and other segments of the population therefore entertain established expectations concerning the behavior and performance of the specialists.[21] When this behavior or its consequences are not consistent with the expectations, among those affected a reaction ensues that may produce an association. Thus we have individuals in the society who specialize in moving goods and persons from place to place. Industrial locations and the forms of our sprawling cities are in part based upon the expectation that this transpor-

[21] See Linton: *The Study of Man*, pp. 272–3.

tation service will be effective, available when needed, and supplied at "reasonable" prices. Breakdowns, failures, and "unfair" pricing practices are likely to produce an association of shippers and travelers to "do something about it." Such efforts to achieve conformity between results and expectations, or other attempts at stabilization, almost inevitably involve at least some recourse to the institutions of government. The tremendous political importance of the association thus stems directly from its basic functions.

The number of such groups in our society is of equal political significance. With an increase in specialization and with the continual frustration of established expectations consequent upon rapid changes in the related techniques, the proliferation of associations is inescapable. So closely do these developments follow, in fact, that the rate of association formation may serve as an index of the stability of a society, and their number may be used as an index of its complexity. Simple societies have no associations (in the technical sense of the term); as they grow more complex, i. e., as highly differentiated institutionalized groups increase in number, societies evolve greater numbers of associations.[22]

An exact count of the number of associations in the United States that have some occasion to utilize the governmental processes is a virtual impossibility. In the first place, the number is constantly changing, and secondly, reliable means of identifying all such groups are not available. Various rough estimates, however, give some idea of the numbers. In 1929 Herring indicated his judgment that a "very conservative" estimate would place the number of groups maintaining representatives in Washington on a continuing basis at "well over five hundred."[23] How many others confined their activities to the States and localities or operated in Washington only on a temporary basis it is impossible to know. That this number had been eclipsed within a decade is suggested by the finding of a Temporary National Economic Committee study that in 1938 there were in the country over fifteen hundred national and regional trade associations, the vast majority of which listed "governmental relations" as one of their primary activities. Comparatively few of these had permanent offices in Washington, of course. The study did not cover an estimated six thousand State and local trade associations that could be expected to engage in governmental activities locally, if not nationally.[24]

[22] Chapple and Coon: *Principles of Anthropology,* p. 435.
[23] Herring: *Group Representation Before Congress,* p. 19.
[24] U.S. Temporary National Economic Committee: *Trade Association Survey,* pp. 2, 26.

The Federal Regulation of Lobbying Act, which is Title III of the Legislative Reorganization Act of 1946,[25] gives a further basis for contemporary estimates. Under this act, generally speaking, registration is required of persons and groups who solicit, receive, or expend money to influence congressional legislation. Because of the ambiguities and loopholes in the legislation, such as the exemption of groups and individuals whose funds are not used "principally" for such purposes, a careful student of the law has concluded that it is impossible to derive from its operation an accurate estimate of the number of organizations engaging in such activity.[26]

An authoritative count of national associations, issued in 1949 by the United States Department of Commerce, gave informative details concerning "approximately 4,000 trade, professional, civic, and other associations." [27] It is estimated that, including local and branch chapters, there were 16,000 businessmen's organizations, 70,000 labor unions, 100,000 women's organizations, and 15,000 civic and similar organized groups of business and professional men and women. The 4,000 national groups on which this document gave detailed information were distributed as follows:

Type of Group	*Number of Organizations Described*
Manufacturers	800
Distributors	300
Transportation, finance, insurance, etc.	400
Other national associations of businessmen	300
Professional and semiprofessional persons	500
Labor unions	200
Women	100
Veterans and Military	60
Commodity exchanges	60
Farmers	55
Negroes	50
Public officials	50
Fraternal	25
Sports and recreation	100
All other fields	1,000
Total	4,000

[25] Public Law 601, 79th Cong., 2d. Sess. (1946).

[26] Belle Zeller: "The Federal Regulation of Lobbying Act," *American Political Science Review*, Vol. 42, no. 2 (April, 1948), pp. 239–71.

[27] U.S. Department of Commerce: *National Associations of the United States* (Washington, D.C.: Government Printing Office, 1949).

They range from the Abrasive Grain Association and the American Bible Society to the Society for the Preservation and Encouragement of Barber Shop Quartet Singing in America (23,000 members) and the Zionist Organization of America. Not all of these are interest groups or associations in the technical sense of those terms, but the list gives some idea of the tremendous number of groups operating in the American scene. Moreover, the report states: "Almost all the organizations listed in this handbook engage in lobbying to varying degrees." [28]

Although these sources are obviously inadequate for a completely reliable reckoning, they do indicate that even a conservative estimate would count in at least four figures the number of associations active at the national governmental level alone.

The evolution of associations does not necessarily proceed at a uniform rate. When a single association is formed, it serves to stabilize the relations among the participants in the institutionalized groups involved. At the same time, however, in the performance of its function it may cause disturbances in the equilibriums of other groups or accentuate cleavages among them. These are likely to evoke associations in turn to correct the secondary disturbances. The formation of associations, therefore, tends to occur in waves.[29] For example, the introduction of machine techniques or new management methods may sufficiently disturb the workers in an industry to produce a union. While it may stabilize or restore the equilibrium of the workers, the effectiveness of the union's demands may so upset the accustomed behavior of the managers or owners that they will develop an association of their own in compensation. Zeller's study of interest groups in New York and McKean's study in New Jersey both indicate the frequency with which the formation of associations stems from the disturbances created by those formed at an earlier date. Such waves are a natural consequence of what is understood as interaction in a highly complex social situation.[30]

The possible ramifications of such waves of association-building are limited only by the extent of the affected interactions, some of which may initially appear to be rather remote. Thus the formation of labor unions, veterans' organizations, and professional associations may be followed by the establishment of parallel or, in a sense, competing as-

[28] *Ibid.*, p. 561.
[29] Chapple and Coon: *Principles of Anthropology*, p. 426.
[30] Zeller: *Pressure Politics in New York*, pp. 8, 51, and *passim*; McKean: *Pressures on the Legislature of New Jersey*, p. 6. Cf. Lundberg: *Foundations of Sociology*, pp. 218–9.

sociations for workers, veterans, or professional men who belong to the Catholic Church, who are of the Jewish faith, or who belong to a particular nationality group. The latter have the effect of stabilizing activity within the parent institution that is threatened by the attractions of associations unaffiliated with it. In this sense, the establishment of an association is an innovation in technique that has effects in tangent institutionalized groups quite as disturbing as do changes in technology. Even the new practices of established groups may have the same effect if they invite or compel other groups to utilize the same methods. Thus Herring has pointed out that the systematic campaigns of woman suffrage organizations in the second decade of this century set the pattern of techniques for what he calls the "new lobby." This phenomenon of organization in waves, together with the influences discussed previously that have stimulated the proliferation of groups, undoubtedly account in part for the dilution and subsequent partial eclipse of the corrupting "lobby barons" and "corporation lobbies" typical of State and national legislative halls seventy-five years ago.[31] The disturbances created by such groups caused the formation of defensive groups and the modification of tactics by the former.

Not all institutionalized groups are equally sensitive to disturbances, of course. As we have already observed, such groups are characterized by a high degree of stability. Those that are particularly stable will maintain their equilibriums in the face of all but the greatest changes in their relations with other groups. Such is the case in those well-managed industrial enterprises that have successfully avoided the establishment of labor unions or that have established a long record of operation without interruption by strikes. The inertia of these groups is such, in fact, that disturbances of disaster proportions may be required to upset the established relationships within them.[32]

Although associations operating as political interest groups may grow out of the tangent relations among institutionalized groups of all kinds, probably the most common in recent years have been those stemming from economic institutions. So common have these groups become and so involved has government activity been with economic

[31] Herring: *Group Representation Before Congress*, pp. 34–8, 41–6, 195.
[32] The role of disasters in the formation and alteration of groups, especially political groups, deserves more investigation than it has received. See John M. Gaus and Leon O. Wolcott: *Public Administration and the United States Department of Agriculture* (Chicago: Public Administration Service, 1940), especially the section on land use (chap. 8), p. 128 ff. See also Stuart A. Rice: *Farmers and Workers in American Politics* (New York: Columbia University Press, 1924), chap. 1.

policy, that many writers have fallen into the error of treating economic groups as the only important interest groups.[33] There are, undoubtedly, a number of reasons for the prevalence of associations growing out of economic institutions, but two that greatly illuminate the general process may be noted here. In the first place, there has been a series of disturbances and dislocations consequent upon the utopian attempt, as Polanyi calls it, to set up a completely self-regulating market system. This attempt involved a policy of treating the fictitious factors of land, labor, and capital as if they were real, ignoring the fact that they stood for human beings or influences closely affecting the welfare of humans. Application of this policy inevitably meant suffering and dislocation—unemployment, wide fluctuation in prices, waste, and so forth.[34] These disturbances inevitably produced associations—of owners, of workers, of farmers—operating upon government to mitigate and control the ravages of the system through tariffs, subsidies, wage guarantees, social insurance, and the like. Protectionist demands in international trade, moreover, have had their equivalent in interstate commerce in the United States.[35] As Herman Finer has observed: "The competitive system depends for its sanction on insecurity. Competitors in the real world . . . do not intend to be insecure." [36]

The second reason for the prevalence of associations stemming from economic institutions is the rapid and extensive change that has occurred in technical methods of industry and in the organization of industrial units. For example, it has been found that in the shoe industry there has occurred within recent years a marked development of associations.[37] Organizations of owners and managers have developed as a means of aiding the adjustment of each enterprise to the vicissitudes of the national market. These have been paralleled

[33] See, for example, Crawford: *The Pressure Boys*; and Stuart Chase: *Democracy Under Pressure* (New York: The Twentieth Century Fund, 1945).

[34] Karl Polanyi: *The Great Transformation* (New York: Farrar & Rinehart, Inc., 1944). See also T. N. Whitehead: *Leadership in a Free Society* (Cambridge, Mass.: Harvard University Press, 1936), chap. 2.

[35] McKean: *Pressures on the Legislature of New Jersey*, pp. 56–7, notes the frequency with which groups besiege the New Jersey legislature for legislation restricting the effects of competition, especially from out-of-state companies. See U.S. Department of Agriculture: *Barriers to Internal Trade in Farm Products* (Washington, D.C.: Government Printing Office, 1939).

[36] Herman Finer: *The Road to Reaction* (Boston: Little, Brown & Company, 1945), p. 185.

[37] This section is based on W. Lloyd Warner and J. O. Low: *The Social System of the Modern Factory* (Yankee City Series, Vol. IV, New Haven: Yale University Press, 1947), esp. pp. 89, 114, 121–3.

by workers' associations (unions). Both, however, have been stimulated by the problems consequent upon the steady absorption of independent factories into a few large regional or national shoe manufacturing enterprises.

For the owners and managers this centralization of the shoe industry has produced a new series of problems concerning financing and marketing that their associations aid in solving. For the workers it has meant that the officials at the top of the hierarchy are total strangers whose names they may not even know. The manager of a local plant is relatively far down in the new organizational structure, and his discretion is sharply limited. He does not make many of the crucial decisions affecting his plant, but merely carries out directives issued by those at the peak of the structure. These orders may be entirely consistent with the logic of the problems directly facing the officials at the top without these officials being in any way aware of the fact that the orders seriously disturb the workers. Since there is no appreciable interaction between workers and their ultimate employers, these disturbances inevitably have produced suspicion and resentment, perhaps wholly unwarranted, of the absent authorities. Equally inevitably, compensatory and defensive interactions among workers have increased and unions have emerged as a means of stabilizing and ordering these relations. As Millis and Montgomery observe: "It is only a labor organization with the structure and the relations of the trade union that can exercise control over matters not of plant or firm origin." [38]

In addition to and accompanying this change in the organization of shoe enterprises, the introduction of machinery has steadily narrowed to the point of elimination the craft skills upon which the industry has been based. These skills had been organized into an elaborate hierarchy and a corresponding structure of rewards had been created in which age and skill were closely correlated. This structure, especially in the context of small, locally owned factories, was not wholly inconsistent with the notions of advancement and improvement that constituted the "American dream." The expanding mechanization, as in other such industries, dissolved this structure of relationships and interactions with the result that the workers "were ready for any mass movement which would strike at those they charged, in their own minds, with the responsibility for their present unhappy conditions." [39]

[38] From *Organized Labor* by Harry A. Millis and Royal E. Montgomery, p. 886. Copyright 1945. Courtesy of McGraw-Hill Book Company, Inc.

[39] Warner and Low: *The Social System of the Modern Factory*, p. 89.

Classifications of Interest Groups

The language of laymen and journalists includes a number of type designations for political interest groups. Everyday discussion, particularly on the editorial pages, usually uses such group classifications as *business, labor, agriculture, veterans,* and the like. Most academic discussion has employed similar lists. Others distinguish groups according to the number of issues in connection with which they are active. Still others use a classification that substitutes for, or adds to, the above a judgment concerning whether the group's objectives are *public* (*unselfish, humanitarian, reform,* and the like) or *private* (*selfish, special,* and so on). By using the classifications made familiar by frequent use in popular discussions, one gains something in simplicity of communication. Such simplicity may be achieved, however, at too high a cost if these terms are used uncritically. Although we shall employ such designations as *farm groups, business groups, labor groups,* and so on, it will be important to bear in mind some of the pitfalls that surround such usage and similar classifications.

The particular danger of a designation like "business" is that it implies a certain solidity or cohesion within the group that may not exist. When the term is used in the midst of interest group conflicts, the group leadership may wish to give this impression. The slogan "What Helps Business Helps You" was a skillful means of suggesting the existence of complete unity among businessmen, and one may take note of this tactic in the political struggle. But when a writer states that "business has been intent upon wielding economic power and, where necessary, political control for its own purposes,"[40] he has become a participant in, rather than an observer of, that struggle. "Business" may be a useful collective term for certain economic behaviors, but the individuals and groups falling under such a heading do not necessarily act as a political unit. "Business" groups are normally found on opposite sides of many political issues such as reciprocal trade legislation, farm subsidies, and minimum wage bills. Careless use of the classification thus may tend to obscure more than it explains.

A corollary of this danger is that one may ascribe an interest to certain groups on an *a priori* basis that may bear no relation to the atti-

[40] U.S. Temporary National Economic Committee: *Economic Power and Political Pressures* (Monograph No. 26, Washington, D.C.: Government Printing Office, 1941), p. 1.

tudes held by the group. When the activity of the group is not consistent with such description, the discrepancy involves the student in the fruitless task of trying to make the evidence fit a misconception. Even where this kind of error is not made, there is a strong possibility that such classification will tend to obscure one of the essential characteristics of the process of group politics, namely, that an individual can affiliate with many potentially conflicting groups. What of the business man whose trade association seeks the aid of troops in the violent suppression of strikes and who at the same time belongs to an active society for the protection of civil liberties? If such affiliations may affect the behavior of individuals, they may equally affect the operation of the groups to which the individuals belong. To obscure this fact, as will be shown in detail in a later chapter, is to cripple one's understanding of the political process.

A further hazard in using classifications of the usual sort is that one may emphasize political relationships at a particular point in time and neglect the dynamic, changing content of a generic process. A dominant group at one point may be inactive or ineffective at another. Women's groups, often placed in a "miscellaneous" category, may be primarily sociability groups, and yet under certain circumstances—if there is a school scandal, for instance—they may become overwhelmingly influential. Over time, furthermore, the relative importance of various groups may be completely transformed by technological and cultural changes of all kinds. As their situations and experiences shift, there will be shifts in individuals' attitudes and interests, regroupings of affiliation that directly affect the relative power of groups. It was quite reasonable for Herring to observe in 1929 that scientific societies were rarely interested in governmental matters.[41] The development of atomic power, the increasing recognition of the importance of basic research in all the sciences, and the increased importance of military considerations in American politics, to mention only a few changes, have combined to give organized scientists a greatly augmented political role.[42] Classifications that neglect such emerging trends or that underemphasize the processes by which they take place are a serious handicap to understanding.

Such classifications, because they are likely to depend upon the names assumed by organized groups and upon certain of the obvious claims the groups make, may lead the student to mistake the self-estimate of groups for their actual significance. He may mistake a fake

[41] Herring: *Group Representation Before Congress*, p. 180.
[42] See, for example, issues of the *Bulletin of the Atomic Scientists*, which began publication in 1945.

or dummy group for the real thing, and so become a victim of the fraud. One who tried to reconcile the Farmers' State Rights League of the early 1920's with other "farm" organizations would have been dealing in fact largely with a group of cotton mill operators who assumed this guise to work against the proposed child labor amendment to the Constitution.[43] It was a group, and its activities were relevant to the inquiries of a student of politics, but its significance would not have been revealed by such classification.

Finally, efforts to distinguish among interest groups on the basis of personal preference, that is, subjective judgments as to their "public" or "private" character, may be an unavoidable part of a citizen's functions, but they have nothing to do with the methods of scientific analysis. They contribute little to a systematic understanding of the political process by whatever methods such knowledge is pursued. The basis of such judgments cannot be reliably communicated, and the results are therefore useless in analysis.

Perhaps the most significant feature of group politics is that it is a dynamic process, a constantly changing pattern of relationships involving through the years continual shifts in relative influence. If it is this aspect that it is most important to describe or, what is the same thing, to understand, then the most significant questions are those that bear directly on this process of change—questions indicating the basis of a more meaningful classification. How do interest groups emerge? Under what circumstances do they make claims upon or through the institutions of government? In concrete situations and over time, what are the internal features of existing groups, the degree of cohesion they command under varying conditions, their resources? How are various groups interrelated, either as organized groups or through the interactions of individual members? In what fashions do groups operate upon the government and its subdivisions? With what frequency and degrees of intensity? What are the mutations of governmental institutions in response to group activity? Obviously we do not at present have the data from which to answer these questions and on which to base a functionally more useful classification of interest groups. As adequate means of measurement are developed, such data may become available. Meanwhile conventional classifications can be employed if their limitations are kept in sight.

[43] Herring: *Group Representation Before Congress*, p. 27. See Crawford: *The Pressure Boys*, chap. 10, for further examples of this sort.

4

Group Origins and Political Orientations

IN THE preceding chapter the origins of interest groups and the circumstances surrounding their orientation toward the institutions of government were indicated as among the factors most relevant to a description of group politics. It was also suggested that the rapid proliferation of associations in recent years, so extensive that "interest group" and "association" are almost interchangeable terms, had been largely responsible for focusing the attention of both layman and specialist upon the role of groups in government. In the course of this discussion the factors involved in the emergence of institutionalized groups and associations were stated in schematic terms. A clearer picture of these crucial political situations will be afforded by an examination of the origins of a number of associations and a statement of the conditions under which they have become involved in the governmental process.

The Rise of Labor Organizations

Perhaps the most instructive examples of the growth of associations and their involvement in government, as previous illustrations suggest, are to be seen in the labor movement. Labor organizations are important not only because they play a significant role in the current scene, but because they embody one of a variety of responses to the innovations (disturbances) that for more than a century have been at the vortex of a rapidly changing society, namely, disturbances in the relationships in economic institutions. These relationships, for centuries stabilized at a relatively simple level necessitating little differentiation of function, have within little more than a century changed so radically that the bonds of habitual behavior by which they had been controlled have been destroyed. The origins of these changes, and of labor organization in the modern sense, lay in specialization, in differentiation of function, making the worker only a producer and not equally owner and merchant of his product. For reasons apparent from previous discussions, the functional differentiation of employer and employee permitted the development of attitudes (interests) peculiar to each. Subsequent and varying disturbances inevitably increased interaction among workers, and the emergence of associations to stabilize these relationships followed.[1] These disturbances, it should be noted by way of caution, were not in the beginning, and have not since been, narrowly economic in the sense that they depended wholly upon wages. Wage demands have usually been symptoms of an unacknowledged need for achieving equilibrium in the lives of workers both within and outside the factory.[2]

Local trade unions in the United States, organizations made up exclusively of wage earners, date from the 1790's. The rise of these associations illustrates in simple and direct fashion the generic processes by which any association is formed. In some instances the disturbing influences were the "merchant capitalists," under the pressure of whose merchandising methods masters were often obliged to cut wages in order to compete for sales. In others the stimulating disturbances were the competition of "foreign" workers, those migratory journeymen who undermined the bargaining position of local artisans. These and other influences, such as the scarcity of skilled workmen, led to the formation of local and intercity workingmen's associations.

In the wavelike fashion discussed previously, the expansion of these workingmen's groups led to the associated opposition of employers, utilizing in considerable measure the institutions of government and particularly the convenient common-law concepts of conspiracy. Reaching a peak in the early 1830's, these efforts on the part of employers were one cause of a series of attempts to fuse all organized workers into one national organization, a trend temporarily halted by the panic of 1837.

[1] See Millis and Montgomery: *Organized Labor*, pp. 2–4. This section relies heavily upon the excellent summary in the first five chapters of this book. Material not otherwise acknowledged is drawn from these pages.

[2] Warner and Low: *The Social System of the Modern Factory*, p. 131. See also Whitehead: *Leadership in a Free Society*, pp. 16–7.

Further efforts toward nation-wide organization were invited by the industrialization and transportation improvements of the two decades before the Civil War. Local organizations were no longer able to control wages and working conditions under the competitive situation these improvements made possible. Slowed by the war, these federative drives emerged with renewed vigor afterwards under the increased tempo of industrialization. For workers, as for many in other phases of American life, the postwar decades were stormy, confused, and filled with contradictions. Until the creation of the American Federation of Labor in 1886 these labor movements were amorphous, lacking in cohesion, and short-lived. Basic to their high mortality was a vagueness of interest, an interest that could not provide a solid and continuing basis of interaction. Differentiation between worker and employer had gone forward rapidly, and the consequences of this and other developments were painfully felt. Yet, despite these changes, the employee, wage-earning position was not accepted as a permanent one; the dream persisted of individual advancement to property-holding, self-employing security. Not even skilled workers, however well organized locally, were fully interactive nationally as such; instead, they saw themselves as part of the amorphous "plain people"—farmers, middle-class employers, and the like. The ill-starred National Labor Union (1866–72) and the considerably more important Knights of Labor, begun in 1869 and past its peak by 1887, had in common a central preoccupation with antimonopoly and other "uplift" matters aiming to eliminate the obstacles to moving out of what was becoming a relatively permanent position in society. The Knights, for example, assumed that "no fundamental disharmony of interest obtained between employers and workers as such" and that the interests of all those who were producers, whether by hand or brain, were virtually identical.[3] Radical in one sense, these romantic and utopian movements were not in harmony with more substantial lines of interest among workers.

The American Federation of Labor, before which the Knights rapidly declined, was in tune with reality in that it was based on a firmer foundation of common interest than that of belonging to the "plain people." This foundation for continuing interaction was the skilled craft. Skilled workers, especially those having the same skill, could interact, not just as workers, but as workers with a particular specialty that they desired to protect from wage cutting and overcrowding. Although the development of the new type of union had

[3] Millis and Montgomery: *Organized Labor*, p. 68.

the effect of distinguishing skilled from unskilled workers, it also necessarily helped to create attitudes accepting a more or less continuing wage earner status. Individualism was de-emphasized by being harnessed firmly to the objective of controlling skilled jobs. Other utopian hangovers continued only in much less important form. Statements issuing from a convention in May, 1886, leading up to the formation of the A.F. of L., indicated awareness of the workable lines of interaction in their emphasis upon the "historical basis" of the craft unions and their preclusive qualifications to "regulate their own internal concerns."[4] Not despite the fact that it included only skilled workers, but because of that fact, the creation of the A.F. of L. marked a revolutionary change: "The 'natural' unit of organization was that of men in the same occupations, possessed of approximately the same skill and technical knowledge and potential underbidders of each other in the absence of collective selling of labor power."[5] The proof of this "naturalness" lay in the continuance of the movement despite the upheavals of the next decade. The A.F. of L. survived troubles of the sort that had regularly crippled or eliminated the predecessors of the new organization.

The success of the A.F. of L. and its international craft unions had reached impressive proportions by the turn of the century. In 1902 their membership exceeded one million. Effectiveness in ordering the relationships of skilled workers, however, provided a stimulus to activity on the part of employers' groups, whose equilibrium was affected. Not only did new organizations of employers develop after 1901, as will be noted later, but a number of them engaged in vigorous defensive action in the form of an open-shop drive on a nationwide basis during the years 1901 through 1908.

The reaction of the A.F. of L.'s membership to these efforts was mixed, but some of its aspects are highly instructive. Control within the constituent unions was increasingly centralized as these circumstances called for hard-hitting tactics in order to hold members and force employer acceptance. Some unions reacted to the open-shop offensive with vigorous insistence on a wider attack on existing economic relationships than was consistent with the A.F. of L.'s "business unionism." These participated in forming a more revolutionary, industrial union movement in 1906, the Industrial Workers of the World. Division of this sort in the face of changes in relationships among groups is continual, as was indicated in Chapter 2. The

---

[4] Quoted ibid., p. 73.
[5] From *Organized Labor* by Millis and Montgomery, p. 77. Copyright 1945. Courtesy of McGraw-Hill Book Company, Inc.

I.W.W., however, never became a real rival to the A.F. of L., since, like similar movements in the past, it was not able to satisfy immediate economic needs of workers and never achieved effective cohesion. It nevertheless had significance and meaning for the future in that it forced the A.F. of L. leadership to contemplate including unskilled workers within its fold.

The most interesting reaction of the A.F. of L. to the open-shop drive and related employer offensives, however, was the development of a measure of political activity. The strictly economic implications of "business unionism" meant avoidance of politics and any reliance upon government. This policy, a reaction against the political movements that had preceded the A.F. of L., had withstood the blandishments of the various socialist parties in the nineties and the efforts of socialists within the A.F. of L. The major influences leading the A.F. of L. to a more active position respecting politics by 1906 included the following: the antiunion efforts of employers, particularly as implemented by the free use of injunctive powers by the courts; the increasing restlessness of the unorganized unskilled workers, partially reflected in the I.W.W., who looked toward legislation as a means of improving their circumstances and who constituted a potential threat to the dominance of the A.F. of L.; the atmosphere of the "progressive" movement; and the tempting success in the elections of 1906 of the organization that later became the British Labor Party. Precedent for this new orientation could be found in State-wide labor organizations four decades earlier. In New York the association that later became the New York State Federation of Labor had since 1864 been primarily concerned with legislative matters, a preoccupation that it has consistently maintained.[6] The change in A.F. of L. policy, however, involved no real abandonment of the tenets of "business unionism," but merely the use of governmental mechanisms to facilitate achieving the established objectives. Legislative requests were largely efforts to free the union from restraints upon the use of its customary methods—particularly from court injunctions and prosecutions under the Sherman Antitrust Act of 1890. Political participation was confined to bipartisan endorsement "to defeat labor's enemies and to reward its friends." Nevertheless, the greater preoccupation with government and politics indicated a significant trend.

These new political efforts of organized labor reached something of a peak with the passage in 1914 of the Clayton Act, hailed overoptimistically by Gompers as a "new magna charta." This act, an amendment to the Sherman Act, seemed to satisfy the major legisla-

[6] Zeller: *Pressure Politics in New York*, pp. 8–9.

tive demands of the unions—relief from the injunction and from the requirements of the antitrust legislation that had been so applied as to limit the rights to organize and to strike. Subsequent construction of its provisions by the courts largely dashed these optimistic first hopes.

The trend toward political activity was strengthened during World War I, though it was not changed in character. The Federation demanded safeguards for union activities in return for its vigorous support of the war. These were so far forthcoming that by 1920 A.F. of L. membership exceeded a record-breaking four million. Government policies led to labor representation in many of the emergency agencies. More important, in those basic industries, like coal mining and railroads, that the government undertook to operate, official sanction was given to the right of workers to organize and bargain collectively.

In the complicated period of the 1920's and 1930's one may discern the operation of two trends in organized labor, not very noticeable prior to 1914, but dominant in the postwar years because of changed circumstances. The first of these was a growing need for the organization of the unskilled and semiskilled workers. The second, closely related, was the demand by organized labor for greater political activity along positive lines and not merely for defensive purposes.

In the background of the increased need to organize the nonskilled workers were a number of novel developments. First, there was the rapid growth of several new or much altered industries, such as automobiles, chemicals, and electrical manufacturing. Along with this growth went rapid technological development involving mass production and the partial or complete elimination of many of the traditional craft skills, so that the relative importance of highly skilled workers was greatly diminished. In these and other lines mergers and combinations within industry occurred at a greatly increased rate, a development that, as was noted in the case of the shoe industry, may constitute a major disturbance in the equilibrium of workers' groups. Paradoxically, in the face of a greatly increased number of potentially organizable workers and conditions of rather general prosperity in the 1920's, which normally favor union growth, the number of organized workers steadily declined, showing a net decrease in every year but one between 1920 and 1930.[7] This decline was due in large measure to the rigidity of established patterns in the A.F. of L., as will be indicated in more detail later.

During this decade associated activity among employers increased

[7] Millis and Montgomery: *Organized Labor*, pp. 162–3.

in compensation for the aggressive advances of organized labor during World War I. The open-shop movement was renewed in somewhat more sophisticated guise than it had displayed at the turn of the century but still was strongly aided by such judicial weapons as the injunction. It was accompanied as well by a wide range of paternalistic, welfare practices. In a number of industries, especially those in which there had occurred an increase in the real income of workers, labor groups did develop, not spontaneously as labor efforts, but under management sponsorship in the form of the so-called company union. The company unions were able, in prosperous times, to stabilize workers' relationships, but they did so by establishing supplementary lines of interaction within the hierarchy of the institutionalized economic group such as the factory; they were not, like the conventional labor union, associations formed around tangential relations between such groups. The company unions were effective in strengthening the existing order within economic groups, making workers "company conscious rather than craft-conscious."[8] It is significant that the means of accomplishing this result was in form more like unionism of the industrial type than like that of the craft skill sort.

When the National Industrial Recovery Act and later the Wagner Act gave sanction to labor organization, unions in all sorts of lines experienced rapid growth. The former legislation, passed in 1933 during the disturbed early months of the first administration of Franklin Roosevelt, involved a gargantuan program of business "self-government." It included a section providing that employees should have the right to organize and bargain collectively through representatives of their own choosing and without employer interference. The National Labor Relations Act (Wagner Act) of 1935 was based on this section, strengthened by provisions deemed necessary to guarantee these rights, notably proscription of the company union and provision of enforcement machinery. The most dramatic union expansion under these statutes occurred in the newer mass-production industries. The "need" for organization in these enterprises is illustrated by the example of the automobile industry:

> The wage earners in many of the plants were . . . ready and often anxious to organize. Complaining of the speed-up, a complicated system of wage payment, absence of job security, an espionage system in some plants, and in general of policies they characterized as those of industrial autocracy, they possessed atti-

[8] From *Organized Labor* by Millis and Montgomery, pp. 159–60. Copyright 1945. Courtesy of McGraw-Hill Book Company, Inc.

tudes and a frame of mind that should be capitalized most effectively by union organizers.[9]

The readiness in fact went so far that rank-and-file membership in the early stages of organization under the C.I.O. undertook strikes despite advice to the contrary from their leaders.

The company unions, however, offered stiff competition to unions of the conventional sort until after the passage of the Wagner Act. It was an ominous fact that in the N.R.A. period A.F. of L. unions invaded the mass-production industries without supplanting the company-promoted and company-controlled union. The number of the latter nearly doubled between 1932 and 1935, and the number of employees covered by them, equivalent to 40 per cent of total "legitimate" trade union membership in 1932, increased to 60 per cent of the total of unionized workers by 1935. This form of organization, moreover, was particularly common in such mass-production industries as iron and steel, chemicals, and transportation. Not until the constitutionality of the National Labor Relations (Wagner) Act was established in 1937 was an effective check placed on the growth of the company-dominated labor organization.

The need for positive recourse to political institutions became increasingly apparent as the mass-production industries were organized. It was foreshadowed in the twenties by the problems of the railroad brotherhoods. These unions became increasingly dependent upon government to enforce the right of collective bargaining and to settle disputes, and consequently needed to protect their stability and their access to governmental institutions through greater political participation. Significantly, they were among the most vigorous backers of the LaFollette presidential candidacy in 1924, which the A.F. of L. endorsed only reluctantly and with much dragging of feet. Conservative unionists were brought to accept more aggressive political action partly by the increased migration of industry during the twenties into areas where low standards and wage levels threatened the higher standards in organized areas.[10] Adequate protection against such competition required action by the national Government. These influences toward political activity were reinforced by the activities of local and state officials supporting employers during industrial disputes. Skill changes in industry were equally influential. The semi-

[9] From *Organized Labor* by Millis and Montgomery, p. 226. Copyright 1945. Courtesy of McGraw-Hill Book Company, Inc.

[10] See Philip Taft: "Labor's Changing Political Line," *Journal of Political Economy*, Vol. 45, no. 5 (October, 1937), pp. 634–50.

skilled and unskilled workers of the mass-production industries were unable to protect their job security through "job control" based on a semimonopoly of entrance into a craft. Well before the advent of the Committee for Industrial Organization in 1935 (later the Congress of Industrial Organizations), established unions in such industries were increasingly convinced that they were confronted with economic forces that could be subjected to control only through the use of governmental mechanisms. Since control of entrance into employment was no longer feasible or appropriate, security had to be sought by other means. With the great expansion of unions of the industrial type after 1935, including as they did great numbers of nonskilled workers in the mass-production industries, increased political activity by labor organizations was inevitable.

A more detailed consideration of the reasons for the split between the C.I.O. and the A.F. of L. will be reserved for a later chapter, but it should be noted that this break (which represents a tendency not peculiar to labor) was a direct consequence of the trends toward industrial unionism and increased union participation in politics discussed above. Changes in the organization and techniques of industry had, by the beginning of the 1930's and perhaps earlier, made organized relationships among workers along plant and industry lines, regardless of skill, far more realistic than organization by craft. That craft organization, which had been made "natural" in the 1880's, was by this time artificial, is evident from the fact that, although workers in industrial unions amounted to only 27 per cent of organized workers in 1933, by the early 1940's the proportion was more than half. These and similar developments also dictated a more aggressive use of national political institutions than was customary for the previously dominant craft type of labor organization. When the established patterns of interaction—that is, the organizational structure —of the A.F. of L. failed to accommodate these new demands, division and the establishment of a rival organization could not be long postponed.

Trade Associations and Related Groups

If we turn to another common interest group, the trade association, a similar process of growth and involvement in government is found. The development and characteristics of the trade association are differentiated responses to many of the changed circumstances that stimulated and guided the emergence of the labor movement. It will be unnecessary to restate these in greater detail than is sufficient to demonstrate the similarity of the basic pattern: that trade associations have emerged in response to changes or disturbances in the habitual relationships (interactions) of groups of individuals and that these associations have had increasing resort to the institutions of government in order to stabilize relationships within and between groups.

Although the antecedents of the modern trade association go back on the local level at least to the guild organizations of master craftsmen and traces of them can be found very early in American history, the beginnings of trade associations of regional or national scope date from the Civil War. By the 1890's they had become so widespread as to be a familiar feature of industrial organization in America.[11] The rapid changes during these decades—technological changes, expanding markets, and painfully sharp fluctuations in the trade cycle—provided the stimulus for this growth. As the unsettling effects of unrestricted competition became apparent and were often accentuated by a rising proportion of fixed to variable costs, and as improved means of communication made contacts among physically separated individuals simpler, firms in the same or similar industrial activities increased the rate of, and regularized the means of, their interaction. Tangent to one another through the market system, these institutionalized groups developed continuing relationships among themselves (trade associations) in response to increased disturbances stemming from the market. The general attitude was put with remarkable frankness by a trustee of the Cement Institute: "The truth is of course—and there can be no serious, respectable discussion of our case unless this is acknowledged—that ours is an industry above all others that cannot stand free competition, that must systematically restrain competition or be ruined. . . ."[12] The same factors that produced the "trusts" and other aspects of what has been called the "combination movement"—pools, market sharing, and price agreements—led in the American setting to the proliferation of the trade association as a specialized form of interaction.[13]

As in the case of labor organizations, the trade association move-

[11] See Clarence E. Bonnett: "The Evolution of Business Groupings," *Annals of the American Academy of Political and Social Science*, Vol. 179 (May, 1935), pp. 1–8. This journal will be cited hereafter as *Annals*. U.S. Temporary National Economic Committee: *Trade Association Survey*, p. 12; Merle Fainsod and Lincoln Gordon: *Government and the American Economy* (New York: W. W. Norton & Company, 1941), chap. 15.

[12] Quoted in Earl Latham: "Giantism and Basing-Points: A Political Analysis," *Yale Law Journal*, Vol. 58, no. 3 (February, 1949), p. 383.

[13] Fainsod and Gordon: *Government and the American Economy*, chaps. 13 and 15.

ment received a vigorous stimulus during the period of American participation in World War I. The responsibility of the government for a suddenly increased measure of economic planning in order to satisfy the needs of war led it to invite and encourage the establishment of associations that could simplify its task of eliciting information and co-ordinated action. Many of the objectives that had led to the establishment of such groups now became governmental objectives, at least for the duration. The larger crisis of international hostilities thus supplemented the older disturbances that had earlier stimulated the movement. The response was striking: an estimate by the Department of Commerce and Labor in 1913 indicated that there were about 240 regional, national, and international trade associations; this number grew to approximately 2000 in 1919.[14] After a decade of fluctuation in the movement, a similar rapid growth took place, again as in the case of labor organizations, during the N.R.A. period. This national effort, growing out of the dislocations of the depression, made the establishment of some such groups essential and promoted a tendency already present both by making trade associations quasi-governmental agencies and by relaxing the restraints of antitrust legislation. A careful study in 1938 indicated that nearly 23 per cent of the associations then extant had been formed in the years 1933–5.[15] Many disbanded following the nullification of the National Industrial Recovery Act by the Supreme Court in 1935, but the period produced a permanent increase in number. That a somewhat similar development occurred during World War II is suggested by a 1949 estimate from the Department of Commerce that there were in that year 2,000 national and regional trade associations. This figure indicates an increase of 500 over the number estimated to be in operation in 1938.[16]

Various cases illustrate the role of government encouragement in the establishment of trade associations. Thus the National Coal Association was founded in 1917 at the suggestion of the Chairman of the Committee on Coal Production of the Council of National Defense in order to facilitate working relationships during World War I between this highly decentralized basic industry and government war administrators.[17] A slightly different situation, in which the stimulus

[14] Herring: *Group Representation Before Congress*, p. 96.
[15] U.S. Temporary National Economic Committee: *Trade Association Survey*, p. 369.
[16] U.S. Department of Commerce: *National Associations of the United States*, p. viii.
[17] Herring: *Group Representation Before Congress*, p. 103.

for association stemmed from disturbed market conditions, although the trail had been blazed by previous interaction under government tutelage, is illustrated by the Sugar Institute. During World War I the Government had closely controlled the sugar industry, producing, incidentally, financial stability and profit for the latter. Following withdrawal of government support in 1919, a somewhat chaotic situation developed, marked by reduced consumption, underutilization of refining capacity, and sharp competitive practices. The year 1927 was a particularly painful one for the refiners, owing in part to reduced consumption following a "slimness" advertising campaign by a cigarette manufacturer. As a direct consequence the Institute was founded in 1928, the initiative being taken, interestingly enough, by those refiners who had been engaging in "unethical" competitive practices. It was dissolved following a court decree in 1936 that found that its price-control activities violated the Sherman Act.[18] Another variant of government influence in the formation of an association is illustrated in the case of the Association of American Railroads. The relatively weak condition of the railroads during the 1920's, aggravated by the development of competing methods of transportation and by the depression, resulted in the establishment in 1933 of a Federal Coordinator of Transportation, the late Joseph B. Eastman, who undertook a series of comprehensive studies of the situation. One of his reports in 1934 indicated that the only alternative to government ownership or enforced consolidation was "a better organization of the railroad industry which will enable them [the managements] to deal collectively and effectively with matters which concern them all." Recognizing the weaknesses of existing railroad associations, a group of railroad executives, after much consultation among themselves and with Mr. Eastman, formed the Association of American Railroads in October, 1934. It was looked to by its members as a means of ending "further talk of government ownership and operation" and "further effort to extend the influence of the government over railroad operations, particularly in the field of management." This membership represented, at least in the formal sense, 99 per cent of the Class 1 railroad mileage, or about 95 per cent of the total railroad mileage in the United States. [19]

Evidence of the reasons for the establishment of trade associations is to be found in the major functions that they have usually performed.

[18] U.S. Temporary National Economic Committee: *Trade Association Survey*, pp. 113–5, 139–42.
[19] U.S. Senate, Committee on Interstate Commerce: *Senate Report No. 26*, Part 2, 77th Cong., 1st Sess. (1941), pp. 22–5.

Although many of the early groups primarily engaged in "innocuous and inconsequential social festivities" that indicate merely an increased rate of interaction, virtually all of them eventually assumed the function of protecting the trade against the rigors of competition and the market, either directly through devices for controlling prices or indirectly through the application of various trading rules.[20] Given the political strength of antimonopoly views and their embodiment in such statutes as the Sherman Antitrust Act of 1890, many agreements to these ends necessarily operated in secrecy. For example, in the early years of the century an association of cottonseed crushers, known as the Sons of Plato, met as a secret fraternal order apparently to fix prices and divide the market. [21] Although this and other such groups were dissolved through government action, less crude efforts to essentially the same ends have been persistent. As a Temporary National Economic Committee study cautiously states: "Mutual restraints of competition . . . are found among the activities of a large proportion of national and regional trade associations." [22] These received the implied approval of the Supreme Court when in 1911 it enunciated the "rule of reason" as a guide in applying the Sherman Act. This "rule," in fact, so softened the restrictions of the act that it gave great encouragement to the growth of trade associations.[23] It provided freer rein to these groups for carrying on the basic functions of relieving the frictions of competition and promoting stability of the market.

In carrying on these activities, trade associations have inevitably and increasingly asserted claims through or upon the institutions of government. There were ancient local precedents for this type of activity. In 1819 a group of writing paper manufacturers met in Boston to prepare a request to Congress for increased tariff protection.[24] In 1922 a National Association of Manufacturers survey of the major trade associations indicated that most of them were actively interested

[20] Leverett S. Lyon, Myron W. Watkins, and Victor Abramson: *Government and Economic Life* (Washington, D.C.: The Brookings Institution, 1939), Vol. I, pp. 274 ff.
[21] Walton Hamilton and Associates: *Price and Price Policy* (New York: McGraw-Hill Book Company, Inc., 1938), pp. 237–8.
[22] U.S. Temporary National Economic Committee: *Trade Association Survey*, p. 346.
[23] U.S. v. Standard Oil Co. of New Jersey, 221 U.S. 1 (1911). Fainsod and Gordon: *Government and the American Economy*, p. 528.
[24] Chamber of Commerce of the United States: *Development of Trade Associations* (Washington, D.C.: Chamber of Commerce of the United States, 1937), p. 5.

in legislation.[25] A more exhaustive study in 1938 revealed that "government relations" in various forms constituted the most important of trade association activities. Of the groups queried, over 80 per cent reported that they engaged in such work, and it was the only field of endeavor that more than half of them rated as of major importance. Moreover, the frequency and importance of these relationships showed only slight variation according to the type of industry covered by the association.[26]

Recourse to the institutions of government results both from the need of these groups for help in furthering their aims and from their closely related need of protection from the activities of economic and political rivals. The use of government in the former connection is easily illustrated. Federal Trade Commission sponsorship of trade practice conferences has materially assisted associations in controlling certain types of competitive practices. Product standardization through the assistance of the Bureau of Standards has been common, and the use of government statistical services for information on the industries represented in these associations and on competing industries has been of general importance. Promotion of legislation consistent with the interests of the group has been a prominent activity.

The efforts of trade associations to obtain the aid of various branches of the government against rivals are perhaps more important than their dependence upon government services like those just described. Inevitably, these efforts have helped to increase the number and political activity of trade associations. For, as we have seen, the work of one political interest group, whether a business association or a group representing some other interest in the society—labor unions, for instance—results in a wavelike development of interest group activity; other groups are created to present different claims and to push opposing policies, and, in turn, still other groups grow up in response to these, and so on. The result, in part, of the proliferation and increased political activity of trade associations and other political interest groups concerned with economic policy has been what is often called "the unparalleled growth of Federal legislation affecting business in recent years,"[27] a growth that has, in its turn, stimulated the development of even more trade associations into political interest groups. Herring, in fact, states that the major reason for the concern of these trade associations with government action has been, not the

[25] Herring: *Group Representation Before Congress*, pp. 100–101.

[26] U.S. Temporary National Economic Committee: *Trade Association Survey*, pp. 22, 26, 31–3.

[27] Ibid., p. 333.

promotion of their own interests *per se*, but the defense of their interests, both by fostering legislation or regulation to control the activities of their rivals and by fighting legislation or regulation that operates to the disadvantage of their members.[28] As changes and disturbances in economic relations have become more severe, trade associations have undertaken, for instance, the kind of action exemplified in the promotion of resale price maintenance legislation by the National Association of Retail Druggists in opposition to the chain stores. For similar reasons such action has also been promoted to an increasing degree by labor groups, farm groups, and others.

An interesting illustration of more purely defensive tactics is provided by the Association of Life Insurance Presidents, the principal trade association in this business. It was founded in 1906, and the major impetus for its organization was a barrage of restrictive legislation by the State governments following an investigation in New York in 1905, the so-called Armstrong investigation. As the association's manager and general counsel put it in 1939, its function was in large measure "to take care of the legislative matters which were flooding the country in the various legislatures." Its activities have been largely defensive; proposed bills examined by the staff, for example, are classified in three ways: those "quite objectionable," those which might "become objectionable" through amendment, and others "obviously of no interest." [29] The United States Brewers Association, among others, was also created primarily to defend its members against government action. Within four months of the inclusion by Congress of a dollar-per-barrel tax on beer in the revenue legislation of 1862, this trade association was formed.[30] The privileged position of some business groups, particularly those with the resources of large-scale enterprise, has under these circumstances forced upon the trade association, along with other types of business group, the function of defending the economic *status quo* with as little modification as possible.

Elaboration of these propositions may more appropriately be reserved for later chapters. The point to emphasize here is that trade associations are organized for reasons that necessarily lead to political activity. For both the associations and their concern with government action are a natural outgrowth of the circumstances attending the establishment of interest groups in the area of economic institutions.

---

[28] Herring: *Group Representation Before Congress*, p. 101.
[29] Zeller: *Pressure Politics in New York*, pp. 48–9; U.S. Temporary National Economic Committee: *Hearings*, Part 10, 76th Cong., 1st Sess. (1939), pp. 4346, 4358, 4360, 4395.
[30] Odegard: *Pressure Politics*, p. 245.

Essentially the same patterns of origin and development seen in the case of the trade associations are shown by the major national federations of such groups—the National Association of Manufacturers and the Chamber of Commerce of the United States.[31] The former of these, one of the most interesting political interest groups in the United States, is not strictly speaking a federation except in one of its subsidiary forms. Its central organization has a membership of individual firms all over the nation. The N.A.M. emerged out of the disturbed conditions of the panic of 1893. At a meeting in Cincinnati in January, 1895, at which Governor William McKinley was guest of honor, the organization was formed. Its entire program then and for the next eight years was concerned with the promotion of American commerce, particularly international trade. During these years the organization remained relatively small and unimportant.

The N.A.M. did not become a particularly significant group until it also became involved in labor questions in 1903. This change in emphasis and the subsequent growth of the organization almost justify the assertion that 1903 marked the beginning of a new association. The point is illustrated by income figures: In 1896, the first full year of the N.A.M.'s operation, revenues amounted to about $30,000 and they did not go much above that level until the shift; in 1904 and subsequent years, however, the association's income was in excess of $150,-000.[32] If one examines such data as the following on the increase in trade union and A.F. of L. membership between 1897 and 1904, a major reason for the change in emphasis in the N.A. M. program will be apparent.[33] The average annual increase in both A.F. of L. and total trade union membership between 1897, when the movement shook off the effects of the depression, and 1904 was over 25 per cent. In some years—such as 1903, significantly enough—it was in the neighborhood of 40 per cent. The total A.F. of L. and independent union membership of more than two million in 1904 represented an increase in excess of 360 per cent over 1897. The increase involved as well a considerable growth in solidarity, since the A.F. of L. proportion of the total membership grew from 60 per cent in 1897 to 80 per cent in 1904. Accompanying these changes, as has been suggested earlier, was a strengthening of controls within the national and interna-

[31] A distinction is often made between the trade association as an organization for dealing with the market and the employers association as a device for activity in connection with the employment relation.

[32] U.S. Senate, Committee on Education and Labor: *Senate Report No. 6*, Part 6, 76th Cong., 1st Sess. (1939), p. 14.

[33] Adapted from Millis and Montgomery: *Organized Labor*, pp. 82-3.

tional unions, a greater subordination of the locals, and vigorous demands for the eight-hour day, higher pay, and the closed shop.

Although it is no doubt incorrect to say that union organization has always preceded association on the other side of the employment relation—employers' groups have tended to form as a result of various circumstances making united action on labor policy desirable[34]—it is nevertheless true that increased strength of workers groups has been one of the circumstances producing such employers associations. The reasons will be apparent if one refers to the basic functions performed by associations in stabilizing relations between tangent groups.

At any event, beginning in 1900 a number of local and State-wide associations of employers developed and carried on vigorous drives for the open shop, which was in a sense a symbol for insistence upon the unrestricted discretion of employers in setting the conditions of work in their plants. General leadership of this movement on a national scale was assumed by the National Association of Manufacturers at its 1903 convention, although national action by a smaller group had been taken in 1901, when the National Metal Trades Association shifted to a strong antiunion policy.[35]

Inevitably the N.A.M. was from the beginning closely concerned with government action. Its continuing concern with the tariff and other trade-promotion policies necessitated such activity, and the new emphasis upon labor relations, particularly following the political reorientation of the A.F. of L. discussed above, increased the N.A.M.'s involvement in government. The federated aspect of the N.A.M. was in part an outgrowth of this preoccupation with political activity. Although its primary membership included only individual firms, to facilitate its activities in labor relations it set up a series of satellite, though nominally independent, groups made up of trade associations concerned with labor matters. The first of these, the Citizens' Industrial Association of America, was formed in 1903 on the base of local employers' groups. It was succeeded in 1907 by the National Council of Industrial Defense (later called the National Industrial Council), which included national groups as well, in the hope that the more inclusive organization would produce better "protection against a constantly increasing demand for . . . legislation" on the part of labor unions.[36] This political activity, paralleled

[34] See Clarence E. Bonnett: "Employers Associations," *Encyclopaedia of the Social Sciences.*

[35] U.S. Senate, Committee on Education and Labor: *Senate Report No. 6,* Part 6, 76th Cong., 1st Sess. (1939), pp. 5–6.

[36] Quoted ibid., p. 15. See also Clarence E. Bonnett: *Employers Associations in the United States* (New York: The Macmillan Company, 1922), p. 374.

by various state organizations,[37] was so direct as to involve unpublicized participation in election campaigns prior to 1913. Publicity on these zealous performances was a by-product of a series of congressional investigations initiated in 1913 by a statement from President Wilson criticizing lobbying activities in opposition to the Underwood tariff bill of that year.[38] Although some of these methods have perforce fallen into the discard, the organization has not deviated from its early interest in the processes of government.

The N.A.M. continued to expand during the second decade of the century, fluctuating somewhat with shifts in the business cycle and the aggressiveness of labor unions. During the post-World War I decade, however, the organization did not grow appreciably. After 1926 its financial position declined, and its memberships soon followed. By 1933 the number of members had dropped about 75 per cent from the peak of 5350 established in 1922.[39]

The reasons for this shift are of particular interest. In the first place, the active membership—and presumably the entire roll, though this cannot be ascertained, since the organization does not release membership lists even to those who pay dues—was limited almost entirely to relatively small firms. The officials represented only those firms presumably not large enough alone to oppose the union organizations as they were then constituted. For the big, mass-production industries, especially those that developed after World War I, were, as we have seen, beyond the grasp of organized labor in the 1920's. Neither the possibility that their workers would become organized nor the threat of labor activity through legislation was enough to bring these corporations into an organization like the N.A.M. Consequently, when the depression hit in 1929 and a number of the small firm members withdrew for reasons of economy, the association suffered acutely.

This situation was dramatically altered after 1933. With the upturn in labor union membership and the organization after 1935 of

[37] For example, McKean: *Pressures on the Legislature of New Jersey*, p. 104, notes that the Manufacturers' Association of New Jersey was formed in 1905 to defeat a workmen's compensation measure; and Zeller: *Pressure Politics in New York*, pp. 51–2, quotes a publication of the Associated Industries (New York) indicating that it was founded in 1914 to resist the "riot of social legislation" in the state legislature at that time.

[38] U.S. Senate, Subcommittee of the Committee on the Judiciary: *Hearings under S. Res. 92*, 63d Cong., 1st Sess., 4 vols. (1913); U.S. House of Representatives, Select Committee on Lobby Investigation: *Hearings*, 63d Cong., 1st Sess., 4 vols. (1913); U.S. House of Representatives, Judiciary Committee: *Hearings*, 63d Cong., 2d Sess. (1914). See Herring: *Group Representation Before Congress*, pp. 43–6.

[39] "Renovation in N. A. M.," *Fortune* (July, 1948), p. 75.

the mass-production workers along industrial lines, and with the passage of national legislation favorable to labor consequent upon a shift in the relative influence of major political groups, the association began again to grow. The new recruits, moreover, included increasing numbers of large corporations in automobile and electrical goods manufacture, chemical products, and similar industries. The "independence" that these firms had easily maintained in the 1920's had been sufficiently threatened to bring them into the fold, and they led in building the membership, especially after passage of the National Labor Relations Act of 1935, up to a claimed sixteen thousand in 1948. [40] The entire association was reorganized in 1933, and since then it has been led primarily by representatives of "big business." Its political activities, moreover, have shown no diminution, but rather a considerable increase.

The second of the major national federations, the Chamber of Commerce of the United States, resembles the trade associations more than does the N.A.M., since, with exceptions to be mentioned later, its formal structure is built upon trade associations and State and local chambers of commerce. The circumstances surrounding the formation of the Chamber in 1912 will be sufficiently clear from what has gone before, and a brief review of the interrelated influences will suffice. The increasingly insistent assertion of interests in opposition to those of many business groups, especially the larger ones, symbolized in the passage of the Sherman Act of 1890 and the fulminations of Theodore Roosevelt, was one influence. The threat implied by the growth and increased political activity of organized labor was a second and closely related influence. Finally, those instabilities of the market that produced the trade associations and the State and local chambers of commerce invited interaction among the economic groups so organized. As these problems increasingly involved nation-wide action and as other groups effectively pressed their demands through the national Government, there emerged both aggressive and defensive reasons for a federation of trade groups based on interests broader than those stemming from the employment relation.[41]

The chamber was not the first attempt at a response of this sort. The National Board of Trade, to whose functions the chamber succeeded, had been established in 1868. Those who prepared its constitution had revealed the nature of the precipitating disturbances when they included the following among the objectives of an organi-

[40] Ibid., p. 72.
[41] Cf. Paul Studenski: "Chambers of Commerce," *Encyclopaedia of the Social Sciences*.

zation of commercial associations: "to secure unity and harmony of action in reference to commercial usages, customs, and laws; and especially . . . to secure the proper consideration of questions pertaining to the financial, commercial, and industrial interests of the country. . . ."[42] Inadequacies in its organization, probably including its failure to affiliate trade associations as well as chambers of commerce, led to its replacement by the chamber.

It is frequently asserted that the Chamber of Commerce was founded as a result of the encouragement of the Government and that it was sponsored by the N.A.M.[43] Such accounts say both too much and too little, because so narrow a set of sources is insufficient to account for an association of the chamber's scope. As in most major inventive developments, social as well as technological, the stimulating circumstances were so general as to produce initiating actions from a number of sources. Prior to 1912 several preliminary efforts had been made by such organizations as the Boston Chamber of Commerce and the Chicago Association of Commerce either to reorganize the National Board of Trade into a more representative body or to supplant it. Among the obstacles to these efforts was the problem of securing appropriate sponsorship. Childs indicates that this problem was solved by a decision to have an organizing meeting called by the President of the United States.[44] Thus the Government's role was a reflection of efforts on the part of a small, initiating group. Persuasion of the President undoubtedly was made easier by his previously expressed desire for an organization that could regularize the relations between the Government and business associations in the field of foreign commerce. In his message to Congress on the subject of foreign affairs, delivered on December 7, 1911, President Taft observed:

In the dissemination of useful information and in the coordination of effort certain unofficial associations have done good work toward the promotion of foreign commerce. It is cause for regret, however, that the great number of such associations and the comparative lack of cooperation between them fail to secure an efficiency commensurate with the public interest. . . . Some central organization in touch with associations and chambers of commerce throughout the country would, I believe, be of great

[42] Quoted in Childs: *Labor and Capital in National Politics*, pp. 8–9.
[43] U.S. Temporary National Economic Committee: *Economic Power and Political Pressures*, pp. 25, 85; U.S. Senate, Committee on Education and Labor: *Senate Report No. 6*, Part 6, 76th Cong., 1st Sess. (1939), p. 33.
[44] Childs: *Labor and Capital in National Politics*, p. 10. The material on the origins of the Chamber is largely drawn from this source.

value. Such organization might be managed by a committee composed of a small number of those now actively carrying on the work of some of the larger associations. . . .[45]

At a preliminary meeting in the Department of Commerce and Labor in February, 1912, the National Association of Manufacturers was represented, along with the San Francisco Chamber of Commerce, the Southern Commercial Congress, the Boston Chamber of Commerce, and the District of Columbia Board of Commerce. This meeting resulted in issuance by the Secretary of Commerce and Labor of an invitation to the organizing meeting in April, attended by about seven hundred delegates. The entire course of this development not only illustrates the circumstances under which such groups emerge but indicates as well the involvement of the association, from its inception, with governmental affairs.

Membership in the chamber is of two general kinds: first, organization members, such as state and local chambers of commerce and trade associations; second, individual and associate members (differentiated on the basis of the amount of dues paid), that is, persons or firms who are also members of an organization that belongs to the chamber. The group was organized at an appropriate moment, for, as in the case of the trade associations, the World War I period gave a considerable boost to its membership. Because the number of organization members has generally fluctuated with the fortunes of the business cycle and these members have thus provided an unreliable financial base, the chamber has from the beginning exerted great effort to build up the other category of membership. Since this policy inevitably means concentration upon obtaining the membership of those best able to pay individual as well as organization dues, it has certain implications for the operations of the chamber. These will be examined at a later point. Despite the sources of its financial strength and the variations in the number of its affiliates, the chamber can make formal claim to representing a considerable proportion of the commercial organizations of the country.[46]

[45] *Congressional Record*, 62d Cong., 2d Sess. (December 7, 1911), p. 75.
[46] Its claimed membership in 1948 was 2932 organization members and 18,891 individual and associate members. (Letter to the author, August 18, 1948.)

The Rise of Agricultural Groups

Turning to associations among farmers, we are confronted with a bewildering array of interdependent movements, an array fully as complicated as that presented by the trade unions and trade associations. The latter developed more or less simultaneously in response to similar conditions and may be reliably discussed collectively, but the history of farm organizations is rather that of a succession of movements of national scope. It is true, of course, that agricultural associations organized around common interests in particular commodities—fruits, vegetables, peanuts, milk, cotton, and the like—are virtually indistinguishable from trade associations. Some of these, such as the National Council of Farmer Co-operatives, the National Co-operative Milk Producers' Federation, and the National Beet Growers Association, either function much like trade associations or are closely affiliated with such business groups.[47] The best over-all picture of farm associations, however, can be drawn from the successive development of three national organizations that are still operating, the National Grange Order of the Patrons of Husbandry, the Farmers' Educational and Co-operative Union, and the American Farm Bureau Federation. All three emerged out of the increased interactions of farmers in response to intense disturbances of their accustomed behavior. All three sooner or later had recourse to the institutions of government as a major means of establishing the desired degree of stability in both intergroup and intragroup relations.

Although agricultural societies are of ancient vintage in the United States and although agricultural interests, especially in the early years of the Republic, have consistently been important in party politics, no differentiated national organization of farmers emerged until after the Civil War. The appearance of such associations at that time is further evidence of the way in which the same general set of rapid changes in traditional relationships may produce proliferation in the forms of group life. Genuine associations of farmers, as distinct from the rather genteel and literary agricultural societies that developed after the Revolution, came with the spread of commercial farming in the North and West after the Civil War. The accompanying specialization exposed farmers to the unpredictable insecurities stemming from changes in the market, accentuated by the discrimina-

[47] For a good popular account of farm organizations and their political activities see Wesley McCune: *The Farm Bloc* (Garden City, New York: Doubleday, Doran & Company, 1943).

tory practices of the railroads and by various speculative activities. By the 1870's the farmers of both East and West found themselves dependent upon the vagaries of marketing institutions, transportation facilities, and prices.[48] It is no accident that the militancy of farmers associations has generally varied inversely with the prosperity of agriculture.

The Grange, as it is usually known, was started in 1867 by seven men, six of whom were government employees, as an educational society for farmers on the pattern of the Masonic order. Although looked on with suspicion by farmers in its early years, it experienced rapid growth during the agricultural difficulties of the 1870's, particularly after the panic of 1873, which had affected farmers in the West as early as 1870. Between 1873 and late 1874 the number of local Granges increased in number from about three thousand to over twenty thousand, paralleling an increase in mortgage foreclosures. At one time, it is reported, Indiana had an average of two Granges for each township in the State.[49] The Grange in its constitution formally eschewed political activity, but in many States the pressure for action was so strong that these groups participated, under another name, in the various farmers' political parties of the middle 1870's. In any case, by 1876 the Grange had restricted the meaning of the term "political" to purely electoral and partisan activity, which it continued formally to avoid. It engaged in other governmental activities, as is indicated by its setting up in 1876 a detailed plan for securing legislation favorable to farmers. It has participated in the governmental process in similar fashion ever since. The Grange reached the peak of its strength of nearly 900,000 in 1875, from which point it declined to a low of 100,000 by the turn of the century. In recent years it has built up to a level of about 800,000. Although nominally national in scope, its principal strength is in New England, New York, New Jersey, Pennsylvania, and Ohio,[50] a concentration that may help to explain the fact that the organization at present assumes a policy position far different from that of its radical youth.

[48] Solon J. Buck: "Grange," *Encyclopaedia of the Social Sciences*. See generally his two books: *The Granger Movement* (Cambridge, Mass.: Harvard University Press, 1913) and *The Agrarian Crusade* (New Haven, Conn.: Yale University Press, 1920).

[49] Orville M. Kile: *The Farm Bureau Movement* (New York: The Macmillan Company, 1921), pp. 14, 17.

[50] U.S. Department of Agriculture: *Farmers in a Changing World: The Yearbook of Agriculture, 1940* (Washington, D.C.: Government Printing Office, 1940), p. 948.

The second of these farm organizations in point of age and the third in size at the present time is the Farmers' Union. It was founded in Texas in 1902 among low-income farmers, a segment of the farm population from which it has drawn a considerable portion of its membership ever since, a fact that has permitted it almost alone among farm organizations to co-operate politically with organized labor. The Union was aimed at the same kind of stability sought by its predecessors. Among the purposes enunciated by its constitution are the following: "To discourage the credit mortgage system. To eliminate gambling in farm products. To secure and maintain profitable and uniform prices for cotton, grain, livestock, and other products of the farm." [51] The Union early emphasized co-operative buying and selling, and many of its enterprises, such as the Farmers' Union Grain Terminal Association, have been conspicuously successful. By 1914 the Union had expanded out of the South into the Middle West and North West, with units in twenty-two States. Although it is organized in about three quarters of the States, its principal strength has been concentrated in the Great Plains from the Dakotas south, where frequent deficiency of rainfall has made farming peculiarly hazardous. In no small measure this concentration may account for the Union's consistently "radical" position on most issues since its inception. [52] By 1920 the Union found that the promotion of co-operatives was an insufficient means of achieving the stability its members sought, and it turned to the promotion of Federal legislation favorable to its program. These efforts were originally directed primarily at securing a government guarantee of the farmer's "cost of production." The Union has been much concerned also with the problems of tenancy and subsistence farming, in which connection it was the sole champion among national farm organizations of the early program of the Farm Security Administration. In the early 1930's several of the State Farmers' Unions, notably in Iowa, sponsored the direct-action Farmers' Holiday Organization, which attempted to strike against low farm prices by forcibly preventing products such as milk from reaching the market. During the early 1920's, probably as a consequence of its political orientation, the Farmers' Union membership reached a peak of over one million. It

---

[51] Quoted in Kile: *The Farm Bureau Movement,* p. 31.
[52] See J. D. Barnhart: "Rainfall and the Populist Party in Nebraska," *American Political Science Review,* Vol. 19, no. 3 (August, 1925), pp. 527–40; George A. Lundberg: "The Demographic and Economic Basis of Political Radicalism and Conservatism," *American Journal of Sociology,* Vol. 32, no. 5 (March, 1927), pp. 719–32.

has declined since then and by now probably includes approximately 450,000 families.[53]

The third of the national farm associations, the American Farm Bureau Federation, is on all counts the largest and most important. It has had an extraordinarily curious history, in large part because of its close relation to government from its beginnings. Although it conforms to the general pattern of association development, unlike those of other such movements its immediate origins apparently were not in the disturbances associated with a sharp deterioration of agricultural markets. They lay rather in the obstacles to increased farm production and efforts to promote more effective control of plant diseases. In 1903 the Department of Agriculture embarked on a demonstration project in Texas designed to teach farmers that cotton could be grown profitably despite the boll weevil, whose ravages had demoralized both farm and business groups in the South. Beginning in 1906 in the South, counties and States began appropriating funds for the support of "demonstrators," or, as they later were known, county agents. In 1914 this development was recognized and regularized nationally by the passage of the Smith-Lever Act establishing a system of grants-in-aid to the State colleges of agriculture in support of a program of extension education in improved farming methods. With this encouragement the county agent system spread rapidly, covering approximately one third of the nation's counties by the beginning of 1915.[54]

Around these county agents there had developed, prior to the inauguration of the national program, a series of local organizations designed both to provide additional funds for the work and to facilitate contacts with the local farmers. On occasion these were sponsored by mail-order houses, railroads, and chambers of commerce as well as by local farm groups. The Smith-Lever Act specifically recognized these groups as a proper source of a portion of the State matching funds necessary to secure the maximum Federal grant. In setting the conditions under which extension work could be organized in a

[53] Accurate figures on farm organization membership are difficult to secure, since several of the organizations are very loosely set up. They are not strictly comparable, moreover, since some count each family as a membership unit, others count each family member or each one over a certain age as a separate unit. See U.S. Department of Commerce: *National Associations of the United States*, p. 477.

[54] Kile: *The Farm Bureau Movement*, pp. 88–9. See also Gladys Baker: *The County Agent* (Chicago: University of Chicago Press, 1939) for a careful analysis of the whole movement.

county, most State legislatures required the establishment of an organized group of farmers as a co-operating body. Some of these specified that such groups should be known as a farm bureau. By 1916 these local groups were generally called county farm bureaus.

The entire movement received a strong stimulus during World War I in the form of additional Federal funds and encouragement for the formation of farm bureaus in order to maximize agricultural production. The exigencies of the war also provided the occasion for rapid federation of the county bureaus, first at the State level and then nationally.[55] With the aid of officials of the United States Department of Agriculture, the American Farm Bureau Federation was launched in 1919–20. Thus when the agricultural boom broke sharply in the fall of 1920, the new federation was a ready vehicle through which farmers might attempt to restore a measure of stability. In no small measure its advantage lay in the established governmental relationships involved in its founding. In many States the county bureaus had a semiofficial status, which, incidentally, they have maintained in a number of instances despite the protests of competing farm groups. In recent years there have been seven States that still require a county farm bureau as a local sponsoring body, although in two of these, Maine and Rhode Island, the farm bureau organization is unaffiliated with the American Farm Bureau Federation. Other State laws require a local sponsoring organization but do not name any specific one. Among the latter are Illinois and Iowa, where formal relationships between the Farm Bureau and the extension services have existed from the beginning; in recent years from one fifth to one third of the funds expended for extension work in these States has come from Farm Bureau contributions. In addition to these two, there are only four States in which nongovernmental contributions to extension work have been in significant amounts in recent years: Connecticut, New York, Kansas, and Missouri. In many others, however, the Farm Bureau has retained the advantages of a semiofficial status even after formal connections with the State and county governments were severed. As a consequence, in part, of these developments, the emphasis in the Farm Bureau program shifted from education to governmental activities, particularly the promotion of favorable legislation, a preoccupation that it has retained ever since. This shift was dramatically symbolized by the formation and operation of

[55] A discussion of the New York federation is contained in Zeller: *Pressure Politics in New York,* chap. 4.

the first "farm bloc" in the 67th Congress (1920–22), in which the Farm Bureau was a major factor.[56] Thus each of the major farm organizations has found recourse to the institutions of government a natural outgrowth of its formation, the more so as the overrepresentation of rural areas in both State and national legislatures has given such interests a special bargaining advantage.

Although the Federation is organized in more than three fourths of the States, the great majority of its members are in the Corn Belt, and the organization tends to reflect the interests of its membership in that section. It has fluctuated somewhat in size, declining rather consistently during the lean years of the 1920's and early 1930's from the high of nearly half a million to which it had climbed in 1921. After 1933 it was able to utilize the agricultural adjustment legislation and the later programs in World War II, as its constituent groups had those of 1917–19, to build its numbers up to one and one-quarter million families, according to recent claims.

Before turning to other types of association it may be appropriate to note that the Federal agricultural extension work mentioned in connection with the Farm Bureau, as well as a number of similar farm programs, has given rise to a whole series of interest groups aside from those of active farmers. A prominent example is the Association of Land-Grant Colleges and Universities, which is made up of the principal officials of the educational institutions benefiting from the series of Federal statutes, beginning with the Morrill Act of 1862, granting aid to agricultural research and education. Interaction among such officials as a result of similar relations with the national government led to the establishment of the association in 1887 as a means of regularizing their tangent relations. Beginning with the second Morrill Act of 1890, the association has undertaken the active promotion of favorable legislative and administrative policies. It has worked closely with the Farm Bureau, especially on matters affecting the extension services, and with other such groups. Some indication of the intimacy of the connection between the association and the Department of Agriculture is provided by the large number of department officials who have served as its officers or as administrators of land-grant colleges. Similar in origin, and in a sense tributary to the Association of Land-Grant Colleges, is the National Association of County Agricultural Agents, formed in 1915, which was one of the

[56] See Kile: *The Farm Bureau Movement*, chap. 14, and the account by an active participant, Arthur Capper: *The Agricultural Bloc* (New York: Harcourt, Brace & Company, 1922).

groups instrumental in the formation of the American Farm Bureau Federation. Such groups have almost invariably developed following the passage of grant-in-aid legislation by the Federal government.[57]

Other Organizational Beginnings

These major occupational groups show the expected patterns of development and readily come to mind as examples, since their origins and history are relatively well documented. Although the evidence is less complete on such groups as the organized professions, it points to the same sort of pattern, with differences only in various particulars of largely minor importance. In the case of the ancient and honorable professions of medicine and the law, of course, the picture is complicated by the fact that these go back to an early and strong guild organization whose traditions have been carried forward through the centuries. These occupations, moreover, have in all ages been close to the institutions of government in the sense that almost invariably they have been subject to a considerable measure of regulation to insure effective and scrupulous discharge of their public trust. The number and importance of the group interests affected by the fashion in which these professional functions are performed have been sufficient to force their regulation by government from an early date. Such regulation usually, if not invariably, has been established at the instance of subgroups in the profession who have utilized the powers of government to chastise their wayward bethren or to prevent those deemed unqualified from gaining access to the professional ranks.

In the United States the oldest continuing groups of this sort are the medical associations. Emerging in the late eighteenth century, they formalized tangent relations dependent in part upon the seedling growth of hospitals and medical schools, and their major concern was with the closely related matters of the quality of professional training and licensing. Typical of these is the Medical Society of the State of New York, established by a law of 1806 that sanctioned the establishment of county societies to examine and license aspiring practitioners and that approved their federation into a State society. Among the primary purposes of this society was the improvement of medical

[57] For a full discussion of this point see V. O. Key, Jr.: *The Administration of Federal Grants to States* (Chicago: Public Administration Service, 1937), chap. 7.

practice through passage of State legislation contributing to that end.[58]

The development of a national organization did not occur until the mid-nineteenth century, when, as in the case of so many national groups, the improved means of transportation and communication permitted a great frequency of contact. Starting as an annual meeting of doctors, the American Medical Association did not achieve a thoroughgoing formal organization until 1901. Among the reasons for this delay undoubtedly is the fact, stemming from the federal character of our political institutions, that the governmental means of carrying out the objectives of professional groups were in the hands of the State legislatures rather than in the domain of the national Government. Despite such handicaps, the American Medical Association included in its membership by 1912 approximately half the doctors in the United States, which proportion has now risen to something over two thirds, a remarkably complete coverage for any widespread group.[59] Moreover, with the increase in Federal appropriations for public health purposes since World War I and with the efforts of various groups largely made up of laymen to use the powers of the national government to foster changes in the organization and financing of medical practice through some form of social insurance, the A. M. A. has become increasingly active in trying to influence national government policy.

The legal profession inherited from its English origins a tradition of organization. Despite this fact there were few important associations of lawyers in America until after the Civil War. In the 1870's such groups began to develop, at first locally and then on a State basis. Typical of the latter is the New York State Bar Association, the first such organization to be formed. Set up in 1876, it was primarily concerned, like the medical societies, with professional standards, though it has also become involved in the organization of the judiciary and other matters closely affecting legal practice. Other State groups were formed rapidly, and by 1888 bar associations existed in three fourths of the States. The American Bar Association was set in operation in 1878 by a group of seventy-three men among whose first official acts, it is significant to note, was the establishment of a committee on legal education and admission to the bar.[60] Although ef-

[58] Garceau: *The Political Life of the A.M.A.*, p. 14; Zeller: *Pressure Politics in New York*, p. 180.

[59] Garceau: *The Political Life of the A.M.A.*, p. 130.

[60] M. Louise Rutherford: *The Influence of the American Bar Association on Public Opinion and Legislation* (Philadelphia: The Foundation Press, Inc., 1937), pp. 8–11; Zeller: *Pressure Politics in New York*, p. 191.

forts were made as early as 1887 to make the national association a federated organization representative of the entire American bar, these have never been entirely successful. An approximation to such an arrangement was achieved in 1936, but the relations between the bar associations at the local, State, and national levels are still slight. Moreover, the American Bar Association has never numbered among its members more than one fifth of the country's lawyers, although the coverage of many of the State and local groups is more nearly complete.[61]

One may well ask a number of questions concerning the peculiarities of lawyers' associations. Why did a national organization emerge so late? Why has it remained relatively weak in its leadership of the State and local groups? Why has the American Bar Association included in its membership so small a segment of the country's lawyers? Not all these questions are immediately answerable, but suggestions concerning some of them will illuminate our discussion of the origins of associations and their orientation toward government.

Despite the predominant role that members of the bar have played in the political affairs of the country since the late eighteenth century, it is apparent that their continuing experiences as lawyers have not been such as to produce interests strong enough to unify them in an effective and inclusive group. As Bryce observed a half century ago, legal practice in America was for long "virtually an open profession like stockbroking or engineering" and consequently has not been marked by "a distinctive character and corporate feeling."[62] This fact may be noted without attempting at this point to explain it.

Probably the delay in establishing a national lawyers' organization is first of all in part a result of the fact that, as in the case of medicine, the matters of training and admission to the profession are the concern of the State governments rather than the national government. Secondly, disturbances of the accustomed habits of the legal profession as such, in the form of legislative efforts to modify common-law rules and to introduce through expert commissions alternatives to the traditional judicial means of settling disputes, are largely a product of the rapid changes in American society since the Civil War. Moreover,

[61] Rutherford: *The Influence of the American Bar Association,* pp. 12, 16–7, 19-34.
[62] James Bryce: *The American Commonwealth* (2d edition, New York: Macmillan & Company, 1891), Vol. II, p. 502. Copyright by Macmillan & Co. and used with the permission of The Macmillan Company. On this subject in general see James Willard Hurst: *The Growth of American Law: The Law Makers* (Boston: Little, Brown & Company, 1950), chap. 12 and esp. pp. 285–94.

these were first felt in the States and not until comparatively recently at the Federal level. Bryce in the 1880's felt it proper to characterize the legislative product of Congress as "scanty," though he noted "an increasing tendency to invoke congressional legislation" in fields in which State action was proving inadequate.[63] The great expansion in the area of affairs covered by congressional consideration, however, dates from the administration of Woodrow Wilson. Such changes affected the practice of law not only directly but also indirectly through the widened jurisdiction and increased work load of the Federal courts.[64]

Although these disturbances were enough to stimulate and sustain a small national bar association, their effect was by no means uniform. A large proportion of most practices remained at the State and local level. Moreover, as the road to success in the law increasingly lay in the direction of specialized corporation practice, those men concerned about changes in the legal profession were likely also to be those primarily engaged in defending large economic groups from attack through legislative and judicial channels. Thus the American Bar Association's self-appointed role as "trustees and guardians of American institutions" was likely to involve the inextricable mixture of these substantive matters with those of a procedural or ethical nature. For those men who have no such practices and for those large numbers for whom the law provides only the most modest means of livelihood, such trusteeship activites are likely to hold no interest. The same situation apparently prevails frequently in the State associations, judging from occasional suggestions that membership is likely to increase only with efforts by the legal profession to improve the economic position of a large proportion of its members.[65] Thus the centrifugal effects of specialized practice and wide income differentials have placed limits on the effectiveness with which bar associations stabilize the relationships of their potential membership and upon the completeness of association among lawyers. However, limited mem-

[63] Bryce: *The American Commonwealth*, Vol. I, p. 348; Vol. II, p. 710. Copyright 1891 by Macmillan & Co. and used with the permission of The Macmillan Company.

[64] George B. Galloway: *Congress at the Crossroads* (New York: Thomas Y. Crowell Company, 1946), pp. 52–3; Felix Frankfurter and James M. Landis: *The Business of the Supreme Court* (New York: The Macmillan Company, 1927), chaps. 2–7.

[65] Cf. Zeller: *Pressure Politics in New York*, p. 194. A highly critical evaluation of the American Bar is contained in Harold J. Laski: *The American Democracy* (New York: Viking Press, Inc., 1948), pp. 564–91.

bership has not prevented the organized segments from becoming deeply involved in the processes of government.

One might go through an almost interminable list of associations in the recognized and self-styled professions further to illustrate the fundamental pattern. People with similar skills that produce similar interests may at any time become an active group. Their interaction is increased in frequency as a consequence of sufficiently prolonged and intense disturbances: changes in techniques, shifts or threatened shifts in economic status, altered relationships or the probability of such alteration resulting from the formation or expansion of other groups, and the like. Development of organized associations follows in order to regularize such interaction and to facilitate stabilization of the group's internal and external relations. In the process of attempting to establish and protect an equilibrium of this sort, the association usually, if not invariably, resorts to the institutions of government. Such resort may be close and continuing or peripheral and intermittent. Teachers, especially public school teachers, are an obvious instance of a group who are a segment of the total government institution, but who have found themselves so poorly articulated with the central decision-making parts of the institution that they have formed associations to compensate for this situation.[66] In recent years, particularly, with the disturbances and maladjustments following upon rapid changes in the business cycle, people engaged in such occupations have found the institutions of government—through licensing agencies and statutory training requirements—a primary means of strengthening the occupation by limiting the number of those who enter it and of controlling unfair or destructive practices invited by economic insecurity and frustration. The statute books of almost any State include provisions for licensing not only the professions already discussed but also public accountants, librarians, nurses, barbers, chiropodists, dentists, embalmers, pharmacists, optometrists, veterinarians, beauty-shop operators, real-estate agents, cleaners and dyers, land surveyors, and many others. McKean reports that in one session of the New Jersey legislature there were efforts to set up licensing laws for bait-fishing boats, beauty shops, chain stores, florists, insurance adjusters, photographers, master painters, and cleaners and dyers. The last-named bill was passed, providing for a board of three members, of which one was to

[66] See Herring: *Group Representation Before Congress*, pp. 172–80; McKean: *Pressures on the Legislature of New Jersey*, pp. 115–20; Zeller: *Pressure Politics in New York*, pp. 156–80.

be the secretary of the New Jersey Dyers and Cleaners Association.[67]

It would be highly misleading if this examination of the origins of representative associations were to include only those of an economic or occupational character. It is true that associations have formed with startling rapidity in the past eighty years upon the tangent relations between institutionalized economic groups. As the preceding pages indicate, the disturbances of established patterns of behavior in that area have been intense and continuing. The very rate at which such associations have been formed testifies to the cleavages and instability concentrated in the economic groups of the society, as well as to the likelihood that for an extended period the struggle for a more stable equilibrium in economic relationships will be a major focus of attention.

Economic groups, however, are not isolated, discrete phenomena, though we may treat them as such for convenience in analysis. Changes directly affecting them will also influence interactions throughout the social web, as scientific discoveries concerning the nature of matter and energy may affect not only relationships involved in the production of energy from conventional sources but also, and equally, the patterns of interaction in religious groups and even in college faculties. Other types of disturbances, moreover, may have their primary focus in other institutionalized groups, only secondarily or insignificantly affecting economic groups. The processes of group politics are not an aspect of economic determinism. As Herring points out in his study of Congress, a large number of noneconomic, nonoccupational groups "have their spokesmen who often equal and sometimes exceed in power the agents of vocations and industries."[68]

As an example of this sort one readily thinks of one of the most powerful associations in recent American history, the Anti-Saloon League, whose activities were a major factor in the country's politics for two decades. The temperance "movement" in the United States did not begin, of course, with this league. The Prohibition Party nominated its first candidate for president in 1872, two years before the kernel unit of the league was formed. The growth and influence of the latter, however, particularly in contrast to other groups in the temperance movement, reflected in part the strength of the institu-

[67] McKean: *Pressures on the Legislature of New Jersey*, pp. 56–7.
[68] Herring: *Group Representation Before Congress*, p. 206. Copyright 1929 by and used with the permission of The Brookings Institution. It is not intended here to assert, of course, that "economic attitudes" are not involved in the functioning of such groups. If institutionalized economic groups are not discrete, neither are other groups.

tionalized groups around whose tangent relations the league was formed. These were primarily the Protestant churches. (The Catholic Church never had a very strong role in the league, though it, as well as other religious groups, has been a source of other associations that have participated in governmental activity.) The circumstances from which the league emerged, moreover, fit the familiar patterns, as did its later activities. The Oberlin (Ohio) Temperance Alliance, out of which the league grew, was formed in 1874 "to deal with a crisis in the local temperance situation." A State-wide organization was set up in 1893, and two years later a number of such groups were merged into the Anti-Saloon League of America, which grew steadily. From the beginning the strategy of the "Ohio idea" was not to secure abstinence pledges from individuals, but to operate through political institutions toward the objective of abolishing all traffic in liquor. It was a political interest group from the start.[69]

Associations of veterans are of a similar sort, the prime contemporary example being the American Legion. Formed at the close of World War I, the Legion was based on tangent relations stemming from service in the armed forces. The small group of men who founded it, themselves concerned about "radicalism" in the United States, might have remained small but for the fact that the chaotic conditions under which the soldiers were demobilized made it difficult for many of them to find jobs and increased the strains inevitably involved in a readjustment to civilian life. Consequently, the association spread with remarkable rapidity. After World War II it took a new lease on life from the similar, though less acute, circumstances of the new veterans, this time aided by its resources as a going organization. Its large membership, reported as over three million, makes it by all odds the most important association of veterans.

Almost from its inception, of course, the Legion has operated as a political interest group. Those familiar with these operations may be astonished to learn that its constitution provides that the Legion "shall be absolutely non-political." Whatever may be said of the rationalization necessary to reconcile this limitation with the Legion's performance, it should be obvious that the circumstances of its growth made it inevitable that the Legion, like many other associations, should work in part through the institutions of government in order to perform its functions. The financial insecurity of many of its members made Legion sponsorship of government financial aid, first in the form of increased pensions for disabled veterans and finally as a bonus for all veterans, unavoidable. Similar conditions also explain its activity in

[69] Odegard: *Pressure Politics*, pp. 1–9.

support of medical care legislation, preference for veterans in government employment, and the like. Regardless of the self-denying phrases in its formal charter, the dynamics of the Legion's existence as an association forced it to become a political interest group.[70]

Women's associations should also be mentioned in this set of groups, since they are both influential and numerous. Herring noted at the time of his study of Congress that women's organizations were second in number only to trade associations.[71] These groups, whose number has certainly not declined, are of three general types. First, there are the women's occupational groups, such as the nurses, home economists, policewomen, and physicians. This category should include also such generalized organizations as the National Federation of Business and Professional Women's Clubs. These are so similar in origin to the equivalent men's or mixed groups that they need not be examined separately.

The second type is the woman's auxiliary to an organization of men, of which examples are the American Legion Auxiliary, the Associated Women of the American Farm Bureau Federation, and the auxiliaries of the various fraternal orders. These groups, which need not be discussed in detail, since their political activity and influence are largely supplementary to those of the male organizations, are of interest primarily owing to the circumstances of their origin. When a men's association is formed, it often has the effect, particularly for its more active members, of reducing the husbands' participation in the family group. In order to compensate for the resulting disturbance, the wives and mothers of the members establish tangent relations with one another that may be formalized eventually in an association which is auxiliary in this sense to the men's association. Thus there was discussion of the desirability of setting up such an auxiliary very soon after the formation of the American Farm Bureau Federation, further stimulated in this case by the development of home demonstration work through the extension services.[72] Interestingly enough, these auxiliary associations usually draw most of their active membership from among middle-aged women whose children are grown, who are childless, or who are single. That is, they draw upon women whose family responsibilities are not sufficiently heavy to provide compensation for reduced interaction with the principal male member of the family. Basic to these groups, moreover, are the funda-

[70] Chapple and Coon: *Principles of Anthropology*, p. 424; Marcus Duffield: *King Legion* (New York: Cape & Smith, 1931).

[71] Herring: *Group Representation Before Congress*, p. 186.

[72] Kile: *The Farm Bureau Movement*, p. 147.

mental conditions that have fostered the development of women's associations of all sorts.[73]

These fundamental conditions are well illustrated in the third type of women's association, the nonoccupational, nonauxiliary group for women only. These are of such widely varying types—ranging from local bridge and reading clubs to national charitable, educational and political societies—that it is perhaps hazardous to group them under the same heading. All, however, have their source in the changes in family functions within the past three generations. Under modern conditions, particularly in urban areas, the family no longer operates as an economic unit to the degree that once was the case. Furthermore, the time consumed in the rearing of children has been considerably reduced by the full establishment of public schools. At the same time a series of labor-saving devices for the housekeeper have lightened the tasks of the middle-class housewife. These changes have reduced the need for patriarchal dominance, have made it inevitable that women of all income classes could engage in full- or part-time activities outside the home, have permitted the development of educational facilities for women fully equal to those of men, and have made it possible for unmarried women to live and work apart from their families without losing status. Such changes lie at the base of a wide number of legal and political reforms, such as the enactment of woman's suffrage. They have also stimulated the development of associations among women similarly affected by the changed circumstances.

Although a large proportion of these groups are purely sociable in character, an impressive number have engaged in community activities necessitating recourse to government action. Obviously, the various movements for removing the legal disabilities of women illustrate these activities; to an equal degree so do the Woman's Christian Temperance Union, the Daughters of the American Revolution, the League of Women Voters of the United States, the Women's International League for Peace and Freedom,[74] and many others. The League of Women Voters may be taken as an illustration. Formed in 1920, it was the offspring of the National American Woman Suffrage Association, which was dissolved following the ratification of

[73] Chapple and Coon: *Principles of Anthropology*, pp. 430–1. It is worth noting that these auxiliaries, through stabilizing family patterns, have the incidental but important effect of increasing the cohesion of the parent association.

[74] Dorothy Detzer, for twenty years the national secretary of this organization, has written her interesting recollections, including a discussion of her political methods, in *Appointment on the Hill* (New York: Henry Holt & Company, Inc., 1948).

the Nineteenth Amendment; it included originally the same group of women. Its new objectives were primarily those involved in the political education of the newly enfranchised voters. These purely educational activities, however, have necessarily included efforts of the league to influence public policy as a political interest group. As we shall have frequent occasion to note, a simple increase in knowledge often has the effect of defining and activating an interest group. In this case the transition was easier because of the habits of political activity established in the struggle for the franchise. The activities of the league have covered a wide range, including such dissimilar policies as civil service reform and international organization for world peace. Although it has never become a very large organization or succeeded in appreciably broadening the class base of its membership to include other than middle-class women, its influence through its educational efforts often is wider than these limitations would suggest.[75]

Finally, among these nonoccupational associations, from which we have selected examples more or less at random, should be included those made up primarily of racial and national minorities. For the many immigrant peoples who have come to American shores, association has been inevitable, particularly for those whose acceptance into the society has been handicapped by their lack of education and their low economic status, and by language differences. Disturbances to their equilibrium have come not only from the fact of migration into a strange country and from the hostility of their reception but as well from such shattering changes in accustomed patterns of behavior as were experienced by most Italians in their sudden shift from an agricultural existence in one country to an urban life in another. To compensate for these shifts by perpetuating as many as possible of the familiar patterns of interaction and to offset or mitigate the effects of nonacceptance by the remainder of the community, both local and national associations have developed. In the latter connection, particularly, these associations of national minorities have become involved in political activities, since through such channels their members have found a means of making a place for themselves in the institutions of the dominant segment of the society, of securing opportunities for advancement in status, and of gaining a measure of stability. That such groups have sometimes carried on activities that other groups in the community have regarded as improper or illegal is merely symptomatic of the incomplete articulation of the patterns

[75] Cf. the comments in Estes Kefauver and Jack Levin: *A Twentieth-Century Congress* (New York: Duell, Sloan and Pearce, 1947), pp. 154–5, 164.

of these groups with those of the "accepted" segments of the population.[76]

Similar disturbances of equal or greater intensity are a part of the continuing experience of racial minorities, especially the Negro. No good purpose will be served here by attempting to detail any of these, since they have been set forth definitively elsewhere, but it is worth noting that, largely in compensation for the disturbances consequent upon discrimination, there are relatively more "voluntary associations" among Negroes than among whites.[77] By no means all of these involve recourse to political institutions, but many of them must; for, as in the case of unassimilated nationality groups, political activity for the Negro, in Myrdal's words, is primarily a means of securing "legal justice—justice in the courts; police protection and protection against the persecution of the police; ability to get administrative jobs through civil service; and a fair share in such public facilities as schools, hospitals, public housing, playgrounds, libraries, sewers and street lights." [78]

Although, for a variety of reasons that need not be examined here, these efforts of the Negro to obtain justice have largely been confined to local areas, they have also operated to some extent at the national level. An interesting, though perhaps minor, example is the March-on-Washington Committee. This remarkable association, led by A. Philip Randolph, the head of the Brotherhood of Sleeping Car Porters, emerged in 1941 and became a mass movement among Negroes, particularly in the North. The disturbances leading to its formation were primarily those stemming from the continued discrimination against Negroes in the mushrooming defense activities. In addition there was the vivid memory of the consequences for Negroes of the migrations and rapid shifts in employment that had attended and followed World War I. The March-on-Washington Committee was intended to organize a mass march on the nation's capital to express Negro determination that the continued discrimination, in particular, should be stopped. Although the march never took place, the movement resulted in the establishment by the President in June, 1941, of the Committee on Fair Employment Prac-

[76] Cf. Whyte: *Street Corner Society*, pp. 272–6; Donald R. Young: *American Minority Peoples* (New York: Harper and Brothers, 1932), pp. 589–91; W. Lloyd Warner and Leo Srole: *The Social Systems of American Ethnic Groups* (New Haven, Conn.: Yale University Press, 1945), chap 9.

[77] Myrdal: *An American Dilemma*, p. 952.

[78] Myrdal: *An American Dilemma*, p. 497. Copyright 1944 by and used with the permission of Harper and Brothers.

tice.[79] Such dramatic examples are rare, but they illustrate both the originating circumstances of such groups and their efforts at working through the institutions of government.

The Inevitable Gravitation
Toward Government

Throughout this chapter it has been stated repeatedly that at various stages in their development, interest groups have become political. In each instance we have noted that they "inevitably" began to make claims through or upon the institutions of government. Why should this be so? We can observe in fact that such groups do operate in this fashion, but why is it justifiable to say that this was "inevitable?"

In the first place, it will be apparent that such a statement implies some special characteristic of interest groups, especially in their contemporary forms. We have seen that many of these groups, the associations, come into being or are activated as a consequence of disturbances—prolonged or intense or both—in the expected patterns of interaction. The associations function to restore a previous equilibrium or to facilitate the establishment of a new one. To a certain extent, depending upon the circumstances, groups can accomplish these goals without recourse to government action—that is, by the successful imposition of claims directly upon another group. An example can be seen in the operations of the early craft unions, which for many years were able to protect their members exclusively by direct claims upon employers. As we have seen, the situation grows somewhat complicated as the sources and effects of the disturbances giving birth to such associations are distributed over wider and wider areas. In response to this development have occurred the amalgamation and federation of local and regional groups into organizations of national and even international scope. In many instances, moreover, the new group still imposes its claims directly without important resort to a mediating institution such as the government.

As our society has become increasingly complex, however, these disturbances have affected not merely the relationships of widely distributed individuals; they have also created a new problem, by placing the means of adjustment beyond the resources of direct action by the groups involved. Thus, for example, disturbances growing out of the

<hr>

[79] Ibid., pp. 851–2. See Malcolm Ross: *All Manner of Men* (New York: Reynal and Hitchcock, 1948), pp. 19–20.

market cannot all be settled directly by trade associations or monopolistic economic groups. These groups must supplement direct action by making claims through or upon some mediating institutionalized group whose primary characteristic is its wider powers. In general, of course, the weaker the means of direct action available to an affected group, the more ready has it been to work through such mediating institutions. For example, farm groups have early resorted to political action, in some cases despite an announced intention to eschew political activity. The early years of the Grange are an illustration. The special characteristic of contemporary interest groups that has "inevitably" forced them to operate in the political sphere is this: unaided by the wider powers of some more inclusive institutionalized group, they cannot achieve their objectives; interest groups of the association type cannot, without such mediation, perform their basic function, namely, the establishment and maintenance of an equilibrium in the relationships of their members.

But why must this institution be the government? Obviously, a second implication of the statement that the political action of interest groups is inevitable concerns some unique feature of modern government. Why should not interest groups seek the mediation of the church or some such institutionalized group other than government? If we go back far enough, of course, we find that the church has generally performed just this function, though in simpler fashion than government does today. The clergy in the New England colonies of the seventeenth century functioned in much this fashion; an even better example is supplied by the medieval Church. It was the primary mediating device of the medieval period, because it comprehended within its jurisdiction all groups in the society, including the state itself. Moreover, interest groups still attempt to gain the aid of the churches, the press, and similar institutionalized groups. What labor union will not try to secure the support of both the church and the press in a dispute with employers? In some enclaves of our society, indeed, where a single church enjoys the support of all or a major portion of the population—for example, Quebec and certain metropolitan cities of the United States—it is still the principal mediator, exercising its control not only over interest groups but even over local governments.

Herein lies the clue to the universal tendency of interest groups to resort to government action in the present day. Such groups will supplement their own resources by operating upon or through that institutionalized group whose powers are most inclusive in that time and place. With such local exceptions as those just noted, that in' stitution today is government. Governments, since the Renaissance, especially national governments, have become the most inclusive power concentrations in Western society, virtually unrivaled by any others. The reasons for this development are beyond the concern of these pages, but the fact is of pre-eminent importance.

The effects of such reliance upon government are cumulative. Just as the direct and indirect efforts of an interest group may disturb the equilibriums of related groups, so its operations through and upon government are likely to force the related groups also to assert their claims upon governmental institutions in order to achieve some measure of adjustment. For example, as we have noted above, the labor movement was drawn into politics in no small measure because of the use of governmental injunctive powers by employers. Both types of groups then attempted to assert their claims through the government.

Government is not simply a neutral force, however, moved this way and that solely by the relative vigor with which competing organized groups are able to assert themselves. Such an explanation is much too simple; the functions of government cannot be described in such narrow terms without ignoring significant aspects of its operations. Elucidation of this point must be delayed for later chapters. It must be mentioned here, however, in order to guard against the too literal reading of Madison's sage observation in essay number 10 of *The Federalist*: "The regulation of these various and interfering interests forms the principal task of modern legislation. . . ."

Summary

The major lines of discussion in this chapter may be drawn together in summary form. We have noted that any groups, including institutionalized groups, may function as political interest groups. At the same time, the increasing complexity of our society and the rapidity with which changes have occurred—creating greater intensity as well as frequency of disturbances—have made the association the most characteristic and pervasive sort of political interest group.

These associations have sprung from disruption of the established patterns of behavior, but these disturbances show wide variety. For example, labor unions and their federations have been the product of the increasing division of labor within industry, the growing differentiation between employer and worker, and the consequent major changes in the status and rewards of both workers and managers. These disturbances have been aggravated by rapid developments in transportation and communication and by the shifts in economic organization that have removed policy-makers in institutionalized economic groups from direct and intimate contact with workers. The disturbances resulting from these changes have produced the alterations in attitudes (interests) necessary for cohesive associations among workers. Finally, the tactics of opposing interest groups and the ineffectiveness of such traditional weapons as a monopoly of skill have led labor unions to make vigorous claims upon and through the institutions of government. Once made, such claims have been continued and expanded in order to strengthen and protect the measure of stability previously achieved.

Trade associations and their federations, on the other hand, have been formed to deal with the disturbances stemming from numerous technological changes and from the accompanying increased effects of market fluctuations. Supplementary causes have been the revolution in communications and the short-run need during war, depression, or other emergencies for organized groups that could supplement the work of government agencies in economic planning. The activities of competing groups and the ineffectiveness of the weapons available to the associations when working alone have led these groups, like the labor unions, to make increasing demands upon and through the government.

The growth of labor and trade associations, and of most others as well, exhibits a wavelike pattern; for the very success of one group in stabilizing its relationships creates new problems for others and makes necessary either new organizations or the extension and strengthening of existing ones.

The farmers' groups examined are in many ways similar to the trade associations (although there are differences in the specific character of the disturbances that stimulate their growth). The relative weakness of the farmer's bargaining position in the market and the relative strength resulting from the overrepresentation of rural areas in State and national legislatures combine to explain the readiness of these groups to resort to the government in order to achieve their objectives. The wide variety of groups that may be labeled agricultural illustrates how many are the segmental interests that may grow up around the activities of government.

Various professional and quasi-professional associations follow a pattern similar to that of other associations; they are founded in common attitudes (interests) that are created, in turn, by the special skills and preoccupations of their members, and they reach formal organization as the result of disturbances in the relationships of their members to one another or to other groups. The extent to which these associations are concerned with legislation or other government action in part reflects the extent to which disturbances have been produced by the political activity of competing groups and in part indicates the stake of these groups, especially lawyers and doctors, in the effective discharge of their professional functions. Such associations usually try to control (stabilize) their membership and their relationships with the rest of the society by seeking legislation defining standards of practice and requirements for admission to the profession.

These broad patterns can be seen equally clearly among a wide variety of nonoccupational interest groups. For fundamental changes in society affect not only the stability of economic relationships but also the interests of almost infinitely many segments of society.

Many of the examples discussed in this chapter, especially the bar associations and the labor unions, suggest that a group's relation to governmental institutions is partly determined by its own internal relationships. It will therefore be appropriate to turn to an examination of the internal relationships of groups.

PART TWO

Group Organization and Problems of Leadership

5

Forms of Organization: Myths
and Realities

"THE labor movement," it has been asserted, "has an internal political life of its own."[1] Organized labor groups have developed counterparts of political parties and have their legislative, executive, and judicial bodies, their representative systems, their factions, their gerrymanders, elections, and campaign oratory. With modifications of type and degree the same observation can be made about all organized associations, for the forms and processes of influence and the influential are common to all organized interaction, not just to the institutions of government. The characteristics of those forms and processes in a nation are among the crucial determinants of strength and importance in the great arena of international affairs, in peace and in war. Similarly, these features of interest groups have much to do with their various roles in domestic politics, and the relations between the two—the political life of a nation and the internal politics of groups contained within it—are close and reciprocal.

These are fairly obvious statements, and yet the realities they suggest are frequently overlooked. We are all familiar with declarations that begin with such phrases as "Business expects . . . ," "Doctors protest . . . ," "Labor demands . . . ," "The veteran insists . . . ," and the like. Even when such declarations are, or can be made, meaningful, they involve certain hidden assumptions, assertions, or conclusions about the political life—and particularly the unity—of the

[1] Robert R. R. Brooks: *When Labor Organizes* (New Haven, Conn.: Yale University Press, 1937), p. 277. Copyright by and used with the permission of Yale University Press.

interest groups designated by such labels. These are at best shorthand expressions, simplifications, which avoid the awkward or embarrassing tasks of indicating which individuals are included under such terms as "business," "farmers," "labor," and the like in a concrete situation and of stating which of them are doing how much insisting, protesting, demanding, and so on. In effect such expressions take it for granted that the degree of cohesion in these groups is perfect. But such an assumption is unrealistic, for the degree of cohesion is of critical importance in determining the effectiveness with which the group operates. It is a product, in large measure, of the dynamic relations existing within the group—of its internal political life. An analysis of the patterns of politics within groups is, therefore, of commanding importance in understanding the role of these groups in the life of the nation.

The Significance of Formal Organization

It is appropriate to begin an exploration of these internal relationships by discussing certain features of formal organization. We must, of course, guard against the danger of mistaking the asserted for the real, of overlooking those very dynamics that are the heart of political relationships. We must not take descriptions of organizational forms at their face value. Nevertheless, a grasp of formal organization is essential to the understanding of a group's internal political life, just as a familiarity with the Constitution of the United States is essential to, though not sufficient for, an appreciation of the country's politics.

The formal organization of interest groups is of particular importance for several reasons. In the first place, formal organization is usually a consequence, and therefore an index, of a fairly high frequency of interaction within a group, as was noted briefly in Chapter 2. For instance, the activity of collecting postage stamps may be very widespread without leading to much interaction among the participants. Even rather frequent interaction within this potential group may remain informal. But when a philatelic society is formally organized, such interaction usually has greatly increased, and the group has achieved a degree of cohesion sufficient for certain purposes, such as making special arrangements with postal authorities for securing specimens of new stamp issues. The degree of a group's cohesion is frequently indicated in its formal organization. For example, although the writing and adoption of the Constitution of the United States indicated an increased measure of cohesion among at least certain elements in the population of the young nation, the provision in Article V guaranteeing equal representation in the Senate, the inclusion of the Tenth Amendment, and other features indicated, at least in general fashion, the limits of that unity.

Secondly, the existence of formal organization in a group suggests a measure of permanence or at least an expectation that the arrangement will be a continuing one.[2] A degree of stability in a group pattern, as we have seen, usually precedes formal organization, and the regularization of such arrangements implies the expectation that they will continue at least as persistently as the circumstances that give rise to the group.

In the third place, formal organization necessarily presupposes acceptance by the participants of a particular division of labor—forms of leadership, distributions of responsibility, and methods of determining policy.

Finally, a particular type of formal organization is in a sense a precipitate of the values shared by the group, at least at its inception. Such values are a function of the personalities and experiences of the participants; but their expression in the form of group organization is affected by the organization and political techniques of other groups. As in military conflict, so in the political process the organization, strategy, and tactics of one combatant in part determine the organization, strategy, and tactics employed by the other. Within this context these values—embodied in agreed procedures—constitute a mold by which the dynamic activities of the group are formed and into which only certain kinds of action can safely be cast. Around these forms, moreover, develop habits of behavior that, like those in institutionalized groups, are resistant to change and that may persist long after their usefulness as a means of guiding group activities has disappeared. These habits may so stifle dissenters within the group—restive because they cannot achieve expression through the habitual pattern—that they invite disunity or revolt.

All these factors—degree of cohesion, expectations of permanence, internal division of labor, and formalized values—intimately affect the survival and influence of the group. If they can be stated even partially through an examination of formal organization, that scrutiny is essential.

One further caution with respect to formal organization should be emphasized if this feature of the process of group politics is to be seen

[2] See Muzafer Sherif: *An Outline of Social Psychology* (New York: Harper and Brothers, 1948), p. 101. Cf. Grace L. Coyle: *Social Process in Organized Groups* (New York: Richard R. Smith, Inc., 1930), chap. 4.

in proper perspective. Organization is merely one aspect of the process. For in the first place, when we speak of the organized dues-paying members of a group, we are not necessarily stating its outer limits. All interest groups have their "fellow-travelers" who may or may not be eligible for formal membership, but who act or interact with actual members with a frequency that in certain types of political situations may be of considerable importance. For example, the American Association of University Professors, which functions as an interest group to defend standards of academic freedom in institutions of higher learning, has never included more than a small fraction of the nation's professors in its formal membership. The unenrolled professors, however, may sympathize with and support particular efforts of the association by refusing to accept an appointment at an institution blacklisted by the organization. Alumni and other interested citizens not eligible for membership may form judgments and even take action concerning a college on the basis of the A.A.U.P.'s recommendations. To the extent that they do, they may be regarded as functional members of the group for the time being.[3]

To say that organization is merely one aspect of the process of group politics implies, secondly, that if organization is to be seen in proper perspective, one must bear in mind that at a particular time those groups formally organized are not the only ones that may be politically significant. In any society there exist interests that, as we noted in defining "interest groups" in Chapter 2, may not at a given moment form the basis of group interaction. These potential interest groups may, however, become actual if events, including the activities of already-organized groups, permit. The interests of the potential groups are usually widespread, though momentarily weak, and as such serve to limit in a general way the behavior of the more apparent participants in politics. The unacknowledged power of such unorganized interests lies in the possibility that, if these wide, weak interests are too flagrantly ignored, they may be stimulated to organize for aggressive counteraction. Thus, although organization is presumptive evidence of strength in the short run, in the long run, especially in a society permitting wide freedom of association, access to power is not confined to the organized groups in the population.[4] For example, there is likely to exist in any community a widespread but unorgan-

[3] The notion of "fellow travelers" is roughly equivalent to the social psychological concept of "reference groups." Cf. Newcomb: Social Psychology, pp. 225–32.

[4] On this point generally see Bentley: The Process of Government, pp. 218–19 and 371–2.

ized attitude that "corruption" in the awarding of public contracts should not exist as a political technique or that it should at least be confined to rather narrow limits. A group that subsists in part upon the rewards of this technique may use it so extensively or indulge in such zealous efforts to assure its success—as by the "purchase" of court and enforcement officers—that the latent counterinterest will assume organized form and compel the confinement of such behavior within more acceptable limits. Such, indeed, seems to be the pattern of the recurring "reform" movements in American municipalities.

Structural Types

Any discussion of the broad types of organization found among political interest groups must necessarily be confined to certain general tendencies. So great is the diversity of types and forms and so imperceptibly do they merge into one another that they almost defy generalization. This state of affairs is not astonishing if one bears in mind the fact that, although all these groups have certain political functions in common, they may also carry on a congeries of related activities, some of them of basic importance to the group, that assume a variety of organized forms. Some of these activities, such as the promotion of craft skills by trade unions, may have been of primary importance only at an earlier stage in the organization's history; yet their impress upon the organizational structure of the group may continue. Vested interests and habits of action grow up around this structure and resist displacement, as anyone familiar with efforts at governmental or corporate reorganization will recognize. Younger organizations, appearing under a different set of competitive circumstances but performing similar basic functions, are more or less free of such group habits. They will frequently assume forms differing in significant detail from older groups of the same kind. Thus, even in a single limited field, such as organized labor, structural forms showing general similarity prove, upon close examination, to be greatly varied.[5]

Perhaps the most useful distinction that can be applied to political organizations in the United States is that between federated and unitary forms. The first is, generally speaking, an organization of organizations, in which powers or functions are divided, formally, at least, between the constituent groups, on the one hand, and the more inclusive organization, on the other. Membership in the larger group

[5] Millis and Montgomery: *Organized Labor*, pp. 244–5.

may be direct or may be indirect—that is, derived from membership in a constituent group—although significant fusions of these patterns occur in some instances. The second is a single organization that may, and usually does, have subdivisions to carry on various functions or stages of functions. Membership is directly in the parent group, and derivative participation in the activities of subdivisions depends upon geographical location, occupational specialization, and so on.

An example of the federated form is, as its name implies, the American Federation of Labor. It is primarily an organization of national and "international" unions, in turn made up of local unions in which the individual holds his membership. The majority of national and regional trade associations can be cited as illustrations of the unitary type. For the most part these are made up of individuals or firms, the difference being of slight significance, who belong directly to the trade association. These groups may, however, be subdivided on a temporary or permanent basis into groups making or selling the same product or units primarily concerned with a specialized phase of trade association activity, such as product standardization or technical research.[6]

The importance of this distinction between the federated and unitary forms of organization may be seen in their influence upon the cohesion, or unity, of the group. Federations tend to have much less cohesion, especially with respect to functions whose importance increases after a distribution of powers is agreed upon. The tendency is strikingly apparent, of course, with respect to activities that have long been the prerogative of the constituent groups but that the logic of events suggests should be assumed by the more inclusive organization. As in the case of government itself, the defense of local autonomy in such circumstances is likely to clothe in the vestments of principle a partially acknowledged desire for inaction on the matter at issue, as well as hostility toward any diminution of the perquisites of a local officialdom. Under these conditions any organization, whether strictly governmental or not, is forced to feel out a dangerous course between, on the one hand, debilitating inaction or localized actions that are self-defeating because mutually inconsistent and, on the other, centralized action that may invite dissolution or an embarrassing nonconformity.

Examples of this kind of problem are not hard to locate, although careful investigations of this aspect of group dynamics are far too few.

[6] A limited number of trade associations are organized on a federated basis. U.S. Temporary National Economic Committee: *Trade Association Survey,* pp. 40 ff.

One case in point is the problem of racketeering in A.F. of L. unions. Although this problem has been less widespread than many hostile treatments would suggest, it has been serious in certain unions and frequently has given a bad odor to the A.F. of L. and to the whole labor movement. Under its constitution, however, the Federation lacks the power to remove an official of an affiliated national union. It may revoke the charter of the national union, but such a drastic step involves a loss to the treasury and possibly a corresponding gain to the rival C.I.O. federation. Even a persuasive program of investigation and publicity has foundered on the rock of concern, whether justified or not, for the traditional autonomy of national unions. When delegates to the 1940 A.F. of L. convention introduced a resolution giving the federation's officers the power of summary removal of union officials convicted of dishonesty, the convention adopted a very much weaker substitute that reaffirmed the responsibility of the national union and confined the federation to using its "influence." It is significant that the A.F. of L. has taken most drastic action in cases of corruption in those locals directly responsible to it and not to national unions.[7]

Many examples indicate that even where constitutional powers permit, action may produce an embarrassing refusal by constituent units to conform. The American Medical Association, which for a variety of reasons has suffered from the diseases of federation less than many groups, has had to countenance open defiance of its policy against compulsory health insurance programs by various State societies and even by some county societies. The national organization once was reduced to petulant complaints that it was not permitted to state its position in the pages of the California Medical Association's journal.[8] The monumentally impressive American Farm Bureau Federation has had similar difficulties. Its Ohio affiliate, a notable example, not only has refused to conform to this federation's policies from time to time, but has even sided with the rival Farmers' Union.[9] Of the many recent examples that could be cited, one is provided by the Utility Workers' Union, C.I.O., which has openly refused to support the national C.I.O. policy of pressing for the extension of publicly owned power projects in the Tennessee, Missouri, and Columbia river

[7] Joel Seidman: *Union Rights and Union Duties* (New York: Harcourt, Brace & Company, Inc., 1943), pp. 117–18. The handling of the problem of communism among C.I.O. affiliates shows the similarities in the problems of the two federations.

[8] Garceau: *The Political Life of the A.M.A.*, pp. 137–47.

[9] McCune: *The Farm Bloc*, p. 188.

valleys and has for this purpose allied itself with the interest groups of the private utility companies.[10]

The fundamental reason for the tendency toward disunity in federated organizations is not obscure, although its ramifications may be highly complex. By acknowledging in formal terms certain spheres of local or constituent autonomy, a federated organization establishes and, as it were, sanctifies subcenters of power. The functions that are assigned as of right to the constituent units, although they may conform to realities at the time the division is agreed upon, become the focus of interaction for subgroups whose interests (or the interests of whose leaders) may not always be in harmony with those of the national group. Where changed circumstances make advisable a centralization of responsibility and a consequent diminution in the power and prestige of subgroup leaders, these formally recognized subgroup interests resist change. Under these circumstances the federated organization may in fact be no more unified than a league of sovereign states unable to act except upon the unanimous agreement of the constituent units.

The A.F. of L., as earlier comments suggest, provides an excellent, though by no means unique, example of this situation. It is a very loose federation of autonomous unions. The chief governing body in fact, though not under the terms of its constitution, is the Executive Council, consisting of the president, secretary-treasurer, and from thirteen to fifteen vice-presidents. Although this body has considerable discretionary authority, its members are, before anything else, established leaders of their own national or international unions, and as such, they exercise a *liberum veto* on any proposals tending to limit their autonomy. This veto power rests on an implied or expressed threat to withdraw a union from the federation, a threat that is by no means an empty one, especially when made by the larger organizations. Since members of the Executive Council are likely to have consolidated their positions within their own unions prior to their service on the Council, any attempt to go over their heads to the rank and file—a procedure not sanctioned by A.F. of L. rules—would be futile. By 1933 this situation was so acute that Lorwin observed: "The principle of trade autonomy has been carried to such lengths as to nullify the capacity of the Federation to perform most of the functions for which it exists. In fact, for some time, the Federation has existed on

[10] The *New York Herald Tribune*, March 9, 1949. See Charles E. Parker: "Utility Employees and Public Opinion," *Public Opinion Quarterly*, Vol. 14, no. 1 (Spring, 1950), pp. 33–9.

suffrance of its larger and more powerful international unions." [11]
This inability of the A.F. of L. to adjust to changed circumstances
was crucial in the split that led to the establishment of the C.I.O. [12]
Although this tendency toward low cohesion is a common feature
of federated structure, it should not be exaggerated or overgeneral-
ized. For one thing, as will be shown in more detail in Chapter 7, a
number of such groups have achieved a very high measure of unity,
partly through the skillful use of a variety of offsetting controls. For
another, subcenters of power rivaling that of the larger group may
develop even in nominally unitary types of organization. Long enjoy-
ment, by subordinate units, of delegated powers and of a sphere of
de facto autonomy can as easily produce resistance to unified central
action as can a constitutional distribution of functions. This situation
is well illustrated in the sphere of government by the stubborn independence of counties, municipalities, and school districts—legally
merely creatures of the State governments—in the face of efforts toward consolidation and redistribution of functions. An instructive example among interest groups is provided by the Association of American Railroads. The system prevailing in the 1930's for sharing charges
for freight moving over more than one railroad, which was a source of
considerable dissatisfaction among some of the members of the association, could not be modified by the national organization. Despite vigorous efforts made in the directors meetings by the representatives of
the dissatisfied Midwestern trunk lines, the matter could be dealt with
only by negotiation between the originating and the forwarding
lines. [13] The patterns of interaction that develop about subcenters
and that come to be accepted by individuals and groups thus can become the means of resisting the assumption or resumption of central
functions by the central authority.

Organizational Elements Affecting Cohesion

Given the general tendency of federated organizations to lack cohesion, we may ask what determines whether or not a particular federation will display this tendency. An exhaustive list of the determin-

[11] Lewis L. Lorwin: *The American Federation of Labor* (Washington, D.C.:
The Brookings Institution, 1933), p. 465.
[12] On this section generally see Lorwin: *The American Federation of Labor,*
chap. 12; Millis and Montgomery: *Organized Labor,* chap. 6.
[13] U.S. Senate, Committee on Interstate Commerce: *Senate Report No. 26,*
Part 2, 77th Cong., 1st Sess. (1941), pp. 26–20.

ing influences would be impossibly long, since the variations among groups are considerable. It would necessitate, also, evaluation of the techniques of leadership for offsetting these disadvantages, which are not the most basic influences upon cohesion and which can be discussed more appropriately in a later chapter, since most of them are common to both structural types. The three most basic factors not dependent upon leadership will be analyzed here.

In the first place, the problem of cohesion almost invariably arises where the constituent units antedate the federal body, as is usually true. In this situation the very fact that organization assumes a federated rather than a unitary form indicates that the interests associated with the individual units are so strong that the inclusive organization cannot absorb the units, but can only take over those functions that they can be induced to relinquish.

On the other hand, as has been noted above, this resistance to central control may be grounded in social facts outside the particular groups. Under the Constitution of the United States, for example, the federal system, especially before the early 1930's, left to the State governments a very large sphere of action. The activities of local and State-wide interest groups were early focused upon the State governments, and, to the extent that these governments still exercise significant power, there is basis for the claims of autonomy by the constituent units of federated groups. That State powers are still important influences upon the cohesion of interest groups is illustrated by the experience of the movement, between 1943 and 1947, for permanent national legislation on fair employment practices. "Co-operating" State committees frequently relegated the financing and prosecution of the campaign for national legislation to a position secondary to the securing of legislation from the various State governments.[14] Yet the effort to operate simultaneously on both the State and the national governments does not necessarily lead to lack of unity. The Anti-Saloon League in its heyday encountered no such difficulties. Though its constituent units were constantly working on prohibition legislation in State and local areas and though a considerable amount of latitude was permitted these for purposes of experimentation, they were subject to close control by the national officers. The League was federal in form, but unitary in operation.[15]

A reason for subunit independence is provided in the case of various

[14] Louis C. Kesselman: The Social Politics of FEPC: A Study in Reform Pressure Movements (Chapel Hill, N.C.: University of North Carolina Press, 1948), pp. 57, 75.

[15] Odegard: Pressure Politics, pp. 12–15.

occupational groups, notably labor unions,[16] by the structure of an industry—the heterogeneity in the conditions under which various firms operate, the character and extent of competition within the industry, and so on. Recognition of these hard facts of localism and decentralization by the founders of the A.F. of L., it is generally agreed, was crucial in facilitating the association of highly independent unions in a single national organization. It is equally apparent that the freezing of these arrangements has in recent years weakened the A.F. of L. as a national group. By way of contrast it is significant that the C.I.O., a number of whose major constituent units had little or no independent existence prior to their association with the newer federation, has achieved a far more compact and powerful national leadership than its older rival.[17] As Brooks has observed: "The condition of any national union or of the labor movement as a whole at a given time represents a compromise between an original condition of separatism on the one hand and the integrating forces of economic life on the other."[18] The character of the compromise, moreover, is dependent in no small measure upon the relative age of the national movement and its constituent units.

In some federated interest groups, notably the American Medical Association, some of the constituent units antedate the federation, while others are of later origin. The A.M.A's organization is somewhat different from that of many federated groups, since doctors who belong to the constituent units are eligible for membership in the A.M.A. *as individuals.* (The pattern thus resembles in many ways that of the Chamber of Commerce of the United States.) The governing arrangements, however, are federal in character; all but a few members of the House of Delegates are elected from the constituent societies, beginning at the county level. Although a large number of the State medical societies considerably antedate the A.M.A., the county organizations originally developed through the efforts of the State societies to unify their memberships. It is not astonishing, therefore, that although both State and national groups have experienced difficulties with recalcitrant units lower in the hierarchy, the centralized powers of the State societies in such situations are more extensive

---

[16] See Brooks: *When Labor Organizes,* chap. 9; Arthur M. Ross: *Trade Union Wage Policy* (Berkeley and Los Angeles, Calif.: University of California Press, 1948), pp. 35–6.

[17] Millis and Montgomery: *Organized Labor,* pp. 7, 71 ff.; Herbert Harris: *Labor's Civil War* (New York: Alfred A. Knopf, Inc., 1940), chap. 5.

[18] Brooks: *When Labor Organizes,* p. 247. Copyright 1937 by and used with the permission of Yale University Press.

and more effective than those of the national body.[19] Timing is not the only influence in such a situation, but it is ordinarily an important one.

In the same general category as the literally federated organizations appear those attempting to co-ordinate specialized activities of a number of other organized groups. By definition these are likely to encounter the handicaps stemming from the prior existence of the constituent groups. A recent and instructive example is the National Council for a Permanent FEPC, which was set up largely as an attempt to co-ordinate a congeries of national organizations. A study of this group from its founding in 1943 through the year 1947 arrives at the conclusion that the National Council's failure in those years was in considerable measure due to these centrifugal aspects of its organization.[20]

A second influence upon the degree of cohesion in federations is the basis upon which their constituent units are organized. This may either recognize and formalize the potential lines of cleavage within the group or utilize some form of association that instead cuts across such lines. The first basis usually involves organizing each unit on the basis of function or specialization, whereas the second utilizes a geographical area as its starting point. Though potential cleavages of major importance within a group may exist along geographic lines, as will be noted below, organization according to function especially tends to encourage interaction growing out of specialized subinterests. Because leadership at the lower levels of the structure is necessarily caught up in these subinterests, the problem of reconciling these potentially conflicting elements is delayed until it reaches the middle or top levels of leadership. The situation is roughly comparable to the one that would develop in the government if legislators were elected by occupational (functional) groups rather than by geographically defined constituencies. Adjustment under such conditions is made more difficult because those assuming responsibility for it are removed from regular contact with the concerns of the rank and file. On the other hand, the nonfunctional, or geographical, basis of organization tends to settle the task of adjusting conflicting subinterests upon the

[19] Garceau: *The Political Life of the A.M.A.*, pp. 14 ff., 118 ff.
[20] Kesselman: *The Social Politics of FEPC*, p. 88. Oliver Garceau reports a similar situation in the American Library Association, in which State committees were so preoccupied with securing State aid that they neglected or were hostile to the A.L.A. drive for Federal aid. *The Public Library in the Political Process* (New York: Columbia University Press, 1949), pp. 185–6.

entire leadership at all levels by emphasizing interaction based on more inclusive shared attitudes. This sharing of the responsibility for compromise will occur unless the subinterests follow geographical lines—a situation that is becoming less and less common in the United States. We must remember, however, that adoption of one of these bases of federation is not altogether a matter of choice. The organization of groups, as we have previously noted, grows out of more or less durable patterns of interaction that necessarily determine the basic structural forms. The choices of founding fathers are confined within relatively narrow limits. This proposition is well illustrated by the A.F. of L., which also typifies the problems emerging from the functional basis of federation. For the reasons already detailed in Chapter 4 it is apparent that in the 1880's the only basis for a viable national labor organization lay in loose federation of national trade unions, especially those built upon common skills. The successive failures of the Knights of Labor, the I.W.W., and the movement for One Big Union in 1919–20 testify to the absence of any genuine choice. The precarious position of even this form of unification is neatly summarized in the remark: "For the first fifteen years of its life the Federation consisted chiefly of Samuel Gompers and a series of annual conventions." [21] Although the organization has gradually achieved a greater degree of unity than this situation suggests, its Executive Council is still limited in the exercise of its extensive powers by the fact that it consists of the ambassadors plenipotentiary of a series of "sovereign" units. The primary loyalties of the hierarchies within the international unions, moreover, are focused on the extension and preservation of these units.

The effect of organizing the primary constituent units of the A.F. of L. according to skill (function) is further highlighted by an examination of two types of secondary organization within the federation that to some extent cut across the dominant functional lines. First of all there are the city centrals and State federations of labor, which constitute a peripheral or vestigial form of geographic organization. City-wide groups of employees, especially unionized employees, date far back in the history of the labor movement. They were as spontaneous a growth in an earlier period of poor communication as national organizations were later, and at the time of the A. F. of L.'s founding, city central unions were almost as numerous as trade unions. Even some of the State federations grew up independ-

[21] Brooks: *When Labor Organizes,* pp. 34–5. Copyright 1937 by and used with the permission of Yale University Press.

ently of any national unit; and their original role in the national organization indicates that they represented an adjustment to some of the realities of the situation that the labor movement was facing in the closing decades of the last century. Since at that time the State legislatures rather than Congress handled most legislation of interest to labor, it was originally provided that the State federations should deal with legislative questions, whereas the national federation should concentrate upon expansion of the organization. This division of responsibility had shifted by the turn of the century. It is significant that the headquarters of the A.F. of L. remained in Indianapolis until 1896 and that they were moved to Washington at the height of the period in which the injunctive powers of the Federal courts were being used against labor activities.[22]

However, the city centrals and State federations have lacked the cohesive basis of interaction provided for the international unions by the skills their members have in common and have never occupied more than a secondary position in the organization. The national organization has encouraged the establishment of city centrals, made up of delegates from local unions in good standing, and of State federations, formed by delegates from city centrals and locals. But these geographic units have been kept in a decidedly subordinate position: they are poorly represented at the annual conventions; they are prevented from encroaching in any way on the jurisdictions of the international unions, as in the restriction forbidding them to call strikes; membership in them by local unions is entirely voluntary; they may not accept or retain a local that has been ousted by its international; they usually include considerably less than the total number of A.F. of L. locals in their areas; and they may not reject the delegates of any A.F. of L. local in good standing. The functions of the city centrals and State federations are primarily political—electoral and legislative—but even in these activities most of them are notoriously ineffective. Their efforts to secure legislation of various kinds have been checked repeatedly by the national organization on behalf of the international unions. Their attempts in many areas to function as electioneering agencies for their more active locals have identified them with particular political parties, thus weakening their influence when that machine is out of power and making them unsatisfactory vehicles for those locals attached to the other major party organization or to bipartisanship. Thus, although the A.F. of L. structure recognizes the desirability of co-ordinating devices such as these geo-

[22] John R. Commons: "American Federation of Labor," *Encyclopaedia of the Social Sciences.*

graphic units, the dominance of the international unions based on function reduces them to comparative impotence.[23]

The other type of secondary organization in the A.F. of L. in part reflects the need to mitigate the effects of the plaguing jurisdictional disputes that occur in the craft unions. This type is made up of the departments of the A.F. of L.—the Building and Construction Trades Department (1908), the Metal Trades Department (1908), and the Railway Employees' Department (1909).[24] Essentially federations or partial amalgamations of international unions, the departments have performed a variety of functions adding up to an attempt to mitigate the consequences of strong particularist tendencies among a collection of closely related trades. Where they have been successful, they have inevitably challenged the international unions. As in the case of the city centrals and State federations, the internationals' claims to autonomy—backed by secession or threats of withdrawal—have limited the effectiveness of these departments, with the possible exception of the Railway Employees' Department.[25] The multiplicity of points of conflict in an organization where power is centered in groups representing a variety of more or less specialized trades inevitably threatens cohesion. The significance of the devices to cut across the functional organization of the A.F. of L. lies less in their effectiveness than in the evidence they supply concerning the need for such unifying forces.

The C.I.O. is organized on essentially the same basis as the A.F. of L.—it is a federation whose constituent units are formed around industries, not geographic areas—and it may eventually show many of the same forms of disunity as the older organization. Although the youth of the C.I.O. makes generalization hazardous, it seems apparent —to cite only one example—that industrial unionism of the C.I.O. type will limit the number of points at which jurisdictional conflicts may occur, but may not avoid them entirely.[26] Just as the age of the superpowers may substitute bigger but less frequent conflicts for the continual minor disturbances of a Balkanized world, so the rivalries of the electrical workers and the automobile workers may surpass those among the building trades in extent, though probably not in frequency. If the C.I.O. largely avoids the disunity implicit in the

[23] Lorwin: *The American Federation of Labor*, pp. 49, 190 ff., 326–7, 346–9, 410, 424; Millis and Montgomery: *Organized Labor*, pp. 302–4.

[24] A fourth department, the Union-Label Trades Department, has functions that are rather different from those of the other three and that do not involve the unifying effort of interest here.

[25] Millis and Montgomery: *Organized Labor*, pp. 279–301.

[26] Ibid., pp. 274 ff.; Seidman: *Union Rights and Union Duties*, p. 63.

THE GOVERNMENTAL PROCESS 126

form of its organization, its continued cohesion will be partly owing to the counterbalancing effect of the fact that the federation and its constituent groups are largely coeval and to such factors as the stronger political drives of an organization deliberately based upon unskilled workers in mass-production industries.[27]

By way of contrast to the labor federations, one may cite a number of examples, one of the most interesting of which is the American Farm Bureau Federation. A federation of geographic units, county and State, it has avoided many, though not all, of the disunities associated with that form. In its early years there was some discussion of the desirability of establishing it as a federation of commodity organizations, such as wheat growers, live-stock raisers, fruit growers, dairymen, and the like.[28] This possibility was never a serious one, however, and there are evident explanations for the fact. The promotional-educational work of the county agents, out of which the units of the national movement grew, as was noted in Chapter 4, necessarily produced patterns of interaction based on areas rather than on commodities as such. Leaders aspiring to use these patterns as elements in a national structure had no choice concerning basic forms. Since these forms had developed out of a program of aiding a large number of commercial farmers throughout the various counties, it was not astonishing that the leaders of these groups at all levels emphasized the interests that farmers could be expected to share regardless of the crops on which they specialized for the market. The period of the 1920's, during which the American Farm Bureau Federation was getting its start, was an auspicious one for this line of development. The uniformly depressed state of agriculture, affecting all the major commodities, made it easier to fuse the problems of all commercial crops into a generalized picture of the plight of "the farmer." The interests of specialized producers have been organized in independent groups such as the National Co-operative Milk Producers' Federation, the American Soy Bean Association, the American National Livestock Association, and the like. Nevertheless, many commercial farmers find it quite feasible to maintain memberships in both the Farm Bureau and one of these commodity associations.

Although there are great advantages accruing to the Farm Bureau from federation on the basis of geographical area rather than of crop specialization, the differences should not be exaggerated. In the first place, areas, especially in agriculture, often have their particularized interests. These may stem not only from crop specialization but also

[27] Cf. Harris: *Labor's Civil War*, pp. 126–8.
[28] Kile: *The Farm Bureau Movement*, pp. 253–5.

from such factors as relative proximity to markets or the availability of cheaper modes of transportation. Whatever their source, they involve the possibility of disunity in a national organization that includes such rivals. In the second place, although federation of units organized according to geographic area facilitates emphasis upon nonspecialized agricultural interests, it is obvious that in agriculture geographic area may correspond closely to commodity unit. Not all farmers in the Corn Belt specialize in corn and hogs, nor are there none but wheat farmers on the eastern Great Plains, but these crops are the primary concern of a great majority of farmers in the areas. County and State farm bureaus in these areas can be expected, therefore, to display some of the characteristics of commodity organizations. In view of the concentration of membership in the American Farm Bureau Federation, mentioned in Chapter 4, it is not astonishing that the interests of the corn-hog farmers of the Middle West have been served by the national organization with more than ordinary solicitude. Organization by geographic units reduces the emphasis upon the claims of such factions, but the difference from a federation of commodity units is necessarily one of degree.

Other illustrations of federations of geographic units may be mentioned briefly. The American Medical Association, for example, finally adopted this form of organization after nearly a decade of experimentation with a modified functional form. Between 1892 and 1901 its principal formal governing body was composed of delegates from the technical sections into which its general meetings were divided. In the latter year, however, it set up a body of delegates representing primarily the State societies.[29] The Chamber of Commerce of the United States, whose organization members are nominally drawn both from associations formed on a geographic basis and from those built on a particular line of business, has found that the former type is an easier as well as a more reliable source of support. The specialization of the trade association stands in the way of its becoming an effective unit in the Chamber's structure.[30]

A third influence upon the degree of cohesion in federated organizations is one that in a sense cuts across the previous two—the adequacy of the powers wielded by the central body. A threat to cohesion frequently occurs where certain of the problems with which a group is concerned cease to be primarily local or regional in scope and become predominantly national. Under such circumstances, an increased measure of centralization in the group is normally required,

[29] Garceau: *The Political Life of the A.M.A.*, p. 15.
[30] Childs: *Labor and Capital in National Politics*, p. 84.

but resistance to an alteration either in the distribution of powers between the federal body and its constituent units or in the basis of federation may assume threatening proportions. Although the attachment of local or subordinate officials to the perquisites of their accustomed positions may be a cause of this lag in adjustment, as we have suggested previously, it is important to look at the factors that facilitate and support their objections. A shift in the scope of a group's problems is ordinarily not sudden and complete, but gradual and partial. Thus at any given point in time the functions of the subordinate unit may still be of considerable significance in the lives of the membership. It is the continuing importance of such local activities, and the consequent degree of intimate, face-to-face interaction, that affords the basis of resistance to centralization. Conflicts of loyalties resulting from such circumstances are the setting for disunity and hesitant inaction. This situation is clearly apparent in the case of the co-ordinating type of federated organization, such as the National Council for a Permanent FEPC. The National Council attempted to co-ordinate units and pre-existing national organizations, but the latter performed for their members a variety of functions that were largely unrelated to F.E.P.C. and were central to the concerns of their membership. The National Council, therefore, had no effective leverage by which to force these groups to co-operate in support of a unified strategy.[31]

Illustrations of these tendencies can be seen in the histories of most federated organizations in the United States, particularly those of organized labor. In the realm of government itself, the halting shift of responsibilities from the State governments to the national government has been impeded by the fact that many State functions are still considered critically important by various groups within the electorate. Such situations reach a maximum of complexity where it becomes desirable to shift a portion rather than the whole of some local function from the State governments to the national government. Public education provides a good example. Here the obvious advantage of increased national financial responsibility appears to conflict, or can be presented as conflicting, with the traditional (and presumably desirable) decentralized responsibility for staffing and curriculum. Significant interaction on the basis of the latter interests may delay the partial transfer of financial responsibility or even prevent the adoption of a compromise.

The experiences of government in these matters are not just illus-

[31] Kesselman: *The Social Politics of FEPC*, chaps. 4–9. Cf. Schattschneider: *Politics, Pressures and the Tariff*, pp. 236–42.

trative of the problem among interest groups. They are equally a part of the latter and in turn, of course, are materially affected by the stresses existing within related interest groups.

The Democratic Mold

Formal organization, as we have noted earlier, indicates the existence of significant values or attitudes within a group, at least at the time of its creation. These attitudes mold the formal structure, which in turn sets channels and limits for the group's activities. Some of these formative attitudes may be peculiar to the group—for example, those regarding craft autonomy that so sharply affected the structure of the American Federation of Labor. Others, however, may be so widely held in the society of which a given group is a part that they are in effect imposed on an organized group from without as well as demanded from within. Such widespread attitudes, in fact, are indicative of potential, or even actual, interest groups that may, or do, exert claims for conformity upon other groups in the society.[32]

Prominent among attitudes of the latter type in our society are those that can be subsumed under the general heading "democratic." The attitudes themselves are vague, but they usually involve approval of such devices as periodic elections of key officials, broad participation by the membership in the group's policy making, either directly or through a system of elected representatives, written constitutions, and the like. These, in fact, become elements without which an organization cannot achieve "respectability" and "legitimacy" in the community.[33] No matter how solidly the rank and file of a labor union may stand behind their leaders, if the latter do not submit to regular elections and periodic "legislative" conventions, they invite censure from other groups and guilt feelings among the membership that may destroy their cohesion. The elaborate efforts of some corporations to give an impression of large attendance at, and active participation in, annual stockholders' meetings provide another example.

Within limits that we will examine later, the organizational structure of political interest groups in the United States has been molded in conformity with the "democratic" expectations of the community, including, of course, most of their members. Some representative examples will illustrate the point.

[32] Cf. Bentley: *The Process of Government*, pp. 218–22.
[33] Cf. Garceau: *The Political Life of the A.M.A.*, p. 18.

Taking first the two national labor federations, we find the clearest instances of "democratic" structural formalities. Both place the formal control of the groups in an assembly of delegates, primarily drawn from the international unions. A typical constitutional provision is the following: "The convention shall be the supreme authority of the Organization and except as otherwise provided in the Constitution, its decisions shall be by a majority vote." [34] Membership in the annual assemblies is based upon rather elaborate systems of representation. In the C.I.O. each international union is entitled to from two to ten members, in proportion to paid-up membership. On a roll-call vote, the internationals cast one vote for each paid-up member. The directly chartered locals and the Industrial Union Councils cast one vote each. The A.F. of L. arrangement is similar. Both organizations show the dominant position of the internationals in the federal structure, the C.I.O. somewhat more sharply than the A.F. of L. if voting arrangements alone are considered.

The annual conventions themselves, at least formally, dispose of a considerable authority. They elect (usually re-elect) the respective presidents, secretary-treasurers, and vice-presidents who make up the governing boards that operate between conventions, called the Executive Committee by the C.I.O. and the Executive Council by the A.F. of L. In addition they elect the members of the convention committees, in which the most important business is initially transacted; this selection, however, amounts to a formal ratifying action, since the president's recommendations for these committee posts are made in advance of the convening of the electoral body.[35]

Such formal arrangements as these are clearly the product of the values and practices of representative democracy, whatever may be the actual operation. They imply broad participation in the affairs of the group, regular answerability to the rank and file by means of annual elections, and some measure of delegate control of the purse strings. The parallel is less clear in financial practice, as the almost hallowed practice of legislative appropriations is not followed. In both federations the governing boards authorize expenditures. Nevertheless, in both groups the taxes on individuals and units—the primary source of the groups' revenue—are fixed in the constitution, and, as is cus-

[34] *Constitution of the Congress of Industrial Organizations,* Article VII, Section 1.

[35] Materials on the organization of the A.F. of L. and the C.I.O. are extensive. A useful summary is contained in Millis and Montgomery: *Organized Labor,* pp. 306–17.

tomary in such cases, auditors' reports are submitted to the annual conventions, though they are not challenged. The peculiarities of financial control in these federations are in part the result of the conflict situations in which these groups have operated, particularly in their early years; these arrangements thus illustrate the molding effect of external circumstances on the organized expression of group values. Because these circumstances are often close to warfare, in which exact knowledge of the group's resources would be a tactical advantage to opponents, individual unions and the federations have been cautious about publicizing finances. The following observations by Philip Murray early in 1940 illustrate the problem as it applies to individual unions:

> The United Mine Workers of America, of which I am vice-president, is one of the older and well established unions. It has virtually every coal operator under contract. . . . Its position is recognized as invulnerable. As a result, every six months the United Mine Workers makes public its financial accounts. The S.W.O.C. [Steel Workers' Organizing Committee, now the United Steelworkers of America] is a new union, still violently opposed by a minority of the steel employers. It does not give out a public financial statement because of the obvious reason that its enemies would distort its meaning and significance for the purpose of maligning and harassing the S.W.O.C.[36]

The limitations on "democratic" control of the purse strings are not peculiar to the labor federations, nor are they most sharply illustrated by these groups. In varying degrees they appear in almost all large modern associations. In this respect and for much the same reasons, as will be noted in the next section, such associations have adopted some of the forms of the modern business corporation, which has been characterized as "an arrangement by which many men have delivered contributions of capital into the hands of a centralized control."[37] These practices are implicitly in conflict with some of the "democratic" forms, as others have noted.[38] The exigencies of operation, the dominance of attitudes reflected in business control patterns,

[36] Quoted in Seidman: *Union Rights and Union Duties*, pp. 191–2.
[37] Adolf A. Berle, Jr. and Gardiner C. Means: *The Modern Corporation and Private Property* (New York: The Macmillan Company, 1932), p. 127.
[38] Cf. Garceau: *The Political Life of the A.M.A.*, chap. 1. Except where otherwise noted, the material in the following paragraphs is drawn from this excellent monograph.

and other factors have given these groups the appearance of a mixture of differing elements. It is almost possible to rank associations and other groups on the basis of the extent of adoption of "corporate" forms. Such is the pervasiveness of the "democratic" preferences in our society, of course, that even the corporation shows their influence, as the semiritual of the annual stockholders' meeting suggests.

Illustrative of an almost balanced mixture of these elements, and of the conflicts that it creates, is the American Medical Association. Like the labor federations, the A.M.A. structure places formal control in an annual assembly, designated in this case the House of Delegates. The house is made up of approximately 175 members, all but a handful of whom are elected for a two-year term by the State societies, the number allotted to each State being proportional to its medical population. Reapportionment takes place every three years, and each State is guaranteed not less than one representative. The remaining delegates are drawn one each from the scientific sections of the society, the medical corps of the military services, and the United States Public Health Service.

The powers of election exercised by the House of Delegates are impressive on paper. It elects the A.M.A.'s president (one year term), president-elect, and vice-president. Although it also elects the secretary, general manager, and treasurer, these normally receive repeated re-elections for a considerable period of years. The house elects a speaker and vice-speaker as its presiding officers, as well as the members of its standing committees. Finally, it elects for five-year terms the nine members of the board of trustees.

This nominal power of election is evidence of the strength in the organization and in the community of "democratic" interests. These are to be seen also in some of the rules of election procedure. A standing rule of the House of Delegates provides that "the solicitation of votes for office is not in keeping with the dignity of the Medical profession, nor in harmony with the spirit of this Association, and . . . such solicitation shall be considered a disqualification for election to any office in the gift of the Association." The rule is apparently observed largely in the breach, and, as will be noted later, its effect may be the reverse of its apparent intent. But the "democratic" expectations of the community that it embodies remind one of the myths surrounding the New England town meeting, or, even more appropriately, the Quaker meeting, since it is assumed that the House of Delegates can reach a consensus on competing candidates without any electioneering by the latter.

The tendency to follow corporation practice in the association is perhaps best illustrated by the board of trustees, which is charged with the powers conferred by law upon a corporate board of directors. The board exercises, without direct control from the House of Delegates, complete authority over the property and finances of the organization. Such vestiges of control of the purse strings as remain to the house are further limited by the participation of the trustees in its deliberations, though without vote. The extent of the trustees' discretion is highlighted, moreover, by the fact that no more than half the association's revenues is normally derived from dues, the remainder coming from investments and the profits of its publishing ventures.

The extent of the conflicting patterns in the A.M.A. is not completely indicated by the control over finances. Nominations for many of the elective positions whose incumbents are nominally chosen by the House of Delegates are made by the officers. The treasurer falls into this category, as do the standing committees of the house, candidates for these positions being nominated either by the president or by the trustees. The purely appointive power in the hands of the officers is also impressive. The trustees appoint all members of the A.M.A. staff, including the members of the important Bureau of Medical Economics, the Bureau of Legal Medicine and Legislation, the editor of the A.M.A. publications, and the business manager. The speaker of the House of Delegates, who is ex-officio one of the trustees, has complete appointive control over the reference and special committees, in which the main business of the house is actually conducted. He has, moreover, almost unlimited discretion in assigning matters to the various committees. Finally, the deliberations of several of these bodies are influenced by the officers through ex-officio membership by members of the standing committees and the paid staff. Thus the reference committee on amendments to the constitution and by-laws includes all five members of the powerful Judicial Council, "supreme court" of the A.M.A., whose members are elected for a five-year term on nomination by the president. The reference committee on legislation and public relations similarly includes the director of the Bureau of Legal Medicine and Legislation.

The conflicts of interest that inevitably intrude upon and occur within the association have become involved in these contradictory tendencies of the organization's structure. Resistance to changes in policy has been facilitated by the restraining character of the "corporate" tendencies,[39] and the obvious inconsistencies between the two

[39] Cf. "The American Medical Association," *Fortune* (November, 1938), pp. 88 ff.

tendencies have permitted the critical and the rebellious to verbalize their efforts in terms of "democracy" against "oligarchy." [40]

If associations in the field of business and industry are examined, clearer evidence appears, as might be expected, of the preponderance of "corporate" practices, though they are somewhat softened by tendencies that appear also to satisfy the claims of "democracy."

This situation is particularly well illustrated by the trade association. Although virtually all such groups hold one or more meetings of the membership each year,[41] the effective as well as much of the legal power in the organization rests with the officers, boards of directors, and the paid staff. Where the general membership plays a contributing part in policy making, it does so largely through committees. The T.N.E.C. study says of the large meetings: "If they are not a manner of performing activity, they are a means by which programs of activity are implemented and fostered. . . ."[42] The elected officers and boards of directors are in a peculiarly strategic position in the setting of policy, since they exercise the formal authority of the group (especially when the association is incorporated, as more than half are).[43] The influence of the officers is further enhanced by their relations with the staff and particularly the paid executive.

The key importance of the paid executive of a trade association has been suggested in forthright terms:

> The selection having been made, the executive can, to no inconsiderable degree, determine the direction and emphasis of the association's program; and the executive in some instances probably has been quite as much a factor in determining the character of the association's program of activity as the nature of the industry, the size of the membership, and other circumstances . . .[44]

His freedom of action, however, is subject to control by the directors, whose influence is increased in a large number of instances by the fact that the executive holds his position only from year to year. Among or behind the directors, moreover, may stand a few large financial contributors whose preferences and recommendations will carry special weight. The T.N.E.C. survey found that nearly half of the national and regional trade associations in 1937–38 received 40

[40] See Garceau: *The Political Life of the A.M.A.*, pp. 23–67.
[41] U.S. Temporary National Economic Committee: *Trade Association Survey*, pp. 33–5 and 384.
[42] Ibid., p. 35.
[43] Ibid., pp. 9, 366.
[44] Ibid., p. 38.

per cent or more of their income from their four largest contributors. This situation is due largely to the common practice of apportioning dues by some measure of size or volume of business. It is worth noting that, although size of financial contribution may be a clue to the actual lines of influence, the formal patterns usually conform to the "democratic" mold. Nearly 90 per cent of the trade associations surveyed by the T.N.E.C. indicated that their formal voting arrangements permitted only one vote per member regardless of size or amount of contribution. Only 14 per cent allotted votes on some other basis.[45]

The same kind of pattern emerges from an examination of the national business organizations. In the case of the Chamber of Commerce of the United States nominal policy control rests in the annual national convention.[46] Delegates to this meeting are apportioned among the organization members, the individual and firm members having no direct voice. This body elects some two thirds of the members of the board of directors, which is the locus of effective control in the association. The board is supplemented, however, by a national council made up of one representative for each organization member, which formally assists in planning the convention and advises and takes part in nominating members of the board of directors. With nearly three thousand organization members in the chamber, this body is not materially more significant than the annual convention itself.

The position and functions of the board of directors of the Chamber of Commerce are clearly of the "corporate" type. This body, numbering about fifty, elects the president and other officers of the organization, designates an executive committee from among its own membership, and appoints the principal officials of the headquarters staff. In addition, the board of directors passes upon all applications for membership, screens proposals submitted for action by the annual convention, and maintains close control over the organization's finances.

The importance of the last-named function is enhanced by the circumstance that the formal sources of policy-making authority are not identical with, nor even representative of, the major sources of financial support. This situation is similar to that in the American Medical Association, but it is more striking. Not only does the chamber, like

---

[45] Ibid., pp. 10, 11, 38.
[46] The following paragraphs are based largely on Childs: *Labor and Capital in National Politics*, pp. 42–8, supplemented by pamphlet material issued by the Chamber of Commerce of the United States.

the A.M.A., derive a sizable income from its publishing ventures, but also, as has been noted in Chapter 4, its income from dues is derived from two different classes of members. The organization members, upon which the representative system in the annual convention is based, supply a relatively small proportion of the chamber's annual income, probably a good deal less than 10 per cent. This situation is the result of a deliberate policy, for the chamber's leadership has felt for a good many years that contributions from individuals and firms provide a firmer financial base than do those from the constituent commercial associations, whose own financial positions are often weak and subject to wide fluctuation. The chamber has thus concentrated its promotional efforts on potential individual and firm members. Although these members must also belong to one of the organization members, they will perhaps display interests divergent from those of the organization members, since they are men and firms financially strong enough to pay dues to at least two associations. To the extent that they do hold different interests, such individual and associate members are more directly, though not formally, represented in the key policy-making units than the constituent associations, whose continued support is less necessary on financial grounds. Such financial structure makes the financial powers exercised by the board of directors of more than ordinary significance.

The Chamber of Commerce thus illustrates sharply the symptoms of "centralized control" characteristic of modern large-scale business organizations, though many features of its formal organization show the impress of the democratic mold. One further feature that conforms to the latter pattern is of particular interest—the referendum. This device is also included in the formal organization of a number of the State medical societies, though it is virtually a dead letter.[47] It is a permissive device in the organization of the National Association of Manufacturers and some labor unions, but is rarely used in either. Its use by the Chamber of Commerce is comparatively active. Decision to hold a referendum on a policy issue is taken by the board of directors, which appoints a special committee to look into the issue and make recommendations. A ballot on the issue, together with the committee's findings and a statement of the arguments counter to those supporting the committee's proposals, is sent to the organization members, each of which has as many votes as it is entitled to in the annual convention. The usual response is a large majority in favor of the committee's suggestions. Whatever may be the functional significance of the device, its existence is a striking instance of the impact of wide-

*Garceau: *The Political Life of the A.M.A.*, pp. 20–2.

spread community practices and values upon a group's formal organization.

Turning to a final example, the National Association of Manufacturers, we find, not unexpectedly, the clearest case of concentrated control, both formal and actual. Even here, however, the influence of "democratic" demands is apparent. Like the associations previously described, the N.A.M. holds its annual convention (called the Congress of American Industry). The policy-making functions of this body are limited, as is illustrated by the fact that its sessions, with few exceptions, are open to members and nonmembers alike.[48] This limitation is further evidenced by the absence of any representative system for the annual convention. Presumably all of the membership—currently claimed at sixteen thousand—could participate directly in its deliberations. This body elects roughly two thirds of the members of the board of directors, which numbers approximately 150, the exact number varying according to the size of the underlying membership. The most direct connection of the association's members with policy formulation, however, is through roughly a dozen standing committees—appointed by the board of directors—which submit recommendations to the board and its policy committees. About four fifths of the elected board members are chosen by a form of geographic proportional representation, the remainder being elected at large by the membership as a whole.

Despite these arrangements, centralized control is rather explicitly provided for in the organization. The board of directors, which has "full authority to effectuate the purposes and policies of the association," exercises the most extensive powers. It elects the president of the organization, chooses its own chairman (by custom the past president), and appoints an executive committee of about two dozen, whose chairman is usually the past chairman of the board. It elects the other officers of the association, appoints the principal members of the paid staff, makes changes in the bylaws, exercises complete authority over the budget, and approves changes in the constitution before they are submitted to the membership.

The nonelected members of the board are the officers, serving ex-officio, and a dozen to sixteen appointees. Among the latter are representatives of the National Industrial Council, a satellite organization

[48] See Alfred S. Cleveland: "N.A.M.: Spokesman for Industry?" *Harvard Business Review*, Vol. 26, no. 3 (May, 1948), pp. 353–71; also his Some Political Aspects of Organized Industry (unpublished Ph.D. dissertation, Harvard University, 1946); "Renovation in N.A.M.," *Fortune* (July, 1948), pp. 72 ff.

of manufacturers' associations whose exact relations with the N.A.M. have never been entirely clear. (The parent group supplies staff and headquarters facilities, and the chairman of the N.A.M. board is chairman of the N.I.C. This offshoot appears to have little or no influence on N.A.M. policy, functioning largely as a channel for spreading the parent organization's views among manufacturers not directly numbered among N.A.M. members.) The elected members of the N.A.M. board are chosen from a slate presented by a nominating committee appointed by the president, who also appoints members of the board to the policy committees, which sift proposals coming to the board and the executive committee.

In summary, the significance of the "democratic mold," which affects all associations and to some degree almost all organizations in our culture is of fundamental importance in the process of group politics. It has a profound relationship to the problem of unity—not only the cohesion of the particular association, but as well the unity of the society of which it is a part. Associations in our culture are expected to be "democratic." This expectation, moreover, represents a sort of hostage to other elements in the community. That is, to the extent that these "democratic" expectations have vitality, they constitute interests. These interests are expressed through groups or, more commonly, are represented by potential groups, the membership of which cuts across that of the associations of narrower compass. Thus, when a conflict occurs within or between groups of the latter sort, a conflict in which the broad "democratic" interests appear to be violated, cleavages within the affected associations may be accentuated. That is, interaction may occur on the basis of these "democratic" interests, and the potential group may become actual and operative. The situation is well illustrated by Garceau's observation concerning the American Medical Association: "It is . . . probable that the official interpretation of medical politics is so dogmatically democratic, not out of conviction, or personal preference, but rather to meet the emotional issue as framed by the economic protest group."[49]

Depending upon the intensity of the supposed violations, the cohesion of the affected associations may be reduced, their influence in the society jeopardized, and their continued existence threatened. These possibilities are a part of the setting of the internal politics of interest groups, which is the primary concern of the next chapter. Be-

[49] Reprinted by permission of the publishers from Oliver Garceau: *The Political Life of the American Medical Association* (Cambridge, Mass.: Harvard University Press, 1941), p. 28.

fore turning to that subject, however, it is appropriate to examine somewhat more closely the origins and character of those tendencies that operate outside the "democratic mold," that furnish an occasion for cleavage and disunity, and that define the problem of interest group leadership. What precisely are these contradictory tendencies? Why do they develop?

The Active Minority

Tendencies toward minority control are not confined to the political interest groups used here for illustration, nor are they peculiar to this type of group. Writers of the most diverse political views and using the most widely variant methods of observation have called attention to the existence in almost all groups of an active minority—identified by such condemnatory terms as "oligarchy" and "old guard" or such approving ones as "public spirited citizens" and "civic leaders." The late Lord Bryce put the situation in these words:

> In all assemblies and groups and organized bodies of men, from a nation down to the committee of a club, direction and decisions rest in the hands of a small percentage, less and less in proportion to the larger and larger size of the body, till in a great population it becomes an infinitesimally small proportion of the whole number. This is and always has been true of all forms of government, though in different degrees.[50]

It is unnecessary here to examine all the varied formulations of this proposition. However, one of these, a book by the Italian Swiss sociologist, Robert Michels, has peculiar relevance to the discussion of political interest groups. Studying the European socialist parties prior to 1914, Michels found that these groups, above all others attached to the "democratic" principle, showed unmistakable evidence of control by an active minority. His central conclusion, stated by him in somewhat flamboyant language as "the iron law of oligarchy," can be summarized in his words as follows: "The appearance of oligarchical phenomena in the very bosom of the revolutionary parties is a conclusive proof of the existence of immanent oligarchical tendencies in

[50] James Bryce: *Modern Democracies* (New York: The Macmillan Company, 1921), Vol. II, p. 542. Copyright by The Macmillan Company and used with their permission.

every kind of human organization which strives for the attainment of definite ends." [51]

Because of some serious limitations in his method, Michels derived from his evidence a series of implications concerning political leadership that are largely untenable and that do not adequately explain the complicated phenomenon of leadership. They need not be dealt with here. In isolating and stating some of the causes of the "oligarchical tendency," however, Michels performed a lasting service. With some modification his formulations will help to answer the question of this section: Why do interest groups develop an active minority in apparent contradiction of the "democratic mold?" Part of the answer has been mentioned in earlier paragraphs; it will be restated in more complete form now.

As Michels has suggested, the fact of formal organization is itself basic to an explanation of the existence of the active minority. Organization, viewed as a standardized, habitual pattern of interaction, implies varying degrees of participation by the membership in the process of decision making. These variations stem in part from the fact that it is virtually impossible for any considerable body of people to solve directly all the problems that may confront it. They represent the fact of delegation, explicit or implicit, of what we may call authority. Thus formal organization creates or recognizes various roles in a group, some of which involve more intimate and direct participation in the solution of the group's problems than do others. It acknowledges at least the rudiments of an active minority.

By way of illustration, the American Medical Association fairly early found that a general meeting of its members was too unwieldy a body for policy determination. Its present House of Delegates was a partial solution. That even this smaller body could handle only a limited segment of the association's delicate external and internal problems was acknowledged in the creation of the board of trustees, the committees, and the paid staff. "If the general meeting could not manage these affairs, no more could the House of Delegates." [52] The same observations can be made about any other such group.

The importance of formal organization in fostering the active mi-

[51] Robert Michels: *Political Parties: A Sociological Study of the Oligarchical Tendencies of Modern Democracy*, translated from the Italian by Eden and Cedar Paul (London: Jarrold & Sons, 1915), p. 14. This translation was republished in 1949 by The Free Press, Glencoe, Illinois.

[52] Reprinted by permission of the publishers from Oliver Garceau: *The Political Life of The American Medical Association* (Cambridge, Mass.: Harvard University Press, 1941), p. 19. See also p. 15.

nority is increased as the group increases in size of membership or variety of functions performed. Trade associations provide a good example. In the manufacture of electric refrigerators there are not many more than a dozen producers in the United States. In the trade association that includes these firms no elaborate formal organization is necessary. Three or four men or firms may act as a leadership group for limited purposes, and a small number of others may function similarly for other purposes, but the differences in participation among all members of the group are not great at any time. The association secretary performs some delegated functions, as do committees of the membership, but he is easily subject to a continuing check. Those dealing with the group can almost as easily reach the whole membership as they can the secretary. In the National Retail Dry Goods Association, however, which includes thousands in its membership, the general manager performs quite different functions. No effective approach to the group is possible except through him and the association's officers.

Berle and Means have called attention to the same situation in the development of minority control in the modern corporation. Their essential thesis, in fact, is that as ownership of corporations has been more widely dispersed, a separation of ownership and control has tended to develop.[53]

Those at the upper reaches of a large organization develop a remoteness from the rank and file that, buttressed by the special managerial skills usually necessary in such positions, approximates insulation from the stresses that may operate at lower levels. This situation has been noted frequently in studies of labor groups. Thus the long tenure of many officers of international unions, as compared with local officials, is ascribed primarily to their being "better insulated from rank-and-file pressure."[54] Their performance is not so directly apparent to the local membership. This remoteness, combined with the discretionary power implicit in delegation, is illustrated in unchallenged efforts by the well-situated minority to take action that does not conform to the decisions or preferences expressed by the rank and file or by their elected representatives. For example, in discussing the

[53] Berle and Means: *The Modern Corporation and Private Property*, pp. 69 ff.
[54] Ross: *Trade Union Wage Policy*, p. 31. Copyright 1948 by The Regents of the University of California and used with the permission of University of California Press. Cf. Philip Taft: "Democracy in Trade Unions," *American Economic Review*, Vol. 36, no. 2 (May, 1946), p. 362; Brooks: *When Labor Organizes*, pp. 260–1; Seidman: *Union Rights and Union Duties*, pp. 47–8.

role of the American Legion's National Executive Committee as a formulator as well as an executor of policy, Gray cites the fact that in 1943 this body reversed a vote of the previous national convention that had censured Hamilton Fish, one of the founders of the Legion, for his alleged assistance to elements deemed hostile to the best interests of the United States.[55]

Two words of caution should be emphasized in discussing the connection between formal organization and the active minority. In the first place, the authority of the active minority as fostered by formal organization is stated as being a matter of degree. It is an error to assume, as Michels[56] and others implicitly do, that delegation is necessarily complete, that it necessarily involves complete renunciation of power by the rest of the group. Although in some groups, under appropriate circumstances, some of which will be discussed in later paragraphs, nearly complete power may be delegated to an oligarchy, in no organization do we consistently find a sharply defined "mass" who merely obey and an equally definite minority who always command. The extent to which this sharp differentiation is approached is a matter for precise determination for individual groups in varying circumstances and not one for easy generalization. One may find, as Garceau has, that as a partial consequence of formal organization one can discern in the American Medical Association the rough outlines of an active minority exercising delegated functions that are extensive and highly discretionary. All initiative, whole and entire, does not, of course, necessarily rest in such minority hands. The interaction that defines the group puts limits on the monopoly of initiative.

In the second place, in order not to overemphasize the influence of formal structure, it is important to bear in mind the suggestion at the beginning of this chapter that formal organization represents a stage in the frequency of interaction of a group. The delegation it necessitates creates opportunities for the exercise of greater authority by leaders, but it also recognizes the authority that has already developed. That is, although formal organization facilitates leadership, leadership precedes this stage of interaction, for differential powers also exist at a stage where the frequency of interaction does not produce formal organization.

Consequent upon organization and influential in fostering the growth of an active minority are the managerial skills that are acquired by those who occupy in the organization positions through

[55] Justin Gray: *The Inside Story of the Legion* (New York: Boni & Gaer, 1948), pp. 167–8, 219.
[56] Cf. Michels: *Political Parties*, pp. 40–4.

which the delegated authority is exercised. Because men in such positions know the "system" and have learned some of the special skills that it demands, and because such posts in most organizations involve some measure of discretion, the occupants enjoy corresponding advantages over the rank and file. They are in possession of manipulative skills and tools not available to the uninitiated. Managerial position is itself a form of power, as many observers have noted. "The social mechanism is . . . so complex that those who are familiar with its working acquire authority on that account, possessing considerable control over those who use the services of the organization."[57]

The effects of occupying managerial positions—whether elective or appointive—may be quite varied. They stem, however, from the specialization, the "know-how," necessary in key positions in a hierarchy. Anyone who has observed a legislature in action will have noted how important to the effectiveness of a bloc is a knowledge of parliamentary tricks. The newcomer in such a setting is almost powerless unless he too learns how to operate the machinery. Tenure of such positions not only permits a tactical manipulative advantage but gives such individuals some control over the flow of ideas to the rank and file.

The effects on the development of an active minority of acquiring managing skills are particularly well illustrated by labor groups. Even at the local union level "the development of a bureaucracy seems almost inevitable irrespective of the philosophy or political outlook of the leadership," and local union leaders enjoy a wide discretion in matters of policy. At the more inclusive level of the international unions, the situation is more striking. As one close observer has put it: "The top executive of a national union exercises tremendous power—and the term 'tremendous' is used advisedly."[58] Such officials and their immediate associates, through their greater familiarity with the organization's affairs, through their power to name the membership of key committees, and through other advantages derived from their position, play a disproportionately large role in determining policy.[59] The situation is similar in a federated national group like the A.F. of L. The Executive Council of that organization determines

---

[57] MacIver: *The Web of Government*, p. 431. Copyright 1947 by Robert M. MacIver and used with the permission of The Macmillan Company. Cf. also Herring: *Group Representation Before Congress*, p. 29.

[58] Taft: "Democracy in Trade Unions," pp. 361-3. Copyright 1946 by and used with the permission of American Economic Association.

[59] Ibid., p. 364; cf. Millis and Montgomery: *Organized Labor*, p. 256; Ross: *Trade Union Wage Policy*, p. 41; Brooks: *When Labor Organizes*, pp. 257-8.

the major business to come before the annual convention; such business is largely transacted in committees led by members of the active minority. Millis and Montgomery indicate as fairly typical a convention of the A.F. of L. in which the chairmen of thirteen out of fourteen convention committees were either A.F. of L. vice-presidents or other major officers. They sum the matter up in the following terms: "Thus it is for the most part the voice of labor as interpreted by the Executive Council that becomes articulate in the legislation of the A.F. of L. The policies of the Federation are essentially those of the official class." [60]

In the National Association of Manufacturers the paid staff constitutes only a segment of the active minority, but they are reported to have more than a little to do with molding objectives and formulating policy, owing to such factors as long tenure in office and knowledge of the affairs of the association. A key figure of this sort was the late James A. Emery, who was counsel and chief legislative representative of the N.A.M. for thirty years; the late Walter B. Weisenburger was executive vice-president for nearly fifteen years; Noel Sargent has occupied various administrative positions, including that of manager of the industrial relations department and secretary of the association, since 1920. [61]

In the American Medical Association, as in the N.A.M., the active minority is made up partly of long-term holders of various elective and appointive positions and partly of its salaried administrators, many of whom have been in the same positions for long periods of time. Dr. Morris Fishbein, who in the eyes of many laymen was the A.M.A., served as the editor of its principal publication for nearly thirty years. The implications of such arrangements are fairly obvious.

For such men, work for organized medicine is a large part of their life, and for some it is their only career. . . . Secretaries, editors, and technicians develop skills which are useful primarily in "organized medicine" as such. It is natural and not wholly unrealistic that, to some commentators, they should appear themselves to be "organized medicine." [62]

[60] From *Organized Labor* by Millis and Montgomery, p. 308. Copyright 1945. Courtesy of McGraw-Hill Book Company, Inc.

[61] Cleveland: *Some Political Aspects of Organized Industry*, chap. 4.

[62] Reprinted by permission of the publishers from Oliver Garceau: *The Political Life of The American Medical Association* (Cambridge, Mass.: Harvard University Press, 1941), p. 49. See also p. 25.

The functions and power of such minorities become most apparent when they are used, not necessarily without reason, to resist either a change in long-established policy or the inclusion of new elements in the minority, or both. For example, a struggle has been carried on in the American Legion since 1945 over the inclusion of veterans of World War II among the major officers. Attempts to make a younger man National Commander have taken place at every postwar convention. One influential legionnaire has been quoted as saying: "After all, this Legion is a billion dollar corporation. You don't just throw something that big over to a bunch of inexperienced boys." [63] Despite the voting strength of the "boys," the elected National Commander is invariably the man groomed and named for the position by the active minority, known in Legion parlance as the king-makers.

In many groups the defensive efforts of those with managerial "know-how" stem from the indirect effects of acquiring such skills. Although those who over the years have learned how to manipulate the elements of a group's organization have thereby gained a means of exercising power, they may also have incapacitated themselves for gaining a satisfactory livelihood by any other means. The doctor who has given all of his time for a decade or more to the activities of organized medicine is in no position to return to active practice. The union leader who for years has not been a factory worker, who has not used the tools of his trade and has become accustomed to the forms and perquisites of union leadership, has disqualified himself psychologically, if not technically and physically, for work at the bench or lathe. To a lesser degree, perhaps, the business man who has spent years as a trade association secretary is not prepared readily to resume a career that he has all but forgotten. Under such circumstances it is not astonishing that some members of an active minority should tenaciously use their skills to perpetuate policies and methods with which their personal fortunes are literally identified.[64]

Other examples could be given at length. In his New Jersey study McKean found in all the groups he studied that control lay in the hands of a small group of officers, among whom the paid officials were an important element. About fifteen directors actually governed the New Jersey State Chamber of Commerce; control of the Manufac-

---

[63] Quoted in Gray: *The Inside Story of the Legion,* p. 171. For a good account of the line-up at the 1947 meeting, see The *New York Times,* August 27, 1947.

[64] Cf. Brooks: *When Labor Organizes,* pp. 260–1; Garceau: *The Political Life of the A.M.A.,* p. 64.

turers Association of New Jersey was in the hands of its secretary and the other officers; an executive secretary controlled the New Jersey Taxpayers Association, allegedly with support from the railroads.[65] The position of the paid executive in many trade associations has already been alluded to. It is well summarized in a statement by the general manager of one such group to the effect that less than a dozen association secretaries "can very largely control the general thought and action of employers' associations of the country." [66] The board of directors and the paid staff are the principal source of program and policy for the Chamber of Commerce of the United States. Even in the Board of Temperance, Prohibition, and Morals of the Methodist Episcopal Church, Herring noted some years ago: "The pronouncements of a few men in a central office are . . . able to direct the thought and actions of a large church body." [67]

A third influence upon the development and maintenance of an active minority is the financial structure of the group. In the groups that Michels studied, he did not encounter this as a major element. Yet he noted that in the socialist parties that needed the contributions of their more affluent members this dependence tended to give such contributors a disproportionate influence in a party's affairs.[68]

The influence of financial structure is far more noticeable in the interest groups examined here, though it is not characteristic of all of them. It is not easily isolated in any group, but in some it is indicated by the close correlation between tenure in key positions and the ability to pay. In the National Association of Manufacturers, for example, 125 corporations, constituting less than 5 per cent of the total membership, between 1933 and 1946 held an overwhelming proportion of the key positions: 63 per cent of the positions on the board of directors, 88 per cent of the positions on the executive committee of the board, 79 percent of the finance committee posts, and 52 percent of the major executive positions outside of the paid staff. This inner group represented primarily large, financially strong firms, and they accounted for a large proportion of the organization's funds. In 1936, for example, approximately 5 percent of the membership contributed just short of half the N.A.M.'s funds. Moreover, although the organ-

[65] McKean: *Pressures on the Legislature of New Jersey*, chap. 4.
[66] U.S. Senate, Subcommittee of the Committee on Education and Labor: *Hearings on Violations of Free Speech and Rights of Labor*, 75th Cong., 3d Sess. (1938), part 17, p. 7431.
[67] Herring: *Group Representation Before Congress*, p. 211. Copyright 1929 by and used with the permission of The Brookings Institution.
[68] Michels: *Political Parties*, pp. 129–31.

ization has asserted that more than four fifths of its members employed less than 500 workers, none of the 125 in the active minority was so small a firm, and nearly two thirds of them employed more than 2,500 workers.[69] If organizational structure in the N.A.M. in a sense defines the key posts occupied by an active minority, the financial structure measurably influences what elements are to occupy them.

Other examples are numerous. In the case of the New Jersey State Chamber of Commerce, the officers have been drawn from firms representing a considerable proportion of the State's corporate wealth. The Manufacturers Association of New Jersey employs a system of choosing its directors from those firms that employ relatively more workers and that have given the organization major financial support.[70] Similar tendencies in many national and regional trade associations have been mentioned in another connection.

Care should be taken to avoid any superficial explanation of this phenomenon, such as the common suggestion that the influence wielded by those who give major financial support indicates a sort of conspiracy on their part. A trade association secretary whose budget is heavily dependent upon the contributions of four or five firms will simply avoid situations likely to offend such members. The more or less continuous representation of these firms in the key policy positions, moreover, will minimize the chances of mistakes of this kind. In some instances the needs of financial strength and stability will indicate solicitous concern for the large contributor. Such considerations have encouraged the Chamber of Commerce of the United States to avoid soliciting chambers of commerce in small cities as organization members, to promote individual firm memberships over organizations, and among firms to solicit primarily those whose credit ratings indicate a capacity to pay dues in significant amounts.[71]

In some situations, finally, the financial structure of a group may operate to strengthen the position of an active minority within it in a manner unrelated to the money contributions of the minority element. In a good many labor unions, for example, the inability of locals alone to support adequate strike funds and research facilities has meant the movement of control to the financially stronger national

---

[69] Cleveland: "N.A.M.: Spokesman for Industry?" pp. 353–71 and his *Some Political Aspects of Organized Industry*, chap. 4; "Renovation in N.A.M.," *Fortune*, pp. 165–6; U.S. Senate, Subcommittee of the Committee on Education and Labor: *Hearings*, 75th Cong., 3d Sess. (1938), part 17, pp. 7503–41 and *passim*.

[70] McKean: *Pressures on the Legislature of New Jersey*, chap. 4.

[71] Cf. Childs: *Labor and Capital in National Politics*, pp. 84–6.

unions. This movement has strengthened the hands of those in control of such top machinery. Then, too, where the entire national union is none too strong financially, cost considerations may necessitate the weakening of some controls on the active minority, such as conventions. Although the annual convention of a labor union or other association is not a profoundly important means of restraining leadership elements, it does afford some opportunity for protest and challenge. Since such meetings are expensive, a financially weak union may be able to stage them only at fairly long intervals. In the interim the freedom of action of those in the key positions is appreciably strengthened and protected.[72]

Financial structure, therefore, may account in various ways for the development and continuance of an active minority within an interest group.

A fourth cause, less important than those already discussed but related to the second and third, is the fact that leadership is time-consuming and only a few can afford to spend the necessary time without remuneration. Michels found the emergence of paid, professional leadership one of the signs of developing minority control;[73] and, in part, this professionalized leadership is a product of the managerial skills, already discussed, that it develops. But these manipulative skills seem to be also a consequence of the professional leader's continuing preoccupation with the affairs of the organization. Even unpaid, nonprofessional leaders acquire such skills as a consequence of spending more time upon, and gaining greater familiarity with, the group's activities than can the rank and file. Professionals can give most of their time to the group because they are paid for it. The nonprofessional leader gives the time that he can spare from the activities by which he secures his livelihood.

In many groups only those with personal financial security and success in the institution to which the association is peripheral can afford the time required of unpaid leaders. In many instances the consequence is a highly conservative leadership, since, because of their status, the leaders have most to lose by any change in existing arrangements. Thus in the Chamber of Commerce of the United States and the National Association of Manufacturers the segment of the active minority that is not included among the professional

[72] Joseph Shister: "Trade Union Government: A Formal Analysis," *Quarterly Journal of Economics*, Vol. 60, no. 1 (November, 1945), pp. 78–112; "The Locus of Union Control in Collective Bargaining," *Quarterly Journal of Economics*, Vol. 60, no. 4 (August, 1946), pp. 513–45.

[73] Michels: *Political Parties*, pp. 40 ff.

leaders and staff is quite naturally drawn from among men whose jobs permit their devoting considerable time to the activities of these groups. Indeed, major corporation executives, from the very nature of the positions they occupy, may find it desirable to engage in the activities of such associations. The leaders of most large corporations today carry an extensive responsibility for managing the company's relations with various outside groups, of which labor unions are only one example. Remembering the functions of the association in stabilizing such relations for individuals and subgroups similarly situated, we can understand why the heads of large companies can afford time for extensive participation in these associations.

The influence, in the American Medical Association, of the fact that unpaid leaders must be men of some leisure has been spelled out in considerable detail. A study of the principal elective bodies of the A.M.A. over a period of fifteen years, and of several of the State societies, has indicated that specialists from the more urbanized areas have held positions of power in numbers out of all proportion to their numbers in the medical population as a whole. Those with long tenure (eight years or more) in their positions were especially likely to fall into this category. In accounting for this characteristic Garceau observes:

> A man must have some margin of wealth and leisure to leave his practice and attend conventions, to say nothing of serving on active operating committees, with trips to the state capital or to Chicago. Politics and the public office that goes with it take time; less it is true, in associational politics than in the politics of the state, but too much for a man in active general practice where substitutes are rivals and there may often, in fact, be no one to care for the community if the doctor goes off on a junket.[74]

The American Legion provides another illustration. As in the A.M.A., so in the Legion, membership on key committees tends to fall disproportionately to those who can afford the leisure necessary for frequent participation in group actions. The necessity for such leisure favors city specialists among the doctors; in the veterans' or-

[74] Reprinted by permission of the publishers from Oliver Garceau: *The Political Life of the American Medical Association* (Cambridge, Mass.: Harvard University Press, 1941), p. 54. This mobility and leisure afforded by a favorable financial situation help to define the active minority in the American Library Association also. See Garceau: *The Public Library in the Political Process,* chap. 4.

ganization it encourages higher military officers, both active and retired.[75]

A fifth influence in the formation of an active minority may be found in qualities peculiar to leaders as persons. We must avoid the implication that the existence of the active minority can be accounted for entirely on the basis of elements outside the personalities of the particular leaders. This is not the place for a thorough discussion of the psychology of leadership; suffice it to say that the matter of leading is better viewed as a relationship between individuals than as a quality that some individuals "have." Nevertheless, it must be recognized, as Gordon Allport emphasizes in his discussion of differential participation, that "talents differ." [76] It then becomes entirely reasonable to suggest that a few members of a group may adequately represent the attitudes and aspirations of the rank and file. Michels discusses the influence of leaders' personalities, though in rather loose terms that associate it primarily with such elements as formal learning and personal prestige.[77] The general point can be illustrated by Garceau's observations on the American Medical Association. He points out that the city specialists who dominate the group's active minority are men already set apart from their constituents by personality and energy. Not that organized medicine provides rewards exactly corresponding to merit, but the successful city specialist is likely to exhibit high energy and differentiating talents of various sorts. Those talents, whether strictly professional or not, that lead to a successful practice are likely also to prove useful in the hierarchy of the organized group, if only because they make their possessor a more skillful spokesman for the group's claims upon other elements in the society. The practice of medicine, moreover, although it is a demanding, and in many cases completely absorbing, enterprise, is for many of its devotees not a complete means of satisfying individual psychological needs. Talent for management in its many forms, and drives for prestige, can be expressed by achieving influential positions in the group.[78] If such men tend to cling to the positions thus acquired and if they persistently defend a system that has been the apparent means of their advancement, one should not be astonished. By so doing, in fact, the active minority may most effectively represent, except in periods of rapid change, the attitudes and aspirations of their constituents, both those

[75] Marcus Duffield: *King Legion* (New York: Cape and Smith, 1931) pp. 110–1.
[76] Gordon W. Allport: "The Psychology of Participation," *Psychological Review*, Vol. 53, no. 3 (May, 1945), pp. 117–32.
[77] Michels: *Political Parties*, pp. 70, 78–9.
[78] Garceau: *The Political Life of the A.M.A.*, pp. 57–67.

who have similar but as yet unrecognized talents and those whose personalities do not require the satisfactions of leadership.

Assent to these representative qualities by the rank and file except in periods of rapid change suggests a sixth influence sustaining an active minority, the influence of custom. As Michels has noted, the holding of an office tends to become a customary right, and an individual will "remain in office unless removed by extraordinary circumstances or in obedience to rules observed with exceptional strictness." [79] These "extraordinary circumstances," moreover, may be long postponed if the official appears to advance the group's interests sufficiently to make his continuance in office a gesture of decent gratitude on the part of his constituents or at least sufficiently to forestall intense dissatisfaction. "Authority," as John Gaus has observed, ". . . follows the successful exercise of function." [80] The authority, it should be added, may be much more extensive than the function so exercised.

Such gratitude is unquestionably one of the keys to the power of the active minority in the American Legion, since these leaders are able not only to champion veterans' benefits in general but also to facilitate the settlement of the individual claims of members. Many a veteran has found a pending claim against the government mysteriously expedited upon his joining the Legion. A similar situation can be noticed in trade associations. For example, the successful promotion of anti-chain-store legislation in the 1930's placed the director of the National Association of Retail Druggists in an almost invulnerable position with his constituents. Edward A. O'Neal, President of the American Farm Bureau Federation from 1931 to 1947, was elevated to the position of a demigod as a consequence of his successful leadership of the organization during these years that produced so marked a change in the economic position of farmers. [81]

In many labor unions gratitude for services presumably rendered supports a customary re-election of officers. On the other hand, although opposition in union elections is exceptional whether they are held in convention or are conducted by referendum, unsuccessful leadership is often as likely to be supported by custom as is one that has gained marked advantages for its group. Taft points out that success in strengthening the union was a poor explanation for the ten-

[79] Michels: *Political Parties*, pp. 50–3, 66–8.
[80] John M. Gaus, L. D. White, and M. E. Dimock: *The Frontiers of Public Administration* (Chicago: The University of Chicago Press, 1936), p. 39.
[81] See Orville M. Kile: *The Farm Bureau Through Three Decades* (Baltimore: The Waverly Press, 1948), pp. 326–8 and *passim*.

ure of the officers of the United Mine Workers in the 1920's and suggests as a more likely cause the decline of the older union districts with the shift of the industry and the consequent movement of the union into areas where the miners had little memory of autonomous locals undominated by the national officers. High membership turn-over, in fact, has been noted by many observers as promoting the customary stability of leadership in a variety of groups.[82]

The nature of the strategic position of a group in relation to other groups in the society suggests a seventh influence that, under appro-priate circumstances, may facilitate the development of an active minority, just as it may affect the character of formal organization. That is, where a group finds itself in more or less open conflict—not necessarily involving violence—with other groups, the need for quick maneuver and discipline will, as Michels observed concerning his so-cialist parties, promote the influence and authority of the few.[83] This pattern is a familiar one in the operation of the government itself, for the executive acquires almost dictatorial powers in time of war or serious domestic crisis. It is further illustrated by the discretionary power exercised by the makers of a nation's foreign policy and by the secrecy that necessarily surrounds much of their work, even in a pe-riod in which a fetish is made of hostility to secret diplomacy. In-terestingly enough, groups attempting to influence the making of foreign policy may be similarly affected by the dynamics of the situa-tion in which they find themselves. A study of interest groups operat-ing on foreign affairs in the United States in the two years prior to Pearl Harbor indicates that "events transpired so rapidly that the ini-tiative was in the hands of a small controlling leadership" in all such groups.[84]

The influence of conflict upon labor groups has been referred to in a slightly different connection earlier in this chapter. Labor unions are a peculiarly appropriate example, since, as many students of the subject have observed, the operation of such groups is closely analo-gous to war and diplomacy. To gain its ends, whether economic or political, a union must give considerable authority to its leadership, the amount varying with a multitude of circumstances affecting the strategic position of the group. As Ross has observed: "The wage pol-

[82] Philip Taft: "Opposition to Union Officers in Elections," *Quarterly Jour-nal of Economics*, Vol. 58, no. 2 (February, 1944), pp. 251-2; Michels: *Po-litical Parties*, p. 85; Childs: *Labor and Capital in National Politics*, p. 256.

[83] Michels: *Political Parties*, pp. 46-9.

[84] John W. Masland: "Pressure Groups and American Foreign Policy," *Pub-lic Opinion Quarterly*, Vol. 6, no. 1 (Spring, 1942), pp. 115 ff.

icy of a union, like the foreign policy of a nation, is a matter poorly
suited to the methods of primitive democracy." [85]

An eighth and final influence facilitating the development of an
active minority involves, not the characteristics of the leading element,
nor the external relationships of the group, but rather peculiar qualities of those who are led. This factor is crucial, and not only because of its observed influence in the operation of interest groups.
It is not an exaggeration to say that what one regards as the verified facts in this area will determine the adequacy of one's theory of
the political process. The loose and uncritical use of such terms as
"mass apathy," for example, leads to conclusions that may be emotionally satisfying but that are seriously superficial. The superficiality
lies in the fact that such statements do not account adequately for upheavals, shifts, and rebellions. They force their holders to resort to
some implied and hopelessly undynamic *deus ex machina* as a means
of explaining the sudden transformation of inert mass into active participants. Here lie the clearest shortcomings in Michels's formulations.
For him the characteristics of the rank and file are not merely the ob-
verse or reciprocal of those of the active minority; they are an independent and continuing influence by themselves. That is, he asserts
that there is an "indifferent and apathetic mass" that has a felt need
for leadership. This felt need derives from the increasing division of
labor and "profound differences of culture and education." It is manifest in "all countries," though "its intensity varies as between one nation and another." [86]

Concerning the American scene Myrdal has made similar and
only slightly less sweeping statements. In a chapter entitled, "The
American Pattern of Individual Leadership and Mass Passivity," he
observes:

> Despite the democratic organization of American society with its
> emphasis upon liberty, equality of opportunity (with a strong
> leaning in favor of the underdog), and individualism, the idea
> of leadership pervades American thought and collective action.
> The demand for "intelligent leadership" is raised in all political
> camps, social and professional groups, and, indeed, in every col-
> lective activity centered around any interest or purpose—church,

[85] Ross: *Trade Union Wage Policy*, p. 38. Copyright 1948 by The Regents
of the University of California and used with the permission of University of
California Press. Cf. Taft: "Democracy in Trade Unions," pp. 359–61;
Shister: "Trade Union Government: A Formal Analysis," pp. 78–112; Brooks:
When Labor Organizes, pp. 257–8.
[86] Michels: *Political Parties*, pp. 54–65.

school, business, recreation, philanthropy, the campus life of a college, the entertaining of a group of visitors, the selling of patent medicine, the propagation of an idea or of an interest.[87]

To this he adds: "The other side of this picture is, of course, the relative inertia and inarticulateness of the masses in America."[88] Aside from the matter of whether such patterns are peculiar to America and the further problem of just how one measures the differences between countries in this respect, about which questions might well be raised, there is plenty of evidence to give some plausibility to these observations. In McKean's study of interest groups in New Jersey he repeatedly notes cases in which activity is confined to a few individuals in a group.[89] In the National Association of Manufacturers, even among those belonging to the key policy-making bodies, participation varies widely. It is estimated that less than half the board members regularly attend meetings and that committee attendance is even lower.[90] In the medical societies lack of participation has been a matter of some concern to the active elements from the very beginning.[91] A similar situation has persistently characterized labor unions, especially at the local level. Millis and Montgomery report that attendance by a quarter of the members of an average local at routine meetings is considered good, and frequently it is less than 5 per cent. They conclude that "there is here, as in political government, the problem of seeming indifference on the part of the rank and file."[92]

The danger in these observations does not lie in the suggestion that the active minority participate continuously in the group's affairs, whereas others do not. This situation is observable. If, as has been noted elsewhere, differing talents in part produce leadership, it is not astonishing that the same kind of factor produces followers. The danger lies rather in assuming that because these two tendencies can be observed in a group at a particular point in time, they identify two sharply distinguished and unchanging subgroups—leaders and mass.

[87] Myrdal: *An American Dilemma*, p. 709. Copyright 1944 by and used with the permission of Harper and Brothers.

[88] Myrdal: *An American Dilemma*, p. 712. Copyright 1944 by and used with the permission of Harper and Brothers. See also chap. 33.

[89] McKean: *Pressures on the Legislature of New Jersey*, chap. 3.

[90] Cleveland: *Some Political Aspects of Organized Industry*, chap. 4.

[91] Cf. Garceau: *The Political Life of the A.M.A.*, pp. 14, 18, 24, 61–7.

[92] From *Organized Labor* by Millis and Montgomery, pp. 246–7. Copyright 1945. Courtesy of McGraw-Hill Book Company, Inc.

We are dealing here with the complicated problems of participation. Far too little of a precise nature is known about this realm of human behavior. It is clear, however, that every individual, for both physiological and psychological reasons, develops a pattern of participation or interaction that is standardized within broad limits both in respect to frequency and type. This standard exists for his behavior as a whole, but in the groups in which he interacts it is subject to wide variation, both from group to group at a particular time and from time to time in any one group. Participation of the membership of a group, moreover, is a matter of degree, scaling down from continuous activity in a few cases to what can be called apathy in a large number. Individuals may move up and down this scale of participation as circumstances inside and outside the group change.[93] Leadership of the group is a rate and type of participation, a relationship with others on the scale.

Thus, although the active minority is characterized by a higher rate of participation than any others in the group and although this rate may be highly stable in a group over a period of time, the roles of leader and follower involve also a dynamic relationship. As Ross says of labor unions, though the rank and file are dependent upon the leadership for guidance,

> This is not to argue that the membership is only a passive tool. It does have a temper, apathetic or militant; it does have a propensity or disinclination to strike; it is highly susceptible to the appeals of rival leaders and of would-be leaders. The relationship with the rank and file remains the most important in the reckoning of the union officials.[94]

The character and operation of this dynamic relationship, of crucial significance in the internal and external politics of groups, is the concern of the following chapter.

[93] See Chapple and Coon: *Principles of Anthropology*, chaps. 3 and 4; Erich Fromm: *Escape From Freedom* (New York: Rinehart & Company, Inc., 1941), esp. chap. 5.

[94] Ross: *Trade Union Wage Policy*, p. 38. Copyright 1948 by The Regents of The University of California and used with the permission of University of California Press.

6

Internal Politics: The Problem of
Cohesion

COMPLETE stability within any interest group is a fiction, albeit one that has technical usefulness in the management of the group. Large or small, national or local, all groups experience continual altercations over policies, involving both ends and means. These disputes both produce, and are reflected in, struggles for leadership.

The nature of these internal political situations and their effects upon the group's success are a function of two interdependent factors, the leadership skills present and the make-up of the membership itself. The attitudes present in the membership define the tasks of the leaders, and the internal political life of the group is made up of a continuous effort to maintain leaders and followers in some measure of harmonious relationship. Such problems are not, of course, necessarily generated from within the group, though they may be. External events, stemming from the activities of other groups or from more impersonal sources, may be the major initiating influences. But these derive their effect from the character of the political situation within the group. As Ross says of the labor union: "The economic environment is important to the unions at the second remove: Because it generates political pressures which have to be reckoned with by the union leader. The effect of any given change depends upon how it fits into the general constellation of pressures." [1]

---

[1] Ross: *Trade Union Wage Policy*, p. 14. Copyright 1948 by The Regents of The University of California and used with the permission of University of California Press.

Cohesion and Overlapping Membership

The internal political problems created by such influences derive basically from a characteristic of group life that is particularly noticeable in complex modern society, namely, that no individual is wholly absorbed in any group to which he belongs. Only a fraction of his attitudes is expressed through any one such affiliation, though in many instances a major fraction. Moreover, this characteristic is true not alone of interest groups but also, as John Dewey, F. H. Allport and others have argued, of all groups in the society.[2] Even the nation at war, the most inclusive and demanding group of our times, has its reluctant patriots, its conscientious objectors, and its traitors. The characteristic is better illustrated within the nation by the fact that an individual generally belongs to several groups—a family, a church, an economic institution, and frequently a very large number of associations, perhaps sixty or seventy for active "joiners" in our society.[3]

The demands and standards of these various groups may and frequently do come in conflict with one another, a situation that is the primary source of the problem of internal group politics. This notion of conflict, however, will be misleading unless the conflict is understood as taking place at various levels from the highly explicit to the subtly implicit. It may be clear and recognized, as when a man who belongs to a local improvement association that is demanding the repaving of a neighborhood street is also a member of a taxpayers' group that is opposing an appropriation for this purpose. At the other extreme it may be a scarcely conscious feeling of incongruity between the moral standards of a family or church and the drive of a trade association for preferred treatment at the hands of public officials. Or the conflict may be merely the sense of rivalry for the time and attention of the member. Whether explicit or implicit, however, each such conflict may have significant implications for the internal affairs of the groups involved. It is an experience that is disturbing and not infrequently painful for the individual; at the same time, and more important for present purposes, it may be critical for the groups, depending upon the number of persons in whom the conflict is occurring, their roles in the groups,

---

[2] Dewey: *The Public and Its Problems*; F. H. Allport: *Institutional Behavior*, chaps. 2 and 5; Rice: *Farmers and Workers in American Politics*, chap. 1.

[3] Chapple and Coon: *Principles of Anthropology*, p. 425; Lundberg: *Foundations of Sociology*, pp. 355–8.

and the manner in which it is resolved. The process is the same, of course, whether we look at its effects on the individual or whether, as in the present case, we are more interested in the impact on the affected groups. As Bentley has put it: "To say that a man belongs to two groups of men which are clashing with each other; to say that he reflects two seemingly irreconcilable aspects of the social life; to say that he is reasoning on a question of public policy, these all are but to state the same fact in three forms." [4] The phenomenon of the overlapping membership of social groups is thus a fundamental fact whose importance for the process of group politics, through its impact on the internal politics of interest groups, can scarcely be exaggerated.

Membership, as noted in the preceding chapter, should not be understood narrowly as including only those who pay dues to a formal organization. Those "fellow-travelers" who share the attitudes characteristic of an interest group must also be reckoned in some degree as participants in it. In fact, as subsequent chapters will indicate, retaining the loyalty of such "members" may be important to the successful achievement of the group's claims. Those in the dues-paying category differ from these in degree, it is true, since financial support is presumptive evidence of more active participation. Both, however, may in varying degrees experience the conflicts of overlapping membership. For example, the American Bar Association and the American Civil Liberties Union are two among the interest groups that attempt to protect and enforce various elements in our constitutional tradition. Both have comparatively small memberships in the narrow sense, yet many people throughout the country share the basic attitudes that underlie these activities, as the propaganda efforts of the groups will indicate. One who shares these sympathies and belongs also to a labor union or employers' association whose claims are being attacked by one of the above-named groups will be as likely to experience some doubts or conflicts concerning these contrary claims as will one who pays dues to two such groups. Or the doctor who is not a member, in the narrow sense, of a labor union, but is sympathetic with the efforts of labor organizations to achieve security for their members through governmental legislation, may experience similar conflict when the American Medical Association and the labor organizations line up against one another over a proposal for governmental health insurance.

[4] Bentley: *The Process of Government,* p. 204. Copyright 1908 by and used with the permission of Arthur F. Bentley.

It is also important in dealing with the concept of overlapping membership to re-emphasize that the moving stream of politics involves not only actual groups but, as has been pointed out in other connections, potential groups as well. Indications of these potential groups are to be found in attitudes widely held, but not at the moment the basis of interaction and claims upon others. Some of these attitudes may be contained in the laws and constitutional provisions of the state, since such enactments presuppose the existence at some time of interests in the community capable of securing their passage. Others may be reflected merely in the unwritten "rules of the game" and moral codes of a people. Looking at the genesis of individual attitudes of this sort, one should note that most of these will have had their origins in group affiliations, perhaps in childhood, that are no longer active but whose influence on behavior is continuing. All of these, like the "anticorruption" interest used as an illustration early in Chapter 5, are likely to be, in Bentley's terms, "wide, weak interests," part of what he calls the "habit background." [5] These are not necessarily embodied in organized groups, but they set some of the limits within which the narrower groups operate. Flagrant violation of the "habit background" by a group will often bring the potential group into active existence and, more important for present purposes, will create a conflict situation for those members of the offending group who share the affected attitudes, whether these attitudes become the basis for a countergroup or not. As one thoughtful observer has put it: "Problems of representative action within a private association also turn upon the extent to which the coercive power of the group seems to promote and conform to the basic beliefs and promises of society, or conflicts with them." [6]

The internal political situation in a group is affected by the extent to which its membership overlaps that of other groups because of the varying effects that such overlapping has, and can have, upon cohesion. Cohesion in turn—along with the related factor of size and those of organization, financing and techniques—is a crucial determinant of the effectiveness with which the group may assert its claims. It is a constantly operating influence that limits the activities of a group and its leaders, not only in critical times but as well when a group presents a front of harmonious unity. It is, in fact, the appearance of harmony in a successful group that may mislead the casual observer

[5] Ibid., pp. 218-9, 372, 374-5.
[6] Avery Leiserson: "Problems of Representation in the Government of Private Groups," *Journal of Politics*, Vol. 11, no. 3 (August, 1949), p. 567.

into treating such a group as a solid, homogeneous unit. A group must approach such a state in some degree if it is to exist at all, but no group fully attains it. As MacIver has observed: "The sense of the common over-rides the differences within the group, but it does not abolish them."[7] For this reason it is important never to lose sight of the group as a set of interactions, as described in Chapter 2; a group is not a mass of physical men, but is rather some of the interactions of certain men, varying in frequency and intensity, increasing, moderating, developing, and declining.[8]

A few illustrations of the effects of the overlapping memberships of groups can be cited here. More detailed cases will be discussed later in the chapter. These effects occur in interest groups of every sort. Thus Ross reports that heterogeneity of membership (overlapping) is a major source of political problems inside a union:

> Nonhomogeneity of membership often gives rise to conflicts of interest; it is one of the most delicate political tasks of the union leadership to reconcile these conflicts in formulating its wage program. The ultimate resolution depends upon (1) the effective political pressure generated by the various [internal] interest groups and (2) the political skill of the leadership.[9]

Such heterogeneity is overtly apparent in many groups. Thus even the National Association of Manufacturers, which has avoided some of these difficulties by defining the type of firm that it will accept as a member, has applied the definition of "manufacturing" sufficiently loosely to include at least one of the large mail-order houses.[10] That there are limits to heterogeneity of membership, however, is obvious. Undoubtedly one reason why a group like the League of Women Voters is confined largely to women of the middle and upper classes is that many of the habits and attitudes of the majority are so strange or so meaningless to a recruit from another class that even similarity of political concern cannot offset them.

Sherif and Cantril report an excellent illustration of overlapping and conflict drawn from a study of the attitudes of coal miners. In

---

[7] MacIver: *The Web of Government*, p. 415. Copyright 1947 by Robert M. MacIver and used with the permission of The Macmillan Company.

[8] Cf. Bentley: *The Process of Government*, p. 211.

[9] Ross: *Trade Union Wage Policy*, pp. 31–2. Copyright 1948 by The Regents of The University of California and used with the permission of University of California Press.

[10] The concept of overlapping is not less applicable where a firm is involved, since it then applies to the key officials who interact in both groups, though not, of course, to the whole firm.

May of 1943 the leadership of the United Mine Workers was threatening a strike that would, if it took place, almost certainly precipitate Government seizure of the mines. The union members were asked whether they favored calling a strike, and they responded two to one in the negative. The primary reason given was the "desire not to let down the war effort, their confidence in President Roosevelt as a man who would give them a square deal." But in spite of this, more than three fourths of the miners also stated that they would go out if the strike were called, because they "wouldn't let their union and their union leaders down." [11]

A rather conventional case is suggested by McKean in his study of New Jersey interest groups. Noting that the Catholic Church was opposed to sterilization of the mentally unfit and that the New Jersey League of Women Voters favored the proposal, he commented: "A loyal Catholic woman who was also an enthusiastic member of the League would find herself in a most unpleasant dilemma, and one of her loyalties would have to give way. Similar conflicts constantly occur. . . ." [12]

A less obvious instance is suggested by Schattschneider's study of the Smoot-Hawley tariff legislation of 1930. So strong was the general attitude over the country in favor of protective duties that groups likely to be disadvantaged by the law engaged in vigorous opposition only when their very existence was threatened. [13]

Under the influence of events the direction and intensity of overlapping and conflict are constantly shifting. These shifts necessarily affect the claims of groups and the relative influence that various groups are able to exercise. Until recent years all of the national farm groups could be counted upon to promote and defend the restrictive taxes upon oleomargarine in favor of butter. As the former commodity has increasingly been manufactured from domestic oils and particularly from soy beans grown largely in sections in or adjacent to the principal dairy areas, groups such as the American Farm Bureau Federation have found it necessary to avoid the issue. A report of their 1948 convention contained the following item:

> The American Farm Bureau Federation withheld action yesterday on the controversial issue of repeal of oleomargarine taxes. The Bureau's resolutions committee debated the question at

[11] Reprinted by permission from *The Psychology of Ego-Involvements* by M. Sherif & H. Cantril, published by John Wiley & Sons, Inc., 1947, p. 380.

[12] McKean: *Pressures on the Legislature of New Jersey*, p. 224.

[13] Schattschneider: *Politics, Pressures and the Tariff*, p. 163 and *passim*.

length but finally wound up voting to take no stand, paralleling procedure at last year's convention.

The organization has heavy membership in areas which produce both butter and vegetable oils used in margarine.[14]

But what happens to the individual in these situations? How are the multiple memberships of a number of persons reflected in the internal politics and the degree of cohesion of the interest groups to which they belong? We must start from the fact that the equilibrium of an individual consists of his adjustment in the various institutionalized groups and associations to which he belongs. Changes in the personnel of these groups, changes in their patterns, and the like, will constantly create mild or strong disturbances; individuals consequently may increase or decrease their activity in existing groups, enter new associations, or drop out of current ones. Both individuals and groups, therefore, are constantly in the process of readjustment.

The conflicts and contradictions that almost inevitably stem from membership in several groups produce disturbances among the affected individuals and groups. Felt conflicts of this sort are painful. They compel the individual to seek a readjustment by altering the character of his participation in the groups or by changing his group affiliations.[15] Research evidence on the effect of such conflicts upon political interest groups is not abundant, but some recent studies provide effective illustrations. Lazarsfeld's study of the 1940 presidential vote in Erie County, Ohio, broke new ground in this as in other respects. Having found religion, urban or rural residence, and socio-economic status as influences predisposing voters toward one candidate or the other, he examined those cases in which the predisposing elements from these three sources were not all in the same direction. These cases involved conflicts similar to those that concern us here, though the data of the study did not permit identification of the organized interest groups that may have been affected. Thus the Catholic (Democratic predisposition) who was of upper socio-economic status (Republican predisposition) was subject to conflicting pressures; so was the rural resident (Republican predisposition) who was of low socio-economic status (Democratic predisposition), and so on. The effect of these cross-pressures or conflicts, as indicated by vot-

[14] Associated Press dispatch from Atlantic City, New Jersey, December 17, 1948.
[15] Sherif and Cantril: *The Psychology of Ego-Involvements*, pp. 5, 290. Cf. also p. 286 of the same volume and literature there cited. Chapple and Coon: *Principles of Anthropology*, pp. 434-5.

ing behavior, by the degree of ease with which the voter came to his decision, and by expressed attitudes toward the election, was to decrease the affected citizen's interest in the election. He escaped from the conflict by withdrawing in effect from participation in the campaign. Citizens with such a low level of interest were most likely to be nonvoters.[16]

A study of the 1944 national vote, using essentially the same methods, confirmed these findings. This set up a five-point scale of political predisposition, using only religion and socio-economic status, ranging from strong Republican to strong Democratic. Those individuals falling at the mid-points of the scale, where the predispositions were in conflict, showed the same lack of interest and tendency toward withdrawal as did those exposed to similar conflicts in Erie County.[17]

A more recent example is described in a study of a number of local unions led by Communist officials but largely made up of Catholics. The study concentrated on attitudes toward American-Soviet relations, concerning which the union members were presumably exposed to conflicting influences from the union leadership and from the Church. Those Catholics in the union who most closely approximated the Communist view "tended to withdraw from the religious fold." Others, like the voters studied by Lazarsfeld, withdrew from the conflict by losing interest in the controversial subject.[18] Those subject to conflict because of their multiple memberships thus resolved it by partly or completely dropping out of one group or by withdrawing from both with respect to the issue that produced the difficulty. The cohesion of the rejected group was affected in the first instance and that of both groups, at least for special purposes, in the second.

It should be possible, by careful observation of the relative frequency of interactions within a wide variety of interest groups, to measure, or at least describe with some accuracy, the effects of overlapping membership upon group cohesion. This possibility has been suggested elsewhere,[19] but so far such studies have not been undertaken in a thoroughly systematic fashion for groups of political importance, although the study of the Communist-Catholic trade union may be regarded as a beginning.

---

[16] Lazarsfeld, *et al: The People's Choice*, chap. 6.

[17] Korchin: *Psychological Variables in the Behavior of Voters*, chap. 5.

[18] Martin Kriesberg: "Cross-Pressures and Attitudes: A Study of the Influence of Conflicting Propaganda on Opinions Regarding American-Soviet Relations," *Public Opinion Quarterly*, Vol. 13, no. 1 (Spring, 1949), pp. 5–16.

[19] Chapple and Coon: *Principles of Anthropology*, p. 38.

Thus, on the basis of the available research evidence, we can set forth with some confidence the kinds of effects to be anticipated from conflicts resulting from multiple memberships. These effects will depend in the first place upon the number of members of the group experiencing the conflict. Where this number is appreciable, the implications for group cohesion will be serious. Where the number is small, the consequences for the group will depend on the roles played by the individual or individuals affected. If these individuals are among the official or unofficial leaders, the effects may be disproportionately extensive, involving the possibilities of temporary or permanent schism; but if the affected individuals are merely a small number of followers, the results may be slight. In the second place, the effects for any particular group will depend upon the way in which the conflicts are resolved. Temporary loss of interest or reduced participation in the group because of a conflict of limited duration may affect cohesion slightly or not at all. If the lowered rate of interaction or the withdrawal becomes permanent, however, the effects may be considerable.

It is at this point that the skills and strengths of the group leadership, to which we shall turn later, become relevant and crucial. Leaders can scarcely control the multiple group memberships of the rank and file, but within limits they can isolate or minimize the effects. The maximization of cohesion in such circumstances, whether to perpetuate the tenure of leaders or to achieve group goals, is the continuing and primary task of leadership in the internal politics of interest groups.

Without precise data on particular groups at particular times it is impossible to predict with accuracy the effects of given conflicts and overlappings of membership in specific situations. Even in the case of a single individual, the likelihood of one group attachment rather than another being dominant at a given time will vary with the circumstances. The determining factors will be relatively apparent, but their precise strengths will not be predictable except by means of close and continuing observation. As Sherif and Cantril observe: "It has become almost a truism by now that group interaction produces differential results in the experience and behavior of individuals participating in a group situation."[20] Thus the communications media have repeatedly been observed to produce differential effects on in-

[20] Reprinted by permission from *The Psychology of Ego-Involvements* by M. Sherif & H. Cantril, published by John Wiley & Sons, Inc., 1947, p. 280. See also p. 382.

dividual opinions, depending upon the pre-existing attitudes of the audience.[21] The consequent behavior is equally variable.

Such obvious points about individual differences have led some writers to an at least implicit modification or rejection of the hypothesis that groups mold the attitudes of their members. Seeing the evidence of partial inclusion and overlapping membership, they infer a mystical individual autonomy reminiscent of sterile controversies over "free will." MacIver, for example, states:

> The individual is never wholly absorbed in his society, wholly responsive to it, wholly accounted for by it. . . . Unlike the cells of the organism the individual is a *self-directing unit*, with some kind or degree of autonomy. His society does not prescribe his every action. Above all, it does not prescribe his every thought. . . . [22] (Italics added.)

Divergent perceptions and differential reactions can be accounted for adequately within the limits of a group hypothesis on the basis of the individual's unique biological inheritance and his unique group experiences. Individual differences do exist and do have their influence upon the patterns of politics, but neither their genesis nor their incidence requires a rejection of the group hypothesis.[23]

The evidence regarding individual differences stemming from multiple group memberships is of further importance in another connection. It challenges the Marxist assumption that class interests are primary and the more common assumption that occupational group interests are always dominant. Both of these oversimplifications are easy ways of avoiding the facts concerning overlapping membership, with serious consequences for an adequate theory of the political process. It would be idle to deny that a large proportion of organized interest groups have a class character.[24] It would be ridiculous also to question the fact that interest groups growing out of occupational similarities are among the most important on the American scene. But it does not follow that either of these forms is invariably dominant,

[21] Bernard Berelson: "Communications and Public Opinion," in Wilbur Schramm (ed.): *Communications in Modern Society* (Urbana, Ill.: University of Illinois Press, 1948), p. 178.

[22] MacIver: *The Web of Government*, p. 412. Copyright 1947 by Robert M. MacIver and used with the permission of The Macmillan Company. See also the discussion of "selfhood" on p. 415.

[23] Cf. Muzafer Sherif: *An Outline of Social Psychology* (New York: Harper and Brothers, 1948), chap. 17.

[24] Cf. Lazarsfeld, *et al.: The People's Choice*, chap. 15.

that all significant political conflict is class conflict or that occupational interests are even usually stronger than others in most individuals. As Mannheim has pointed out:

> There are no absolute class antagonisms and the Marxist theory takes the marginal situation of an absolute clash as the normal one. Clashes which in one configuration seem to be irreconcilable may march together in another situation. Whether they cooperate, or whether they prefer revolutionary methods, will depend, among other factors, on future clashes and past experiences.[25]

A most interesting recent study of class as a psychological phenomenon finds no absolute differences between the identified classes in the United States, but rather testifies, in temperate terms, to the existence of narrower affiliations that cut across class lines: "The imperfect correlation between class identification and conservatism-radicalism would thus seem to be in some part due to a conflict of interests."[26] There may come a time when Mannheim's "marginal situation" will exist in the United States, but an explanation of politics must account for the whole plot and not merely for one of the climaxes.

That occupational groups can be basically affected by interests not derived from the occupation is clear from the fact that they of necessity accept the "democratic mold," discussed in the preceding chapter. Furthermore, the heterogeneity of membership that causes internal difficulties in all such groups tempers the claims of an occupational interest through the process of internal compromise and adjustment. As Herring has noted in discussing the nonoccupational groups: "Their presence serves to illustrate that the supplemental system of representation in this country is not just a congress of economic classes, but a democratic evolution in which ideas, doctrines, and even creeds have their spokesmen who often equal and sometimes exceed in power the agents of vocations and industries."[27] Nor is this a strange state of affairs. The evidence from simpler cultures indicates that a society may give a very low precedence rating to a group interest that objectively has high economic value to them. [28]

---

[25] Karl Mannheim, quoted in MacIver: *The Web of Government*, p. 281.

[26] Richard Centers: *The Psychology of Social Class: A Study of Class Consciousness* (Princeton, N. J.: Princeton University Press, 1949), p. 204.

[27] Herring: *Group Representation Before Congress*, p. 206. Copyright 1929 by and used with the permission of The Brookings Institution.

[28] Cf. Linton: *The Study of Man*, pp. 427–31.

The stability of the body politic in the United States does not rest on such a thin foundation as that suggested by the theories of class conflict or the dominance of occupational interests. The foundation is stronger, and perhaps unfortunately for the observer, the political process itself is more complex, than such simple propositions would suggest. As Bentley says in referring to this complexity:

> The very nature of the group process (which our government shows in a fairly well-developed form) is this, that groups are freely combining, dissolving, and recombining in accordance with their interest lines. And the lion when he has satisfied his physical need will lie down quite lamb-like, however much louder his roars were than his appetite justified.[29]

Cohesion and Rebellion

The problem of cohesion is a crucial one for the political interest group. Other factors bear upon its capacity to assert its claims successfully upon other groups and institutions in the society, but the degree of unity in the group is probably most fundamental in determining the measure of success it will enjoy. In turn, as the preceding section has indicated, the cohesion of the group is intimately affected by the phenomenon of overlapping membership. But this factor is not the only determinant of cohesion: the geographic dispersion of the group will be influential, for, even in this day of rapid communication over long distances, the scattered group is likely to be less unified than one in which the members can interact face-to-face more or less frequently; within the group struggles for leadership that follow clique lines and do not contain any appreciable policy content may be influential; size, though not an entirely independent factor, may be significant, since an increase in size increases heterogeneity and thus the likelihood of disunity; the differential impact of external change, closely related to group heterogeneity, may be of importance, since changes in technology and attitude outside a group will seldom affect all members of the group at the same rate and with the same intensity; finally, the political skill of the leadership may be significant, for it can go far toward minimizing the threats to cohesion from all these sources.

Although overlapping membership, therefore, is not the only de-

[29] Bentley: *The Process of Government*, p. 359. Copyright 1908 by and used with the permission of Arthur F. Bentley.

terminant of cohesion, it is fundamental, and it is peculiarly important for an explanation of group politics in the larger society—for answering the question: How does a stable policy exist in a multiplicity of interest groups? The answer can only be asserted at this point, as its elaboration must wait for subsequent chapters. In essence, however, it is that the fact that memberships in organized and potential groups overlap *in the long run* imposes restraints and conformities upon interest groups on pain of dissolution or of failure. We should add, of course, that in the long run a complex society may experience revolution, degeneration, and decay. If it maintains its stability, however, it may do so in large measure because of the fact of multiple memberships.

Evidence on the internal struggles resulting from overlapping memberships and related factors is not easy to secure. Since unity and the appearance of unity are essential ingredients in a political formula for group effectiveness, most groups are careful to reveal as little as possible to the outsider concerning such internecine struggles. They tend, therefore, to adhere to the old political maxim that one should never handle a hot poker on the front porch. The effectiveness of this device is indicated by the tendency of many observers to take these groups at their own estimate, to accept unquestioningly their own protestations of unity, to avoid the question of cohesion. However elusive the evidence, nevertheless, the question of internal politics is central, for as Garceau has observed: "The most baffling problems of democratic government are to be found not in legislatures or executives, not even in group alignments and conflicts, but in the internal politics of the . . . groups upon which the whole system has turned out in large measure to rest." [30] To illustrate our explanations there is available even to the casual observer a wealth of general evidence, and in a few cases we have rather complete data on internal group conflicts. To some of these we shall now turn.

One of the most instructive struggles of this sort has been taking place within the American Medical Association over the past decade or so. The A. M. A., whose formal organization has been discussed in the preceding chapter, is as a professional society peculiarly the object of widespread public expectations in such matters as ethical standards, dedication to improving the lot of all men, and loyalty to the "rules of the game" that are widely espoused in the community. Because it is

[30] Reprinted by permission of the publishers from Oliver Garceau: *The Political Life of The American Medical Association* (Cambridge, Mass.: Harvard University Press, 1941), p. 13. This book has been primarily relied upon for material on developments up to 1939.

associated with the strongly valued symbol of the "man in white," the group and its members are endowed with a prestige and authority out of proportion to their numbers in the community so long as the accompanying expectations are not sharply violated.

The tranquillity of this group has been disturbed during the past two decades by changes, originating largely outside it, including altered demands upon its members by other groups. These demands have been centered upon eliminating the marked contrasts in the quality of medical care available to different income levels and regions of the United States. They have involved a challenge to the traditional pattern in which medical practice has been organized—the relationship between a doctor and a patient who called him when he was needed and, presumably, when his services could be paid for. This challenge in turn was aided by two additional disturbances to the accustomed pattern: first, the increased population mobility has decreased attachment to the "old family doctor," for a family is likely to have had several doctors, one in each of the communities in which it has successively resided; second, the growth of specialization in medical practice has led many, including physicians, to the conclusion that the most effective treatment could be given patients if a number of such specialists engaged in joint practice in a single clinic.

Accommodation to the demands emerging from these and related changes has been guided in part by the American Medical Association and its active minority. Unskillful adjustment or blind resistance to the effects of change has called the methods of the active minority into question, both within and outside the profession, on the basis of those "democratic" elements in the habit background to which associations in this culture are expected, by both members and outsiders, to conform—especially those associations whose members enjoy professional status. A crisis of this sort was dramatized in 1938 when the United States Government brought a subsequently successful antitrust suit against the American Medical Association and its constituent society in the District of Columbia for denying membership, and therefore the hospital facilities upon which a modern doctor is heavily dependent, to a number of doctors retained by an association of government employees. This association was set up to provide medical services for members and their families on a prepayment basis.[31] Significantly for present purposes, the Group Health Association, as this prepayment association of government employees is known, was aided in its difficulties by several distinguished members of the A. M. A.

---

[31] American Medical Association v. U.S., 317 U.S. 519 (1943).

who were sympathetic with the experiment despite its inconsistency with the then existing requirements of the A. M. A.

The threat to cohesion in a situation of this sort is clear. The strength of the active minority is threatened from within if it is convicted, in the eyes of some of its membership and of outside groups, of violating the widespread attitudes making up what was designated in Chapter 5 as the "democratic mold," or what Bentley calls the habit background. The effectiveness of the group is reduced in relation to outside groups, moreover, if the practices and pronouncements of the leadership are successfully contradicted and resisted by some of its members in collaboration with opposing groups. The more prominent these resisting members are in their own right, the more apparent it becomes that the association does not "speak for" its following in an authoritative fashion. The position of the active minority is in turn further threatened from within if, for reasons such as these, the group is handicapped in asserting its claims upon other groups. Under such circumstances the association may cease adequately to perform its functions of adjustment and may be threatened with schism or dissolution.

From conditions of this sort there was formed within the American Medical Association in 1937 a loosely organized group of doctors who called themselves the Committee of Physicians for the Improvement of Medical Care. This was an élite element in the A. M. A., led by such men as the late Dr. Hugh Cabot of Boston. Their espoused program was vague, but it amounted to a demand for a freer hearing within the organized profession for alternative means of organizing and financing medical care. It was thus in effect a minority element claiming the protection of the "democratic" habit background. Although it has grown in numbers over the years without any vigorous efforts at promotion, it has not set itself up as a rival to the A. M. A., and its affiliates retain their A. M. A. memberships. Its function has been rather to force a change in the position taken by the A. M. A. on matters of medical organization and financing by threatening the association's internal cohesion and external effectiveness. As Garceau commented shortly after the committee was formed: "The whole tactic has been to serve as a symbol rather than to muster the maximum potential strength." [32]

The efforts of the Committee of Physicians were early subject to rebuke by the controlling elements in the A. M. A., but it is signifi-

[32] Reprinted by permission of the publishers from Oliver Garceau: *The Political Life of The American Medical Association* (Cambridge, Mass.: Harvard University Press, 1941), pp. 148–9.

cant that minor modifications in the latter's practices were forced by protests and threats of rebellion from portions of the membership outside the committee. Thus it is reported that the committee was for a time obstructed by the policy of keeping divergent viewpoints on such matters out of the pages of the A. M. A. *Journal*, until "several state journals had blasted unmercifully at the AMA's policy" on this score.[33]

Various other signs of dissension have appeared within the A. M. A., many of them about the person of Morris Fishbein, long-term editor of the *Journal* and until 1949 unofficial spokesman of the active minority. At its San Francisco meeting in 1946 the House of Delegates adopted a resolution interpreted in some quarters as a curb on his activities.[34] But the most dramatic developments have occurred as a result of the recent efforts to set up a program of compulsory health insurance in the United States. The Committee of Physicians has been active in connection with this and other legislative proposals, taking a public position opposed to that of the A. M. A.'s dominant elements.[35] Others within the association, moreover, though not necessarily in sympathy with all of the committee's commitments, have swelled the chorus of open opposition.

This conflict reached something of a climax in December, 1948, when the House of Delegates adopted a policy authorizing the county societies to assess each member twenty-five dollars for a fund to be used in opposing the compulsory health insurance measure revived following the 1948 elections.[36] Opposition to the assessment developed almost at once, and the objections were made public. A group of 136 members of the A. M. A. made public a letter to Dr. Fishbein that suggested the extent of the conflict. Its public release implied that the faction expected to find the machinery of the association unresponsive if the protest were made through the A. M. A.'s regular channels, and indicated extensive restiveness based on differing perceptions of the changes leading to the proposals for compulsory health insurance. More important, since the document specifically opposed compulsory insurance, it suggested the degree of dissatisfaction stemming from the loss of prestige that the A. M. A. had suffered in com-

[33] Reprinted by permission of the publishers from Oliver Garceau: *The Political Life of The American Medical Association* (Cambridge, Mass.: Harvard University Press, 1941) p. 99.

[34] The *New York Times*, July 3, 1946.

[35] For an example see U.S. Senate, Committee on Education and Labor: *Hearings on a Bill to Provide for a National Health Program*, 79th Cong., 2d Sess. (1946), pp. 982–1016.

[36] The *New York Herald Tribune*, December 3, 1948.

petition with other interest groups in the community. It is appropriate to quote certain passages from this letter:

> Numerous comments by medical colleagues in various parts of the country have convinced the undersigned physicians that a large segment of the medical profession is not in sympathy with many policies and actions of the American Medical Association on the extension of medical care. The $25 assessment levied in executive session upon all members of the association will place several million dollars at the disposal of its officials. . . .
>
> If the funds are to be used for propaganda and legislative lobbying instead of developing a comprehensive medical care program we are heartily opposed to the levy and shall refuse to pay it and we urge all physicians with a sense of responsibility for the future of American medicine to register their protest. The significance of stand-pat propaganda will not escape the public. . . .
>
> We believe that the fundamental failure of the A. M. A. in its attitudes and policies bearing on the general problem of medical care has been its unwillingness fully to acknowledge the need for improvement and to seize this particularly favorable opportunity to come forward with a comprehensive, constructive program which would be of clear advantage to the public as well as to the profession itself. Further, we believe that in the present crisis the obvious direct way to avoid an all-inclusive compulsory health insurance and to make secure the valuable features of our present system is for the association to develop a program that will be manifestly so considerate of the needs of the people and at the same time so eminently fair to the interests of the physicians that it will command general approbation.[37]

In response the A. M. A., through the editor of the *Journal*, rebuked the protestors as men in "plaster towers." As in the attacks on the Committee of Physicians, the editor dismissed the faction as being teachers, or men who "spend most of their time teaching." Presumably the teaching and research men in medicine have been more sensitive to disturbing changes because of differences in their experience as individuals and as a group. Using the low esteem in which teaching is held by men of affairs in the culture, the A. M. A. has in both instances attempted to isolate them from the main body of practicing

[37] Ibid., December 12, 1948.

physicians, especially the general practitioners, by classifying them as trouble-making, impractical dreamers.[38]

A twelve-point program announced by the A. M. A. in February failed to satisfy the insurgents, even after a conference with A. M. A. officials. Moreover, invoking the symbol of unity, which is characteristic generally of interest groups and particularly of the A. M. A., the trustees and officers rebuked the protesters for "an unfortunate disservice to the cause of the medical profession of the United States." They further asserted that the controversial levy was to be used, not for "legislative lobbying," but for "education." [39] These tactics seem to have been designed to prevent further desertions rather than to win back the dissidents, since the latter could notice in the official "explanation" of the assessment distributed to all members that three of the four objectives listed dealt with: disseminating widely "material exposing the fallacy of a compulsory sickness insurance program;" stimulating "lay" groups, presumably to oppose the measure; and retaining the public relations firm of Whitaker and Baxter, who "successfully directed the campaign of the California Medical Association to defeat the socialized medicine program sponsored by the Governor of California." The fourth point covered "stimulation of voluntary prepayment . . . plans . . . ." [40]

Other groups joined in the protest, including members of the Committee of Physicians and Dr. Channing Frothingham, member of that group and chairman of the relatively new Committee for the Nation's Health, made up of doctors, labor leaders, businessmen, and clergymen, which supports the compulsory insurance proposal.[41] Some of the constituent county societies made their objections formal. Thus the Medical Society of the County of Kings, N. Y., defeated the proposed assessment by a narrow margin, and it was hotly contested in other county societies. In the midst of this situation Dr. George Lull, A. M. A. secretary, felt called upon to assert that 85 per cent of the organization's membership would support the assessment, basing his prediction on returns from "300 to 400" of the 2,000 county societies.[42]

The effects of the conflict began to appear in April with the

[38] Ibid., February 14, 1949. For evidence of more drastic sanctions against rebellious members, see ibid., April 15–16, 1949.

[39] Ibid., February 19, 24, 1949.

[40] "An Explanation of the $25.00 Assessment Voted by the A.M.A. House of Delegates," letter to A.M.A. members, undated.

[41] The *New York Herald Tribune*, February 21, 25, 1949.

[42] Ibid., February 19, 1949.

announcement of the disbanding of the National Physicians Committee for the Extension of Medical Service. This body was set up shortly after, and is not to be confused with, the Physicians Committee for the Improvement of Medical Care, though the similarity of the names seems more than coincidence. This committee, which had operated with the blessing of the A. M. A., had announced in January that it was going to continue operations at the official request of the A. M. A. and despite the A. M. A.'s increased activity after the December assessment,[43] but in April its explanation for ceasing operations was "the Medical Association's decision in December to set up its own agency to take over the work of the national committee." [44] A more plausible explanation might be that its rather crude propaganda efforts had widened the cleavage within the A.M.A. Thus in its appeal for funds from doctors in January, the National Physicians Committee enclosed as an illustration of its work a copy of the "Dan Gilbert Washington Letter" sent to Protestant ministers and all newspapers, which it presented as "one of the few really vital pronouncements of an age." [45] The quality of this letter, subtitled "Prophetic News-of-the-Month," can be indicated by a few excerpts. Addressed to "Dear Christian American," it stated in part:

> I am addressing this appeal to my fellow-ministers of all churches at the very time that the strongest pressure is being mobilized behind the proposal for "compulsory health insurance" by Federal enactment. This is not "socialized" medicine, strictly speaking. It is worse than that. It is political medicine of the most sordid kind.

> Christ taught the separation of church and state. I do not believe the political authority has any more business "socializing" the medical profession than it has our churches.

> As a minister of the Gospel, I am preaching against this monster of Anti-Christ—political medicine. I am urging Christian believers everywhere to work and pray that our beloved land may

[43] National Physicians Committee for the Extension of Medical Service, letter to doctors, January, 1949.

[44] The New York Times, April 17, 1949. This committee was reported to have spent more money during the first nine months of 1948 than any other group registered under the Federal Regulation of Lobbying Act, of which about half came from twenty-nine drug manufacturers.

[45] National Physicians Committee for the Extension of Medical Service, letter to doctors, January, 1949.

be delivered from the blight of this monstrosity of Bolshevik bureaucracy.[46]

That the A. M. A. should have been embarrassed by this sort of material, especially under the circumstances then prevailing, and that such propaganda would have threatened to strengthen existing dissident factions, seems entirely reasonable.

A second major development came at the annual A. M. A. convention in June, 1949. At that time the House of Delegates approved what newspapers characterized as a "muzzling" of Dr. Fishbein. This was evidently an appropriate description, for the announcement forbade the editor to speak on all controversial subjects, to hold press conferences except on scientific matters, to write his regular column in the *Journal*, or to publish editorials without the approval of the executive committee. (It is an interesting illustration of the origins and character of an active minority, however, that this action should have required elaborate justification, since Dr. Fishbein was formally a paid member of the staff and, as such, legally subordinate to the elected officials.) That this move represented a more complex adjustment within the active minority than was apparent on the surface was indicated by the contradictory statements concerning the move that were issued by various A. M. A. officials. Thus Dr. R. L. Sensenich, retiring president, said that it merely reflected the routine measures that are taken to prepare for the retirement of a person who has served his office long and faithfully. The measures themselves scarcely seem so routine, and the statement to the House of Delegates by Dr. Elmer Henderson, chairman of the board of trustees, indicates some of the more fundamental reasons. He stated:

> The board of trustees is aware of the criticism of the editor, coming from within and from without the profession. The board recognizes that the public has come to believe that the editor is a spokesman of the association. The membership undoubtedly wishes the elected officials to speak authoritatively on all matters of medical policy.[47]

How this controversy eventually works out and what is to be the fate of compulsory health insurance proposals are unimportant for an understanding of the group process in politics. It is highly unlikely,

[46] *Dan Gilbert's Washington Letter: Prophetic News-of-the-Month,* 511 Eleventh Street, N.W., Washington, D.C., December, 1948.
[47] The *New York Herald Tribune,* June 7, 1949. This paragraph is based largely on this report.

for a variety of reasons, that the A. M. A. will formally split into two or more independent associations. But it is obvious that the conflict, taken in connection with its ramifications outside the group, has forced, and probably will continue to force, the active minority in the A. M. A. to modify its policies and practices. It is not significant, furthermore, to determine whether the changes mentioned in the paragraphs above constitute basic shifts in policy or whether they are merely a face-lifting operation—guided by the association's public relations counsel—designed to confuse the dissidents and their sympathizers. Only in so far as the facts, whatever they are, become the subject of a continuing conflict, are they essential to the political analysis. Moreover, even if the changes amount merely to a redressing of the show window, it is significant that such changes were deemed necessary.

The A. M. A. thus illustrates the seriousness of such conflict for both the cohesion and the external effectiveness of a group. One will find no better example of the interdependence of the internal and the external aspects of group politics. A moderate conclusion concerning the A. M. A. situation could well be phrased in the terms Garceau used some years ago: "Techniques and policies developed over a generation have failed to keep the group united in opinion and effort. Even a surface harmony has vanished; and it has finally vanished in such a dramatic eruption as to diminish the group's prestige and repute with the public." [48] Technological changes and related shifts in attitudes in society required adaptations and modifications in the activities of the association's active minority. The failure adequately to develop these adjustments produced dissident factions within the group, their make-up largely depending upon differences in the multiple memberships of the dissenters. The subsequent conflict threatened the position of the association and its active minority both from within and from without. Medicine now had at least two voices in the forum of government, and it was no longer possible to say that doctors or even all competent doctors supported the position of the society. In consequence the A.M.A.'s general influence progressively declined. This decline in turn further increased the internal unrest. Violation of "democratic" and similar interests widely held in the

[48] Reprinted by permission of the publishers from Oliver Garceau: *The Political Life of The American Medical Association* (Cambridge, Mass.: Harvard University Press, 1941), p. 152. In a somewhat similar instance of revolt within the American Library Association, the author notes that leadership skill has operated so that "the opposition has never broken out to impair openly the pressure tactics of the association." See Garceau: *The Public Library in the Political Process*, p. 178; see also chap. 4, *passim*.

community thus clearly provided a threat to the group's unity. Ultimately the resulting dissent forced at least apparent changes in the active minority's policies and practices—changes necessary if the active minority were to retain its control and if the association were to regain the ground it had lost.

It is significant that in at least two other national professional associations schisms or secessions have occurred under circumstances roughly the same as those that produced the Physicians Committee. Within the American Dental Association the conflict over health insurance gave rise in 1946 to a Dentists Committee for the Passage of the Murray-Wagner Bill.[49] The setting up of the National Lawyers Guild in 1936 in competition with the American Bar Association provides a parallel somewhat less close. The Guild is an independent association rather than a minority group demanding to be heard, and the secession took place from an association far less cohesive under any conditions than the American Medical Association.[50]

A second major example of internal conflict, one which has been rather fully documented, is that within the American labor movement, particularly the struggle leading to the splitting off of the C.I.O. from the A.F. of L. Much of the setting for this conflict and the factors producing it have been discussed in the two preceding chapters. These need not be repeated here, but the main lines of the struggle can be sketched in to illustrate the operation of internal politics.

The heterogeneity of membership that produces conflict in all groups is particularly striking in labor movements. Differences in occupational setting, differences in the relations to the market of various occupations and industries, plus many other factors seem to accentuate the effects of overlapping membership and to produce lines of cleavage around which struggles rage with varying degrees of intensity. Even the constituent unions, especially in the United States, have experienced internal conflicts of sufficient severity to oblige them to resort to the courts for settlement in a large number of cases.[51] Although most union members are lethargic about union affairs, they

[49] U.S. Senate, Committee on Education and Labor: *Hearings on a Bill to Provide for a National Health Program*, 79th Cong., 2d Sess. (1946), pp. 1036 ff.

[50] Esther L. Brown: *Lawyers and the Promotion of Justice* (New York: Russell Sage Foundation, 1938), pp. 146–53. Cf. Hurst: *The Growth of American Law*, chaps. 12 and 13, esp. pp. 359–66.

[51] Philip Taft: "Democracy in Trade Unions," *American Economic Review*, Vol. 36, no. 2 (May, 1946), pp. 366 ff.

may entertain strong expectations about the functions the union is to perform for them. For the organization to survive, these expectations must be reckoned with by the union leadership, both in dealing with the employer and in relations with more inclusive bodies in the labor movement. As Ross has noted: "The policies adopted by particular unions do not represent different degrees of enlightenment but different ranges of choice and cannot be understood until we recognize the primary importance of organizational survival as the central aim of the leadership." [52] In these circumstances, he continues, the labor leader is confronted with "a battery of political pressures," each of which derives "from some interest group which is concerned that the formal purpose of the institution be interpreted in a manner favorable to itself." Included among these groups, in addition to employers and agencies of the government, are the rank-and-file members, union officials at higher and lower levels of organization, and other unions. [53]

Such is the setting, as related in Chapter 4, out of which the A.F. of L. emerged and in which its troubles occurred. We have already seen that by the late 1920's the industrial unit had become, for numerous reasons, the "natural" basis of organization for a large segment of labor. But response to the new needs by the A.F. of L. would have involved the disruption of a great many vested relationships throughout the entire structure. The A.F. of L. was, and is, its constituent international unions; its ruling body was, and is, a collection of ambassadors from them. Introduction on a large scale of a new basis of organization would have threatened the dominant position on the Executive Council of these internationals built along craft lines, even of those whose memberships would not have been thus reduced. They were unable to contemplate happily their prospective eclipse in the federation, despite the fact that it had been amply demonstrated that craft unions could not organize the new mass industries. As Millis and Montgomery observed concerning the problem of recasting union forms, it "is different from setting up a logical scheme on paper." Even when such reorganization means merely the amalgamation of craft unions, it "jeopardizes the office holders; it involves financial readjustments . . . ; it runs counter to

[52] Ross: *Trade Union Wage Policy*, p. 16. Copyright 1948 by The Regents of The University of California and used with the permission of University of California Press.
[53] Ross: *Trade Union Wage Policy*, pp. 25-6. Copyright 1948 by The Regents of The University of California and used with the permission of University of California Press.

the sentiments of loyal members; it may let down the bars established by craftsmen and permit new types of workers to compete for the old craftsmen's jobs." [54] As we have seen, the A.F. of L. was set up organizationally to permit the craft unions to protect such established relationships. In the conflict over industrial unionism these arrangements worked with ultimate effectiveness.

Autonomy of its constituent units has been the hallmark of the A.F. of L., and the C.I.O. split is only the most dramatic of the conflicts that union independence has recently encouraged. During the early phases of that struggle, in fact, and unrelated to it, the Building and Construction Trades Department, afraid of intended changes in the department and of efforts to elect new officers, refused to seat delegates to its 1934 convention from unions that had been accepted by its Executive Council. Circumstances permitted the A.F. of L. president to declare this action invalid, with the support of the convention, but the issue was deadlocked until the 1935 A.F. of L. meeting. [55]

For the advocates of industrial unionism, the issue was not a trifling one. They were largely the leaders of those unions already organized along such lines, and as such they were disturbed by the continued failure to unionize the major mass-production industries, such as steel, automobiles, and electrical machinery. Many of their semi-skilled workers were threatened by the spread of company unions in such areas. Moreover, their members were restive under the ineffectual political activity that characterized the A.F. of L. Their organizations, as was indicated in Chapter 4, needed a new and more intimate participation in the processes of government. Although the personality of the principal leader of the industrial union forces, John L. Lewis, had a good deal to do with the timing of the split and the failure to compromise, the conflict itself stemmed from deep divergencies in attitude between industrial and craft union forces—divergencies produced by differences in the patterns of multiple membership. The conflict was inevitable; the split was an incident.

The problem of the A.F. of L. thus was, in the then existing state of its internal political arrangements, almost the insoluble one of "how to organize the workers in industries almost entirely untouched by unionism into the most suitable type of organization without encroaching upon the jurisdictions already claimed by, and conceded

[54] From *Organized Labor* by Millis and Montgomery, p. 277. Copyright 1945. Courtesy of McGraw-Hill Book Company, Inc.
[55] Ibid., pp. 295–6.

to, the national and international affiliates [of the A.F. of L.]." [56] The initial efforts of the Executive Council following the stimulus to organization provided in the early years of the New Deal, was to establish federal unions (directly affiliated with the A.F. of L.) along semi-industrial or plant lines. Both the industrial union proponents within the federation and the members of these new unions generally assumed that the latter would be fused into industrial unions, since their members largely lacked the attitudes compatible with craft organization. However, "the craft unions began to assert their jurisdictional claims to workers in the newly organized plant unions."

At the San Francisco convention in October, 1934, several resolutions were introduced by the partisans of industrial unions, and they expressed considerable resentment at the dilatory efforts of the A.F. of L. Executive Council in pushing organization and at the tenderness with which that body considered the claims of the craft unions. Dividing among the established crafts those of the new converts who could be claimed by the craft unions would and did threaten the cohesion of the new locals and, therefore, the spread of industrial unionism. A verbal compromise was reached at this meeting—a compromise that each side construed as it chose and that merely postponed a showdown. The next year at Atlantic City a group of leaders of the industrial union cause set up the Committee for Industrial Organization on the grounds that the Executive Council had ignored the meaning, in their terms, of the 1934 compromise. At this time the craft union forces roundly defeated a minority committee report, in itself an unusual development, that put the issue sharply by calling for organizing the mass production industries along industrial lines "regardless of claims based upon the question of jurisdiction" in industries where craft skills were not predominant.

This was rebellion, but not secession. The interests of the incipient industrial unions and those of the craft unions were different to the extent that the institutionalized economic groups to which they were peripheral differed, as they sharply did. But the members of both retained certain shared attitudes respecting the labor movement as a whole that did not immediately sanction either formal secession or formal expulsion. The loyal active minority in the A.F. of L. was challenged, however, because the establishment of the Committee for Industrial Organization removed from the Executive Council the initiative in organization matters. There was raised the specter of "dual

[56] From *Organized Labor* by Millis and Montgomery, p. 203 and 205. Copyright 1945. Courtesy of McGraw-Hill Book Company, Inc. The material for this section is drawn largely from this source, pp. 203–19.

unionism," which is the equivalent of original sin not only in the labor movement, but, as we have previously seen, in all organized interest groups. Since, however, the threat to unity and to the dominance of the active minority was greater than in the case of the A.M.A. and the Committee of Physicians, the countermeasures were also more severe, quickly going beyond mere rebuke.

The Executive Council, fearing the effects of "dual unionism," asked that the Committee for Industrial Organization disband by January, 1936. When the dissolution did not occur, formal charges against the participating unions were filed and their officers called to trial. With the approval of the 1936 A.F. of L. convention, at which the rebellious unions were not represented, suspension of the C.I.O. unions was approved. Formal expulsion, it is interesting to recall, did not occur until 1938, two and one-half years after the split first took place, and then only after the failure of numerous efforts to negotiate a peace between the factions.

Among the less dramatic consequences of this division in the labor movement, but more important as an illustration of the chastening and limiting effects of such conflicts, are the new developments in A.F. of L. organization methods. Following the withdrawal of the C.I.O. and the Supreme Court's validation of the National Labor Relations Act in 1937, the Federation greatly intensified its organizing efforts. Moreover, it considerably diluted the strictly craft criteria that had been the chief source of the final split.[57] Similarly, the vigor with which the C.I.O. participated in politics and legislation on the national scene forced the A.F. of L. to forsake the limited and defensive political position it had normally held and to support various kinds of social legislation concerning which it had previously been largely inactive.

Though this conflict was undoubtedly the most spectacular in the history of the A.F. of L., it is not an isolated phenomenon. Conflicts and struggles of varying degrees of bitterness are inherent in the internal political life of interest groups, for the reasons outlined earlier in this chapter. Their failure to be revealed in the public prints may mean low intensity of disagreement or effective use of the organization's machinery to adjust or suppress divisive influences, but not the absence of disagreement. Particularly in election years those groups accustomed to endorse candidates openly or by implication are likely to show division. Early in the campaign of 1948, for example, the President of the A.F. of L. announced that his organization would

[57] Ibid., pp. 222–3.

never support the Republican ticket. Officials of the powerful team-sters' union promptly announced that Mr. Green was not speaking for them, adding that this union did not "share Mr. Green's views on this matter and will abide by its decision to consider the entire national picture at a delegate assembly." [58]

Nor is the C.I.O. proof against such threats to unity, though its form of organization and related factors minimize certain of the cleavages that have plagued its rival. One instance has previously been cited.[59] Another, which illustrates nicely the interdependence of external and internal issues, especially for a group actively operating through or upon government, involves the attempt to repeal the Taft-Hartley Act in the Eighty-first Congress (1949). The C.I.O. leadership, obliged, as all political leadership at times must, to compromise its demand for an outright repeal, was accused by its left wing, allegedly dominated by Communists, of "selling-out." The Executive Board's resolution repudiating these charges significantly observed that "in the legislative process there is room for alteration in any bill." [60] In order to maintain unity against its left wing, moreover, the C.I.O. moved to revoke the charter of the United Farm Equipment and Metal Workers of America for defiance of an order of the Executive Board.[61] The claims to autonomy of the constituent units in a federated group raise problems in the C.I.O. as well. At the 1949 convention of the United Automobile Workers, which would stand to gain from the dissolution of the Farm Equipment Workers union, objections to endorsing the action of the C.I.O. Executive Board were based on the assertion that its decision violated union autonomy.[62]

Although it would serve no useful purpose to go into great detail concerning similar struggles within other interest groups, evidence of such conflicts is abundant. So-called business groups may be highly unified on those rare occasions when the foundations of private property are openly attacked, but under other circumstances multiple memberships in varied and competing institutionalized economic groups and associations produce cleavages of significant proportions. It is generally recognized that the superficiality and generality of the programs put forward by the Chamber of Commerce of the United States are due largely to the heterogeneity of the membership

[58] The New York Times, June 27, 1948.
[59] Chapter 5, p. 117 and note 10.
[60] The New York Herald Tribune, May 16, 19, 1949.
[61] Ibid., May 15, 19, and 20, 1949.
[62] Ibid., July 12, 1949.

that it claims.[63] Its affiliated units do not necessarily keep in line with its policy pronouncements. On the other hand, as was pointed out in Chapter 5, because the chamber is not financially dependent upon these affiliated units, a threat of withdrawal by one or more of them does not carry the same weight as a similar threat in one of the labor federations.

The National Association of Manufacturers, often popularly assumed to be a monolithic political force, perhaps because of its advocacy among its following of "unit thinking and unit action," has probably achieved a maximum of unity because its political efforts have been largely defensive in character. Nevertheless, it has experienced criticism from its rank and file for its opposition to the renewal of price-control legislation in 1946 and for the dominance of "big business" in the organization's affairs. Its leaders admit, moreover, the necessity for internal compromise on policy matters in order to achieve effective unity.[64]

Groups that attempt, like the Chamber of Commerce, to speak for "American business" or "American industry" as a whole, both members and nonmembers, are at great pains to avoid situations in which the interests of "little" business differ sharply from those of "big" business. They have, for example, left to the specialized trade associations the struggles between the retailers and the chain stores and mail-order houses. From time to time, however, cleavages of this sort have come out in the open and have resulted in the formation of competing groups,[65] more often than not shortlived. For example, in the spring of 1946 during the struggle in Congress over the renewal of price-control legislation, to which both the Chamber and the N.A.M. were opposed, there appeared a group calling itself the New Council for American Business. An outgrowth of the Business Men for Roosevelt organization that participated in the 1944 presidential campaign,

---

[63] Cf. Paul Studenski: "Chambers of Commerce," *Encyclopaedia of the Social Sciences;* Childs: *Labor and Capital in National Politics,* p. 110; Herring: *Group Representation Before Congress,* p. 94; McKean: *Pressures on the Legislature of New Jersey,* chap. 4.

[64] Alfred S. Cleveland: "N.A.M.: Spokesman for Industry?" *Harvard Business Review,* Vol. 26, no. 3 (May, 1948), pp. 360, 366–7; "Renovation in N.A.M.," *Fortune* (July, 1948), p. 73.

[65] See Oliver Garceau: "Can Little Business Organize," *Public Opinion Quarterly,* Vol. 2, no. 2 (Summer, 1938), pp. 469–73. Useful materials on this question will be found in the hearings before the Senate Special Committee to Study and Survey Problems of American Small Business, 77th–80th Congresses (1941–48), and The House Select Committee on Small Business, 79th and 80th Congresses (1945–48).

the New Council asserted that "business is not properly represented by the N.A.M. and the U.S. Chamber of Commerce."[66] The group claimed its support from among "small" businessmen who are "more vulnerable to a depression than big N.A.M. people."[67] Although its exact membership is unknown, the roster of its officers suggested an additional line of cleavage accounting for the group's existence, namely, that between the manufacturing and large commercial enterprises and the service and light consumer goods enterprises. Most of the officers were engaged in businesses of the latter sort, the list covering the manager of a broadcasting station and newspaper in Utah, an industrial designer, a sound equipment manufacturer, a plastics processor, and a perfume manufacturer. This group raised a competing, if feeble, voice in opposition to the chamber and the N.A.M. Other businessmen's groups, such as the Committee for Economic Development, have had a somewhat similar origin.[68]

The same kind of situation prevails in particular lines of commercial activity. Thus some years ago the public relations director of the American Bankers Association, in explaining why the association had not undertaken a nation-wide publicity campaign, cited "the diversity of viewpoints among bankers as to the type of material which should be released." He noted that "the approach of country banks to their public is different from that which would be acceptable to the big-city banks." He continued: "Banks which emphasize the virtues of local independent unit banking, and competing banks which have developed large branch systems might find it difficult to participate in a common campaign . . . . Some banks are willing to participate in a general campaign, others are not."[69]

Trade associations reveal similar cleavages and conflicts, these occasionally going so far that separate associations are formed within a given industry for the small and the large units or the "independents" and the "chain" units.[70] The Temporary National Economic Committee's survey of trade associations examined the reasons for the dis-

[66] *Advertising Age*, May 6, 1946.

[67] *Washington Daily News*, April 25, 1946.

[68] See, for example, the speech of the president of Johnson and Johnson, praising the C.E.D. and related groups and condemning the N.A.M., reported in The *New York Times*, July 10, 1947. Cf. also Burton Bigelow: "Should Business Decentralize Its Counter-Propaganda," *Public Opinion Quarterly*, Vol. 2, no. 2 (Summer, 1938), pp. 321–4.

[69] Gurden Edwards: "Banking and Public Opinion," *Public Opinion Quarterly*, Vol. 1, no. 1 (Spring, 1937), p. 24.

[70] U.S. Temporary National Economic Committee: *Trade Association Survey*, p. 4.

banding of a large number of such groups. Significantly, one of the most important of these reasons in the 1930's was the tendency of the rather rigid legal sanctions of the N.R.A. to accentuate existing but partially hidden cleavages. The report states: "Because it attempted to bring to bear the sanctions of law in enforcing standards of conduct, the N.R.A. undoubtedly tended to sharpen and bring to the surface the underlying conflicts of interest between members of an industry." [71] Other reasons were heterogeneity of interest resulting from large numbers in an industry, inability to co-operate, division within an industry on policies toward labor unions, similar divisions arising from geographic differences in wage rates, and differences in marketing and distributing methods.

Schattschneider cites a number of instances in which actual or incipient conflicts within trade associations prevented such groups from taking any part in the hearings on the Smoot-Hawley tariff bill of 1930. [72] Even a comparatively well-disciplined trade group like the National Association of Retail Druggists has experienced struggles of various types. A federated organization, its constituent State units threatened open rebellion when the national organization moved to absorb some of their functions. In its long struggle with the chain stores, moreover, differences have emerged between druggists in urban and rural areas, the latter being somewhat less subject to the competition of the chains. [73]

Associations of farmers show the same symptoms. The tendency for State units of the American Farm Bureau Federation to deviate from the latter's policy positions has been mentioned in the preceding chapter. [74] This "independence" of local and State units helped cause the failure of early farm movements, and the sectional differences of interest that underlay these divisions largely account for the disintegration of the "farm bloc" in the 1920's, following its initial successes. [75] A more recent subject of dissension is, of course, the legislative struggle over the repeal of discriminatory taxes on oleomargarine. Within recent years the principal ingredients of this product have become cottonseed oil, soy bean oil, and oil derivatives from cattle. The production of each of these commodities is of major importance in areas of

[71] Ibid., p. 14.

[72] Schattschneider: *Politics, Pressures and the Tariff*, pp. 154 ff.

[73] *American Druggist*, October, 1937, p. 5; *Business Week*, September 20, 1937.

[74] Cf. D. C. Wing: "Trends in National Farm Organizations," in *Farmers in a Changing World*, 1940 *Yearbook of Agriculture*, p. 973.

[75] Herring: *Group Representation Before Congress*, p. 112; see also his article: "Farm Bloc, United States," *Encyclopaedia of the Social Sciences*.

the country where the Farm Bureau finds much of its support, but so is dairying. In consequence, to avoid an open split, to avoid making members choose between the federation and these commodity groups, the Farm Bureau, as noted in an earlier paragraph, took no stand on the proposed repeal of the taxes. A parallel cause of disagreement is the struggle since 1945 over a new Government farm price program. At the 1948 convention of the Farm Bureau, disagreements between delegates from the South and from the Middle West over whether to endorse the retention of a rigid price formula that would maintain cotton prices or to support the flexible price legislation enacted by the previous Congress so threatened to disrupt the convention that the question was referred to the association's board of directors in an effort to achieve a compromise.[76]

A less prominent case of a slightly different sort developed within the Association of Southern Commissioners of Agriculture, a normally solid sectional interest group, when its secretary filed a brief with the State Department in December, 1946, opposing the negotiation of reciprocal trade agreements with eighteen foreign countries. Considerable doubt was cast, once this action was made public, on the legality of the secretary's action, and it was soon apparent that at least he did not speak for a unanimous group. Will Clayton, then Under-Secretary of State for Economic Affairs, released a statement containing repudiations of the brief by the commissioners in Alabama, North Carolina, South Carolina, and Kentucky. Whether the secretary of the Association of Southern Commissioners had complied with the by-laws of his organization is less significant than that his action produced a conflict that apparently weakened the group's influence on the issue in question.[77]

The American Legion affords examples of conflict growing out of overlapping membership. Thus Gray reports that following the denunciation of General Omar Bradley, a popular military leader in World War II and then head of the Veterans' Administration, by National Commander John Stelle, a wave of rank-and-file protests flowed into the national headquarters. He also reports that it was this form of protest that obliged the Legion leaders to reverse the position they had taken shortly after World War II opposing Federal legislation in support of publicly financed low-rent housing. The Legion's policies toward organized labor, however, provide an example of more long-

<hr>

[76] The *New York Herald Tribune*, December 16, 1948. Kile, in *The Farm Bureau Through Three Decades*, p. 390, indicates that the A.F.B.F. is still bothered by sectional cleavages.

[77] The *New York Times*, February 2, 1947, letter from W. L. Clayton.

run significance. Since its founding the veterans' association has not been known for its identification with labor unionism. On the contrary, there is considerable evidence that at least in its early years the members of many of its local posts were used as strikebreakers. Yet inevitably the Legion includes within its ranks a large number of veterans who are also members of labor unions, as the uniforms in a picket line indicate. In a manner suggestive of the origins of the Physicians Committee, a number of such individuals have within recent years formed a subgroup within the Legion, presumably to force upon the leadership a more balanced position in union matters. Calling itself the National Conference of Union Labor Legionnaires, this group reportedly includes nearly 150 posts with 130,000 members and a separate headquarters in Chicago. Between 1940 and 1943 its leaders fought for and secured the establishment of a Labor Relations Committee within the fold of the Legion. Again like the Physicians Committee, the National Conference has been treated as a dissident group by the Legion leadership, one whose activities skirted the dread borders of dualism, although no open effort has been made to expel its units. Nevertheless, in December of 1945, Legion authorities declared that the National Conference was without "any legal authorization or existence within the structure or under or pursuant to the Constitution of the American Legion." [78]

Instances in other groups can be cited almost indefinitely. Herring, for example, noted some years ago that the American Council on Education, because of its heterogeneous membership, had had difficulty in selecting projects acceptable to its following. It had found it impossible up to that time to take an unequivocal stand on proposals to create a Federal department of education.[79] Even the Anti-Saloon League, strongly united by skillful leadership and its fanatical concentration on a single question, had its internal difficulties. Co-operation with some of the Protestant churches, the secret of its strength, was not always smooth and involved, as did other aspects of its activities, considerable internal politics.[80]

[78] Gray: *The Inside Story of the Legion,* pp. 125, 162, and 180–3.
[79] Herring: *Group Representation Before Congress,* p. 179.
[80] Odegard: *Pressure Politics,* pp. 15–22.

7

Internal Politics: The Tasks of Leadership

THE tasks of interest group leadership are set by the inevitable conflicts within the group that emerge largely from the overlapping of group memberships. Preservation and strengthening of the group's cohesion become the prime objectives of the active minority, for without cohesion the group becomes ineffective, and without a measure of effectiveness either the leadership must change or the group must cease to exist. It does not follow, of course, that the group must maintain a consistent or growing membership. In fact, as some of the examples in the preceding chapter suggest, frequently one way—often the only way—of retaining a measure of unity in a majority may be through the secession or expulsion of a rebellious minority. Clearly, however, a following must remain, tolerably unified and effective.

The Nature of Leadership

These observations, like others in previous chapters, imply certain propositions about the nature of leadership that at this point should be made explicit. Leadership is a subject, particularly as it deals with politics, that has long been mired in a morass of mysticism and superficiality. With a few notable exceptions there are few empirical data on political leaders that throw much light on the subject. In recent years, however, observation of leadership in small groups has provided a number of well-validated propositions that have general application.

The principal feature of these propositions about leadership is that they grow out of concentration, not solely upon individual personalities identified as leaders, but upon the relationships observed to exist between such persons and those identified as followers. Under these circumstances a leader can be viewed as an individual who initiates most of those actions—verbal or otherwise—to which the others in the group respond. It should be noted that this relationship must be persistent, that the leader and followers must behave in this fashion more or less consistently through time in the particular group. It should be noted also that the leader need not always initiate all actions involving members of the group. In fact, the most successful leader responds in private to the actions of individuals who are among his followers in the group—that is, he "takes advice" from individuals but "gives orders" to the group.[1]

This emphasis on relationship places in its proper context what is referred to as the power of a leader. Power *is* the relationship, not something external to it. As Lasswell has pointed out:

> Power is an interpersonal situation; those who hold power are empowered. They depend upon and continue only so long as there is a continuing stream of empowering responses.[2]

Or, in MacIver's terms:

> Social power is in the last resort derivative, not inherent in the groups or individuals who direct, control, or coerce other groups or individuals. The power a man has is the power he *disposes*; it is not intrinsically his own. He cannot command unless another obeys. He cannot control unless the social organization invests him with the apparatus of control.[3]

It appears, then, that leadership is a functional relationship. Are there no "traits" that leaders can be said to "possess" that distinguish them from followers? Both psychological and sociological studies of leadership long assumed the existence of some such elements and sought to isolate and identify them. The weight of current opinion is summarized in a recent paper in which the author says: "No single trait or group of characteristics has been isolated which sets off the leader from the members of his group."[4] It follows then that, as

[1] Chapple and Coon: *Principles of Anthropology*, pp. 59, 60, 330–1.

[2] Harold D. Lasswell: *Power and Personality* (New York: W. W. Norton & Company, Inc., 1948), p. 10. Copyright by and used with the permission of W. W. Norton & Company, Inc.

[3] MacIver: *The Web of Government*, pp. 107–8. Copyright 1947 by Robert M. MacIver and used with the permission of The Macmillan Company.

[4] William O. Jenkins: "A Review of Leadership Studies with Particular Reference to Military Problems," *Psychological Bulletin*, Vol. 44, no. 1 (January, 1947), pp. 74–5.

Sherif has stated it, "there is no leadership quality as such; it is relative to the situation." [5] As the situation is changed, the qualities necessary to leadership change, and relationships within a group also change. The situation, moreover, may in some instances be defined in highly personal terms. An illustration is afforded in Edward J. Flynn's account of the changed position of the formal leadership of Tammany Hall in the 1920's following the death of Charles F. Murphy and the succession of Judge George W. Olvaney:

> Neither Mayor Hylan nor Governor Smith felt any personal allegiance to Judge Olvaney. While Mr. Murphy lived, both realized that he had been largely responsible for their elevation to high office. After his death, the Mayor and the Governor each began to deal with the separate organizations in the counties rather than with the leader of Tammany Hall, which lowered the prestige and greatly diminished the influence of Tammany.[6]

Although the conception of leadership as a functional relationship rules out the possibility that all leaders have in common certain "traits" that set them off from followers, it does not imply that in particular instances there will be no differences between leaders and led. These differences, however, are specific to the situation. The requirements for successful leadership in any group or institution are likely to vary through time, depending upon the internal and external circumstances in which the group is operating. At any particular point in time, it follows that the qualifications for leadership of various groups and institutions will differ sharply. One whose personality and skills are appropriate to group leadership at one time may be completely inadequate at another, and one who is a successful leader in one group may perforce become a follower in another. One group situation may demand physical strength and courage, another oratorical skill, another intellectual acumen, another facility at negotiation, and so on. A man may, moreover, be a successful leader simultaneously in a num-

---

[5] Sherif: *An Outline of Social Psychology*, p. 458; see also p. 101. Copyright 1948 by and used with the permission of Harper and Brothers. Cf. Jenkins: "A Review of Leadership Studies," p. 75; Irving Knickerbocker: "Leadership: A Conception and Some Implications," *Journal of Social Issues*, Vol. 4, no. 3 (Summer, 1948), pp. 23–40; Ralph M. Stogdill: "Personal Factors Associated with Leadership: A Survey of the Literature," *Journal of Social Psychology*, Vol. 25 (1948), pp. 35–71.

[6] Edward J. Flynn: *You're The Boss* (New York: Viking Press, Inc., 1947), p. 49. Copyright by and used with the permission of Viking Press, Inc.

ber of groups whose requirements are similar, but it does not follow that he may achieve that status in any group to which he belongs and at any time. These propositions have been well summarized in a recent paper:

Leadership is not a quality which a man possesses; it is an interactional function of the personality and of the social situation. A leader is a member of a group on whom the group confers a certain status, and leadership describes the role by which the duties of this status are fulfilled. The effectiveness of the role depends upon the functional relation between the individual attributes of the man and the specific goal of the group at any moment. It is natural that some individual attributes of skill and personality will be generally effective though they will not confer upon their possessor universal leadership status.[7]

As the preceding sentences suggest, the group, reflecting the situation in which it operates, exerts in the long run a control over the fortunes of aspiring leaders. It has been proposed in some quarters that leadership can be measured in quantitative terms by a ratio between the frequency with which an individual initiates actions in a group situation and the frequency with which he responds to the initiative of others. Control by the group can be indicated by the fact that when this ratio is exceeded or when the basis of it is changed, the leader-follower relationship will be dissolved.[8] Essentially the same notion can be indicated in simpler terms by saying that the occupant of a leadership position is the object of expectations on the part of other members of the group—expectations that become stronger as the leadership position becomes more inclusive. One who fails to live up to those expectations, or a sufficient number of them, will drop to a less important position in the group's structure, or will be dropped from the group entirely. As Lasswell has observed: "The act of entering an 'office' is to appear at the focus of attention of those who are predisposed to expect and demand rather definite modes of conduct

---

[7] Cecil A. Gibb: "The Principles and Traits of Leadership," *Journal of Abnormal and Social Psychology*, Vol. 42, no. 3 (July, 1947), p. 284. Copyright by and used with the permission of the *Journal of Abnormal and Social Psychology* and the American Psychological Association, Inc. Cf. also Sherif: *An Outline of Social Psychology*, p. 101; and Harold D. Lasswell: *Politics: Who Gets What, When, How* (New York: McGraw-Hill Book Company, Inc., 1936), chap. 8.

[8] Chapple and Coon: *Principles of Anthropology*, p. 36–7.

from the office-holder."[9] This control relationship is supported by some of the results of Sherif's experiments with the autokinetic phenomenon, described in Chapter 2, in that a leader who changes his norm sharply after the group norm has been established may not be followed by the others.[10] It is also one of the major points in Whyte's study of street-corner gangs.[11]

The control of the group over the leader, however, also varies somewhat with the situation. An association in its early stages, for example, may be completely dominated by its leaders, but when it has become organized, their discretion is sharply limited. As Sherif has put it:

A movement may be initiated at the outset by a handful of determined leaders who know the discontent and restlessness of the people to whom they appeal. But once the movement starts to acquire a definite leader-and-membership structure and gets under way, the leader is no longer free to stop or alter the course of action as his whims dictate.[12]

How wide the leader's discretion can be is variable. The notion of membership control does not mean that the leader has no discretion. It suggests only that he must be aware of the limits imposed by membership expectations and must be careful not to overrun them.

Some measure of discretion, in fact, is an essential consequence of certain previously noted features of the internal politics of groups. The expectations of various factions in a group may not be entirely consistent with one another, as the evidence on overlapping group memberships would lead us to expect. The leader's task then is further complicated by the necessity of reflecting these divergent expectations roughly in proportion to their strength within the group, by compromise if possible, by "favoritism" and "inconsistency" if necessary. As Ross has observed it in union negotiations: "An important aspect of the leadership function is reasonably to ensure that every interest group which can exercise effective political pressure is repre-

* Lasswell: *Power and Personality*, p. 63. Copyright 1948 by and used with the permission of W. W. Norton & Company, Inc.

[10] See citation in note 15, chap. 2, and Sherif: *An Outline of Social Psychology*, pp. 162 ff.

[11] Whyte: *Street Corner Society*, pp. 40, 41, and *passim*. Cf. Kesselman: *The Social Politics of FEPC*, pp. 37–9, for an example in an interest group.

[12] Sherif: *An Outline of Social Psychology*, p. 420. Copyright 1948 by and used with the permission of Harper and Brothers. For testimony on this phenomenon in labor unions, see Ross: *Trade Union Wage Policy*, p. 41; Brooks: *When Labor Organizes*, p. 258.

sented in the bargaining process."[13] At times, as some of the examples cited earlier suggest, this task will become impossible, in which event schism and disunity will threaten. The leader who unhappily finds himself in this position may be labeled "weak," a judgment that may be thoroughly superficial. Although he may in fact be unable to effect a reconciliation among conflicting expectations in the group because of failure adequately to employ skills and devices readily available to him, it is also possible that the most skillful maneuvering would not be able to disguise the completeness of the contradictory demands upon him. Bentley has somewhat overstated, but nevertheless makes, the essential point when he observes: "Weak leadership is primarily the outcome of quarreling interests, not vice versa." [14] One can apply to all associations, not just the labor unions of which Ross was speaking, the comment that revolts by the rank and file are less likely to indicate "vigorous democracy" than "internal demoralization."[15]

Some Techniques of Leadership

It will be obvious that the bulk of the data upon which these propositions about leadership rest are drawn from relatively small groups not formally organized. This limitation does not detract from the usefulness of these propositions, for if they are psychologically valid for that stage of group life antecedent to formal organization, they are also likely to be appropriate to more formalized situations. Human behavior is not basically different in these two stages of group life, which, as has been noted before, blend imperceptibly one into the other.

The fact of formal organization appears to provide some differences in degree, however, which have an important bearing upon the techniques of leadership in organized interest groups as compared with small, informal groups. These differences can perhaps best be illuminated by asking why it is, if there exists this functional control rela-

[13] Ross: *Trade Union Wage Policy*, p. 33. Copyright 1948 by The Regents of The University of California and used with the permission of University of California Press. Cf. Eli Ginzberg: *The Labor Leader* (New York: The Macmillan Company, 1948); C. Wright Mills: *The New Men of Power: America's Labor Leaders* (New York: Harcourt, Brace & Company, 1948), chaps. 1–5 and *passim*.

[14] Bentley: *The Process of Government*, p. 229–30. Copyright 1908 by and used with the permission of Arthur F. Bentley.

[15] Ross: *Trade Union Wage Policy*, pp. 39–40.

tionship between leaders and followers, that organized groups retain in positions of power and follow the directions of men who are at best mediocre? The possible answers to such a question are complex. Among other things, they have something to do with the intensity of the shared interests in the group, a low intensity permitting greater tolerance of incompetence. They may also involve the extent to which leadership relations with members and outside groups have become stabilized and routinized, thereby permitting an acceptable performance by a mere time-server. But they also stem from the fact of formal organization itself.

Office in an organized group is a status, as has been indicated earlier—a position of importance in the group about which membership expectations cluster. As such it is symbolic of the unity of the group, of the functions that the group performs in the lives of the members. In other words, the office itself has prestige. The membership of a group that has adequately performed its functions will for this reason accept the existence of such statuses, even though those who occupy them do not play their roles perfectly. Unless these deficiencies become intolerable, dissatisfied members will respond to the initiatives of an office, even though they would not follow those of the office-holder in informal situations. Especially if the group is highly institutionalized, they will confine open resistance to the formalized processes of election and appointment that the group has established and, for long periods, may not even directly participate in such processes despite the shortcomings of the leaders.

In the course of maintaining cohesion and of perpetuating itself, the active minority can manipulate and exploit such aspects of formal organization. The services performed by the leaders, the forms of the group, and the characteristics of its members can be utilized by the leaders to modify hostility, to delay replacement, and to eliminate or postpone revolt. It is significant in this connection, as others have noted, that the counteroffensive against labor unions embodied in the Taft-Hartley Act of 1947 was aimed not directly at the benefits secured by organized labor, such as minimum wages, improved working conditions, and the like, but at the organization and structure of the unions themselves, what Ross calls the "institutional privileges" of the unions.[16] It is equally significant that a large proportion of the union rank and file apparently responded defensively without knowing the exact provisions of the legislation. Direct attacks on the benefits of unions would have provoked wide hostility; attack on

[16] Ibid., p. 24.

union structure produced a similar reaction where the union structure was working well enough to permit the members to identify themselves with it. These observations raise the topic of the techniques of internal political leadership. The techniques we will discuss are a selected rather than an exhaustive list of leadership skills. Moreover, in some cases they indicate merely tendencies of leadership activity and not separate acts. Finally, as the discussion will imply, they are not all common to all groups, but are possible in most groups depending on the situations in which leaders find themselves.

These devices can be divided roughly into two types: those that, because of their general impact on the membership, tend to maximize cohesion; and those that more directly serve to perpetuate the existing active minority. A number of the latter type have been discussed tangentially in Chapter 5 in explaining the reasons for the existence of the active minority in organized groups. Primarily of the first type, but involved in the second as well, is the highly generalized device of internal propaganda, or to use a term less emotionally colored, internal publicity. It is a major means, sometimes the only one that group leaders use, to develop those consistent responses of members to leaders' actions, responses that are the basis of leadership. (It may operate, of course, upon all segments of the "membership," both dues-payers and "fellow-travelers.") Such efforts may consist of printed media, face-to-face contacts with limited segments of the membership, the annual conventions, and the like. As Millis and Montgomery have observed of the internal publicity efforts of the A.F. of L., which are manifold, they "assist in building up and maintaining morale as well as in molding union opinion and shaping union policy."[17] This result is possible because the active minority is in a position largely to regulate the flow of ideas concerning the organization and its policies to members more or less prepared by their identification with the group to accept an authoritative view of both.[18] These effects of leadership control of the channels of communication within the group may be accentuated where the mem-

[17] From *Organized Labor* by Millis and Montgomery, p. 311. Copyright 1945. Courtesy of McGraw-Hill Book Company, Inc.

[18] For varied illustrations see the following references, among others: Childs: *Labor and Capital in National Politics*, pp. 69–70, 110–35; Herring: *Group Representation Before Congress, passim;* Odegard: *Pressure Politics,* chap. 1; Earl Latham: "Giantism and Basing Points: A Political Analysis," *Yale Law Journal,* Vol. 58, no. 3 (February, 1949), pp. 394–7; McKean: *Pressures on the Legislature of New Jersey,* chap. 4; Millis and Montgomery: *Organized Labor,* pp. 255–9.

bership is large and sufficiently dispersed, so that individuals seldom have direct communication with one another except through rigidly formal means. In such circumstances a condition of "pluralistic ignorance" may exist, in which many individuals question what is presented as the group position, but each assumes that he is unique in that respect and fails to act upon his doubts for fear of ostracism.[19]

The American Medical Association, as in so many other instances, provides an excellent example of the use of internal propaganda. Its active minority operates through various means, but most persistently through the pages of the weekly *Journal*. Especially on matters not involving the scientific aspects of medicine, such as those that have recently disturbed the group's unity, the busy doctor, almost completely absorbed in his practice, is particularly easily guided in his opinions by the utterances of the organized group. The *Journal* has much the largest circulation among medical publications, and the technical material filling the bulk of the magazine has an authoritative quality, especially for the general practitioner, that gives its editorial section added prestige. Exploiting this situation, the active minority has rarely afforded an opportunity for heterodox views, or even such disconcerting news as the British Medical Association's endorsement of compulsory health insurance, to reach the members of the profession. "The job of the editor is to get the one-party line across to the members and see that they keep to the line." [20] Perusal of the *Journal's* pages indicates a preoccupation with the device of repetition to achieve this end. The recent output of the A.M.A. has repeatedly emphasized the threat involved in health insurance ("It is not possible to socialize the means for paying for medical care without simultaneously socializing the quality and quantity of the product of medical care") and the vast resources of the opposition ("The funds raised by the assessment are relatively small compared with the millions of dollars available to the government for its all-out effort to secure compulsory sickness insurance").[21] The *Journal* achieves added influence, moreover, from the tendency of many of the publications of the State societies to say nothing on a controversial question of "medical economics" until the *Journal* has spoken and then

[19] Cf. David Krech and Richard S. Crutchfield: *Theory and Problems of Social Psychology* (New York: McGraw-Hill Book Company, Inc., 1948), pp. 388–9.

[20] Reprinted by permission of the publishers from Oliver Garceau: *The Political Life of The American Medical Association* (Cambridge, Mass.: Harvard University Press, 1941), p. 98.

[21] The quotations are from "Explanation of the $25.00 Assessment," cited above, note 40, chap. 6.

not infrequently to use material prepared for them in the bureaus of the central organization. Similar services, in fact, are provided for the busy doctor asked to speak on a medical subject of general concern, in the form of ghost-written speeches, pamphlets, and the like. Such practices are apparently also well established in the American Dental Association. It has mailed regularly to its constituent societies material and even speeches "to be given at a special or regular meeting of your society," and apparently has only rarely opened its pages to contributions favoring compulsory health insurance.[22]

The National Association of Manufacturers, the Chamber of Commerce, trade associations, and similar groups attempt to achieve similar results, although with somewhat less complete effectiveness. The N.A.M., in addition to its publishing, has its annual Congress of American Industry, which, more than most such gatherings, is a means of spreading the word rather than determining it. It also maintains a special membership relations division described by one of the association's officials as a means of establishing a party line for businessmen too busy to ascertain the "facts" for themselves.[23] Similarly, the American Legion has placed great emphasis on its internal publicity efforts from the beginning, its publicity agency in the central headquarters being a key unit in the organization. As Duffield has pointed out, this development was natural, since "the interest of a large body of ex-soldiers can be maintained, and that of non-members acquired [presumably in view of the effects of overlapping membership] only if the name of the Legion is constantly kept before their minds."[24] As in other such efforts, much of the burden of this activity is aimed at denouncing the sins of dissenters and at keeping disagreements out of the general channels of public information.

A device that must be classified with internal propaganda in most instances, although it superficially would not appear so, is the referendum. This is a widely employed instrument in chambers of commerce, trade associations, labor unions, and professional associations. By this device a question of public policy on which the association is to take a stand is sent to the members or constituent societies, frequently to-

[22] U.S. Senate, Committee on Education and Labor: *Hearings on a Bill to Provide for a National Health Program,* 79th Cong., 2d Sess. (1946), pp. 1037–78.
[23] Alfred S. Cleveland: "N.A.M.: Spokesman for Industry?" *Harvard Business Review,* Vol. 26, no. 3 (May, 1948), p. 360.
[24] Marcus Duffield: *King Legion* (New York: Cape and Smith, 1931?), p. 299.
Cf. also Gray: *The Inside Story of the Legion,* pp. 34–5, 97, 172–4.

gether with arguments on both sides of the issue. The recipients are to indicate their choice of policies on a ballot. The practice has been particularly used by the Chamber of Commerce of the United States. It is classed along with propaganda because judgments of it almost universally are that it serves primarily to emphasize unity, to give sanction to a previously determined decision, and, by the appearance of wide rank-and-file participation in policy forming, to strengthen the group internally and make it more effective externally. That little more than a majority of the membership may participate is not remarkable; this proportion is roughly comparable to the percentage of voters who participate in the election of a president of the United States. The propagandist element in the referendum lies elsewhere. As has been observed concerning the chamber's procedure:

> The questions are answered by organization [constituent society] members and often by organization secretaries, who may or may not consult their group before replying. In either case the matter is given only cursory consideration. Furthermore, the questions are frequently framed in the referendum in such a way that there can be little doubt in the mind of the representative of the average chamber as to how he should vote upon them.
>
> The secretary of a local chamber ordinarily draws up resolutions which obtain automatic endorsement. Committee reports are drawn up hastily, usually by the secretary of the organization, whose business it is to see that no action is recommended which may stir up a controversy and cause a loss of members.[25]

An almost classic example of the referendum device, or a variant of it, was its use shortly after the war by the N.A.M., although this organization uses the practice rather infrequently. Prior to initiating its campaign against the postwar continuance of price controls, the N.A.M. sent to 10 per cent of its member firms the question: "Do you believe that price controls hamper the production of manufactured goods?" Less than half of the addressees replied, though most of them in the affirmative. But the leadership used these results as justification for its advocating the immediate removal of all price controls. Yet not only were few members consulted on the subject, but no opportunity was given the rank and file to indicate whether they thought price controls necessary even if they "hampered production."

[25] Studenski: "Chambers of Commerce," *Encyclopaedia of the Social Sciences*, Vol. III. Copyright 1930 by The Macmillan Company and used with their permission. Cf. Childs: *Labor and Capital in National Politics*, pp. 158–70; Herring: *Group Representation Before Congress*, pp. 86–92.

That this case is somewhat extreme is perhaps indicated by the evidence that the incident provoked some internal controversy.[26]

Similar examples might be cited from other groups. Thus Ross concludes that "the essential function of the strike vote and the referendum is to demonstrate the solidarity of the union in support of its leaders." [27] In the American Medical Association it is rarely used, but "even its organization . . . suggests that the referendum may often be intended more as a technique for eliciting member participation and for demonstrating group solidarity than as an escape from entrenched organs." [28]

Policy determination, if it is not to reveal disunity, must be guided by the active minority. The referendum in interest groups is an instrument of guidance rather than the reverse.

A second device available to leadership for keeping its group cohesive and maintaining its control is the use of actual sanctions against recalcitrant individuals or factions. These sanctions may range widely in severity from informal expressions of disapproval to more serious punishments. In a good many groups, however, depending upon their formal structure and the effectiveness with which the leadership has produced general acceptance of a party line, effective sanctions may be completely unavailable. If an individual belongs to many associations, no one of which exercises control over his livelihood or his emotional equilibrium, he may withdraw from one and substitute another without material disturbance to his peace of mind.

The A.F. of L., for example, has virtually no sanctions to employ against its constituent international unions or against individuals. Suasion and propaganda have had to be its principal weapons against its constituent unions; these failing, it has had to accept, as a federal body, the fact of disagreement. The suspension and subsequent expulsion of the C.I.O. unions was a rare occurrence made possible because the precipitating issue did not involve the usual question of union autonomy. The C.I.O., on the other hand, for reasons indicated in Chapter 5, has been able to censure more readily leaders of its constituent unions for deviations from majority policy in political and

[26] U.S. House of Representatives, Committee on Banking and Currency: *Hearings on H. Res. 5270*, 79th Cong., 2d Sess. (1946), Vol. 1, p. 814. Cf. Cleveland: "N.A.M.: Spokesman for Industry?" pp. 366–7.

[27] Ross: *Trade Union Wage Policy*, p. 38. Copyright 1948 by The Regents of The University of California and used with the permission of University of California Press.

[28] Reprinted by permission of the publishers from Oliver Garceau: *The Political Life of The American Medical Association* (Cambridge, Mass.: Harvard University Press, 1941), p. 21; see also p. 20.

other matters, and to revoke the charters of unions that have defied the Executive Board.[29] The individual unions of both federations, however, have more extensive powers over their locals and particularly over individual members. In some instances expulsion from membership can occur for such vaguely defined offenses as slandering the union or its officers and discussing union business outside a regular meeting. Such expulsions, frequently meaning deprivation of a means of livelihood, have often resulted in litigation over the limits of lawful expulsion from private groups.[30]

The situation varies widely in types of business groups. Thus the N.A.M. has no sanctions upon its members, but, like many other such groups, must rely upon propaganda to achieve conformity.[31] Within trade associations the existence of disciplinary authority depends upon such factors as the structure of the particular industry and the objectives of the group. Most trade associations may formally require adherence to standards of conduct, but these are frequently so ill-defined as to make them virtually unenforceable. Moreover, as has been pointed out in an earlier paragraph, insistence upon enforcement such as occurred under the ill-starred N.R.A. may produce such cleavages as to disrupt rather than unify the group.[32] Moreover, it is generally true that sanctions may be effective in a situation central to a group's major objectives, yet ineffective in connection with functions regarded as more nearly peripheral.

In a closely knit profession like medicine, where reputation is crucial to a successful practice and where access to hospitals and other medical institutions is essential, sanctions can be effective, particularly

[29] The *New York Herald Tribune*, May 20, October 27, 1949.

[30] Philip Taft: "Democracy in Trade Unions," *American Economic Review*, Vol. 36, no. 2 (May, 1946), pp. 366 ff.; see also his "Judicial Procedure in Labor Unions," *Quarterly Journal of Economics*, Vol. 59, no. 3 (May, 1945), pp. 370–85; Zacharia Chafee, Jr.: "The Internal Affairs of Associations Not for Profit," *Harvard Law Review*, Vol. 43, no. 7 (May, 1930), pp. 993–1029; cf. "Equitable Jurisdiction to Protect Membership in a Voluntary Association," *Yale Law Journal*, Vol. 58, no. 6 (May, 1949), pp. 999–1006.

[31] Cleveland: "N.A.M.: Spokesman for Industry?" p. 367; McKean: *Pressures on the Legislature of New Jersey*, chap. 4.

[32] U.S. Temporary National Economic Committee: *Trade Association Survey*, pp. 5, 14, 106; see particularly chap. 4 for a discussion of the sanctions employed by the Sugar Institute against both members and outsiders. For a discussion of these problems in the press, radio, and motion picture industries, see Commission on Freedom of the Press: *A Free and Responsible Press* (Chicago: University of Chicago Press, 1947), chap. 5, esp. pp. 69–76. Cf. also Latham: "Giantism and Basing Points," pp. 395–7, for sanctions available to the Cement Institute.

against individuals. Both social and economic pressures can operate with maximum effectiveness at the local level. Where, therefore, as in the A.M.A., the local and State units are closely tied in with a national organization (in spite of its federal form), sanctions may keep the rebellious in line. Even in this situation, however, expulsion or censure will not deter those whose reputations are already established, as is evidenced by the activities of the members of the Committee of Physicians. The effectiveness of group sanctions involving partial or complete ostracism varies directly with the offender's aspiration or objective need to retain his position in the group. The application of sanctions in instances where these needs are not great may actually backfire, as in the instance that resulted in antitrust prosecution of the A.M.A. and its District of Columbia affiliate. In the spring of 1949, considerable furor was caused in Congress when it was reported that one of the doctors who had openly opposed the medical association's assessment to fight compulsory health insurance had been "punished." A Louisiana doctor who had served as a consultant to the Arkansas State Board of Health had been invited to speak at a postgraduate pediatrics course at the University of Arkansas School of Medicine. When it was discovered that he had signed the letter of protest against the A.M.A. assessment, both appointments were canceled at the request of the Arkansas State Medical Society and the Pulaski County Medical Society. Reports of the incident caused denunciations and threats of investigation on the floor of the United States Senate that probably did more harm to organized medicine than the punishment did to the rebel doctor.[33] Although expulsion and boycott, organized to operate through hospitals and medical equipment manufacturers as well as doctors, will often work against the obscure individual, they are weak and rarely used against whole units of the association.[34]

In some groups sanctions are available but rather limited in usefulness. In the American Legion, for example, individual posts are forbidden to take a position on national issues without going through the channels of the national organization; but the only sanction enforcing this rule is the expulsion of the posts that refuse to conform. Although such measures have been taken from time to time, their use on a large scale would be more destructive of cohesion than the tolerance of deviations. It is doubtful, for example, whether they

[33] The *New York Herald Tribune*, April 15, 16, 1949.
[34] See Oswald Hall: "The Stages of a Medical Career," *American Journal of Sociology*, Vol. 53, no. 5 (March, 1948), pp. 327–36; Garceau: *The Political Life of the A.M.A.*, pp. 95–117.

would be employed against the large and well-established Conference of Union Labor Legionnaires, distasteful though its activities might become to the active minority.[35]

In exercising sanctions, it should be noted, a group may be using powers delegated to it from the Government to regulate the behavior of a profession or other calling. In order to maximize cohesion, to punish deviants, and, in some instances, to restrict entrance into the occupation, some occupational groups have secured from State governments the power to require membership in the group as a condition of carrying on the employment and to impose punishments for violations of the group's approved standards of practice. Examples of this guild, or "closed shop," situation are numerous, though the phenomenon has never been studied in sufficiently systematic fashion.[36]

One of the most interesting but little-known instances is that of the so-called integrated bar. In striking contrast to medicine, the legal profession in the United States has been notably lacking in cohesion, as can be seen from the fact that the national lawyers groups, such as the American Bar Association, include only a fraction of the country's lawyers in their membership, although State and particularly local associations are more completely representative. The reasons for this lack of cohesion are not altogether clear, but conjecture leads to the suggestion that American lawyers identify themselves more closely with those interests that characterize their specialized practices than with the interests of lawyers as such, especially when a lawyer is in effect a full-time employee of an institutionalized economic group. A labor lawyer, for example, interacts more frequently with, and is likely to share more interests with, his union clients than with a lawyer engaged primarily in corporation practice. Furthermore, as has been frequently noted, American lawyers have largely ceased to function as officers of the court, after the ancient tradition of the English bar, and have become more completely the servants of their clients.[37]

Whatever the causes of this lack of cohesion, there has been a movement for more than thirty years in the States to establish the integrated bar. Sometimes called the self-governing, inclusive, incorporated, or statutory bar, the movement proposes that membership in the State bar association be required of all lawyers practicing in the

[35] Cf. Gray: *The Inside Story of the Legion*, pp. 174–5, 180–9.

[36] But see Louis Jaffe: "Law Making of Private Groups," *Harvard Law Review*, Vol. 51, no. 2 (December, 1937), pp. 201–53; McKean: *Pressures on the Legislature of New Jersey*, pp. 56–7.

[37] Cf. A. A. Berle, Jr.: "Modern Legal Profession," *Encyclopaedia of the Social Sciences*.

State, and that the bar association be designated as an official body to enforce codes of legal ethics and to admit aspirants to the bar. Beginning with a proposal from the American Judicature Society in 1914, this idea has been promoted by the American Bar Association since 1920. The movement has spread slowly and its successes have been confined primarily to the younger States west of the Mississippi, but there is recurring demand for the adoption of the plan among lawyers in the older States of the East.[38] The significance of the development for the present purposes, of course, is a group's use of the compulsive powers of government to compel membership in the group and to enforce conformity with the group's standards of practice.

Closely related to the devices of internal propaganda and sanctions is the technique of using services performed by the active minority, or those under its direct control, to compel the loyalty of individual members and constituent groups. Internal propaganda ("information") may be one of these services, and the real or alleged existence of others may provide much of the content of internal propaganda. The withdrawal or withholding of such services may operate as a potent sanction upon deviant behavior. The American Legion, for example, has from its beginnings maintained for its members welfare and relief services the withdrawal of which may have this effect. Moreover, as a result of its intimate collaboration with, not to say domination of, the Veterans Administration, the Legion is in a position to facilitate its members' claims to the various benefits dispensed through this agency. Because the Legion member is likely to find his petitions threading the toils of the bureaucracy rapidly and without significant effort on his part, whereas the nonmember may find his ensnared by them, the greatest power that the Legion has over its individual members is its ability to help them in such circumstances.[39]

This use of the services of an active minority to compel membership loyalty is a common feature of cohesive trade associations. Thus the credit given to the executive secretary of the National Association of Retail Druggists by its members for securing the passage of State and national anti-chain-store legislation made him a sort of demigod, unchallenged by rivals, and enabled him to run the N.A.R.D. in a manner to suit his own taste. If an association is federally organized, moreover, such devices may be employed to restrain the constituent societies. Thus after the failure, noted elsewhere in this chapter, of

[38] Brown: *Lawyers and the Promotion of Justice*, pp. 284–7; Hurst: *The Growth of American Law*, pp. 292–3, 365–6.
[39] A. A. Berle, Jr.: "American Legion," *Encyclopaedia of the Social Sciences;* Gray: *The Inside Story of the Legion*, pp. 175–7.

the effort in 1937 by the national organization of the retail druggists to take over the functions of the State societies, the N.A.R.D. began to set up various service bureaus to "aid" the State societies in their efforts.

Such services are a notable feature of the American Medical Association's operations as well. Not only does the A.M.A. provide the individual doctor, who may be too busy to prepare materials himself, with ghost-written speeches and pamphlet materials, but its State societies also perform various functions of great value to the members. Principal among the latter is the provision of defense in malpractice suits, which the non-member physician finds difficult to handle successfully. The national organization, moreover, ties the State societies more closely to its policies by the services that it performs for them. Most interesting of these is the co-operative medical advertising bureau, which is the source of advertising for the great majority of the State journals and therefore of major financial importance for them. This service constitutes a hidden weapon of great importance, since, if medical equipment manufacturers are reluctant to sell to a practitioner who is *persona non grata* to the A.M.A., they are even less likely to buy advertising space in the journal of a State society that is in revolt. "To the degree that the state societies profit by the system they are loath to bite the hand that feeds . . . ." [40] In addition the A.M.A. headquarters aids the legislative activities of the State society by following and advising on pending State legislation, and its officers are quick to aid the constituent groups in any sort of crisis, especially one of a political nature.

In the labor movement the opportunities for the national federations to use services as a lever upon members and constituent units are not great. But, as in the constituent unions themselves, where the central organization assumes some or all of the responsibility for organization drives and their financing and for the payment of various individual benefits, power goes with the assumption of the function. Sometimes these services have been initiated with just this objective in mind. Thus Taft cites a case in which an international union set up a death-benefit program for the purpose of ensuring local conformity to national orders to end illegal strikes or face suspension. [41]

[40] Reprinted by permission of the publishers from Oliver Garceau: *The Political Life of The American Medical Association* (Cambridge, Mass.: Harvard University Press, 1941), p. 124. See also pp. 103–4, 121–6.

[41] Philip Taft: "Understanding Union Administration," *Harvard Business Review*, Vol. 24, no. 2 (Winter, 1946), p. 250. Cf. Brooks: *When Labor Organizes*, p. 251.

The usefulness of services in compelling loyalty to the group are effectively pointed out by Kile. Discussing the problems of the American Farm Bureau Federation, he observes: "Providing plenty of services and plenty of activities should go far toward making the Farm Bureau such an intimate part of each member's life, that he would no more think of dropping out than he would think of having his children drop out of school."[42]

A fourth device for maintaining cohesion, one often of great importance, is the requirement of secrecy, the use of the executive session or the off-the-record debate. Secrecy, as has often been observed, is in varying degrees imposed by many institutions and groups in all societies. It may offset some of the effects of overlapping membership by confining interaction to the particular group during the period of participation and by emphasizing the existence of attitudes and activities known and shared only by the initiates, the latter particularly in the rituals of fraternal societies.[43] Secrecy may further enhance cohesion, suppress differences, and preserve the appearance of unanimity before competing elements inside and outside the group, by adjusting disagreements and effecting compromises in a setting free from the stresses that arise when the withdrawal of original demands is recorded and internal cleavages are made public. Of the practice in the A.M.A. Garceau observes: "The basic attitude of the active minority appears to be that differences of opinion are dirty linen."[44] In view of the importance of cohesion and the appearance of unity for the successful imposition of claims upon outside groups, this position is natural and, with varying degrees of intensity, almost universal.

Functionally somewhat related to secrecy is a device that we discussed briefly in Chapter 3 as an example of the tendency of association formation to occur in waves. To reduce the effects of overlapping membership and to maintain cohesion, an established group may recognize the emergence of new interests and associations competing for the attention and support of its membership by setting up parallel or competing associations, after the fashion of the company unions established by employers to compete with the trade union. These new associations may satisfy the emergent need but are under the control of the parent group. Perhaps the best examples of this phenomenon are

[42] Kile: *The Farm Bureau Through Three Decades*, p. 394. Copyright 1948 by and used with the permission of Orville M. Kile.

[43] Chapple and Coon: *Principles of Anthropology*, p. 423.

[44] Reprinted by permission of the publishers from Oliver Garceau: *The Political Life of the American Medical Association* (Cambridge, Mass.: Harvard University Press, 1941), p. 77.

provided by the Catholic Church. The development of associations such as labor unions, veterans' groups, and youth organizations like the Y.M.C.A. threatened to divide the loyalties of many Catholics. These groups, however, were a response to felt needs in the society, and their functions could not be opposed as such. The establishment of the Catholic War Veterans and the Catholic Youth Organization, to mention only two examples, recognized the functional needs and provided a means of satisfying them without serious threat to the cohesion of the Church. In this country the Church has not established its own labor unions, although it has attempted to reach a similar objective through the American Association of Catholic Trade Unionists.[45]

The sponsorship of competing associations is akin to, but not identical with, the efforts of established groups to protect their cohesion from the attractions or attacks of alternative groups by "infiltrating" and controlling the leadership of the latter. Such tactics have commonly provided "fronts" for the Communist party, but they have also been a means of choking off opposition to entrenched political "machines" in a fashion approximating the practices of totalitarian regimes in other lands. Domination of overlapping and potentially disruptive associations may be an effective alternative to the open sponsorship of "kept" groups.

Other devices that may be utilized by the active minority for their effect on the membership in general need not be discussed in detail. Sufficient mention has already been made in Chapter 5 of the "democratic mold" to indicate that in most instances some means of apparent participation in the affairs of the group by a large fraction of the membership is almost inevitable. The annual convention, the elaborate structure of committees that characterizes most associations, devices for consultation with the membership, such as the referendum discussed above—these and other elements establish the form, if not always the fact, of widespread member participation. The auxiliary organization, usually of women, is another device employed by some groups to strengthen the cohesion of the parent association. These techniques have been discussed in Chapter 4 and need not be further analyzed here.

A number of techniques whose principal effect is to perpetuate the control of an existing active minority have been discussed in accounting for the existence of minority leadership; they need not be

[45] Paul Blanshard: *American Freedom and Catholic Power* (Boston: The Beacon Press, 1949).

repeated here. A few that were not discussed in Chapter 5 should be mentioned, however. When one examines these devices, the most nearly universal is the formal or informal succession to positions in the active minority through co-optation. The system of indirect election of principal officers, common to so many organized groups, is itself a means of assuring a minority element that such positions will be filled by persons it regards as "sound." So long as the intermediate electing body is controlled, moreover, criticism of the system and the leadership can be suppressed. Of similar character is the custom, notably in the National Association of Manufacturers, of establishing a *cursus honorum* among the top elective positions, so that the most important of such spots are filled by men whose acceptability to the active minority is high. (In the N.A.M. a one-year term as president of the group is followed successively for similar periods by the chairmanship of the board of directors, chairmanship of the executive committee, and chairmanship of the finance committee.)

The active minority almost by definition is likely to have control of the nominating machinery and to constitute a decisive influence in group elections. Its backing is desirable if not essential to the success of an individual aspiring to important position in the group. In consequence, the known recalcitrant is not likely to have his way made easy by getting the support of the active minority. An example is provided by the American Legion: "If a Legion official is inclined to differ from the organization's policies, he must keep his differences to himself or he will not get ahead in the organization; troublemakers are not named on committees nor rewarded by being supported for high offices." [46] The Legion is not unique in this respect. "In a controversy between an officer and a member or a group of members, the advantage is on the whole with officials. They are the leaders and politicians with followers and retainers throughout the union." [47] The active minority, moreover, will use minor positions in the hierarchy to locate and test prospective recruits to more important office. Garceau, for example, reports that A.M.A. officials attend the meetings of State and some county societies partly in order to identify prospective leaders. Those aspirants who are "sound" may be aided to more advanced standing by appointment to reference committees of the House of Delegates, where their capacities are further

---

[46] Marcus Duffield: *King Legion* (New York: Cape and Smith, 1931), pp. 110–1.

[47] Taft: "Democracy in Trade Unions," p. 364. Copyright 1946 by and used with the permission of American Economic Association.

tested.[48] Some groups, such as the Legion, even carry on formal training schools for future leaders.[49]

Manipulation of the electoral machinery in various ways may supplement the devices for selection of leaders by co-optation. Although these manipulations normally differ little from the practices used in public elections, some of them are of peculiar interest. The A.M.A.'s statutory ban on electioneering, mentioned in Chapter 5, serves a triple purpose. It facilitates an appearance of unanimity, since many nominees are unopposed. It pays lip service to an almost mystic democratic notion that a choice of leaders emerges spontaneously from the meditations of a large body, like Athena from the brow of Zeus. Finally, of course, it permits preconvention, behind-the-scenes maneuvering by the active minority to control nominations and elections.[50] Somewhat similar procedures exist at the local level, and occasionally the accusations emerging from these practices are like those made in elections to public office. In the New York County Medical Society, where a nominating committee presents one name for each office to be filled, an election contest occurred in 1949 for the second time in more than a decade. When the independent slate lost by a wide margin, the press reported that the defeated candidates were considering demanding an investigation of the society's election procedures on the grounds that irregularities had occurred in the counting of votes and in the rules governing the voting.[51]

Manipulation of the machinery for policy declaration is of similar importance. This may vary from phrasing policy statements with a nice ambiguity that will allow the leaders maximum discretion and avoid internal dissension to more forthright repressive measures. It may involve no more than the securing of agreement among a few key leaders prior to a convention, so that opposition from the floor is leaderless and can be isolated.[52] Or it may depend upon the careful domination of committees in which real conciliation of differences takes place subject merely to ratifying action by a body of larger size. In the American Medical Association the reference committees serve this function in the House of Delegates. Appointed by the speaker and frequently including members of the staff and officers, these committees may hold hearings and by other means assess the strength of

[48] Garceau: *The Political Life of the A.M.A.*, pp. 18, 127.
[49] Gray: *The Inside Story of the Legion*, pp. 172–3.
[50] Garceau: *The Political Life of the A.M.A.*, pp. 82, 84.
[51] The *New York Herald Tribune*, May 26, 1949.
[52] Cf. Seidman: *Union Rights and Union Duties*, pp. 48–9, for a discussion of such arrangements in union conventions.

various viewpoints in the House of Delegates in such fashion as to disguise controversy and to assure acceptance of their work by the delegates. As in other legislative bodies, the speaker's discretionary power to choose the committee to which a resolution is referred can effectively prevent any but the leaders' views from being presented in open debate. These arrangements ordinarily operate smoothly in the national body; similar ones are even more effective in the State and county societies.[53]

Finally, mention should be made of the device of utilizing conflicts with outside groups, usually with the aid of internal propaganda, to increase cohesion and to strengthen the position of the active minority. In Chapter 5 it was pointed out that outside threats to a group could have much to do with the development of an active minority. The threat may not be real or may be grossly exaggerated, of course. In observing competing groups one encounters with amusing regularity a tendency of leaders on both sides to inflate the strength, organization, and finances of the opposition. The alleged omnipotence of "big business" is a familiar theme, but the compliment is as frequently paid its opponents. For example, a vice-president of the N.A.M. recently exhorted a group of public relations executives to exert more effort to defend the "American system of free individual enterprise against spreaders of unrest and fanatical collectivists" who, he said, "are much better organized, financed and united in their drive" than the defenders of the system.[54] Whether the threat is genuine or not, if it is perceived as real by the members of the group, it is likely to have the anticipated effects. Although this use of conflict assumes a minimum measure of pre-existing cohesion in the group as well as a negligible amount of overlapping with the opposed group or groups, it appears to be, as Williams has asserted, "one of the most important general principles of group dynamics."[55] Within limits conflict may be exploited by group leaders to strengthen and perpetuate their control.

[53] Garceau: *The Political Life of the A.M.A.*, pp. 68–95.

[54] The *New York Times*, February 7, 1947. For a similar case see L. C. Crain and A. B. Hamilton: *Packaged Thinking for Women* (New York: National Industrial Conference Board, 1948).

[55] Robin M. Williams, Jr.: *The Reduction of Intergroup Tensions: A Survey of Research on Problems of Ethnic, Racial, and Religious Group Relations* (Social Science Research Council, Bulletin No. 57, New York: 1947), p. 58. Cf. MacIver: *The Web of Government*, p. 415; Warner and Low: *The Social System of the Modern Factory*, p. 131; and Millis and Montgomery: *Organized Labor*, p. 99.

Conclusion

Instability, in varying degrees, is endemic to political interest groups. It may be produced and fostered by a large number of influences, but the most significant of these is the necessarily divided loyalty of the individual, all of whose interests are never completely represented by any one group. All men in a complicated society have a wide variety of memberships in competing groups and potential groups.

This fact sets the problem of internal politics, which is to achieve the maximum cohesion possible in the situation in which the group exists. This problem is also, and incidentally, a matter of continuing the existing leadership of the group in the privileges that its status provides. This consideration is secondary, not for moral reasons, but because the make-up of a particular leadership element depends primarily upon the group's situation and only secondarily upon the leaders' skills. Leadership is not a quality possessed by individuals, though some personalities are obviously better adapted than others to a variety of leadership roles; rather, it is a functional relationship between people in a given setting.

The group's strategic position among other groups, the character of the overlapping attachments of its members at a particular point in time, and the skills of the leadership largely determine the group's cohesion. Its cohesion will in the long run profoundly affect the extent to which the group is successful in exerting its claims upon other groups in the society.

PART THREE

The Tactics of Influence

8

Group Interests and Public Opinion

A PRIMARY concern of all organized political interest groups in the United States is the character of the opinions existing in the community. Group leaders, whatever else they may neglect, cannot afford to be ignorant of widely held attitudes bearing upon the standing and objectives of their organizations. Estimating the direction and incidence of public opinions, moreover, goes hand in hand with more or less continuing efforts to guide and control them. In fact, almost invariably one of the first results of the formal organization of an interest group is its embarking upon a program of propaganda, though rarely so labeled, designed to affect opinions concerning the interests and claims of the new group. Although this phenomenon is not peculiarly modern, its relative importance in group politics has so increased in the twentieth century as to make the whole pattern of interest group activity appear different in kind. It is this change that is at the base of Herring's distinction between the "new lobby" and the "old lobby" of corporation representatives, "patronage brokers," and behind-the-scenes "wire-pullers" that characterized legislative operations in the nineteenth century.[1]

To explain adequately the reasons for this greatly increased preoccupation with public opinion on the part of political interest groups would require a book in itself. Without elaborate investigation, however, it will be apparent that we are discussing one of those complicated and highly significant shifts in the means of political influence that reflect changes in the structure and techniques of the society as a whole. This shift is akin to those changes in the organization and operation of the political party in the Jackson period, at-

[1] Herring: *Group Representation Before Congress*, pp. 30–41, 59–61.

tendant upon the expansion of the suffrage from a narrow class base to one including nearly all white males. In the one case as in the other, changes in the distribution of political participation required new political techniques. This fact is clear enough in the case of the Jacksonian revolution, but what were the changes in political participation at the beginning of this century? White manhood suffrage had been fully operative for roughly fifty years. What then dictated the increased solicitude for the opinions of broad sections of the populace and made propaganda "the strongest weapon in the arsenal of the lobby"? [2]

The basic causes of the change are essentially those discussed in Chapter 3 in accounting for the proliferation of interest groups, particularly associations, in modern America. The growing interdependence of a complex society, the instability of institutionalized groups, which produced stabilizing associations on their periphery, and the revolution in communications technology underlie both phenomena. The rapid increase in the number of interest groups, especially those exerting their claims through the institutions of government, led to extensive changes in the forms and frequency of political participation. The ballot box, the political party organization, and, possibly, a personal visit with an elected representative were the only means of political participation for a worker prior to the rise and political orientation of the national labor movement. With the latter development, a significant alternative means has become available. For citizens in other walks of life similar associations have also provided supplementary channels of political activity. The extent and significance of these new means of political participation have been inadequately explored by social scientists as yet, but it is clear that these developments have led to the emphasis that modern interest groups place upon public opinion and propaganda. Being almost inevitably minorities in the total population, organized interest groups must find some means of allying themselves with other groups and of mobilizing their "fellow-travelers" if they hope to compete successfully for the attention and indulgence of other groups and of government institutions. The state of public opinion affects the limits to which such alliances can extend, and propaganda is a major means of mobilizing support and of securing allies.

This use of propaganda is merely an extension of its function as outlined in Chapter 7 in discussing the techniques of internal control. There internal propaganda was presented as a means of promoting

[2] Herring: *Group Representation Before Congress*, p. 60. Copyright 1929 by and used with the permission of The Brookings Institution.

among the group membership the consistent responses that are the basis of effective leadership within the group. External propaganda also seeks to secure acquiescence, but it attempts to win the consent of a portion of the population more extensive than the formal, dues-paying membership of the group. If the broad conception of group membership suggested at the beginning of Chapter 6 is recalled, the connection with public opinion will be clear. The limits that define formal membership in a group are necessarily somewhat arbitrary. No sharp barrier separates the dues-paying members from the "fellow-travelers;" the two are distinguishable only by different rates of participation, and particular individuals may move from one category to another easily and frequently. Beyond the "fellow-travelers," from the viewpoint of the active minority, are the potential sympathizers, the neutral, the indifferent, the actively hostile, and gradations in between. With all but the hostile segment the function of propaganda is essentially the same, to secure acquiescence to the leadership and the claims of the group. Whether all such potentially friendly segments of the population are actually solicited at a particular moment depends upon circumstances at that time. Moreover, a somewhat different approach may be made to each of these segments in recognition of the different patterns of multiple membership and, consequently, different attitudes existing within them.

Propaganda directed toward the hostile segment can be understood best if considered in the context of competing groups, in each of which the leadership exercises some authority over formal members and "fellow-travelers." If each such competing group is attempting to widen the area of its leadership, then each will attempt to weaken the opposing effort in that direction and to confine the opposition to as small and weak a segment as possible. Where the competing interests are not organized, propaganda is less necessary, and the "wire-pulling" methods of the "old lobby" may be sufficient. Where competing interests are organized, propaganda is essential.

Thus the factors that have contributed to the proliferation of organized interest groups in the United States have also necessitated the increased concern of these groups with public opinion and propaganda, after the fashion of the "new lobby." Other events, frequently designated as causes of this development, are probably less fundamental and are as much reflections of the altered pattern of political participation as causes of it. At most they constitute immediate rather than underlying causes. Thus the 1911 reform of the rules of procedure of the House of Representatives broke the power of a controlling clique and gave interests not represented, or inadequately represented by the clique, a more satisfactory chance to influence policy. Although this change helped the new groups, it could not have occurred without a prior change in the techniques and relative strength of groups over the country. Similarly the practice firmly established since 1900 of holding public hearings before congressional committees on all legislation of major importance improved the position, especially the propaganda position, of the newer groups and reflected their developing strength. The adoption of the Seventeenth Amendment in 1913 was similarly significant in making the Senate accessible to groups previously denied any appreciable opportunity to influence that body. Finally, the 1913 House and Senate investigations of lobbying to defeat the Underwood tariff bill, the first major hearings of this type, marked a turning point in the techniques and relations of political interest groups in the United States. They discredited the "old lobby" and its methods, but it is more significant that the very existence of the investigations revealed the strength of competing groups. If the National Association of Manufacturers, the principal target of the hearings, subsequently abandoned or modified its wonted techniques, it did so not from remorse, but from the necessity of altered methods to meet the competition of other groups and interests. A minority in numbers, it has increasingly been forced since the organization of effective competing groups to utilize propaganda on a broad scale in order to achieve its objectives.[3] In highlighting the N.A.M.'s predicament the 1913 investigations provide the perfect illustration of the factors causing the increased importance of public opinion and propaganda in latter-day group politics.

Public Opinion and Propaganda

Before proceeding further it is necessary to give some attention to what is meant by the terms "public opinion" and "propaganda." Both, and particularly the former, have become so much a part of everyday speech that they have acquired a congeries of figurative and highly emotionalized meanings that are useful for polemics and poetics but are the despair of precise communication. Notions about public opinion, of course, have an ancient lineage in the thought of the Western world, running back to the earliest speculations about the nature of the political process. Explicit formulations of the concept did not become frequent until the intensification in the eighteenth and nineteenth centuries of movements toward broader popular participation

[3] See the Congressional hearings cited above in note 38, chap. 4.

in the government of the national state. Among important political philosophers Rousseau was apparently the first to use the phrase.[4]

This is not the appropriate place for a history of concepts of public opinion, but it will be helpful to discuss a few features of the term that are a part of common usage and that weaken it as a tool of analysis. These include at least the implicit assumption that public opinion is a collective entity, almost a supernatural being, that becomes "aroused," makes "demands," and issues judgments, like some benevolent minotaur. Even where the term is not quite so personalized and it is acknowledged that the only beings involved in the matter are individual humans, it is frequently implied that the product that emerges from the thinking and interaction of individuals is a disembodied force qualitatively superior to the view of any participant individual or individuals.[5] Thus an idea or proposal is "put to the test in the arena of public opinion" or is "brought to judgment before the bar of public opinion," by which means its essential merits allegedly are determined. Or a distinction may be attempted between "real" and "apparent" public opinion, the former being more rational (from the observer's viewpoint).

Such figures of speech are adequate for ordinary discourse, but they lead only to difficulties in an attempt at precise analysis. Consequently, one can identify as belonging to another academic period a statement like the following from James Bryce: "Towering over Presidents and State governors, over Congress and State legislatures, over conventions and the vast machinery of party, public opinion stands out, in the United States, as the great source of power, the master of servants who tremble before it."[6] Under the influence of developments in psychology such as those associated with the name of Freud and in partial consequence of the revelation of the role of propaganda in World War I, the non-rational aspects of opinion became accepted among students of the subject. With the demand for more verifiable methods of studying social phenomena, moreover, the nineteenth-

---

[4] See Paul A. Palmer: "The Concept of Public Opinion in Political Theory," in *Essays in History and Political Theory in Honor of Charles H. McIlwain* (Cambridge, Mass.: Harvard University Press, 1936), pp. 230–57. Also, Francis G. Wilson: "Concepts of Public Opinion," *American Political Science Review*, Vol. 27, no. 3 (June, 1933), pp. 371–91.

[5] For a good discussion of these fictions and fallacies, see F. H. Allport: "Toward a Science of Public Opinion," *Public Opinion Quarterly*, Vol. 1, no. 1 (January, 1937), pp. 7–23. Cf. Bentley: *The Process of Government*, chap. 8.

[6] Bryce: *The American Commonwealth*, Vol. II, p. 255. Copyright 1891 by Macmillan & Co. and used with the permission of The Macmillan Company.

century rhapsodic approach to public opinion, typified by Bryce, has largely disappeared from the academic literature, though not from the press and the hustings. Conceptualized in such obscure or metaphysical terms, public opinion cannot be analyzed, but, like the risen and the fallen angels, must be treated as a matter of faith and authority.

We can best approach the analytical view of public opinion by dividing the concept into its component segments, and in explaining the term "public" the most satisfactory starting point will be the view of John Dewey.[7] Positing the obvious fact that some human actions have consequences for others who are not immediate participants in the actions, he conceives of the public as those "others" who perceive these consequences. These consequences, it is important to note, may be viewed by the members of the public as more or less adverse or more or less favorable. Thus the public of a group may be thought of as an aggregate of individuals who are aware, or who can be made aware, of various possible consequences of the group's actions, including its propaganda. These actions, it should be noted, may be actual or merely contemplated, "real" or merely alleged. Moreover, they may stem from the threatened or manifest actions of another group upon the group in question.

It will be apparent that there is a connection between this conception of a public and that of an interest group. Broadly viewed, an interest group is a segment of a public that shares a similar view of, or attitude toward, the consequences under discussion. It may be merely a potential interest group, of course, or an actual one if its members attempt to "do something" about the consequences. When it has become organized, moreover, a major function of the organization is to speed up and sharpen its members' perceptions of the consequences of actions (events) occurring or impending in the environment and related to the group's interests. Thus the public that exists around a given tariff policy may be very large and diversified, including importers, exporters, domestic producers, the employees of each, consumers, and so on. Some persons in these categories may not perceive the consequences of the policy. Of those who do, some will take a more or less favorable and some a rather unfavorable view of the consequences. Those included in a trade association of domestic producers may be made quickly aware of possible consequences through the organized interest group, which will also attempt to persuade other segments of the public to support or not oppose their

<hr/>

[7] Dewey: *The Public and Its Problems*, pp. 12–17.

view of the situation. Others not included in such a group may form one on the basis of their shared view.

In the United States a public rarely, if ever, includes the whole of even the adult population. Depending on the circumstances, a varying proportion of that population is unaware of even the most generally significant events and their consequences. Neither a World Series nor a presidential election is sufficiently dramatic to become known to all the citizens of the country. Opinion surveys have amply demonstrated the existence of what has been called a "hard core of chronic know-nothings" who are not aware of events concerning which even the most extensive information has been provided.[8] For example, more than a year after the establishment of the United Nations, one third of the adult population were not sufficiently aware of its existence to be able to give the simplest explanation of its purpose, even in such terms as "to keep the peace," and at as late a date as October, 1948, one quarter of the population were still in that position.[9]

Because of this varying proportion of "know-nothings," it is inaccurate and misleading to speak of "the public" in any continuing, general sense. The public is always specific to a particular situation or issue. From the viewpoint of an organized interest group, "the public" overlaps to some extent the publics of other groups with which it is competing or is allied on the political stage. This kind of overlapping, as the preceding chapter indicated, is the setting for both "internal" and "external" group propaganda.

Opinion may be thought of in the simplest terms as the expression of an attitude on an issue or proposition. An individual may be said to have an opinion not only if he has expressed an attitude but as well if he can express one when called upon to do so. Thus he may volunteer an opinion in a discussion with his associates or may supply one upon request from an interviewer, although he may not have expressed the particular opinion previously. Opinions, of course, develop and change, as do the attitudes that they express. Without completely restating the argument presented in Chapter 2, we may recall that group affiliations of various sorts are the source of attitude-forming influences; that the family is in point of time and even of impor-

[8] See Herbert H. Hyman and Paul B. Sheatsley: "Some Reasons Why Information Campaigns Fail," *Public Opinion Quarterly*, Vol. 11, no. 3 (Fall, 1947), pp. 412–23.

[9] Social Science Research Council: *Public Reaction to the Atomic Bomb and World Affairs* (Ithaca, N. Y.: Cornell University, 1947), pp. 166–7; Survey Research Center: *Attitudes Toward United States-Russian Relations* (Ann Arbor, Mich.: Survey Research Center, University of Michigan, 1948), p. 46.

tance the primary affiliation of this sort, especially concerning the society's basic institutions; and that such attitudes are altered by experiences and by shifting group loyalties.

Public opinion, therefore, consists of the opinions of the aggregate of individuals making up the public under discussion. It does not include all the opinions held by such a set of individuals, but only those relevant to the issue or situation that defines them as a public. Public opinion, it follows, is strictly speaking specific to a particular set of conditions.

The implications of this conception of public opinion are various: they all stem from the fact that public opinion in one situation or at one point of time will have different characteristics from that in another situation or at a different time. It has sometimes been said that public opinion is majority opinion. This definition is inaccurate not only because the minority is also a part of the public whose opinions are being discussed but also because there may be no majority opinion. The existence of a majority is not a prerequisite for public opinion, but a characteristic, like its size and the size of the minority or minorities, to be determined by reasearch. As Harwood Childs has put it: "The degree of unanimity is not a condition of the existence of public opinion, but an aspect to be investigated." [10]

Some other aspects to be investigated are suggested by the familiar fact that the political effectiveness of a segment of public opinion may bear little or no relation to its size. Thus to describe adequately public opinion in a given situation we want to know the relative intensity with which the various opinions are held. Because political situations develop and persist through time, we also want to know the relative stability of such opinions. For similar reasons it may be important to determine the amount of knowledge on which opinions are based, the degree of rationality they display, and the like. Finally, we may want to find out to what extent various opinions involve a willingness and ability to act upon them. Willingness to act is a simple variable; ability may comprehend a number of factors, such as the extent to which individuals holding similar opinions are able to communicate with one another through the press and radio, whether they belong to or are represented by organized interest groups, and the like. The political importance of these structural or action aspects of public opinion in specific situations and in general can be suggested by two examples. Schattschneider's distinguished study of the passage of the Smoot-Hawley Tariff Act of 1930 revealed that the adequacy

[10] Harwood L. Childs: *An Introduction to Public Opinion* (New York: John Wiley & Sons, Inc., 1940), p. 48.

of means of communication among individuals and firms with similar views of the proposals was of major importance in the relative effectiveness with which such views were brought to bear on the legislature.[11] In studying public opinion on certain foreign policy problems, the University of Michigan's Survey Research Center found that those who belonged to organizations in which foreign affairs were discussed—10 per cent of the population—were more likely to be well informed on such matters than those who did not belong.[12]

These aspects and others of a similar sort are characteristics or dimensions of public opinion that will vary through time and in different circumstances. Take a simplified example: suppose research indicates that at a certain time the public concerned with a threatened strike in the steel industry includes only half the population, within which opinion is divided into segments no one of which constitutes a majority. Two opposing opinions are held with considerably greater intensity than the others and are equally well informed. They are both represented by organized interest groups, one of which has better access to the press and radio. The other minority opinions are based on little knowledge, are not significantly organized, and appear relatively unstable. Now suppose that at a later time public opinion on the same issue displays a quite different configuration. Four fifths of the adult population now is aware of the threatened strike, and one of the several opinions on the subject is held by a majority. Among the majority intensity varies considerably; it is more uniformly high among those holding the principal minority view. Knowledge of the "facts" in the dispute is similarly distributed, but in the majority is not closely correlated with intensity. The majority view is represented by one principal organized interest group allied with several minor ones. Together they receive dominant attention in the mass communications media. The principal minority view has not changed significantly with reference to any of the observed characteristics, but the lesser minority opinions have all but disappeared. At both points in time the various opinions on the issue can also be described in terms of their distribution among regions, population concentrations of various size, the age, sex, occupation, and income segments of the country, and the like.

Although not all characteristics (dimensions) of the sort mentioned in the example above are yet subject to effective measurement, social scientists over the past several years have made great strides in this

[11] Schattschneider: *Politics, Pressures and the Tariff,* pp. 123–5, chap. 4.
[12] Social Science Research Council: *Public Reaction to the Atomic Bomb,* pp. 202–3.

direction.[13] The tools for precise description are so far developed that it is no longer necessary to discuss public opinion in terms of the vague, unverified speculations of earlier periods. Out of an accumulation of carefully designed analyses made under specified conditions it will be possible to develop generalizations concerning the characteristics of public opinion with respect to *types* of issues and in various *kinds* of situations. Only in such verified, conditional statements is it accurate to talk about public opinion as a generalized phenomenon.

"Propaganda" is a term that has not only acquired various figurative meanings but has also become chiefly derogatory in its connotations. Its application to a statement usually means that the message is believed to be malicious, interested, and partially or wholly false. However, the word has not always been so used. Originally it referred to the process of disseminating a particular faith, religious or political. Since World War I it has been in bad odor in consequence of the revelations after the end of hostilities that the various belligerent Governments, in their efforts to win the support of neutral nations, demoralize the enemy, and encourage the home front, had indulged in a considerable measure of distortion and fabrication. Widespread denunciation of such practices was a not unreasonable reaction.

Such a view of propaganda has limited usefulness, however, because it prevents one from recognizing that attempts to persuade large numbers of people constitute a basic process in our kind of society. Where social complexity has fostered a diversity of attitudes and where widespread agreement is frequently necessary for effective action, organized efforts to influence and control attitudes are inevitable. In this sense propaganda is simply a kind of communication and is morally neutral. The means and ends of particular propaganda efforts may be more or less good or bad, true or false, honest or dishonest, depending on one's basis of judgment. As a social process, however, propaganda is no more a matter of morals than is the process of buying and selling.

There are numerous definitions of propaganda in this neutral sense, the particular merits of which need not be discussed here.[14] For pres-

[13] See, for example, Hadley Cantril et al.: *Gauging Public Opinion* (Princeton, N. J.: Princeton University Press, 1944); Samuel A. Stouffer et al.: *Studies in Social Psychology in World War II*, 4 vols. (Princeton, N. J.: Princeton University Press, 1949–50); Lazarsfeld et al.: *The People's Choice*; and the items cited in note 9, above.

[14] See, for example, Leonard W. Doob: *Propaganda: Its Psychology and Technique* (New York: Henry Holt & Company, Inc., 1935), pp. 89 ff.; Harold D. Lasswell and Dorothy Blumenstock: *World Revolutionary Propaganda* (New York: Alfred A. Knopf, Inc., 1939), pp. 9 ff.; Paul M. A.

ent purposes propaganda will be considered as any attempt, by the manipulation of words and word substitutes, to control the attitudes and consequently the behavior of a number of individuals concerning a controversial matter.

Two aspects of this definition require brief comment. In the first place, although the principal instrument of propaganda is the manipulation of words, spoken or written, it is frequently supplemented by gestures, pictures, and other symbolic elements. The artful grimace of a skilled orator and the flag carried by a group of marching pickets are as much means of propaganda as the spoken or written word. In the second place, it is useful to think of propaganda as dealing with the controversial not only because the concerns of political interest groups inevitably are of that order but also because the restriction permits a rough distinction between propaganda and education. No interest group in the United States admits that it is engaging in propaganda. Because of the unsavory connotations of the term in popular usage, only one's opponents use propaganda. One's own group is engaged in "education," a term of favorable connotation, or in "informational work," a term of more neutral character. Under the present classification, however, virtually all such activities of political interest groups should be regarded as propaganda. Following Lasswell, the term "education" is properly confined to the transmission and reinforcement, by words and related means, of attitudes and skills that are accepted in the society under examination. Thus, to promote a favorable attitude toward individualism would be education in the United States, but propaganda in the Soviet Union. To train people in the principles of aerodynamics would be education in both places.

The Tactics of Propaganda

The basic propaganda techniques used by political interest groups are not unique, but are shared with all other elements in society that attempt to influence the attitudes of large numbers of people. Nor, it should be added, are many of these techniques peculiarly modern, since most political situations or problems of our time are essentially those of the Greek city-state, even though they are described in other terms. It is the technology of the mass communication media, with their broad coverage, their elaborate organization, and their suscep-

Linebarger: *Psychological Warfare* (Washington, D. C.: Infantry Journal Press, 1948), pp. 39 ff.

tibility to monopolistic control, which primarily distinguishes the propaganda of the twentieth century from that of earlier periods.[15]

It should also be emphasized, in the face of popular tendencies to believe otherwise, that propaganda is not an independent political device that can function effectively apart from other political skills. This fact is obvious enough in military propaganda, where "psychological warfare" is employed against an enemy as a supplement to other weapons designed to weaken his will to resist. The supplementary character of propaganda is less commonly accepted in the realm of peacetime politics. Nevertheless, it functions here in conjunction with techniques of negotiation, adjudication, bribery, and violence as a support to these and other political skills, not as a substitute.

To assume the independence of propaganda as a political device, to assume that where propaganda exists it is effective, is to invite failure in political analysis, for such an assumption tends to take the propagandist at his self-assigned value and to that extent makes the analyst himself a victim of the propaganda. For example, one may observe and recount the details of a propaganda effort by an interest group, note its extensive coverage in the mass media, examine and evaluate the appeals it uses. Such an account says nothing about the effectiveness of the propaganda effort. Even if the propagandist achieves the attitude changes he seeks, unless these are represented by appropriate organizations that can use them at the key points of policy determination, the campaign as a whole may fail. For example, propaganda efforts on behalf of the continuation of price control in the period of reconversion after World War II were, on the evidence of the opinion surveys, able to secure the agreement of a large majority of the adult population.[16] But to have based an estimate of the prospects of the legislation solely on that evidence, however sound, would have been naive. Propagandists, in their zeal to impress clients with their skills, frequently use coverage as an index of a campaign's success.[17] The political analyst knows that this is only a part of the picture.

As a consequence of the inevitable dependence of a propaganda

[15] See Bruce L. Smith: "The Political Communication Specialist of Our Times," in Bruce L. Smith, Harold D. Lasswell, and Ralph D. Casey: *Propaganda, Communication, and Public Opinion: A Comprehensive Reference Guide* (Princeton, N. J.: Princeton University Press, 1946), pp. 64–5. Cf. William Albig: *Public Opinion* (New York: McGraw-Hill Book Company, Inc., 1939), pp. 286–90.

[16] See *Public Opinion Quarterly*, Vol. 9 (1945), pp. 369–70, 517–8; Vol. 10 (1946), pp. 278–80, 633–4.

[17] For some strikingly naive examples of this practice see Philip Lesly: *Public Relations in Action* (Chicago: Ziff-Davis Publishing Company, 1947).

effort upon the other political instruments with which it is associated, there are various circumstances under which propaganda must play a comparatively minor role in the political activities of interest groups. For example, if the decisions taken in a legislative body are crucial to group success, and if that body is the product of a gerrymandered or "rotten borough" system that greatly overrepresents one group at the expense of another, propaganda on the merits of an issue may be relatively unimportant, though the underrepresentation itself may later become an issue and the subject of propaganda. The handicapped groups fail despite the most skillful propaganda efforts, and the favored side may achieve its purpose without using such techniques. A related and equally common instance of the unimportance of propaganda may occur where the public concerned with a particular issue is extremely small and where it is not likely to be extended materially either by the publicity attached to the controversy or by the immediate consequences of the way in which the conflict is resolved. Thus the proposed alteration of a railroad freight rate on a particular commodity may be known to a public not much more extensive than the railroad managements and the producers. If neither the denial nor the approval of the change is likely materially to affect a larger public, propaganda will play a minor role in the settlement. A proposed excise tax on a luxury product not widely used in the community might be dealt with in similar fashion.

Such limitations on the role of propaganda are, of course, subject to change over a period of time. Changes in both formal institutional arrangements and the size of a public are likely to encourage such shifts, as was suggested early in the chapter. For example, until fairly recent years the affairs of organized labor were of concern to a fairly limited public, and the propaganda efforts of such groups were concentrated primarily in the channels afforded by the labor press and periodicals. With the development of such practices as industry-wide bargaining, the consequences of which are apparent to a large segment of the population, and particularly with the increased resort of labor groups to government as an instrument for exerting their claims, such organizations have found themselves obliged to deal with a public of mass proportions. When a national labor group runs full-page advertisements in the metropolitan press and purchases time on the radio networks, propaganda has assumed increased importance as a means of managing the affairs of the group.

Because the particular propaganda devices employed by interest groups are as varied as the situations in which they operate, a discussion of propaganda tactics perhaps can best be organized around the principal psychological elements in a propaganda effort and the pitfalls faced by the propagandist in dealing with each.[18] In necessarily simplified terms these elements can be thought of as three stages in the propaganda process: (1) ensuring perception of the words and symbols presented by the propagandist; (2) stimulation of pre-existing attitudes appropriate to the propagandist's aim; and (3) production of a resulting new or modified attitude that will lead to the act the propagandist desires.

The problem of ensuring perception can be indicated quite simply. If the propagandist is to have a chance to exercise influence, his "message" must at least be seen or heard by his intended audience. Like the door-to-door salesman, unless he is able at least to get his foot in the door, the difficulties of the later stages in the process are of no relevance to him; he has already failed. The problem arises from the fact that in a complicated society no individual can possibly take cognizance of all the stimuli (messages) that compete for his attention. He cannot, obviously, read all the books, magazines, and newspapers available to him nor listen to all the radio programs.

Although the problem of perception can be stated in such simple terms, it is not easily solved. The propagandist for an organized interest group, however, has certain advantages in attempting to solve it. If his principal objective is to influence his membership, he faces less difficulty than if he is trying to reach an unorganized public. The act of formally joining the group is evidence in itself of a willingness to give some attention to communications from the group's leaders. Membership in an organization may in fact make one feel a sort of compulsion to see and hear messages issued by the group. Thus the specialized journal of a trade association or professional organization is more influential with its audience than is a publication of larger and more general circulation. Evidence on the point is supplied by Lazarsfeld's study of the presidential vote in 1940 in Erie County, Ohio:

> As a source of influence, the specialized magazine designed for a
> special-interest audience rivalled the general mass magazine. The
> latter have many times the coverage of the former but they are
> relatively less effective in changing people's minds. The special
> ized magazine already has a foot in the door, so to speak, because
> it is accepted by the reader as a reliable spokesman for some

[18] This section is based largely upon Doob: *Propaganda*, chaps. 7–11. Numerous alternative formulations are available, such as Krech and Crutchfield: *Theory and Problems of Social Psychology*, chap. 9.

cause or group in which he is greatly interested and with which he identifies himself.[19]

This advantage with which the specialized publication can approach its reader-members obviously affects more than the problem of ensuring perception, as later paragraphs will indicate.

With those on the periphery of the group the propagandist may have no special advantage, owing to the effects of their multiple memberships. Those belonging to conflicting groups may be equally receptive to opposing messages. Those belonging to alternative groups may find their time largely taken up by the demands of these, particularly if the attitudes involved are more central to their personalities. In these circumstances the propagandist's problem of securing perception is great. It is exceeded only when he is attempting to extend the limits of his public to include the indifferent or when he is trying to change its composition by winning over the hostile.

In these circumstances the skillful propagandist will use one or more of a variety of devices to assure perception of his message. In the first place, he may employ an attention-getting symbol that depends for its effectiveness upon attitudes, designated "auxiliary attitudes" in Doob's terminology, that are not necessarily related to the attitude change he wishes to achieve. The most familiar example of this device is the commercial advertiser's use of an attractive young female's portrait in his copy. Her charms catch the eye, but the attitudes they arouse do not directly influence the observer to buy from the brewing company that pays her salary. More commonly in interest group propaganda the attention-getting device not only catches the eye or ear but also arouses attitudes that are related to the ones the propagandist wishes to develop. Take, for instance, the picture of an undernourished, ragged, and dirty child used by a group that wishes to change this nation's foreign policy as it affects the country in which the child lives; or note the picture of the good, gray family doctor at the bedside of an ailing child, used by a medical society in its efforts to defeat health insurance legislation. In the second place, the propagandist dealing with a complicated or subtle matter may simplify it in a few phrases or a slogan, so that a layman will grasp the point and feel that he is master of the subject. This technique commonly occurs in group propaganda concerning the complex fields of public finance and government regulation of industry. The subtleties of both these

[19] Lazarsfeld *et al.*: *The People's Choice*, pp. 135–6. Copyright 1948 by and used with the permission of Columbia University Press.

fields were dramatically simplified in the slogan "What Helps Business Helps You," widely used by the Chamber of Commerce and other groups in the 1930's. Similar complexities are buried by the leftist slogan "Production for Use and Not for Profit." In the third place, the propagandist usually will repeat his message in different media and at different times so that as many people as possible will see or hear (perceive) it.

Such techniques will maximize the possibility of ensuring perception, but they are by no means infallible. Particularly in dealing with those whose existing attitudes are hostile, the propagandist is likely to find that his message is neither seen nor heard. For example, in their 1940 voting study Lazarsfeld and his associates found that even those who had not decided how to cast their ballots but whose social characteristics indicated a predisposition toward one party or the other exposed themselves predominantly to material consistent with those predispositions. "Voters somehow contrive to select out of the passing stream of stimuli those by which they are more inclined to be persuaded. So it is that the more they read and listen, the more convinced they become of the rightness of their own position." [20]

If the problem of perception suggests that even the most skillful propaganda is neither infallible nor omnipotent, this impression is reinforced when one examines the second stage of the propaganda process. In this phase the propagandist's symbols, if they are successful, arouse in the audience pre-existing attitudes that are related favorably to the aim of the campaign. Lest this point seem to be too obvious to mention, it should be observed that probably more propaganda efforts of all kinds fail at this point than at either of the other stages. For the propagandist must deal with people as they are. In John Locke's words: "Whatever flatterers may talk to amuse people's understanding, it never hinders men from feeling." [21] They are not blank pages on which he can write as he will, but rather organisms that have already acquired attitudes, that are disposed to act in certain ways as a result primarily of what they have experienced and learned. Perceiving the propagandist's message, they will see it in relation to those pre-existing attitudes that are aroused by it. What the resulting attitude will be depends in large part upon what kind of predispositions are activated.[22]

[20] Lazarsfeld *et al.*: *The People's Choice*, p. 82. Copyright 1948 by and used with the permission of Columbia University Press.

[21] John Locke: *Of Civil Government*, chap. 7, par. 94.

[22] Cf. Marie Jahoda and Eunice Cooper: "Evasion of Propaganda: How Prejudiced People Respond to Anti-Prejudice Propaganda," *Journal of Psychology*, Vol. 23, no. 1 (January, 1947), pp. 15–25.

The unskilled amateur and the zealot are likely to fail at this point because they are ignorant of the kinds of attitudes that their wishful symbols will arouse. They assume that most of their audience will react as they themselves would, that pre-existing attitudes of their audience are essentially identical with their own. What Linebarger says of war propaganda is applicable to all types: "The propagandist must tell the enemy those things which the enemy will heed; he must keep his private emotionalism out of the operation."[23] Nowhere is this point better illustrated than in Lasswell's study of Communist propaganda in Chicago in the 1930's. This propaganda was skillful in a limited tactical sense, but its uncongenial symbols were so rigidly adhered to as to arouse, not hatred of the existing system, but attitudes supporting American patriotism and individualism, which not only weakened the revolutionary movement but also strengthened the existing structure by providing a target for the release of hostilities.[24]

One does not have to look exclusively to war or revolutionary propaganda to find instances of the faulty assumptions of propagandists and their consequent failures to arouse appropriate related attitudes. The Republican campaign of 1936 involved the most lavish outpouring of propaganda recorded of any presidential campaign up to that time.[25] In addition numerous business groups put out a large volume of material implicitly aimed at discrediting the Administration. That these efforts had not sufficiently reckoned with the prevailing attitudes in the country is indicated by a particularly candid comment on the election by two advertising men: "Had business successfully sold its philosophy, therefore, an incidental result would have been, at the least, the reduction of Roosevelt's margin of victory. Almost everyone concerned in the public relations movement sensed this. . . ."[26] If the "philosophy" was not "sold," it was because the propaganda had not successfully activated attitudes favorable to its aim.

The great strength of the Anti-Saloon League in its heyday, as Odegard has indicated, was its ability to utilize a wide range of existing attitudes so closely related to its objective that it needed only to arouse them to be effective. Concentrating its efforts upon the saloon, which few were disposed to defend as such, rather than upon the con-

[23] Linebarger: *Psychological Warfare*, p. 27.

[24] Lasswell and Blumenstock: *World Revolutionary Propaganda*, pp. 247–358.

[25] See Ralph D. Casey: "Republican Propaganda in the 1936 Campaign," *Public Opinion Quarterly*, Vol. 1, no. 2 (April, 1937), pp. 27–44.

[26] S. H. Walker and P. Sklar: "Business Finds Its Voice," *Harper's Magazine* (March, 1938), p. 428.

sumption of liquor in general, the league was able to call up in its audience attitudes toward sin, suffering, and corruption that could be related appropriately to attitudes toward saloons and the liquor trade. The saloon was presented as a means of corrupting children, as a cause of broken homes, and as the headquarters for crime, vice, and crooked politics. Its abolition would be in keeping, therefore, with a variety of widespread attitudes, even among those who would not support a compulsory policy of total abstinence.[27]

The most obvious way of dealing with pre-existing attitudes, of course, is to alter the message so that it will arouse those appropriate to the aim being pursued. Although this fact is apparent, the significance of such alteration is easily overlooked. Changing the message to meet the character of existing attitudes may mean the modification as well of the aim that the propagandist originally held. When the Reciprocal Trade Agreements Act was first before the Congress in 1934, opposition to the legislation was largely open and direct, that is, it objected to tariff reduction. When the act was up for renewal in 1937, however, its opponents apparently confronted a different pattern of attitudes. The program, however minor its actual achievements, had been widely accepted. The tacit assumptions in favor of protection that had threatened the proposal in 1934 and that had formed the background of previous tariff increases,[28] had been changed. Opposition appeals in 1937 and subsequent years, therefore, less frequently condemned tariff reduction directly and more often objected to the procedures by which reductions were achieved. Representative of this position in 1937 was the stand of the National Grange, whose spokesman expressed himself as in favor of the general objectives of the program, but as wanting Senate ratification of each agreement as a treaty under the Constitution.[29] Presumably unable or unlikely to get the desired response through symbols openly advocating tariff protection, these groups instead attempted to utilize attitudes concerning unconstitutional methods and executive aggrandizement. Adoption of the requirement for Senate ratification would have weakened the movement for tariff reduction, albeit less effectively than outright repeal of the trade agreement legislation. The signifi-

[27] Odegard: *Pressure Politics*, p. 38. For a full discussion of the symbols used by the Anti-Saloon League, see pp. 40–72.

[28] Cf. Schattschneider: *Politics, Pressures and the Tariff*, pp. 141 ff.

[29] U. S. Senate, Committee on Finance: *Hearings on H. J. Res. 96*, 75th Cong., 1st Sess. (1937), pp. 483 ff. This illustration is obviously oversimplified, since it leaves out of account such variables as the make-up of the congressional committees and the increased prestige of Secretary of State Hull, champion of the trade agreements program.

cance of the altered tactics is itself considerable, however. By conceding, in effect, that the issue was how to effect trade agreements rather than whether to lower protective duties, opponents of these agreements found themselves obliged to discuss their position in terms of its possible effects on an accepted public policy. The propaganda aim had become the restriction of an established program rather than its elimination, and this change had come about at least in part because of the changed attitude pattern faced by the proponents of tariff protection.

As the above example suggests, the propagandist will often find it appropriate to use symbols that will arouse attitudes associated with the "rules of the game," as they were designated in Chapter 6. If marshalled on his side, these rules are highly useful to him, for they are widely accepted in the community, they are comparatively stable, and many individuals attach great importance to them. The ambiguity that stems from their being "general" rules and that permits their evocation in connection with numerous contradictory situations increases their advantages.

Illustrations of these advantages can be seen in the propaganda of the American Medical Association against compulsory Federal health insurance. It depended in part upon the assumptions, probably valid, that many Americans are opposed to widespread socialization of the economy, fear proposals that are regarded as "alien," disapprove of excessive government expenditures, dislike invasions of their privacy, and expect doctors to be motivated by the highest humanitarian ideals. These attitudes were aimed at by appeals such as the following: that the proposed measure is "socialization;" that if medicine is "socialized," other phases of American life will follow ("If the doctors lose their freedom today—if their patients are regimented tomorrow who will be next? YOU WILL BE NEXT!"); that health insurance had its start in Germany, where all occupations were socialized, and has spread to England, which is following the same path; that "socialization" in Germany led to the atrocities that Nazi doctors committed against the occupants of concentration camps; that the program would require the addition of over a million employees to the government payroll who would "siphon off medical funds;" and that the establishment of local administrative boards would destroy personal privacy in medical matters ("Under this system your health record becomes a public record—and privacy goes out the window.").[30] The

---

[30] Quotations are from a pamphlet entitled "The Voluntary Way is the American Way," issued by the American Medical Association, National Education Campaign (Chicago, 1949).

health insurance scheme thus was presented as alien and immoral, the appeals utilizing attitudes not confined to health and medical matters, but likely for other reasons to be "central" in the personalities of many in the public.

An instance of the same sort is an advertisement sponsored by a group of private power companies and published in a number of national magazines in the fall of 1949. Perception is facilitated by a half-page photograph capitalizing on the current interest in football and showing a referee carrying a football against a group of players, the referee being aided by the field judge, who is improperly blocking a possible tackler. The text reads in part:

> What goes on here?
> Referee makes first down—or did he really just miss it? Field judge blocks out the nearest tackler—or was it clipping? If the officials call 'em—and play too—what kind of game is that?
> You wouldn't stand for that sort of thing on a football field—but it happens every day in the electric light and power business. Government not only regulates the electric power companies—but is in competition with them at the same time.

This advertisement is an example of how a highly complicated subject can be simplified to give the layman all he needs to know to feel initiated. And its central appeal is almost literally to the "rules of the game," a generalized attitude favoring fair play.

In a good many situations the interest group propagandist can count on arousing without much difficulty attitudes favorable to his aim. These may be both continuing attitudes supporting the "rules of the game" and ones of a less fundamental sort that are currently dominant because of some immediate situation. This kind of situation can be illustrated by the full-page newspaper advertisements that appeared following the announcement in September, 1949, of a government antitrust suit against the A & P grocery chain. This was a civil suit instituted in consequence of a successful criminal antitrust prosecution begun seven years earlier. The advertisements appealed to a continuing sense of fair play by indicating that the suit was simply a penalty upon initiative and efficiency. (It is significant that the prosecution was not described as the United States Department of Justice or the Attorney General of the United States acting under the direction of the President of the United States, but as "the antitrust lawyers from Washington.") With relatively high current food costs a matter of concern to many citizens, moreover, the suit could be presented as certain, if successful, to result in an increase in prices.

Such favorable circumstances are by no means always present, however. As a result of experiences widely spread through a public, of events beyond the control of an interest group, or of opposing propaganda, unfavorable attitudes may be more easily activated. Under such circumstances announcement of the identity or aim of the interest group is likely to produce results contrary to those sought for. Consequently, the alert propagandist will conceal his identity or his aims or both. This concealment may continue indefinitely if conditions seem to require it. Thus Odegard reports that because of the bad reputation of the alcoholic beverage industry, partly earned and partly the product of temperance propaganda, the United States Brewers Association in its struggle against the extension of prohibition set up fake organizations over whose impressive names its messages were carried.[31] The Farmers' States Rights League of the 1920's, which purported to express Southern farmers' views on the proposed child labor amendment to the Constitution, was in fact an association of cotton textile manufacturers in the South. Revelation of their identity would have weakened the acceptability of their propaganda.[32] Much of the propaganda of the National Electric Light Association in the 1920's was of this character. Particularly their efforts in the schools and colleges on behalf of privately owned utilities, such as subsidizing and influencing the content of textbooks, would have failed at once if the association's part had been openly acknowledged.[33]

Concealment of aim or identity or both often may be continued, on the other hand, only until the propagandist has been able, or thinks he has been able, to create related attitudes that are favorable to his group and its aims. Or the propagandist may have no very definite aim in mind for some time. He may be interested immediately in developing attitudes of a favorable sort that he can utilize at some future date when one of a number of eventualities occurs. Such is

[31] Odegard: *Pressure Politics*, chap 9.

[32] Discussed in Herring: *Group Representation Before Congress*, pp. 27–8. This type of organization should not be confused with the fake or "paper" groups whose only function is to provide a living for their employees and whose following, aside from the contributors who are their victims, is nonexistent. Examples of these can be found on pp. 25–7; also see Crawford: *The Pressure Boys*, chaps. 4 and 10.

[33] See Ernest Gruening: *The Public Pays: A Study of Power Propaganda* (New York: The Vanguard Press, 1931); Jack Levin: *Power Ethics: An Analysis of the Activities of the Public Power Utilities in the United States, Based on a Study of the U. S. Federal Trade Commission Records* (New York: Alfred A. Knopf, Inc., 1931); U. S. Federal Trade Commission: *Utility Corporations*, Senate Document 92, 70th Cong., 1st Sess. (1927). The summary report of this investigation is in part 71–A.

the principal function of what is known as "institutional" advertising, and it is a primary concern of the professional public relations man. Much of the propaganda of the National Electric Light Association, especially that made through the schools, was of this long-range sort. Attitudes favorable to the private ownership of electric power facilities were to be developed in children so that proposals for extended regulation or public ownership would at some later date fall on deaf or hostile ears. Since the American Telephone and Telegraph Company is a public utility subject to government regulation and, therefore, necessarily involved in the political process, it engages with its subsidiaries in a considerable volume of such anticipatory advertising. It is less interested in selling telephone subscriptions than in convincing its public of its excellent management, effective service, and moderate charges. The bland or indulgent attitudes fostered by such advertising are expected to be useful at a future date in rate controversies, labor disputes, and struggles against the threat of public ownership.[34]

An almost classic case of the temporary concealment of aim and identity, of the skillful use of related attitudes, and of other aspects of successful group propaganda, is the battle over the California chain-store tax in 1935–6.[35] In 1935 the California legislature approved a license tax on retail stores, steeply graduated according to the number of stores owned. The tax was consequently a serious threat to the large regional and national chains. The proposed legislation was to be passed upon by popular referendum, but not until a year later, and the availability of this period of time determined the chains to attempt to defeat it. They retained the services of a public relations firm, which immediately set out to find out the nature and extent of the attitudes with which they had to deal. An opinion survey indicated that 60 per cent of the voters favored the tax. A study of the newspapers showed that only fifteen per cent of the press stories on the subject were favorable to the chains. Special interviews with segments of the chains' public—employees, landlords, suppliers, bankers, and customers—revealed various kinds of hostile attitudes. In particular they found that farmers, fruit growers, and the farmers' co-operatives distrusted the chains. These were politically important elements in the State.

Under these circumstances it was obvious that an immediate large-

[34] See N. R. Danielian: *A.T. & T.: The Story of Industrial Conquest* (New York: The Vanguard Press, 1939), chaps. 12–14. For a somewhat similar case, see Thomas S. Green, Jr.: "Mr. Cameron and the Ford Hour," *Public Opinion Quarterly*, Vol. 3, no. 3 (Fall, 1939), pp. 669–75.

[35] Summarized in Walker and Sklar: "Business Finds Its Voice," pp. 428–40.

scale campaign against the tax, openly sponsored by the chains, would have little value. Before that could be attempted, the existing pattern of attitudes would have to be altered, preferably by means not easily identifiable with the aims of the propaganda. Almost at once, therefore, the chains quietly let it be known, without mentioning the tax, that their employees' wages and working conditions were to be improved. An offer was made to close the stores on Sundays if the independent stores would follow suit. (Both of these offers are good examples of how to vary propaganda to fit the attitudes and preoccupations of different segments of a public.)

The key opportunity to engage in temporarily concealed propaganda came with a huge peach surplus in the winter of 1935–6, which threatened large losses to growers, since the canners could not possibly absorb more than a fraction of the crop. The growers formed an association, as might have been expected in the circumstances, the California Peach Stabilization Committee. This group, apparently on its own initiative, appealed to the chains for help. The publicity from this growers' committee dramatized the seriousness of the crisis, so that it was widely known before the activities of the chains were revealed. The stores put on a series of weekly drives that resulted in eliminating the surplus with a profit for all concerned. Aside from these drives, the publicity on the problem was issued entirely by the growers. None of it mentioned the coming referendum.

At the end of ten months an opinion survey indicated that the distribution of voters' attitudes had almost completely changed. Press stories, moreover, by this time were favorable to the chains in 79 per cent of the cases. At this point, therefore, the direct attack on the proposed tax, minor during the preceding ten months, became open and full-scale. The main slogan, distributed by every conceivable means, used the referendum proposition's ballot number: "22 is a Tax on You. Vote no." At the time of the legislature's action this appeal would have been futile; now it could be counted upon to be perceived and generally in favorable terms. At the elections in November, 1936, the referendum proposal was defeated in fifty-seven of the fifty-eight California counties. Without giving the propaganda effort full credit for the outcome, one can agree that propaganda skill must have been of importance.

The purpose of stimulating appropriate related attitudes is to produce new or modified attitudes that in the third stage will lead to the action (or inaction) desired by the propagandist. As in the other stages, no propaganda is at this point completely invulnerable. Because individuals inevitably differ from one another, the successful stimulation of related attitudes may in one person produce the desired new tendency to act but in another may produce an attitude almost irrelevant to the propagandist's object. Even when the appropriate new attitude is produced, it may not be strong or stable enough to result in action. Or the new attitude may be inconsistent with another of equal strength, and the individual will "lose interest" in the disputed area and take no action in order to avoid pain stemming from conscious inability to make a choice. This withdrawal has been observed in the Catholic members of a Communist-led labor union on questions of American-Soviet relations.[36] It has also appeared in the behavior of voters who "lost interest" and failed to vote when they were unable to reconcile conflicting influences in their environment.[37]

This "sphere of unpredictability," to use Doob's term, is seriously affected by the passage of time. Excepting perhaps the situation in which a mob is being urged to attack, there is inevitably some lag between the formation of a new attitude and the time at which action is desired. In this period the new attitude, if it is not sufficiently strong or central to the individual's preoccupations, may simply deteriorate. Or events and experiences in the interim period may weaken or destroy it. These may be events in the usual sense, such as the solution of the peach-surplus crisis in the California tax case described above. Or they may be the propaganda of some competing group.

For the propagandist of a political interest group timing is peculiarly important in the third stage of the propaganda process. Unlike the propagandist on the home front in time of war, he is not engaged primarily in bolstering already existing attitudes. Such reinforcement is rather the task he undertakes in "internal" propaganda to his "members." In "external" propaganda he is dealing with the potential sympathizers, the neutrals, and the hostile elements in his public. With the hard core of his members he may concentrate on reinforcing existing favorable attitudes, relying on the latter to handicap if not prevent the perception of competing messages. With the others he may see his efforts nullified by an unforeseen event or by an opponent's propaganda. These others are by definition more or at least equally susceptible to opposition messages, as the earlier discussion of perception has indicated.

For example, look at the task of an interest group attempting to promote Federal legislation requiring that grants-in-aid for education be so utilized by the States as to assure equal facilities for children of

[36] Martin Kriesberg: "Cross-Pressures and Attitudes," *Public Opinion Quarterly*, Vol. 13, no. 1 (Spring, 1949), p. 9.
[37] Lazarsfeld *et al.*: *The People's Choice*, pp. 45–9, 56–64, 67–9.

all races. The group will probably ignore the clearly hostile elements in the public and concentrate on the supposed neutrals. It must do at least this much, since it is already in a handicapped position in that its aim is to make a change in an existing set of arrangements. It can work on various humanitarian attitudes, can attempt to demonstrate the consequences of inadequate Negro education in the South for the Northern cities to which Negroes are migrating, and so on. The matter is a difficult one on which to get widespread support in the North, both because it is not a central concern of most citizens there and because of moderately latent anti-Negro prejudice in that section. Suppose, however, that the proponents have been able to make some headway along the lines indicated and are asking people to write their congressmen urging support of the bill. At this point the opponents can weaken this newly-won support, not by a direct appeal to prejudice, but by a more acceptable appeal relying indirectly on the prejudice. Thus, they can argue that education is a local matter concerning which the Federal Government should not dictate or, in effect, that this is a problem that need not concern people outside the South. By introducing an acceptable rationalization for inaction at the crucial point, they can take advantage of the inherent instability of the new attitude and confine support of the proposal to the limited ranks of confirmed "members." [38]

For obvious reasons the third stage of the propaganda process is particularly hazardous in long-range campaigns where revelation of the aim of the propaganda must be delayed or must remain implicit. Take a corporation that desires the defeat of an incumbent president of the United States. Although it may use a number of means to its objective, its own advertising cannot openly advocate the election of an opponent. Federal law forbids any corporation to make "a contribution in connection with any election at which presidential and vice-presidential electors . . . are to be voted for. . . ." A corporation's own advertising, therefore, cannot do more than imply its position by opposing particular policies or types of policies. In this respect its own propaganda is handicapped in comparison with those groups that may take a position on policy and follow up with a direct appeal to vote for a particular candidate.

Where the aim of the propaganda cannot be made explicit until some future date, the likelihood that desired action will not be taken is probably roughly proportionate to the length of the period of concealment. Even if appropriate attitudes are developed, the variety of

---

[38] See Kesselman: *The Social Politics of FEPC*, esp. chaps. 11 and 12, for data suggestive of this sort of pattern.

unforeseeable events is likely to be such that the results of a long-range campaign of this sort are completely unpredictable. For example, the concealed propaganda efforts of the National Electric Light Association (now the Edison Electric Institute) to prevent further public ownership and regulation of electric power facilities were not outstandingly successful when their sponsors most needed them. These efforts may have had some effect for nearly a decade during the 1920's in reinforcing existing attitudes hostile to socialization in general and in developing attitudes favoring private ownership of utilities on the grounds of efficient management. But these attitudes were seriously weakened by the combined effect of three almost simultaneous unanticipated events. The first was the Federal Trade Commission investigation of utility corporations that in 1928 and 1929 revealed the details of this propaganda and over the next six years followed with reports on other practices of the utilities. The second was the stock market crash of 1929, which in peculiarly dramatic form invited disclosure of the inflated character of many holding company structures and the dubious practices of those who controlled them to the disadvantage of investors not "in the know." Finally, the depression and widespread unemployment of the 1930's greatly reduced, at least for the time being, the proportion of the non-investor population opposed to further government activity in the utilities field. Here was precisely the kind of situation with which the private ownership propaganda was presumably designed to deal. Possibly the propaganda may have contributed to restricting the area of increased government intervention. It was unable, however, following these events to produce widespread opposition to the marked strengthening of Federal regulatory powers or to the extension of public ownership of generating and distributing facilities in the decade after 1930.[39]

The propagandist has a number of means for dealing with the hazards of the third stage of the propaganda process, none of which is infallible. Thus to avoid deterioration of the new attitude that he has, or presumes he has, developed, he may attempt to reinforce it by frequent repetition. Where he has indeed succeeded in creating the attitude he desires, repetition may be effective, other things remaining the same. But other things often perversely change, and if the experiences of a public are inconsistent with a newly learned attitude, no amount of repetition of a propaganda message will prevent its deterioration. To use an obvious example, although slogans depicting

[39] Cf. Fainsod and Gordon: *Government and the American Economy*, chap. 10.

Herbert Hoover as the "Great Engineer" and the "Great Humanitarian" could be repeated in 1928 to reinforce attitudes favorable to the Republican presidential candidate, after the events of 1929 through 1932 not only could they not be repeated with effect, but in fact they became a weapon for the opposition. The unqualified power of repetition in propaganda was asserted by the late Adolf Hitler early in his political career;[40] its most vigorous champions, however, are in the ranks of the commercial advertisers. They defend it, though not without reservations, for very good reasons. For instance, in a society that engages in a sort of ritualistic tooth brushing, people are disposed to buy a dentifrice of some kind. That attitude is well established; it will survive wars and depressions. Capturing and holding a body of consumers for a particular brand is, therefore, likely to depend in part on the frequency with which the brand-name is seen and heard. Hence the need for repetition. Political propaganda of all sorts, however, is more complicated. Attitudes associated with a particular "brand" of politics are often highly unstable because they are conceived of as producing highly differentiated results. The political message, in a sense, means more, is seen as having more important consequences. The political propagandist is the slave of events, and in his equipment repetition is of secondary value.

A second device the propagandist can use to protect the attitudes he has encouraged is that of counterpropaganda, that is, an effort to break down attitudes potentially or actually in conflict with the ones he desires, especially those fostered by his competitors. The value of this technique, as of many others, depends upon timing. If the propagandist attacks the efforts of an opponent too early, he may simply facilitate the spread of the opposing message. He not only commits himself to fighting on his opponent's grounds, but he gives the opposition more prominence than they might win for themselves. If he waits too long, however, he may find himself confronted with attitudes sufficiently firmly held so that counterpropaganda will do more harm than good. For people treat certain of their attitudes and stereotypes as part of themselves, and an attack on such dispositions is reacted to as an attack on their persons. It is only while a matter is still debatable for a considerable proportion of the public that counterpropaganda can be utilized to good effect. Thus it is reasonable, while the project is still controversial, for the National St. Lawrence Project Conference to denounce the current support for the St. Lawrence seaway and power project as stemming from the efforts of a

[40] Adolf Hitler: *Mein Kampf* (New York: Reynal and Hitchcock, 1939), pp. 238 ff.

"small and relatively unimportant group of steel interests" to prevail upon the Government "to protect their investments in the Labrador-Quebec iron ore fields." [41] It would be unwise, on the other hand, for a group opposing the extension of governmental welfare activities to attack, or appear to attack, those segments of existing services that are already widely accepted, such as unemployment insurance. When the National Association of Manufacturers a few years ago viewed with alarm the danger to a balanced Federal budget from grants-in-aid to the States, it aimed its attacks primarily upon proposed programs. Its spokesman specifically stated that the association was not opposed to such "long-established" programs as those involving agricultural experiment stations, highways, the National Guard, and the land-grant colleges. Open attacks on the latter would have increased the strength of the groups opposing the N.A.M.'s position. [42]

Counterpropaganda is a poor substitute for a strong positive appeal. By aiming his message at as many common and dominant attitudes as possible, the propagandist may best avoid the danger that the resulting attitude will deteriorate or change before appropriate action occurs. Therefore, if his message contains as many elements of prestige as possible, he will render his audience more susceptible of the action he desires. For prestige is the power of some objects and persons to be disproportionately influential with most people in a given setting. As Doob has pointed out, the propagandist is somewhat akin to the hypnotist in that the latter's success is partially a function of his prestige for his subject. [43] The propagandist to the home front in time of war can often gain acceptance for the most unlikely stories because he is in command of some of the most powerful prestige symbols in the society, those of the nation and, usually, of the church. [44]

The interest-group propagandist is usually not in so enviable a position. He will, nevertheless, make every effort to include dominant prestige symbols in his message. The commercial advertising during World War II was full of messages depicting the contributions of various groups to the national effort. The pages of any current magazine will contain announcements that the latest gadget is an achievement of "science," and everything from patent medicines to perfumed

[41] The *New York Herald Tribune,* March 7, 1949.
[42] The *New York Times,* May 21, 1947.
[43] Doob: *Propaganda,* pp. 132–3.
[44] Cf. Harold D. Lasswell: *Propaganda Technique in the World War* (New York: Alfred A. Knopf, Inc., 1927), esp. chap. 4; James R. Mock and Cedric Larson: *Words That Won the War: The Story of the Committee on Public Information, 1917–1919* (Princeton, N.J.: Princeton University Press, 1939).

mouth wash and condensed milk is "prescribed" in the advertisements by men in white with clinical mirrors strapped to their heads. In matters that are more strictly political, most groups attempt to use the prestige of their distinguished members. Staff assistants may prepare the statements that are heard before congressional committees, but, in order that such speeches may be carried in the press and with the maximum effect, they are frequently read by men of distinction among the officers and members.[45] The American Medical Association's alternative to compulsory health insurance is presented as "the American Way." When the National Association of Manufacturers and other trade associations opposed the renewal of price-control legislation in 1946, they made elaborate efforts to present themselves as speaking for "small business," a symbol that has more prestige than, or avoids the negative prestige of, "big business." [46] It was his prestige as a former President of the United States that was in part the reason for inviting Grover Cleveland to become the first manager and general counsel of the Association of Life Insurance Presidents in 1906. The life insurance companies' efforts to influence legislation had recently been severely criticized by a committee of the New York legislature, and the association needed all the prestige it could acquire if it was to be successful.[47]

Prestige attaches not only to persons, objects, and institutions, but also to majorities. In most political situations, what "everybody" is doing or thinking not only can't be wrong but also has a presumptive claim to being right. The tendency to submit or conform to behavior that gives what Doob calls an "impression of universality" is utilized by the group propagandist wherever possible. The Anti-Saloon League's campaign for congressional passage of a prohibition amendment included a strong drive for new dry territory in the States, which would suggest an overwhelming wave of prohibition sentiment, and maps showing territory (but not necessarily densely populated territory) that had adopted such legislation had an important place in the propaganda.[48] Schattschneider has remarked upon the "peculiar charm" that the phrase "90 per cent" had for group witnesses in the tariff revision of 1929. Some claimed to speak for larger segments of

[45] Cf. Herring: *Group Representation Before Congress*, pp. 92–3.
[46] See U.S. Senate, Committee on Banking and Currency: *Hearings on Extension of Price Control and Stabilization Acts*, 79th Cong., 2d Sess. (1946), pp. 392 ff.
[47] See U.S. Temporary National Economic Committee: *Hearings*, Part 10, 76th Cong., 1st Sess. (1939), pp. 4346 ff.
[48] Odegard: *Pressure Politics*, pp. 56 and 156.

their alleged constituencies, and most stated that these segments were unanimous in their views, but the most frequent assertion was that the spokesman represented "ninety per cent" of an industry's firms, or of its output, or of its capacity.[49] Presumably that base was selected that would most easily produce the magic figure. The American Legion's propaganda has usually made much of the size of its membership, giving the impression that its leaders speak for a unified membership inclusive of most veterans.[50] The American Medical Association faced a loss of prestige from the publicized resistance of some of its members to its assessment for the 1949 campaign against compulsory health insurance. To minimize this loss, as noted in Chapter 6, the association released an estimate that 85 per cent of its membership would pay the assessment of twenty-five dollars.[51] The impression of universality this statement was supposed to create would presumably both induce some of the doubting doctors to pay up and persuade some portions of the public that the A.M.A. was speaking for almost all doctors. These and hundreds of other examples are tributes to the power of the band wagon.

To maximize the prestige elements in his message as well as reduce the likelihood that competing symbols will be perceived by his audience, the propagandist may make use of censorship and related devices. Censorship is the withholding of certain elements in a situation either by the propagandist or by someone under his influence who can control a medium of communication. It "leaves out" the disadvantageous symbols in order to avoid the danger of propaganda failure if the full evidence is revealed. A related device is distortion, that is, the shifting of relative emphasis among elements of a "full" account. Of the same type is fabrication, either by the invention of a situation or by the embellishment of a "real" one with convenient but fanciful additions. These are common techniques, though by no means as common as they are thought to be by those who define propaganda in such terms. The sponsor's aims and identity are fairly often concealed, as previous examples have suggested, and the omission or distortion of the "facts" in a situation is frequent. In commercial advertising, of course, this technique is common enough to call for a good many pages in the regular reports of the Federal Trade Commission.

Censorship and related techniques, however, will fail unless they

[49] Schattschneider: *Politics, Pressures and the Tariff*, pp. 243 ff.
[50] Duffield: *King Legion*, p. 299.
[51] The *New York Herald Tribune*, February 19, 1949. Cf. Harold B. Clemenko: "What is the A.M.A.?" *Look*, October 11, 1949, pp. 27–32.

provide what Lippmann has called a "barrier between the public and the event." If independent access to evidence concerning a controversial situation is available, either through competing communications or through direct experience, it is futile to attempt censorship and risky to distort or fabricate. Even in time of war censorship is a limited weapon. The Japanese Government in World War II followed a consistent practice of suppressing full news of their losses. Even after the devastating air raids on Japanese homeland cities, the authorities minimized damage and fabricated accounts of American losses. But the Japanese civilians were experiencing these raids, either directly or through the accounts of evacuees, and they could observe flights of American planes coming over and returning virtually intact. By the end of the war, consequently, at least half the civilian population no longer believed the official accounts of the raids. As would be expected, moreover, rumors, often highly exaggerated, took the place of accurate official communications.[52]

Interest groups rarely are able to prevent independent access to information about events of any widespread significance. The National Electric Light Association in the 1920's apparently tried to influence or control every conceivable channel for the flow of information, but with limited and temporary success.[53] Less extensive efforts appear from time to time. John Gunther reported that the only group that openly attempted to influence him in preparing his book on the United States was an electric power company.[54] Attempts at censorship are common, but they are of limited value in a setting of competing propagandas and contradicting experience.

Whatever the devices used, propaganda as a form of communication must be made available as efficiently as possible to the public in whom the propagandist is interested. He must, therefore, select those channels or media with which his intended audience is most likely to come in contact. Within those media he must choose those channels that can be expected to reach various segments of his public. An exhaustive treatment of the media cannot be undertaken here, for it would require at least a volume by itself. The subject is one of increasing concern to social scientists and others, and the literature in

[52] U.S. Strategic Bombing Survey: *The Effects of Strategic Bombing on Japanese Morale* (Washington, D.C.: Government Printing Office, 1947), chap. 10, esp. p. 125.
[53] Carl D. Thompson: *Confessions of the Power Trust* (New York: E. P. Dutton Company, 1932), p. 330.
[54] John Gunther: *Inside U.S.A.* (New York: Harper and Brothers, 1947), p. 746.

the field is rapidly growing.[55] Two observations are of particular importance here, however. First, the media and particular channels within them differ significantly from one another. Book readers differ in number and in more important characteristics from those who read only newspapers. As noted earlier, the specialized periodical is more effective than the magazine of general mass circulation. Those media that most closely approach direct personal contact between propagandist and audience are likely to be most effective.[56] These and other generalizations emerging from research mean that the success of the interest group propagandist depends in no small measure on his skill in selecting the appropriate media and channels for his efforts at communication. Second, although the volume of modern propaganda is largely a result of the revolution in means of mass communication, the mass media are not the only, or necessarily the primary, ones used by political interest groups. In addition to the daily and periodical press, books, radio, and the motion picture, there are a number of supplementary or alternative media available. The educational system of the country is obviously one of these. Its importance is indicated in part by vigorous, periodic efforts to keep various types of controversial material out of the schools.[57] Churches, in addition to being interest groups themselves, may be of great value as channels of propaganda. One of the great assets of the Anti-Saloon League in its heyday was its access to the pulpits of many Protestant churches, through which it could solicit members and contributions and even campaign in favor of candidates it supported in elections.[58] The public library may also serve as a supplementary channel.[59]

Various portions of the mechanisms of government may serve as supplementary media. For example, the party platform and a candidate's speeches may function as channels for propaganda and also as means of getting attention in the mass media. The public hearings of legislative committees, whatever their formal justification, perform somewhat the same functions and have the advantage of permitting groups to play their parts directly rather than through intermediaries.

---

[55] See, for example, the titles in Smith, Lasswell, and Casey: *Propaganda, Communication, and Public Opinion*, pp. 255–350, 361–5.

[56] Berelson: "Communications and Public Opinion," in Schramm (ed.): *Communications in Modern Society*, pp. 172–6.

[57] See Bruce Raup: *Education and Organized Interests in America* (New York: G. P. Putnam's Sons, 1936).

[58] Odegard: *Pressure Politics*, pp. 94, 190–4.

[59] See the publications of the Social Science Research Council's Public Library Inquiry, especially the summary volume, Robert D. Leigh: *The Public Library in the United States* (New York: Columbia University Press, 1950).

The variety of less obvious, though scarcely minor, channels of communication is considerable. Group "members" may be highly useful as means of communication, especially since the personal quality of dissemination by word of mouth gives them greater effectiveness than media such as the press. Petitions with long lists of signatures are vastly overrated as means of influencing directly the decisions of public officials. Their value is far greater as a means of getting propaganda to signers and potential signers. Since they involve active roles for both circulator and potential signer, there is greater likelihood than in more passive situations that their messages will be learned.[60] The initiation of rumors, which in some situations travel faster and farther than "information" distributed via institutionalized media, may be useful, particularly for communications that for one reason or another are denied access to other channels. The study of political propaganda thus inevitably involves the examination of every means through which organized efforts at communication may take place.

Variations in Propaganda Advantage

The discussion of the tactics of propaganda has indicated some of the reasons why the process is fallible. Because propaganda is neither an independent nor an absolute weapon, circumstances give a relative advantage to some groups over others, and as these settings change, the distribution of advantage is altered or reversed. These favorable circumstances should be taken up in some detail, especially as they affect political interest groups, if the dynamics of group propaganda are to be made clear.

A propagandist of any type enjoys the maximum of advantage when his audience is confronted with events that are ambiguous, whose "meaning" is not clear. The members of a public are then not easily able to decide in what terms the events are to be "understood;" in the psychologist's words, responses to the events are not well "structured;" that is, they are not closely tied in with stable cognitive and attitudinal patterns in individual personalities. People in such circumstances are suggestible because they feel a need for "clarification;" they are receptive to an explanation that makes sense to them in terms of some of their existing attitudes and beliefs.[61] Such conditions

[60] See Gordon Allport: "The Psychology of Participation," *Psychological Review*, Vol. 53, no. 3 (May, 1945), p. 119.
[61] See Krech and Crutchfield: *Theory and Problems of Social Psychology*, pp. 346–9, 358–9.

often provide opportunities for groups otherwise at a disadvantage, since established standards of judgment no longer adequately account for experience.

One of the most humorous and at the same time dramatic illustrations of behavior in an ambiguous situation is described in Cantril's study of the "invasion from Mars" of March 30, 1938. On that evening one of the radio networks presented a dramatic version of H. G. Wells' *War of the Worlds*. An apparently standard musical program was interrupted by news of the landing in New Jersey of a Martian rocket ship whose unlovely occupants were rapidly and inexorably spreading death and destruction throughout the area in which they were moving. The "news" broadcast included comments and appeals from fictitious scientists and public officials, plus all the other trappings of radio coverage of a significant news event. The result was a panic among many listeners, especially those who tuned in too late to hear the introduction to the program. "Long before the broadcast had ended, people all over the United States were praying, crying, fleeing frantically to escape death from the Martians. . . . At least a million of them were frightened or disturbed." [62] People behaved in such hysterical fashion because they believed the "news;" many listeners believed the report because the situation was temporarily unstructured and would have been "meaningless" otherwise. Having, under these circumstances, no standard of judgment that would demonstrate that the broadcast was only a play, they were amenable to the suggestion in the account itself that the invasion was a fact. Lending plausibility to such reactions were: the realism of the drama, which named places and even streets with which the victims were familiar; the fact that entertainment programs had recently been interrupted rather frequently for news of the Munich crisis; the authority of the "scientists" and "public officials" who confirmed the disaster.

The revolutionary propagandist lives for the situation in which lack of structure or "meaning" has reached its virtual ultimate. A series of disastrous military defeats, the collapse of an economic system, and similar events occurring singly, serially, or in combination profoundly affect the lives of most of a population. They require explanation; there is a need to "understand" in some satisfactory fashion. But the disasters have undermined the prestige of the usual sources of authoritative explanation, such as the government, the church, and the leaders of the economy. Many people are thus

[62] Hadley Cantril: *The Invasion from Mars* (Princeton, N.J.: Princeton University Press, 1940), p. 47.

open to the suggestions of revolutionary propagandas that "clarify" the situation and identify those "responsible" for it.[63] Such circumstances, in which he cut his political teeth, warrant Hitler's famous observation that the masses more easily accept a big lie than a small one.[64] Only when events have subverted most familiar standards of judgment, so that they fail adequately to structure events, do such explanations assume plausibility.

The role in group politics of the unstructured situation is not confined to wars, revolutions, and Martian invasions. Many less dramatic events lack a stable "meaning" for the publics concerned with them. A sharp and extensive increase in unemployment occurs. Who is "responsible?" What shall be done? There is a rapid rise in the cost of living. Why? What will control it? A foreign government defaults on its debts to the United States. What is the "explanation?" A civil war occurs abroad that seems to alter the strategic positions of the great powers. Why did it happen? What does it mean? Who was "responsible" for America's defeat at Pearl Harbor? A major strike takes place that affects the daily lives of millions. What is the "cause?"

Such questions as these illustrate the recurring situations in which ambiguity affords an opportunity for the group propagandist. Particularly when the impact of events greatly increases the size of the public concerned with an activity, many people are included in the public whose experience gives the events no adequate structure. They are affected by the developments, know that they are, and are receptive to propagandas that give these events "meaning." They are suggestible.

The field of foreign affairs illustrates this situation well.[65] Psychologically remote and complicated, for many people, it is an area in which events may rather suddenly produce an expanded public. Stereotyped explanations of the "Wall Street" and "perfidious Albion" variety compete for ascendancy. Where these appear inadequate, more novel simplifications may be persuasive if they are adequately related to existing attitudes.

Dramatic examples of the same kind are available in the area of domestic policy. A quarter of a century before the New Deal, various individuals and small groups were calling attention to the dangerous depletion of the country's soil resources through misuse of land and

[63] Cf. Lasswell: "The Strategy of Revolutionary and War Propaganda," in Wright, editor: *Public Opinion and World Politics*, pp. 187–221.
[64] Hitler: *Mein Kampf*, p. 313.
[65] See Harold H. Sprout: "Pressure Groups and Foreign Policies," *Annals*, Vol. 179 (May, 1935), pp. 114–23; Gabriel A. Almond: *The American People and Foreign Policy* (New York: Harcourt, Brace & Company, 1950).

consequent erosion. At least as early as 1909 scientists in the Department of Agriculture were pointing to the general stake in the management of private as well as public lands. But the conservation movement of the day was largely concerned with sealing up the remaining public lands against private exploitation, not with the management of all land. The prevailing "explanations" for our large national income supported a policy of individual exploitation of land held in fee simple absolute and denied any other policies a significant hearing. They remained dominant until the disastrous dust storms of the early 1930's greatly enlarged the public concerned with land use and, together with the other economic developments of the period, cast doubt upon previous standards of judgment. For by then these standards provided an inadequate structure for the experience even of the urban resident of New Jersey, whose sky was darkened by tons of topsoil blowing from the Great Plains. New explanations could gain some hearing when, as John Gaus has put it, there developed a "catastrophic situation in which prevailing attitudes were sufficiently blasted to permit the new ideas to be applied." [66] The ambiguity inherent in a national crisis thus affords opportunity for shifts in the relative influence of groups.

Even though unstructured situations broaden the possibility of a kind of free-for-all among competing groups, they do not give all groups an equal opportunity. In nonrevolutionary circumstances, in fact, they may have only a slight effect upon what kinds of groups may reasonably bid for support. These inequalities in the opportunities open to groups, of course, depend in large part upon the structure and values of a given society. A group's position in this society affects the success of its propaganda and its ability to utilize most of the other resources of influence. As Robin Williams has observed in a penetrating essay: "There are definite possibilities and limitations as to the control which can be achieved by any given agency or group with a certain position in the social structure, with certain funds and personnel at its disposal, with particular authority and power, with defined channels of communication, and so on." [67] The position of a group in the social structure can be roughly equated with the extent to which its objectives and methods are congruent with the prevailing values of the society, and the degree of influ-

---

[66] John M. Gaus: *Reflections on Public Administration* (Tuscaloosa, Ala.: University of Alabama Press, 1947), p. 16. For a good discussion of this development, see Gaus and Wolcott: *Public Administration and the United States Department of Agriculture,* pp. 116–37.

[67] Williams: *The Reduction of Intergroup Tensions,* p. 11.

ence that it can exercise through propaganda depends, as we have seen, upon its ability to utilize and to associate itself with these prevailing attitudes. Groups that enjoy high status in the society can best succeed in thus invoking for their purposes the values and attitudes that are held by most of the population. They carry the prestige that goes with such status.

The structure of American society could not be set forth here, even if the materials for such a statement were available, which they are not. Nevertheless, certain features of that structure are sufficiently apparent to illustrate the differential propaganda advantages that stem from them. The groups and individuals that enjoy most prestige in a society are those that are given major credit for the most highly valued achievements of the society; their status is high. In the United States for more than a century the greatest of these achievements have been the settling of the continent and the revolutionizing of techniques of production. Because of their close association with these developments, the groups that can be subsumed under the loose heading "business" have in varying degrees throughout our history occupied a status of the highest order. As Kluckhohn has observed: "This has been a business civilization—not a military, ecclesiastical, or scholarly one." [68] These tendencies have been shared in considerable measure with all of western Europe, but they have been more nearly dominant in the United States. Penalties for such things as fraudulent speculative ventures were for some time markedly lighter in the United States, for example, than in England.[69] Combinations and associations of businessmen have met with some restrictions in the United States, but such regulation has been mild in comparison with the hostilities that have retarded the development of labor unions, whose aspirations could easily be viewed as infringing upon the prerogatives of those generally if not explicitly regarded as their "betters." Even within the early labor movements, as was indicated in Chapter 4, attachment to the dominant attitudes weakened cohesion and limited revisionist efforts. Differential propaganda advantage is not hard to verify when a President of the United States could proclaim: "The man who builds a factory builds a temple." [70]

Advantages accrue also to other types of groups that are well situ-

---

[68] Clyde Kluckhohn: *Mirror for Man: The Relation of Anthropology to Modern Life* (New York: Whittlesey House, McGraw-Hill Book Company, Inc., 1949), p. 229.

[69] Cf. Miriam Beard: *A History of the Business Man* (New York: The Macmillan Company, 1938), p. 696; see generally chaps. 24, 26, 27.

[70] Calvin Coolidge, quoted ibid., p. 754.

ated in the status structure of the society. Physicians, who a few short centuries ago occupied the position of barbers, are now very differently placed. Aided by association with both the prestige and the achievements of science, "men in white" enjoy a respect that gives them influence disproportionate to their numbers in the population. Their groups accordingly command special propaganda advantages. Some other professional groups—those of churchmen and lawyers, for instance—also derive advantages from the high status of their members, although it may not be quite so exalted. Teachers' groups, similarly, may often find useful the favorable attitudes toward education.

The advantageous position of such élite groups offers a clue to their insistence that they are not engaged in propaganda. The values and programs that they espouse have but lately become controversial. Such groups propagate a "faith" that until recently has gone largely unchallenged, and from their standpoint they are propounding ancient truth—education, not propaganda.

Since such advantages derive from the structure and values of the society, élite groups change with changes in the society. The values that give such groups their power provide a frame of reference by means of which most members of society interpret experience and anticipate the future. When experience can no longer be understood in such a frame of reference, it changes, the values change, and the positions of the formerly privileged groups are changed. In vastly oversimplified terms, we may say, for example, that Americans generally would acknowledge that the growth and economic health of the entire society was due to the untrammeled initiative of business enterprises; and that left largely to themselves these enterprises would provide maximum economic welfare in the future as they had in the past. But since World War I, at least, the experiences of many have not squared with these explanations and expectations. Urban slums, denuded forests, waves of widespread unemployment, and the like have called these ideas into question and have induced changes. Adherence to the ancient formulas is no longer automatic. There is room for rival explanations and for modification of the prestige of the formerly ranking groups.

Such changes do not come about overnight, and in the process the threatened groups enjoy the continuing advantage of established status. The values and attitudes underlying their advantageous position do not change completely or at a uniform rate. Consequently, the opportunities deriving from them are not withdrawn at a stroke. Unaffected or largely unmodified attitudes can be invoked to protect the claims of a group even when its previous élite position has been modified. So long as such attitudes remain, defensive groups enjoy an advantage over their challengers, who cannot command such allegiances and who cannot, as will be pointed out in a later chapter, as easily gain entrance to the institutions of government. It is not astonishing, therefore, that trade associations and various institutionalized business groups have engaged in propaganda largely aimed at protecting established attitudes and positions. Twenty years ago Herring noted that trade associations active in Washington were chiefly engaged in defensive activities. Throughout most of its history the National Association of Manufacturers has, in its propaganda and through other means, executed a series of retreats to prepared positions. The American Medical Association since the early 1930's has performed a similar maneuver. It obstructed all plans for prepaid medical care in the 1930's in the name of protecting professional specialization from any lay control. Confronted with defeat on this front, it has recently espoused these voluntary plans as the American alternative to "socialized medicine" in the form of compulsory health insurance. Throughout such retreats, however, these groups have been able with varying degrees of success to delay change by invoking established attitudes that their status permits them to utilize.

A group's position in the society has other implications for propaganda advantage, not the least important of which is financial. In most societies status and prestige are closely correlated with income. That is, both prestige and money are among the rewards for persons and groups occupying high position. Such persons and groups can raise money relatively easily both because their supporters have it and because, in a good many instances, giving them money is a source of vicarious prestige to the giver. Money is not the only variable determining the influence of a group, but, like formal organization, it is highly significant. It buys printing presses and typewriters, pays for telephone calls and traveling expenses. It buys time and space in the mass media of communication and secures the services of people who can devote most of their energies to advancing the claims of the group. Other things being equal, position is a determinant of financial strength, and affluence facilitates propaganda activities.

Position and prestige also facilitate the formation of alliances among groups. As an early paragraph in this chapter suggested, such alliances are inevitable because most organized political interest groups are minorities. In a society that frequently uses majority rule as a technique in making decisions, groups often find it essential to make alliances in order to assert their claims effectively. Alliances are a means of enlarging a public, and the facilities of allied organizations are channels through which a friendly group's propaganda may flow. Like the specialized press, such channels have for the membership of the allied group a prestige and influence greater than that of any "outside" group. Access to these channels, therefore, reduces the hazards facing an outside group. (Alliances, of course, are equally significant in strengthening a group's demands upon the key points in government policy determination. In fact, if an alliance provides for nothing more than propaganda assistance, it is almost certainly going to be weak and relatively ineffective. This aspect will be taken up in a later chapter.) A group's position materially affects the ease with which it can form such alliances. On most matters, for example, the American Farm Bureau Federation and the Chamber of Commerce of the United States would find it easier to secure allies than would the Congress of Industrial Organizations.

Examples of allied propaganda efforts are numerous. A typical one is provided by the Cement Institute. This trade association recently found itself in disfavor in a number of quarters, because it was suspected of maintaining uniform prices throughout the cement industry. To "neutralize the growing acidity of the environment," as one observer put it, the group felt obliged to win over the leadership of various peripheral groups. These presumably could then be counted upon to disseminate the Institute's "line" among their following.[71] Included among these groups were building-materials dealers, contractors, manufacturers of concrete products, and industrial groups whose practices were similar to those of the Institute and thus liable to the same sort of criticism.

The National Association of Manufacturers, being a fairly vulnerable minority and lacking a mass following of its own, has made a variety of alliances with groups having equal prestige and larger publics, such as the Chamber of Commerce, the American Federation of Labor, the Grange, and the American Retail Federation. Similar alliances with a number of trade associations have been formalized in the N.A.M.'s satellite organization, the National Industrial Council, discussed in Chapter 5. A somewhat less formal understanding was reportedly developed between the N.A.M. and the American Legion in 1940. This arrangement established a co-operative committee to carry on "educational" activities, including the distribution of N.A.M. literature through the Legion's hierarchy.

[71] This example is drawn from Earl Latham: "Giantism and Basing-Points: A Political Analysis," *Yale Law Journal*, Vol. 58, no. 3 (February, 1949), pp. 383–99 at p. 395.

The position of the Legion is instructive. As a veterans' organization it has prestige both with its members and with many outsiders, and it has a large public. Its officials, consequently, are the targets for a good deal of persuasive "lobbying" by other groups. The claims of the successful suitors in some instances may correspond more closely to the attitudes of the Legion's active minority than to those of the rank and file, although they may not be very important to either. In any case, the more important point is that "mutual-aid" relationships are established that may be useful to both parties unless the prestige of one is so low as to constitute a handicap. Each group presumably has some influence that it can trade, and even the Legion is not so large that it can be independent of alliances.[72]

Before we can generalize about which political interest groups will enjoy propaganda advantage, we must analyze carefully all of the factors determining such advantage. It is particularly important to analyze the influence of a group's status in the society, for an oversimplified and misleading explanation of the significance of particular propagandas will result if the effects of this and other factors are not examined critically. We can see the importance of such analysis by examining a widespread theory that in the United States and similar societies "business" groups always enjoy a controlling advantage as interest groups. It is argued in effect that because "business" groups (both associations and institutionalized groups) occupy and enjoy the perquisites of high status, they tend to control all the significant governmental decisions in the United States. Some even assert that this "business community" is so highly organized that it can act as a unit controlled by a handful of individuals and in a fashion inimical to "democratic" institutions. This assertion, like the theory as a whole, of course covers much more than the sphere of political propaganda.

Some of the documents in which this argument is presented constitute little more than broadsides on behalf of opposing interests and should be viewed merely as a portion of the stream of propaganda in group politics.[73] Others, however, purport to be serious and disinterested analyses of the politico-economic process and must be reckoned with as such.[74] One of the most thorough and provocative of these

[72] Gray: *The Inside Story of the Legion*, pp. 76–8, 83, 102–4.
[73] One book can be cited as representative of this type: George Seldes: *One Thousand Americans* (New York: Boni and Gaer, 1947).
[74] Notably Brady: *Business as a System of Power*, including the foreword by Robert S. Lynd. See also U.S. Temporary National Economic Committee: *Economic Power and Political Pressures*.

publications is Robert A. Brady's *Business as a System of Power*. Although Brady's thesis, as others have noted,[75] is not completely clear, the argument proceeds somewhat as follows. The social relationship that we call property includes, in part, the power of owners to control the behavior of other people. This power increases as property is concentrated, so that if one is an owner "one can coerce, bend others to one's will, withhold, restrain, settle the fate and alter the fortunes of growing numbers of non-owners without, and increasingly against, their consent." Because "fee simple is related to private monopoly as youth is to age, as acorn to oak," there has been throughout the capitalist world an increasing concentration of business ownership and control.[76] The epitome of this centralization is the "peak" association (*Spitzenverband*), represented in pre-Hitler Germany by the *Reichsverband der Deutschen Industrie*, in pre-Fascist Italy by the General Confederation of Italian Industry, in Japan by the *Zaibatsu* and their organizations, in pre-Vichy France by the *Confédération générale de la Production Française*, in Britain by the Federation of British Industries, and in the United States by the National Association of Manufacturers. Emphasis is placed on the manufacturing "peak" association because it sets the path for trade associations, cartels, and other "peak" associations.[77] Despite differing "historical environments," the development of "business centralization" has been parallel in all these countries.[78] "Within Germany, Italy, Japan, and France these bodies made the critical decisions without which the final destruction of democracy could not have taken place." Because "nothing fundamental in history, program, structure of organization, or social outlook divides clearly the policies of the *Spitzenverbände* within the 'totalitarian' countries from those of the liberal-capitalist states," democracy in the latter is seriously threatened. It is acknowledged, however, that "monopoly-oriented business . . . can dominate government only through control over the thinking processes of the mass of the people who dwell at the base of the social pyramid." [79]

In the United States there is a considerable measure of evidence to

[75] See the review by Charles A. Beard: *American Political Science Review*, Vol. 37, no. 2 (April, 1943), pp. 329–30.

[76] Brady: *Business as a System of Power*, p. 296. Copyright 1943 by and used with the permission of Columbia University Press.

[77] Ibid., p. 16.

[78] Ibid., pp. 5–6.

[79] Brady: *Business as a System of Power*, p. 320. Copyright 1943 by and used with the permission of Columbia University Press.

support this contention. Reasons have already been cited for the high prestige enjoyed by "business" activities in our society and for their favored position in the conventional myth patterns. A large proportion of legislators and others in political life accept, at least in some measure, these patterns and the behaviors they imply. The favored position of "business" groups is furthered by the existence of an economic system under which businessmen's confidence and expectations of profit are of crucial importance to the health of the economy.[80] Moreover, there has been a marked tendency in many, if not most, sectors of the economy toward monopolistic organization. At the same time greater unity of outlook among the top policy makers of the large economic units has been encouraged by overlapping directorates, by associations, and by other forms of interaction not directly connected with their enterprises. Power is involved in these as in all social relationships, and monopoly power of any sort always involves the possibility of a subversion of democratic processes, for it can be used to deny free access to the points where key decisions are made. The large aggregations, through their concentration of economic power, may have direct and indirect influence over the smaller ones, and their leaders may exercise a good deal of influence over their own and others' managerial and production personnel.[81] As related in an earlier chapter, officials of large corporations have frequently taken over the leadership of associations growing out of business relationships.

The concentration of control, moreover, extends to the media of communication. The Commission on Freedom of the Press recently called this control "the outstanding fact about the communications industry today" and summarized the situation in the following terms:

> In many places the small press has been completely extinguished. The great cities have three or four daily newspapers each, smaller cities may have two; but most places have only one. News-gathering is concentrated in three great press associations, and features are supplied from a central source by syndicates. There are eight majors in motion pictures, four national radio networks, eight to fifteen giants among magazine publishers,

---

[80] Cf. John Maynard Keynes: *The General Theory of Employment, Interest, and Money* (London: Macmillan & Company, 1936), pp. 148–9.

[81] On these developments generally, see U.S. National Resources Committee: *The Structure of the American Economy, Part I*, esp. chap. 7, "The Organizational Structure," and chap. 9, "The Structure of Controls."

five to twenty-five big book houses. Throughout the communications industry the little fellow exists on very narrow margins, and the opportunities for initiating new ventures are strictly limited.[82]

Since these enterprises are usually "big business" themselves, it is not startling that those who control them share many of the views of executives of large corporations in other fields. Illustrations appear from time to time indicating the distortion or suppression of content by most of the media in a fashion favorable to various "business" groups.[83]

Evidence such as this lends plausibility to the general thesis advanced by Brady and others, but it is not conclusive. Hasty generalization is not in order; we cannot responsibly conclude from evidence of the existence of influence that the influence is dominant or controlling, unless there is adequate evidence to support this conclusion. Not only are data of the latter sort not available, but also there is a good deal of information that would lead to a more moderate conclusion.

As the material in Chapter 6 indicated, business groups are faced with problems of internal cohesion no less than other groups in the society.[84] Differences of interest and multiple memberships create obstacles to unified action here as well as elsewhere in the society. Brady himself admits that organized business has difficulty in finding a "collective mind" and a "collective will," although he assumes its ability to blunder into decisions destructive of democracy.[85] The rapid decline in N.A.M. membership after 1929, admitting that the dominant elements in the organization in that year were not the same as those after 1933, suggests a certain peripheral quality in the members' attachments, since affiliation apparently was dispensable in a period of economic adversity. Such obstacles to cohesion are, of course, subject to variation. Under the impact of strong claims that appear to challenge the bases of the property relationship itself, they may be reduced at least temporarily to a minimum. Key states this point about as strongly as the existing evidence will permit when he suggests: "It may be . . . that over the past 40 or 50 years the forces unifying

---

[82] Commission on Freedom of the Press: *A Free and Responsible Press*, p. 37. Copyright 1947 by the University of Chicago and used with the permission of The University of Chicago Press.

[83] See, for example, Seldes: *One Thousand Americans*, p. 241.

[84] See items cited in notes 68 and 69, chap. 6.

[85] Brady: *Business as a System of Power*, p. 3.

business—the labor movement and the expansion of governmental services and costs—have introduced into business generally a discipline that represses political expression of its inner conflicts of interest." [86] The conflicts exist, however, and they may be repressed without being eliminated.

If it is argued that, despite these difficulties, concentrated economic power has its way, there are a number of instances that just do not fit the hypothesis. In the field of communications we haven't the facts to prove or disprove the allegation. As a thoughtful newspaper editor recently put it: "We simply do not know what difference diversified ownership as against concentrated ownership makes in what people read, hear over the air, and see on the screen." [87] In governmental policy making a representative case suggests that in many instances political effectiveness is in inverse proportion to the average economic strength of the members of a group. As the result of a reciprocal trade agreement with Switzerland before World War II, Swiss watch movements cased in the United States largely dominated the American wartime market, since the three large American manufacturers were completely engaged in making precision instruments for war use. Through the American Watch Manufacturers Association the latter succeeded toward the close of the war in urging a renegotiation of the Swiss agreement. The opponents of renegotiation were not only the firms that case Swiss movements, but also watch retailers, who at that time had no American movements to sell. The result was that a new agreement was made, but it involved no significant changes in the tariffs on Swiss movements.

The matter seems to boil down to the fact that at least on the American scene there are significant differences between economic and political power. Lynd has observed: "Power is no less 'political' for being labeled 'economic' power." [88] But, although this point is acceptable, it does not follow that a distinction between types of power is without value. Power, as earlier sections have indicated, is an aspect of a social relationship. If the relationships involved in the institutions labeled "economic" are in significant measure different from those involved in "political" institutions, then we may speak of

[86] V. O. Key, Jr.: *Southern Politics in State and Nation* (New York: Alfred A. Knopf, Inc., 1949), p. 476.

[87] Herbert Brucker: *Freedom of Information* (New York: The Macmillan Company, 1949), p. 73.

[88] Robert S. Lynd: "Foreword" to Brady: *Business as a System of Power*, p. viii. Copyright 1943 by and used with the permission of Columbia University Press.

different forms of power. Nor is it illegitimate to speak of the institutions as separate. As MacIver says:

> We cannot simplify the issue and claim with the Marxists that economic power is always primary in capitalistic society and that political power is both its offspring and its servant.
>
> . . .
>
> The economic strength of any group or class is no longer, as it tended to be under feudal conditions, the measure of its political strength.[89]

The relationships involved in economic institutions rest upon the function of buying and selling goods and services. Especially when control over portions of the function is concentrated, there is no denying that it can be coercive, withholding and granting rewards for conformity to a desired type of behavior. This point, however, is not the issue. All power, in whatever form, may be coercive.

Whatever may be true of countries where political participation is narrowly limited, in the United States the relationships productive of political power depend upon eliciting consent from a heterogeneous mass of people—not an aggregation of individuals, but, as this book has gone to some pains to elaborate, an overlapping congeries of groups, organized and potential.

Relationships in the economic and political spheres differ, even when the holders of power in the two may to some extent be identical. These relationships differ both in the techniques that leaders must employ and in the expectations and demands of those who participate in the institutions. We simply do not expect the same things of the United States Government as we do of the United States Steel Corporation. When the holders of power in one sphere enter the other, they do so on the latter's established terms, including both techniques and expectations.

It is likely, therefore, that economic power can be converted into political power only at a discount, variable in size, which perhaps accounts for some of the heat and frustration generated in corporate directors' meetings off and on over the past twenty years. As Merton has put it: "Men with power to affect the economic life-chances of a large group may exert little interpersonal influence in other spheres:

---

[89] MacIver: *The Web of Government*, pp. 91–2. Copyright 1947 by Robert M. MacIver and used with the permission of The Macmillan Company. Cf. Charles E. Merriam: *Political Power* (New York: McGraw-Hill Book Company, Inc., 1934).

the power to withhold jobs from people may not result in directly influencing their political or associational or religious behavior." [90] The National Association of Manufacturers (and other economic groups) in attempting to control political decisions must engage in the compromises and concessions required by the techniques and expectations dominant in the political sphere. They must do so not only because of the demands of those whom they aspire to lead, but also because many of these demands are just as strongly held by business men themselves. Especially in the area of political techniques— the whole fabric of elections—such demands rest upon values that are widely dispersed and the strength of which should never be underestimated. Violation of them would generate group protests supported by many N.A.M. members. The occupational allegiance is no more exclusive here than among others in the society. Those who will not or cannot accept the going discount rate and make the requisite adjustments must suffer reduced effectiveness or failure. Thus the record of the N.A.M. over fifteen years has been largely a history of successive defensive retreats: witness its ineffective opposition to the Social Security Act, the Securities Exchange Act, the Reciprocal Trade Agreements Act, the Public Utility Holding Company Act, and others.[91] The discount, or the importance of it, is further illustrated by the dominant, though largely implicit, assumption underlying most of its propaganda, that the limits upon "business" leadership are due to public "ignorance" or to "false propaganda," which need only "correction" in order to be reversed.

Although it is correct, therefore, to say that "business" groups in the United States currently enjoy special advantages in the use of propaganda and in other political efforts, it does not follow that they are or must be dominant or exclusive or unchanging. It *may* be but it is not *necessarily* appropriate to predict that:

> Just as the giant corporation takes on as an incident to its growth a definite political significance as a wielder of power over increasing numbers of people and their interests, so it is inevitable that the N.A.M. should in its much larger sphere be

[90] Robert K. Merton: "Patterns of Influence: A Study of Interpersonal Influence and of Communications Behavior in a Local Community," in Paul F. Lazarsfeld and Frank N. Stanton (eds.): *Communications Research 1948–1949* (New York: Harper and Brothers, 1949), p. 217.

[91] Note in Seldes: *One Thousand Americans*, pp. 243–4, the admission that the allegedly controlled press has on numerous occasions failed in its "efforts to mislead the people."

transformed, as it grows and expands, into a community force
ever more politically potent and politically conscious.[92]

The going discount rate on the political claims of such groups may
restrict them to a more modest position.

Summary

The process of group politics is such that no organized groups can
afford to be indifferent to public opinion. Moreover, the same influences which have led to a rapid multiplication of organized interest
groups in America have also caused an increased concern with public
opinion. This concern inevitably is reflected in efforts to guide and
control opinion through propaganda. Public opinion in this sense is
not to be conceived of as a collective and essentially rational entity,
but as an aggregate of the more or less rational opinions held by
those individuals who, on a given issue make up the "public." In addition to the degree of rationality, a number of other "dimensions" of
opinion are involved in describing it adequately.

Propaganda is to be regarded as a morally neutral process of influencing attitudes and behavior. Propaganda of any sort, including that
by political interest groups, is not a device which can function independent of other political skills. For this and for other reasons the
propaganda of interest groups is fallible and frequently ineffective.
Among the major additional reasons for the impotence of propaganda in particular situations are the failure of the target population
to perceive the group's message at the time and in the way the
propagandist intended it to be perceived, the failure of the group's
message to arouse appropriate attitudes, and the failure of the propaganda to produce the particular action it aims at. Within limits an
interest group may use a variety of technical skills to minimize these
obstacles.

Not all the hindrances to successful propaganda are subject to a
group's control. Because propaganda must rest upon and use pre-
existing attitudes, certain groups at any time enjoy special propaganda
advantages. Ambiguity or lack of stable "meaning" in a set of events
affords advantages of this sort. The status or prestige of the sponsoring
group is a similar factor. In the American system "business" groups
have long enjoyed the advantages of superior status, along with other

[92] Brady: *Business as a System of Power*, p. 217. Copyright 1943 by and
used wtih the permission of Columbia University Press.

attributes of power. For this reason it is sometimes assumed that such groups are certain to be dominant in propaganda and to manipulate the political system invariably in their favor. Although movements toward monopoly and concentration have greatly centralized economic power, when monopolists attempt to convert such power into political influence, especially through propaganda, it is subject to a discount of varying size. Propaganda advantages are not stable, and forms of power are not completely interchangeable.

9

Interest Groups and Political Parties

"POLITICS," according to Max Weber, ". . . means striving to share power or striving to influence the distribution of power, either among states or among groups within a state." [1] Such a view of the political process is a particularly helpful one if we are to understand the tactics of group influence upon and through the institutions of government. It suggests the importance of viewing these institutions in their proper perspective as power relations and of going beyond their formal, legalistic aspects.

It may seem unnecessary to insist that political institutions are essentially power relationships, since most sophisticated readers will acknowledge that legal and constitutional structure provides an incomplete statement of the governing process. And yet, so strong is our awareness of the standardized, formal aspects of government—especially a government to which we owe allegiance—that we easily fall into the error of a simplified, stereotyped picture of the process: the legislature adopts policy, the executive approves and administers it, the courts adjudicate controversies arising out of it—only these things, always in this order, constitute the process of government and where such is not the case, it ought to be. Although this account may be something of a caricature, a close reading of almost any textbook on American government will indicate that it is not a gross distortion. The standard procedure in such expositions is to take the legal formalities as the theme and to treat everything else as variation.

A clearer picture of reality is not likely to be provided merely

[1] Max Weber: "Politics as a Vocation," in H. H. Gerth and C. Wright Mills: *From Max Weber: Essays in Sociology* (New York: Oxford University Press, Inc., 1946), p. 78. Copyright by and used with the permission of Oxford University Press, Inc.

by reversing the standard procedure and "debunking" the formalities. Constitutional structure affords a convenient framework for exposition, as the arrangement of chapters in this section assumes; moreover, formalized governmental relationships are a major part of the picture, even though they are not the whole of it. We shall be on safer ground, therefore, if we keep constantly in mind the element common to both "theme" and "variations," namely, the interactions of men. These, in Bentley's phrase, constitute our "raw materials," [2] whether we are talking about political parties, legislatures, executives, courts, or interest groups.

An institution, as Chapter 2 indicated, is a pattern of interaction different only in degree from other group patterns in a society. It involves a relatively high degree of formality and stability, to mention only two characteristics, but its basic ingredients, interactions among men, do not differ in kind from those of other groups. Constitutional and other legal documents testify to the formality and stability of political institutions. They may even describe the pattern with considerable accuracy. More frequently, however, they provide only a partial account or indicate merely key elements of ritual that may bear more upon what is expected to take place than upon what actually occurs. In any case, an accurate description of the institution cannot assume either the sufficiency or the irrelevance of the formal legal framework. It must be built up from observation of the interactions of the men who participate in it. As Bentley has said, by way of illustration: "A discussion of the work and defects of a state legislature carries one nowhere as long as the legislature is taken for what it purports to be—a body of men who deliberate upon and adopt laws." [3]

The lasting value of Lincoln Steffens' classic "muckraking" studies of American cities and States in the first decade of the century lies in his insistence on this point. His articles, which fall far short of forming a systematic account of the political process, were nevertheles based almost entirely on direct observations of the behavior of people involved in politics. From these he derived his telling patterns of State and local politics, and his diagrams bore little or no relation to the organization charts of the "forms" of State and local government.[4] One need not endorse his conclusion, "that the form of gov-

---

[2] Bentley: *The Process of Government*, chap. 6.

[3] Bentley: *The Process of Government*, p. 163. Copyright 1908 by and used with the permission of Arthur F. Bentley.

[4] For example, see the diagram of Greenwich, Connecticut, at p. 596 of *The Autobiography of Lincoln Steffens* (single volume edition, New York: Harcourt, Brace & Company, Inc., 1931).

ernment did not matter; that constitutions and charters did not affect essentially the actual government." [5] One cannot deny, however, the implication that the realities of governmental structure are grounded in the persistent interactions of men.

The Basic Objective: Access

A second introductory point must be made before turning to the principal subject of this chapter. Weber observes: "He who is active in politics strives for power either as a means in serving other aims, ideal or egoistic, or as 'power for power's sake,' that is, in order to enjoy the prestige-feeling that power gives." [6] In the governmental activity of interest groups both motives are frequently at work, but the former is perhaps more often dominant. Whichever is operating at a particular point in time, however, power of any kind cannot be reached by a political interest group, or its leaders, without access to one or more key points of decision in the government. Access, therefore, becomes the facilitating intermediate objective of political interest groups. The development and improvement of such access is a common denominator of the tactics of all of them, frequently leading to efforts to exclude competing groups from equivalent access or to set up new decision points access to which can be monopolized by a particular group. Toward whatever institution of government we observe interest groups operating, the common feature of all their efforts is the attempt to achieve effective access to points of decision.

Key decision points may be explicitly established by the formal legal framework of the government, or they may lie in the gaps and interstices of the formal structure, protected by custom or by semi-obscurity. One key point may be at the president's elbow as he writes his message on the state of the Union; another may be in a smoke-filled room at a nominating convention; and a third almost literally may be in a legislative committee chairman's coat pocket, into which it is desired to slip a bill to prevent its being considered by the Congress. To describe the relative ease with which various groups gain access to such points of decision and to analyze the exploitation of such access through time is another way to describe the governmental institutions involved.

[5] Ibid., p. 409.
[6] Gerth and Mills: *From Max Weber*, p. 78. Copyright 1946 by and used with the permission of Oxford University Press, Inc.

The importance of access to the machinery of government is formally recognized in the Constitution itself. Thus the First Amendment provides: "Congress shall make no law . . . abridging . . . the right of the people peaceably to assemble, and to petition the government for a redress of grievances." This provision, it should be noted, although an important safety valve, is a minimum guarantee and is essentially negative in character. Although Congress may not formally restrict access, the facts of the social structure, including established procedure, internal group politics, and the like, afford relatively greater ease of access to some groups as compared with others. Such will be a recurring theme of the next several chapters, but it may clarify the point to explore here some of its more general aspects.

Perhaps the most basic factor affecting access is the position of the group or its spokesman in the social structure. We encountered this element when discussing relative propaganda advantage in the preceding chapter. It is equally important here and for the same reasons. The deference accorded a high-status group not only facilitates the acceptance of its propaganda but also eases its approach to the government. Its petitions and claims may even in some instances appear less as demands or supplications and more as flattery of the official of whom a favor is asked. Such is likely to be the case when the legislative representative of a major corporation, of the American Bar Association, or of the Chamber of Commerce of the United States approaches a junior member of the legislature or an aspiring administrator. Even an official who shares the attitudes of a competing group may be flattered into aiding one of these high-status organizations. Even where flattery is not an influence, the high-status group is aided by the large proportion of key officials—legislative, executive, and judicial—whose class backgrounds are such that they have similar values, manners, and preconceptions.

Instances of difficulty of access owing to handicaps in status are not hard to find. It is only within recent years that labor organizations have been able to expect a hearing from most government officials, and their opponents have not necessarily experienced a corresponding diminution of their ease of access. In the years since the creation of the Department of Labor in 1913, the labor unions' nominal spokesman in the president's cabinet has not infrequently been unwelcome to labor groups or even hostile to their expressed interests. A more subtle example is to be found in Schattschneider's examination of the position of the importers in the hearings on the tariff act of 1930. The nationalistic attitudes prevailing in the dominant protectionist atmosphere meant that importers were "excluded from influence by the logic and psychology of the protective system." Summarizing the position of the importer, he concludes: "He is the agent of foreign interests that have no standing in court, and does business on suffrance, continuing only until challenged. His opposition is taken for granted, discounted in advance, and if he is heard, it is with irritation." [7]

Much of the importance of status in relation to access is summed up in the popular observation that it is important to "know the right people." But put in this way access appears to involve a much more fluid set of relationships than may actually be the case. An individual's or a group's status in the actual as well as the formal structure of relationships in the society may determine whether the "right people" can be identified and whether access will be permitted when they are known.

Mythology to the contrary, access is not just a matter of initiative on the part of the petitioner. Whyte illustrates this point effectively at several points in his study of "corner-boys." He notes, for example, that as the Federal relief organization became established after the early days of the New Deal, "the powers of local politicians in dealing with relief were progressively curtailed." It did not follow, however, that the matter was "out of politics;" rather, "the pressure had to come from higher up in the political hierarchy." The politically active wife of a State senator from the district that included the "little Italy" that Whyte studied was able to continue to get her husband's constituents into W.P.A. positions only because she was able to deal directly with the U.S. Senator. "If she had not such connections, she could have accomplished very little." [8] The "right person" was known in this case. Moreover, he could be reached.

A more complicated example will illustrate the consequences of not having access to the "right person." The playing of softball by a number of "corner-boys" in a small park had resulted in broken windows in an adjacent building owned by an important bank. An official of the bank talked to the park commissioner of the city, who ruled that the older boys might not play softball in this park. Enforcement of this order not only stopped isolated games, but also

---

[7] E. E. Schattschneider: *Politics, Pressures and the Tariff*, pp. 161–2. Copyright 1935 by Prentice-Hall, Inc.

[8] Whyte: *Street Corner Society*, pp. 196–7. Copyright 1943 by the University of Chicago and used with the permission of The University of Chicago Press.

jeopardized a softball league of sixteen teams that was just being organized. Four separate attempts were made to get the authorities to build a protective fence and thus permit cancellation of the ruling. The first three failed because the positions of the applicants were not such as to give them effective access. First, the corner-boy organizer of the ball league and an older friend who had met the park commissioner approached the latter and were rebuffed. Second, one of the directors of the local settlement house talked to the bank official in charge of the property, but without success. Third, the same director talked with a local politician who had some contact with the park commissioner and who agreed to speak to that official. The park commissioner was as resistant as before. Finally, the settlement-house director approached the alderman and one of the mayor's secretaries. Although the first approach brought no results, a second, which involved a personal call on the alderman by the director and the sixteen team captains, was ultimately successful. Both the alderman and the mayor's secretary, impressed by the votes which the ball teams represented, went to the mayor, who directed the park commissioner to build the fence. Whyte says of the situation:

> In this case the corner boys were not able to deal directly with the park commissioner. There was too big a gap between their positions. [The local politician] could talk with the comissioner, but he could not give him an order. [The alderman] was not interested in acting for [the settlement-house director] until he realized that he was part of a well-knit organization, which in this case included . . . sixteen corner-boy leaders, and all their followers. Then he and [the secretary] acted upon the mayor. . . . [The alderman] had made his connections through [the secretary]. Both men were in a position to exert pressure upon the top point in this legislative hierarchy, and, when they did, the course of action initiated by [the corner-boy organizer] was brought to a successful conclusion.[9]

Access here depended on more than the initiative of the original petitioner.

The evidence indicates that the corner boys' problem of status and access represents the political process in microcism, although the volume of evidence on the point is not great. The problem is at the heart of Schattschneider's distinction between "insiders" and "out-

[9] Whyte: *Street Corner Society*, pp. 247–50. Copyright 1943 by the University of Chicago and used with the permission of The University of Chicago Press. Bracketed words inserted for proper names.

siders" at the tariff hearings. Notice of the hearings and proposals was very unevenly distributed among the political interest groups —associations and firms—affected by them. He describes the consequences in the following terms:

> Some groups did not have warning of proposals affecting them adversely, while others, more strategically situated, were able to induce the committees to adopt their proposals without opposition or adequate criticism. Substantially, the contrast is between 'insiders' who knew very much and 'outsiders' who knew very little. . . . The groups which knew their way about knew also where to go for information on their own initiative and knew how to get it.[10]

The connection between access and status is indicated by the fact that many of those groups whose notice was adequate were "influential" groups kept posted by members of Congress. Many congressmen were careful of the interests of the groups important in their home districts, assisting them in many ways in addition to providing notification. Thus Senator Smoot, chairman of the Senate committee hearing the testimony, was generally regarded as the designated representative of the beet sugar group. Senator Bingham of Connecticut appointed an official of the Connecticut Manufacturers' Association as his own secretary during the period. These cases were not exceptional.[11] Their frequency underscores the significance of access and its dependence upon superior status in the prevailing structure of relationships.

The privileged treatment of "insiders" in legislative deliberations suggests a second basic aspect of effective access. In addition to status, the extent to which the interest is effectively organized is an important variable. For example, the individual business firm that is not accustomed to acting upon government, except in routine matters of taxation and the like, is likely to lack the established connections that would apprise it of developments such as those involved in proposed tariff legislation. By way of contrast, a public utility more or less continuously subject to action through government is organized both to learn of developing proposals and to act effectively concerning them. Its established connections with government are likely to include points of access. The individual business firm that belongs to an association, trade or otherwise, may be con-

[10] E. E. Schattschneider: *Politics, Pressures and the Tariff*, pp. 165–6. Copyright 1935 by Prentice-Hall, Inc.
[11] Ibid., pp. 175–84.

siderably better off than it would be without such affiliation. The association, in performance of its function of maintaining equilibrium in the relationships between its members and other groups, will provide notice of threats to such equilibrium and will have developed means of access to protect it. The tariff revision of 1929–30 again provides an illustration:

> Highly organized groups having legislative agents and staffs permanently located in Washington, with experience in former tariff revisions, and able to disseminate knowledge through the industry by way of trade publications and mailing lists, react to notice . . . (provided by a general press release) more sharply and decisively than groups lacking these advantages.[12]

The relation between group organization and access is not, it should be noted, a matter just of being organized but equally of being organized appropriately for the problem at hand. Nor should the term "organization" be understood narrowly. It should include the existence of established means of learning about impending changes. Cohesion among members sufficient to give force to their claims would be equally essential, as in the case of Whyte's settlement-house director and his sixteen team captains. Even the distribution of members geographically may be significant. Thus one of the weaknesses of the importers in fighting the Smoot-Hawley Tariff was their concentration in New York City.[13]

Finally, the skills and other qualifications of the group's leaders and agents are a crucially important variable. This last organizational factor explains the special qualifications characteristic of the representatives of political interest groups in their dealings with government. The considerable proportion of former members of Congress among such agents has frequently been noted by critics inside as well as outside legislative halls. Former congressmen are of great use to interest groups, but not primarily because they are granted the privilege of appearing on the floor of the House or the Senate. Should this courtesy be denied, as has been suggested from time to time, it would not seriously curtail the usefulness of such persons as agents. The ability to walk onto the floor of the Senate or the House of Representatives is a tactical advantage, but it is not the primary value of their services. This privilege is largely symbolic of the position such men have in government circles, of their connections, and of

[12] E. E. Schattschneider: *Politics, Pressures and the Tariff*, p. 165. Copyright 1935 by Prentice-Hall, Inc.
[13] Ibid., pp. 160–1.

their knowledge of the complexities of "getting things done" in legislative and other governmental institutions. Their stock-in-trade is access. It was not strange, therefore, that the A.F. of L. should have approached former Senator Burton Wheeler in 1948 when it was seeking a director for its political activities.[14]

The importance of the skills of the successful group agent is further indicated by the large number of Washington newspaper-correspondents, and newspaper men stationed in State capitals who enter such employment. In the process of covering governmental units over a period of years for a newspaper or press association, correspondents acquire the knowledge and the connections that give them access. Former officials and employees of executive departments and agencies, including the independent commissions, are an equally valuable source of group agents. A man who has headed or has been an important policy-maker or technician in an administrative agency has usually acquired the ingredients of access, particularly in dealings with that agency.[15]

Such qualifications are, of course, not a guarantee of effectiveness, nor are they the only ones that permit access. Any combination of skills and position may be valuable. It is, for example, a well-known fact that many corporations and law firms have found it expedient to have among their officers persons of some prominence from both political parties in order to gain access to government leaders regardless of which party is in power.

The Meanings of "Political Party"

The political party has come to be thought of as the instrumentality through which choices are made among aspirants for office. Access to this instrumentality, therefore, may be important to a political interest group, although, for reasons that will become apparent in succeeding pages, it cannot be the only, and may not be the most important, point of access to government. Group connections with the parties may be of the same type as those with other parts of the machinery of government; the latter may be either supplementary to, or alternative to, the contacts with party organizations.[16]

Whatever else it may be or may not be, the political party in the

[14] The *New York Herald Tribune*, February 5, 6, 1948.
[15] For examples of these kinds of relationships, see Herring: *Group Representation Before Congress*, pp. 53–9; Crawford: *The Pressure Boys*, chap. 2.
[16] Cf. Bentley: *The Process of Government*, p. 400.

United States most commonly is a device for mobilizing votes, preferably a majority of votes. (The phrase "most commonly" is necessary here because in many so-called one-party States the weaker party organization may carefully avoid winning majorities in order to enjoy the perquisites of patronage and the like that stem from and depend upon a continued minority position.[17]) As a vote mobilizer a party must be an "alliance of interests"—to use Herring's phrase[18] —as we can see if we recall the conception of interest as equivalent to attitude. The procurement of votes then must obviously depend upon the successful appeal to a variety of dominant attitudes.

An example will demonstrate that such has always been the case. The gubernatorial election of 1787 in Massachusetts, following Shays's Rebellion, provided an early popular recognition of the activity of divergent interests. Following that election John Hancock, the winner, champion of the insurgent debtor elements, and Governor Bowdoin, by a narrow margin the defeated candidate of the more "substantial" voters, each submitted to the *Massachusetts Centinel* an analysis of the returns. Behind the bitterness of some of the classifications lies a significant acceptance of differences in electoral behavior stemming from divergence of interests. In Bowdoin's analysis he claimed for himself by substantial margins the physicians, clergymen, lawyers, independent gentlemen, merchants and traders, and printers. He also claimed more than half of the tradesmen, though he asserted that the bulk of Hancock's support came from this group and the "laborers, servants, etc." Hancock, whose breakdown of the vote appeared three days after Bowdoin's, gave his opponent the total support of "usurers, speculators in public securities, stockholders and bank directors, persons under British influence," and one individual whom he classified under "wizards." All of his own support, he asserted, came from "merchants, tradesmen and other 'worthy' citizens"—a few of whom voted for Bowdoin—and "friends of the Revolution." [19]

As the preceding paragraph suggests, the interests aroused in support of a candidate may be represented by potential rather than actual interest groups. The parties or other parts of the machinery of

[17] Cf. Key: *Southern Politics*, chap. 13. This condition is by no means confined to the South.

[18] Pendleton Herring: *The Politics of Democracy* (New York: Rinehart & Company, 1940), p. 55.

[19] Cited in Peter H. Odegard and E. Allen Helms: *American Politics: A Study in Political Dynamics* (1st edition; New York: Harper and Brothers, 1938), pp. 24–5.

government may reflect such interests, even though the latter have not reached the stage of formal organization. In a simple society with a small and relatively homogeneous electorate, the party may serve this function without difficulty. Such circumstances, in fact, probably would indicate the adequacy in eighteenth-century England of Edmund Burke's frequently quoted definition of a political party as a "body of men united, for promoting by their joint endeavors the national interest, *upon some particular principle in which they are all agreed.*" With the vast expansion in the size of the electorate over the past hundred-odd years, both as an absolute number and as a proportion of the adult population, and with the equally vast multiplication of interests and of the disturbances that precede and follow their growth, the party task has become much more difficult. Partly because many of these interests are no longer so automatically reflected by the parties, they are more frequently represented by actual rather than merely potential groups. That is, in order to exert their claims through or upon the institutions of government, including the parties, more interests have tended to become organized.

Some observers have interpreted the multiplication of organized political interest groups as evidence of the failure or decline of the political party in the United States.[20] These, however, would not seem to be the most meaningful terms in which to state the situation. Clearly a change has taken place, a change in the character both of the interactions composing political parties and of those constituting the political interest groups. The initiative in promoting particular policies is apparently assumed more frequently by the latter, although precise evidence on the point is not available. But the functional relationship between the parties and interest groups remains the same. With limited local exceptions, some of which will be discussed shortly, no interest group or alliance of such groups has supplanted the party as a device for mobilizing majorities. The two types of group are still interdependent. The search for understanding, therefore, must concentrate upon the precise nature of the interactions, upon the character of this interdependence.

Serious difficulty is encountered in an effort to analyze the relations between parties and interest groups because the term "political party" has so many different meanings in this country. By "meanings," of course, we refer to the range and variety of behaviors that are called "political party" in different circumstances.

[20] See, for example, Rice: *Farmers and Workers in American Politics*, chap. 1; E. E. Schattschneider: *Party Government* (New York: Farrar & Rinehart, Inc., 1942), chap. 8.

Even if one considers only the two major parties, the behavior patterns are fluid and inconsistent. The term does not have the same meaning at the national, State, and local levels of government; it may not have the same meaning in two States or in two localities; finally, in the nation, in a single State, or in a single city the term may not have the same meaning at one point in time as at another, in one campaign year and in the next. It usually means in election campaigns something very different from what it means when applied to activities in a legislature. Less is known on the subject of these variations than would be desirable, but it is obvious that it is risky to speak of the relationships between political interest groups and "the political party," since such relationships will vary in part according to differences in the behavior that constitutes the party in different places and at different times.

The protean character of political parties will be apparent if the major political parties are examined as national aggregations. Herring has suggested that "the organization of the party on a national scale is most accurately envisaged in terms of a network of personal relations." [21] He is not simply restating the obvious fact that all organizations are patterns of interpersonal relations. Rather, he means that the organization of the so-called national parties does not have much continuity of pattern, regardless of the persons who occupy various positions in the formalized structure. At a given period the organization is composed of the temporary, shifting relationships that a man or a handful of men have been able to establish with other individuals throughout all or part of the country. The formal, paper structure shows a hierarchy of committees running upward from the local voting precincts through the county, the State, and the senatorial and congressional campaign committees to the national committees. Actual lines of authority, however, do not correspond to this paper structure. The key men in the national party may not even be members of any of these committees. Even if some or all of them are, however, a committee at one level ordinarily has no control over one at the next lower level in the paper structure. The various committees actually are largely autonomous and are arranged in parallel, rather than in a hierarchy—units which become associated in temporary collaboration for the period of a campaign or a series of campaigns.

The principal function of a national party organization is to elect a president of the United States. The nucleus for this quadrennial

[21] Herring: *The Politics of Democracy*, p. 204.

organization consists of the leaders who have been primarily responsible for nominating the candidate; to this core is added as many State and local leaders and committees as possible. Thus the nucleus of the organization for the Roosevelt campaign of 1932 was made up of those leaders whose support Farley and others had been able to secure before and during the nominating convention at Chicago. Farley became chairman of the national committee, as the nominee's choice and according to tradition, but the campaign effort operated through the members of the committee only to the extent that effective relationships could be established between them and those close to Roosevelt. Such relationships, on the other hand, might be developed outside the committee structure with any individuals who appeared to have a significant following among the voters or local leaders. In such circumstances it is not news when a national committeeman is revealed as being in opposition to the president's program. When the press in 1949 made much of the hostility of the Arkansas national committeeman, a doctor, to President Truman's health insurance proposals, they were implying a most inaccurate picture of the national committee's role.[22]

By way of contrast, in the Republican presidential campaign of 1948, the national chairman, though selected by Dewey, was not a member of the candidate's inner circle, and he had little or nothing to do with running Dewey's campaign. Based on such variable personal relationships, the national party organization of both major parties must be rebuilt, for all practical purposes, every four years, in some cases even when the president is running for re-election. When the candidate is seeking his first term in the office, rebuilding of the organization is extensive and inevitable.

The character of the national party was particularly sharply revealed in the Democratic campaign of 1948. Several of the leaders of the "Dixiecrat" party were members of the Democratic national committee, including Governor J. Strom Thurmond of South Carolina, the "Dixiecrat" nominee for President. Some of these resigned from the committee, but Thurmond, backed by the South Carolina Democratic committee, refused to do so. He was displaced only when the national chairman recognized a new committee in the State.[23] In four States of the South, moreover,—South Carolina, Alabama, Mississippi, and Louisiana—the "Dixiecrat" candidates were listed on the ballot as the nominees of the Democratic party. In

[22] The *New York Herald Tribune*, April 16, 1949.
[23] Ibid., September 3, 10 and October 30, 1948; The *New York Times*, September 19, 1948.

one, Alabama, the names of President Truman and Senator Barkley were not even included on the ballot.[24] Reconstruction of a national party organization does not usually include such dramatic developments, but those in 1948 were distinctive only in degree.

One result of the kaleidoscopic pattern of national party organization is that the relationships that produce the vote for a president in a State or locality may be quite different from those that elect senators and congressmen, to say nothing of governors. In such circumstances it is accurate to say that the effective constituencies of the two sets of officials are different and even conflicting. The political interest groups supporting them are correspondingly different. The consequences for harmony between the president and Congress on matters of legislation, which will be explored in another chapter, are obvious. It is this sort of situation, in fact, that explains why interest groups, as Bentley and others have noted, encounter different degrees of resistance to their claims in the two houses of Congress and in the presidency and why they therefore work primarily through one or the other of these channels, whichever is more receptive.[25]

The meaning of the term "political party" is even more obscure if the behaviors so designated are examined at the State level. Lack of correspondence between the constituencies of State and national officers is only one aspect of the matter. In certain States at certain times correspondence may be quite close, yet it may be virtually nonexistent in the same States at other times. In most States the pattern of activity that is given the label "party" involves securing the support of a majority of voters for at least some of the candidates running for office under the party banner, but in some this function is in no sense implied by the term. The major political parties in the States sometimes operate as units of a national organization, whereas at other times they go their own way; they are always autonomous. At some times and places they stage a co-ordinated assault upon every major elective office in the State; at others, each nominee makes a completely independent effort without help from a State party.

The factional struggles for control of a State party are not just clique rivalries, devoid of content. Depending on what faction is dominant and on the extent of its dominance, the party is likely to vary in the functions it performs and in the interests that it represents. For example, in recent years the so-called Grundy faction

---

[24] There is a good discussion of these and related events in 1948 in Key: *Southern Politics*, pp. 329–44.
[25] Bentley: *The Process of Government*, pp. 344 ff.

of the Pennsylvania Republican party has been made up primarily of elements in the rural counties and small towns rather than those in the major cities of Philadelphia and Pittsburgh. When it is dominant and its men are the nominees for all the State-wide offices, the organized support it receives in the major cities at the general election is likely to be *ad hoc* and improvised, or reflective of the habitual responses of voters to a party label. Nominees on the State-wide slate who are not of this faction need to develop their own organization support in the election, as the dominant faction may not provide assistance and may even quietly aid the candidate of the opposition party. Moreover, when control of the State organization falls to the Grundy faction, the interests having access to the State party are likely to be quite different from those dominant in the urban centers.[26]

Unified State parties, in which vigorous efforts are made in support of all candidates under the party label, sometimes do exist, but other "meanings" of State parties are perhaps more typical. V. O. Key's revealing study of politics in the South provides abundant demonstration. He shows that in many of the one-party States the party organization is primarily a device for securing representation in the councils of the national Democratic party. It rarely conducts a campaign, and control of the organization is neither a weapon in primary elections nor an objective; the official party is, in Key's phrase, "neutral, not partisan." On the other hand, where a single faction—such as the Byrd machine in Virginia, the Crump faction in Tennessee, or Huey Long's machine in Louisiana—has achieved control of the State, command of the State party organization is sometimes significant. In such circumstances the party, or its dominant faction, may wage a primary or election campaign for a fairly complete State ticket. On the whole, however, primary campaigns in the South tend to be separate and independent for each office. Campaigns for each of the Federal, State, and local offices avoid formal connection with each other. Therefore most candidates must build personal organizations from scratch at the outset of each campaign, since even the successful organizations hold together only loosely after a campaign and supporters easily move from faction to faction. Furthermore, the lone aspirant seeking, for example, a seat in the State or Federal legislature, cannot look to a State party headquarters for organizational or financial help. He is on his own. Looking for financial and other forms of assistance, he is likely to be more

[26] See, for example, W. H. Lawrence's article in The *New York Times*, February 12, 1950.

easily accessible to interest groups, especially those with ample funds, than are candidates running on an integrated ticket.[27]

Comparable studies of States outside the South are not available, but the fugitive evidence from numerous sources suggests that in some States in other sections, State parties show a pattern similar to the dominant pattern in the South and that in all States there is wide variation in their significance. This condition would seem to be a logical result of, among other things, the variety of methods used for nominating candidates. Conventions, open primaries, closed primaries, nonpartisan primaries, "cross filing," and "multiple nominations" are symptomatic of wide differences in the behaviors collectively designated by the term "party" in various States. It is scarcely likely that these activities are more than roughly similar in New York, where all State-wide candidates are selected in party conventions, and in California, where the primary system will permit such candidates to win the nominations of both major "parties." Thus in 1946 Governor Earl Warren, Republican candidate for vice-president of the United States in 1948, was the gubernatorial nominee of both the Republican and the Democratic "parties" in California. Who and what are "Republicans" and "Democrats" under such arrangements it is difficult to discover.[28]

The heterogeneity of political parties in the United States is at its peak in the localities—cities, counties, legislative and other election districts. At this level the party may be a unified organization capable of executing a co-ordinated campaign inclusive of all offices for which "party" nominees are running. Probably more often the candidate in each local constituency must organize a purely personal following that for all practical purposes becomes the party organization in that election district. When no such candidate presents himself, the party organization simply does not exist in the locality. This situation is particularly common in congressional districts, but it is not peculiar to them.

The local party organization at various times and places may be effectively tied in with the State and even the national organizations. As indicated earlier, however, the local organization is not therefore

---

[27] Key: *Southern Politics*, pp. 387–92, 395–405, 477.

[28] An exhaustive body of evidence on variations of this sort is presented in Clarence A. Berdahl: "Party Membership in the United States," *American Political Science Review*, Vol. 36, nos. 1–2 (February, April, 1942), pp. 16–50, 241–62. See also his "Some Notes on Party Membership in Congress," *American Political Science Review*, Vol. 43, nos. 2–4 (April, June, August, 1949), pp. 309–21, 492–508, 721–34.

necessarily subordinate. It may be, in fact, the controlling element in the State party and synonymous with the national party in a particular State. Thus in Illinois the Cook County (Chicago) Democratic organization has long been the dominant force in the State party and usually has acted for it in the party councils at the national level. At times, however, its hegemony has been challenged by a governor or United States senator whose personal following may be more extensive and may even include some of the elements nominally part of the Cook County organization.

Party organizations in the localities are often almost completely autonomous. Gosnell's studies in Chicago, for example, disclosed the astonishing ease with which ward and precinct leaders were able to move with their supporters not only from one party faction to another but occasionally even from one party to another.[29] Any well-disciplined faction from the precinct on up is likely to show independence. Such groupings may be the building blocks of more inclusive organizations, but they are exceedingly fractious and unruly ones. Moreover, the governmental officials whom they elect to State and national office are tied directly to these local constituency organizations, whether the public officials have made, or are made by, the district parties. Such officials are attached only tenuously to any more inclusive aggregation. The activities of local party workers of the Eighth Congressional District of Virginia in the election of November, 1944, were a particularly open illustration of independence, but they were not remarkable in any other respect. These workers were urging those coming to the polls to "Vote for Howard Smith (Democrat) for Congress and Dewey for President." More cautious ones confined themselves to "Vote for Howard Smith for Congress and your choice for President."

The causes for the independence of local party units are many and complicated. Detailed examination of them lies outside the scope of this book, since our present concern is primarily to call attention to the way in which these variations in party structure must be accompanied by similar variations in the relations between parties and interest groups. It is obvious, of course, that these relations significantly reinforce localism and factional independence in the parties, even though they may not have produced such diffusion of control. The diversities that have always underlain and sustained the Federal system, the separate election of the president, an election system rigidly tied to the calendar, under which a member of

[29] Harold F. Gosnell: *Machine Politics: Chicago Model* (Chicago: University of Chicago Press, 1937), chaps. 2–4.

Congress must face his constituency on a given date, usually without dramatic national issues to reduce his dependence upon purely local demands—these are among the causes of localism in the party system.

As might be expected, the tendencies toward State and local independence are buttressed by various legislated arrangements. Thus the Hatch Acts of 1939 and 1940, whether or not properly designated "clean politics" acts, have had the effect of weakening any nationalizing tendencies in the party system. The first of these forbade partisan activity by Federal employees, excepting assistant heads or higher officials of executive departments. This ban was extended in the 1940 legislation to State officials principally engaged in activities financed wholly or partly from Federal funds. These laws therefore discouraged the formation of partisan electoral relationships around the chain of administrative relationships running from the president and the cabinet down into congressional constituencies. It is significant that they are apparently less effective against State officials connected with State and local party organizations, though paid with Federal funds, than against persons directly included in the Federal bureaucracy. That is, they have weakened the centripetal forces in the national party system without discouraging the centrifugal ones.

The Hatch Act of 1940 also placed rigid and hopelessly unrealistic limits on the amounts of money national political committees might spend and on the amounts individuals and groups might contribute to them. Although these restrictions have had no effect on total expenditures, they have almost certainly reduced the financial dependence of State and local party organizations upon the titular national leadership.[30]

The localized loyalties in party organization can further be traced to the interest-group character of these units. The motives for participating in an electioneering machine, particularly at the local level, are often almost devoid of ideological or policy content. As in the case of other interest groups in the society, participation may be an end in itself. To be "one of the boys," to belong to the group, to identify with a dramatic leader, and the like, may satisfy deep-seated psychological needs in the individual almost regardless of what the group is doing. Where this element is not the exclusive feature of the local party organization, it is still likely to be of importance. The incentive to "belong" is usually supplemented and reinforced by the distribution of patronage and other spoils through

[30] Cf. Louise Overacker: *Presidential Campaign Funds* (Boston: Boston University Press, 1946), chap. 2.

party channels. For many participants spoils may become the more important element, but the feature of simple "sociability" is never entirely missing.[31]

In his study of the Philadelphia Republican organization Kurtzman observes:

> The committeeman is, for the most part, not interested in facts or the truth; he wants to know what the instructions of the ward leaders are so that he may pass them along to his voters. In one of the Philadelphia wards the chairman of the executive committee thought that it would be a good idea for someone to explain to the committeemen the 12 amendments to the State Constitution that were to be voted on by the voters of the city and state at that election, so that the committeemen might understand them and explain them to the voters. One lawyer, a committeeman, volunteered to make the proper explanations. . . . When he was finished some committeemen began asking questions. One member arose and said, "I think it is a waste of time to discuss these amendments when we do not know what ones we are going to support or oppose. We are not interested in their provisions, we want to know how we are going to vote on them."[32]

There could hardly be a better illustration of the restricted motivations of many local party participants.

Local relations of sociability and patronage are established social patterns around which have developed definite expectations. They will, therefore, be defended by their participants against disturbance from whatever source. This characteristic is the central feature of the local party organization as a political interest group. The party claims patronage and spoils of various kinds, control of the electoral machinery, and freedom from intrusions and restraints threatening its solidarity, whether from national party leaders or from reform movements. In other words, the party organization, State or

[31] Cf. Harold D. Lasswell: *Psychopathology and Politics* (Chicago: University of Chicago Press, 1930), esp. chap. 5. Roy V. Peel's significant study: *The Political Clubs of New York City* (New York: G. P. Putnam's Sons, 1935), indicates the relative importance of "social" activity in these organizations. See particularly pp. 160–77, 179–90. Cf. Georg Simmel: "The Sociology of Sociability," translated by Everett C. Hughes, *American Journal of Sociology*, Vol. 55, no. 3 (November, 1949), pp. 254–61.

[32] David H. Kurtzman: *Methods of Controlling Votes in Philadelphia* (Philadelphia, 1935), p. 35. Copyright by and used with the permission of David H. Kurtzman.

local, is not only a vehicle for various interest groups but is in a sense in competition with any of them that seek to change the behavior patterns it encompasses, whether by direct attack upon its claims or by efforts to force conformity to national programs and direction. In this respect the local party is subject to the same problems of internal politics and external effectiveness as other groups.

One illustration of the complexity of the relations between interest group and party is provided by the minor or "third" party in the United States, discussion of which has been omitted from the preceding paragraphs. These groups, of which there are dozens on the national and local scenes, uniformly represent elements that cannot establish or maintain adequate relationships with the major parties. Sometimes they are groups that have split off from one of the major party organizations because the latter have not effectively represented the interests of a factional element. Thus the American Labor Party in New York split off from the Democratic organization in the city in 1936 for a variety of such reasons, including the failure of Tammany to work for the re-election of President Roosevelt.[33] At other times they are groups that have emerged outside of the major parties with interests and claims which the latter cannot or do not reflect. The Socialist and Communist parties are obvious illustrations.[34]

Frequently minor parties have made serious attempts to produce electoral majorities for a candidate or a slate of candidates. Where they have succeeded, usually they have been the spearhead for a concentrated local or sectional interest. In such cases, in fact, the minor party has occasionally held a local balance of power between the two major organizations or has actually become a "major" local party, with significant repercussions on the national scene. The Populist party of the 1890's illustrates this state of affairs.[35]

Local success at the polls has usually resulted in the absorption of a minor party by one of the majors. That is, when the minor party has developed extensive support for its claims, the major parties find it expedient to accommodate these demands. Many other minor parties never reach this point of influence and in fact make little effort at

[33] See Hugh A. Bone: "Political Parties in New York City," *American Political Science Review*, Vol. 40, no. 2 (April, 1946), pp. 272–82.

[34] See generally Nathan Fine: *Labor and Farmer Parties in the United States, 1828–1928* (New York: Rand School, 1928); William B. Hesseltine: *The Rise and Fall of Third Parties: From Anti-Masonry to Wallace* (Washington, D.C.: American Council on Public Affairs, 1948).

[35] See John D. Hicks: *The Populist Revolt* (Minneapolis, Minn.: University of Minnesota Press, 1931).

electioneering, but instead use the nomination of candidates as a propaganda device that eventually may win them access either to the major parties or to the government itself. This situation was amusingly illustrated on election night, 1948, when Norman Thomas, perennial Socialist candidate for president, quipped in a radio interview that his election returns would be available in "early editions of *The World Almanac*." Such "parties" essentially are weak political interest groups that adopt this form of activity because they cannot command access to government through other means.

The meanings to be attached to the term "political party" are thus extremely varied. What activities are implied by the designation depends upon the time and place, the level of government, and the section of the country involved. Viewed from the national level the so-called party system gives an impression of disorganization, if not of unrelieved chaos. Such an impression is not strictly accurate, but it is apparent that the national party at any given time is fluid and unstable, consisting more of temporary personal alliances than of continuing institutionalized relationships. It follows that relations between political parties and other political interest groups will be similarly protean. The appropriateness of the political party as a means of group access to government proper will depend, therefore, not only upon the claimant groups involved but also upon the characteristics of the party at the particular time, place, and level of government under discussion. Generalization in the area is hazardous.

Declarations of Party Policy

In view of the amorphous character of American political parties it is not easy to assay the importance of official "policy declarations" for the activities of political interest groups. Given the shifting alliance patterns, the localism, and the factional independence that distinguish the parties, especially as viewed nationally, can any policy statement, however "official," be regarded as an indication of future performance? If declarations cannot be so interpreted, what importance do they have, if any?

The most familiar policy declaration, of course, is the national party platform. Probably the commonest view of it, moreover, is that it is meaningless, that, like the platform of a railroad car, it is something to get in on rather than something to stand on. The platform is generally regarded as a document that says little. binds no one, and is forgotten by politicians as quickly as possible after it is adopted. Admittedly there is much to justify such a view. Considered as a pledge of future action, the party platform is almost meaningless and is properly so regarded by the voters. If it is a document intended for popular consumption, moreover, it has no very extensive audience. The evidence collected by the American Institute of Public Opinion in the 1948 campaign is probably typical. Approximately one third of the adult population claimed to have read all or part of the Republican platform, less than 10 per cent saying they had read all of it. The figures were virtually the same in the case of the Democratic platform. The estimated proportion of nonreaders, roughly two thirds of the adult population, was probably low rather than high, given the familiar reluctance to admit one's deficiencies in the performance of civic duties.[36] The platform is not, therefore, a significant campaign document. Does it have another function?

If all party organizations suddenly ceased preparing and issuing platforms, the party system would not be noticeably affected, for admittedly the platform is not the keystone of all party arrangements. Yet it does have functions of some significance. A hint concerning these is perhaps contained in the fact that professional politicians and political interest groups pay more attention to the platforms of the national conventions than to those in the States, where platforms in most instances are adopted after the party's nominees have been selected in the primaries.

Search for the significance of the platform is not aided by raising the essentially false issue of whether an electorate passes on issues or on men. These alternatives are not real. An electorate cannot select officials completely without reference to the policies they reflect nor pass upon policies in complete disregard of the men who are to act upon them. Even where an apparently "issueless" politics exists, such as Key observed in Arkansas, it is characterized by an effective electorate that is highly homogeneous and concerned primarily with selecting the "best men" to carry on policies on which a consensus has already been reached.[37]

It is the very interdependence of policies and men that suggests the importance of the national party platform. The significance is to be found, however, not in the words of the document taken at their face value, but in the process by which these verbal formulations

---

[36] *Public Opinion Quarterly*, Vol. 12, no. 3 (Fall, 1948), pp. 559–60.

[37] Key: *Southern Politics*, pp. 184–95. Cf. Bentley: *The Process of Government*, pp. 424–5.

are arrived at.[38] For present purposes this process can be examined from two points of view, that of the party as an electioneering device and that of the political interest groups. (This division is, of course, arbitrary, since many of the leaders and delegates at the convention are also members or representatives of interest groups.)

From the standpoint of the party as a vote-getting mechanism, writing a platform is part of the process of forging a coalition of leaders and factions that can nominate a candidate and carry on a nation-wide election campaign. These factions represent clusters of interests directly or estimates of the interests that must be accommodated if the faction is to stage a successful campaign and win or maintain leadership in its area. Given the loose, confederative character of the major national parties, some equivalent of this process is essential. An alliance strong enough to nominate a presidential candidate cannot be constructed without some means of registering and testing the strength and compatibility of factions and suballiances. Consequently, various elements in the parties begin to consider platforms some months before the conventions. These factions may be concerned primarily with promoting the fortunes of aspirants for the nomination. Or they may be concentrating on forging a subordinate factional alliance capable of winning concessions in the form of both policy and patronage in return for support of such aspirants. The fusion, growth, and elimination of these groupings proceeds up to and through the convention to the denouement of the nomination. Test-points for the groupings are provided by the votes that organize the convention and authorize the machinery for appointing the chairman of the resolutions committee, by the revisions of the dominant faction's platform proposals in the resolutions committee, and by the debate (if any) and vote on the adoption of the platform by the full convention. In the nominating procedures that follow, further important alignments and realignments occur, with the result that the nominee may represent a faction that did not dominate the resolutions committee. He may proceed, from this point of view quite understandably, to distinguish his position from that in the platform. Thus in 1928 Al Smith as nominee effectively repudiated the platform plank on prohibition. The earlier stages of constructing an alliance are important, however, as means of testing, demonstrating, and, therefore, augmenting or reducing the strength of the principal factions. When a bolt occurs it reflects the inability of the dissident faction to achieve, by compromise and negotia-

[38] Herring: *The Politics of Democracy*, pp. 230 ff.

tion, the influence its members demand in the selection of the nominee and, by implication, in the policies that the nominee will promote. The platform is thus an outward sign, visible to those who can see below its manifest ambiguities, of the elements constituting the faction dominating that stage of the nominating process.

When an incumbent president is seeking renomination, the process is sharply different in degree. His forces are usually able to organize the convention and to dictate the platform draft on which the resolutions committee's negotiations will be based. Modifications in the proposed platform, however, will still indicate alterations in the alignment of forces supporting the president. Because of his ability to organize the convention, however, opposing factions will be less likely to attempt to draft their own platforms than they would be if a new nominee were to be selected. Under these circumstances the party coalition already exists, and the platform-writing process may strengthen it but is not needed to create it.[39] The process then is of little more importance than it is in the States where it is not needed to effect an electioneering organization.

From the standpoint of the political interest groups, the significance of preparing a platform lies primarily in the evidence that the negotiations provide concerning what groups will have access to the developing national party organization. Interest groups ordinarily will seek the insertion of planks that are as explicit as possible. The well-known ambiguity of such documents, however, is not in itself a matter of concern to them. Only if ambiguity or silence indicates reduction or denial of access to the coalition and its nominees will a group become alarmed.

Interest-group leaders are aware that the real settlement of the issues they are concerned with, even within the party, will take place later; in the platform they seek tentative assurance of a voice in that settlement. To maximize this assurance political interest groups normally seek recognition in the platforms of both major parties. This policy is a logical consequence of the fact that the major national parties are essentially devices for electing the president, rather than instruments for operating the government. Most proposals for national legislation need the votes of legislators from both parties if they are to be enacted, especially where extraordinary majorities are necessary, as in the case of treaties and constitutional amendments. These bipartisan efforts are also a result of the preoccupation of interest groups with their claims; they seek to exert demands through or

[39] Ibid., pp. 234–7.

upon the government and they must consequently utilize any peripheral group or institution that will contribute to that end.

Group activity in the construction of party platforms also has some propaganda values for the group. Appearance before the resolutions committees of the conventions and recognition of a group's claims in the platforms may provide useful content for both internal and external propaganda. Especially where platform planks are a step toward inclusion of the group's claims in party campaign propaganda and in candidates' speeches, they have promotional value for the group. Finally, postelection propaganda that treats a platform plank as a pledge of legislative and presidential action may have some value for a group's effectiveness if the group is well organized, if it is cohesive, if its working alliances with other interest groups are effective, and so on. The concern of political interest groups with platform writing, therefore, is in some respects similar to, or even identical with, that of various party factions, but it often involves additional considerations of a different sort.

The most obvious group activity in the building of platforms occurs, of course, in the hearings before the resolutions committees or in the debates on minority reports before the full convention; but it is not by any means the most important. For a variety of reasons some interest groups, actual and potential, need not appear in such formal fashion in order to achieve recognition. In a situation of international crisis such as that existing when the conventions of 1940 approached, the major interests, organized and unorganized, are sufficiently apparent to obviate any possibility that they will be ignored in the platform. In less dramatic circumstances significant groups are involved in the preparation of various of the factional drafts drawn up prior to the conventions. If such a faction succeeds in organizing the convention, formal appearance by the favored group before the resolutions committee may be entirely unnecessary. For example, the Roosevelt forces were in touch with the American Farm Bureau Federation and other influential agricultural groups well before the 1932 convention; these groups were assured access to the nominee regardless of their appearance before the resolutions committee.[40] Furthermore, under normal conditions a large number of a convention's leaders and delegates will also be leaders or "members" of important political interest groups; the more important these leaders are in the party councils, the less likely it is that the group will need to appear formally before a resolutions committee in order

[40] Kile: *The Farm Bureau Through Three Decades*, pp. 185 ff.

to be recognized. It is not clear, for example, exactly what role the late Sidney Hillman played in the Democratic convention of 1944. He was not a delegate, but it is evident that he was at one and the same time an important convention figure and head of the C.I.O. Political Action Committee. The Pennsylvania Manufacturers Association scarcely needed to appear formally before the resolutions committee at the 1924 Republican convention in support of its tariff plank, since its president, Joseph R. Grundy, was one of the leaders of the Pennsylvania delegation. It seems likely, in fact, that interest groups are relatively weak and uninfluential if they must rely exclusively on appearances before the resolutions committees in order to secure recognition in the platforms.

Platforms are the most common declarations of party "policy," but there are others that deserve at least some mention. Group efforts to secure pledges from particular candidates and party committees have something of this character, but they need not be examined closely at this point. Within recent years both national parties have held some interelection conferences that have had some of the earmarks of platform proceedings at the quadrennial conventions. In 1937 the Republicans set up a program committee that issued its report early in 1940.[41] In the summer of 1949 both parties held conferences in Iowa concerning new farm programs, the Democrats at Des Moines in June and the Republicans at Sioux City in September. These conferences and others of the same type bear a strong resemblance to the less-publicized factional maneuverings preceding the nominating conventions and have similar significance. In this instance the Democratic effort was to "sell" the Administration's farm program, the so-called Brannan Plan. It was significantly boycotted by the leaders of the American Farm Bureau Federation and the National Grange. These groups, along with the National Farmers Union, were prominently represented in the testimony at the Republican meeting.[42] Especially in the case of the party "out of power," these meetings and declarations are probably properly considered in the same category with platforms and preconvention factional maneuvers related to platforms.

[41] See Ronald Bridges: "The Republican Program Committee," *Public Opinion Quarterly*, Vol. 3, no. 2 (April, 1939), pp. 299–306.
[42] The *Washington Post*, September 21, 1949.

10

Interest Groups and Elections

SINCE access to the institutions of government is basically a matter of relationships with individuals who occupy governmental positions, political interest groups inevitably have a stake in the matter of who is to occupy the offices with which they are concerned. While this stake is not confined entirely to elective positions, the latter are a major consideration both as points of policy determination and as means of filling important appointive offices. Since the nominating process, whether by convention or by primary, usually reduces the field of aspirants from a very large number to a few, interest groups are equally likely to make it an object of concern.

Groups and Nominations

In view of the obvious significance of the nominating process, it is astonishing that we know almost nothing of a systematic character about how nominations are made and about the role of groups in connection with them. The formalities, of course, are set forth in all elementary textbooks. The evidence on what occurs prior to this stage, however, is virtually nonexistent.[1] Consequently, the most that we can do here is to engage in a kind of extrapolation from our general knowledge of the nature of political interest groups, aided by stray bits of evidence appearing in the press, in memoirs and biographies, and in similar documents. Until systematic research is done, we can only presume.

Group activities influencing the nominations of presidential can-

[1] But see C. H. Wooddy: *The Chicago Primary of 1926* (Chicago: University of Chicago Press, 1926), esp. chap. 2.

didates have been touched upon in the discussion of platform writing by factions in preparation for the national conventions. Similar efforts probably are made to influence nominations for almost all elective positions at all levels of government. In the localities, to be sure, some of the offices may be of moment to no organized political interest group except the party organization itself. Some, in fact, may lack even this attraction and, like the office of fence viewer in a New England town, may have to be filled by the process of conscription rather than of elimination. These are exceptions, however, and even the normally unattractive office may assume importance under changed circumstances—boundary disputes in connection with a public improvement, for instance, might make the fence viewer a controversial and significant figure.

The specific activities of interest groups in influencing nominations can be reduced to two types, not necessarily alternatives to one another. First, the group may promote the fortunes of an aspirant through the party machinery, whether through the primary, the caucus, or the convention, either to secure organization support or, where that is nonexistent, to gain the advantages of a party label. Where one or two well-organized parties exist in the area, this technique is similar to the maneuvers among rival factions, or to the negotiations with a dominant faction, that occur in platform writing at some levels of the party organization. Where party ties are not persistent but loose and temporary, the interest group itself may provide the organizational and financial sinews of a nomination effort. This situation is common enough in the unstable factional arrangements characteristic of much of the South,[2] but it is not unknown elsewhere. In some, perhaps many, congressional districts in the North, party organization is so nearly nonexistent that no man will seek the nomination unless he is confident of building a personal organization or of having available to him the machinery of one or more interest groups, whether for use in a primary fight or in a general election.[3] The group's organization virtually becomes the party under these conditions.

Second, the group may influence nominations by inducing members to vote in the primaries for those whose records, backgrounds, or promises best meet the claims of the group. In this case the group may take no part in selecting aspirants to run in the primary but

[2] Key: *Southern Politics*, p. 416.
[3] Cf. E. E. Schattschneider: "Party Government and Employment Policy," *American Political Science Review*, Vol. 39, no. 6 (December, 1945), pp. 1152–4.

merely promote the fortunes of the ones who are most acceptable. Such activity may be open—that is specific endorsements may be
made—or it may be more concealed. Concealed promotion typically
involves merely listing the qualifications, records, and pledges of
candidates and relying upon the members to vote in accordance with
the group's policies without the necessity of explicit endorsements.
In the same category belong efforts to increase registrations or voting
in primaries. Thus when a labor group or a civic organization em-
barks on a campaign to maximize registrations or primary voting, we
can usually assume that it will work primarily among those in the
population most likely to vote as the group's interests indicate.
The motive may not be apparent, of course, even to those participating in the drive.

Whether the group engages in open endorsement of prospective
nominees depends on various internal and external factors. For example, open support will be dangerous, if not impossible, for a group
whose following overlaps with several different party factional groups
and personal cliques. An endorsement then invites cleavage and disunity in the group. Nor can a national or state-wide group, federated
or not, safely endorse a local primary aspirant seeking to become a
representative in Congress or the State legislature unless the local
group will "go along." Thus opposition to a hostile candidate becomes
more nearly feasible than positive support of a friendly one. A record
patently hostile to a group's claims can easily produce consolidated
opposition to a candidate, as the history of labor union politics demonstrates. Less clear-cut situations create difficulties, however, since local
attachments and tactics may then prevail over State or national
strategy.[4]

It is likely that whether nomination activity is open or not depends on outside factors as well as upon the internal influences just
discussed. Where the group's prestige in the community is not high,
open election activity of any sort may harm rather than aid the
favored candidate. Race-track and gambling interest groups are deeply
concerned with nominations in many States, for example, but their
efforts are largely behind the scenes. Similarly, if the group is in
danger of becoming politically isolated should its nomination ac-

[4] For examples at the State level see Eugene Staley: *History of the Illinois
State Federation of Labor* (Chicago: University of Chicago Press, 1930), pp.
413-25 and *passim*. See Sidney Hillman's testimony on the C.I.O. Political
Action Committee in 1944 primaries in U. S. House of Representatives, Committee to Investigate Campaign Expenditures: *Hearings*, 78th Cong., 2d Sess.
(1944), part 1, pp. 8 ff.

tivities fail, it may keep these quiet or more commonly take no part at all. Only the group with no other hope of access can risk openly backing a likely loser.

The particular form taken by group activities in influencing nominations is a matter of tactics. Looking at the broad character of political interest groups, we can be certain that all these activities have the same general objective. This was put in particularly candid terms some years ago in a letter from the Georgia representative of the Association of Life Insurance Presidents to one of his superiors: "the method is to interest ourselves in key men before they are elected, help them to get elected, and then they owe us something instead of our owing them. That is the whole secret." [5] Access is most certain when it is established early.

Not all circumstances are appropriate to the successful operation of interest groups in influencing nominations, nor are all interest groups, as previous paragraphs have suggested, equally able to engage successfully in such activity. Where party organizations are strong and access to them has not been established by other means, the resources needed to influence slate makers may be considerable. A sizable and cohesive block of votes is one such resource. The Anti-Saloon League provides an illustration. The cohesiveness of this group was such that it had effective weapons against any party organization that ignored its demands concerning nominees. On occasion it placed independent candidates in nomination when the dominant factions in both parties responded unsatisfactorily to its claims. If this action forced one of the party organizations to change or to reconsider policy commitments, the League candidate would withdraw from the race. Precisely this maneuver occurred in the 1924 campaign for United States Senator from New Jersey.[6]

Campaign contributions may be an alternative or an additional requirement. Where the local party organization is not extensive, the availability of group members as speakers and canvassers may be influential. These are almost certainly among the reasons why labor organizations have had a voice in nominations in many constituencies in recent years.

In place of, or in addition to, such sources of leverage, an interest group may derive influence from an established view that particular positions are peculiarly the concern of a given group or that they are, in a sense, under the protection of that group. Thus in

[5] U. S. Temporary National Economic Committee: *Hearings*, part 10, p. 4403.
[6] Odegard: *Pressure Politics*, p. 88.

many States and localities having an elective judiciary, the bar association is widely regarded as entitled to a say in the nomination of judicial candidates and to the right to make public judgments concerning the qualifications of men nominated for the bench by the party organizations. This power is not necessarily great, and it does not go unchallenged, particularly when the courts are deeply involved in policy controversy, as they were when the labor injunction was being used so freely in the early years of this century. Judges exercise real political power, and their personal allegiances are a matter of concern to all interest groups. Nevertheless, the special relations between bench and bar may give the latter, if fairly cohesive, an advantage in the nomination of judges.[7]

The formal legal structure of the nominating procedure may significantly affect the role of interest groups in nominations. Where the open primary and cross filing are used, as in California, with the resulting weakness and volatility of party organizations and factions, the nomination of various candidates may be a matter of the direct activity of interest groups and alliances of such groups. These groups may assume complete responsibility for nomination papers, propaganda, canvassing, and mobilizing the primary vote as well as the vote in the general election. Nomination is then almost solely an affair of interest groups, and the party becomes almost completely an abstraction.

Participation in nominations, like other aspects of group technique, is certain to be profoundly affected by the status that a group occupies in the social structure. The importance of status has already been noted in discussing differential propaganda advantages, and it pervades the entire problem of access. Its importance here lies in the fact that favorably situated groups may not need to engage in nominating activity in order to gain access to legislative, executive, and judicial policy makers. Their "members" almost inevitably figure prominently among the names on any slate. In other words, the attitudes they represent are so strong in the community that almost any successful nominee is accessible to them.[8] Business groups in most urban areas of the country occupy such positions, as do the Farm Bureau Federation, in the Corn Belt and comparable areas, unions

[7] See Rutherford: *The Influence of the American Bar Association*, pp. 155–61; E. M. Martin: *The Role of the Bar in Electing the Bench in Chicago* (Chicago: University of Chicago Press, 1936).

[8] Cf. Key: *Southern Politics*, p. 416. Stephen K. Bailey: *Congress Makes a Law: The Story Behind the Employment Act of 1946* (New York: Columbia University Press, 1950), pp. 148–9, 185–92.

such as the United Mine Workers in some constituencies, and many other groups both broad and narrow. Automatic access may be available to inclusive groups, such as chambers of commerce, and even to particular firms or families, as the Lynds' Middletown studies have indicated with respect to the "X" family and its enterprises. Such assurance, in fact, goes a long way toward explaining the tendency of such groups in a bipartisan or bifactional constituency to contribute money to both partisan organizations in a gesture of impartiality.

From the standpoint either of party organization or of interest group, the accessibility of a nominee is not the sole consideration; his ability to get himself elected is of equal importance. The group does not desire access to a person, but to a position that commands a measure of institutionalized power. The nominee is useless to the group unless he is elected. In some constituencies almost anyone can win if he marches under the dominant party banner. At various times in other constituencies the strength of one candidate may be so great that he carries along most others on the party ticket almost regardless of their qualifications. The latter, in the popular phrase, "ride in on the coat tails" of the former. Under still different circumstances the nominee stands by himself, relying on his own influence and following, to the practical exclusion of a party organization and of others on the same ticket.[9] In any of these situations, however, the nominee's individual strength as a vote-getter is never irrelevant; it is always significant in some measure.

To the extent that the effectiveness of a nominee is based on his personal influence in a constituency, the group's control over him may be limited. There is, however, almost nothing in the way of empirical evidence to test this proposition. As the discussion in Chapter 7 suggested, an adequate body of theory concerning the general nature of leadership is developing, but detailed, systematic studies of the workings of interpersonal influence are few, and in the strictly political sphere they are still more rare. One of the most suggestive for present purposes is Merton's exploratory investigation of patterns of influence in a local community.[10] He found that all those recognized

[9] Although the only intensive investigation of this type of situation is V. O. Key's *Southern Politics*, it is, like many patterns he discusses, probably fairly common in areas outside the South.

[10] Robert K. Merton: "Patterns of Influence: A Study of Interpersonal Influence and of Communications Behavior in a Local Community," in Lazarsfeld and Stanton (eds.): *Communications Research, 1948–1949*, pp. 180–219. Cf. Whyte: *Street Corner Society*, pp. 263 ff.

as "influentials" belonged to more formal organizations than did the general run of the population. Leadership apparently involves participation in a variety of groups. Those "influentials" whose interests were largely confined to the local community tended to belong to organizations that primarily provided the means of establishing personal ties in quantity, and the following of such leaders was based upon personal relationships of sympathetic understanding. Most important, these "local influentials" were more likely to hold elective political positions than the "cosmopolitan influentials," who were significantly interested in the world outside the local community and whose following was based on their wider experience and specialized skills.

If localized personal attachments are assumed to be the characteristic basis of support for officials elected from local constituencies—State and national legislators as well as municipal officials—what significance has this assumption for interest groups and parties? Precisely how and in how many ways interest group leadership may be tied in with such "local influentials," we do not know. It would seem likely that an important, if not exclusive, basis of access to such persons would depend upon the group leaders' ability to fit into, to become part of, a local pattern of interpersonal loyalties. Once established, such relationships would help explain the resistances that national, especially federated, organizations meet in their efforts to shift the political attachments of their local affiliates. Within the party the situation is likely to be similar. The local vote-getting abilities of a nominee may make him virtually independent of State and national party organizations, as well as of State and national interest group organizations. For both party and group leaders at higher levels, therefore, alternative channels of control may be sought that do not operate through the nomination and election process. These would include the withholding of patronage and the denial of support for the local rebel's policy proposals. Alternative channels would also include access to the local recalcitrant through cliques, through friendship and work groups into which the elected official moves, whether in the legislature, the executive, or the judiciary. Recalcitrant local leaders may be moved or removed through these and similar means, but if they are succeeded by men whose base of support is of a similar type, the solution is likely to be temporary.

Although our knowledge of the nomination process is too limited to permit confident generalization, from the standpoint of political interest groups nominating activity can best be regarded as one of many alternative means of securing access. Whether participation in nominations is important to a particular group and how a group participates will depend upon the group's internal politics, its position in the constituency, the character of the party organization, patterns of influence in the constituency, and the nature of the formal, legal procedures governing nominations and elections.

"Keeping Out of Politics"

When we turn to actual election campaigns, data on the role of political interest groups are more nearly adequate, perhaps largely because such campaigns are inevitably more in the open and more fully reported than the nominating process. It is also true that official and unofficial investigations focus more commonly on elections than on nominations. Evidence from such sources seems to indicate that more interest groups participate at this as compared with the earlier stage, or at least that they function more openly. A variety of factors account for this state of affairs, but an obvious and basic one stems from the fact that the election normally offers fewer alternative choices than are available before the field has been narrowed by nomination. It is far less risky to wager on the outcome of a race between two contestants than to try to pick the winner from a field of three or four or twenty. To have backed the winner before he was nominated is likely to pay high dividends in access, but to have backed one of his unsuccessful opponents is even more likely to result in lonely isolation.

Although interest groups rather generally participate in elections, they are usually timid about admitting it. Most, in fact, place a high premium on what is known as "keeping out of politics." The American Legion, for example, professes to adhere to its constitutional requirement that it be "absolutely non-political." Nevertheless, it has exerted a continuing influence in politics, particularly at the local level, but to some extent in more inclusive arenas as well.[11] The kind of "politics" that most groups claim they are "keeping out of" is apparently a special one. The phrase obviously does not mean that such groups are indifferent about the persons placed in official position. It certainly does not indicate that they are unconcerned with legislative enactments, administrative determinations, or judicial decisions. These affect and reflect the claims and counterclaims of interest groups to such an intimate extent that, as Chapter 4 in-

[11] Cf. A. A. Berle, Jr.: "American Legion," *Encyclopaedia of the Social Sciences.*

dicated, almost all groups are inevitably involved in this kind of "politics" in some measure.

"Keeping out of politics" primarily means avoiding complete identification with any one political party organization or faction. In some instances it implies keeping clear of any such identification. But it does not mean refraining from all involvement in governmental affairs. David Dubinsky, head of the International Ladies' Garment Workers' Union, illuminates this point in a statement concerning the political activities of labor groups: "Labor should be a social pressure group, pushing its views on great social questions, lobbying for progressive legislation, keeping our society in balance. *Labor must be in social politics not in party politics.*" [12] (Italics added.)

Avoiding any commitment, especially an open or continuing commitment, to a particular party organization or faction is generally characteristic of interest group politics. The reasons for this policy are numerous and complicated. The most commonly cited explanation is that the formalities of the Constitution of the United States, especially the distribution of powers under the federal system and the separation of powers—legislative, executive, and judicial—which obtains at all three levels of the governmental structure, make partisanship unwise.[13] (Here is one more illustration of the channeling influence of formal structure, whether within the group or in the polity as a whole.)

The existence of the federal system means that a nation-wide group may have to be concerned with as many as forty-nine different jurisdictions, perhaps even more, since some major cities exercise significant powers under constitutional provisions for "home rule." If at the national level the group becomes completely identified with one national party, not only is it handicapped when the opposition comes to power in Washington, but it may deny itself access to the other party in the States in which the latter is dominant. A party, as we have seen, is a loosely knit organization, but there are usually connections between the forces supporting members of Congress and those behind governors and State legislators. Open and continuing identification with one of these forces may easily cost more than it gains. At the national level, moreover, and in varying degrees in the State legislatures, party discipline is so nearly nonexistent that few legislative decisions are made strictly along party lines. Friendly leg-

---

[12] Quoted in Mills: *The New Men of Power*, p. 163.

[13] Cf. A. N. Holcombe: *The Political Parties of To-Day* (New York: Harper and Brothers, 1924), chap. 2; Herring: *Group Representation Before Congress*, pp. 47–50.

islators of whatever party are thus the principal concern of most interest groups; they have nothing to gain and everything to lose by
consistent partisanship. A group interested in promoting a constitutional amendment can afford even less to be partisan, since the extraordinary majorities usually required cannot ordinarily be produced
by a single party. It is unlikely that one party can control two thirds
of the seats in each house of Congress and majorities of each house
in three quarters of the State legislatures.[14]

The centrifugal influence of the federal system may be in process
of modification. The sharp extension of Federal authority since the
1930's, with the effective though tardy blessing of the Supreme
Court, may be shifting sufficient power away from the States to make
group partisanship on the national level more advantageous and less
hazardous than in the past. The basic difficulties are likely to remain,
however, since the States' spending and taxing powers will continue
to have sufficient importance to require the concern of national
as well as State and local interest groups.

The separation of powers has a similar significance at the various
governmental levels. Where the party designation of the executive is
not shared by the majority of both houses of the legislature, a group
ordinarily will have little to gain from casting its lot with one major
party. Even where one party nominally controls both legislature
and executive, moreover, discipline is normally so weak that the
group identified with the majority party may enjoy no special advantages from being so.

The more complex reasons for the tendency of interest groups to
"keep out of" partisan politics are to be found in the internal politics of the particular groups and their strategic position in the political arena. These can be classified under three heads: first, the conceptions of the electoral process held by group members; second, the
relation between partisanship and cohesion; third, the risks of political isolation involved in partisanship.

All three of these to some extent, but particularly the first, are affected by the degree to which group members—and consequently
the groups as units—are psychologically disposed toward partisan activity by the group. To what extent do their conceptions of

[14] In the Eighty-first Congress, the Senate's vote on Republican Senator
Lodge's proposed amendment changing the method of allocating electoral votes
within the States is illustrative. For the amendment were 64 Senators (three
more than the required two thirds): 46 Democrats and 18 Republicans. The
opposition was made up of 4 Democrats and 23 Republicans. See *Congressional
Record*, 81st Cong., 2d Sess., February 1, 1950, p. 1307.

the group and of the electoral process make partisan activity seem "proper"? Is it "right" for group leadership to tell the members to back a particular party or, for that matter, a particular candidate? Is such political activity what the group was "set up to do"? Is it a "proper" means for asserting the claims of the group? The answers to questions such as these can indicate the degree to which members are psychologically ready for partisan activity. This degree of readiness will vary from group to group and from time to time within a particular group, but there is circumstantial evidence of a general disposition against partisanship. Most suggestive is the rather deferential lip service that is paid to being an independent voter rather than a partisan. Consistently one fifth to one third of the voting population regardless of social status classify themselves in opinion surveys as independents.[15] The significance of this tendency is increased when we find evidence that most self-styled independents actually vote in a highly partisan manner.[16]

The fact that, although most voters are in fact partisans, many of them are unable to admit it, does not contradict the tendency, noted in Chapter 2, for groups to achieve a high degree of homogeneity in their candidate preferences. It is one thing for a group to arrive by informal processes at a fairly uniform preference for one candidate—or even one party—over another. It may be a quite different thing for the group's leadership openly to announce support of one party and opposition to another.

The effectiveness of groups that do participate in election campaigns will be taken up later. Here we are interested in the influences that encourage or prevent such activity. Empirical data on this point are sadly lacking, but presumptive evidence can be adduced from the behavior of a number of groups, notably the labor unions and federations. It is a common observation that such groups are likely to accept leadership and discipline during a strike but to display no such unity in electoral behavior. To most people discipline in the process of collective bargaining seems natural, since collective bargaining is "what labor organization is for." Precisely. Not only the outsider but also the union member tends to look upon collective bargaining and the strike as the proper sphere of union activity and upon election activity, especially partisanship, as outside this sphere. This

[15] See, for example, *Public Opinion Quarterly*, Vol. 12, no. 3 (Fall, 1948), p. 564.
[16] Cf. Hadley Cantril and John Harding: "The 1942 Elections: A Case Study in Political Psychology," *Public Opinion Quarterly*, Vol. 7, no. 2 (Summer, 1943), pp. 222–41.

attitude is a consequence, in the C.I.O. as well as the A.F. of L., of a particular set of economic assumptions and of a particular wage theory that holds to the collective bargain backed by the threat of a strike as the best means of improving the position of wage earners.[17]

Until partisan political activity takes a major position in the implicit wage theories of labor unions, union discipline will dictate when the worker will strike, but not how he will vote. Mills refers to this fact when he observes that "labor unions as organizations and as memberships are oriented only in the economic sphere." He comments further:

> If a labor leader begins to work for a political act not immediately and obviously involving an economic gain for his membership, immediately he will be accused of working for personal glory and selfish power. If he takes a longer-run political chance, he may get into short-term economic trouble with his members. . . .[18]

Mills's own evidence, moreover, indicates that this limited view of the union role is not peculiar to the rank and file. According to his findings, labor leaders do not consider party affiliation a means of achieving policy preferences.[19] Unless the electoral process and partisan activity are viewed by a group as within its legitimate sphere, it will tend to "keep out of politics."

The cohesion of the group is obviously both a cause of, and an effect of, the extent to which the group accepts a partisan role. The degree of unity sets limits on permissible partisanship, and involvement in party politics is likely to affect cohesion. We have here, of course, an example of the effects of overlapping membership. Individual political partisanship is an attachment formed early and likely not only to persist through a lifetime but also to be handed down from generation to generation.[20] Within a group, therefore, cleavages along party lines are a constant threat unless partisanship is accepted as merely a group tactic. Even in the simple matter of endorsing a candidate rather than a party, therefore, leaders will move cautiously until assured of fairly cohesive support. Sidney Hillman's testimony in 1944 before the House Campaign Expenditures

[17] This point has not been fully explored by the labor economists, but see Millis and Montgomery: *Organized Labor*, p. 317.

[18] Mills: *The New Men of Power*, p. 236. Copyright 1948 by and used with the permission of Harcourt, Brace & Company, Inc.

[19] Mills: *The New Men of Power*, p. 174.

[20] Cf. Cantril and Harding: "The 1942 Elections," pp. 222–41.

Committee is illustrative. Concerning the activities of the C.I.O.-P.A.C. he asserted not only that the national organization did not "endorse senatorial, congressional, State, or local candidates," but also that its endorsement of President Roosevelt was not made until "substantially all of the C.I.O. international unions and the great majority of its State councils had already acted, so that the action of our committee merely recorded the unanimity of their opinion." [21] Similarly, the A.F. of L.'s only outright endorsement of a presidential candidate, its reluctant support of LaFollette's independent candidacy in 1924, occurred only after considerable insistence from the rank and file and after the dominant factions in the two major parties had coldly rejected its claims. The more normal pattern is bipartisanship, which, as Lorwin has said concerning the A.F. of L.'s practices, "is a way to screen political disunity." [22]

In the less cohesive federated groups, such as the A.F. of L., bipartisanship at the national level or among the leadership of the international unions is often the result of a diversity of local partisan attachments. Such diversity in the Anti-Saloon League maximized the power of the national organization in legislatures, even though it meant supporting candidates who were "dry" politically but "wet" personally.[23] In the A.F. of L. it has meant an equally bizarre set of alliances whose usefulness is almost exclusively local and not infrequently more useful to the local party organization than to the national union.[24] Such local and specialized attachments, as might be expected, are highly resistant to efforts at change from above. Key reports that in Tennessee the Memphis A.F. of L. council, tied to the Crump machine, put up resistance of this sort in 1948. When the Tennessee League for Political Education endorsed Gordon Browning, the anti-Crump candidate for governor, the head of the Memphis council stated that this action hadn't "anything to do with Memphis." [25] Less colorful but equally significant events of a similar sort occurred elsewhere in the 1948 campaign. When William Green, President of the A.F. of L., announced in June that the federation would never support Dewey, the leadership of the huge Teamsters Union immediately made it clear that he did not speak

[21] U. S. House of Representatives, Committee to Investigate Campaign Expenditures: *Hearings*, 78th Cong., 2d Sess. (1944), part 1, p. 8.

[22] Lorwin: *The American Federation of Labor*, p. 425.

[23] Odegard: *Pressure Politics*, p. 87.

[24] Cf. Millis and Montgomery: *Organized Labor*, pp. 304–5; Key: *Southern Politics*, pp. 73, 100, 658.

[25] Key: *Southern Politics*, p. 73, n. 25.

for them. The A.F. of L. did not endorse Truman; rather, some of its leaders formed the Committee of Labor Executives for the purpose. When the C.I.O. Executive Board in August voted 35 to 12 to support Truman, Philip Murray was quoted as saying: "There isn't any way under the constitution of the C.I.O. that you can make a decision of this sort mandatory. Any union still may exercise its right to do what it wants." [26] The same observation was made in substance by Sidney Hillman in 1944.[27]

Under these circumstances it is not astonishing to find, as Mills did in his 1946 study of A.F. of L. and C.I.O. national union leaders and heads of the State and city councils, that labor leaders are found in the following of most major candidates and all major parties. Although a majority of those in his sample said they were registered Democrats, a significant proportion, especially among heads of the national unions, claimed bipartisanship. Significantly, he suggests that the problem of cohesion imposes this view on such leaders:

> Since the affiliations of the lower leaders, not to mention members, are mixed, it is often more advisable for the top leaders, who have the task of holding the union together, to be non-partisan. In this way they can mediate between local endorsements and the complex and protective tie-ins of the various organizations.[28]

The threat of partisanship to cohesion is not simply a result of the overlapping membership between interest group and party. The causes may be much more subtle. As we have said previously, for example, the widespread attitudes toward the medical profession in and out of the group—attitudes indicative of a potentially heterogeneous group—probably would not permit that body to engage in open partisanship or open electoral activity on an extreme scale. Doctors aren't expected to act that way. If the suspicion of legislative politics has threatened the group's cohesion and influence, participation in electoral politics might be fatal.

The danger of becoming politically isolated is a very real threat stemming from partisanship, from not "keeping out of politics." As

[26] The *New York Times,* June 27, 1948; The *New York Herald Tribune,* August 26, September 1, 1948.

[27] U. S. House of Representatives, Committee to Investigate Campaign Expenditures: *Hearings,* 78th Cong., 2d Sess. (1944), part 1, p. 23.

[28] Mills: *The New Men of Power,* pp. 171–3. Copyright 1948 by and used with the permission of Harcourt, Brace & Company, Inc.

Schattschneider has put it: "Isolation is the extreme peril to be avoided by any interest at all costs. . . ." [29] This "peril" has two facets. In the first place, open identification with a party which turns out to be the loser is likely to weaken or block the group's access to elected officials. Some measure of bipartisanship thus becomes a sort of insurance. Having some access to both sides may thus be preferable to an all-or-nothing arrangement. It appears that hedging in this fashion is not confined to the familiar sort of interest groups. Key has noted that in South Carolina the low-country factions or "rings," not knowing which candidate will win in State campaigns, will officially support one candidate but at the same time designate a member to back another, so that "if their favorite does not win, the local group will have a man with access to the victor to plead local matters." [30]

Isolation resulting from open endorsement of a losing ticket has significance (and partisanship, *per contra*, has advantages) only if party lines are important in the determination of policy. Although legislative voting follows party lines in some State legislatures, it does not ordinarily in the Congress. A national party, in fact, is chiefly significant as a device for electing the president. Consequently, on the national level the temptations toward partisanship and the dangers of isolation occur principally in campaigns for the presidency. These dangers are usually great enough so that a group will hesitate to take sides unless it is fairly certain that access to one of the candidates is likely to be denied anyhow and nothing is to be lost by backing his opponent.

An excellent illustration can be seen in the dilemma of the American Farm Bureau Federation in 1928. Coolidge had twice vetoed the McNary-Haugen farm relief measures, in 1927 and again in 1928, which the Farm Bureau had backed. Even before the nominating conventions a good many members of the group wanted to give open support to the party that would promise to enact the measure. At the Republican convention the Farm Bureau got an unsatisfactory reception by the platform committee, on top of which the convention nominated Herbert Hoover, who was more objectionable to the group than Coolidge himself. When the Democratic platform committee gave the desired promises, the issue was clear. "But," as Kile says, "how could farm bureau leaders in the midwestern battleground states fight effectively, while at the same time avoiding the appearance of

---

[29] Schattschneider: *Party Government*, p. 86.
[30] Key: *Southern Politics*, p. 139, n. 6.

'dragging their organizations into politics?'" Continuing with his account:

> The solution finally worked out to utilize the organization's county machinery without involving the state officials too much, was to set up an independent farmers' campaign organization committee in each of the midwestern states and in each county insofar as possible. This was called the 'Independent Agricultural League' and it adopted the slogan 'Vote as Farmers, not Partisans.'
>
> The Democratic National Committee turned the organization job over to George Peek and put up the necessary money.
>
> In a further effort to protect the Farm Bureau from the disastrous effects of active partisan politics, state farm bureau men undertook to stick to platforms and principles rather than talk party politics. . . .
>
> It was admittedly a ticklish situation and one not at all relished by President Thompson and many members of his board.[31]

As might be expected, this tactic threatened upheavals in some of the State Farm Bureaus. Despite this fact, however, and despite the election results, which in this instance demonstrated that established party attachments were stronger than group demands, cohesion was not seriously impaired. Nevertheless it is significant that in 1932, when circumstances were far more auspicious, the Farm Bureau did not repeat its 1928 efforts:

> With farm feeling running so high against Mr. Hoover, and with Mr. Roosevelt definitely favoring so much of the farm organization's program, it was not easy to avoid direct endorsement of the Democratic candidate, with all that implies. But the 'battle of ballots' was kept on a non-partisan basis and the Farm Bureau was 'kept out of politics.'[32]

The second facet of the "peril" of isolation is that partisanship may handicap groups in their efforts to gain allies for purposes of

[31] The account is drawn from Kile: *The Farm Bureau Through Three Decades*, pp. 147–51 at p. 149. Copyright 1948 by and used with the permission of Orville M. Kile.

[32] Kile: *The Farm Bureau Through Three Decades*, p. 188. Copyright 1948 by and used with the permission of Orville M. Kile.

legislation and propaganda. Groups that avoid partisanship themselves are likely to be equally chary of open alliances with other groups that are regularly partisan. Such alliances are important in pressing demands for legislation, and they involve some exceedingly strange combinations; but they are unlikely to be entered into if they threaten to produce cleavages within one of the participating groups or to reduce its chances of independent access to political leaders. The partisan label is likely to involve such threats.

Constitutional arrangements in the United States, the character of American parties and of individual attachments to them, the problem of group cohesion, and the exigencies of group strategy in the legislative arena all combine to discourage political interest groups from open identification with particular parties. This is strikingly apparent on the national level. With variations it applies as well to the States.

Groups in Election Campaigns

Strategic considerations not only discourage groups from openly identifying themselves with a particular party but also are responsible for keeping some groups entirely out of election campaigns, even in a non-partisan role. In addition, those groups with small memberships, those whose members are thinly spread over a number of constituencies, and those representing interests which are comparatively peripheral even to their members will be likely to find any sort of election activity unrewarding. Finally, those nonprofit or "educational" groups that enjoy tax-exemption are usually reluctant to jeopardize that privileged status through election activities, although some of them are not so cautious.[33]

However one defines participation in election campaigns, it is clear that a very large number of groups do participate in them. Since such partisan activity as occurs is mostly confined to presidential campaigns, its purpose is usually simple. It is designed to put in power a faction or bloc of elected officials, including the chief executive if possible, who will be receptive to the group's claims. Whether or not these efforts begin as early as the nomination of candidates, they usually involve three supplementary types of activity: (1) supplying

[33] See, for example, the interrogations concerning the activities of the Committee for Constitutional Government and the Constitution and Free Enterprise Foundation in U. S. House of Representatives, Committee to Investigate Campaign Expenditures: *Hearings*, 78th Cong., 2d Sess. (1944), part 2, pp. 377–556.

their members with information concerning the records and pledges of candidates, with or without explicit endorsements; (2) contributing in various ways to a candidate's campaign; (3) getting out the vote among their members and sympathizers.

Perhaps the simplest and most common form of group participation in elections is publicizing for their members and sympathizers the political records of incumbent candidates. If the candidate is a legislator this means a tabulation of his recorded votes on measures considered important by the group leaders. Although this is the classic procedure of the A.F. of L. and other labor organizations, it has also been followed by such widely divergent groups as the National Association of Manufacturers, the Anti-Saloon League (now known as the Temperance League of America), and the League of Women Voters.

Nominees seeking an office for the first time, and sometimes also those running for re-election, are asked, as an alternative or supplement to their records, to commit themselves on governmental policies in which the group is interested. They may be given a written questionnaire or a personal interview, and the results are ordinarily publicized among the group's following. The group may confine its queries to one or two matters, as the Anti-Saloon League did, or it may cover a wide range of difficult and controversial issues. For example, in 1946 the Illinois State Industrial Union Council (C.I.O.) sent all candidates for the State legislature a questionnaire covering a series of proposals, including the following: a State wage and hour act, a State labor relations act, a State fair employment practices bill, a State anti-injunction bill, amendments to workmen's compensation and unemployment compensation legislation, housing legislation, a State constitutional convention, changes in the primary law, legislative redistricting, veterans bonus proposals, public education, assistance to the aged and to handicapped children, and revision of civil service laws. Such requests, when the results are made public on any considerable scale, can prove very awkward for the nominee, especially one whose effective constituency is heterogeneous: failure to respond is construed as hostility, ambiguous responses may be similarly interpreted, and specific pledges may antagonize competing interest groups.

In addition to attempting to secure pledges on policy from the candidates and to publishing the incumbents' records, the group may or may not endorse specific candidates. Whether it does or not is, in any case, of relatively slight importance, since if the members are aware of the group's claims, they will usually be able to choose among candidates in accordance with these demands. Avoidance of endorsement probably implies in most cases nothing more than a concern for the niceties of "keeping out of politics" and for the cohesion of the group.

Although evidence on the point is slight, to say the least, it is probable that the effectiveness of endorsements, whether open or implied, varies greatly. The size of the group in a constituency, and its cohesiveness and consequent ability to induce its members to follow these endorsements at the polls, are determining influences. The effectiveness of endorsement, express or implied, also depends upon the extent to which it is accompanied by other forms of electoral participation. For example, it appears that C.I.O.-P.A.C. endorsement of some candidates for Congress in 1946, unaccompanied by effective mobilization of the vote on election day, constituted a sort of political "kiss of death." Endorsement gave the opposition forces an issue and activated their supporters without sufficient offsetting benefits to the endorsee.[34] Situations of this kind illustrate the point that publication of records and pledges, without supplementary participation of a tangible sort, has little political effect. Standing alone this device is subject to a very heavy discount at the polls and provides only the most tenuous basis for access to the elected official.

The second type of group participation in elections, contributing to a candidate's campaign, is a complicated one. Not only are the forms of contribution various, but the meanings they have in the relationships between candidate and group are not easily discerned. The most obvious form of contribution, of course, is a gift or loan of money from a group or group member to a candidate. Such contributions are an inevitable part of an election system that is only partially supported by public funds. Election campaigns, especially over large constituencies, are not the most economically operated undertakings in the country, but they are expensive under any circumstances. Unless a candidate is that rare political specimen, namely, a man able to finance his campaign out of his own pocket, he is likely to welcome financial assistance from a group or any other source whose character is not such as to constitute an obvious political liability.

To what extent and in what amounts organized interest groups provide monetary aid to candidates' campaigns is not known. The published and unpublished reports on campaign expenditures, even

---

[34] Cf. Hugh A. Bone: *American Politics and the Party System* (New York: McGraw-Hill Book Company, Inc., 1949), pp. 146–9; *The New Republic*, November 18, 1946, pp. 656–7.

in Presidential campaigns, are casual and incomplete in the extreme.[35] In the course of political campaigns and group rivalries, investigating committees occasionally produce embarrassing but inconclusive evidence on the point. From time to time these disclosures have resulted in legislation nominally restricting the practices of certain groups. A spate of such investigations at the turn of the century produced a typical reform association, the National Campaign Publicity Association, whose efforts on behalf of the "rules of the game" were at least partly responsible for Federal legislation in 1907 forbidding corporations and national banks to contribute financially to presidential and congressional election campaigns. Three fourths of the States carry similar provisions on their statute books. Efforts to restrict the influence of labor groups produced in 1943 the war-time Smith-Connally Anti-Strike Act, which forbade trade unions to make such contributions. This prohibition was extended in the Taft-Hartley Act of 1947 to any "contribution or expenditure" by a labor organization in connection with national elections. In 1937 a congressional committee went so far as to propose a ban on contributions "from all organizations, associations, or enterprises, incorporated or unincorporated, whose aims or purposes are the furtherance of group, class or special interests."[36]

If contributions to presidential campaign committees are representative, most monetary contributions are made, at least nominally, by individuals rather than by organized groups.[37] We know, however, that such organized groups as the Anti-Saloon League, State manufacturers associations, trade associations, labor unions, and others have made a more or less regular practice of contributing to campaign funds. Furthermore, it can be presumed that many of the contributions nominally coming from individuals actually represent groups with which they are affiliated, especially corporations and to some extent labor organizations. In some cases, moreover, these gifts move through the hands of several individuals, so that, by the time they reach a candidate or campaign committee, it is virtually impossible to identify the original source. The activities of Joseph R. Grundy of

[35] The standard references on the subject of campaign expenditures are James K. Pollock: *Party Campaign Funds* (New York: Alfred A. Knopf, Inc., 1926); Earl R. Sikes: *State and Federal Corrupt Practices Legislation* (Durham, N. C.: Duke University Press, 1928); Louise Overacker: *Money in Elections* (New York: The Macmillan Company, 1932). See also Miss Overacker's periodic articles on the subject in the political science journals and her *Presidential Campaign Funds*, previously cited.

[36] *House Report No. 151*, 75th Cong., 1st Sess. (1937), p. 135.

[37] Cf. Overacker: *Presidential Campaign Funds*, chap. 1.

Pennsylvania in his heyday are illustrative of the complexities of this kind of relationship. He was not only a key member of one major faction of the Republican party but also an official of the Pennsylvania Manufacturers Association and a producer of wool yarn. The latter commodity was protected in the 1920's by very high tariff rates, a fact that helped account for, and was a result of, his deep involvement in successive tariff revisions. When Grundy acted as fund raiser extraordinary for the Republican party in Pennsylvania, both for the national ticket and for individual members of Congress, it was not always clear exactly what interests were represented by his important middleman position.

Despite the obscurity surrounding the sources of funds, students of campaign finance are agreed that monetary support comes from a very small proportion of the electorate in any constituency. The rank-and-file voters do not contribute significantly and may be unwilling to do so.[38] It is particularly important, therefore, to inquire into the meanings which these donations have for the relationships between candidates and the few who supply money.

The easiest assumption to make is that an understood *quid pro quo* in legislative or administrative policy is involved. This is often the case, and many of the more dramatic revelations about campaign finance support the assumption.[39] The Caraway Committee investigating lobbying activities reported to the Senate in 1929 a judgment of this sort concerning the fund-raising efforts of Joseph R. Grundy in the 1928 Republican congressional and presidential campaigns:

> It need not be said that the services so rendered gave him a standing among his political associates in both Houses of Congress not to be ignored in a study of the influences affecting its legislation, not to speak of the consideration likely to be accorded him in other branches of the Government.[40]

[38] Early in the 1948 campaign the American Institute of Public Opinion put the following question to a sample of adults: "If you were asked, would you contribute five dollars to the campaign fund of the political party you prefer?" Only 29 per cent answered affirmatively. *Public Opinion Quarterly*, Vol. 12, no. 3 (Fall, 1948), p. 564.

[39] See, for example, C. H. Wooddy: *The Chicago Primary of 1926* and *The Case of Frank L. Smith* (Chicago: University of Chicago Press, 1931). See also U. S. Senate, Subcommittee of the Committee on the Judiciary: *Hearings on Lobby Investigation*, 71st Cong., 1st, 2d, and 3d Sess., 72d Cong., 1st Sess. (1929–32).

[40] *Senate Report No. 43*, part 3, *Congressional Record*, 71st Cong., 2d Sess., December 10, 1929, p. 352.

In this sense the contribution is essentially a bribe. An ancient and recognized, if not legitimate, place among political techniques is occupied by bribery. More prevalent at some times and places than at others, it is probably never entirely absent from the social scene.[41] It is a means to privilege for those who have money to spend and stakes to defend. Without denying these facts, however, it is correct to say that this assumption by itself provides a grossly over-simplified and inaccurate picture of campaign contributions.

As Key has observed, the semicontractual theory of contributions thrives on the dearth of evidence and the projective tendencies of most observers.

> Most speculation in this vein has been by professors and news-paper reporters, persons to whom $25 is a wad of money, and it is doubtful that they achieve a sophisticated comprehension of the motivation, attitudes, and expectations of persons who can blithely throw $5,000 in the pot to help elect old Joe, a college classmate, a drinking companion, and a fellow Rotarian, without being any the poorer.[42]

Undoubtedly a great many contributions have their basis in such purely personal considerations. Even when more explicit expectations are aroused they may amount to no more than an assumption that a particular candidate, because of his background and position in the community, is likely to share certain attitudes with the donors, is a "sound" man who will "see things our way."

Except where a donation is purely a matter of personal friendship, the central objective of contributions is access to the power of the elected official. Such access may mean merely the representation in legislative and executive circles, of a general point of view toward government policies, or it may mean an "inside track" on lucrative contracts or jobs. It may imply merely a chance to argue a particular point of view or it may signify effective leverage for or against administrative or legislative action respecting taxes, regulation, and the spending of public funds. It may indicate that the recipient is virtually the agent of the donor or merely that the latter has hopefully climbed aboard the band wagon of an obvious winner.

Even where a *quid pro quo* apparently is involved, the meaning of the arrangement is not always clear. Public utilities, insurance com-

---

[41] See H. D. Lasswell: "Bribery," *Encyclopaedia of the Social Sciences*.
[42] Key: *Southern Politics*, pp. 470–1.

panies, railroads, and similarly vulnerable enterprises may receive from candidates and committees requests for contributions that closely approximate extortion. Under other circumstances an appeal for funds may simply be the act of a sympathetic candidate whose visible resources are not adequate to meet the anticipated costs of a campaign. Kesselman reports that the relatively impecunious National Council for a Permanent FEPC received a good many applications of the latter sort, one from Senator Chavez, the principal leader of the movement in the Senate.[43]

Since most financial contributions come from among the few who have money to spare, all interest groups are not equally able to make them. Corporations and other institutionalized economic groups are probably the most important source of funds, directly or indirectly. Representing or overlapping with some of these are a small number of affluent families. Relatively few interest groups of the association type are in a position to be important contributors. In some cases such action might threaten their cohesion as much as endorsements of parties and candidates. Excepting those set up for campaign purposes, associations more frequently do not have the financial resources for expenditures beyond what is directly required by their central functions.

It is undeniable that the standard pattern of campaign financing places certain handicaps upon the political activities of groups whose funds are small. In addition the salaries of elected officials in most State and local governments are so small that candidates sympathetic to such groups are not likely to be recruited. The A.F. of L., in fact, was recently reported to be considering a system of supplementary payments to State legislators endorsed by the group so that more labor sympathizers could afford to occupy legislative positions.[44] Presumably this proposal was modeled after the practice followed until recently by British trade unions.

Financial handicaps should not be exaggerated, however. Either of two candidates may be adequately accessible to many groups not in a position to contribute. Contributions, moreover, are not the only means of access, and financial donations are not the only form that contributions may take. We have already taken up some of the alternative means of contributing in discussing the indirect means of influencing nominations. Publicizing the records and pledges of candidates may be a contribution of considerable value, with or without

[43] Kesselman: *The Social Politics of FEPC*, p. 81.
[44] The *New York Times*, February 13, 1949.

endorsement.[45] If a group is already engaged in internal propaganda, as most associations are, there is no additional expense incurred by the inclusion of material designed to influence the voting preferences of members. For little additional cost such materials can be spread widely over a constituency. Efforts of this sort, especially where the group is a large one, may be fully as important as a direct monetary donation; they can be contributions in fact, whatever they may be legally.[46]

Where two candidates are identified with quite sharply differentiated policies, propaganda that on its face is wholly concerned with the issues may contribute significantly to the success of the aspirant whose position on the issues is similar to the propagandist's. Various campaigns in the United States have involved issues of that sort—the presidential races in 1896 and 1928, for instance, and, since the advent of the New Deal, a considerable number of local and State as well as national elections. Under such circumstances there has been a strong tendency for interest groups to contribute propaganda to one side or the other. Such propaganda has the disadvantage that it cannot openly support the candidate identified with the policies defended by the sponsoring group, for only by maintaining a "nonpartisan, nonpolitical" façade can the group avoid threats to its internal cohesion and minimize the effects of the low prestige of openly one-sided appeals among undecided voters. Some of the propaganda of labor groups like the C.I.O.-P.A.C. has been of this type.[47] The "What Helps Business Helps You" campaign by the Chamber of Commerce of the United States in 1936 is an excellent illustration.[48] Much of the propaganda of the National Association of Manufacturers and that of various State and local business groups fits into the same category. In 1940 the Committee for Constitutional Government carried on a campaign against more than two terms in the White House for "any" president. Under examination by a congressional committee the group asserted that this campaign was not "political," since they "did not come out against any

[45] Kesselman: *The Social Politics of FEPC*, pp. 200–1, gives several instances in which such aid was solicited by candidates supporting permanent F.E.P.C. legislation.

[46] In U.S. v. C.I.O., 335 U.S. 106 (1948), the Supreme Court somewhat ambiguously held that such activity by a labor organization was not a "contribution or expenditure" under the Taft-Hartley Act of 1947.

[47] See the pamphlet, "This is Your America," reproduced in Joseph Gaer: *The First Round* (New York: Duell, Sloan & Pearce, 1944), pp. 17–44.

[48] Cf. John W. O'Leary: "The 'What Helps Business' Campaign," *Public Opinion Quarterly*, Vol. 2, no. 3 (Fall, 1938), pp. 645–50.

particular candidate." The obvious contributory objective was more frankly stated in another connection by one of the group's officers: "If we did not have any political effect, either on the election of candidates or on legislation, we might as well fold up." [49]

Propaganda services by no means exhaust the list of nonmonetary contributions. Groups may, for example, without charge supply a candidate with their highly valuable membership and mailing lists or in other ways facilitate his solicitation of money and votes. They may permit their meetings to become important opportunities for candidates to appear and make themselves known not only to those present but to those reading newspaper stories of the event. They may offer their meeting halls with little or no charge, and they may lend the time of technicians without charge. These and other tactics illustrate the point that money is not the only, and may not be the most important, form in which groups may contribute to election campaigns.

The various kinds of contributions blend imperceptibly into the third type of group participation in election campaigns, getting out the vote. For convenience this is treated as a separate type of activity, but it cannot be distinguished sharply from the other two. All such efforts have at least the implicit objective of maximizing the vote for the favored candidate or party. Not all groups, however, attempt the laborious and time-consuming task of ringing doorbells and getting voters to the polls.

The available evidence suggests that whether or not a group attempts to get the vote to the polls is a function primarily of the group's size, the geographic distribution of its members, and its cohesion. Its financial resources may be important, but they need not be decisive. Like many local party committees, interest groups have found that an effective job of mobilizing voters need not depend upon money if other influences are favorable. It is unlikely, for example, that the National Association of Manufacturers could engage in this type of function, even if it wished to. Its fifteen or twenty thousand members are too few and too widely distributed over the country to do this work effectively, even supposing the cohesion of the group were sufficient for the task. (It might be added that the roles that such individuals play in their communities probably would not permit this kind of activity.) The resources of the N.A.M. members can better take the form of monetary contributions to party committees and similar satellite organizations.

[49] U. S. House of Representatives, Committee to Investigate Campaign Expenditures: *Hearings*, 78th Cong., 2d Sess. (1944), part 7, pp. 388, 406.

The old Anti-Saloon League is perhaps the prototype of associations capable of mobilizing voters. Its membership was large, well distributed over a great many constituencies, and cohesive, if not fanatic. It operated through local voters' committees, since its whole effort was primarily concerned with the voters. It not only imitated but in some instances all but supplanted the most efficient party organizations. It was Odegard's judgment of the group that "seldom has a political machine worked with such efficiency and dispatch." [50]

The outstanding examples of efforts to get out the vote on a national scale in recent years have been those of the labor organizations, especially the C.I.O.'s Political Action Committee, but including A.F. of L. equivalents, the most recent of which is Labor's League for Political Education, formed in 1947. Where these associations have been effective, they have drawn upon their large, unified, and well-distributed memberships to form local canvassing committees, largely on a volunteer basis. In recent elections they have not only put on registration campaigns but have also rung doorbells, provided transportation to the polls, supplied "sitters" for voting mothers of small children, and provided other important if humdrum services. In some areas, especially in the 1944 elections, they have been given more credit for getting out a big Democratic vote than are the official party organizations. Their own membership is so large, twelve to fifteen million, that concentration upon it alone is a political task of major importance. Significantly, the International Ladies' Garment Workers Union, one of the A.F. of L.'s largest affiliates, has announced that it will establish for just this purpose a system of "political shop stewards," whose tasks will include getting union members to register and vote. [51]

A variety of groups have made efforts to get voters to the polls on a local or State-wide scale from time to time. The American Legion has done so, primarily when issues like the veterans' bonus have been at stake. In some instances, as earlier paragraphs have indicated, the county Farm Bureaus have been used for this purpose when special agricultural issues have been in question. Key reports that in Alabama the Farm Bureau, often working closely with the State Extension Service, has engaged in this sort of electioneering. [52] Retail liquor dealers are an almost traditional channel of such activity. In California, where party organizations are notoriously weak, the power of "Artie" Samish, journalistically dubbed "the Secret Boss

[50] Odegard: *Pressure Politics*, p. 94.
[51] The *New York Times*, June 12, 1949.
[52] Key: *Southern Politics*, pp. 55–6.

of California," is said to rest on the State's forty or so thousand liquor licensees. His technique, it is reported, is not to contribute to election campaigns, but to run them.[53] The number of liquor dealers and their cohesiveness, especially when control of liquor licensing is in question, make them an ideal vehicle through which to turn out the vote.

Results at the Polls

The standard popular statement of the role of organized political interest groups is that because they constitute highly disciplined blocs of voters who will do the bidding of their leaders at the ballot box, they are able to bend elected officials to their wills. The chief weapon of such groups is alleged to be the threat of opposition at the polls, before which the candidate for re-election trembles and to which the aspirant for office pledges respect and submission.

We are not yet ready to discuss the relationships between interest groups and officeholders, but we may inquire into the effectiveness of such groups at the polls. Are they able to carry out their threats and promises? Under what conditions are their threats and promises put into effect at the polls?

The crude theory of democratic politics implicitly assumes that each voter behaves, or should behave, as an isolated unit. Thinking logically and without bias about an election, he is supposed to cast his ballot unaffected by any other influences. Any contrary behavior is aberration or pathology. This notion assumes that the voter, like the classical economic man, is an independent individual. His vote, like the decision in the market of classical economic theory, is isolated and rational, not capable of controlling majorities and the distribution of power any more than the decisions of an individual business man control prices and the pattern of production. Neither such an oversimplified theory of democratic politics nor the theory of the classical economists treats as anything but a troublesome exception the effects of group affiliation and group behavior in the market place and at the ballot box. The atomistic individual unit is the rule; all else is exceptional.

It is unnecessary here to review the evidence found by Lazarsfeld and others, presented in Chapter 2, that contradicts the idea that voting is an atomistic act. In essence this evidence indicates that

[53] Lester Velie: "The Secret Boss of California," *Collier's Magazine*, August 13, 1949, pp. 11 ff.; August 20, 1949, pp. 12 ff.

people who are similarly situated and associate with one another tend toward homogeneity in their candidate preferences. Face-to-face groups like the family and less intimate ones like trade unions tend toward maximum homogeneity in this respect.[54] These data, as an earlier paragraph has suggested, effectively challenge the individualist assumption concerning voting. However, they do not demonstrate clearly the effect of organized interest groups. The evidence does not tell us the extent to which members' votes are "deliverable," that is, can be led to such agreement. It is one thing to observe that aggregations achieve through informal processes a high measure of political homogeneity; it is quite another to say that the leaders of groups can control the choices that the members will make. Certainly they can be influential. But when and how much?

We have already seen, in Chapter 6, that the incompatibility of political predispositions, the result of multiple memberships, prevents unanimity in a group's voting preferences. It seems likely, therefore, that the effectiveness of a group at the polls is a function of its cohesion at that time. Whether the degree of unity will be sufficient depends upon whether a sufficient proportion of the members identifies itself strongly enough with the claims of the group and sees them as being intimately affected by the outcome of an election campaign. Then multiple memberships in competing groups, in other political parties, or in the following of an established politician will not be predominant. Then, also, it may be possible to minimize the proportion of nonvoters in the group.

Presumptive evidence is available to support the proposition that the unity of a group's vote depends upon the perception by the membership that dominant group claims are at stake in election results. Like much of the data in this general field, however, the evidence is not entirely adequate. A crude analysis of the C.I.O.-P.A.C. record in the congressional elections of 1948 is instructive.[55] The Taft-Hartley Act of 1947 was one of the major issues in this campaign. Aimed primarily at union organization rather than directly at such worker benefits as minimum wages, maximum hours, and the like, this legislation tended to put the "deliverability" of union votes to the test. In the 1948 election the C.I.O.-P.A.C. endorsed 215 can-

[54] See above, chap. 2, pp. 22–3, and Helen Dinerman: "1948 Votes in the Making—A Preview," *Public Opinion Quarterly*, Vol. 12, no. 4 (Winter, 1948–9), pp. 585–98. Cf. Frederick Mosteller *et al.: The Pre-Election Polls of 1948* (New York: Social Science Research Council, Bulletin 60, 1949), pp. 227–37.

[55] Mosteller *et al.: The Pre-Election Polls of 1948*, pp. 231–6.

didates for House seats, of whom 144 were elected. Of these successful candidates, 64 were members of the preceding Congress, all but
seven of whom were on·record as having voted against the Taft-
Hartley Act. Of the remaining 80, 74 replaced members of the
previous Congress who had voted for the objectionable labor legislation. The following table summarizes some of the information on
these successful candidates.

Successful Candidates Endorsed by C.I.O.–P.A.C.,
U.S. House of Representatives, 1948 *

Total	Number of endorsed candidates winning seats that were held by another party:		
	During preceding term	During preceding 3 terms	That received 55% or more of major party vote in 1946
144	61 **	26 ***	22

* Source: Frederick Mosteller, *et al.*, *The Pre-election Polls of 1948*
(New York: Social Science Research Council, 1949), pp. 233-4.
** Excludes 15 seats in Illinois, which was redistricted in 1948.
*** Two preceding terms for 4 seats in New York and 2 seats in Penn-
sylvania, since these States were redistricted after 1942.

These figures take no account of the group's efforts in the primary,
and they do not indicate the extent to which this group was responsible for the changes indicated. Despite these and other shortcomings,
however, the data, particularly the evidence on the shifts from one
party to another, do give some support to a conclusion that the
group's efforts were fairly effective. Such shifts, occurring in districts held by the losing party through two war-time and the first
postwar elections and in districts carried in 1946 by 55 per cent
or more of the major-party vote but lost in 1948, indicate that
the changes in 1948 were of major importance. Presumably the
C.I.O.-P.A.C. efforts had something to do with them.

A quite different conclusion is presented by an earlier and more
dramatic test of leadership strength, John L. Lewis's endorsement of
Willkie in 1940, on whch he staked the presidency of the C.I.O.
All the evidence on this effort indicates that it was an almost complete failure. The C.I.O. was a relatively young organization at that

time, but several of its unions, including Lewis's United Mine Workers, were highly unified. Nevertheless, the loyalty to the union and the discipline easily established under the conditions of collective bargaining could not in that election be transferred to the political sphere. Lewis's leadership was segmental, largely limited to the processes that the subordinate leaders and the rank and file regarded as "proper" for union activity. Overlapping memberships between the union and the political party as well as between the union and the following of Franklin Roosevelt were too strong. Furthermore, many workers were loyal to subordinate C.I.O. officials, a large proportion of whom supported Roosevelt. Although there is some evidence of increased nonvoting in 1940 in strong C.I.O. areas, indicating the effects of conflicting loyalties, Lewis's political influence in such areas, even those where the miners were concentrated, was not appreciable.[56] Mills has stated the general point well: "Even the most potent labor leader cannot necessarily count on union members to follow his decisions about political candidates. Unions are not now set up that way; motives for joining and being good members are not primarily political." [57] Cohesion for one purpose does not necessarily involve equal cohesion for another.

Key has analyzed the effects, as indicated in election returns, of congressional hostility to the American Legion's bonus demands. He compared the fortunes of members of the House of Representatives who had voted to sustain presidential vetoes of such measures with those of congressmen who voted to override them just before the elections of 1922, 1924, 1928, 1930, 1934, and 1936.[58] His findings indicate that the most important variable was whether or not a congressman carried the label of the party against which the political tide was then running. The Legion's general effect on the outcome was almost completely negligible.

Although cohesion appears to be a determining influence upon a group's effectiveness at the polls, certain external factors should also be mentioned. One of these is our system of elections by the calen-

[56] Irving Bernstein: "John L. Lewis and the Voting Behavior of the C.I.O.," *Public Opinion Quarterly*, Vol. 5, no. 2 (Summer, 1941), pp. 233–49. Cf. H. F. Gosnell: *Grass Roots Politics* (Washington, D.C.: American Council on Public Affairs, 1942), pp. 29–32.

[57] Mills: *The New Men of Power*, p. 180. Copyright 1948 by and used with the permission of Harcourt, Brace & Company, Inc.

[58] V. O. Key, Jr.: "The Veterans and the House of Representatives: A Study of a Pressure Group and Electoral Mortality," *Journal of Politics*, Vol. 5, no. 1 (February, 1943), pp. 27–40.

dar, regardless of whether there are issues of a national character on which voters may express a preference. Especially in the nonpresidential elections, members of Congress are likely to face their constituencies on matters of largely local concern. A highly cohesive and geographically concentrated political interest group is given a particular advantage under such arrangements, especially if party organization is weak.[59] A second external factor, which may operate in presidential elections, is the electoral college system, under which all of a State's electoral vote goes to the candidate winning a plurality of the popular vote, thus giving a minority of unified voters a chance to exert a disproportionate influence on the outcome. In the large, pivotal States this influence may have a significant effect on the national result, a point stressed by the proponents of reform in the electoral college system.[60]

The effects of interest group activity upon the outcome of elections are thus highly variable. They are, moreover, easily exaggerated. The difficulty of obtaining incontrovertible evidence that a group has wielded influence at the polls facilitates this tendency toward overestimation of the group's effectiveness. It is precisely in the inconclusiveness of the evidence on group activity in elections, in fact, that the significance of such activity may lie. In their pursuit of access to elected officials, interest groups are in a position to exploit the major difficulty faced by both politician and academician in obtaining evidence. A fairly good *prima facie* case for a group's unity at the polls may be every bit as useful as a substantial one. Moreover, it may be effective both before and after an election. A group that can point to activities suggesting a contribution to the election results is not likely to be turned away by a recently elected official. Before an election a politician's estimate of his chances, like a stock-market investor's estimate of prospective yield, is likely to have only a slight basis in reliable knowledge of the persistence of trends and the effects of his decisions upon them. His data are always insufficient, and the less adequate they are, the more sensitive he may be to the claims of a group that may be able to affect the outcome. The imponderables in a politician's estimate of his chances are, of course, by no means the only factors governing access, but

<hr>

[59] See the testimony of W. Y. Elliott before the Joint Committee on the Organization of Congress: *Hearings*, 79th Cong., 1st Sess. (1945), part 4, pp. 951–73.

[60] See *Senate Report No. 602* on S. J. Res. 2, 81st Cong., 1st Sess. (1949), pp. 13–4.

they are likely to play a part. To that extent the absence of evidence provides a rationale for a group's efforts at the polls, almost regardless of their decisiveness.[61]

Conclusion

Interest group activity in the various stages of elections—nominations, declarations of policy, and election campaigns—is one type of political technique available to such groups. Utilized effectively, it is one means of access to key points of policy determination, but by no means the only one. Viewed as technique, group election activity is not essential to the effective assertion of claims upon or through the government. As later chapters will indicate, moreover, it is not by itself a sufficient guarantee of effective access.

Satisfactory data on group activity of this sort are scant and spotty, but they indicate fairly clearly that the advantages that groups can derive from election activity depend on a multitude of variable factors. Some of these are internal and others are external to the group. Cohesion of the membership is crucial in several respects and it appears to vary through time in any group, depending upon whether there are at stake issues that will arouse the maximum loyalty to group claims and upon whether members accept election activity as an appropriate means of asserting such claims. The status of the group in the community, among other external factors, affects both the form and the effectiveness of participation in the election process. The structure of the federal system has an important effect upon what a group can gain from election activity, depending somewhat on the character of the claims it wishes to assert. Other legal arrangements of a less fundamental kind may be equally influential—the legal framework, for instance, in which nominations take place or the statutory arrangements under which party machinery operates.

[61] Key gives an excellent illustration of the bargaining advantage that a group may derive from fairly perfunctory electoral activity. An Arkansas Representative who ran for the U. S. Senate had supported the Farm Security Administration, an agency set up to benefit farm tenants and bitterly fought by the Farm Bureau. The Representative's support of the F.S.A. was "an action that should have won him votes in a state whose white farmers were more than 50 percent tenants—if they voted. Yet his defeat, the Farm Bureau bureaucracy could claim, came from the publicity they gave to his farm security votes." Key: *Southern Politics*, p. 186, n. 4.

The varying nature of the political party at different times and different places significantly conditions the kind of election activity engaged in by interest groups. Variations in the completeness of party organization, the incidence of localism, differences in the interest-group character of local party organizations, and the extent to which the party is a governing as well as an electioneering device invite or discourage various forms and degrees of group election participation. Before reliable generalizations concerning such activity can be made, a good deal more information on variations of this sort is necessary.

11

The Dynamics of Access in the
Legislative Process

"EVERY opinion," Mr. Justice Holmes observed in one of his great dissents, "tends to become a law." [1] In thus adumbrating his conception of the legislative process Holmes pointed to a distinctive feature of modern representative government. Especially in the United States, the legislature, far more than the judiciary or the executive, has been the primary means of effecting changes in the law of the land. In consequence, the legislature traditionally has been the major focus of attention for political interest groups. Though this interest in legislation has not been an exclusive preoccupation, the established importance of group activities in legislatures is reflected in a popular synonym for the political interest group, the word *lobby*. Though for tactical reasons many groups profess slight or no concern with lobbying, legislative activity has been for the layman the distinguishing feature of the political interest group.

It follows that access to the legislature is of crucial importance at one time or another to virtually all such groups. Some groups are far more successful in this pursuit than others. Moreover, access is not a homogeneous commodity. In some forms it provides little more than a chance to be heard; in others it practically assures favorable action. Some groups achieve highly effective access almost automatically, whereas it is denied to others in spite of their most vigorous efforts.

It will be appropriate, therefore, to begin an exploration of the

[1] Lochner v. New York, 198 U. S. 45 (1905).

role of groups in the legislative process by examining some of the factors that affect the kind of access that various groups are able to achieve. For the sake of convenience these may be divided into two types: first, a set of formal, structural factors whose importance will be readily apparent; second, a set of informal determinants whose effect is somewhat more subtle but of at least equal significance.

Governmental Structure and Differential Access

The formal institutions of government in the United States do not prescribe all the meanderings of the stream of politics. They do mark some of its limits, however, and designate certain points through which it must flow whatever uncharted courses it may follow between these limits. Such is the character of formal organization in any setting, as Chapter 5 has suggested. Although the effect of formal structural arrangements is not always what its designers intended, these formalities are rarely neutral. They handicap some efforts and favor others. Debate over proposals to eliminate such a ritualistic bit of procedure as the electoral college, for example, reveals the fact that, although no one knows the exact consequences that would follow if it were to be abandoned or modified, a change would affect various segments of the community unequally. Such, inevitably, is the influence of formal structure.[2]

Access is one of the advantages unequally distributed by such arrangements; that is, in consequence of the structural peculiarities of our government some groups have better and more varied opportunities to influence key points of decision than do others. Take as an example the provision for equal representation of States in the Senate of the United States. This has allowed agricultural interest groups that are predominant in many thinly populated States more points of access in the Senate than urban groups whose members are concentrated in a few populous States. Thus, were it not for this structural provision, the United States would not have been so solicitous for the sugar beet or silver-mining interests as it has been over the years. It is obvious, moreover, that a group such as the American Farm Bureau Federation, which can cover a great many rural States, can gain readier access than urban groups concerning any matter on

---

[2] Cf. Pendleton Herring: "The Politics of Fiscal Policy," *Yale Law Journal*, Vol. 47, no. 5 (March, 1938), pp. 724–45.

which it can achieve a satisfactory measure of cohesion. It is less obvious, but equally important, that an urban group whose interests are such that it can ally with the Farm Bureau derives an advantage in access over another urban group whose claims are such that it cannot effect an alliance of this sort. The National Association of Manufacturers and various trade associations, among others, have been the beneficiaries of such combinations.

Similar advantages, gained from the way in which the boundaries of legislative districts are drawn whether by legislatures or by constitutions, can be observed throughout the governmental system. They are clearly observable in the House of Representatives, many of whose districts, even in relatively urban States like Illinois, are defined by State legislatures in which rural groups predominate. The State legislatures, of course, show similar patterns.[3]

The existence of the federal system itself is a source of unequal advantage in access. Groups that would be rather obscure or weak under a unitary arrangement may hold advantageous positions in the State governments and will be vigorous in their insistence upon the existing distribution of powers between States and nation. As the advantage of access shifts through time, moreover, groups shift from defenders to critics of the existing balance. At the turn of the century, for example, the insurance companies were active in Washington to get the Federal Government to take over the regulation of insurance, despite the obstacle of an adverse Supreme Court decision handed down shortly after the Civil War. Since the Court in 1944 altered the prevailing doctrine, the insurance companies have been equally vigorous in the opposite direction, at least in so far as they have tried to gain exemption from the Sherman Antitrust Act.[4] A somewhat complicated symptom of a similar state of affairs is suggested by the contrast between argument and behavior in connection with the Tydings-Miller Act of 1937. This legislation, sponsored principally by the National Association of Retail Druggists, exempted from the provisions of the Sherman Act contracts fixing resale prices on goods sold in interstate commerce, provided that they were resold in a State which permitted such contracts. Proponents of the

---

[3] Cf. McKean: *Pressures on the Legislature of New Jersey*, chap. 2 and p. 112; C. E. Merriam, S. D. Parratt, and A. Lepawsky: *The Government of the Metropolitan Region of Chicago* (Chicago: University of Chicago Press, 1933), chap. 28.

[4] *Paul v. Virginia*, 8 Wallace 168 (1869). See Edward B. Logan: "Lobbying," supplement to the *Annals*, Vol. 144 (July, 1929), p. 6. *U.S. v. South-Eastern Underwriters Association*, 322 U.S. 533 (1944).

measure argued that it was simply a means of permitting the individual States to regulate their own affairs. When the law was passed, however, the N.A.R.D. set up an unofficial *national* board through which uniform contracts between manufacturers and retailers could be approved and administered. The policy was a national one, but the druggists' access to the States was more effective once the Federal antitrust hurdle was eliminated.[5]

The separation of powers, especially between the legislature and the executive, and the accompanying system of checks and balances mean that effective access to one part of the government, such as the Congress, does not assure access to another, such as the presidency. For the effective constituencies of the executive and the members of the legislature are not necessarily the same, even when both are represented by men nominally of the same party. These constituencies are different, not simply because the president is elected from the whole country rather than from a particular State or congressional district, although this fact has significance under a system characterized by loose party discipline, but rather because within any State or district, for various reasons, the organized, active elements responsible for the election of a senator or representative are not necessarily the same as those which give the State's or district's support to a candidate for president. This situation is accentuated at the national level by the staggered terms of senators, representatives, and president. A senator elected at the same time as a president must face re-election in an "off" year, and vice versa; a representative must "go it alone" at least every four years. In consequence, as Herring has put it, "Most congressmen are still independent political entrepreneurs."[6] The representative, the senator, and the president each must give ear to groups that one or both of the others frequently can ignore.

An admirable illustration of this situation is the fact that four successive presidents—Harding, Coolidge, Hoover, and Franklin Roosevelt—found it possible to veto veterans' bonus legislation passed by the Congress, although on each occasion approximately four fifths of the House of Representatives chose to override the veto. Somewhat the same circumstance is indicated by the periodic group demands that reciprocal trade agreements should be submitted to the

---

[5] See U.S. Federal Trade Commission: *Report on Resale Price Maintenance* (Washington, D.C.: Government Printing Office, 1945), pp. 62, 145–6, 149
[6] Pendleton Herring: *Presidential Leadership* (New York: Farrar & Rinehart, 1940), p. 27. Copyright by Pendleton Herring and used with the permission of Rinehart & Company, Inc.

Senate for ratification as treaties. Such requests imply less effective access to the executive than to the maximum of thirty-three senators sufficient to reject a treaty.

As the preceding paragraphs suggest, access to points of decision in the government is significantly affected by the structure and cohesion of the political parties considered not just as electioneering devices, but as instruments of governing within the legislature. A single party organization that regularly succeeds in electing an executive and a majority in the legislature will produce one pattern of access to the government. The channels will be predominantly those within the party leadership, and the pattern will be relatively stable and orderly. A quite different pattern will be produced if the party is merely an abstract term referring to an aggregation of relatively independent factions. Then the channels of access will be numerous, and the patterns of influence within the legislature will be diverse, constantly shifting, and more openly in conflict. Party discipline provides the power to govern because it permits stable control of access to the points of policy determination.

It is no novelty to observe that in the United States political parties, particularly on the national scene, correspond more closely to the diffused than to the disciplined type of structure. Because the legislator's tenure in office depends on no overarching party organization, he is accessible to whatever influences are outstanding in his local constituency almost regardless of more inclusive claims. Whether he carries the label of the majority or the minority party, he finds himself now in the majority and now in the minority on legislative votes. Majorities rarely are composed of the same persons in votes on successive measures. They are likely to be bipartisan or, more accurately, nonpartisan.

The dominant character of access and of influence under the American system is well stated in the remark of a Texas Representative in response to a query concerning his motives in advocating the repeal of Federal taxes on oleomargarine: "If I were from the South and were not interested in a market for my people, I would indeed be unworthy to represent my people. Of course I am interested in the right of the cotton farmer to sell his seed. . . ."[7] Diffusion of access has its ramifications as well. During the struggle over the McNary-Haugen farm "relief" bill from 1924 through 1928 President Coolidge was hostile both to the measure and to its principal group sponsor, the American Farm Bureau Federation. Vice-

[7] U.S. House of Representatives, Committee on Agriculture: *Hearings on Repeal of the Oleomargarine Tax*, 80th Cong., 2d Sess. (1948), p. 36.

President Dawes, however, gave "support and assistance," to quote the words of the group's president, that were "of the utmost importance." [8]

Advantages of access are likely to go to the group that can accentuate and exploit the local preoccupations of the legislator. Many corporations and trade associations have long made use of this tactic although the exact forms have been various. Railroad companies have worked through lawyers and doctors retained in the States and counties in which they practice to reach influential supporters of State and national legislators, as have other corporate enterprises. The Association of Railway Executives, predecessor of the Association of American Railroads, organized such a device in a rather complete form. As outlined by one of its officials:

> I had it in mind putting into effect a plan whereby we would be advised as to who are the influential men behind the several Congressmen, and the further thought that we might be able through personal contact or by the careful distribution of literature to influence in a perfectly proper way the judgment of the men upon whom the several Congressmen rely for support and advice.[9]

Such a system has never been more completely organized than it has been by the Iowa Farm Bureau Federation. Although the group does not openly endorse candidates for election, after the election it sets up committees of five members in each legislative district, whose function it is to capitalize upon local support. The qualifications of the members of these committees, according to Kile, are four in number: (1) they must be "willing to put Farm Bureau policies ahead of any personal interest;" (2) they must be from the same party as the successful candidate; (3) they must be men who "individually helped get the candidate elected;" and (4) they must be "politically potent in the district." [10] A very similar plan of organization to exert local influence has been employed by, among others, the National Association of Retail Druggists. The Federal Trade Commission has described it as "the most important device"

---

[8] Kile: *The Farm Bureau Through Three Decades*, p. 146.
[9] U.S. Senate, Committee on Interstate Commerce: *Senate Report No. 26*, 77th Cong., 1st Sess. (1941), part 2, pp. 51–3. Cf. Danielian: *A. T. & T.: The Story of Industrial Conquest*, pp. 321–5.
[10] Kile: *The Farm Bureau Through Three Decades*, pp. 381–2. Copyright 1948 by and used with the permission of Orville M. Kile.

used by the association in its efforts to secure passage of desired legislation.[11]

Such is the effect of our disintegrated national party structure upon access. Although this structure may be in process of gradual change in the direction of greater integration and central control, as some competent observers believe,[12] conclusive evidence of this shift is not at hand. We can be sure, however, that an altered party structure will be reflected in an altered pattern of group access to the Congress.

The effects of party structure upon group access to many of the State legislatures are similar to its effects upon access to Congress. The channels of approach for various groups are numerous and varied, as in Congress, except in those cases where an individual party leader or faction has been able to impose a high degree of discipline upon the rank and file. In the heyday of Boss Platt, access to the legislature of New York was available primarily through him, usually at a price.[13] When in 1935 the Governor of Florida established temporary dominance over the State legislature, the Association of Life Insurance Presidents found that it could not even gain admission to legislative committee hearings until it had persuaded the Governor of its point of view.[14] Other States, such as New York and New Jersey, have quite consistently shown a pattern of party government quite different from that at the national level.[15] Where the party structure is integrated and the legislators are under discipline, access is channeled and is more available to those groups upon which the party as a whole, rather than the individual legislator, is dependent.

Once it has established access, by whatever means, a group will exert tremendous efforts to retain the structural arrangements that have given it advantage. An illustration is afforded by the struggle over the adoption of the Twenty-first Amendment repealing the Eighteenth. When the prohibition amendment was submitted, the Anti-Saloon League favored the method of ratification by the State leg-

[11] U. S. Federal Trade Commission: *Report on Resale Price Maintenance,* pp. 64–6.
[12] Cf. E. E. Schattschneider: *The Struggle for Party Government* (College Park, Md.: University of Maryland, 1948), pp. 28–9.
[13] Cf. Logan: "Lobbying," p. 5.
[14] U.S. Temporary National Economic Committee: *Hearings,* part 10, pp. 4380 and 4758.
[15] Cf. McKean: *Pressures on the Legislature of New Jersey,* chap. 2; Warren Moscow: *Politics in the Empire State* (New York: Alfred A. Knopf, Inc., 1948), *passim.*

islatures, since it had built up its access to most of those bodies and could be sure that the weapons at its disposal would assure favorable action by the required number of States. When the repeal proposal was passed by the Congress in 1933, however, the method of ratification by conventions called especially for the purpose was specified for the first time in the history of amendments to the Federal Constitution. This means was employed in order to get around the established access of the league.

All the factors of a structural character that result in the unequal distribution of access among interest groups operating upon a legislature need not be discussed in detail. We must, however, even in this rough sketch, discuss one additional type, closely related to the structure of the party system—the structure of the legislature itself, including legislative procedure and the committee system. Legislative structure and rules of procedure are by no means neutral factors in respect to access. As Schattschneider observed with reference to the Smoot-Hawley Tariff Act of 1930: "Legislation cannot be understood apart from the manner in which it is made." [16]

No legislative assembly of whatever size can, of course, carry on its activities without some internal division of labor, without methods of setting the order of business, or without means of regulating the process of deliberation. The procedures for selecting those to whom the leadership of an assembly is entrusted, for example, have a direct bearing upon the kind of access to the legislature that various groups may be able to achieve. Thus the practice in Congress and most of the States of assigning committee memberships and designating their chairmen on the basis of seniority gives a special advantage to groups having access to members from "safe" constituencies who are likely to look with hostility on the demands of the less established groups. Organizations whose membership is concentrated in "close" districts, where the incidence of change and the consequent demands for adjustment are high, are less easily able to establish access to committee chairmen.

Whoever sets the timetable of a legislature and determines how long debate on a measure shall continue has a significant control upon access. This power, of course, is one of the principal means by which the British Cabinet leads the House of Commons. In American State legislatures a unified party leadership, both legislative and executive, may enjoy similar dominance, and in that case effective access will be through such leadership. In the Congress, and at

[16] E. E. Schattschneider: *Politics, Pressures and the Tariff,* p. 13. Copyright 1935 by Prentice-Hall, Inc.

times in all of the State legislatures, control of the timetable lies with a loosely integrated collection of men belonging to the majority party, sometimes acting in consultation with the minority leaders. In the Senate this scheduling function is performed by the floor leader, his aides, and the chairmen of the standing committees. The party Steering Committee and its Policy Committee are nominally a part of this machinery, but their importance is slight. In the House the timetable is set by the Rules Committee, the floor leader, the Speaker, and the chairmen of standing committees. The Steering Committee is of as little functional significance as in the Senate. Depending on the nature of the legislation to be considered and on the skill of the leadership, the legislators who determine the schedule may work in concert, or they may operate at cross purposes. In the latter case the legislative timetable is a compromise or emerges from a test of strength among these various points of power, a process in which the president, if he is of the same party, may play a significant role.[17] Groups with access to parts of this machinery have a privileged influence upon the legislative program, especially if their objective is to obstruct rather than to promote a particular bill.

Both the power to limit debate and the practice of permitting unlimited debate on a measure have significance for the degree of access that various groups achieve. In the House of Representatives, where limitation on debate is customary, it usually takes the form of adopting a special rule reported by the Rules Committee. Practically all major legislation in the House is handled under this sort of procedure, which sets both the terms and the duration of debate. The Committee is thus in a position either to block or to expedite action on a bill, and access to its membership is a crucial advantage. Such access is likely to go disproportionately to established groups dominant in "safe" constituencies, since the seniority of all members of this committee is high. For example, in the Seventy-seventh Congress, elected in 1940, no member of the Rules Committee had had less than four consecutive terms of service, and the average number of such terms represented on the Committee was just under seven. Thus most of the members came from districts that had made no change in their representation since before the onset of the New Deal. A similar advantage accrues in the Senate to any defensive group that has access to even a small bloc of members. Under that body's practice of unlimited debate, such

[17] Cf. Floyd M. Riddick: *The United States Congress: Organization and Procedure* (Manassas, Va.: National Capitol Publishers, Inc., 1949), chap. 6.

a minority can "talk a bill to death" through the filibuster, effectively preventing action by the Senate as a whole. In some cases this result has been achieved by one member alone. Although the Senate has had since 1917 a rule permitting closure of debate, it is rarely applied, and the effective veto power of a Senate minority remains virtually unchallenged.

Finally, the enormously complicated and technical rules under which debate is carried on in legislative chambers have an important influence upon relative access. In the first place, the rules themselves are not neutral; witness the heat frequently generated by an attempt to change them. At the beginning of the Eighty-first Congress in January, 1949, a successful effort was made to modify the House rules so that committee chairmen could call up bills that the Rules Committee failed to report out. The significance of such a modification was indicated both by the activity in the House and by the attention given the amendment in the press.[18] But groups gain advantages in access not just from the substance of such procedural regulations. They may derive tremendous advantage if their representatives, whether in or out of the legislative halls, have a mastery of the ins and outs of parliamentary procedure. Like the technicalities of legal procedure in courts of law, procedural arrangements may be used as often to delay and obstruct action as to facilitate it. Thus the ability to command the services of a skillful parliamentary tactician may be the key to effective access to a legislature.

Reference has already been made to legislative committees, and in the next chapter we shall give close attention to their functions. At this point it is necessary, however, to indicate that the place of committees in a legislative body has important effects upon the degree of access that various groups can achieve. It is as accurate today as it was nearly three quarters of a century ago when Woodrow Wilson published his little classic, *Congressional Government*, to say that, although the Congress as a whole formally legislates, the real policy determination takes place in the standing committees.[19] Both because of the volume and the complexity of the problems coming before a modern legislature and because of the size of such bodies, they have had to leave the most important part of the examination, if not the preparation, of legislation to smaller

[18] *Congressional Record*, 81st Cong., 1st Sess., January 3, 1949, pp. 10–11, A. 3–4, A. 6, A. 7 (daily edition).

[19] Woodrow Wilson: *Congressional Government* (Boston: Houghton Mifflin Company, 1885), p. 56 and *passim*.

units. Under the British system this function is performed primarily by the Cabinet, which is strictly speaking a committee of the legislature. Relatively minor use is made of other standing committees. In the Congress of the United States the sifting of legislative projects is pre-eminently the function of the committees, primarily the standing committees. Neither house, with rare exceptions, considers any measure that has not first been acted upon by one of these nominally subordinate bodies. Refusal to report a bill from a committee usually dooms the proposal. But perhaps the most significant feature of the system is that, although many major measures are altered by the Senate or the House after a committee has reported, both houses usually follow closely the recommendations of their committees. Few bills are passed in a form substantially different from that given them at the committee stage.[20]

The effect that this system of committees has upon access stems not only from the relative finality of their actions but also from the comparative independence that they enjoy. These bodies are subject to little or no co-ordinating influence from any source. A committee majority, or even its chairman alone, effectively constitutes a little legislature, especially in so far as it blocks action on a proposal. Therefore access to a committee majority or even to a chairman may give a group effective advantage in the legislature itself, to the virtual exclusion of its competitors.

The role of committees in the State legislatures varies widely. In some their place is roughly similar to that of the congressional committee, whereas in others it is sharply different. One general difference is that, since State legislative sessions are shorter and less frequent and since many State legislators perform their duties on a part-time basis, there is usually less opportunity for prolonged committee consideration in the States. In some States, New Jersey, for instance, the committees are of no significance, except as graveyards for bills, since control by the party leaders is pervasive. Access to the committee under such circumstances is almost meaningless.[21] In other States the committee function appears to be quite similar to that in Congress. Thus a study of several legislative sessions in Maryland and Pennsylvania shows that well over 80 per

---

[20] Cf. Riddick: *The United States Congress*, pp. 3, 153; Herring: *Group Representation Before Congress*, pp. 250–1; Paul D. Hasbrouck: *Party Government in the House of Representatives* (New York: The Macmillan Company, 1927), pp. 74–5.

[21] Cf. McKean: *Pressures on the Legislature of New Jersey*, pp. 47–9.

cent of the committee reports were accepted outright by these legis-latures.[22]

This evidence would suggest that committees in Maryland and Pennsylvania were indeed "little legislatures" and that access to them was crucial. Although such undoubtedly was the case in some instances, in these same two States there were other regularities that lay behind the acceptance of committee reports. The legislators followed the committees, to be sure, but the latter were dominated by chairmen who in turn co-operated closely with the governors and other legislative leaders.[23] Similar evidence on the New York legislature indicates that State legislative committees and their chairmen enjoy much less freedom of action than their congressional counterparts. Political management by an informal conference of legislative leaders determines the content of major bills, not the individual committees operating independently.[24] Under such circumstances access to the legislature is not assured merely by establishing relationships with individual committeemen or chairmen. Lines of access tend to be integrated rather than diffused; consequently, the tactics of groups and relative advantage among them can be expected to show a pattern quite different from that characteristic of the Congress.

Aspects of formal structure, therefore, are significant determinants of the channels of access to legislatures, national and State. They afford advantages to some groups and impose handicaps upon the efforts of others to achieve influence in the legislature. Formal structure both reflects and sustains differences in power. It is never neutral.

The Role of Knowledge and the Effects of Overlapping Membership

Governmental structure is not the only factor creating advantages in access to the key points of decision in the legislature. It is the most obvious, but perhaps not the most important. The politician-legislator is not equivalent to the steel ball in a pinball game, bumping passively from post to post down an inclined plane. He is a human being involved in a variety of relationships with other human beings.

[22] C. I. Winslow: *State Legislative Committees: A Study in Procedure* (Baltimore: The Johns Hopkins Press, 1931), pp. 7, 112 ff., 139.

[23] Ibid., pp. 118–21, 137. Cf. Robert Luce: *Legislative Procedure* (Boston: Houghton Mifflin Company, 1922), pp. 493–4.

[24] Joseph P. Chamberlain: *Legislative Processes, National and State* (New York: D. Appleton-Century Company, 1936), p. 90.

In his role as legislator his accessibility to various groups is affected by the whole series of relationships that define him as a person.[25] Most of these relationships, however, cannot be identified by viewing the legislator as a creature of the statute book. We need not go into the complicated area of motives to account more fully for differences in accessibility by observing such continuing relationships, remembering that their stability is as important an element in the equilibrium of the individual legislator as are predictable relationships in the well-being of any other human.

One important factor among the informal determinants of access is created by the legislator-politician's need of information and the ability of a group to supply it. Any politician, whether legislator, administrator, or judge, whether elected or appointed, is obliged to make decisions that are guided in part by the relevant knowledge that is available to him. In this deciding, however, the politician is in a position analogous to the late Lord Keynes's stock-exchange investor, whose knowledge of the factors that will govern the future yield of an investment is necessarily partial or even negligible.[26] The politician also must rely on somewhat conventionalized assessments of trends, corrected by new information about the relevant facts.

The politician is in continuous need of current information because he is at the mercy of the changes as they occur. Like a college president, a politician, especially an elected politician, is expected to have a judgment on all matters ranging from the causes of an outbreak of Bang's disease among the local livestock to the latest strategy of the Kremlin. He must make decisions on many of these questions, decisions on the content of his public statements, on the causes and persons he will champion, on how he will vote on a roll call.

The penalty for numerous or conspicuous decisions made in ignorance or in neglect of relevant available knowledge is disturbance in the politician's established relationships. The disturbance may be minor and temporary or serious and lasting. It may be reflected in a diminution of "reputation" or in a threat to his leadership position in party, faction, or other group. Finally, it may lead to defeat at the polls, a penalty that no elected official can be expected to welcome. Forced to make choices of consequence and to minimize serious disturbances in his established relationships, the legislator is constantly in need of relevant information. Access is likely to be

---

[25] See Newcomb: *Social Psychology*, chap. 10 and *passim*.
[26] Keynes: *The General Theory*, pp. 149 ff.

available to groups somewhat in proportion to their ability to meet this need.

For purposes of discussion the knowledge required by the politician may be divided into two types: technical knowledge that defines the content of a policy issue; and political knowledge of the relative strength of competing claims and of the consequences of alternative decisions on a policy issue. Any group may be in a position directly or indirectly to supply information of either type.

Representative of the first sort of knowledge is the specialized information about industry conditions that a trade association can provide for the politician, whether legislator or administrator. Almost any group is likely to regard knowledge of this sort as a major part of its stock-in-trade. Those who are preoccupied with moral judgments of group politics, in fact, normally treat the supplying of such information as a "legitimate" group activity. A measure of access almost inevitably accompanies the ability to provide this type of information. Where competing claims are not present, and where available knowledge of the likely political consequences suggests that the legislator will be little affected whatever decision he makes, technical information may control his decision. The politician who comes from a "safe" district, confronted with an issue of no moment in his constituency, is in a position to act upon what he regards as the "merits" of an issue, to act like what the ward heeler calls a "statesman." Especially where official sources of information are deficient, command of technical knowledge may provide access for groups that can supply the deficiency, especially if other influences are operating in their favor.[27] Thus McKean noted that the absence of a legislative reference library, the impossibility of retaining technical staff on a legislator's salary, and the failure of the State Government to provide such services as information on the progress of pending bills, gave privileged access to groups in New Jersey prepared to perform such functions.[28]

The second type, political information, is of at least equal importance. Many familiar expressions, such as "keeping one's ear to the ground" and "mending fences," testify to this fact. The legislator, as anyone knows who has had even an amateur's brush with politics, can never know enough in this sphere. Who are behind this measure? How well unified are they? What dormant elements in the constituency will be stirred up if the proponents' claims are acceded

---

[27] Cf. V. O. Key, Jr.: "The Veterans and the House of Representatives," *Journal of Politics*, Vol. 5, no. 1 (February, 1943), pp. 39–40.
[28] McKean: *Pressures on the Legislature of New Jersey*, pp. 203–5.

to? Will there be a later opportunity to pacify them? For questions such as these there is rarely a final answer, but the legislator often must act as if there were. Where the situation remains obscure, his behavior may be ambiguous. Thus he may vote to kill a bill by sending it back to committee, but when that motion is lost, he may change his position and vote for the measure's passage. It may be easier to defend such apparent vacillation than to face the consequences of an unequivocal stand.

In politically ambiguous circumstances, and they are common, a group that can give the legislator an indication of the consequences of supporting or opposing a measure is likely to win his ear at least in some degree. Such "information," of course, is rarely taken at face value, since most groups find it expedient to exaggerate their influence and the cohesion of the rank and file. It is up to the legislator to apply a discount rate that seems appropriate. In some instances his knowledge of his constituency is such that he knows immediately how to evaluate such claims. In others he must be aided by trusted advisers, who may themselves, in consequence, become the objects of petitions from various interest groups. The evaluation of group claims may itself be a puzzling task, although a politician of any skill can often see through assertions that are largely pretense. Yet because pretense and exaggeration are common, a group may gain advantage in access if it is presented by agents who have a reputation for candor and realism. Few elected politicians are in a position requiring no reliable political knowledge.

The desire for information may not be the only informal factor leading the legislator to make himself accessible to particular interest groups. He is not simply a machine for calculating odds and acting on the most favorable ones. When he assumes office he does not cut himself off from all previous connections and divest himself of the attitudes he has acquired up to that time. The prevailing myths may hold that he does so or should do so, but to accept such folklore literally is to fall victim to the institutional fallacy, to look at formalities and to ignore relationships. As John Dewey has put it: "Those concerned in government are still human beings. They retain their share of the ordinary traits of human nature. They still have private interests to serve and interests of special groups, those of the family, clique or class to which they belong." [29] Such was essentially the point argued by Madison in the following passage from *The Federalist, No. 10:*

[29] Dewey: *The Public and Its Problems,* p. 76. Copyright 1927 by and used with the permission of Henry Holt & Company, Inc.

No man is allowed to be a judge in his own cause, because his interest would certainly bias his judgment, and, not improbably, corrupt his integrity. With equal, nay with greater reason, a body of men are unfit to be both judges and parties at the same time; yet what are many of the most important acts of legislation, but so many judicial determinations, not indeed concerning the rights of single persons, but concerning the rights of large bodies of citizens? And *what are the different classes of legislators but advocates and parties to the causes which they determine?* (Italics added.)

Madison concluded that legislators must inevitably have interest affiliations, and not infrequently we find evidence that members of Congress also assume so. Thus in 1929 the Senate committee investigating tariff lobbying criticized the head of a series of "paper" associations for pretending to an influence that he did not have. After commenting on his lack of technical qualifications, the committee added as further evidence of his fraudulent position: "He is on terms of intimacy with no Member of Congress so far as your committee has been able to learn." [30]

Since an elected representative cannot give up his already existing attitudes and relationships, the legislature and various political interest groups inevitably overlap in membership. Any of the latter that can claim members in the legislature will thus enjoy a measure of privileged access. Other influences aside, the value of this means of access will vary with the number of such members and with the importance that they attach to such affiliation. It is well known, for instance, that the organized bar has had advantages in access to State and national legislatures in consequence of the number of lawyers elected to those bodies. The American Legion usually can list among its membership one third to one half the members of Congress, in addition to Cabinet members and even the President. Not all of these are equally accessible to the Legion, but at least a portion of them are likely to be readily so. Similarly the Chamber of Commerce of the United States constitutes, as one author has put it, "an unofficial functional constituency of the federal legislature" in consequence of having several of its members in the Congress. [31]

Where the claims of a group are or can be made sufficiently cen-

---

[30] *Senate Report* 43, 72d Cong., 1st Sess., *Congressional Record*, December 20, 1929, p. 994.

[31] Cf. Gray: *The Inside Story of the Legion*, p. 99. Paul Studenski: "Chambers of Commerce," *Encyclopaedia of the Social Sciences*.

tral for its members in the legislature, the latter can be formed into a "bloc" that is expected to act as a unit on as many as possible of the issues of concern to the group. At its height such was the "farm bloc" of 1921–2, which included a quarter of the Senators (14 Republicans and 10 Democrats) and a similar but less well defined segment of the House. Though a minority of both houses, it held a balance of power for the better part of four years.[32]

The National Rivers and Harbors Congress, whose membership overlaps with that of a variety of other groups, including Congress, has acquired almost as much influence in the area of its claims. It is made up of contractors and State and local officials, members of Congress, and, ex-officio, officers of the Army Corps of Engineers. The loyalties uniting this group have demonstrated their strength on many occasions. When the Rivers and Harbors Congress announces its opposition to the recommendation of the Hoover Commission that the flood control and rivers and harbors activities of the Corps of Engineers be transferred to the Department of the Interior, it is in effect announcing the opposition of a "bloc" to any effort to implement the suggestion. When Representative William M. Whittington of Mississippi testified in 1945 before a Senate committee in opposition to a proposal to establish a Missouri Valley Authority, he spoke not only as a member of Congress and as chairman of the Flood Control Committee of the House, but as vice-president of the National Rivers and Harbors Congress and vice-president of the related Mississippi Valley Flood Control Association.[33]

The variety of uses to which such multiple memberships can be put is almost infinite. The legislator who is a "member" of an active political interest group may, better than anyone outside the legislature, observe and report on developments within the legislative body and its committees; he may act as the group's spokesman on the floor;

---

[32] E. Pendleton Herring: "Farm Bloc," *Encyclopaedia of the Social Sciences*, and *Group Representation Before Congress*, pp. 122–4; Kile: *The Farm Bureau Movement*, pp. 188 ff. Not infrequently men have entered the legislature after serving as officials of interest groups. Before he was Governor and Senator, Styles Bridges was the paid secretary of the New Hampshire Farm Bureau Federation (Kile: *The Farm Bureau Through Three Decades*, p. 386).

[33] The *New York Times*, April 10, 1949. See U.S. Commission on Organization of the Executive Branch of the Government: *Task Force Report on Natural Resources* (Washington, D.C.: Government Printing Office, 1949), esp. pp. 79–88, 98–9, 149–82; Robert de Roos and Arthur Maass: "The Lobby That Can't Be Licked," *Harper's Magazine* (August, 1949), pp. 21–30. The hearings on the M. V. A. are effectively discussed in James M. Burns: *Congress on Trial* (New York: Harper and Brothers, 1949), pp. 94–7.

he may attempt to persuade key committee members; he may save the group postage by allowing it the use of his franking privilege; and so on. A few examples will suggest the range of relationships. When the retail druggists and their allies were attempting in the 1930's to secure passage of price-maintenance laws, full use was made of retailer-legislators, according to the manual on the subject issued by the National Association of Retail Druggists. In Iowa the druggists who were members of the legislature met as a group and selected the persons who were to sponsor the measure. In the State of Washington the bill was introduced by a collection of legislators, "several of whom were or had been in the retail business and knew the meaning of predatory price cutting. Such men needed no prodding when it came to arguing the bill on its own merits." [34] Much the same procedures are followed by the veterans' organizations. The Legion distributes among its members in the Congress the responsibility for sponsoring its measures, and it supervises the tactics they employ. During the bonus drive of the 1930's the key member of the Veterans of Foreign Wars in Congress was Representative Wright Patman of Texas. He spearheaded the V.F.W.'s effort to secure immediate cash payment of the bonus. [35] When the tariff revision of 1929–30 was in process, Senator Bingham of Connecticut placed on the payroll of the Senate the assistant to the president of the Connecticut Manufacturers Association. The latter not only advised Senator Bingham, but accompanied him to the meetings of the Senate Finance Committee, which prepared the measure, as an "expert" on tariff matters. [36]

An important possibility to bear in mind in connection with the effect of a legislator's group memberships upon his accessibility is that the willingness to aid a group's claims need not involve any overt act on the part of the group, any "pressure" on the legislator, and it need not involve formal membership in the group. A legislator-politician no less than any other man has, as we pointed out in chapter 2, lived his life in a series of environments, largely group-defined. These have given him attitudes, frames of reference, points of view, which make him more receptive to some proposals

[34] U. S. Federal Trade Commission: *Report on Resale Price Maintenance*, pp. 52 ff.

[35] Cf. Herring: *Group Representation Before Congress*, p. 222. Veterans of Foreign Wars, 35th National Encampment: *Proceedings*, House Document 45, 74th Cong., 1st Sess. (1935); U. S. Senate, Finance Committee: *Hearings on Payment of Adjusted Compensation Certificates*, 74th Cong., 1st Sess. (1935).

[36] *Senate Report 43*, part 1, 71st Cong., 1st Sess., *Congressional Record*, October 26, 1929, p. 4922.

than to others. As a specialist in politics he may be in possession of information that obliges him to choose between his preferences as a successful upper-middle-class lawyer and the demands of a group of militant workers in his constituency. But in the absence of such conflicts, and even in the face of them, he is likely to be most accessible to groups or proposals that stem from sources comparable to those from which his own attitudes have been derived. Many, if not all, such legislators will insist in all sincerity that they vote as their own consciences dictate. They may even resent any effort from an otherwise acceptable group to force a particular decision from them. This is true; however, whether they are "liberals" or "conservatives," urbanites or country boys, their "consciences" are creatures of the particular environments in which they have lived and of the group affiliations they have formed.

Under such circumstances the notion of group "pressure" has limited value. Bailey makes this point extremely well in his discussion of the attitudes of those members of Congress who were on the joint conference committee that produced the Employment Act of 1946 in its final form. In accounting for the strongly hostile position of Senator Buck of Delaware, Bailey refers to Buck's close connections with the Du Pont family, including his marriage to the daughter of T. Coleman Du Pont. No overt group act was necessary to secure Buck's vote against the measure, for, as Bailey observes, "It was not the pressure of Du Pont *on* Buck but the pressure of Du Pont *in* Buck which was at work." [37] Similarly it is scarcely necessary for an organized interest group to take overt action among members of Congress from the South in order to secure their votes against F.E.P.C. legislation and the like. Access for this point of view is assured in most cases by the attitudes which Southern legislators hold without prompting.

We encounter here again the fact that interest groups operate in a hierarchy of prestige. Some groups, as we have seen previously, enjoy a prestige which makes it unnecessary for them to participate actively in elections. Such high status groups are likely to acquire favorable access to the legislature for the same reasons. A politician need not himself be a member of the Chamber of Commerce of the United States to listen with respect to the testimony of a business leader who is pleading its case. Among the attitudes he is likely to have acquired in the average constituency are ones involving deference toward those groups that enjoy high prestige in

[37] Bailey: *Congress Makes a Law*, p. 192. Copyright 1950 by and used with the permission of Columbia University Press. See also pp. 148–9, 182.

the country as a whole. In the legislative process, as in other aspects of politics, groups are affected by their position or status in the society.

In this connection some reference should be made to what is widely referred to as the "social lobby." An informal influence upon access, it provides material for the more lurid exposés of legislative life and lends itself to treatment in eye-catching headlines. Popular impressions to the contrary, there is no reason to revise Herring's judgment that the influence of this device is "decidedly secondary."[38] If the minor importance of the "social lobby" is not forgotten, however, examination of the phenomenon will provide instructive illustrations of the informal determinants of relative access.

The "social lobby," a technique rather than a type of group, is a device to create a feeling of obligation on the part of the legislator toward individuals who have established sociable relations with him through entertaining him and his family. It uses social intercourse to develop multiple memberships, on the not unwarranted assumption that in a conflict situation the face-to-face relations of the "social lobby" will be dominant.[39] It is harder to refuse someone who has been kind to you than to turn away a more or less complete stranger.

If the attempted seduction is successful, it probably works best with the new legislator who is just taking up residence in a strange community.[40] Having been a fairly large frog in a comparatively small pond, he suddenly finds the situation reversed. He may be disturbed by the abrupt interruption of his accustomed social relationships and feel the need for adequate substitutes. These may be supplied by the dinner and golf games of a "social set" or by the poker games and other diversions offered by an interest group representative. The implied penalty for sharp political disagreement is ostracism from the friendly group, and the legislator may quite unconsciously find himself avoiding this penalty by conforming. Reinforcement in this direction may come from the legislator's wife and daughters. They too need satisfactory personal relationships in the new community; once established these may involve none of the conflicts which the legislator himself feels, and the sanction then becomes the more unpleasant. Especially if the ladies are "socially ambitious," exclusion from "important" social functions may be acutely

[38] Herring: *Group Representation Before Congress*, p. 40.
[39] Cf. Lazarsfeld *et al.*: *The People's Choice*, chap. 16, esp. pp. 153–5.
[40] McKean found that the "social lobby" was almost nonexistent in New Jersey because most legislators commute to the capital from their homes (*Pressures on the Legislature of New Jersey*, p. 192).

painful. The rationale of the device is suggested by the Georgia representatives of the Association of Life Insurance Presidents in a report on the 1933 session of the State legislature. Accounting for their expenditures, they say in part: "This money has been spent in invitations to those of whom we wished to make friends, and seeing that their wives and daughters were looked after properly and courteously. . . ." [41] At its crudest the "social lobby" amounts to simple bribery, as the following case suggests. A new member of the House of Representatives, assigned to a committee considering a power bill, struck up a friendship with a "newspaper correspondent" to whom he had been introduced at a small luncheon. He did not know that the introduction was by prearrangement, nor did he develop suspicions as the men and their wives became quite intimate, the two couples enjoying dinners and week-end excursions together, and the genial "journalist" drawing the congressman and his wife into a new set of friendships. The "reporter" and wife even aided in redecorating the legislator's apartment. After this kind of thing had gone on for some time, the "journalist" one day dropped in at the congressman's office, stated his attitude toward the power bill and his assumption that the legislator also opposed the measure. When the congressman announced that he favored the bill and would not be dissuaded, the pleasant social relations between the two couples ceased completely. [42]

Normally the technique is more subtle, along the lines of the following statement by a former State legislator:

> The legislator who remains aloof will find himself, if not quite ostracized, at least not "one of the gang," and will constantly be surprised at an unexpected solidarity on the part of a majority of his colleagues for or against a pending measure. His surprise will be dissipated when he learns that the night before the "gang" were at an entertainment at a downtown hotel, where probably the subject of legislation was not even mentioned, but in some subtle way an understanding was reached as to what was expected of those present as all around "good fellows." [43]

[41] U.S. Temporary National Economic Committee: *Hearings*, part 10, p. 4770.
[42] Reported in Logan: "Lobbying," p. 53.
[43] Henry Parkman, Jr.: "Lobbies and Pressure Groups: A Legislator's Point of View," *The Annals*, Vol. 195 (January, 1938), p. 97. Copyright 1938 by and used with the permission of The American Academy of Political and Social Science.

Part of the subtlety in this case, of course, depended upon the clique structure within the legislature itself, to which we shall turn shortly.

Although the "social lobby" illustrates a type of informal overlapping membership, the reasons for its comparative unimportance are fairly obvious. In the first place, the successful politician, like other leaders, is likely to be a person whose pattern of interpersonal relations is fairly flexible and thus not readily subject to the sanction of ostracism. Secondly, since positions of power within the legislature customarily are occupied by experienced legislators rather than by newcomers, the seductive technique must operate in a limited field. The old hand does not need the flattery of the "social lobby" for his personal happiness; he may, in fact, favor a gathering by his presence rather than be favored by an invitation to it. Excepting, therefore, the occasional newcomer and the rare legislator who is undisturbed by bribery, the "social lobby" is at most a means of reinforcing the preferences already held by various members of the legislative body. Even among these it may not prevail over other devices in a legislative situation where opposing influences are present.

An important implication of the various multiple memberships of legislators is that their interactions with interest groups are not just one-way relationships. The popular view is that the political interest group uses the legislator to its ends, induces him to function as its spokesman and to vote as it wishes. As we have already seen, this is not an inaccurate view. But it is incomplete. In most of the examples discussed above the legislators were not subject to overt "pressure." They did not necessarily act in anticipation of group demands but rather behaved as persons in official position whose views of the pending legislation for various reasons approximated those of organized and potential interest groups. When a legislator arouses organized groups in connection with a proposal that he knows will involve them or when he solicits their support for a measure which he is promoting, the relationship becomes reciprocal. Even in connection with the development of a single bill from conception to enactment, the initiative may lie alternately with legislator and with group, including other outside influences.

The Employment Act of 1946 furnishes a good example of such reciprocal relationships, as Bailey's study indicates.[44] Perhaps because this legislation involved few concrete deprivations or indulgences and is, therefore, not entirely typical of many controversial

[44] Bailey: *Congress Makes a Law*, chaps. 3, 5, 7, and *passim*. For some good examples of this see Burns: *Congress on Trial*, pp. 19–23.

measures, it highlights the use that members of Congress may make of a variety of interest groups. The impetus for the bill came in part, to be sure, from the National Farmers Union. Much of the drive behind the measure, however, was supplied by the most important of the Senate and House sponsors and their aides. These solicited the support of a diversity of groups and welded them into what Bailey dubs the "Lib-Lab Lobby." Some of these interest groups in turn attempted to win over other members of Congress and officials of the executive branch, so that it became difficult to determine who was influencing whom. Certainly, however, it was no simple, one-way pattern of group demands upon legislators. On the opposition side as well, moreover, testimony against the measure was solicited by members of Congress. In particular, Representative Carter Manasco of Alabama, chairman of the House Committee on Expenditures in the Executive Departments, to which the bill was referred, took the initiative in mobilizing opposition witnesses.

Overlapping memberships of legislators, therefore, give privileged access to the interest groups involved, whether the membership is formal or of the "fellow-traveler" variety. Such membership does not mean simply that the legislator is "used" by the groups in a one-way, conditioned-response relationship. As "parties to the causes which they determine," legislators may equally function as leaders of the interest groups with which they identify.

The Group Life of the Legislature

We have seen that formal governmental structure and various informal group-legislator relationships give some groups advantages over others in achieving access to the legislature. These factors are productive of patterns of interaction that affect legislative decisions. A third factor that also regulates access is the pattern of relationships within the legislature itself. We are concerned here more than in the earlier paragraphs with access not merely to the individual legislator, but to the legislature as a unit. Such a body is not properly conceived of as a collection of individual men, unorganized and without internal cohesion. Nor is it any better accounted for exclusively in terms of the formal, legal structure of the legislature. A legislative body has its own group life, sometimes as a unit, perhaps more often as a collection of subgroups or cliques. It has its own operating structure, which may approximate or differ sharply from the formal organization of the chamber. When a man first joins such a body, he enters a new group. Like others, it has its standards and conventions, its largely unwritten system of obligations and privileges. To these the neophyte must conform, at least in some measure, if he hopes to make effective use of his position. The claims and imperatives of his other group attachments must be accommodated and adjusted to those of a new one. This conformity is facilitated by the fact that the new group commands some of the means of satisfying the demands of the outside groups with which the new legislator identifies himself; the adjustment is also strengthened by the morale, the *esprit*, in the legislative body.

The morale of legislative groups is often marked, even when mutual confidence of the members is not productive of the most widely approved results. As one discriminating student of the legislative process has put it: "In general, the *esprit de corps* displayed by legislative bodies, especially the smaller ones, is probably not rivaled by any other formally organized, self-governing body. There seem to be factors inherent in the legislative process which are conducive to the production of good morale." [45] The factors productive of legislative morale are rooted in the continuing interpersonal relationships among the members, which are initially grounded in the common experiences they have had in reaching and holding elective office. Politicans of quite different opinions and of at least nominally opposed political party are likely nevertheless to understand and respect a colleague's fears and triumphs. Like old veterans of a military campaign or like the alumni of a college athletic team, they speak a language which the uninitiated can never quite understand; they have had roughly parallel experiences that set them a little apart from those whose struggles have been of a different order. These commonalities help to support the conforming influences of the legislative group. "Smoke-filled cloakrooms and bars where one can rub elbows with his colleagues who have shared experiences with him and who know what he has been through to get there and stay there, are assimilating and conditioning grounds." [46] The relationships of a legislator with his fellow legislators do much to moderate the conflicts inherent in the legislative process and to facilitate the adjustments without which the process could not go on. Skill

[45] Garland C. Routt: "Interpersonal Relationships and the Legislative Process," *Annals*, Vol. 195 (January, 1938), p. 130. A unique study, this article reports on a systematic observation of the Illinois Senate. Cf. Harold F. Gosnell: *Democracy: The Threshold of Freedom* (New York: The Ronald Press, 1948), p. 233; Luce: *Legislative Assemblies*, chaps. 14, 18, 24, and *passim*.

[46] Gosnell: *Democracy*, p. 234.

in handling such relationships, moreover, generates influence that is reflected in leader-follower patterns within the chamber. Legislative skill, usually acquired only after considerable experience in the law-making body, creates its own following; less experienced or overly busy members will often be guided by the skilled veteran when a vote is called for and in a fashion that cannot be explained simply in terms of party loyalty or of the trading of votes.

The pattern of interpersonal relationships in the legislature may closely approximate the formal structure of floor leaders, whips, and committee chairmen. Whether it does or does not, however, the tyro who reaches the capitol breathing fire after a vigorous campaign soon finds that he can accomplish nothing until he learns how to get along with his colleagues. The acknowledged leaders of the body, whether they are the formal ones or not, can help the newcomer to advance himself and his projects at a modest price in conformity and recognition of reciprocal obligations. The conformity and recognition of obligations, moreover, involve some acceptance of the notion that the ramifications of some of the claims he espouses will, if the claims are unmodified, reach beyond the groups for which the new legislator speaks. The consequences of the demands he voices may affect his colleagues and the legislature as a group. He becomes more or less conscious of the need not to "upset the apple cart." Failure to learn the ways of the legislative group, to "play ball" with his colleagues, is almost certain, especially in a large body like the U.S. House of Representatives, to handicap the proposals in which the freshman legislator is interested and to frustrate his ambitions for personal preferment.[47] The group life of the legislature thus may temper the claims of an interest group, since the legislator-spokesman must reconcile such demands with his role within the chamber. Even the established and skillful legislative leader rarely rides roughshod over his colleagues.

The political interest group whose spokesman "belongs" to the legislative group, who is "one of the boys," enjoys an obvious advantage in access to the legislature, especially if the representative is one of the acknowledged leaders of the chamber. Correspondingly, a group is handicapped if its only connections are with a maverick or a newcomer. It is not enough for the legislator to be a member, in some sense, of the interest group or even to be in a position of formal power. He must "belong" within the legislature as well.

[47] Cf. Riddick: *The United States Congress*, pp. 89, 102; and Routt: "Interpersonal Relationships and the Legislative Process," p. 131.

Although the pattern of relationships within the legislature thus affects the access of interest groups, it is important not to assume that these interactions produce an integrated, hierarchical structure. They may, but the life of the legislative group as of others may as easily involve a loosely allied collection of cliques. Where a measure of integration is achieved in one chamber, moreover, it may not extend to the other. The group life of a legislature may bear little or no likeness to cohesive party government. As Woodrow Wilson said of the power of the Rules Committee and the Speaker of the House of Representatives before the 1911 revolt: "It integrates the House alone . . . ; does not unite the two houses in policy. . . . It has only a very remote and partial resemblance to genuine party leadership." [48] Party government is a form of legislative group life, but it is not the only or the most common form in the United States.

The Influence of Office

The influences we have discussed thus far come close to accounting for the relative access of interest groups to the legislature, but they are not complete. Formal structural aspects of government, the legislators' various group "memberships," and what we have called the group life of the legislature do not tell the whole story. In addition to these, the fact of holding public office is itself a significant influence upon the relative access of the groups. Not unrelated to the group life of the legislature, the influence of office is of sufficient importance to deserve separate and extended treatment.

In Chapter 2 we had something to say about the positions or statuses that an individual occupies in his society and about norms of perception and behavior that he derives from his experiences in the society. These concepts were treated as determinants of the ways in which an individual knows, interprets, and behaves in his society. Looking more closely at these statuses, we can conceive of a whole society as a system of interrelated positions that people occupy, each individual normally filling a great many. For each recognized status in a society there are norms that prescribe more or less definitely how the occupant is to behave toward persons in related statuses. These prescribed ways of behaving are known as roles. Thus a woman who occupies the status of mother in a given society performs a certain role, that is, she behaves as a mother in prescribed ways toward her

---

[48] Wilson: *Congressional Government*, preface to the 15th edition, p. ix.

children, her husband, her children's grandparents, teachers, friends, and others in related positions.[49]

Public office, including that of a legislator, is such a status. It hardly should be necessary to make this point were it not that its implications are so easily overlooked. When a man enters a legislative position he takes on a new role that is prescribed for him by the society. His success as a legislator depends in large part upon how well he performs that role.

Some parts of the public official's role he has been learning since early childhood, for any youngster early though dimly begins to pick up what it "means" to be a government officer. As he has matured, his understanding of the behavior prescribed for a legislator has been sharpened. He has learned to engage in some of these behaviors in other positions that he has occupied, particularly if he has consciously aspired to be a member of the legislative body. Some requirements he has learned in the course of election campaigns. Others, those toward his colleagues in the legislature, he is likely not to learn until after he has become a member of that body, as the preceding section suggested.

The norms that define a role do not specify all the things that the occupant of a particular status shall do. They require some behaviors and forbid certain others; still others are a matter of the officeholder's discretion; that is, they are permitted under appropriate conditions but are not essential. These required and forbidden behaviors, it is important to bear in mind, are defined by norms that are socially determined; one might call them the standardized expectations of those who are aware of the particular status. Some of these behaviors are, of course, specified in legal enactments, such as corrupt practices legislation and the constitutional right of petition.

As the existence of these formal, legal definitions suggests, these behavioral norms are not neutral. Whether or not they are embodied in statutes and constitutions, they are activities about which many people in the society feel very strongly; that is, these norms are associated with values the violation of which will cause disturbances of varying degrees of seriousness and will be punished in various ways—by impeachment, imprisonment, execution, ridicule, defeat at the polls, insult, lynching, and so on.

Not all behavioral norms are unambiguous. The legislator does not always "know what is expected of him" in a given situation, because in his constituency, unless it is remarkably homogeneous in every re-

---

[49] For a thorough discussion of this point see Newcomb: *Social Psychology*, chap. 8 and *passim*. The material in this section relies heavily on this source.

spect, various groups—organized and potential—will interpret his behavior in different ways. What is important to one segment may be
irrelevant to another; what is bribery to one may be charity to another; some may be able to distinguish between "honest and dishonest graft," and others not; some may be sufficiently organized and
cohesive to "remember" his actions for a long time, whereas others
are not. Especially if the legislator aspires to move from a smaller
to a larger and more heterogeneous constituency—from State legislator to governor, from Representative to United States Senator—what
an existing constituency regards as a proper concern for one's supporters may appear to voters in the larger area as narrow parochial-
ism. Hence is derived the importance of the forms and sources of
knowledge that we discussed earlier in the chapter.

But many of the norms defining the legislator's role are relatively
unambiguous, and these are the ones in which we are primarily interested here. These are included in what we referred to as
the "rules of the game" in Chapter 6. The legislator is expected
to avoid open partiality to the contested claims of a small minority;
he must at least appear to be solicitous for the vocal needs of his
constituents, but he is expected in some measure to look beyond his
constituency; he must defend the orderly procedures of political settlement; he must support the political and civil freedoms involved
in a fair trial, in petition, in speech, press, and assembly. These,
along with many others, not only define his role but represent the
substance of prevailing values without which the political system could
not exist. As Kluckhohn has said in a broader context: "A system
of beliefs, profoundly felt, is unquestionably necessary to the survival
of any society. . . ."[50]

It is, of course, obvious that the "rules of the game" are not invariably adhered to, that they are not accepted universally or with
unvarying vigor in all parts of the society at all times. But it does
not follow that they are not powerful. The protests of those who
denounce "the government" for lapses and deviations, in fact, testify
to the power of "the rules." The ability of a small group, speaking
in defense of such values, to exercise influence out of all proportion to the size of its paid-up membership has the same significance. These norms, values, expectations, "rules of the game"—call
them what you will—largely define the institution of government
along with other institutions of the society. For the legislator they

[50] Kluckhohn: *Mirror for Man*, p. 248.

set the approximate limits within which his discretionary behavior may take place. Accounting for the observation that "legislation will, on the whole, be more equitable than the legislators are themselves as private individuals," Myrdal puts his finger on this connection between norms and institutions in what we call democracy: "In their institutions they have invested more than their everyday ideas which parallel their actual behavior. They have placed in them their ideals of how the world rightly ought to be. The ideals thereby gain fortifications of power and influence in society." [51] When an individual achieves a widely recognized status such as legislative or other public office, these norms are usually brought to a sharp focus in the rites of oath-taking and investiture. Such ceremonies and rituals serve notice upon the individual and those about him that he has entered upon a new role with new rights and obligations. The norms are reaffirmed and intensified by a variety of devices and situations, including his continued participation in the legislative group. Honorific modes of address, public ceremonies, parliamentary ritual, and imposing public buildings have the function, among others, not only of reaffirming the loyalties of the governed, but also of strengthening and redefining the roles of the governors. [52]

The standards expected of those holding public office, the role of legislator, thus have an important influence upon the relative ease with which political interest groups gain access to points of decision. It does not follow that in every decision he makes the legislator is consciously aware of norms defining his role. It is entirely reasonable to assume, in fact, that the widely recognized norms are given little explicit consideration in daily policy decisions. These decisions constitute the discretionary segment of the legislator's role, and this discretion may be very wide. The existence of the required and the forbidden aspects of the role, however, means that those groups representing the expected or disapproved behaviors will be privileged or disadvantaged, respectively, in the matter of access. Occasional disregard of individual rights, for example, may have little effect upon the legislator's position. Flagrant and continued neglect, however, will provoke demands in the name of the abused norms, demands that are likely to gain privileged access. In the great majority of instances the successful legislator has so learned his role that groups

[51] Myrdal: *An American Dilemma*, p. 80. Copyright 1944 by and used with the permission of Harper and Brothers.

[52] See Charles E. Merriam: *The Making of Citizens* (Chicago: University of Chicago Press, 1931).

whose demands clearly require the forbidden behaviors will get a cold reception. It is within these limits that the competing demands of political interest groups are given a hearing.

Conclusions

The degree of access to the legislature that a particular group enjoys at a given moment is the result of a composite of influences. These determining factors will include the peculiarities of formal governmental structure and of the political party as a legislative instrument, such informal influences as the knowledge-supplying functions of the group and the character of the legislator's group affiliations, the formal and informal structure of the legislative body, and the influence of the standardized expectations in the community concerning the behavior of a legislator. Depending on the circumstances and the relative importance of these factors in a given situation, some groups will enjoy comparatively effective access, and others will find difficulty in securing even perfunctory treatment. As conditions change, as some of these influences become more and others less potent, the fortunes of group claims upon the legislature will rise or decline.

The most important implication of this multiple-factor conception of the dynamics of access is that the legislature is not just a sounding board or passive registering device for the demands of organized political interest groups. The legislature as a part of the institution of government embodies, albeit incompletely, the expectations, understandings, and values prevailing in the society concerning how the government should operate. These expectations may cover now a wide and now a relatively narrow range of behavior; they may be fairly explicit or highly ambiguous. Although the legislator's role is in part defined by limited expectations and norms prevailing in his constituency and in the interest groups with which he identifies himself, it is also the creation of the norms more widely recognized in the society. Partly because his role as a legislator inevitably gives him a specialized kind of experience from which he learns the limits of his behavior, partly because he has learned some of these norms as a member of the society, he cannot behave simply and completely as a vehicle for organized group demands.

It does not follow from the argument in this chapter that the widespread expectations about the legislature alone account for differences in ease of access or for all features of the legislative product. It is easy enough to identify cases in which the standardized expectations are ignored. The norms of official behavior inevitably partake of the quality of myth, of professed values. On the other hand, they are also operating values that affect all legislative behavior in some measure and that place limits upon both the methods and the content of group demands upon the legislature. In a stable political system the competing demands of organized interest groups are meaningless unless they are viewed in the context of these limiting and defining norms.[53]

A second implication of this conception of the dynamics of access is that "pressure," conceived as bribery or coercion in various forms, is scarcely the distinguishing feature of interest groups in the legislative process. Such coercion is frequently attempted, of course, and it often has an observable effect. "Pressure" of group upon legislator, however, is at most one aspect of technique, one among many different kinds of relationships that exist within the lawmaking body. As indicated by the evidence we have examined, the belief that the relationship between groups and legislators is a one-way, coercive relationship simply does not explain the observed behaviors. The institution of government, as later chapters will further demonstrate, is not so passive and cannot be understood in such oversimplified terms.

[53] This is one of the central points in Bentley's argument (cf. *The Process of Government*, pp. 361 and 372), although it is frequently overlooked. MacIver, for example, claims: "To Bentley . . . a legislative act is always the calculable resultant of a struggle between pressure groups, never a decision between opposing conceptions of the national welfare." (*The Web of Government*, p. 220. Copyright 1947 by Robert M. MacIver and used with the permission of The Macmillan Company.) This appears to be an inaccurate and unfair statement of the Bentley position.

12

Techniques of Interest Groups in the Legislative Process

ALTHOUGH access is the fundamental objective of group activities in the legislature, it is in a sense the minimum objective. Once achieved, access provides an opportunity to maneuver, a chance to use established relationships and the procedures of the legislative body to give effect to the group's claims. But access must be made effective, and an important determinant of the interest group's success is, therefore, the skill with which it and its "members" in the legislature are able to exploit their position. This is a matter of techniques.

There is no single formula, no simple chronology of devices that all effective groups use in standard fashion. Implicit in the notion of degrees of access is the additional fact that tactics within the legislature are tremendously varied. Because the position of no two groups is precisely identical and because the resources of any single group are in part altered by the presence of other groups operating in the same area, techniques appropriate at one time may be inappropriate or unavailable at another. Moreover, the formal and informal characteristics of legislatures—national, State, and local—differ and change. While it would be comforting, therefore, to be able to present a sort of manual, a "how to do it," of group legislative techniques, the complexity of the legislative process will not permit it. Our method rather will be to look at various legislative procedures, primarily those in the Congress, and to judge their significance in relation to activities of interest groups.

The Defensive Advantage and the Size of the Public

The commonest popular notion of the interest group operating in the legislature is that of an organization which is trying to promote something, a favorable subsidy, an increased appropriation for a governmental service, a protective licensing arrangement, or what not. This notion is accurate enough in a good many instances. In fact, Schattschneider's study of legislative tariff-making in 1929 and 1930 concluded that the interest groups most actively involved were those that favored the policy of tariff protection and wanted an increase in the duties directly affecting themselves.[1] On some occasions high-tariff demands were the only kinds made upon the Congress.

The promotional activities of interest groups, however, should not blind us to the fact that a very large proportion of group activity is merely defensive or preventive. Whether one looks at efforts to redistribute the tax load, to alter market practices, to restrict the exploitation of natural resources, to equalize opportunities for public education, or to accomplish any of hundreds of other objectives through the processes of government, one will find a large share of group activity dedicated to preventing any change in the existing order of things. Where there are groups whose claims involve a change, there are as likely to be others more or less vigorously defending the *status quo*. In itself this observation is not very startling. Its importance lies in the fact that such defensive groups frequently enjoy special opportunities in the legislative process.

The defensive advantage stems from two sources: first, the strength of established relationships in the society; second, the opportunities for delay or obstruction offered by existing legislative procedures. Turning to the first of these, we see it is obvious that any change in governmental policy involves an alteration of existing relationships within the society, the severity of the change being slight or drastic depending on the policy involved. Thus a decision to restrict the use of injunctions in labor disputes alters the relative strength and changes the interrelations of unions and management; a proposal to change the tax structure threatens to revamp the pattern of income distribution and hence the behaviors of various categories of taxpayers; a program to regulate the private exploitation of natural resources modifies, in effect, the property titles of persons owning

[1] Schattschneider: *Politics, Pressures and the Tariff*, pp. 106 ff.

such resources; a plan to create a public park in a congested slum area involves altering the behaviors and relationships of tenement owners, slum dwellers, and those remaining in the neighborhood after the improvement; a proposal to legalize gambling under government supervision threatens the established relationships of those engaged in illegal gambling, of "co-operating" enforcement officers, of the owners of other forms of commercial amusement, and of various church groups.

Established relationships offer varying degrees of resistance to disturbances, whether from governmental action or from other sources. Especially within institutionalized groups, as we noted in Chapter 2, patterns of established relationships are particularly likely to withstand disturbance. This is true not only because many individuals have become accustomed to the patterns of behavior affected, but also because the patterns may include roles highly valued by large segments of the community. The business corporation has been such a favored group in the United States and in opposition to the labor union, which has not yet fully achieved such a position of legitimacy, it normally enjoys defensive advantages.

The second advantage for defensive groups results from certain characteristics of American legislative structure and procedure. The bicameral organization of our typical legislature and the constitutional separation of powers operate, as they were designed, to delay or obstruct action rather than to facilitate it. Requirements of extraordinary majorities for particular kinds of measures and the absence of limits on the duration of debate have a like effect, as do numerous technical details of the parliamentary rules. Finally, the diffuseness of leadership, and the power and independence of committees and their chairmen, not only provide a multiplicity of points of access, as Chapter 11 illustrated, but also furnish abundant opportunities for obstruction and delay, opportunities that buttress the position of defensive groups. Something of the variety of such opportunities is suggested by a letter from the legislative committee of the Georgia Underwriters Association to the Association of Life Insurance Presidents in 1935. The letter promises "that we shall try to kill anything inimical, and if anything gets through of that description it is simply because we cannot stop it by any method known to us or any proper practice which we have at hand." It further sets forth what some of these methods were:

It has been our practice for years:
1—To try to persuade the author of a bill, either before its

introduction or after introduction and reference to a Committee, to withdraw same. This has worked oftener than might be thought.

2—We make effort in advance . . . to have friends on the Committee and to have meetings at the proper time and under favorable environment. This has frequently worked out.

3—If we do not succeed in getting a bill adversed, we try to introduce another bill, hoping that the whole thing will wind up in a row, to be plain about it. This has worked out at this session, and I will add in passing that we have one man . . . to get up and say that he does not believe in taxing life-insurance premiums at all and create a diversion in that way.

4—If a bill passes either house and goes to the other house, we try to repeat the above tactics.

5—At this session, particularly, we have considerable confidence in the Governor's statement that he will veto any tax increase.[2]

The degree of defensive advantage that a particular group may enjoy is not a fixed quantity. To state that a group has superiority because of its defensive position is to say something about its tactical or strategic resources in the political scene. The strength of established social relationships and the peculiarities of legislative structure and procedure, as we have just seen, are part of this setting. An additional influence, which may augment or restrict the other two, is the size and disposition of the public that is aware of the issue at stake. In other words, whether or not a defensive group is able to capitalize upon vested relationships and procedural obstructions will depend on the size and intensity of the opposition to it. The dimensions of the public will vary according to the issue and to the intensity of the disturbances or threatened disturbances that may have aroused the opposition.

It is an obvious but reluctantly acknowledged fact that individuals and groups are not equally and continuously active in governmental matters, any more than individuals are within the organized interest groups to which they belong. Participation is variable and uneven. The outsider's ascription of an "interest" to an individual or group is usually a poor basis upon which to predict political activity.[3] Any explanation of the legislative process or any other as-

[2] U.S. Temporary National Economic Committee: *Hearings*, part 10, p. 4767.
[3] Witness the evidence on this point in Schattschneider: *Politics, Pressures and the Tariff*, chap. 3.

pect of politics that does not recognize the inevitability of this fact will be inadequate. It will simply be accepting as fact the myth of omnivigilant citizenship, the picture of the nation as a sort of continuous town meeting with perfect attendance. The myth, of course, has its uses, since the feeling that "everyone ought to be interested in government" helps to provide the basis upon which an individual or group whose claims and protests are being ignored may increase his or its political support.

In a whimsical protest against those who make a business of trying to turn the myth of universal participation into fact entitled "Whom Do We Picket Tonight?" the author inquires: "Wouldn't a really healthy citizen in a really healthy country be as unaware of the government as a healthy man is unaware of his physiology?" [4] Without taking the words literally, we can see a considerable validity in the implications of this question. All the conceivable adjustments between all citizens cannot be made simultaneously and openly through the processes of government. The political system would not stand the strain. As Schattschneider observed in commenting on the variable activity of groups in tariff legislation: "If all groups affected by the legislation exerted an appreciable influence on Congress, the contests on each point in the bill would assume proportions so formidable, and the convulsion become so alarming, that action would be inconceivable; indeed, our politics would need to be quarantined against an agitation so disturbing." [5]

In any legislative session, especially in the Congress, there are likely to be two or three or perhaps half a dozen proposals that receive extended debate, that are given exhaustive coverage in the media of mass communication, and for which the public is of maximum size. For most of the remaining several hundred acts of Congress in a given session and for many of the detailed provisions of the widely publicized acts, the public is extremely small. Many of these acts and paragraphs of acts, it is true, affect directly only a small proportion of the population. Most enactments, however, touch immediately the fortunes of far more citizens than are aware of them in the legislative stage. For example, congressional definition of the terms on which the government will guarantee housing mortgages, exemption of railroad rates from the provisions of the antitrust statutes,

[4] Joseph Wood Krutch: "Whom Do We Picket Tonight?" *Harper's Magazine*, March, 1950, p. 67.

[5] E. E. Schattschneider: *Politics, Pressures and the Tariff*, p. 122-3. Copyright 1935 by Prentice-Hall, Inc.

and establishment of a quota on sugar imports from Cuba will likely be known to a public far smaller than the number of persons affected by the legislation. The technical nature of many such measures may make it unlikely that any very large public will be aware of them, but various circumstances, including group activity, may create an unexpectedly large public around even the most complicated legislation. The same kinds of influences may equally confine the public to very small proportions. Whether a defensive group is able to exploit the advantages of its position or not will depend in part on the size of the public concerned at the time.

The well-organized, cohesive group that enjoys skillful leadership is unlikely to be found outside the public concerned with even the most technical legislation related to its interests. This awareness, particularly on the part of its active minority, is one of the consequences of effective organization and of continued existence as a political interest group. Thus such groups as trade associations and corporations already subject to regulatory statutes are likely to be persistently aware in detail of policy proposals affecting them. These would include corporations and associations in public transportation, electric power, insurance, and similar businesses.

Assured inclusion in a variety of publics is one of the rewards of organization and is one of the advantages that the organized has over the merely potential interest group. The former is able to influence legislative technicalities not only of a substantive, but also of a purely procedural nature. It may even create a public for a minor feature of legislative technique, such as, for example, removing the anonymity of the nonrecord vote. Thus in 1921 the American Farm Bureau Federation was one of the groups seeking legislation to permit the production of cheap fertilizers at the government plant at Muscle Shoals, Alabama. The measure was defeated in the House of Representatives by a voice vote rather than a roll-call vote, so that it was presumably impossible to tell which members of Congress had supported and which had opposed the Farm Bureau's position. On the day after the House vote, however, the Federation officials sent a letter to each House member; it alleged undue influence by the fertilizer manufacturers, referred to the organization's interest in the Muscle Shoals legislation, and in the last paragraph said: "We regret that the vote yesterday was not one of record. In order that we may do justice both to Representatives in Congress and to our membership, will you kindly notify our Washington Representative, Mr. Gray Silver, 1411 Pennsylvania Avenue—whether you voted for or against this proposition." [6] No small part of the effectiveness of an interest group is its ability to include its members in the public for any measure bearing on their interests and its capacity to be "articulate about legislative detail." [7]

The leadership of a group, whether it is on the defensive or not, will try to control the size of the public on a given measure in order that the composition of the public may be as favorable to its position as possible. The most obvious means of control is, of course, propaganda, its objective being not only to activate those already in the public but also to increase the size of the supporting segment of the public by recruits from outside. Enough has been said on this general point in Chapter 8 to make further detail scarcely necessary here. One or two additional facts need to be pointed up, however. Where there is any real possibility of materially extending the dimensions of a given public, the group that expects to benefit must usually be able to identify itself with some widely held objective even though the immediate benefits of the advocated legislation will be narrowly distributed. Of course, some proposed legislation may be opposed or supported by a sufficient number of groups to make the public inevitably quite large. And when it is, the ability to speak in terms of "the public interest" is even more important. It is, for example, one of the assets of groups representing the owners and operators of the American merchant marine that their projects for government subsidies can usually be defended as part of a national defense program. [8] In debating the highly controversial proposals in 1946 to continue wartime price controls, groups on both sides based their appeals on alleged concern for "the public interest." [9] Where groups on one side of an issue find it difficult to argue in terms of "national interest," the opposition has everything to gain by extending the public through propaganda. This device may be available to offensive as well as defensive groups, but the latter are probably somewhat more easily able to use it, especially if they can speak in the name of a large but momentarily weak potential interest group.

[6] Quoted in Kile: *The Farm Bureau Through Three Decades*, p. 97. Copyright 1948 by and used with the permission of Orville M. Kile.

[7] Bailey: *Congress Makes a Law*, p. 182. Copyright 1950 by and used with the permission of Columbia University Press.

[8] Paul M. Zeis: *American Shipping Policy* (Princeton, N. J.: Princeton University Press, 1938), p. 207 and *passim*. Cf. Pendleton Herring: "The Politics of Fiscal Policy," *Yale Law Journal*, Vol. 47, no. 5 (March, 1938), p. 725.

[9] See U.S. Senate, Committee on Banking and Currency: *Hearings on Extension of the Price Control and Stabilization Acts*, 79th Cong., 2d Sess. (1946).

The way in which a public may be expanded by a defensive group may be illustrated by the efforts in 1947 and 1948 to oppose a group of sheep raisers and cattlemen who were working through the American National Livestock Association and the National Woolgrowers Association to extend their grazing privileges on certain public lands. The immediate issue was an administrative policy of the United States Forest Service, but the attack on this policy was part of a general effort to weaken Federal controls over grazing on public lands and to reduce government land holdings in many parts of the West. The two stockmen's associations and their affiliated State associations had excellent access to the Congress. The key members of the subcommittee of the House Committee on Public Lands, which conducted hearings on the stockmen's charges, not only represented States in which Federal landholdings are large, but also were themselves stockmen. In addition, at some of the hearings Senator Robertson of Wyoming, a stockman, sat with the House subcommittee apparently by courtesy. On the side of the Forest Service was a series of groups, including the Izaak Walton League, the Dude Ranchers' Association, mining companies, and others concerned with protecting water supplies. In all probability the latter would have been strong enough to defeat the stockmen, especially as several local stock raisers' groups openly refused to go along with the attack. This outcome was virtually assured, however, when the plans of the two national stockmen's associations were reported prematurely in articles in several national magazines, supplemented later in both magazines and newspapers by accounts of the hearings conducted by the House subcommittee. These disclosures had the effect of expanding the public on the controversy and strengthening the defensive groups through alleging two sorts of violations of the "rules of the game": First, the stockmen's claims were effectively presented as attempts to indulge a single, limited group to the detriment of a number of collectively more inclusive groups; second, the methods of the stockmen and of the subcommittee were presented as devious, partial, and unfair. These efforts enlarged the public, activated overlapping memberships, and reinforced certain widespread expectations concerning the roles of public officials.[10]

Another instructive illustration of the expansion of a public, this

[10] Bernard DeVoto: "The West Against Itself," *Harper's Magazine* (January, 1947), pp. 1–13, "Sacred Cows and Public Lands" and "The Easy Chair," *Harper's Magazine* (July, 1948), pp. 44–45, 108–12. Lester Velie: "They Kicked Us Off Our Land," *Collier's Magazine*, July 26, August 9, 1947, pp. 20–1, 72–3. U.S. House of Representatives, Subcommittee of the Committee on Public Lands: *Hearings on H. Res. 93*, 80th Cong., 1st Sess. (1947).

time by a group on the offensive, was provided by the efforts to increase the size of the public supporting the recommendations of the Hoover Commission on Organization of the Executive Branch of the Government. In the past the public on such proposals has been small, owing largely to the technicality of the issues, and it has been dominated by organized groups resisting any change in their relations with various segments of the executive branch of the government. With the issuance of the Hoover Commission proposals a new interest group, the Citizens Committee for the Hoover Report, was formed to increase the size of the public and to provide more cohesive support for the reorganization. It could not defeat some of the better established groups, such as the National Rivers and Harbors Congress, but its persistent propaganda efforts developed a larger public and more support for the Hoover Commission proposals than any earlier program of administrative reorganization has received.[11]

As the foregoing examples suggest, attempts at controlling the size of the public through restriction are also an aspect of group technique. Avoidance of publicity and efforts at censorship of the communications media are one means to this end. In the drive for resale price maintenance laws in the States in the 1930's the National Association of Retail Druggists' State committees avoided newspaper publicity for fear of being charged with "price fixing." Propaganda was directed only at persons already known to be sympathetic with the program. It is significant that in none of the fifteen States that had passed such laws by 1937 was there significant organized opposition to the measure. In at least one State censorship of hostile newspaper articles was achieved by threats to withdraw advertising.[12] Among the major reasons for the success of the sugar-beet growers and processors in securing protective legislation have been their intensive effort within a limited public and the largely effective avoidance of any considerable increase in its dimensions. These groups have been able to maintain, as one analyst described it, "acceptance of the assumption that a few hundred acres planted to sugar beets and a factory or two to process them make any state *ipso facto* a

[11] The American Institute of Public Opinion announced in March, 1950, that 39 per cent of a national sample had heard of or read about the Hoover Commission report and that 31 per cent indicated a clear understanding of the purpose of the Commission. This is an impressively large proportion, if taken at its face value. (*Public Opinion Quarterly*, Vol. 14, no. 2 [Summer, 1950], pp. 376–7.)

[12] U.S. Federal Trade Commission: *Report on Resale Price Maintenance*, pp. 57–9.

'Beet State' and automatically place its congressional delegation in the beet sugar bloc." [13]

But avoidance of publicity is not the only or even the most important means of controlling the size of a public through restriction. We noticed earlier that the technicality of many legislative provisions tends to limit the public to the technicians and the organized groups directly affected. This limitation is often inevitable. The difficulty of creating a sizable public on technical matters, however, may be used deliberately by an interest group to restrict the public concerned with its defensive or promotional efforts. Such restriction may be effective even in connection with substantive legislation. Thus, as we have noted in an earlier chapter, the proposals enacted in the Taft-Hartley Act of 1947 had the effect of restricting both the size and the composition of the public. Concentrating not upon the wages, hours, and working conditions of employees, but rather upon the "institutional privileges of the union," the legislation minimized opposition both from within and from outside the ranks of organized labor.[14]

Of all the means of using technicality to restrict the size of a public, none are more commonly used than appropriation bills and tax legislation. Such measures are inevitably technical; they are unlikely on most occasions to have a very large public even though fiscal policy is at the very heart of the governing process and through it deprivations and privileges are distributed throughout the society. Moreover, such measures must be passed in one form or another if the government is to carry on its functions, so that if a group's claims can be worked into these bills, they may have a privileged chance of enactment. This is not so likely if the chief executive, like the governors of most of the States, has the power to disapprove individual items within a measure (the so-called item veto), but the president of the United States has no such power. Even if a group's claims cannot be converted into tax rates or the language of appropriations, they may be placed as a "rider" on financial legislation. The rules of most legislative bodies forbid such practices, but they are often breached.[15] Faced with a rider on an appropriation measure, the presi-

[13] William H. Baldwin: "Pressure Politics and Consumer Interests: The Sugar Issue," *Public Opinion Quarterly*, Vol. 5, no. 1 (Spring, 1941), pp. 102–10 at p. 105.

[14] Ross: *Trade Union Wage Policy*, p. 24. Copyright 1948 by The Regents of the University of California and used with the permission of University of California Press.

[15] Chamberlain: *Legislative Processes*, pp. 167–9.

dent is reluctant to issue a veto at the expense of delaying the availability of funds to carry on a government service.

Because of its technicality and its consequent small public, the appropriation bill frequently serves as a second line of group defense. For the public aware of the passage of an appropriation act is
frequently neither as large nor composed of the same groups as that
concerned with the passage of enabling legislation. A long and
skillful campaign based on maximizing a public and on numerous
group alliances, perhaps aided by a dramatic crisis or disaster, like
the campaigns leading to the passage of State antitrust laws in the
1880's and 1890's or to the land conservation measures of the
1930's, succeeds in getting enabling legislation on the statute books.
Then the supporting combination may disintegrate. Within the remaining public those whose activities are to be restricted by the
statute constitute a relatively larger and more active segment. Under
such circumstances the program can be all but repealed by restricting
appropriations to the point where enforcement cannot be financed or
by threatening such restrictions unless administrative interpretation of
the legislation conforms to the demands of the remaining active elements in the public. It is not without significance that the stockmen's
groups referred to earlier in this section used the appropriations device to weaken the effect of the Taylor Grazing Act of 1934 and
threatened the same tactics in their brush with the Forest Service.

The size and disposition of the public on a given measure thus
materially affect the relative advantage enjoyed by the groups involved. Where these are defensive groups, they may already enjoy
certain advantages from the fact alone. The character of the public
may augment that superiority or may operate to the advantage of
the opposing groups. As circumstances alter, the initiative may pass
again to the defensive groups through the appropriations process.

Alliances and Logrolling

Although a group may easily enjoy advantages in position and in the
size and disposition of the public concerned with its claims, rarely
can any single group achieve its legislative objectives without assistance from other groups. Occasionally, to be sure, a proposal is so
noncontroversial that if the sponsoring group secures access to a handful of legislators, it meets with no further obstacles except those
of accident or indifference. That is, its public is homogeneous, and
there is no considerable likelihood that an expansion of the public

will make it less so. Even in this enviable position, however, a group may fail unless there is strong enthusiasm behind its claims. Even if it is not opposed, it may be ignored unless it can get assistance from other sources.

Although the collaboration of different groups is present in some measure in any legislative system, it is particularly characteristic of a legislative body such as the Congress, in which leadership is diffused, unintegrated, and more or less continually shifting. The mutual assistance of interest groups is a means of forging a structure of leadership where the political party does not provide it.

The two principal forms of mutual assistance among interest groups are alliances and logrolling. These are not always clearly separable and are normally supplementary, but they illustrate somewhat different tendencies in the legislative process. The alliance, whether formal or informal, involves the development of a common strategy among several groups in pursuit of a policy which bears some substantive relation to the interests of each. Thus the aggregation of labor unions, the American Veterans Committee, the National Association for the Advancement of Colored People, the National Farmers Union, the National Lawyers Guild, and others, which worked in more or less coordinated fashion for the passage of the Employment Act of 1946, constituted an alliance.[16] Logrolling, on the other hand, involves a group's giving support to a proposal that may bear no relation or only the most tenuous relation to its own objectives; in return it receives similar support from the group it has assisted. The most familiar form of logrolling is in connection with appropriations for local improvements such as flood-control works and harbor development, but the practice is not limited to such projects. Irrefutable proof of its use in other connections is seldom available, but presumptive evidence is common, as in a farm organization's support of continued subsidies for American ocean shipping. Logrolling is a form of trading operation for which access is the coin.

Few groups find no need for the devices of mutual assistance. Even the powerful Anti-Saloon League engaged in alliances. It probably never would have achieved the power it held in its prime without its tie to the Protestant churches and, despite its concentration upon the evils of the saloon, it entered alliances on other projects which bore some relation to prohibition, such as woman suffrage. The League's whole balance-of-power strategy was an example of logrolling in a highly developed form.[17]

[16] Bailey: *Congress Makes a Law*, chap. 5.
[17] Odegard: *Pressure Politics*, pp. 85–90.

Alliances may be continuing and comparatively formal arrangements or they may be temporary and informal, and the same group may be involved in both types. Thus the National Association of Retail Druggists was a leading force as early as 1916 in the American Fair Trade League, an alliance of retail groups promoting resale price maintenance. An illustration of its more transitory connections is a letter from the N.A.R.D. general manager to the Eastman Kodak Company in 1938 offering the association's aid in securing a higher tariff on foreign film in order to permit Eastman to continue to sell on price maintenance contracts.[18] At times these alliances begin as formal arrangements, associations of interest groups, such as the National Council for a Permanent FEPC. At others they develop from casual alliances into a continuing joint legislative committee for coordinating strategy on agreed proposals, such as the New York State Conference Board of Farm Organizations.[19]

Circumstances and events may encourage or permit the most unlikely alliances among groups that customarily are in opposition to one another or that seem to have relatively little in common. Thus in 1949 when Paul Hoffman, head of the Economic Co-operation Administration, and Vice-Admiral William Smith, chairman of the Maritime Commission, suggested a relaxation of the legislative requirement that half of all E.C.A.-financed cargoes be carried in American ships, they met such an alliance. Both the C.I.O. and the A.F. of L. maritime unions collaborated with the National Federation of American Shipping in opposition to the proposal.[20] Agricultural depressions historically have been the occasion for alliances between groups promoting increases in the price of silver and farm groups sympathetic with an inflationary monetary policy.[21] McKean notes a number of instances in which circumstances in New Jersey pro-

[18] U. S. Federal Trade Commission: *Report on Resale Price Maintenance,* pp. 44 ff., 135–7.
[19] Kesselman: *The Social Politics of FEPC,* chap. 2. For a comparable case see Fred W. Riggs: *Pressures on Congress: A Study of the Repeal of Chinese Exclusion* (New York: Kings Crown Press, 1950). Cf. Zeller: *Pressure Politics in New York,* pp. 123–8. Herring: *Group Representation Before Congress,* pp. 97, 168, 178, 188 ff., 208 f., 217 ff., 231–4, gives numerous examples of temporary and continuing alliances. For instances of co-operative alliances among trade associations see U.S. Temporary National Economic Committee: *Trade Association Survey,* pp. 40–2.
[20] The *New York Herald Tribune,* February 9, 1949.
[21] Allan S. Everest: *Morgenthau, the New Deal, and Silver: A Story of Pressure Politics* (New York: Kings Crown Press, 1950), pp. 3, 38–9, and *passim.* Everest notes (p. 56) that the first Agricultural Adjustment Act weakened the cohesion of the silver forces by easing the financial situation of farmers.

duced alliances among usually conflicting groups. The adoption and repeal of the sales tax in that State in 1935 produced a number of these on each side of the issue; proposals to tax and regulate motor truck transportation had the allied support of the railroad unions and the railroad corporations; despite "broad and deep" conflicts among professional groups in the State, they produced a continuing alliance, in the form of the Conference of Professional Societies, to maintain "independence" for the State licensing and examining boards.[22]

Although circumstances may produce a joining of group forces in the legislature, the evidence for an alliance is not always clear. A case in point is the so-called Cox Committee investigation of the Federal Communications Commission in 1943 and 1944, of which more will be said later. The immediate origin of this Select Committee of the House was the F.C.C.'s daring to turn over to the Department of Justice evidence of criminal malfeasance on the part of Representative Eugene Cox of Georgia. Ample support for the resolution authorizing the investigation was available from Cox's position as the second ranking Democratic member of the House Rules Committee and from factors associated with the group life of the legislature. In the background, however, were influences of undefined strength stemming from the broadcasting networks, which recently had been censured by the F.C.C. for their contractual relations with their outlet stations, from the telephone and telegraph companies, which had recently been subject to F.C.C. investigation, and from disappointed applicants for radio broadcasting licenses.[23]

There are limits to the ease with which normally incompatible groups can become allied, even in the most informal fashion. As we noted in Chapter 8 in discussing alliances for propaganda purposes, the prestige or status of a group in the society affects the ease with which it is able to make such arrangements. Thus the American Medical Association was likely to experience little trouble in its ef· forts to establish cooperative relationships with the American Legion, farm groups, and others in opposition to compulsory health insurance.[24] The Association of American Railroads has been able to effect useful alliances with various chambers of commerce, for example, to get bills introduced in Congress apparently at the request of

[22] McKean: *Pressures on the Legislature of New Jersey,* chaps. 3 and 6.
[23] Robert D. Leigh: "Politicians vs. Bureaucrats," *Harper's Magazine* (January, 1945), pp. 97–105.
[24] The *New York Times,* February 6, 1949; The *New York Herald Tribune,* April 4, December 9, 1949.

the chambers of commerce, but actually prepared by the A.A.R.; it has made similar arrangements with shippers' organizations. The railroads put on a campaign in 1945 to secure passage of legislation overriding a Supreme Court decision and exempting from the provisions of the antitrust statutes railroad rate agreements approved by the Interstate Commerce Commission. In the hearings on the measure it took fifteen pages of fine print merely to list the organizations that appeared or sent statements in support of the railroads' demands.[25] If a group lacks or loses a position of "respectability," its prospects of gaining allies are poor, and it is threatened with the perils of isolation. Where, as in the legislative process, a majority of those eligible and voting is an accepted means of settling claims, the inability to effect alliances is a serious handicap.

Given the importance of alliances in the legislative process, a skillful sponsoring group or leader will avoid drafting or interpreting legislation in terms which will facilitate opposing alliances. A major reason why the legislative drafts that eventually became the Emergency Price Control Act of 1942 contained no provision for ceilings on wages was that any such proposal would have facilitated an alliance between certain farm groups and most labor unions. The former were already hostile to the measure, and the addition of the labor opposition would seriously have jeopardized the passage of an effective bill.[26] It is significant that the demise of wartime price control in 1945 and 1946 was assured almost certainly as a result of interpretations of the statute that consolidated an effective alliance among the National Association of Manufacturers, the National Retail Dry Goods Association, the National Automobile Dealers Association, and groups opposed to placing a ceiling on the price of raw cotton.

The necessity of forming and the process of negotiating alliances may have other important effects in the political process. In the first place, the need to acquire support may result in the elimination or modification of group claims which obstruct agreement. To the extent that such adjustments are effected outside the formal institu-

[25] U.S. Senate, Committee on Interstate Commerce: *Senate Report No. 26,* 77th Cong., 1st Sess. (1941), part 2, pp. 54–9. U.S. House of Representatives, Subcommittee of the Committee on Interstate and Foreign Commerce: *Hearings on H. R. 2536,* 79th Cong., 1st Sess. (1945). Cf. Key: *Politics, Parties, and Pressure Groups,* pp. 110–12.

[26] Cf. Burns: *Congress on Trial,* pp. 82–90, for a discussion of the legislative history of this measure. There were, of course, special economic reasons for not placing general controls on wages at this stage in the mobilization of a war economy.

tions of government, the stability of the system is promoted. In the second place, the efforts at achieving alliances, even when not wholly successful, may permit a group to disseminate information to the leaders of another group on a measure that otherwise might arouse opposition and antagonism. Thirdly, the alliance-forming process may have the important political effect of broadening the focus of attention of the groups involved. The range of issues on which a stand is taken by many of the larger political interest groups, such as the American Farm Bureau Federation, the Chamber of Commerce, and the labor federations, is impressive in this respect. The forging of alliances may be only one of the factors producing, for example, extensive discussions of the Marshall Plan in the deliberations of the A.F. of L. and the C.I.O., but it is almost certainly involved. To the extent that alliance-forming requires such widening of a group's concerns, it may have significant "educative" and unifying effects throughout the political system.[27] A group in need of alliances may have to accommodate as heterogeneous a collection of demands as does a political party.

Logrolling is often viewed, not as a device of group collaboration, but merely as a parliamentary maneuver engaged in by legislators. Enough has been said in the preceding chapter to indicate that one cannot adequately define a legislative body without considering the group attachments of its members. Although logrolling is a technique employed by legislators, it is used on behalf of groups, organized and potential. It may be in fact largely supported by the group structure of the legislature itself. In any case, logrolling is one of the points at which effective access pays off. Such trading commonly is a means of securing the necessary signatures on a petition to discharge a committee from further consideration of a measure that is being pigeonholed. Or a committee chairman may require a trade of votes as a condition of reporting a bill to the floor. A group or interest that has achieved access to a number of legislators, so that its claims command their primary loyalty for the moment, has something to trade in its efforts to achieve a majority. The practice of logrolling may give significant leverage to relatively small groups. The device may also have the positive consequence of making it difficult to ignore completely any minority group that has a measure of access. A group that has no significant national electoral power may find its protection in the trading of legislative votes.

An excellent illustration of logrolling, which also reveals the

[27] On this point see Almond: *The American People and Foreign Policy,* pp. 150–1, 235–6.

distinction between it and the alliance, occurred in connection with appropriations in 1940 for unemployment relief and farm parity payments. During that session the Farm Bureau's supporters in Congress had been in opposition to representatives from some of the Eastern cities on these two measures and on others. Neither had sufficient reliable votes on these bills to assure it a majority in the House. Under the leadership of Mayor LaGuardia of New York and President O'Neal of the Farm Bureau, an arrangement was made during the voting on parity payments in the House of Representatives. The votes of a number of urban congressmen on that measure were exchanged for those of certain representatives from farm areas on general relief appropriations.[28]

"Logrolling," as Bentley observed, "is a term of opprobrium . . . because it is used mainly with reference to its grosser forms."[29] It is presumably these grosser forms that from time to time have led majorities in State legislatures and constitutional assemblies to define the practice as a crime or as an offense punishable by forfeiture of office; the Mississippi constitution of 1890, for example, required legislators to take an oath that they would not trade votes. Fundamentally, however, the trading of support is a technique for the adjustment of interests. These interests must be adjusted in some fashion. They are not abstractions; rarely are they merely transient whims. If they are not satisfied by logrolling and related devices, they are likely to be submitted to settlement through less orderly techniques or through dictation, for which, by way of the myth of majority rule, such practices as logrolling are an alternative. When we speak of interests in this connection we do not mean merely organized interest groups, but all interests represented in the legislature. Just as a legislator from the Iowa corn belt does not feel as strongly as his colleague from Cape Cod about the fortunes of New England fishermen, so at any given point in time the demands of other and less explicit interests—those of party, of the legislative group, and of the expectations that in general define the legislator's role—are not felt with equal strength by all members of a legislature. All, including these broad, relatively unorganized interests, must achieve adjustment and recognition through vote trading and related techniques. The very essence of the legislative process is the willingness to accept trading as a means.

[28] Kile: *The Farm Bureau Through Three Decades*, pp. 275–6.
[29] Bentley: *The Process of Government*, p. 370. Copyright 1908 by and used with the permission of Arthur F. Bentley.

The Use of Standing Committees

Legislative committees are usually thought of as a useful and efficient means of dividing the labor of law making, of sifting projects of law before they are acted upon by the whole body. This indeed is the committee's characteristic function and, as we have already seen, it is a necessary result of the large size of deliberative assemblies and of the volume and complexity of matters coming before them. As the preceding chapter has also indicated, these committees, in proportion to their importance in the parent body, have considerable influence upon the degree of access to the legislature attainable by various groups. Where committees are strong and independent, as in the Congress of the United States, effective access to them is equivalent to privileged influence in the legislature itself. In such circumstances it follows that influencing of committees becomes an important part of the technique of interest groups. It is this use of legislative committees by interest groups that we shall now explore.

In interpreting the operation of legislative committees as a reflection of group activities we must be cautious and tentative for two reasons. In the first place, this approach has rarely been a major focus of empirical research on the "little legislatures," although it has often received some peripheral attention. Many of the observations in the following paragraphs must therefore be rather hypotheses than established generalizations. Secondly, the uses that can be made of any particular committee are certain to vary considerably from time to time. We have already seen that access to the legislature or to its subordinate units is highly complex and variable. Similarly the susceptibility of a committee to the demands of any group will vary with changes in the membership of the committee, with shifts in the formal and informal structure of the legislature, and with variations in the political circumstances under which legislative proposals are handled. Generalizations about committees, therefore, must be made with such limiting conditions in mind.

When one refers to legislative committees one usually has in mind the standing committees. Although there are at least two other kinds of committees at which we shall want to look, the standing committees and their functions bulk largest in the political scene. These are the bodies designated when committees are referred to as "little legislatures." As such they have a political task of the utmost difficulty and importance. Especially with respect to measures whose effects are likely to be widely or intensely felt, the standing committee's recommendations are not likely to be followed unless it performs its task skillfully. In pigeonholing a measure and particularly in preparing to report a bill favorably, a committee must judge what is sometimes called "the temper" of the legislature and the country concerning a proposal.[30] In other words, a committee must, whether its majority is actively supporting a bill or not, estimate the relative strength of the interests involved in the measure and judge the political viability of the project with or without modifications; it must make such judgments keeping in view all the technicalities that most modern legislation involves.

Controversy may follow a measure from its consideration in a committee room to the debate upon the floor of a legislative chamber. It may do so merely because a minority insists upon a last-ditch—though perhaps hopeless—fight. Or a controversy on the floor may be caused by lack of political skill within the committee. Or it may reflect the fact that interests lacking adequate access to the standing committee have better access to the legislature through other channels and have chosen to assert their most vigorous claims in the larger body. Nevertheless, the tendency, as we have seen previously, is for the standing committees to set policy that the whole legislature usually follows. In so doing the committee's grasp of the political forces involved must be complete.

The crucial decisions of a committee normally take place in executive session, at which private citizens and the press are customarily not present. It is here that amendments and modifications, drafts and redrafts reflecting different formulas for meeting the claims involved in a measure are worked out, and it is in such sessions that the fate of most bills is sealed. Committee actions in these sessions may, in some instances, be merely ratifications of decisions taken previously by a strong chairman. A chairman may and frequently does arrogate to himself a decision of this sort, especially a determination to shelve a measure. In such cases the chairman himself is performing the political function of estimating relative strength that is normally performed by the committee as a whole. Upon such one-man decisions, of course, the multiple elements influencing access are at work. The chairman is not an automatic registering device: his skills and his preferences will both be displayed in the result. Whether action is

[30] Cf. Chamberlain: *Legislative Processes*, pp. 63 f.

by the whole committee or by the chairman, the technical staff of the unit may play a role, sometimes a crucially important one. Bailey concluded that in the case of the Employment Act of 1946 "the staff became the central mechanism for mobilizing widely-dispersed intellectual resources and a coalition of pressures, public and private, behind the legislation." [31]

Since significant committee action, whether by the chairman alone or by the whole membership, occurs in executive session, this is one of the points at which the effectiveness of access is tested. Unless a group has a degree of access that assures it representation in the executive sessions of the committee, in one if not both houses of the legislature, the group's achievements are likely to be limited. It should have access directly to the chairman, the rank-and-file membership, or the staff, particularly if it is trying to smother a proposal. On the other hand, if it is seeking to modify or restrict the provisions of a bill, indirect access to other important members of the chamber may be equally effective. Part of the task of the standing committee in developing a measure that is politically viable is to take into account the claims expressed through any significant cluster of legislators. In a bicameral legislature such as the Congress, this reckoning must take notice of patterns of access not only in the chamber to which it reports, but in the other as well. Moreover, since the president's veto power gives him a significant part in legislation, a committee must reckon with interests that have superior access through him. The object may be to avoid a veto or to make concessions in the legislature that will assure a majority large enough to override the president's objections.

To be most effective, both direct and indirect access to the committee must have been established before, preferably long before, the executive deliberations begin. Moreover, direct access must be a good deal more than perfunctory. When we have stated in the preceding paragraphs what a committee majority or chairman must take into account if an acceptable measure is to be written, we have assumed that the committee sponsors want such a bill, that access is close and intimate. Lacking such intimacy, failure of a measure on the floor of the chamber, though it may appear to result from lack of skill on the part of the committee or its chairman, may actually result from an artful effort to defeat a measure without having to take responsibility for its defeat. Just as the declared opponents may amend a bill so as to make it unacceptable to a portion of its proponents,

[31] Bailey: *Congress Makes a Law*, p. 78. Copyright 1950 by and used with the permission of Columbia University Press.

just as a legislator may vote for a bill in full hope and confidence that it will be vetoed, so a nominal sponsor may by lack of zeal in perfecting a measure, escape the conflicting claims being made upon him. A group cannot use a committee or its chairman unless its relations with them are dominating and preclusive, a situa·tion that, as we noted in Chapter 11, is not easily achieved.

The Use of Public Committee Hearings

If the crucial decisions of a standing committee are made in executive session and if reliable access makes certain that key committee members shall have made up their minds long before the session, what function is performed by the public hearing? Of what use is this device either to interest groups or to the governing process in general? That the public hearing is not just a meaningless vestige is suggested by the fact that it is not of ancient vintage. The general practice of holding hearings on most major legislation before the Congress, except appropriation bills, dates only from the early years of the twentieth century. The right to be heard before a committee is only customary and not legally or constitutionally guaranteed.[32]

The functions or uses of the public hearing can be listed in three categories.[33] First, the hearing is a means of transmitting information, both technical and political, from various actual and potential interest groups to the committee. This is the most familiar function, but probably the least important. From the standpoint of interest group or committee member, as we shall have occasion to see in more detail later, the hearing is usually a haphazard and unsatisfactory device for giving and receiving information. This is one function of such proceedings, but it alone would not account for their continued vitality. A second use is as a propaganda channel through which a public may be extended and its segments partially consolidated or reinforced. A third function is to provide a quasi-ritualistic means of adjusting group conflicts and relieving disturbances through a safety valve. The last two uses merit examination in some detail.

Before considering the public hearing as a propaganda channel, it is worth noting that the public hearing has become an accepted

[32] Herring: *Group Representation Before Congress*, p. 41; Luce: *Legislative Procedure*, p. 143.

[33] Cf. Bailey: *Congress Makes a Law*, pp. 109–10; Chamberlain: *Legislative Processes*, pp. 79–80; Luce: *Legislative Procedure*, pp. 142–8; Winslow: *State Legislative Committees*, p. 84.

practice in the Congress during a period in which an increasing number and variety of interest groups, particularly associations, have been attempting to achieve access to the government in general and to the legislature in particular. General introduction of the public hearing, as we noticed in Chapter 8, was a consequence of the proliferation of interest groups and of the challenge to established interests that their claims constituted. Open hearings satisfied the forms of the democratic "rules of the game" even when they did not immediately grant the benefits of real access.

The value of a hearing as a propaganda channel is that it is an event. It is news. Especially when the participants are prominent or the testimony involves startling revelations or sharp conflicts, the event is likely to receive generous coverage in the media, principally the news media. Even when the "show" doesn't receive the full treatment by klieg lights and motion-picture cameras, it is likely to be covered by the press services. As a means by which a group may "break into print" and reach a wider, nonmember, public, a well-staged hearing has real advantages. At some points in the development of a measure, in fact, the primary purpose of hearings lies in their propaganda value. It is unlikely, for instance, that when hearings on a compulsory health insurance measure were first held in the Seventy-ninth Congress (1945–6) Senator Murray and the other sponsors expected in the near future to report a bill to the floor of the Senate. Rather these hearings, as a kind of trial balloon, served both to reveal the sources of opposition and support and to extend the public concerned with the issue.

Examples of the propagandist use of standing committee hearings on proposed legislation can be found in any newspaper, but the citation of a few may be helpful. In the dying days of the Office of Price Administration in 1945 and 1946, the Small Business Committee of the House, under the chairmanship of Congressman Patman of Texas, was the forum and sounding board for the alliance of groups which were attempting to defeat the renewal of price-control legislation.[34] The farm organizations, notably the Farm Bureau, have regularly attached considerable importance to hearings before "their" committees. Relations between farm groups and the House and Senate agriculture committees have long been so close that a declared opponent of one of the major farm groups is not likely to be placed on these committees by either party. In the 1920's the farm groups

[34] U.S. House of Representatives, Select Committee on the National Defense Program and its Relation to Small Business: *Hearings*, 79th Cong., 1st Sess. (1945), part 5.

had to use such hearings to promote their demands for government aid, and they still value them. For example, in the winter of 1939–1940, when an attempt was made to amend agricultural credit legislation without giving the Grange and the Farm Bureau what they regarded as adequate opportunity to express opposition, the hearings before the House Agriculture Committee were reopened, reportedly on the insistence of these two organizations.[35]

That most public hearings tend to be at least as much a matter of propaganda as of persuading or informing the committee is also indicated by the use that some of the major organized interest groups make of their "big names." When the Chamber of Commerce of the United States or a major trade association wants to make effective use of a hearing, witnesses usually are not drawn from the staff, although the latter may be technically better informed, but from among the more prominent members. The staff may and often do brief the headliners. It is the prominent witnesses who make the news, however, not the technicians. The same practice is normally followed by the labor federations and by other groups. It is frequently possible, in fact, to tell from the importance of the witnesses at a hearing whether a group is making an all-out or only a token effort on a measure. If the C.I.O., for example, merely files a written statement or sends a relatively obscure employee, the priority rating of the bill probably is low. If its president testifies, however, it is likely that the organization considers it important for the newspapers to be able to carry headlines with Philip Murray's name to catch the reader's eye.

The general character of a group's access to a committee can also be observed from the conduct of the hearings. A sympathetic committeeman can do much through his questioning to emphasize the group's views, just as a hostile one may obscure the point by interruptions and obtrusive questions. The partiality of the chairman and the character of the groups he has invited, as compared with those he has merely permitted to testify, may also be revealing. However, the hostility of committeemen may not succeed in obstructing the propaganda channel provided by the hearings, as a sharp clash with a group's witnesses may be just the kind of newsworthy event that receives extensive treatment in the media. This phenomenon is not something peculiarly modern. The abolitionists in Massachusett capitalized on such an encounter before a committee of the General Court in 1836. The committee was conducting hearings on a re-

[35] Kile: *The Farm Bureau Through Three Decades*, p. 259.

quest from Governor Edward Everett for an antislavery resolution. According to the account of Harriet Martineau, the not impartial English critic:

> The chairman and another of the five were evidently predetermined. They spared no pains in showing it, twisting the meaning of expressions employed by the pleaders, noting down any disjointed phrase that could be made to tell against those who used it, conveying sarcasms in their questions and insult in their remarks.
>
> . . . .
>
> The abolitionists held a consultation whether they should complain to the Legislature of the treatment their statements had received, and of the impediments thrown in the way of their self-justification. They decided to let the matter rest, trusting that there were witnesses enough of their case to enlighten the public mind on their position. A member of the Legislature declared in his place what he had seen of the treatment of the appellants by the chairman, and proposed that the committee should be censured. As the aggrieved persons made no formal complaint, however, the matter was dropped. But the faith of the abolitionists was justified. The people were enlightened as to their position; and in the next election they returned a set of representatives, one of whose earliest acts was to pass a series of anti-slavery resolutions by a majority of 378 to 16.[36]

Almost regardless of what happens during or after a session, the fact of a public hearing itself may perform the function of easing group conflicts and of relieving disturbances in and among interest groups. Appearance before a legislative committee is a form of activity that may have significant compensatory value. Within an interest group an insistent faction may be mollified by a spokesman's appearance before a committee even if no very concrete results are produced. The public hearing, as we have observed before, fits in with the democratic "rules of the game"; it conforms to the procedural expectations of the community. For the rank-and-file members, especially those whose involvement in the group's claims is limited or whose overlapping interests include an attachment to "democratic" methods, the public hearing may facilitate acceptance of almost any legislative product because it has been arrived at "in the right way," because "everyone" had a chance to be heard.

[36] Quoted in Luce: *Legislative Procedure*, pp. 147–8, from Harriet Martineau: *Retrospect of Western Travel* (1838).

Direct proof of the importance of the quasi-ritual function of the public hearing is not available, but evidence can be adduced concerning it. Writing on the basis of his many years as a legislator in Massachusetts and as a member of Congress, Robert Luce stated: "In my own opinion not the least, and perhaps the greatest, of the advantages of public committee hearings is their service as a safety-valve." [37] The casual attitude of many legislators and the spotty attendance by committee members at many such hearings further suggests the importance of the cathartic function. Something more than the legal requirements were indicated by a State legislator when, in response to a complaint that a hearing could not be held for want of a quorum, he replied: "You don't have to have a quorum; this is only a hearing." [38]

Statements by interest groups themselves support, at least by implication, the notion of the safety-valve function. An example is a revealing report on the tactics of the Association of American Railroads, written in 1934 to the president of a major railroad by its general counsel. After outlining a plan for railroad executives to deal directly with individual Representatives and Senators, the counsel reported the views of the association's principal staff officer as follows:

> Hearings before the Committees are largely matters of scenery to satisfy the public and . . . the effective work cannot be accomplished in the appearances of members of his staff before Committees. In his judgment the effective work in opposition to bills harmful to railroads can only be done through personal interviews with Congressmen conducted by men personally acquainted with the Congressmen they interview and for whom the interviewed Congressmen would have a feeling of respect and confidence.[39]

Although this comment partly reflects the position of a defensive group interested in preventing action, it is probably not atypical.

The importance of the ritualistic use of the hearings for the release of tension does not mean, of course, that a committeeman never makes his decision on the basis of such testimony. The public hearing is not without significance as a means of informing legislators, but this is probably not its primary function. For the group which enjoys satisfactory access to members of a legislative body, a hearing

[37] Luce: *Legislative Procedure,* p. 146.
[38] Winslow: *State Legislative Committees,* p. 85.
[39] U.S. Senate, Committee on Interstate Commerce: *Senate Report No. 26,* 77th Cong., 1st Sess. (1941), part 2, p. 63.

is not the best place to attempt persuasion. A representative of the Association of Life Insurance Presidents expressed this point in a letter to his superior in which he said: "It is much easier to handle one man or two men alone than it is to argue with a whole committee and it is impossible to argue with the whole house." [40]

The Use of Conference Committees

The device of the conference committee in the Congress is an important one, and, from the group viewpoint, its uses are closely related to those of the standing committee. These joint bodies, appointed to iron out differences on a given measure after it has been passed by both chambers, are a reflection of the diffusion of leadership in the Congress. In those State legislatures where a highly integrated party leadership exists, the conference committee is little used except in connection with minor legislation, since the party leaders agree among themselves on the provisions of major bills. [41] In the Congress only a small proportion of all acts pass through the conference device, but this number is likely to include many of the most important measures. The connection between the conference committee and the standing committees is the practice in both chambers of appointing as members of the conference committee the chairman and the ranking majority and minority members of the standing committees that have handled the bill.

The group use of conference committees is a function of their power and prerogatives as well as of their ties to the standing committees. While the managers technically are supposed to deal only with the differences committed to them and in some instances are under fairly explicit instructions, they often go beyond these matters to delete or alter portions of the bill or even to insert new provisions. One reason why they are able to do this is that their central function is to arrive at an acceptable compromise, which necessarily may require the trading of points on sections not formally in dispute. Equally important in the discretion of managers is the fact that the reports of such committees are highly privileged; they may be brought up for a vote in either house at almost any time.

[40] U.S. Temporary National Economic Committee: *Hearings*, part 10, p. 4401.
[41] Cf. Chamberlain: *Legislative Processes*, p. 252; Ada C. McCown: *The Congressional Conference Committee* (New York: Columbia University Press, 1927), p. 20.

By practice, moreover, they cannot be amended from the floor, but must be accepted or rejected in their entirety. Given the rush of business under which such reports may be received, the fact that few members of the legislature may know the nature of the changes made, and the difficult choice between accepting objectionable changes and getting no bill enacted, the tendency is to accept the conference report.

Despite rules to the contrary, the conference managers have a good deal of discretion. The greater the differences between the measures passed by the two houses, the greater that discretion. Not infrequently, in fact, the dominant members of a standing committee and the interests having access to them design their strategy with an eye to the opportunities for last-minute changes provided by the conference report. These opportunities are likely to be available principally to a group that wants to emend a bill, but they are not confined to that use. For example, the bills dealing with standards for wages and hours that passed the House and the Senate, respectively, in 1938 were so different that the Fair Labor Standards Act that emerged from the conference was, as Administration strategists had planned, markedly different from either of them.[42]

The attempts of groups to influence a conference committee are likely to show in full measure the many elements that go to make up effective access. The committee is rarely accessible to groups in any formal way: it was a notable exception when in 1941 the legislative agent of the Farm Bureau was permitted to appear before the conference committee that handled a bill to extend the life of the Commodity Credit Corporation.[43] The occasional exception serves to emphasize the point that the only groups that have a voice in the conference are those that have established their access to its members long before. Because of the comparative secrecy of the proceedings, however, and the usual mandate to arrive at a compromise, the clique patterns within the legislature and the awareness of the legislative role may permit effective access by a variety of interests, organized and unorganized.

[42] Burns: *Congress on Trial*, pp. 80–1. Cf. McCown: *The Congressional Conference Committee*, p. 16.
[43] He was arguing for the extension of parity payments to non-basic crops. Cf. Kile: *The Farm Bureau Through Three Decades*, pp. 280–1.

Committee Investigations

From the standpoint of a study of group technique the most dramatic and frequently the most important work of committees is public investigation. Most committee work, of course, includes a certain amount of inquiry; but we refer here to the full-dress investigation, complete with public hearings. When this is conducted by a standing committee or one of its subcommittees, it is an extension of the practice of public hearings that we have already discussed, although the standing committee, when investigating, need not have a bill before it. The prototype of the investigating committee, however, is the special or select committee of either house or the joint committee set up to examine an issue or a broad area of the society. (The commission made up of distinguished laymen, officials of the executive branch, or a combination of these and members of Congress performs functions closely akin to those of the special investigating committee but will not be considered separately. The Temporary National Economic Committee created in 1938 and made up of members of Congress and executive branch officials is one example. Various Federal Trade Commission investigations authorized by the Congress, such as the F.T.C. probe of the public utilities between 1928 and 1934, are other examples. Significantly, the F.T.C. investigation of the utilities was a substitute for one by a special Senate committee.)

The distinctive function of the investigating committee, like that of the public hearings on proposed legislation, is to create or extend the public for a particular interpretation of the situation or area being examined. Incidentally, it may serve to transmit information to the committee and members of Congress generally, particularly concerning the strength behind an insistent group claim. Sometimes this may be its primary use, as it was of the Joint Committee on the Organization of Congress in 1945 and 1946. A similar use may also be made of the junket type of investigation, which is principally informative if it is anything but recreational. The investigating committee also may primarily or partially have the function of relieving disturbances stemming from a disaster or other event of similar proportions, in which case the inquiry may result in legislation or may merely constitute a response to a fairly general expectation that the Congress should "do something." Most commonly, however, the investigating committee is used for what one student calls "social leverage." [44] As Robert K. Lamb, experienced investigator for a number of such committees, put it: "In my estimation a congressional investigating committee has one of the greatest responsibilities in American Government today. It is an educational institution both for Congress and the American people second to none." [45]

Inevitably the investigating committee is a powerful vehicle for group attack and defense, although the group need not necessarily be organized. Group interests regularly initiate, guide, and exploit such inquiries, even though they may not be recognized as doing so. Whether one attempts to draw a distinction on the basis of one's own interest-group affiliations between "progressive" and "destructive" inquiries, or lumps all together as part of the same type of process, the context of rival interests is inescapable. The attempted distinction is itself a reflection of the group process. Lamb's characterization of the "destructive" inquiry is in objective terms equally applicable to his "progressive" type, although the group interests involved are not the same. The following covers virtually all investigations, provided we bear in mind the fact that "pressure" is not the only manifestation of the relationships between legislator and group:

> The pressures exerted by various groups for the creation of such . . . special committees . . . find a ready response among a limited number of members of Congress. These pressures do not diminish once such committees are created. On the contrary there then begins an intensive drive to support and direct the campaign of such a special committee, and one who is experienced in observing these processes can often forecast by the stories in certain papers what these Congressional committees will shortly undertake." [46]

The essential features of congressional investigations are two: first, these inquiries are an attempt to deal with or to exploit disturbances of a crisis or semicrisis character; second, they attempt to do this by developing for certain groups and group practices a public

---

[44] M. Nelson McGeary: *The Developments of Congressional Investigative Power* (New York: Columbia University Press, 1940), p. 31. The other standard references on this subject are: Ernest J. Eberling: *Congressional Investigations* (New York: Columbia University Press, 1928) and Marshall E. Dimock: *Congressional Investigating Committees* (Baltimore: The Johns Hopkins Press, 1929). Cf. Hurst: *The Growth of American Law*, pp. 79–81.
[45] U.S. Joint Committee on the Organization of Congress: *Hearings*, 79th Cong., 1st Sess. (1945), part 4, p. 1018.
[46] Ibid., p. 1017.

in which the preponderant elements will disapprove of these groups and practices for apparently violating general expectations and "rules of the game." Their aim is to demonstrate or effectively to allege that there is a connection between the disturbances and the groups and practices attacked. The process is essentially the same whether the disturbance is fabricated or fortuitous, whether the target is a scapegoat for or a cause of the disturbance. As Medill McCormick declared to the Senate in support of a resolution designed to investigate railway labor unions during the strikes of 1920: "What is needed . . . is some body of men which may bring the facts to public attention. There is no other possible means of mobilizing that public opinion which may induce the men to return to work." [47] The purpose was not to make a disinterested inquiry, but to convict.

Congressional investigations of administrative agencies are not inconsistent with the pattern. During the nineteenth century, in fact, most congressional investigations were directed toward units of the executive branch.[48] With rare exceptions they exploit or adjust a disturbance by attacking the agency and directly or indirectly certain of the interests it reflects. A case in point is the investigation of the Forest Service, mentioned earlier in the chapter, by a subcommittee of the House Committee on Public Lands. Though the effort was unskillful, it was aimed at exploiting throughout the public-land States various resentments against the Forest Service so as to convict it of favoritism, discrimination, and incompetence.[49] Such inquiries are often a more or less direct attack upon the president and some of the factions and groups supporting him. Such investigations often proliferate during times of emergency, reflecting the disturbances caused both by the emergency itself and by the shifting of relationships and powers in consequence of executive action.

An elaborate example of the investigation of administrative agencies is the work of the House Select Committee to Investigate the Federal Communications Commission (Cox Committee) of 1943 and 1944. As noted earlier, the immediate disturbance was personal (the delivery of evidence against Cox to the Department of Justice), so that the committee had to engage in a "fishing expedition" to locate publishable charges. These eventually included everything from incompetence and waste of the public funds to obstruction of the

[47] Quoted in McGeary: *The Developments of Congressional Investigative Power*, p. 30.

[48] George B. Galloway: "The Investigative Function of Congress," *American Political Science Review*, Vol. 21, no. 1 (February, 1927), pp. 47–70.

[49] See above, note 10.

war effort and illegal censorship of radio communications.[50] The hearings, when they were started, were designed to reach the headlines with these charges, as a casual reading of the record will reveal. The strategy was also indicated by a memorandum describing effective hearing procedure distributed to the members of the Committee by its general counsel. This document read in part:

> Decide what you want the newspapers to hit hardest and then shape each hearing so that the main point becomes the vortex of the testimony. Once that vortex is reached, adjourn. . . .
>
> Do not permit distractions to occur, such as extraneous fusses with would-be witnesses, which might provide news that would bury the testimony which you want featured.
>
> Do not space hearings more than twenty-four or forty-eight hours apart when on a controversial subject. This gives the opposition too much opportunity to make all kinds of countercharges and replies by issuing statements to the newspapers.
>
> Don't ever be afraid to recess a hearing, even for five minutes, so that you keep the proceedings completely in control so far as creating news is concerned.[51]

Although this is an unusually candid statement, the tactics described are not unrepresentative of other investigating committees.[52] In this case the technique was employed in such clumsy fashion that the investigation backfired, and the committee rather than the F.C.C. was discredited, but the objective was apparent nonetheless.

Perhaps the simplest and most direct examples of investigating committees are the so-called lobby investigations. Although these might appear to be rather generalized inquiries, they are in fact as specific as investigations of any other type. On four occasions during this century full-dress lobby investigations have been undertaken in the Congress, although numerous other committees have dealt with the subject as well. On each of these four occasions the committees have been authorized to look extensively into group activity in connection with legislation, but both the origins and the targets have been more circumscribed. In 1913, investigations were conducted by com-

[50] U.S. House of Representatives, Select Committee to Investigate the Federal Communications Commission: *Hearings*, 78th Cong., 1st and 2d Sess. (1943, 1944).

[51] Quoted in Leigh: "Politicians vs. Bureaucrats," p. 102.

[52] Cf. the testimony of Robert K. Lamb before the Joint Committee on the Organization of Congress, cited above, note 45.

mittees in each house as a result of group activity in connection with the Underwood Tariff Act of that year. Each of these inquiries focused on groups working for increases in tariff rates, and the principal target of both was the National Association of Manufacturers.[53] The tariff again was the occasion, this time the Smoot-Hawley revision of 1930, for a Senate inquiry between 1930 and 1932. Conducted by a subcommittee headed by Senator Caraway of Arkansas, it jumped off from charges of improper arrangements between the Connecticut Manufacturers Association and Senator Hiram Bingham and in its meanderings covered a variety of groups pushing for tariff increases.[54]

The third spate of lobby investigations, one by each house of the Congress, began in 1935 as part of the struggle over passage of the Public Utility Holding Company Act. These two investigations reflected somewhat opposing interests, although the occasion for the inquiries was the same. One week after the House defeated the so-called "death sentence" clause of the holding company bill, it passed a resolution authorizing the Rules Committee to investigate activities for and against the measure. The Rules Committee, dominated by elements hostile to the President, spent most of its time exploring the activities of Administration spokesmen, although it later gave passing, though not particularly unfriendly, attention to the utilities' efforts.[55] Three days after the House resolution the Senate created a special committee headed by Hugo L. Black. It was authorized to look into all lobbying activities on the measure, but at the outset it confined itself almost exclusively to the holding companies and related groups.[56] Its revelations on this score were in no small measure responsible for the passage of the Public Utility Holding Company Act with its "death sentence" provision.

The last in the series of lobby investigations was an inquiry by a select committee of the House authorized late in 1949. This body

[53] U.S. Senate, Committee on the Judiciary: *Hearings on Maintenance of a Lobby to Influence Legislation*, 63d Cong., 1st Sess. (1913); U.S. House of Representatives, Select Committee on Lobby Investigation: *Hearings*, 63d Cong., 1st Sess. (1913).

[54] U.S. Senate, Subcommittee of the Committee on the Judiciary: *Lobby Investigation Hearings*, 71st Cong., 1st, 2d, and 3d Sess., 72d Cong., 1st Sess. (1929–31).

[55] U.S. House of Representatives, Committee on Rules: *Hearings on Investigation of Lobbying on Utility Holding Company Bills*, 74th Cong., 1st Sess. (1935).

[56] U.S. Senate, Special Committee to Investigate Lobbying Activities: *Hearings*, 74th Cong., 1st and 2d Sess., 75th Cong., 3d Sess. (1935–38).

nominally was to examine the need for revision of the Federal Regulation of Lobbying Act of 1946, but the impetus for the investigation stemmed from efforts to defeat public housing legislation, and real estate and private housing groups were among its initial targets. Significant of the divergent claims upon such an inquiry is the fact that the authorizing resolution passed the House only after the Rules Committee had inserted a provision directing the select committee to include an examination of the lobbying activities of executive agencies.[57]

The intent and, in some cases, the effect of each of these inquiries was to demonstrate that particular groups or particular categories of groups had attempted to influence legislation by methods that appeared to violate the "rules of the game." Their use as weapons is evident from the fact that the committees made no effort to deal with all groups associated with a given disturbance, although the amendment to the resolution authorizing the 1949 House investigation reflects *competing* interpretations of such a disturbance. Announced in general terms, these investigations were distinguished by special preoccupations. Intended by their sponsors not as detached inquiries but as demonstrations, they could not be expected to deal even with a representative cross-section, but only with particular interest groups.

This view of lobby investigations as weapons rules out the notion that their meaning and importance are to be found only in the legislation that results from their efforts.[58] A lobby investigation and most other investigating committees are primarily means of altering the power position of interest groups; by their demonstrations they tend, when successful, to redistribute propaganda advantages, to restrict certain kinds of group practices, and to alter "memberships." The La Follette committee, for example, investigating from 1936 through 1938 various kinds of violations of the "rights of labor," undoubtedly did much to increase the "membership" and improve the propaganda position of labor unions, with equivalent adverse effects upon opposing groups.[59] These things investigating committees

---

[57] U.S. House of Representatives, Select Committee to Investigate Lobbying Activities: *Hearings,* 81st Cong., 2d Sess. (1950). The *New York Herald Tribune,* May 19, 1949.

[58] Cf. Edgar Lane: "Lessons from Past Congressional Investigations of Lobbying," *Public Opinion Quarterly,* Vol. 14, no. 1 (Spring, 1950), pp. 14–32, a good review despite the author's view that the major "lesson" is that such efforts should contribute to an "improved system of regulation."

[59] U.S. Senate, Subcommittee of the Committee on Education and Labor: *Hearings,* 74th Cong., 2d Sess., 75th Cong., 1st, 2d, 3d Sess. (1936–38).

can accomplish whether or not they issue a formal report or become the source of legislation. Some of these ends, in fact, may be accomplished, at least in part, merely by the threat of a congressional investigation.

Although investigating committees are weapons in the group struggle, they are not necessarily instituted as a result of "pressure" from particular groups nor do the beneficiaries include only certain organized interest groups. While their sponsors are likely to "belong" to the benefited groups or to party factions that stand to gain advantage from the disclosures, more than this is usually involved. Hyperactivity on the part of interest groups in the legislature often causes a disturbance to the personal relations within that body and to the effectiveness with which its members are able to play their expected roles. The investigation or threatened investigation may be a means of restoring a threatened pattern within the law-making body.

It is worth remembering, moreover, that the strategy of most legislative investigations is to denounce groups and practices in the name of widespread but largely unorganized interests reflected in expectations concerning official behavior and in the "rules of the game." With varying effectiveness the public investigation serves to reinforce these expectations and to reassert the values on which they rest. This may be a far more important function than producing formal legislation and systems of regulation.

The public hearing, whether before a standing committee or a special committee, is one of the points at which the cohesion of a group makes a difference in its political position. It is less important that a group include in its membership all eligible persons than that it include all the active eligibles and that they adhere to one view. These hearings often are stacked in favor of one side of an issue and hostile committee members may make it difficult for a witness to get his views across, but neither of these handicaps is as severe as the expressed hostility of a minority within the group for which a witness is allegedly speaking. We have already noted the difficulties that this kind of internal dissension has produced for the American Medical Association, although these have not yet been crippling. Even the monumental Farm Bureau has been hampered from time to time by opposition within the ranks for which it claims to speak. In 1937, when hearings first were held on what subsequently became the Agricultural Adjustment Act of 1938, the draft—known as the Farm Bureau bill—was not supported by the Grange, the Farmers Union, and other agricultural groups. For this reason the chairmen of the Senate and House agriculture committees both decided against reporting out a bill in that session. As the latter stated it: "In view of the differences of opinion among farm interests as to the provisions which new farm legislation should contain, the committee feels that further study should be given before general farm legislation is reported." [60] When the Farm Bureau and the Grange in 1942 were resisting the imposition of price ceilings on farm products without general controls on industrial and other wages, the open opposition of the Farmers Union to this resistance was awkward. O. M. Kile, the not entirely disinterested historian of the Farm Bureau, described the circumstance in the following terms:

> The membership of the Farmers Union was relatively small and its influence slight as compared with the Bureau and the Grange, but it was most confusing to members of Congress and the press, and very embarrassing to the large farm groups, to have this apparent conflict of views in farm organization circles.[61]

Disunity in a public hearing is usually conspicuous.

Committee Appointments and the Reference of Bills

Because of the importance of various types of committees in a legislature like the Congress, it is inevitable that the organized interest groups will be deeply concerned with the membership and jurisdiction of committees. A group's concern will extend to all the members, but particularly to the chairman. His influence upon legislation is likely to be crucial, since he can block a bill almost at will, arrange the agenda of the committee, stack the hearings by giving disproportionate time to one side, and affect the chances of the bill by the skill with which he handles it on the floor of the chamber or as one of the two principal managers in a conference committee. The chairman's dominance in most committees means, further, that his aid is necessary if public hearings are to be used to attack or restrain administrative agencies that are subject to the committee's scrutiny.

[60] Quoted in Kile: *The Farm Bureau Through Three Decades*, p. 239.
[61] Kile: *The Farm Bureau Through Three Decades*, p. 293. Copyright 1948 by and used with the permission of Orville M. Kile.

If a group has adequate access to the party leaders, it may be able to influence the selection of members to fill committee vacancies, especially if the group has established a sort of prescriptive right to veto appointments, such as the Farm Bureau ordinarily has on appointments to the congressional committees on agriculture. Since congressional chairmanships with rare exceptions are acquired on the basis of seniority, however, a group can scarcely influence the choosing of a committee chairman except by having a hand in all appointments to a committee or by threatening or accomplishing the defeat of an objectionable chairman at the polls. In the States, where the seniority rule is not adhered to as rigidly as in Congress, access to the legislative leadership may be highly effective in controlling committee chairmanships.[62] Because of the importance of the personnel of standing committees in the Congress, however, interest groups are not inactive in attempting to influence the selection of chairmen. For example, the Association of Railway Executives, a predecessor of the Association of American Railroads, was highly active in 1933 in trying to secure appointments to the Rivers and Harbors Committee of the House for legislators pledged to oppose inland waterway development in competition with the railroads. The same group made every effort to prevent Burton K. Wheeler's succession to the chairmanship of the Senate Committee on Interstate Commerce, without success.[63]

It should not be forgotten that members of Congress, as aspiring legislators and as "members" of interest groups, are themselves deeply concerned with their committee assignments. Depending on their position in the legislative group, legislators may be able themselves to obtain appointments to the committees in which groups to which they "belong" are interested. The combination of group backing, access to the legislative leadership, and position in the structure of the legislative group may be highly effective in controlling assignments to committees.

Few groups, as the examples in the preceding paragraphs suggest, can afford to be concerned with only one committee in each house. Even where a group's interests fall completely within the jurisdiction of a single subject-matter committee, which is rare, it normally is af-

---

[62] Cf. Chamberlain: *Legislative Processes*, pp. 85–8. For some examples of group influence in designating chairmen and members of committees in the States, see U.S. Temporary National Economic Committee: *Hearings*, part 10, pp. 4415, 4774.

[63] U.S. Senate, Committee on Interstate Commerce: *Senate Report No. 26*, 77th Cong., 1st Sess. (1941), part 2, pp. 62–3.

fected by at least one other committee and in the House of Representatives by two others. It is unusual for a group to be able to ignore the appropriations committees, whether it is seeking expenditures or attempting to prevent them. Most of the work of these units is done in subcommittees, and the selection of these is as significant as the appointments to subject-matter committees. In the House of Representatives the situation is further complicated by the position occupied by the Rules Committee. Because of its almost unrestricted power to block or facilitate legislation, it is an object of concern to both defensive and offensive groups. The kind of rule under which a bill is sent to the floor, moreover, setting the terms of debate and the admissibility of amendments, can be of critical importance. Since, in addition, the price of reporting a bill from the Rules Committee may involve the insertion of amendments other than those recommended by the subject-matter committee, the position of the Committee on Rules is pivotal.

Whether an interest group has achieved effective influence over a committee or not, the decision to refer a bill to one committee or another is a critical one. The reference of bills in the Congress is done by the parliamentarian in each chamber acting, at least formally, under the authority and supervision of the presiding officer. Decisions on reference are subject to appeal to a vote of the chamber. The discretionary element in these decisions stems from the inevitable vagueness with which committee jurisdictions are defined. Many bills, particularly the extensive and controversial ones, might be referred to any one of at least two standing committees. If one of these is accessible to one set of interest groups and the other to a different set, the significance of a choice between them is considerable. Because the decision on reference is subjct to appeal, the presiding officer's discretion is not complete, but it is important. Access to him, either through his own group "memberships" or through the internal structure of the legislature, is an advantage that may seriously affect the disposition of an interest group's claims.

The legislative history of the Employment Act of 1946 provides excellent examples of the importance of committee reference. In the Senate the bill was referred "not by accident" to the Committee on Banking and Currency, chaired by Senator Robert F. Wagner, who could be fairly certain that a majority of the members would follow his support of the proposal. Before this body the bill received sympathetic and friendly treatment. In the House, however, the sponsors of the measure through oversight allowed it to go to the Committee on Expenditures in the Executive Departments. Because this committee was heavily weighted against the proposals contained in the bill, its course through the House was stormy. Had the measure been sent to either of two other House committees, "the story of the Full Employment Bill might have been markedly different." [64]

The Avalanche of Mail

One of the most widely accepted popular notions of interest-group technique in dealing with the legislature is that spectacular results can be achieved by deluging members of Congress with letters, postcards, petitions, and telegrams. Groups frequently urge members to participate in such activity, supplying the names of Representatives and Senators and giving sample wordings for letters and wires. The press frequently reports such avalanches of paper in stories on a highly controversial legislative measure with the implication that the sheer bulk of these communications has a significant bearing on the legislator's decision.

Filling up the legislator's mailbag is essentially a crude device, a shotgun technique which may only wound where a rifle would kill. It does not follow that Congressmen pay no attention to their mail. Most of them watch it closely. They are, as we have said before, in search of technical and particularly of political information. Their mail gives them some clues of this sort. On an issue on which a legislator has no preference of his own and does not know the wishes of key elements within his constituency, the volume and tone of his mail may be decisive. There may even be times when the legislator counts the number of "pros" and "cons" and votes with the majority. But when he does either of these things, one fact is clear: the usual channels of access to him are empty or silent; the normal structure of his relationships within and outside the legislature gives him little or no guidance.

Even when mail, telegrams, and petitions do influence the vote of a member of Congress on a highly controversial measure, it is likely that they are merely augmenting or supplementing other influences whose access to him is established and whose relative political strength he knows. In other words, he applies a discount factor to the avalanche. A study of the votes in 1939 of 96 members of the House of Representatives on repeal of the arms embargo found a low correlation between these votes and congressional mail. It concluded

[64] Bailey: *Congress Makes a Law*, p. 151. Copyright 1950 by and used with the permission of Columbia University Press. See also pp. 100 ff., 151 ff.

that over half the members of Congress voted against the preferences expressed through the mailbags.[65] The discount rate on congressional mail is probably the product of two factors: first, the ease with which "inspired" communications, including petitions, can be identified permits the legislator to ignore statements from persons whose views are not individualized and, therefore, probably not strongly held; second, his experience leads him to the conclusion that the letter-writing, telegram-sending public is not representative of the electorate.

The clues to "inspired" mail and telegrams are many. Identically worded messages are the easiest to detect. They may take the form of resolutions adopted by a series of constituent groups or units allied to an interest group. Or they may be form messages sent by individuals but obviously coming from a single source. (The group gets volume in this way, as the slightly involved are unwilling to sit down to write a message in their own words and the timid may not know how to address a legislator, but in so doing it sacrifices the appearance of genuineness.) Or the messages, individualized or standardized, may come in batches from different towns on successive days, indicating the movements of some guiding spirit. Such communications are clearly futile if they don't even come from the legislator's constituency. Bailey gives an example of an especially transparent effort to support the Employment Act of 1946. The unfriendly chairman of the House Committee on Expenditures in the Executive Departments, Carter Manasco of Alabama, received hundreds of identically worded postcards on which the signers said they would vote against him if his committee did not report out a strong bill. All the cards, however, were postmarked Brooklyn, New York![66] The "inspired" category also includes most petitions, since almost any politician knows that it is easy to get people to sign such documents and equally easy for them to forget that they have done so.

The available objective data appear to justify a legislator's belief that the letter writers are a special breed.[67] Most significantly, the usual letter writer is likely to write in opposition to a measure

[65] Lewis E. Gleeck: "96 Congressmen Make Up Their Minds," *Public Opinion Quarterly*, Vol. 4, no. 1 (Spring, 1940), pp. 3-24.

[66] Bailey: *Congress Makes a Law*, pp. 95-6.

[67] Cf. Gleeck: "96 Congressmen Make Up Their Minds," pp. 3-24; also Rowena Wyant and Herta Herzog: "Voting Via the Senate Mailbag," *Public Opinion Quarterly*, Vol. 5, nos. 3 and 4 (Fall and Winter, 1941), pp. 359-82, 590-624. The latter of these is an analysis of 30,000 letters received by 14 Senators on the Selective Service Act of 1940.

rather than in support of it. Moreover, such communicants seem to have a chronic addiction to this activity, for repeated opinion surveys indicate that little more than 10 per cent of the electorate has ever written a member of Congress on any subject whatsoever. Finally, the legislator who sees little or no correlation between the structure of influence apparently represented in his mail and the structure he believes politically important in his constituency, is likely to pay little attention to the claims of the former. As Representative, later Senator, Kefauver of Tennessee put it, the letters that really count "are those from people who count." [68]

Skillful interest groups, therefore, make limited use of letters, telegrams, and petitions. Thus the National Association of Retail Druggists early concluded that a communication from one or two personal or political friends is "of far greater value than a hundred letters or telegrams from persons unknown to the legislator." [69] The avalanches of mail may be fairly effective as internal propaganda, they may suggest to the members of a group that its staff is "on its toes," and they may even indicate to the legislator that a group has at least sufficient cohesion to put on a letter-writing campaign. But as means of influencing a legislator's vote they have been greatly exaggerated.

Conclusion

The techniques utilized by interest groups and their "members" in the legislature to enhance and exploit the degree of access that a group has been able to achieve are enormously complicated and varied. The diversity of relationships that culminate in the successful assertion of group claims upon and through the legislature is impressive, including not only those within groups, but also arrangements between groups and relationships with legislators, committees, and committee staffs as well as with elements in the executive branch. Each completed legislative act represents a unique amalgam of these elements.

The complicated procedure of a body like the Congress and the strength of established relationships in the society as a whole tend to give an advantage to the group that is on the defensive in the legis-

---

[68] Kefauver and Levin: *A Twentieth-Century Congress*, p. 182. Chapter 13 of this little book gives a number of examples of messages from constituents and their effect.

[69] U.S. Temporary National Economic Committee: *Trade Association Survey*, p. 337.

lative struggle. This superiority, however, may be augmented or diminished as fortuitous circumstances or skillful manipulation broaden or narrow the public on a given legislative proposal and alter its composition. The organized group may thus be able to ensure the inclusion of its members in any public to which its claims are related and to participate in legislative decisions to the extent of its political strength.

A prime reason for the complexity of the legislative process in the Congress and various of the State legislatures is the absence of an integrated and continuing leadership. The diffusion of power within the legislature, the multiple lines of access, and the diverse means of leverage make an inherently complex process still more complicated. Under such circumstances, logrolling and alliances between groups—inevitable elements in a process that relies upon the device of majority rule to settle differences—become a means of compensating for the diffusion of power. Similarly the importance of the committee system in such a legislative body furnishes a very powerful channel for interest-group activities. The standing committees and investigating committees of both houses and the committees of conference, all of which have developed in our bifocal legislature, are points of power that must be cultivated with skill and watched with persistence both to advance and to protect the claims of a political interest group. Such techniques and those involved in achieving access to points of decision in and outside the legislature are more significant than such conspicuous but crude devices as letter and telegraph campaigns and petitions.

A theme running throughout this presentation of the legislative process and the parts that interest groups play in it is the assumption that even a temporarily viable legislative decision usually must involve the adjustment and compromise of interests. Even where virtual unanimity prevails in the legislature, the process of reconciling conflicting interests must have taken place—though perhaps at an earlier stage wholly or partly outside the legislature and the formal institutions of government. When this happens, the legislature merely registers the decision, as the Congress did in its declaration of war after Pearl Harbor. But the controversial legislative projects—for this is what makes them "controversial"—cannot be handled in this way; they involve more than the refinement of details, and consequently the process of compromise is nearer the surface in the legislature and is more apparent.

Legislative compromise is not an end in itself, however. It is rather a means of so adjusting conflicting claims upon the government that the underlying expectations about the governing process, some of them written in constitutions and statutes and more of them unwritten, will not be sharply and irretrievably violated. These expectations concerning the "rules of the game" themselves are interests, largely unorganized but overlapping more or less insistently those that appear in more obvious form. These expectations must constitute a fairly coherent part of any viable legislative decision. The coherence may not always be close, and the particular composite may not be stable, but the approximations must be fairly close on the average if the system is to survive.

The attempts to harmonize group demands and widely held expectations may produce a pattern of policy superficially lacking in rationality. They may produce a fiscal or other economic policy that is intrinsically self-contradictory, being, for example, partly inflationary in a time of inflation, or partly deflationary in a time of depression. The early New Deal agricultural policies, restricting production and at the same time easing the terms of agricultural credit and developing techniques for raising more produce per acre, involved such contradictions. Whatever violence they did to the economist's abstracted formulas, however, they had a more inclusive rationality. For a sizable and organized segment of the population they were a means of reaching a closer conformity between governmental policies and deep-seated expectations about the political process.

The imperative of compromise among groups, between group demands and the "rules of the game," explains various aspects of the legislature process not explicitly treated in this chapter. One of these is the ambiguity of many legislative formulas. The variety of meanings that can be read into the verbal formulations and other behavior of governmental officials is often derided by those who project their own interest affiliations upon the whole polity. But ambiguity and verbal compromise may be the very heart of a successful political formula, especially where the necessity for compromise is recognized but is difficult to achieve in explicit terms. Ambiguity may postpone or obviate the necessity for a showdown and as such has an important political function.[70]

Legislative debates also are frequently ridiculed as meaningless. Admittedly they have some part in the process of parliamentary maneuver, as in the case of the filibuster, but is that their only function? Persuasion can scarcely be one, since it is rare that any speech in

---

[70] See the examples of ambiguous verbal compromises in the conference committee on the Employment Act of 1946 in Bailey: *Congress Makes a Law,* p. 223–5.

Congress changes a vote on a basic issue, although one may win supporters on a minor point. The chief function of debates is rather as a part of the process of adjustment. Like the ritual of public hearings and the ambiguities in legislative compromises, formal debates facilitate acceptance of the final decision, not necessarily by the immediate participants but by those on the periphery. A Supreme Court opinion setting forth its reasons for concluding that a convicted murderer has had a fair trial does the condemned man no good, but it calms those who otherwise might rise in his defense.

It is not altogether out of place to think of a legislature like the Congress as a court from which petitioners seek indulgences and redress of grievances. As a seat of power it is one of many points to which appeals can lie from disturbances in the society at large or from acts of judicial courts and administrative agencies. Especially in a loosely integrated system like that in the United States, the legislative process offers an interest group alternative means of effectively asserting its claims. This process has long since out-classed that of the common-law courts as a means of declaring the law. In recent years it has been somewhat restricted through the growth of administrative discretion in the wake of the increased complexity and technicality of group relationships and adjustments. Any administrator knows, however, that the legislature still is an alternative line of approach to a policy decision, one of many means of appeal from his own determinations for groups with effective access to the law-making body. It is in consequence of the strength of the legislative channel that few administrative agencies are in fact separate from the legislature and that many such agencies are more closely tied to the legislature and its committees than to superiors in the executive branch. The nature of these relationships and the part that interest groups play in them are the concern of the following two chapters.

13

The Ordeal of the Executive

THE most characteristic feature of twentieth-century government in the United States, as in other modern nations, is the size and importance of what is usually known as the executive branch. When we think of the activities of government, those most likely to occur to us are the day-to-day functions of executive agencies: collecting taxes, protecting lives and property, running schools, constructing highways, promoting public health, setting railroad rates, supervising the relations between management and labor, providing protection against the financial hazards of unemployment and old age, operating parks and other recreational facilities, handling mail, building dams, protecting markets, and licensing radio stations, to mention only a few of those that deal with the internal concerns of the country.

Since the turn of the century the number of functions performed by government has increased at a tremendous rate. Looking at the Federal government alone, a rough index of this growth is provided by figures on government employment. In the first four decades of this century the population of the continental United States increased by roughly 75 per cent. During this same period the number of civilian employees of the executive branch of the Federal government increased by nearly 300 per cent.[1]

The rapid accretion of executive functions is more sharply suggested by a partial list of the fields in which Federal governmental activity was nonexistent, or very nearly so, prior to 1900. Such a list would include: social security and related services; the regulation of

---

[1] U.S. Bureau of the Census: *Historical Statistics of the United States, 1789–1945* (Washington, D.C.: Government Printing Office, 1949), pp. 25, 294.

trade practices; control of television, radio, telephone and telegraph; ownership and regulation of electric power facilities; the promotion and regulation of commercial air transport; the provision of credit to farmers; the control of farm production and the many aspects of agricultural marketing; public health activities; parcel post; regulation and protection of collective bargaining; housing and home mortgages; regulation of the wages and hours of labor; regulation of stock exchanges and the public sale of securities; insurance of bank deposits; and the production and use of atomic energy.

The importance of the executive branch, however, does not derive simply from its size or from the variety of its activities. It is of far greater significance that the operation of these activities necessitates choices among alternative lines of action, the exercise of discretion. Statutes may broadly guide, but they cannot precisely determine, all or even most of the day-to-day decisions of executive officials. The impact of these discretionary decisions may be very broad, as in the declaration of a national emergency and in the granting of an export loan of several million dollars, or it may be fairly narrow, as in the allowance of a particular deduction on an individual income tax return and in the tightening of specifications for materials to be used in highways built with Federal funds. Both the newer and the expanded older functions of government create the necessity for a large measure of administrative discretion, and the tendency is toward the widening of such powers rather than toward their restriction.

Reasons for the expansion of the discretionary powers of the executive branch are many, but they all stem from a single factor: technical complexity. "Government today is largely a matter of expert administration." [2] Even its comparatively routine activities require specialized knowledge and skill, often in very high degree. Because these functions are technical and because they take effect in a rapidly changing and highly interdependent society, their exercise requires more or less constant adjustment to changing circumstances and adaptation to unusual situations. In view of the tremendous volume of changes that must be made in the course of applying statutes, alterations cannot all be made through the slow-paced processes of a legislature. Even a legislative body possessed of the relevant technical knowledge could make only a fraction of these decisions. Within the frequently very broad limits of the authorizing statutes, therefore, officials of the executive branch formally make a very large proportion

[2] From *Public Administration and the Public Interest* by Herring, p. 23. Copyright 1936. Courtesy of McGraw-Hill Book Company, Inc.

of the significant policy choices in the fields that government touches.

The knowledge and technical skill required of officials of the executive branch also have a significant by-product. Because of their qualifications and as a result of rather continuous, detailed contact with the problems of a given activity, administrators have become a primary channel for initiating and refining policy determinations made in the legislature itself. The same factors that have fostered administrative discretion have also given executive officials an important part in developing the statutes under which they operate. The Congress of the United States today rarely enacts a piece of legislation without its first being referred to one or more units of the executive branch for comments and recommendations. Frequently such reference may occur even before the bill is introduced. In the States essentially the same trend is also observable.[3]

The propositions presented in the preceding paragraphs are becoming generally known if not enthusiastically welcomed. Not so widely appreciated is the fact that along with these changes has come an inevitable increase in the play of interests throughout the executive's activity in legislation and discretionary administration. The accretion of executive functions is in large measure due to what we described in Chapter 4 as the gravitation of interest groups toward government. With rare exceptions the assertion of interest-group claims upon and through the institutions of government results in an expansion of administrative activities. The influences that have produced a proliferation of interest groups, particularly associations, in this century have in consequence added to the functions and the discretionary authority of executive agencies. These interests need not be organized, and, as we argued in Chapter 11 in discussing the relations between legislators and groups, the interactions between groups and public officials do not consistently involve a one-way, "pressure" type of relationship. As Bentley has stated it: "Some of these group activities will be noted by the government almost before they have clearly formed themselves, and will be brought to success through the discretion of the government on its own initiative, acting of course in a representative capacity."[4] The interests exist, but they may be led and accommodated by their "members" in the government

---

[3] Cf. Riddick: *The United States Congress*, p. 420; Chamberlain: *Legislative Processes*, pp. 276 ff. See Elizabeth Scott and Belle Zeller: "State Agencies and Lawmaking," *Public Administration Review*, Vol. 2, no. 3 (Summer, 1942), pp. 205–20.

[4] Bentley: *The Process of Government*, p. 410. Copyright 1908 by and used with the permission of Arthur F. Bentley.

before they become the basis for continuing interaction. In any case a consequence usually is an enlargement of executive functions.

Administrative activity, both in influencing the passage of legislation and in the discretionary application of statutes, necessarily involves significant components of power. Interest groups tend to concentrate about any locus of power able to affect appreciably the objectives that the groups seek to achieve. They work through any point of decision to which they have access, and they thus inevitably seek to influence the administrative process. To approach an understanding of the political process, therefore, we must examine the relationships that define the executive branch and explore the behavior of interest groups, organized and potential, in connection with such relationships.

The Role of the Chief Executive

The presidency of the United States is at once the most important and the most complex position in the governmental mechanism. Embodying the national myths and pervaded with tradition, yet imperfectly defined by law and peculiarly reflective of the personality of the incumbent, the presidency defies precise characterization. It is more than the office described in the legal formalities, and it is less than the symbol created of myth and legend.[5]

The Constitution provides: "The executive power shall be vested in a President of the United States of America." It makes him the formal chief of state in dealings with other nations; it makes him a unique representative by giving him, along with the Vice-President, a nation-wide constituency; and by arming him with a veto power and by directing him to "give to the Congress information of the state of the Union, and recommend to their consideration such measures as he shall judge necessary and expedient" it has permitted him to become a significant source of legislative leadership. Above and beyond these powers, the exigencies of rapid change and of social complexity and the accretions of custom have surrounded the presidency with a series of widely held expectations that are fully as exacting as if they were obligations defined by law. The expectations have been summarized by Louis Brownlow in his discerning little book, *The President and the Presidency*, under four headings: first, the president is expected to be "the general manager of the en-

[5] Cf. Louis Brownlow: *The President and the Presidency* (Chicago: Public Administration Service, 1949), pp. 14–15 and *passim*.

tire machinery of government;" second, he must "so manage the governmental machinery that we have good times and not hard times, and that the diverse sections of the economy be kept in reasonable balance;" third, he must be "a faithful representative" of the nation, a symbol, not only in matters narrowly political and economic, but with respect to more inclusive values, aspirations, and "rules of the game," ranging from the faith affirmed in the Declaration of Independence to "the necessity of contributing to the Community Chest;" and, fourth, the president is expected to "keep us at peace" with other nations and, when that proves impossible, "lead us to victory." [6]

The common denominator of the powers and demands focused upon the president is that he must take the lead in effecting a continuous adjustment of the diverse interests within the nation, including not only the organized and limited interests but also the widely held interests and "rules of the game" that are only partly reflected in organized groups. He must do so, moreover, not only in the name of the "rules of the game" but to the end of their greater strength and glory. He can operate only within limits and under constitutional restraints, and he must so act as to enhance the vitality of those very restraints. His obligations are heavy, but their effective discharge depends as much upon persuasion as upon force and legal authority.

One aspect of the process of effecting group adjustments through the presidency was taken up in our discussion of the national political party in Chapter 9. Winning a major party nomination and a presidential election rests upon building and operating an organization of local and State cliques that represent or are supplemented by a variety of political interest groups. By reason of their part, tacit or overt, in his reaching the White House, these party cliques and interest groups will enjoy privileged access to the president. Other groups of which the incumbent president is a "member" will enjoy a similar advantage. A president no less than any other man has acquired a more or less unique set of attitudes in the course of his social experience, and the groups that reflect these interests will most easily gain his ear. He must be particularly careful, however, to retain the support of those elements that were influential in his election. If he aspires to another term in the office, this policy is elementary common sense. Even if he does not seek re-election or does not wish to be able to name his party's candidate for the succession, how-

* Brownlow: *The President and the Presidency*, pp. 62–72. Copyright 1949 by and used with the permission of Public Administration Service.

ever, he cannot approach the expectations imposed upon him unless he retains substantial factional and group support. Alternative lines of political action, notably through the Congress, are available to groups dissatisfied with their treatment by the chief executive. The more extensively they use these alternatives, the less effectively he is able to play his role.

The president's partisanship and partiality among groups must be kept within limits, however, despite the need to maintain cohesion among the elements that helped him to power. The process by which he is nominated and elected inevitably gives some groups better access to him than others can command, but as the dominant symbol of the nation, he cannot be completely identified with a segment of it. The president is chosen "in a partisan political fight," as Brownlow describes the process, but paradoxically "we acclaim him President of all the people and then instantly develop a distaste for his doing anything that even smacks of the partisan." [7] His behavior in the White House must appear to affirm the unity of the nation, whatever license he is permitted as a candidate. This expectation of impartiality is one of those determinants of group access that in discussing legislators in Chapter 11 we called the influence of office. The expectations surrounding the presidency are even more insistent and more effective in determining access. Both its prominence and its symbolic functions make the presidential office a more important molder of its incumbents than any other in the nation, possibly excepting only the Supreme Court. To enter upon the presidency from any other position in the society is to alter the whole fabric of one's accustomed relationships. The incumbent of the White House must satisfy the requirements of a living symbol.

The measure of detachment imposed on a president by his position as chief of state is not necessarily a handicap. The obligation to remain minimally accessible to all legitimate interests in the society can supply him with a measure of independence and a persuasive power that effectively supplements his formal authority. Such supplementary power is crucial, moreover, as both his formal powers and his party position are insufficient to assure his approximating the expectations imposed upon his office.

The "bundle of compromises" that make up the American Constitution is nowhere more sharply seen than in the powers of the president. He is vested with an undefined executive power, but the agencies of executive action exist only by act and suffrance of the Con-

[7] Brownlow: *The President and the Presidency*, p. 49. Copyright 1949 by and used with the permission of Public Administration Service.

gress; they can operate only with such funds as the legislature provides and under such limitations as the Congress may impose; and the Senate shares the president's power of appointment and his discretionary authority in diplomatic matters. The president's actions and those of his nominal subordinates in the executive departments are subject to legislative investigation at any time.

The magnificent ambiguities of the Constitution, without which it would not have been a viable plan, have left the president inadequately equipped with formal powers sufficient to discharge the functions expected of him. It is never clear as a matter of law or as a matter of fact whether he or a transient majority in the Congress is to exercise control over the units of the executive branch. The separation of powers and the system of checks and balances leave open a series of alternative approaches to the government; a number of key points of decision are established in parallel with no formal, solid basis of hierarchy among them. Informal, extralegal means may provide a measure of superordination and subordination, but the way is always open for an interest group to operate through the Congress or the president alternatively, to play one off against the other, to destroy a fragile hierarchical arrangement and fabricate a transitory substitute. These ambiguities are reflected in popular attitudes that are often markedly ambivalent concerning one or another of the presidential functions. "The president is titular head of the nation, chief legislator, and chief representative, as well as chief executive; we do not necessarily support him in all roles at the same time." [8]

Potential differences between the president and a majority of the Congress are further guaranteed by the calendar system of elections and the arrangement of staggered terms. The difficulty is not merely that a majority of Congress or of one chamber may carry a party label different from that of the president. It is rather, as we noted early in Chapter 11, that the effective constituencies of the president and members of Congress may be very different, that the relationships that elect a congressman from a given area may not be the same as those that give the area's vote to a presidential candidate even when both men have the same party designation. Some measure of correspondence between the two constituencies existed during the first three decades under the Constitution, when the congressional caucus nominated presidential candidates. The caucus system gave the president a continuing basis of support in the factional leadership of Congress, even if the actual election fell to the House of Representatives.

[8] Herring: *Presidential Leadership*, p. 3. Copyright 1940 by Pendleton Herring and used with the permission of Rinehart & Company, Inc.

Nomination of the president in the party convention, a practice that has prevailed since Jackson's day, does not "provide stable support for executive leadership" of the Congress.[9]

The consequences of dissociation of presidential and congressional constituencies are accentuated by the methods of selecting the leadership of the legislative body. Reliance upon seniority to designate committee chairmen, presiding officers, and floor leaders means that this leadership is oriented primarily toward the interests whose strength lies in the "safe" constituencies. The electoral majority of the president, however, must be built disproportionately upon the elements of strength in "doubtful" areas. Although the total combination supporting his candidacy is motley, political ties are most easily established with the newly chosen members of Congress whose influence in the legislature is minimal. Interest groups with privileged access to the Congress are likely, therefore, to be quite different from those that find a sympathetic reception in the White House. It is this difference in access that gives substance to Bentley's observation: "The history of the presidency . . . has been the history of interests which chose it as their best medium of expression when they found other pathways blocked." [10] Given the expectations that are focused upon the presidency, the indispensable qualification of a successful White House incumbent is that he be able to lead the Congress. He may need other skills as well, but without this ability he can accomplish nothing. He cannot even manage the executive branch unless he can gain from the legislature a minimal acceptance of his leadership. The times may permit the quiet abdication of a Coolidge, but even he found some use for the White House breakfast with legislative leaders. In the critical years that have been characteristic of the twentieth century an aggressive leadership has usually been demanded. With little or no accretion of formal means of influencing the Congress, presidents since Theodore Roosevelt have had to weave a fabric of leadership relations with the legislature from whatever materials they could find. To a remarkable degree these relations have been a reflection of the personal characteristics of the president.[11]

[9] Herring: *Presidential Leadership*, pp. 5–6. Copyright 1940 by Pendleton Herring and used with the permission of Rinehart & Company, Inc.

[10] Bentley: *The Process of Government*, pp. 344–5. Copyright 1908 by and used with the permission of Arthur F. Bentley. Cf. pp. 351, 367.

[11] Cf. Brownlow: *The President and the Presidency*, pp. 123 ff.; Edward S. Corwin: *The President: Office and Powers* (New York: New York University Press, 1940), pp. 264–81; Herring: *Presidential Leadership*, pp. 10 ff.

The president's leadership of the legislature depends heavily upon his symbolic supraparty position. Although he cannot completely ignore the pleas of partisanship, he must play upon the multiple memberships of both fellow party-members and nominal opponents in order to effect winning support for the causes he is championing. He may use his fellow party-members wherever possible, but he cannot depend upon them, since the support for their presence in the Congress may bear little relation to his popular support and their party position implies no intent to make the party an instrument for governing, let alone for presidential governing. Even similarity of interest affiliation is a slim reed to rest upon, for if a member of Congress must be re-elected largely through arrangements of his own creation, if he is to be a political entrepreneur, he must exhibit some independence.[12]

Nowhere is the highly personal character of the president's leadership of the Congress more in evidence than in the realm of party. If those who carry the same party label are in a majority in the legislature, they will organize both chambers and can control procedure. Although the ties of party are weak, such a majority position gives the chief executive a chance to influence the way in which procedures are employed to advance some legislative proposals and to restrict others. Whether he uses this chance is not a matter of formal power but of his skillful representation of group interests in personal relations with legislative leaders. If the president does not capitalize on the opportunity offered by a legislative majority's procedural controls, it is not unlikely that these will be used against him.

The crisis faced by the Seventy-third Congress at its opening in 1933 had much to do with the amicable relations that then prevailed between the President and the legislature. The claims that most insistently demanded recognition were apparent to both. Nevertheless, it was in no small measure the personal skill of Franklin Roosevelt that permitted him to lead the Congress through an assortment of Democratic legislators, most of whom were from the South and reflected interests divergent from those to which he was most sensitive. Such skill has been a factor in every instance of successful presidential leadership in Congress since Jefferson's inauguration; it is part of the equipment the president's role requires. If the interests

[12] Cf. Pendleton Herring: "Executive-Legislative Responsibilities," *American Political Science Review*, Vol. 38, no. 6 (December, 1944), p. 1163, for the relation between administrative determinations and a congressman's standing in his constituency.

that exert their claims upon the government are to reach harmonious adjustment, the multiplicity of means of access must be guided and controlled through the relationships between the president and legislative leaders.

Presidential Executives or Congressional Executives?

The variety of lines of access to the government that have developed through the separation of powers and the clashes and deadlocks that normally occur between the president and the legislature encourage a competition between them for control of the operating agencies of the executive branch. Such a struggle has been fought more or less from the beginning,[13] but as the discretionary powers delegated to administrative units have grown, its importance has increased. The ambiguities of the Constitution are such that there can be constant dispute over whether control of administrative decisions is to take place directly through the authorizing and appropriating functions of the legislature or through the executive power with which the president is vested.

Because the interests that enjoy privileged access to the legislature are not ordinarily the same as those to which the president is most sensitive, the administrative agencies are exposed more or less constantly to competing and frequently incompatible demands. Despite the "awesome terms" in which the formal powers of the chief executive are formally described, he can have no confidence that the conflict will be resolved in his favor.[14] The position of the administrative official is consequently a most delicate one. The bureaucrat may be withdrawn and aloof under some systems, but in the American scene, especially at the national level, he is often as exposed to changes in the pattern of power as any elected official. His position, moreover, may be far more vulnerable. The conflict resulting from what Herring calls "the presidential versus the congressional theory of responsibility for administrative action" may not often be open and declared, since on both sides the consciousness of role implies the imperative of compromise. Nevertheless, the difference between the

[13] W. E. Binkley: *The Powers of the President* (Garden City, N. Y.: Doubleday, Doran & Company, 1937), pp. 296–8.
[14] V. O. Key, Jr.: "Legislative Control," in Fritz Morstein Marx, editor: *Elements of Public Administration* (New York: Prentice-Hall, Inc., 1946), pp. 339, 349.

two theories "lies like a submerged reef," and the administrator cannot ignore it.[15]

The struggle over which influences shall control administrative agencies is reflected, often very sharply, in the cabinet, though it is by no means confined there. It is inherent in the make-up of the cabinet, for, although nominations to his "official family" are rarely rejected, the president's choices are not free. His selections to head the great "clientele" agencies, such as the Departments of Agriculture, Labor, and Commerce, must be acceptable to the principal interest groups affected, and in some cases are virtually selected by them. The Senate will not necessarily reject a cabinet appointee unacceptable to the affected groups, but both the president and the secretary are likely to suffer unless he is or becomes *persona grata* to these groups. In these and other cabinet appointments the president must satisfy the claims of factions within the coalition that has nominated and elected him. He must recognize the dominant interests in various sections of the country in which an agency's functions are important, as those of the Department of the Interior are to the arid West. Where he wishes to emphasize his role as a unifying national symbol, he may have to include the opposition party, as Franklin Roosevelt did in 1940 by appointing Henry L. Stimson as Secretary of War and Frank Knox as Secretary of the Navy. If the president composes his cabinet exclusively of personal supporters and sympathetic minds, he may secure loyal counsel, but he will sacrifice influence with the Congress and with interest groups.[16]

Consciously or unconsciously the members of the cabinet will "speak for" the elements that have had to be considered in their selection, some as vigorous "members" of these interest groups and others reluctantly as personal adherents to the president's cause. It is not just that different points of view will be expressed, but in many cases competing claims and aspirations will be asserted. Under the circumstances, the cabinet is primarily a means of consolidating the president's political strength and only secondarily an advisory council for the development of policy. Presidents who have aspired to fulfill the expectations focused upon the office and who have been able to meet the requirements of the role have paid little or no attention to the

[15] Herring: "Executive-Legislative Responsibilities," p. 1157. Cf. Norton E. Long: "Power and Administration," *Public Administration Review*, Vol. 9, no. 4 (Autumn, 1949), pp. 257–64; Paul H. Appleby: *Policy and Administration* (University, Ala.: University of Alabama Press, 1949).

[16] Herring: *Presidential Leadership*, p. 100. Cf. Key: "Legislative Control," p. 355.

cabinet as a general council. They could not. There are additional reasons why cabinet meetings are so confined to trivialities that they are generally regarded as a waste of time, but the factors that control cabinet appointments are probably the most fundamental.[17]

The president must use his department heads, or rather their influence with legislators and with interest groups, as Lincoln successfully used a cabinet including two men who had been his competitors for the White House. He must compromise and defer as well as dominate, but he cannot be guided by such a motley council. Individually they must have access to him, and such access is valuable. The efforts of various interest groups to achieve cabinet rank for the heads of agencies with which they deal indicates the importance of getting the president's ear even in a formal way. Efforts to achieve departmental status for an agency, however, may be guided quite as much by a desire to achieve independence of the president as by a solicitude for closer integration with his program. The ambiguities concerning the dominance of legislative or presidential control over the administrative agency ordinarily give more room for maneuver to one of cabinet rank than to one of subordinate position.

The continuing, unanswered question of where the responsibility for administrative action shall lie and the expediencies that consequently must guide the president's cabinet appointments turn department heads in varying degrees into political opponents. The institutionalized relationships between an established agency and its attendant interest groups and legislators may make even a personal supporter act as the president's "natural enemy" when he heads a major department. For, as Appleby says of the president: "He acts subject to subordinates dealing directly with Congress and playing off Congressional forces against Presidential power."[18] The situation is an old one. When John Adams retained the cabinet that he had inherited from Washington, he was surrounded by men who felt themselves responsible to the President's political enemy, Alexander Hamilton, then a private citizen. More recent examples are numerous. Henry C. Wallace, Harding's Secretary of Agriculture, "co-operated actively" in the effort of the Farm Bureau and the

[17] Herring: *Presidential Leadership*, pp. 92 ff.; cf. Henry L. Stimson and McGeorge Bundy: *On Active Service in Peace and War* (New York: Harper and Brothers, 1947), pp. 44, 561–2, and *passim*; Arthur W. Macmahon and John D. Millett: *Federal Administrators* (New York: Columbia University Press, 1939), pp. 4–5.

[18] Appleby: *Policy and Administration*, pp. 113–14. Copyright 1949 by and used with the permission of University of Alabama Press.

"farm bloc" of 1921 to force the Administration's hand. In 1942 the Secretary of Agriculture, Claude Wickard, quietly supported a Farm Bureau amendment to pending price-control legislation, although Roosevelt opposed it. Jesse Jones, as Secretary of Commerce and head of the Reconstruction Finance Corporation, operated with almost complete independence of Roosevelt, thanks to his following among important business elements and among the members of the Texas delegation in Congress and their allies.[19]

The president's constitutional power of removal has little relevance to his control over his cabinet. There are no legal limitations upon his power to discharge a department head, whatever restraints may apply to his removing others of his appointees. But if the president is not free to choose whom he will as department heads, he is equally constrained in their removal. Any member of the cabinet who is strong enough with groups in and out of the Congress to act in a fashion independent of the president's wishes can be removed from office only at a political price. The opposition of the interest groups and legislators with whom an official is affiliated may make the price too high, unless the president can gain more strength than he loses by the action or unless he can weaken the offending official's following before taking action. Roosevelt did not drop Jesse Jones from the cabinet until there was gossip indicating that the Secretary of Commerce had not supported the national ticket in the 1944 campaign.[20] When Truman asked for Henry A. Wallace's resignation as Secretary of Commerce in 1946, he lost less support in Congress and among interest groups outside than he would have if Secretary of State Byrnes had resigned in protest against Wallace's public statements. But a skillful department head who maintains strong support among the interest groups affected by his agency and among members of Congress can be virtually free to ignore the preferences of the chief executive.

Just as the president cannot use his removal power freely, he cannot take a position on every major controversy over administrative policy, not merely because his time and energies are limited, but equally because of the positive requirements of his position. He cannot take sides in any dispute without giving offense in some quarters. He may intervene where the unity of his supporters will

[19] Kile: *The Farm Bureau Through Three Decades*, pp. 101–2; Herring: "Executive-Legislative Responsibilities," pp. 1159–60.

[20] See, for example, *Business Week*, January 27, 1945, p. 16, and I. F. Stone: "Wallace In, Jones Out," *Nation*, Vol. 160, no. 4 (January 27, 1945), pp. 89–90.

be threatened by inaction; he may even, by full use of the resources of his office, so dramatize his action as to augment the influence he commands. But he cannot "go to the country" too often, lest the tactic become familiar and his public jaded. Rather than force an administrative issue, he may choose to save his resources for a legislative effort. The effectiveness of a group's access to the president, therefore, is always subject to a priority rating that may be set by him or by circumstances. He must preserve some of the detachment of a constitutional monarch.[21]

The president's decision to intervene or not in a conflict over administrative policy reflects a choice among competing interests, including those reflected in widely held expectations concerning the other aspects of his role. Thus when Franklin Roosevelt during World War II avoided taking sides in controversies that had implications for the extension or consolidation of the New Deal and concentrated on matters directly affecting strategy and war production, he was emphasizing his role of commander in chief and chief of state. He narrowed his role partly because his time and energy were limited and partly because his information on conflicts within the executive branch was inadequate, but also probably from deliberate attention to being "Dr. Win-the-War."

The president's necessary detachment from numerous issues of administrative policy inevitably imposes a large measure of independence upon department heads, whether or not they are personally attached to his policies. Moreover, it increases the concentration of organized interest-group effort upon administrative agencies, either directly or through legislators and congressional committees. The department head must handle relations with interest groups and their congressional spokesmen largely on his own, knowing that if he gets into difficulty he may have to solve it without aid from the White House. In turn the cabinet officer's tactical position imposes a similar detachment from many intradepartmental problems. This detachment helps to insulate bureaus and divisions from the lines of presidential policy and to increase control of administrative action by way of the Congress. On a matter of any considerable controversy the head of an administrative agency, whether at the cabinet, bureau, or even divisional level, must repeatedly choose between "faithfully going down the line of presidential policy" at the risk of antagonizing competing interests with effective access to the legislature and acting in opposi-

[21] Herring: *Presidential Leadership,* pp. 111–12; Key: "Legislative Control," p. 344.

tion to the president in order to preserve harmonious relations with key elements in the Congress.[22]

The patterns of interaction among officials of the executive branch do not necessarily show a dominant hierarchical pattern reaching its apex in the presidency. Even in noncontroversial activities the patterns may not take this form. The equilibrium reflected in lack of controversy may be founded, not on executive leadership, but on an accepted practice of responding to the initiative of organized interest groups, to elements in the legislature to which these have effective access, or to both. Within limits this situation is an inevitable and, from any point of view, a desirable consequence of delegated authority. It is quite reasonable, for example, that there should be close and cordial relations between the Chicago Board of Trade and the local employees of the U.S. Department of Agriculture who help administer the laws regulating trading in grain futures; it is also reasonable that many matters of administrative policy should be settled without recourse to the formal hierarchy of the department of the executive branch generally.[23] It is equally appropriate that administrative agencies accept a measure of guidance from members of Congress. Such relationships can "promote stability and continuity in policy."[24] Patterns of this sort occur in governments other than the American, as we pointed out in Chapter 1.

The peculiarities of the system of control over administrative agencies in the United States appear when a controversy, a conflict between interest claims, arises. Then it is never certain whether the pattern of decision will be set via the lines of interaction between administrators and the interest groups with access to key points in the legislature or whether it will emerge from the channels of what is usually thought of as the formal hierarchy. Organized interest groups with privileged access either to the legislature or to "superior" points in the executive will attempt to make one or the other of these patterns dominant. Legislators and administrators who are acting for organized groups or for unorganized interests involved in a policy controversy will attempt to strengthen whatever lines of influence they possess in and outside the executive branch. A department head or a chief executive may find in standing aloof from

[22] Key: "Legislative Control," pp. 344–6. Cf. Wayne Coy: "Basic Problems," *American Political Science Review*, Vol. 40, no. 6 (December, 1946), p. 1129.
[23] Cf. David B. Truman: *Administrative Decentralization* (Chicago: University of Chicago Press, 1940), pp. 175–7 and *passim*.
[24] Key: "Legislative Control," p. 346.

some policy conflicts a higher expediency than in committing his full resources to achieving a dominant position. The outcome of a policy controversy, therefore, may not represent a test of the full potential of either side. In any case the movement to a decision may be either "horizontal" through the legislature or "vertical" through the executive. In many instances the decisive relationships will reflect a compromise the details of which are obscure even to the close observer. The continuing pattern of administrative controls in the United States is a composite of alternations, a "maze of criss-crossing relationships." [25]

The President and the Army Engineers

Perhaps the most astonishing example of formal, "vertical" responsibility to the president and actual, "horizontal" control by elements in the Congress is the Army Corps of Engineers. This division, not only a unit in the executive branch but one presumably subject to the president as commander in chief of the army, considers itself responsible directly to Congress, and its operating relationships fully confirm that view.[26] The civil functions of the corps—river and harbor development and flood control works—involve local improvements of considerable interest in congressional constituencies, and these are the basis of the close relationship. The corps has undertaken river development work since the early years of the Republic, when it was the only source of trained engineers in the government. One of the principal reasons for its remaining active in this work is, in the words of a Hoover Commission report, its "excellent relations with local interests and Congress." [27]

Since the growth of multiple-purpose water development projects beginning in the 1920's, the Corps of Engineers has been increas-

[25] Herring: "Executive-Legislative Responsibilities," p. 1159. On this whole problem see Herbert A. Simon, Donald W. Smithburg, and Victor A. Thompson: *Public Administration* (New York: Alfred A. Knopf, Inc., 1950), esp. chaps. 18, 19.
[26] The material on the Corps of Engineers has been drawn primarily from U.S. Commission on Organization of the Executive Branch of the Government: *Task Force Report on Natural Resources* (Washington, D.C.: Government Printing Office, 1949), esp. appendices 1, 2, 5, 7; see also Robert de Roos and Arthur A. Maass: "The Lobby that Can't Be Licked," *Harper's Magazine* (August, 1949), pp. 21–30.
[27] U.S. Commission on Organization of the Executive Branch of the Government: *Task Force Report on Natural Resources*, p. 66.

ingly involved in jurisdictional conflicts with other agencies concerned with water resources, notably the Bureau of Reclamation in the Department of the Interior. Within the executive branch various measures have been attempted to adjust these conflicts, including direct intervention by the president, but without notable success. The basic situation is stated baldly in a remarkable passage in the Hoover Commission's *Task Force Report on Natural Resources*: "As a result of the Corps' position that it is responsible directly to the Congress, the President does not have sufficient executive power to enable him to establish a policy and formulate a coordinated Federal water development program." [28]

The Hoover Commission recommended the transfer of the corps' water development work to a new Water Development and Use Service in the Department of the Interior. Its task force saw the only impressive argument against such a proposal in the "intense opposition" it would produce and added: "There is no need to emphasize the powerful local and congressional support for the corps." [28] The opposition was not long in developing. The recommendation itself was adopted over the objections of a minority. Senator McClellan of Arkansas, a prominent member of the National Rivers and Harbors Congress, and Carter Manasco, former Representative from Alabama, entered an impassioned dissent. It was equally significant that the Secretary of Defense, James Forrestal, felt obliged to abstain "from participation in the discussion and formulation of this recommendation." [30] It was most unlikely that either the president or the Congress would take steps to implement it.

The strength of the relationships between the Corps of Engineers and the Congress rests on a number of factors. Its projects seem to have vote-getting significance in congressional districts from Maine to California. These congressional interests, plus those of contractors and local officials, are organized in the National Rivers and Harbors Congress, which we discussed briefly in Chapter 11. The financial arrangements that the corps has made in connection with the projects it has built have favored various other groups and have assured the corps of their support. Thus the large land owners and water users who profit from increased land values produced by drainage projects and dam construction for which they pay little or nothing have a

[28] Ibid., p. 83.
[29] Ibid., p. 67.
[30] U. S. Commission on Organization of the Executive Branch of the Government: *Reorganization of the Department of the Interior* (Washington, D.C.: Government Printing Office, 1949), pp. 10, 81–9.

THE GOVERNMENTAL PROCESS   412

reason for championing the corps. The corps' opposition to charging tolls on waterways it has developed has established it with groups who use these facilities. Finally, its advocacy of privately owned lines for the transmission of electric power from its dams has been welcomed by the private electric utility groups.

The Corps of Engineers in its civil functions has been almost completely independent of the commander in chief of the army even in time of war. A particularly striking example of the conflict this *de facto* independence leads to is the struggle over the so-called Kings River project in the Central Valley of California.[31] When this controversial project was initiated, the Bureau of Reclamation had been engaged in a continuing basin-wide program of providing more adequate water for the arid southern portion of the valley, partly through using surplus water from the northern end and partly through storing the run-off from the southern Sierras for irrigation and protection against occasional flood damage. The Kings River project fell in the latter category. A local water users' organization in 1937 asked both the corps and the bureau to investigate the needs of the Kings River area, with the apparent intention of supporting the proposal that gave its members the most benefits with the least cost to themselves. During 1939 and 1940 efforts were made within the executive branch and by President Roosevelt personally to prevent publication of the two reports until they could be reconciled. Through accident or design these efforts so far failed that in February, 1940, the Congress received the two separate studies of the Kings River area.

Differences between the two plans in their attractiveness for various interest groups stemmed from the corps' view of the project primarily as a matter of flood control and from the bureau's conception of it as principally an irrigation project planned to fit in with the whole Central Valley program. The bureau plan included limitations on the acreage owned by irrigation beneficiaries (a matter of importance in an area of many large holdings), checks on land speculation, Federal operation of the Kings River works, electric power development with government-constructed transmission lines connecting with those in other parts of the Central Valley project, and a sizable cost allocation to irrigation benefits repayable by the beneficiaries. The corps' plan provided for no acreage limitations, no restraints on land speculation, local operation of the works, no electric power construction but provision for later private development of power resources,

[31] U.S. Commission on Organization of the Executive Branch of the Government: *Task Force Report on Natural Resources,* appendix 7, pp. 149–82.

and a small cost allocation to irrigation benefits. Small wonder that the bulk of the organized local interest groups favored construction by the Corps of Engineers.

Early in 1940 the President made a decision, which he made known in a letter to the Secretaries of War and the Interior, that the Kings River project was primarily an irrigation matter and should be constructed by the Bureau of Reclamation. The bureau and the organized and unorganized interests supporting it had privileged access to President Roosevelt, whose attachment to multiple-purpose water projects under government control was of long standing. The corps had better access to the Congress. At hearings before the House Committee on Flood Control in 1940 and 1941, therefore, the Corps of Engineers advocated its plan without mentioning the President's policy. In the latter year this policy was reaffirmed at a cabinet meeting and in letters to the Secretary of War and to the chairman of the House committee. This action apparently had the effect of keeping the project out of the final version of the 1941 flood control measure. Because of the war no appreciable change in the situation occurred in 1942 and 1943.

In 1944 the President's budget contained an item for preliminary construction activity by the Bureau of Reclamation. It was eliminated by the House Appropriations Committee, restored by the Senate committee, and finally cut out in the conference committee. Meanwhile, the House Committee on Flood Congrol again took steps to authorize construction by the Corps of Engineers. To forestall such action Secretary Ickes (Interior) wrote to Secretary Stimson (War) reviewing the record of the President's policy, and President Roosevelt again wrote Representative Whittington, chairman of the House committee. At the hearings the corps spokesman presented the documents from Secretary Ickes, but the remainder of his testimony did not differ from that on earlier occasions. The Committee on Flood Control reported favorably on the Corps' proposal, and the House passed it. Chairman Whittington, however, apparently felt obliged to reply to the President's letter, stating the project was predominantly a matter of flood control.

Before the 1944 flood-control bill was taken up by the Senate Commerce Committee, President Roosevelt, apparently angered by the behavior of the corps, sent a sharp memorandum to Secretary Stimson, the full text of which was as follows:

> I want the Kings and Kern River projects to be built by the Bureau of Reclamation and not by the Army engineers. I also

want the power generated at projects built by Army engineers to be disposed of by the Secretary of the Interior. I hope you will see that the rivers and harbors and flood-control bills include provisions to effectuate these.[32]

The Secretary of War sent the President's memorandum to the chairman of the Senate committee with a covering statement that showed the essence of caution. He said: "I enclose herewith copy of memorandum I have just received from the President with respect to changes he wants in the rivers and harbors and flood-control bills now pending before your committee. I accordingly recommend that your committee give its earnest consideration to the desires expressed in that memorandum."[33] He then briefly indicated the deletions and amendments necessary to meet the President's wishes. The spokesmen for the Corps of Engineers not only did not support the President's position, but vigorously insisted that the project was primarily a matter of flood control. The Committee and the Senate followed suit.

The denouement came a year later. Both the bureau and the corps had been authorized to undertake the Kings River project, the former by the Secretary of the Interior and the latter by the Flood Control Act of 1944. Neither had an appropriation for preliminary work. The President's budget, submitted in January, 1945, contained a request for the bureau and none for the corps to undertake this project. The appropriation acts passed in the next few months reversed those positions.

No clearer demonstration could be found of the conflict over control of an administrative agency. Despite its location in the War Department, the Corps of Engineers was virtually independent of the chief executive. The actual pattern of its dominant relationships was a "horizontal" hierarchy with its apex in the House and Senate committees, not a "vertical" hierarchy leading to the president. The elements of presidential power were discernible however. These were shown not only in the *pro forma* letters from the Senate and House committee chairmen, but in certain concessions in the Flood Control Act of 1944, concessions extracted by the President and the groups he supported. Furthermore, President Roosevelt, supposing that he had wanted to pay the price in legislative and group opposi-

[32] Ibid., pp. 167–8.
[33] U.S. Senate, Committee on Commerce: *Hearings on Flood Control*, 78th Cong., 2d Sess. (1944), p. 11.

tion, undoubtedly could have punished the chief of the corps for insubordination, as President Truman punished a chief of naval operations, Admiral Denfeld, by relieving him of his position after his testimony before a committee of Congress.

The Kings River case also illustrates the ticklish position of the department head. Secretary Stimson's behavior was correct, but apparently not vigorous in its support of the President. Had he opposed the corps more actively, he too might have paid a heavy price, as he had learned more than thirty years before when he was Secretary of War in Taft's cabinet. In 1912 he had relieved Major General Fred C. Ainsworth of his position as Adjutant General and had ordered him court-martialed for insubordination. Ainsworth had had powerful backing in Congress, based in part on his handling of rivers and harbors projects. Stimson and Bundy have pointed the moral in the most explicit terms: "The relief of Ainsworth was more than a personal affront to his congressional friends; it was a direct challenge to the whole concept of congressional government. . . . For their audacity in this attack on congressional power, Stimson and [the Chief of Staff, General Leonard] Wood paid the price of constant conflict." [34] In the midst of World War II Stimson apparently chose not to pay such a price for executive control of the Corps of Engineers.

It is important to bear in mind the fact that the relationships governing the Corps of Engineers are not unique, although they are not altogether typical. Such cases are not confined to the military. Whatever the statutes may allow, the president cannot reorganize and reassign the functions of many administrative agencies. The actual powers are not in his hands. The same is even more true of department heads. The Secretary of Agriculture, for example, has normally had greater statutory freedom to reorganize his department than have most cabinet officers. But if he attempted to make changes significantly affecting some of the older bureaus, he would meet heavy opposition and would succeed only at a price, if at all. [35]

[34] Stimson and Bundy: On Active Service, p. 37.

[35] See Gaus and Wolcott: Public Administration and the United States Department of Agriculture, pp. 265–6. Cf. U.S. President's Committee on Administrative Management: Report of the President's Committee (Washington, D.C.: Government Printing Office, 1937), p. 35; U.S. Commission on Organization of the Executive Branch of the Government: General Management of the Executive Branch (Washington, D.C.: Government Printing Office, 1949), pp. 31 ff.; Task Force Report on Departmental Management (Washington, D.C.: Government Printing Office, 1949), pp. 5 ff.

"Independent" Regulatory Establishments

The relationships surrounding the so-called independent agencies, not ably the regulatory agencies, differ only in degree from those of the executive units we have been discussing. It is apparent from what has been said thus far that complete subordination to the chief executive, even of agencies legally a part of the executive branch, is rare. On the other hand, despite statutory and constitutional restrictions on the chief executive, notably through limitations on his power of removal, the "independence" of regulatory and other commissions is relative rather than absolute. Members of regulatory commissions are not the only officials who are actually highly independent of the chief executive. In a good many of the States, for example, where the executive branch is not even formally integrated and many of the principal administrative officers who in the Federal government would be appointed by the president are directly elected, such officials are often fully as independent as the "independent" commissions.[36] Few, if any, of the devices for making an establishment independent, however, cannot be circumvented under the appropriate conditions. Party and personal loyalties may create a high degree of interdependence. The legislature's appropriation acts and powers of statutory revision can always be used to enforce changes in agency policy. Staggered terms may be meaningless if the same faction holds control long enough to appoint the majority of a commission. Even restrictions on the chief executive's removal power can be nullified if he follows a device adopted by Calvin Coolidge of requiring an undated letter of resignation as a condition of appointment.[37]

Since the so-called independent regulatory agency has become common in American government, the measure of independence permitted these agencies must have some political usefulness. Some idea of the "independent" agency's significance should be gained, therefore, from an examination of the conditions under which it has been adopted as a form of administrative organization. Generalization about these conditions is hazardous, but we can be certain that an

---

[36] See James W. Fesler: *The Independence of State Regulatory Agencies* (Chicago: Public Administration Service, 1942).

[37] Robert E. Cushman: *The Independent Regulatory Commissions* (New York: Oxford University Press, 1941), chap. 10 and *passim*; Herring: *Public Administration and the Public Interest*, p. 96; James W. Fesler: "Independence of State Regulatory Agencies," *American Political Science Review*, Vol. 34, no. 5 (October, 1940), pp. 944–5.

understanding of the reasons for the widespread use of this form, like those accounting for any other governmental phenomenon, will be found in the distribution of power among the interests concerned with the policy entrusted to the "independent" agency.

We may note to begin with that virtually all "independent" agencies reflect the necessity for the authorization by a legislature of some continuing body to carry on a semidiscretionary activity that the legislature could not feasibly carry on itself. Whether the matter is the setting of railroad and public utility rates, the licensing of beauticians and radio broadcasters, or the regulation of trade practices, the detail and technicality are such that a legislative body cannot practically perform these functions itself. Nor could they be handled any better by the courts. The question then becomes: Why was this type of organization selected to undertake these kinds of responsibilities? Why were these problems not added to those of the agencies formally subordinate to the chief executive? These questions are almost irrelevant to the early experiments with "independent" commissions in the States in the 1870's and earlier, since these commissions were independent only in that they were substitutes for clumsy, direct regulation by the legislatures. Governors were largely figureheads, and integration of the State executive activities was not practiced or sought. The earliest commissions were, in fact, little more than *ad hoc* committees designated by the legislature primarily to collect information.[38] Railroad politics, which provided the occasion for these experiments, always contained political dynamite; such commissions, like the early permanent State commissions of the so-called "weak" type, were compromises by which the legislature agreed to do something, but not very much, to restrict the excesses of the railroads. When the Grangers secured the establishment of "strong" commissions, beginning in Illinois in 1869, they were setting up an *executive* agency, one with power. (The first Illinois commission, in fact, was instructed to report to the governor.)

The common denominator of the latter-day movement for commissions (and especially for their "independence") seems to have been a matter of defensive strategy. Groups reconciled to a regulatory statute have preferred the independent commission as the least objectionable device: the organized and unorganized interests with privileged access to the chief executive and the regular departments are usually fairly apparent; but it is never clear which interests in-

[38] The best single source on the early history of the State commissions as well as on their development at the Federal level is Cushman: *Independent Regulatory Commissions*, chap. 2 and *passim*.

itially will have such access to a new agency that is expected to act with some of the detachment of a court. Experience indicates, however, that the regulated groups will have more cohesion than those demanding regulation, that they can therefore keep close track of the work of the commission, and that consequently little will be done by a commission beyond what is acceptable to the regulated groups.[39] Even when groups have sought regulation, such as the licensing of occupations, the commission has been regarded as the most appropriate form for their purposes because it assures privileged access for the initiating group.

As early as 1887, when the Interstate Commerce Commission was established—the first Federal body of this sort unless one counts the Civil Service Commission—such defensive considerations were probably influential, though this presumption cannot be proved. For the railroads, although they had resisted regulation, had learned to live with the State commissions, and, especially with the waning of the Granger movement, had even secured modifications in some of the State statutes. Their access to these commissions had improved. At the same time the State commissions appeared to have satisfied sufficiently some of the more insistent demands of groups hostile to the railroads, so that the device had an acceptable measure of prestige with most of the congressional proponents of Federal regulation. Independence of the executive was not yet an issue. In fact, the I.C.C. originally was set up within the jurisdiction of the Secretary of the Interior.

Subsequent expansion of the commission device has shown this consistent feature, the acceptance of the form for the defensive advantage it gives the regulated groups. More than twenty-five years passed before a second Federal commission was established. In the period from 1887 to 1914 the Interstate Commerce Commission had achieved a remarkably widespread and not entirely warranted prestige. It had acquired some of the Supreme Court's atmosphere of sacred infallibility; in fact, the two were sometimes classed together in debates on subsequent regulatory measures.[40] This acceptance of the I.C.C. helped to make further use of the same type of agency an acceptable compromise when active interest groups forced additional regulatory legislation.

Regulatory agencies such as the I.C.C., particularly after the beginning stages when the vigor of groups supporting their legislation has

[39] Cf. Herring: *Public Administration and the Public Interest*, p. 213.
[40] Cushman: *Independent Regulatory Commissions*, p. 155.

declined, cannot assume the detachment of a court. Except for a few matters on which all agree, their every act, if it amounts to anything, is at least as explosive as a judicial decision that upsets established concepts and practices. Even judges, not excluding those with tenure during good behavior, have had repeated occasions to learn that such decisions break the calm of the court room and involve them deeply in politics at its fullest. Regulatory activity is as certain to affect and to arouse interest groups when carried on by a commission—or by an agency under the direction of the chief executive—as when attempted by a legislature. Such activity will reflect the relative strength of competing interest groups; it is "a continuation of the legislative process." [41] The significant difference between an "independent" agency and one clearly part of the executive branch is that the latter may somewhat more readily reflect the relative standing of the organized and unorganized interests responsible for the passage of a statute.

The more undefined and imprecise the policy determinations reached by the legislature in passing a statute, the more certainly will the activities of an enforcing commission have to reflect a *modus operandi* worked out with the regulated groups. The history of the Federal Trade Commission is a case in point. Set up in 1914 to eliminate "unfair methods of competition," it was "expected to interpret under a vague mandate from Congress an issue concerning which there was no stable consensus." [42] One of its first important efforts was an investigation of the food industries, undertaken in 1917 at the request of President Wilson, principally the meat-packing industry. "The sweeping character of this investigation and the bold changes suggested caused a political backfire almost fatal to the commission." [43] The incident produced one of the few instances in which a regulated group has sought the jurisdiction of an executive department rather than that of an independent commission. Largely through the efforts of the meat packers, the Packers and Stockyards Act of 1921 gave the supervision of the industry to the Department of Agriculture rather than to the Federal Trade Commission. With the weakening of the groups responsible for the 1914 legisla-

[41] From *Public Administration and the Public Interest* by Herring, p. 218. Copyright 1936. Courtesy of McGraw-Hill Book Company, Inc.
[42] From *Public Administration and the Public Interest* by Herring, p. 117. Copyright 1936. Courtesy of McGraw-Hill Book Company, Inc.
[43] From *Public Administration and the Public Interest* by Herring, p. 119. Copyright 1936. Courtesy of McGraw-Hill Book Company, Inc.

tion, restrictive court decisions, and presidential appointment of less aggressive commissioners, the commission gradually came to terms with the strongest elements in its public and attempted to "help business to help itself."[44] A marked sign of the change came in 1938, when advertising and patent medicine groups succeeded in giving the commission jurisdiction of misleading advertising of food, drugs, and cosmetics rather than the Food and Drug Administration, which was then located in the Department of Agriculture.[45]

The defensive value of the commission form is not determined by whether or not "good men" serve on the body. The best of intentions cannot prevent the necessity for administering vague and developing policy in the context of the interests before the enforcing officials. A commission formally independent of the chief executive and expected to assume the detachment of a judical body is more likely to be primarily accessible to organized elements among the regulated than is an agency in the executive branch; it can less easily command the resources of the presidency for defending its policies; and it is less readily accessible to some of the interests that reach the chief executive.

A regulatory agency normally cannot operate a controversial statute effectively without the support of the chief executive. This it may not get if it is within the executive branch; it is even less likely to get it as a formally independent body. The political survival of an independent commission depends upon its reaching a *modus vivendi* with the regulated. Because other interests may have a larger voice in the arrangements made by an executive agency, "independence" for the regulators has a defensive advantage for the regulated.

This defensive advantage is clearly apparent in the many State bodies set up independently to license occupations. The standard pattern, whether it involves doctors or barbers, lawyers or undertakers, is for one or more associations in a given occupation to secure the passage of a compulsory licensing statute administered by an independent board made up of officials nominated by the association. The enforcement process amounts to using the legal authority thus gained to restrict entry into the occupation, to defend authorized practitioners from competition, and to protect occupational standards from deterioration. In New Jersey such boards have been completely supported by fees, uncontrolled by the State budget, and have op-

[44] Ibid., chaps. 7 and 8.
[45] See "The New Food, Drug, and Cosmetic Legislation," *Law and Contemporary Problems*, Vol. 6, no. 1 (Winter, 1939), especially Milton Handler: "The Control of False Advertising Under the Wheeler-Lea Act," pp. 91–110.

erated as "little governments, responsible to nobody." [46] Like the regulatory commissions of the more familiar sort, these bodies are "taken out of politics" only when they are confined to noncontroversial activities and are exposed to a limited, homogeneous public.

Once a set of relationships between regulated and regulators has been established, the resources of "independence" will be fully employed to defend the existing regulatory pattern against disturbance or disruption. Efforts are made through the chief executive and the legislature to secure as appointees to a commission men who will be easily absorbed into the existing patterns of access. These efforts may be facilitated by statutes that define the background and connections that candidates must possess, but success will not depend on such provisions. The regulators and the regulated ordinarily will co-operate to resist proposals of a statutory character that aim at changing the existing pattern of access. Many of the railroads of the country might welcome release from all governmental regulation, if that were politically feasible, but they will resist any change in the existing pattern that threatens to disturb established relationships with the Interstate Commerce Commission. It is no surprise, therefore, when the Association of American Railroads announces its opposition to the creation of a Department of Transportation under an official in the president's cabinet.[47] Such defensive efforts are not peculiar to independent agencies, as we have already seen. They gain political strength, however, from acceptance of the notion of "independence" and from the prestige of Supreme Court dicta supporting it. The obstacles to assigning the activities of the independent commissions to executive departments are not constitutional in the strict sense. They reflect rather the existing balance of interest groups.[48]

Vehicles for Legislative Influence

In the preceding pages we have spoken of "congressional control," using this as a convenient shorthand term. One should not forget, however, that the diffusion of leadership within the legislature is

[46] McKean: *Pressures on the Legislature of New Jersey*, p. 148. Cf. Fesler: "Independence of State Regulatory Agencies," pp. 943–4; Leiserson: *Administrative Regulation*, pp. 115–18.

[47] The *New York Herald Tribune*, March 27, 1948.

[48] See the opinion of Mr. Justice Sutherland in Rathbun v. United States, 295 U.S. 602 (1935). Cf. Cushman: *Independent Regulatory Commissions*, p. 451.

such that a term of this sort really refers to control by individual senators, representatives, and committees, and by interests having effective access to them. "The actions of Congress are in the great majority of instances those of a single member, or two, or a handful —actions which their colleagues ratify or to which they raise no objection." [49]

The struggle over who shall control the executive branch, moreover, emerges only when events have activated opposing interests some of which have privileged access to the legislature while others have such access to key spots in the executive branch. These interests may be opposing factions in either of the major national parties; rarely they may be the legislative group opposing the president and his immediate circle; they often may be unorganized groups whose interests are shared by either the president or legislative leaders, and the interests may involve substantive policy or defense of the "rules of the game" or both; finally, in a good many cases the opposing forces are made up of organized groups, especially of the association type.

When a conflict emerges each participant, as in similar conflicts within the legislature, may try to expand the public involved in the controversy in the expectation that the proportion supporting its position will be greatly increased. On this score the facilities available to the president are normally far greater than those available to his opponents. The most notable change in the power of the president since the beginning of the twentieth century has been the enhancement of his ability to command a large public for his actions and utterances.[50] Under these circumstances the interests working primarily through the legislature are likely to be at their strongest when they can utilize devices which are so technical or so awkward for the president to handle that they cannot easily be attacked openly. A few examples of such devices will illustrate the point.

Appropriation bills, as we noted in Chapter 12, are a peculiarly useful means of affecting policy without much likelihood of expanding a given public. Such bills, like tax legislation, are technical, involved, and supremely dull reading. An obscure passage, however, may say more about the lines of responsibility within the government than a ream of formal organization charts. Especially in the Federal

[49] Key: "Legislative Control," p. 342. Cf. Appleby: *Policy and Administration*, p. 9.

[50] See Brownlow: *The President and the Presidency*, chap. 4, and Corwin: *The President*, chap. 7. Cf. Harold J. Laski: *The American Democracy* (New York: Viking Press, Inc., 1948), pp. 72 ff.

government, because the president lacks the authority to veto particular items in a measure passed by the Congress, an appropriation act can be the vehicle for a variety of controls on administrative action. For example, the fact that the Secretary of the Interior can by law authorize a project proposed by the Reclamation Bureau suggests that this agency has considerable discretion. However, the practice of making detailed, itemized appropriations for the Bureau means that the restrictions upon it are considerable.[51] Appropriation bills have required executive agencies to notify congressional committees of all decisions concerning the size and location of government hospitals—presumably to permit overruling such decisions.[52] A 1944 appropriation act required the Secretary of the Navy to secure from the House and Senate Naval Affairs committees approval of the terms of all land transactions.[53] The Farm Bureau has tried to use the appropriation bills for the Department of Agriculture as a vehicle for eliminating the field offices of the Soil Conservation Service, which it regards as rivaling the county agents.[54]

Controls through appropriations committees and other such bodies may be so informal as almost to escape detection by the observer. Reports from appropriations committees to the Senate and House may include instructions to the agencies involved, and in the course of hearings admonitions may be given an agency representative by the committee, usually the chairman, that are likely to be regarded as binding. Even lump-sum appropriations frequently are made with tacit and implicit understandings between executive officers and members of the legislature concerning the administrative policies that will be followed.[55]

These devices produce a variety of continuing contacts among legislators—particularly committee chairmen—and administrators and interest groups. Informal clearance may be secured before deviating from understandings previously reached with a committee. Similar

[51] U.S. Commission on Organization of the Executive Branch of the Government: *Task Force Report on Natural Resources*, p. 82.
[52] Appleby: *Policy and Administration*, pp. 9–10.
[53] Key: "Legislative Control," p. 342.
[54] See testimony of Edward O'Neal in U.S. House of Representatives, Subcommittee of the Committee on Appropriations: *Hearings on the Agriculture Appropriation Bill for 1947*, 79th Cong., 2d Sess. (1946), pp. 1627–36.
[55] On this whole subject, see Arthur W. Macmahon: "Congressional Oversight of Administration: The Power of the Purse," *Political Science Quarterly*, Vol. 58, nos. 2 and 3 (June and September, 1943), pp. 161–90, 380–414. Cf. Arthur W. Macmahon, John D. Millett, and Gladys Ogden: *The Administration of Federal Work Relief* (Chicago: Public Administration Service, 1941), p. 280.

relationships may be established with authorizing committees as well. The latter are always ready to summon an executive officer to justify a decision he has made, and the ever-present possibility is as likely to influence his actions as the actual summons. Approval by the key members of such committees may be sought before taking discretionary action of various kinds.

During World War II the Chairman of the House Naval Affairs Committee, Representative Carl Vinson of Georgia, was so frequently consulted by the top military and civilian officials of the Navy Department that he was known among many of the junior officers as "the permanent Secretary." His influence stemmed not only from his position but also from the duration of his contacts with the Navy and from the extent of his knowledge. He had been a member of the Naval Affairs Committee since early in the 1920's and had been chairman since 1931, so that he had had longer continuous association with the problems at the top reaches of the department than any of the admirals or key civilian officials. The sweep of his detailed knowledge was amusingly illustrated from time to time in committee hearings. A member of the committee would direct a question of fact to an admiral or official of the secretary's office. Before the witness could get the answer from one of his attending staff, the chairman frequently answered the query himself. After the unification of the armed services following World War II, Vinson, as Chairman of the House Committee on the Armed Services, apparently established similar relations with the Army and Air Force. Commenting on the extent to which he made major military decisions, a Washington journalist described Vinson as "Admiral of the Ocean Seas, Field Marshal of the Armies and, as to the air, Wing Commander of Everything."[56]

Executive appointments subject to legislative confirmation are another means by which various interest groups exercise inconspicuous control through the legislature. We have touched this point earlier in discussing the president's cabinet members. The difficulties are fully as acute in connection with other appointments subject to confirmation by the Senate, and with the expansion of Federal activities in recent decades these difficulties have increased.[57] The newer functions, with the powerful discretionary authority they often create,

[56] William S. White: "Carl Vinson Has Been Unified, Too," The New York Times Magazine, September 10, 1950, p. 12.

[57] For an insightful discussion on this subject see Arthur W. Macmahon: "Senatorial Confirmation," Public Administration Review, Vol. 3, no. 4 (Autumn, 1943), pp. 281–96.

are an object of concern to a variety of interests. Both those who have supported the functions and those who have opposed them seek to influence the choice of key personnel in order to ensure effective access to points of decision. These groups are supplemented and frequently represented by party groups and factions within the States and congressional districts. The latter wish not only to take care of their members and supporting interest groups but also to prevent the use of executive appointments, particularly those outside of Washington, to build up competing factions.

The subtle element in this control device lies not in the legislative body's refusal to confirm, but in the care taken by an appointing officer not to nominate anyone likely to be rejected. Given the power of confirmation and the practice of "senatorial courtesy," the president will avoid the rebuke of rejection, and he cannot easily publicize his objections to the prior restrictions on his choice. Refusal to recognize these restrictions will often reveal the actual lines of control in the government. An outstanding example of this occurred in Alabama in 1947. Governor Folsom, acting for the small farmers of the State, nominated a set of officials to serve, until confirmed, on the board that supervises the agricultural Extension Service. When the board passed a resolution sharply critical of the Extension Service for its failure adequately to assist small farmers and for its relations with the State Farm Bureau, officials of the Extension Service and the Farm Bureau worked through the legislature to prevent confirmation of the Governor's appointees.[58]

Among other devices that similarly effect control by legislative elements and their group affiliates are legislative investigations of recalcitrant administrative agencies. Little need be added to what has been said on this topic in Chapter 12. It should be noted, however, that such investigations can exploit the diffused controls over the executive branch by playing one administrative agency off against another. One of the devices of the Cox Committee investigation of the Federal Communications Commission in 1943 was an attempt to capitalize on the desire of elements in the Army and the Navy to take over some of the Commission's functions by alleging that the F.C.C. was handicapping rather than aiding the country's war effort.[59] Like the demand for extension of the power to confirm personnel, many investigations of administrative agencies reflect the

[58] Key: *Southern Politics*, pp. 55–6.
[59] See U.S. House of Representatives, Select Committee to Investigate the Federal Communications Commission: *Hearings*, 78th Cong., 1st Sess. (1943), part 1, pp. 9–42 and *passim*.

struggle to gain privileged access to the administrators of new functions. In the same category also belong two other congressional practices: that of reserving the power to overrule executive determinations by concurrent resolutions not requiring the president's signature,[60] and that of enacting legislation for limited terms and thus requiring an appeal to Congress for a renewal of authorizing legislation. Both of these devices have been used with increasing frequency in recent years.

Under the circumstances described in the preceding paragraphs it becomes obvious that the legislature's assignment of functions to administrative agencies does not eliminate the play of interests that we recognize in the legislative process. It represents little more in the way of legislative withdrawal from policy determination than did the development of the power of standing committees. The diffusion of leadership in the legislature has its counterpart within the executive branch. Aided by the formalities and ambiguities of the separation of powers, interest groups produce a complex and often unstable structure of controls that as frequently has its apex in the legislature as the president. As Arthur Macmahon and his collaborators said of one element in that structure: "The seeming increase of the President's authority through appointments at the various levels of administration tends, when accompanied by the requirement of senatorial confirmation, actually to reduce the administrative leadership of the President." [61] Lines of control tend to follow those of continuing interaction and personal obligation. The growth of the executive does not necessarily result in a commensurate increase in the power of the chief executive. To assume that it does is to misinterpret the basic features of our governmental system.

Lines of Executive Influence

It is apparent that there are powerful centrifugal forces operating within the executive branch and that the many points of access to it are not necessarily controlled by the chief executive. But though the executive branch does not present as simple a pattern of hierarchy in operation as the formal statements and organization charts might sug-

[60] See John D. Millett and Lindsay Rogers: "The Legislative Veto and the Reorganization Act of 1939," *Public Administration Review*, Vol. 1, no. 1 (Winter, 1941), pp. 176–89.

[61] Macmahon, Millett, and Ogden: *The Administration of Federal Work Relief*, p. 270.

gest, the chief executive is not without means of influencing the actions of administrative units and officials. Access to the governor or president is not sought by interest groups simply out of habit; the means of leadership in the hands of these officials are not negligible. The president's roles as chief executive, chief legislator, chief of state, and commander of the armed forces are real, not nominal. If he is in fact not always the apex of control patterns within the government, neither does he consistently hold a peripheral or subordinate position.

While we are examining some of the means of executive influence upon the administrative agencies of the government, we must remember that these cannot be sharply divided into administrative and legislative. Regardless of immediate incidence, any increase in the strength of the chief executive is reflected throughout the government. His increased control over administrative agencies gives him closer command of the points of access to administrative decisions. It both facilitates and is dependent upon augmented influence in the legislature. An enlargement of the president's legislative leadership, or that of the members of the legislature who are accessible to the interests that guide him, has similar—though not equivalent—repercussions within the executive branch. The lack of equivalence is attributable to the separability of his various roles. That is, congressional acceptance of his leadership in foreign policy may not affect the congressional ("horizontal") controls on waterway construction. Nevertheless, because his is a single office and his roles are interdependent, the skills and credits he acquires in one area can be used for trading and compromise in another. Similarly a president completely discredited in foreign affairs is likely to be troubled with greater "independence" on the part of his administrative subordinates in various other fields.

The most obvious but not the most important of the means of executive influence is the power to appoint and remove officials. Some of the limitations on this power have already been discussed and need not be repeated here. It is proper to note, however, that patronage is not without significance as an executive tool. Effective handling of appointments in the early months of Franklin Roosevelt's first term contributed to his dominance of Congress and occasionally enabled him to ignore certain established interest-group relationships. When the Economy Act was before the House of Representatives in March of 1933, the veterans' organizations were strong enough to prevent the Democratic caucus from making a party measure of the provision authorizing the President to reduce payments to veterans.

They were not able, however, to prevent a majority of the Democrats from supporting the provision on a record vote.[62] Ordinarily the expenditure for veterans was settled by the Veterans Administration, congressional committees, and such groups as the American Legion. The Veterans Administration in this instance was obliged to relinquish some of its independence of the president.   ·

One reason for the difficulty presidents have experienced in controlling their nominal subordinates is lack of information. Despite his impressive formal powers, the president often simply does not know what is going on in the executive branch, unless or until open controversies occur. This ignorance may be made less serious if he has continuing facilities for aiding him both in securing such information and in acting upon it. Among the foremost developments in the securing of information for the president have been the growth since 1921 of the functions performed by the Bureau of the Budget and the development of other units of the Executive Office of the President since 1939.[63]

Prior to the passage of the Budget and Accounting Act of 1921 the president had almost literally nothing to do with the process of appropriation. The financial relationships of administrative agencies were, for all practical purposes, directly with congressional committees, interest groups being of course deeply involved at all stages. Giving the president responsibility for preparing a budget,—a significant delegation of power,—forced these relationships into a new pattern. The Bureau of the Budget, a presidential agency whose director is appointed without Senate confirmation, became charged with reviewing and revising all requests by the executive branch for funds before the president sent them to the Congress. The interest groups previously concerned with such requests were not eliminated nor, it need hardly be said, were the activities of congressional appropriating committees. But both the executive agencies and interested groups were obliged to operate through additional channels to which other and competing interests also had access. The independent

[62] Cf. Chamberlain: *Legislative Processes*, p. 268.
[63] See Fritz Morstein Marx: "The Bureau of the Budget: Its Evolution and Present Role," *American Political Science Review*, Vol. 39, nos. 4 and 5 (August and October, 1945), pp. 653–84, 869–98; Louis Brownlow and others: "The Executive Office of the President: A Symposium," *Public Administration Review*, Vol. 1, no. 2 (Winter, 1941), pp. 101–40; Don K. Price: "Staffing the Presidency," *American Political Science Review*, Vol. 40, no. 6 (December, 1946), pp. 1154–68; Herman Somers: *Presidential Agency: The Office of War Mobilization and Reconversion* (Cambridge, Mass.: Harvard University Press, 1950), chap. 7 and *passim*.

power of the agencies and their group allies was not eliminated, but they were obliged to reckon with the interests more effectively represented in the presidency and to seek improvement in their own relationships with the president. Combined with a measure of Budget Bureau control over the expenditure of appropriations, the growth of the presidential budget has meant a marked increase in the president's control of the executive branch. Moreover, to the extent that appropriations approximate the president's requests, his role in legislation is also enhanced.[64]

The evidence is abundant that "horizontal" relationships between executive agencies and Congress have not been eliminated by the executive budget, although they have been modified. Their strength is often anticipated by both president and budget officers. If cuts are made that are sufficiently severe, it is easy enough for an executive official to appeal to the appropriating committee. A sympathetic legislator can even invite the testifying official in the committee hearings to criticize the Budget Bureau's recommendations; the official allows his arm to be twisted, observes certain meaningless amenities usually involving the assertion that he is expressing only his "personal" opinion, and then defends his original request. Since the committees prefer to deal with officials at the bureau and divisional level, the official's testimony may also be in effect an appeal from the budget decisions of his departmental superior.[65]

Sometimes the president instructs executive officials not to try to get more funds from Congress than the budget recommends.[66] Though most executive agencies do not openly appeal to Congress from the budget recommendations of the president,[67] organized interest groups with access to the legislature are not so inhibited. These may act on their own initiative, since Budget Bureau actions are usually an open secret in Washington, or they may act at the request of the official whose appropriation has been threatened. In a few instances execu-

[64] On this point see Robert H. Rawson: "The Formulation of the Federal Budget," in Carl J. Friedrich and Edward S. Mason (eds.): *Public Policy* (Cambridge, Mass.: Harvard University Press, 1941), pp. 78–135.

[65] For example, see U.S. House of Representatives, Subcommittee of the Committee on Appropriations: *Hearings on the Agriculture Department Appropriation Bill for 1946*, 79th Cong., 1st Sess. (1945), part 2, p. 10; *Hearings on the Agriculture Department Appropriation Bill for 1947*, 79th Cong., 2d Sess. (1946), pp. 16, 68, 1229.

[66] See *The New York Herald Tribune*, January 9, 1947, for a report on such an order.

[67] See Macmahon: "Congressional Oversight of Administration," pp. 408–11; Price: "Staffing the Presidency," p. 1158.

tive officials have publicly requested action by such groups.[68] The executive budget system has increased the importance of access to the president and has strengthened his controls over the executive branch, even if it has not eliminated the importance of other points of access to the appropriations process.

A significant but less important function performed through the Budget Bureau is the clearance of all legislative recommendations from executive agencies to the Congress, whether they have originated in the agency or have been referred to it by a congressional committee. The Bureau reports whether the recommendation is in accord with the president's program, and the agency must so indicate in any report that it transmits to the Congress. Although the procedure is a useful source of information, clearance has little additional significance if the agency is in a position to ignore the president's "program." The Corps of Engineers, for example, has consistently given favorable recommendations on rivers and harbors and flood-control projects regardless of the Budget Bureau's actions.[69] Where the majority in Congress, and thus the chairmen of committees, are not of the president's party, moreover, a Budget Bureau declaration that an agency bill is not in accord with the president's program is likely not to hinder and may assist in passage of the legislation. Though it is informative and may guide an agency that is receptive to presidential leadership, the clearance procedure cannot reveal or control the informal, personal relations among administrators, groups, and legislators.[70] The recommendation and preparation of legislative measures by administrative agencies reflect the increased importance of the executive branch; the limitations of clearance procedure reveal its lack of integration.

Other elements in the Executive Office of the President, such as the Council of Economic Advisers set up under the Employment Act of 1946, have made contributions, some minor and some ap-

---

[68] See The New York Times, August 27, 1947, for testimony of the deputy chief of naval operations for logistics before the national defense committee of the American Legion, asking the latter to support the Navy's appropriation requests for the next fiscal year.

[69] U.S. Commission on Organization of the Executive Branch of the Government: Task Force Report on Natural Resources, pp. 98–9.

[70] On this subject generally see Edwin E. Witte: "The Preparation of Proposed Legislative Measures by Administrative Departments," in U.S. President's Committee on Administrative Management: Report With Special Studies (Washington, D.C.: Government Printing Office, 1937), pp. 361–77; U.S. House of Representatives, Select Committee on Lobbying Activities: Hearings, 81st Cong., 2d Sess. (1950), part 1, pp. 129–51.

preciable, to the strengthening of the president's relations within the executive branch. They need not be discussed in detail.[71] The development of which they are a part, however, has made access to the presidency increasingly important to organized groups.

The reorganization and reallocation of functions, either within the executive branch or within particular agencies, can be a means of strengthening the chief executive's lines of influence over his nominal subordinates. Not that the president necessarily acquires more formal power from administrative reorganization; though he might do so if, for example, an independent regulatory commission were assigned to one of the executive departments or if the powers of the Comptroller General, whose position is the epitome of independence, were modified. Basically, however, the reasons for reshuffling agencies within the executive branch are: the creation of new relationships and the alteration of the relative importance of old ones—changes that can be expected to affect the discretionary actions of the agencies whose relationships are altered. The policy decisions of an executive unit are significantly influenced by its pattern of relationships with interest groups, with legislators, and with other executive units. A reshuffling of units may make significant changes in these established interactions.

An example will illustrate this conception of administrative reorganization as an effort to affect an agency's policy decisions by changing the structure of influence of which it is a part. When the Pure Food and Drug Act was passed in 1906, the administration of the statute was assigned to the Department of Agriculture largely because of the accidental fact that the legislation's chief proponent within the executive branch was Dr. Harvey Wiley, at that time chief of the department's Bureau of Chemistry. (The passage of the Pure Food and Drug Act, by the way, is itself an instructive study in interest-group politics.) As might be expected, the Department of Agriculture is particularly accessible to groups of food producers; so are the authorizing committees of the Congress and the appropriations subcommittees that handled the Food and Drug Administration's activities along with those of the rest of the department. As a result, when the Food and Drug Administration attempted, for example, to stop the practice of shipping apples in interstate commerce without removing the residue from sprays harmful to human beings, the apple growers had relatively easy access to the department and to the subcommittees handling the department's (and the Food and

---

[71] For a review of these developments see Somers: *Presidential Agency*, chap. 7, and the literature there cited.

Drug Administration's) appropriations. At the same time the Food and Drug Administration tended to give special attention to the misbranding and adulteration of insecticides and fertilizers, practices opposed by the farm groups to which the agency was exposed.[72] An expected consequence of transferring the Food and Drug Administration to the Federal Security Administration in 1940 was the modification of such relationships. The established interests impinging upon the agency could not be eliminated, but their relative access to the Food and Drug Administration, through the parent agency and congressional committees, might be altered by locating it in a different spot and under a different set of committees to which additional or competing interests would have better access.

Control by the president was not clearly of importance in the Food and Drug Administration case, although differential access to him was reflected in the reorganization order. The significance of reorganization as a means of strengthening the chief executive's administrative control, however, lies in the possible effects of altering legislative and intra-executive relationships, including interest-group relationships; such changes create differences in relative access, strengthening the influence of those interests operating most effectively through the president.

Administrative reorganization has many results, but the most basic is its effect in altering relationships upon which relative access depends. The effort to shift lines of access has been a continuing feature of the successive efforts at executive reorganization, particularly those attempted in the Federal government since 1932. In all cases these have been efforts by interest groups, including not only the stereotyped "pressure" groups but also groups of professional students of public administration and unorganized interests reflected in such terms as "economy" and "efficiency." They have tried to strengthen the president's position, that is, to alter the lines of access to the executive branch and to strengthen the interests that have privileged access to the chief executive.[73] It is relative access that is at stake in the struggles over legislation authorizing executive reorganizations or disapproving presidential reorganization plans.

[72] Cf. Gaus and Wolcott: *Public Administration and the United States Department of Agriculture*, pp. 176–7; Herring: *Public Administration and the Public Interest*, chap. 14; Harvey W. Wiley: *The History of a Crime Against the Food Law* (Washington, D. C.: 1929).

[73] See Avery Leiserson: "Political Limitations on Executive Reorganization," *American Political Science Review*, Vol. 41, no. 1 (February, 1947), pp. 68–84, esp. pp. 69–70.

The limitations on the power of the president or department head to reorganize executive functions have been noted earlier in this chapter. They stem from the strength and vitality of established "horizontal" relationships among executive agencies, elements of the diffused leadership in the Congress, and associated interest groups. Without changes in all of these, such relationships will remain strong. As we noted at the beginning of this section, the state of the president's controls over the executive branch and his leadership of the legislature are interdependent. The "independence" of the Corps of Engineers, the Veterans Administration, the Interstate Commerce Commission, and the Forest Service, to mention only a few examples, is not likely soon to be altered by executive reorganization. Only the growth and consolidation of strong overlapping and opposing interests and the related weakening of the interests most closely associated with these agencies are likely to produce changes in such sectors. Though the passage of reorganization acts in 1939, 1945, and 1949 demonstrates the presence of a measure of leverage and the possibility of effecting some changes through exploiting overlapping memberships and expanded publics and through altering expectations concerning the executive, reorganization remains a limited avenue of presidential control over access to the executive.[74]

It should be noted in passing that the struggles over reorganization of the executive branch illustrate the fact that the political process rarely, if ever, involves a conflict between the legislature and the executive viewed as two monolithic and unified institutions. The actual competing structures on each side are made up of elements in the legislature and in the executive, reflecting and supported by organized and unorganized interests. Some of the latter more or less continuously have better access to majorities in the Congress and thus can be spoken for in the name of the whole legislature; the others are similarly situated in the presidency. It is only in this sense that the two institutions are in conflict. Although it is reasonable to use the term "president versus Congress" as a shorthand way of referring to the struggle, the conflict cannot be understood if the observable patterns of interaction are lost from sight.

An important supplement to other lines of executive influence is to be found in the tremendous publicity resources of the chief execu-

---

[74] The congressional committee hearings on the reorganization acts of 1939, 1945, and 1949 and on the plans submitted under them are a mine of evidence supporting the interpretation presented here. The activities of the Citizens Committee for the Hoover Report deserve careful examination from this point of view.

tive. It is one of the marks of the growth of executive leadership that the presidency, as we have noted earlier, has become a prime source of national news. Moreover, because the president so frequently makes news, he is given increased opportunity to make it. Because the presidential press conference has become a "must" for every important newspaper and for all the press and radio services, the questions asked during them give the president a chance to comment on an almost infinite variety of governmental issues. Press conference statements, "fireside chats," "whistle-stop" tours, personal appearances before the Congress, ceremonial addresses, and any number of other occasions can be used to give support to interests and issues he wishes to champion. Most of these may be thought of as primarily affecting pending or projected legislative proposals, elections, and diplomatic issues, rather than control of the executive branch. Though this is partly true, there are appreciable effects within the executive agencies from many such utterances. The president's roles, as we have said before, are not wholly separable. Moreover, his taking sides on a legislative issue is rarely irrelevant to at least some of his nominal subordinates.

The propaganda effect of presidential publicity is not only to broaden a public but also to exploit the overlapping memberships in a public, including those of administrative officials and legislators as well as private citizens. A pronouncement on foreign policy is likely to weaken the relationships of executive subordinates who oppose his policy or to force them "underground." A denunciation of particular "pressure groups" or "lobbies" is as likely to be a warning to administrative officials as a challenge to opponents in the legislature. Even the "independent" commissions are not proof against such measures. Cushman cites two occasions on which President Hoover announced the policy he thought the Interstate Commerce Commission should follow and the commission "reluctantly yielded." Noting that the president has no legal authority to enforce his pronouncements, Cushman concludes that "if . . . the orders are made public they may be exceedingly effective." [75]

In some instances the effect of the president's publicity resources may be enhanced if he shares them. He can create news and political support for the demands he champions if he can embody them skillfully in recommendations from very prominent and reputedly neutral private citizens. This is one of the most significant uses for the little-studied *ad hoc* presidential commission, of which the Com-

[75] Cushman: *Independent Regulatory Commissions*, pp. 680–2, 685–6.

mittee to Investigate the Rubber Situation, appointed by Franklin Roosevelt in 1942, is a prime example.[76]

Because of the seizure of rubber-producing areas by the Japanese, it became imperative in 1942 not only to step up means of manufacturing synthetic rubber, but to conserve existing stocks in manufacturers' plants and in use. The conflicting organized interests were reflected both in the legislature and in the executive. They included: major rubber companies chary of losing patent rights and marketing advantages; oil companies anxious to develop a new use for petroleum, but hostile to gasoline rationing to conserve rubber; agricultural groups interested in producing rubber from grain alcohol; whiskey producers reluctant to lose supplies of grain alcohol; the Rubber Reserve Company, subsidiary of the R.F.C.; the Office of Price Administration; the Petroleum Administration for War; the Senate Committee on Agriculture; and others. When these elements were at loggerheads the President might have cracked down directly, but he was weakened by unwelcome legislation shaping up in Congress and by the probable unpopularity of a gasoline rationing program. Instead he appointed a committee headed by Bernard Baruch and two prominent and unimpeachably disinterested scientists and college presidents, Karl T. Compton and James B. Conant. It was the strength that the prestige of these three men gave to any presidential action that ensured the establishment of an acceptable rubber program and permitted the silencing, at least temporarily, of the contending interests.[77]

The limitations of the presidential commission are inherent in its chief advantage, namely, that it is *ad hoc*. Its prestigeful members cannot easily be identified with any of the competing elements, except the president, because they are not a continuing agency. It is an unusual device, however, and one that derives much of its value from that fact. Like the other publicity opportunities available to the president, it cannot be used on every issue of control that

[76] The only extensive effort to study these devices is Carl Marcy: *Presidential Commissions* (New York: Kings Crown Press, 1945). See esp. pp. 49–53, 67–9. Cf. the comments concerning Franklin Roosevelt's Advisory Council on Social Security in Herring: *Presidential Leadership*, pp. 121–4. For a study of a similar kind of device at the State level see William T. R. Fox: "Will the Public Support a Merit System?" *Public Opinion Quarterly*, Vol. 3, no. 1 (Winter, 1939), pp. 117–23.

[77] See Marcy: *Presidential Commissions*; U.S. Bureau of the Budget: *The United States at War* (Washington, D.C.: Government Printing Office, 1946), pp. 293–7; James W. Fesler *et al.*: *Industrial Mobilization for War* (Washington, D.C.: Government Printing Office, 1947), Vol. I, pp. 377–9.

comes before him, even if the matter is susceptible to such treatment, without the device losing much of its charm. Only issues of top priority can be played for the front page; it will take time and unusual circumstances before the Corps of Engineers reaches that position on the list.

Finally, times of great emergency, whether economic depressions or wars, have usually generated a vast increase in the president's powers. Both his legislative and his administrative leadership are widely accepted as long as crisis lasts and catastrophe does not occur. No better illustration can be given of the interdependence of the controls within the two areas. If he is followed as chief legislator and commander of the armed forces, his controls within the executive usually are sufficient. The interests he espouses are dominant. This is not a matter of law or of the constitution, for as Herring has observed: "Presidential powers in times of emergency really rest upon the imperative of events. Legal considerations have little meaning." [78] Emergency situations permit the president to capitalize upon the multiple memberships of legislators and of a large public. He can thus reduce the effectiveness of access enjoyed by competing interests. In more tranquil times the chief executive is merely one of several points of access to the powers of government, including the executive branch, although his responsibilities may be more extensive.

[78] Herring: *Presidential Leadership*, p. 16. Copyright 1940 by Pendleton Herring and used with the permission of Rinehart & Company, Inc.

14

The Web of Relationships in the Administrative Process

———◆———

THE executive branch of government in the United States normally exhibits a diffusion of leadership and a multitude of points of access comparable to that in the legislature. The preceding chapter has demonstrated this point; it has also indicated that these characteristics of the legislature and the executive are not so much parallel as they are interdependent. Dispersed leadership and multiple points of control within one branch reflect and reinforce similar patterns in the other. This conclusion, drawn from an examination of the actual relationships existing within the two branches, emphasizes the disadvantages for purposes of understanding the political process of accepting too literally the formal separation of legislature from executive.

Provisions of the Constitution of the United States did attempt to separate fairly sharply the executive from the legislative "powers," and this formal separation has continued to be an important influence upon the political process, but the actual practice of government has produced during the course of nearly two centuries a variety of devices for avoiding the literal application of such formal doctrine. These circumventing devices give the government the appearance of a protean aggregation of feudalities that overlap and crisscross in an almost continual succession of changes. Some of the lines of control within these subsystems terminate in the presidency, some in elements within the legislature, and some in persons or groups legally "outside" the government; a few lie in the hands of "subordinate" executives; many more involve all of these in collegial arrangements so informal as to be but dimly recognized even by the chief participants. Most of these lines are at least potentially in dispute. With the passage of time and under the impact of changed circumstances within the society, the lines of control may shift and some of the subsystems spread and grow stronger while others narrow and decline. These changes may be gradual and almost unnoticed or they may be sudden and stormy.

Throughout the system, whatever patterns of control may be dominant at a given point, we observe the activities of organized interest groups. If we focus our attention again on the functions that fall within the formal boundaries of the executive branch, the significance of these groups immediately comes into question. What is their role in the fortunes and decisions of administrative agencies? To what extent are the latter pawns, directly or indirectly, of such interest groups? In other words, what are the factors that affect or control the discretionary judgments of administrative officials? What determines effective access to executive agencies?

Access to the executive, as to the legislature, is not simple. It is the product of a multitude of conflicting and complementary influences the relationships among which are subject to almost infinite variation.[1] Some of these influences are more or less peculiar to the activities we call administrative; others are common to all segments of the government. Often they reflect and depend upon the influences that have access to other key points of governmental decision, notably the legislature. Because of this derivative element and because relative access to the legislative body is the product of a complex of influences, the role of organized interest groups in the administrator's decisions may reflect all the forces that entered into the legislative enactment that authorized his work. Were the element of discretion wholly absent from his decisions and were the relative strengths of the factors that influenced the legislature completely stable, the administrator would simply mirror the elements that went into authorizing statutes. Since, however, the growth of the executive has stemmed from conditions that also required increased executive discretion, and since the kinds of activities authorized by the legislature could not be finally determined by statutes alone, group access to administrative bodies does not follow automatically from the fact that the group operated effectively upon the legislature.

[1] On this whole problem one may consult with profit the thoughtful and instructive essay by Merle Fainsod: "Some Reflections on the Nature of the Regulatory Process," in C. J. Friedrich and Edward S. Mason (eds.): *Public Policy* (Cambridge, Mass.: Harvard University Press, 1940), pp. 297–323.

The Character of the Legislative Mandate

The administration of a statute is, properly speaking, an extension of the legislative process. In looking at the role of interest groups in the administration of any given statute we may well inquire what it is that the administrator is extending. In other words: What were the influences which played a part in creating the function? What kind of "mandate" was given the administrator by the legislative majority? What were the interest groups associated with passage of the statute? Which ones were organized and how cohesively? What kinds of alliances and trading operations helped achieve passage of the legislation? To what extent was the enactment the product of a struggle among party factions? The answers to questions such as these will define the political task facing the administrative agency in carrying out the legislative mandate.

In order to state the administrative task in as realistic terms as possible, we should note two other elements in the process by which the legislation authorizing the work of an agency is enacted. In the first place, although it is convenient to assume for purposes of discussion that the administrative function to be analyzed is a new one, if it is not, we must examine the degree of correspondence between the influences that produced the original statute and those that effected the amending legislation. In the second place, whether or not the function is a new one, we must take account of the role that the administering agency played in its authorization. Was the proposal initiated by or with the assistance of the administrative unit? The skills and discretionary powers of administrators normally make them participants in legislation related to their activities, as we have noted earlier. The character of this participation has a significant bearing upon access, if only because the initiation of a law implies a commitment to a particular line of policy.

Perhaps the most basic influences defining the nature of the mandate received by the administrator are the degree of controversy attending the passage of the authorizing legislation and the character of the opposing contestants—their cohesion, resources, and points of access elsewhere in the governmental institution. Whether controversy surrounds a project of law is often equivalent to whether the function proposed is a regulatory one or a matter of service to some segment of the community. Thus the great bulk of the legislation administered by the Department of Agriculture, at least until about 1920, authorized services to farmers—the distribution of seeds, the development and dissemination of improved production methods, weather forecasts, assistance in marketing, and the like. Similarly, the activities of the Veterans Administration are almost exclusively services for former members of the armed forces and their dependents. The important element in these, however, is not the character of these activities as services, but the comparative lack of controversy surrounding their assumption. Considerable controversy has surrounded the enactment and therefore the administration of programs designed to perform services for groups and subgroups, such as labor unions and subsistence or tenant farmers, who have not so impressive a status in the community or so high a degree of organization as commercial farmers or veterans. Similarly, regulatory legislation is often born in conflict, but not always. As the preceding chapter has shown, a statute such as an occupational licensing law is nominally regulatory but may be sought by the professions affected and may be enacted without significant opposition. Or a regulatory statute may be accepted by the regulated as an alternative to a more objectionable policy, such as public ownership.

The importance of controversy is that, regardless of the preferences of the administrator, a viable administrative project "requires a positive balance of political support over political opposition."[2] A program that lacks such a balance can scarcely be administered. Illustrations of this point are numerous; it was well put by a spokesman for the railway brotherhoods at the hearings in 1926 on the railway labor bill: "The most valuable feature of this law is the fact that it represents the agreement of the parties, that they will be under the moral obligation to see that their agreement accomplishes its purpose, and that if enacted into law they will desire to prove the law a success."[3] Where the element of basic controversy is missing, the relative access of the affected interest groups is likely to be clearly defined, and the administrator's task is eased, whether or not he invokes "moral obligation."

Even if the statute has emerged from a bitter controversy, the relative access of the contending interest groups to the administering agency will be clear, other things being equal, if their cohesion re-

[2] Simon, Smithburg, and Thompson: *Public Administration*, p. 462. See generally the discussion of the struggle for administrative existence and related topics in chapters 18–22 of this volume.

[3] U.S. House of Representatives, Committee on Interstate and Foreign Commerce: *Hearings on H. R. 7180*, 69th Cong., 1st Sess. (1925), p. 21. Quoted in Chamberlain: *Legislative Processes*, p. 66.

mains comparatively stable. The development of viable administrative policy will then involve slight difficulty. The administrator's relationships with interest groups in such a situation are likely to be more or less ready-made. The groups that were strong enough to secure passage of the legislation continue to be dominant in the process of its execution. Such is a possible, but not invariable, situation.

However, many statutes, notably regulatory measures, emerge out of a legislative struggle in which the position of the contending groups is essentially unstable. Such is commonly the case where the executive and legislative leadership that has delivered a measure has been speaking for an unorganized, largely potential interest group or a loose alliance of organized groups among whose claims the measure at issue is peripheral rather than central. Once such a measure is passed, the governmental officials—including not only those who piloted the enactment but also the administrators—must act in effect as the leaders (active minority) of an interest group if the organized elements in the opposition are not to secure the advantage and to achieve privileged access to the administering agency.

The representation of an unstable, unorganized interest is the essence of what Bentley calls "demagogic leadership," using the term in its literal sense of a popular leader rather than in the pejorative one of an insincere manipulator.[4] The leadership involves what might be called a direct relationship with the "members" of the interest group, whose interactions on the basis of the interest are not sufficiently frequent or stabilized to produce an intervening organization and whose multiple memberships, on the same account, are a constant threat to the strength of the claim. Such groups tend to disintegrate and leave the field to more cohesive groups.

Examples of the effects of instability in affected groups upon the work of administrative agencies are numerous. In some measure this kind of situation is likely to be met by most new agencies that have not yet worked out stable relationships with the groups among their clientele. No more notable instance of this sort can be cited than the Stabilization Act of 1942. This legislation, amending the Emergency Price Control Act of 1942 to provide for control of farm prices, was enacted only after Franklin Roosevelt's famous ultimatum to the Congress on September 7: "In the event that the Congress should fail to act, and act adequately, I shall accept the responsibility, and I will act."[5] The reason such a provision had not been included in the original act lay in the resistance of the Farm Bureau and asso-

[4] Bentley: *The Process of Government*, pp. 231–4.
[5] *Congressional Record*, 77th Cong., 2d Sess., September 7, 1942, p. 7044.

ciated groups. The President was able to overcome this opposition by exploiting the multiple memberships of Farm Bureau adherents and of congressmen and by adding the strength of a large potential group to the strength of the few supporting organized groups. The potential group included those responsive to "win-the-war" appeals and those with anti-inflation interests; most of this new source of support depended upon the demagogic relationship, adherence to the President as a popular leader. This was, however, an unstable base upon which to administer the legislation. The program was viable only through constant efforts, primarily on the part of the administrators, to maintain some cohesion among supporting elements and by continual adjustments with organized interest groups whose dominance in the administering process was a constant possibility. The latter, in fact, rendered the program unadministerable when the cohesion of the supporting groups was ruptured by the ending of the war and by the death of the popular leader.[6]

Very similar developments have often occurred in connection with regulatory legislation of the more conventional sort. Thus when a spectacular failure on the stock market causes a discrediting of large-scale financial operators as a result of serious losses to small investors, a demagogic leadership is able to secure passage of regulatory laws. When the administrator takes over, however, the essentially unstable supporting element begins to lose such cohesion as it possessed, and the organized opposing groups are better able to achieve effective access. This access may be secured directly or may be gained via the legislative process of appropriation or restrictive amendment. Or the threat of amendments and appropriation cuts may be effective in enforcing policy changes upon the agency. Organized minority elements with access to key points in the legislature are thus in a position to make their claims felt in the administration of the act. It takes majorities to pass legislation, but, as we have seen elsewhere, a minority under our system may have sufficient nuisance value to affect executive policy. It is in such circumstances that one expects to find a rash of congressional investigations of administrative agencies or threats of such probes.

Under such circumstances the administrator cannot be guided solely by the formal grant of power in a statute or executive order. Even recourse to the legislative debates, hearings, and committee reports may not tell him what he can do, since the crucial relationships may no longer be those that the documents outline. The record may

[6] See Harvey C. Mansfield and associates: *A Short History of O P A* (Washington, D.C.: Government Printing Office, 1948), pp. 315–8 and *passim*.

describe the intent of the forces that effected passage of a measure, but it will be of little help to the administrator if those forces no longer command dominant strength. The administrator in such circumstances is in "politics" and cannot help it. Either he will find means of maintaining the strength of supporting groups, or he will have to accept some of the demands of the opposition elements. If he does neither, attacks upon his incompetent administration will mount, possibly aided by disillusioned segments of his previous supporters, and his position may become untenable. If he resigns or is eased out, his successor is likely to be a man who can represent more readily the new alignment of interest groups or at least recognize the differences that can exist between the balance of forces that produce a legislative enactment and the array of interests with which he is confronted.[7]

The administrator's position in controlling the access of competing interest groups is made the more difficult if the terms of his mandate from the legislature are highly ambiguous. As we noted in the closing paragraphs of Chapter 12, such ambiguities may be an inevitable product of conflict in the legislature. Where compromise in the legislative stage is the alternative to temporary failure and where the imperative to compromise is accepted by some participants as a means of avoiding the open frustration of expectations widely held in the community, the terms of legislative settlement are almost bound to be ambiguous. Such compromises are in the nature of postponements. The administrator is called upon to resolve the difficulties that were too thorny for the legislature to solve, and he must do so in the face of the very forces that were acting in the legislature, though their relative strength may have changed. Note that it is not the ambiguities in the law that make difficult the question of what groups shall have privileged access to an administrator. Almost all legislative declarations are ambiguous in part. It is rather the causes of the ambiguity that make the difference.[8] If the administrator holds out for an interpretation of these controverted ambiguous provisions that is not in itself a compromise, he invites the affected groups either to denounce his "dictatorial" methods and his "unscrupulous assumption of powers not granted to him" or to expose his "sell-out" of the "public interest."

Ambiguity, it should be added, need not be the outgrowth only of

[7] See Appleby: *Policy and Administration, passim;* Avery Leiserson: "Interest Groups in Administration," in Marx (ed.): *Elements of Public Administration,* pp. 315–6; Norton E. Long: "Power and Administration," *Public Administration Review,* Vol. 9, no. 4 (Autumn, 1949), pp. 257–64.

[8] Cf. Herring: *Public Administration and the Public Interest,* chaps. 7–13.

the political situation in the legislature. The quasi-legislative circumstances in which the chief executive finds himself may be productive of similar formulas. When the fledgling National Defense Mediation Board collapsed with the resignation of the C.I.O. members in November, 1941, Roosevelt came face to face with such a situation. The cause of the resignation had been the Mediation Board's refusal to grant a union shop arrangement to workers in the so-called "captive" coal mines. When Pearl Harbor made a means of wage stabilization economically and politically imperative, a conference of employers and union officials was called to work out an agreement. They deadlocked over the union shop, although agreement was reached on all other issues. The President "accepted" their recommendation that a War Labor Board should be created, and the executive order creating it made no mention of the touchy subject.[9] "The War Labor Board," as the administrative historians put it, "thus entered on its work without any clear instructions . . . from Congress or the President." It was only the War Labor Board's adoption of the compromise formula of the "maintenance of membership" clause that permitted the agency's survival, although the compromise itself was not unproductive of controversy.[10]

What the administrator is forced to seek is a means of converting the controversial into the routine. This conversion may be largely achieved, except in the kinds of situations noted above, by the legislative declaration. The administrator then inherits an adjustment among conflicting interests, a mandate, within the terms of which he must operate as long as the respective forces retain the relationships arrived at in the legislative stage. No question arises concerning what groups shall enjoy what measures of access to the administrative agency.[11]

The settlement of relative access to the determinations of an administrative agency, whether arrived at during or subsequent to the development of the legislative mandate, may not display the activities of organized interest groups in day-to-day administration. As relationships to the surrounding interests become routinized, the overt assertion of group claims may virtually disappear. New grants of power may be made by the legislature to expand the activity, and most

[9] Executive Order No. 9017, January 12, 1942, *Federal Register*, Vol. 7, p. 237.
[10] U.S. Bureau of the Budget: *The United States at War*, pp. 194–6. In a sense, of course, the President made a decision on the union security issue in his choice of "public" members of the board.
[11] Cf. Leiserson: *Administrative Regulation*, p. 14; Bentley: *The Process of Government*, pp. 293, 454.

decisions concerning it may be taken at a relatively low level in the agency structure. However, it is not accurate to conclude that because the work becomes routine the program has lost its political character, that is, its setting in an environment of organized and potential interest groups.[12]

Administrative operations under a mandate may lose their routine, accepted character in two kinds of circumstances. In the first place, a determination by even a comparatively unimportant official may violate the written and unwritten adjustments among the interests affected and invite a reopening of the whole issue. The normal procedure may be for such a decision to be appealed up the administrative hierarchy. Or circumstances may be such that the whole adjustment must be remade, through elections, parties, and legislature as well as the executive. A judge or a green policeman, for instance, may attempt the literal enforcement of ordinances against gambling. The previous extralegal adjustment may have tolerated gambling if carried on in limited areas. Vigorous enforcement may require a complete resettlement of the issue. Such a situation threatened to develop in some States in the 1930's when the Association of Railway Executives, acting largely through apparently innocent agents, prevailed upon many local enforcement officers to attempt a strict observance of the casually enforced laws concerning the overloading of highway trucks. Use of these laws as a competitive device upset the prevailing adjustment between the trucking companies and the police, threatening to bring into the open the issue of the relations between rail and truck transportation.[13]

The second circumstance that may upset the routinized relations between administrative agencies and interest groups is a change in the environment, technological, economic, or political, that alters the relative strength of affected groups in marked fashion. We have already pointed out, in Chapter 8, that such changes might make a sharp difference in the relative propaganda advantage of competing groups.[14] Environmental changes may improve or weaken other sources of strength as well as propaganda. Administrative determination and environmental changes, both of which may upset routine relations, may in fact be closely interdependent. Thus the administra-

[12] Paul Appleby: "The Influence of the Political Order," *American Political Science Review*, Vol. 42, no. 2 (April, 1948), pp. 272–83, and his *Policy and Administration*, pp. 10 ff.

[13] U.S. Senate, Committee on Interstate Commerce: *Report No. 26*, 77th Cong., 1st Sess. (1941), part 2, pp. 8–18.

[14] Cf. Fainsod: "Some Reflections on the Nature of the Regulatory Process," pp. 304–6.

tive determination that disturbs the equilibrium previously established among affected interests may be an effort to adjust the agency's group relations to changes in relative group strength without recourse to other points of decision in the executive, the legislature, or the electorate.

The possibility of disturbance to the established relationships and understandings that make up the routine activities of administration is never absent, although it is more likely in connection with newer governmental functions. The mandate of the legislature as interpreted in the process of administration, and as modified by court decisions, is never wholly stable. Even such apparently remote activities as those of technical research may become sufficiently controversial to disturb the setting of group relationships in which they are carried on. "Research policy is made in a political context." [15] Research too must reflect an established adjustment among group interests if it is to be carried on. Whether or not an administrative agency can do particular types of research is in part a reflection of the relative position of the group interests that impinge upon the agency. The investigation of such subjects as the comparative nutritive value of butter and oleomargarine,[16] systems of farm tenancy, methods of industrial pricing, grade labeling of consumer goods, rank-and-file attitudes toward interest-group claims, and the internal operation of labor unions invites controversy. The incautious initiation of studies in such areas, to say nothing of their publication, may, as easily as a change in rules and regulations, disrupt established patterns of access and invite the reinterpretation of the legislative mandate either by superiors in the administrative structure or by controlling elements in the legislature or by both.

The Influence of Office

It is all too easy in examining the kinds of relationships between groups and administrators to conclude that the difficulties encountered by the latter in arriving at stable patterns of interaction make

[15] Charles M. Hardin: "Political Influence and Agricultural Research," *American Political Science Review*, Vol. 41, no. 4 (August, 1947), p. 671. See also his "The Bureau of Agricultural Economics Under Fire: A Study in Valuation Conflicts," *Journal of Farm Economics*, Vol. 28, no. 3 (August, 1946), pp. 635–68. Cf. Gaus and Wolcott: *Public Administration and the United States Department of Agriculture*, pp. 50–1.

[16] See Wesley McCune: "The Oleomargarine Rebellion," *Harper's Magazine* (December, 1943), pp. 10–15.

them pawns of the dominant organized groups. Some of the more dramatic instances tend to support such an interpretation, and in certain cases it is certainly applicable. No responsible account of the governmental process, however, would generalize from such examples. Most allegations of that sort, as we have observed repeatedly, represent an author's participant role in the political process, his identification with, or "membership" in, certain allegedly disadvantaged groups, rather than a complete analysis of the elements at work. Such allegations have political significance, often of a very high order, but they are not diagnoses. There are many other elements, many other interests that modify and restrict the claims of organized clientele groups upon administrative agencies. Depending upon time and circumstances, the influence of these other factors may vary from the negligible to the very strong, but they cannot be ruled out on an *a priori* basis.

In discussing the variables affecting access to the legislature, in Chapter 11, we spoke of the legislator's acceptance of widely held expectations about the proper role of the elected lawmaker. We called this factor "the influence of office." The occupant of an executive position in the government is no less exposed to such expectations than is the legislative politician. He too has learned, before he entered upon his position, some of the expectations concerning his role, including such matters as "loyalty" to the chief executive; he too has entered his position through certain semi-ritualistic procedures, varying in formality with the prominence of his post, including commissioning, oath-taking, fingerprinting, and, more recently, investigation of his loyalty. All these mark his initiation to a new role with special claims upon him. His role also, depending upon its importance, is made up of behaviors that are required, others that are forbidden, and still others that are permissible.

We have seen that the administrative official is constantly attempting to move his activities from a level of controversy to one of acceptance or to maintain the routine character of his operations once they have developed to that point. The relationships that he establishes and maintains and the procedures he uses are not a separate and independent system. Partly because group access to the legislature is in varying degrees affected by the influence of legislative office, the mandate that the administrator receives, explicit or ambiguous, involves express and implied expectations concerning his official behavior in applying the statute. Some of these are purely technical, of course, such as the assumption that he will base his judgments on data that are as accurate as possible. Others, however, are much broader. They assume, for example, that his operations will be in keeping with the written and unwritten "rules of the game," that they will meet both legal and traditional standards of "fairness." They further assume that the activities of the administrative agency will fit into the established though ambiguous, partially conflicting, and gradually shifting understandings or traditions concerning the powers and procedures of the various levels and branches of government and of the institution as a whole.

The continuing characteristics of the government in any society are the product of a gradual evolution. This statement is fairly obvious. It is not so readily recognized, however, that the development and modification of these characteristics reflect the claims of interest groups, organized and unorganized, that have achieved access to the governmental process. The Constitution of 1787, including the first ten amendments, was not only a compromise product of the efforts of a collection of able men; it was also and more significantly the reflection of many demands and expectations concerning governing, some transitory and some lasting, some contemporary and some of ancient lineage, some held narrowly and some widely valued in the society. That many of the stipulations in that document are fully operative nearly two centuries later speaks for the skill with which they reflected certain of the strong and lasting interests in the society. Foremost among these provisions are those preventing arbitrary punishment and restrictions on speech and press. The persistence of some of the cumbersome and largely formal practices, moreover, testifies to the effectiveness of the principal features as a framework within which the adjustment of interests can take place. Successful operation may give even the more awkward provisions of a constitutional system a position of prestige.

The continuing characteristics of the institutions of government as certainly reflect interest groups today as they did to begin with. The strength of the broad general interests supporting the "rules of the game" varies, and the claims based upon them change from time to time as do the strength and the claims of other political interest groups. These persistent interests are not invariably dominant, and, although they are widely shared at any given point in time, they are not held universally throughout the society. These notions of fair play are represented largely by unorganized or potential groups; the generality of their acceptance is such that their claims do not require organized expression except when these notions are flagrantly violated or when they are in process of alteration. In a sense one may think of the principal governmental leaders—legislative, executive, and judicial—as the leaders of these unorganized groups. Part of the official's task is the regular representation of these potential groups in the actions of government. If officials fail to do this adequately, alternative leaders in or outside the government may attempt to organize a following and seek adequate expression of the interest either through the established processes or through violence. In Bentley's words: "When government, as the representative of the 'absent' or quiescent group interests, is distorted from this function to any noticeable extent by the concentrated pressures of smaller group interests, . . . we see the formation of a group interest directly aroused in opposition to the interests which have gained objectionable power." [17]

The broad general interests, whether organized or not, must have a measure of access to the determinations of an administrative agency. The survival of an administrative activity is as certainly dependent upon the adjustment of these as of the more narrowly supported interests that confront an agency in organized form. It does not follow that an administrator in making a decision consciously thinks of himself as a guardian of the constitutional understandings of the American people. Depending upon the nature of his position, he may or may not do so. The influence of these largely unorganized interests is normally of a more unconscious character, however. As Paul Appleby has said in describing the preparation of the budget in the closed hearings at the Bureau of the Budget: "It is not made in a public arena, but the public is somehow well represented. This is one of the most mystifying of governmental phenomena." [18] The influence of the widespread unorganized interests upon the highly routinized activities in which they and other impinging interests are not matters of controversy is likely to be completely unconscious. In more controversial situations the administrator knows that he can reject or modify the claims of more narrowly based but highly organized interest groups that clearly conflict with the demands of office. This he can do as long as he has direct or indirect means of reaching and arousing the threatened interests. Various means of communication may serve him, or he may derive support from other elements in the government itself, including the courts, the legislature, and other officials in the administrative hierarchy. Whether he relies upon propa-

[17] Bentley: *The Process of Government*, pp. 454–5. Copyright 1908 by and used with the permission of Arthur F. Bentley.
[18] Appleby: "The Influence of the Political Order," p. 281.

ganda means or upon superiors in the governmental structure will depend upon his position, upon his skills, and upon the strength and cohesion of the opposing interests.

Recruitment and the Administrator's Group Memberships

When the claims of organized interest groups and the demands of office are not in obvious opposition or when the conflict is primarily between two opposing organized groups, privileged access to the administrative agency is not merely a result of the relative strength of the opposing groups but is also a reflection of the administrator's group memberships. One of these is the agency of which he is a part. Agency membership is an important affiliation, but it is not the only one. We shall defer discussion of it until later. Here we may observe that the notion of the administrator as a neutralized public servant without conflicting motivations is an illusion. This view most closely approximates reality in times and places in which administration is almost completely routinized and the deliberate adjustment of interests is not of major concern. The public official "is not a blank sheet of paper on which the organization can write what it wills."[19] As a human being he comes to his position with group affiliations and preferences, and he forms additional ones during his tenure.

These "memberships," like those of the legislator, need not be formal. They may be relationships of the "fellow-traveler" variety, yet be none the less influential. The hostility of General DeWitt, commanding general of the army forces on the West Coast at the time of Pearl Harbor, toward persons of Japanese extraction was of crucial importance in the effectiveness in 1942 of the campaign for the compulsory evacuation from that area of all Japanese nationals and Americans of Japanese ancestry.[20] Presumably it was the recognition of this kind of factor that induced a congressional majority in 1943 to insert in the act appropriating money for the Office of Price Administration a proviso that officials determining policies and prices must have had at least five years of responsible "business" experience. This "antiprofessor" clause assumed that those who had "met a pay-

---

[19] Simon, Smithburg, and Thompson: *Public Administration*, p. 78.
[20] Morton Grodzins: *Americans Betrayed: Politics and the Japanese Evacuation* (Chicago: University of Chicago Press, 1949), pp. 297–8, 362, and *passim*.

roll" would be more sympathetic than academic economists toward the claims of regulated groups.

The sources from which administrative personnel are recruited, particularly those officials exercising discretionary authority, thus have a bearing upon the question of differential access. We have already seen the importance that organized interest groups attach to the recruitment of officials at the cabinet level. In the lower echelons the impersonal procedures of the civil service system have largely eliminated overt influences of this sort. Even within the civil service system of recruitment, however, nonpolitical selective factors often determine the kinds of "memberships" that will be found in particular agencies. Observers can include in the "farm bloc" many of the officials in the Department of Agriculture, along with members of Congress and groups such as the Farm Bureau, because some of the group "memberships" of the two are identical. The Farm Bureau does not necessarily place its people in the department, although it may provide the men for some of the high-ranking posts. Selective recruitment most frequently works more subtly. In the Department of Agriculture, for example, a high proportion of the administrators share the rural background of the organized farm groups and their "members" in Congress. They have in many cases been trained in the land-grant colleges of agriculture, a powerful interest group within the department's clientele, and some have been drawn from, or anticipate moving to, the staffs of these institutions. For the man trained in agricultural economics, soil chemistry, agronomy, animal husbandry, or some similar specialty, the activities of the department offer a highly attractive career. As administrators such individuals are likely to share many of the unspecified assumptions of the organized farm groups that come before them and are likely to be more sympathetic to specific claims from such groups than persons recruited from different sources.[21]

In some agencies the formal memberships of officials have an important effect upon the relative access of groups. It is highly probable, for example, that the well-established influence of the American Legion in the Veterans Administration stems in part from the number of Legion members in key posts within the V.A. Such recruitment may be a matter of deliberate policy, especially in agencies created during emergencies. These agencies usually need not only to recruit staffs immediately conversant with technicalities involved in the new function but also to secure the immediate co-operation of various in-

[21] Cf. Gaus and Wolcott: *Public Administration and the United States Department of Agriculture*, pp. 16–17.

terest groups. During the depression emergency of the 1930's and in World War II, recruitment from affected groups was a common practice. It was formally established in the structure of the short-lived National Recovery Administration. During World War II most war agencies did not use trade associations and similar bodies directly as a means of mobilization, but recruitment from the ranks of corporations and related groups was general. Two such agencies, however, the Office of Defense Transportation and the Petroleum Administration for War, for all practical purposes incorporated the respective industry organizations into the government and relied upon them to administer those segments of the economy.[22]

Policy-determining administrative boards and commissions are often staffed with an eye to the group memberships of the appointees. As we noted in Chapter 13, this policy may be a matter of statutory requirements that more or less severely restrict selections to the members of particular interest groups.[23] More often it is a reflection of group access to the appointing authority. For example, one of the members of the Tariff Commission from 1921 through 1925, a period during most of which this body had the authority to adjust import duties, was a man who both before and after his term on the commission was an official of the United States Potters' Association. He had also been employed by other interest groups, such as the wool growers, which were notably reluctant to have their high protective duties lowered.[24]

In their effect upon the access of interest groups, some of the most important "memberships" of administrative officials are those in professional and skill groups. Partly because the American public administrator, even in the Federal service, often is not certain that he can pursue an entire career in government employment, he is likely to maintain his connections with groups in his occupational field, groups that include persons in private as well as public employment. Or where a measure of continuity and professionalism in a public employment has developed, associations of public officials have grown up. Among these are such groups as those formed by the public school teachers (notably the National Education Association), the Association of Official Agricultural Chemists, the National Associa-

[22] U.S. Bureau of the Budget: *The United States at War*, pp. 127, 158–9, 284 ff.

[23] Leiserson: *Administrative Regulation*, chap. 4.

[24] *Senate Report 43*, part 2, *Congressional Record*, 71st Cong., 1st Sess., November 11, 1929, p. 5394. Cf. Herring: *Public Administration and the Public Interest*, chap. 6.

tion of Marketing Officials, the International City Managers Association, and many others.[25]

The significance of such group memberships is varied. Excepting those situations in which the official is charged with the regulation of the professional group, however, they reflect claims upon the public official that may be in competition with those of groups directly affected by the agency's activities. In this sense professional memberships tend to operate in a fashion similar to that of the influence of office. As Gaus and Wolcott observed the effect of such affiliations in the Department of Agriculture: "One important influence on the work of the public official. . . is his desire to stand well professionally under the scrutiny of his colleagues in terms of professional standards and of his contribution to the subject generally." [26]

The competitive claims of professionalism may not always expand the official's horizons, however. An organized group of officials may be the means of protecting indirectly the access of other interest groups by acting to prevent any reduction in the powers and perquisites of its members. Or, operating as an employee association, it may be concerned primarily with effecting claims for more generous remuneration and improved working conditions. Even under these circumstances, however, it still may have an important effect upon access. Where clientele groups have been able to achieve advantages in access by holding out the prospects of eventual employment at 'better salaries in groups outside the government, gains in pay and working conditions, from whatever source they derive, may strengthen the detachment of the public employee.[27]

Identification with the Administrative Unit

Membership in the legislature, as we pointed out in Chapter 11, tends to set a man somewhat apart from others who have not had that

[25] U.S. Department of Commerce: *National Associations of the United States*, p. 561, indicates that there were about 75 national organizations composed wholly or in large measure of governmental officials. Public Administration Clearing House: *Public Administration Organizations: A Directory* (Chicago, 1948) lists 566 organizations, of which 130 are made up of public officials.

[26] Gaus and Wolcott: *Public Administration and the United States Department of Agriculture*, p. 392. Copyright 1940 by and used with the permission of Public Administration Service. Cf. Fritz Morstein Marx: "Administrative Ethics and the Rule of Law," *American Political Science Review*, Vol. 43, no. 6 (December, 1949), pp. 1119-44.

[27] Herring: *Public Administration and the Public Interest*, pp. 61 ff. and 221, discusses cases of this sort in the Bureau of Internal Revenue.

experience and to expose him to competing claims from the legislative group, claims supplementing the influence of expectations concerning public office. Essentially the same phenomenon may occur in an administrative agency.[28] Any reasonably stable and continuing executive unit constitutes such a group, or is composed of a galaxy of such groups, as a condition of survival. These, like other groups, exact a measure of conformity as the price of acceptance. Any person entering such an organization, at whatever level, is more or less subject to its claims if he wishes to "belong" to it or to lead it. Once accepted, he comes to identify the goals and claims of the unit as in some degree his own. Among those claims may be a body of unwritten rules defining the proper way of handling the claims of various groups outside the unit. Identification with an agency and its goals can be a regulator of access.

No experience in Washington during World War II was more amusing or more predictable than that of the businessman who joined the staff of the War Production Board or the Office of Price Administration breathing fire against the "bureaucrats" and their creations. If he stayed for any length of time he often found himself defending the agency or his part of it against critics, resisting demands from outside sources with a vigor he had but lately denounced, and explaining to his friends in the business world that he had not "sold out" and that they did not understand what the agency was up against.

Such changed behavior is partly the result of joining and being accepted by a new group. But transformations of this sort are not devoid of positive content. The administrative unit is not separated from claimant groups simply by the more frequent interactions occurring within the agency. Basic to these interactions is a kind of experience different from that of persons belonging to "outside" groups. This experience involves a different kind of problem, including relationships in the hierarchy, with the courts, and with budget and personnel agencies; it may involve different skills, broader bodies of data, and new frames of reference. Such experiences provide in part the means of controlling the access of political interest groups and of modifying their claims. It is this aspect of identification with an agency to which Gaus and Wolcott refer when they speak in the

---

[28] Simon, Smithburg, and Thompson: *Public Administration*, use essentially this notion as one of their organizing concepts. See especially chaps. 3–5 and the literature there cited, including Roethlisberger and Dickson: *Management and the Worker*, and Chester I. Barnard: *The Functions of the Executive* (Cambridge, Mass.: Harvard University Press, 1938).

course of their study of the United States Department of Agriculture of observing "the influence that the analysis of concrete problems has upon the participants." It was their conclusion that "there is a logic inherent in the facts that breaks down the subjective views of those entering upon inquiry, whether the problem be one of land use in the Plains, or the marketing of a commodity, or the relation of farm to other forms of credit." [29]

In the continuing agency these specialized experiences are often productive of insights into the problems of the subject-matter area with which the unit is concerned, and these insights are likely to emerge in plans for new kinds of governmental action that may or may not require legislative approval. As we noted in our discussion of propaganda advantages in Chapter 8, such plans may remain in the proposal stage until a crisis or a change of Administration or both create a political situation in which support for the plans can be secured. Appleby refers to such a facilitating situation when he observes: "A liberal administration . . . gives more room to imagination, boldness and ingenuity than does a conservative administration. It tends to give principal attention to movement toward objectives newly seen. The conservative administration tends to give principal attention to the support of objectives long familiar." [30] Whether an administrative agency's proposals are immediately put into effect or not, however, the fact of their development testifies to the proposition that the group existence of an executive unit may permit it to impose positive controls on the access of interest groups. The emergence of such proposals illustrates and in part explains the important fact that an administrative body is not necessarily a passive transmitter of interest group claims.

We noted at the beginning of our discussion of the executive branch (Chapter 13) that a by-product of the discretionary power born of technical complexity is the tendency for the executive to initiate innovations and modifications in the statutes. The specialized experience of the administrator is basic to this initiative. It is commonly the immediate source of proposals. Where technical competence is combined with the skillful adjustment of claimant interests or is encouraged by a favorable political context, the executive agency finds itself in a position to exercise genuine political leadership. John

[29] Gaus and Wolcott: *Public Administration and the United States Department of Agriculture*, p. 285. Copyright 1940 by and used with the permission of Public Administration Service.

[30] Appleby: *Policy and Administration*, p. 129. Copyright 1949 by and used with the permission of University of Alabama Press.

Gaus succinctly states the elements in the role as follows: "Authority . . . follows the successful exercise of function; the rôle of the administrator is to achieve a reconciliation of the interests involved, and requires the winning of consent by the accumulation of exact and relevant knowledge."[31] Policy initiation by the administrative agency, whether it is the State Department, the Bureau of Animal Industry, or the Public Health Service, is a function of technical specialization combined with effective reconciliation of group claims. It both depends upon and springs from the factors that give the administrative unit its existence as a group.

Where the leadership of the administrative unit has been well established, interest groups may be placed in the position of petitioners rather than claimants. Evidence of this kind of relationship is available, if not abundant. For example, in 1935 President Roosevelt asked the Federal Trade Commission to give him its opinion on the desirability of enacting resale price maintenance legislation along the lines of the Tydings-Miller bill that had recently been introduced into the Congress. Even after an adverse reply had been forwarded to the President and by him to the Congress, the National Association of Retail Druggists made strenuous efforts through various State governors to get the Commission to change its recommendation.[32] The leadership position of executive agencies is further suggested by the congressional committee practice of referring to them for comment bills relevant to their activities. Although these comments are not necessarily followed by the legislators, they are governing in enough cases to make organized groups try to persuade the agency to take the positions the groups desire.

Groups within an executive agency may or may not coincide with the formal organizational units. Moreover, identification with the unit may not extend very vigorously beyond the particular bureau or division. Almost any executive employee will think of himself to some extent, however, as a part of a large department of the executive branch, and of the government of the United States. Skillful political leadership by the chief executive can strengthen these broader loyalties, as can programs of in-service training, promotion policies,

[31] John M. Gaus: "The Responsibility of Public Administration," in Gaus, White, and Dimock: *The Frontiers of Public Administration*, p. 39. Cf. Lane Lancaster: "Private Associations and Public Administration," *Social Forces*, Vol. 13, no. 2 (December, 1934), pp. 283–91, and Mary Parker Follett: *Creative Experience* (New York: Longmans, Green & Company, 1924).

[32] U.S. Federal Trade Commission: *Report on Resale Price Maintenance*, pp. 63–4.

and the like. These are possibilities, however, not certainties. Where loyalties to the smaller and the more inclusive organizations are in conflict, it is by no means certain that the latter will prevail. The situation then is essentially one of overlapping membership, in which the outcome of conflict is uncertain.

It follows that identification with the administrative unit may serve to rigidify established lines of access at the same time that it gives the agency something more than a passive role in policy. Reinforced by statutes, legislative committee practices, and organized group claims, loyalty to the unit may strengthen the agency "independence" discussed in Chapter 13. Where the unit needs the prestige and influence that an administrative superior's status may provide, it may not seek "independence." But if the prestige of the subordinate unit is at least equal to that of the nominal superior, "independence" may be considerable.[33] The point is well illustrated by a story, current in Washington some years ago, about a probably apocryphal incident concerning the Department of Justice and the F.B.I., which some people know is a part of that department. During a period when all Federal employees were required to show identification badges in order to be admitted to government buildings, the Attorney General, arriving at the Department of Justice building on a Sunday, was embarrassed to discover that he had failed to bring along his identification badge and could not produce it for the building guard, who refused him admittance. Commending the man for his efficiency, the Attorney General explained his identity and indicated that an exception might be made in this instance. The guard replied: "I don't care if you are J. Edgar Hoover himself, you can't get into this building without a badge."

Formal Devices for Group Adjustment

As earlier sections of this discussion have suggested, administrative operations may call into being a variety of more or less formalized means through which access to administrators' decisions may be controlled either from within the agency or from without. We shall examine briefly the implications of some of these under three general headings: (1) advisory committees, (2) administration by interest groups, and (3) propaganda by administrative agencies.

[33] The problems of conflicting loyalties within a large organization are well discussed in Simon, Smithburg, and Thompson: *Public Administration*, pp. 96–102.

Basically the creation of advisory committees marks a recognition of those "rules of the game" in the United States that prescribe that individuals and groups likely to be affected should be consulted before governmental action is taken. Such consultation is in most cases a prerequisite to the action's being accepted as "fair." It is an acknowledged part of our jurisprudence, and the courts have been exceedingly reluctant to sustain administrative actions that do not provide interested parties with proper notice and an opportunity to be heard. Not only is the requirement of consultation likely to be more or less automatically observed by administrative agencies in order to maximize support; the obligation is frequently explicitly written into particular authorizing statutes or into laws of general application, such as the Administrative Procedures Act of 1946. The latter, partly in consequence of the prestige of judicial processes and the judicialization of such bodies as the Interstate Commerce Commission, extends many of the requirements of traditional court procedure to the actions of administrative agencies.[34]

Formal consultative arrangements and provisions for advisory committees have been written into a great many statutes, and a great many more advisory bodies have been established by order of agency executives. During World War II both the Office of Price Administration and the War Production Board, the former partly under legal requirement and the latter entirely by administrative action, were dotted with industry and labor advisory committees. When the Congress established the Office of War Mobilization and Reconversion in 1944, it provided for an advisory board of twelve members, three each from business, agriculture, labor, and the "general public."[35]

It is difficult to generalize about so protean a device as the advisory committee. Where the initiative for the establishment of such units is taken by the agency, however, it is likely that the basic purpose is to facilitate acceptance of the agency's actions by the groups repre-

[34] See George Warren, editor: *The Federal Administrative Procedure Act and the Administrative Agencies* (New York: New York University Law School, 1947); Frederick F. Blachly and Miriam E. Oatman: "Sabotage of the Administrative Process," *Public Administration Review*, Vol. 6, no. 3 (Summer, 1946), pp. 213–27; Walter Gellhorn: *Federal Administrative Proceedings* (Baltimore: The Johns Hopkins Press, 1941).

[35] See Carl H. Monsees: *Industry-Government Cooperation: A Study of the Participation of Advisory Committees in Public Administration* (Washington, D.C.: Public Affairs Press, 1944); Edythe W. First: *Industry and Labor Advisory Committees in the National Defense Advisory Commission and the Office of Production Management* (Washington, D.C.: Civilian Production Administration, Special Study No. 24, 1946); Somers: *Presidential Agency*, pp. 102–8; Leiserson: *Administrative Regulation*, chap. 6.

sented on such bodies. In some instances the creation of advisory committees represents a granting of the forms of influence without much in the way of substance. Such lack of power has normally been a feature of "consumers" advisory committees and it characterized many of the labor advisory systems in the World War II emergency agencies.[36] In such circumstances the advisory committee may perform only the kind of safety-valve function earlier ascribed to the public hearing before legislative committees. In other instances the device can be a means of injecting the technical knowledge of the represented groups into the process of administrative policy determination. More important, it can identify probable lines of opposition. It can minimize hostility both by modification of the projected policy and by placing groups under some obligation to defend or at least not to oppose policies that they have had some share in setting. Finally, under skillful leadership the advisory committee can be a means of inducing the represented groups to run interference for the agency both in the legislature and with the remainder of its public. In short, the device is one for "keeping administration out of politics" by formalizing access and by restricting the area of controversy.

Where the advisory committee is established by law, as was the advisory board in the Office of War Mobilization and Reconversion, the intent may be similar to that discussed in the preceding paragraph. But in many cases the intent, if not the result, is to guarantee privileged access for the interests represented. The more restrictions are placed upon the appointing official's selections, the firmer the guarantee. In some instances this assurance may come close to giving the represented groups a controlling veto over agency policies. Such apparently was the purpose of the advisory committee provisions of the 1947 Hope-Flannagan Act to develop agricultural research. These went far toward making administration of the act independent of all influences except those of the interest groups on the committee.[37]

When considerable discretionary authority is given to an administrative agency working in a new field of the kind entered by agencies created in war and depression emergencies, advisory committees established by law or by executive action may be demanded by less strongly established groups to protect their claims. Such demands partly explain the creation of the system of labor advisory committees in various of the emergency agencies of World War II. These demands were also influential in the creation of the advisory board in

[36] See, for example, Persia Campbell: *Consumer Representation in the New Deal* (New York: Columbia University Press, 1940).

[37] Hardin: "Political Influence and Agricultural Research," pp. 671, 673–4.

the Office of War Mobilization and Reconversion, for when its predecessor, the Office of War Mobilization, had been set up by executive order in 1943, it had been seriously criticized by some labor groups because it lacked such an advisory body. Sometimes, furthermore, a group's insistence on being granted advisory status may be defensive in a larger sense. By becoming identified with the handling of critical national problems a group may gain prestige and propaganda advantage, as the war-time advertising of many industrial organizations indicates. Such identification may be sought by labor groups and others whose status is not secure in order to protect or improve their positions. For this prestige is virtually the only advantage the group gains from identification if, as in the O.W.M.R. advisory board, it is given no real opportunity to participate in determining agency policies.[38]

If the establishment of an advisory committee, whether by law or by executive act, restricts effective access to designated groups, the agency's freedom of action may be sharply reduced. The only way for the administrator to avoid this outcome in a controversial situation is to limit the committee to a purely nominal role. If he succeeds in doing so, however, the groups represented on the committee are less likely to feel committed to the policies for which support is needed. This dilemma is inherent in the use of the advisory committee in any controversial sphere. If the advisory committee is to facilitate acceptance of an agency's action, the key groups must be represented by high officers or representatives selected by them; the group officers, to retain influence in their groups, are likely to be insistent upon the claims of their constituencies.[39] On the other hand, where an agency is operating in areas of no great controversy and where the internal politics of a group permit, representatives on an advisory committee may develop a real "membership" in the agency group which overlaps with that in the interest group. In case of conflict the former may not be entirely rejected. If interest-group claims are strongly pressed, however, the agency may not be able to keep the committee in a peripheral position. Such was the experience of the War Manpower Commission in World War II with its Management-Labor Policy Committee. The committee effectively "supplanted the Commission itself as the main forum for policy discussions." During the 1942 controversy between Commission Chairman Paul McNutt and the committee in connection with proposed national service legislation,

---

[38] Somers: *Presidential Agency*, pp. 102–8.
[39] Ibid., p. 104. On this general point see also Philip M. Selznick: *TVA and the Grass Roots* (Berkeley, Calif.: University of California Press, 1949).

McNutt acted without the committee's advice and informed its members that they had no legal standing that entitled them to consultation except at the chairman's option. The labor members of the committee forced the inclusion of a provision in a later executive order on the Commission requiring the chairman to consult with the committee before taking any action.[40]

For the well-established group with effective access to a chief executive or to the legislature, the advisory committee and similar devices of consultation may be more a handicap than an advantage. If the committee serves its function of facilitating acceptance of agency policies, the result may be an embarrassing restriction on the group's freedom of action and upon its leaders' political position within the group. Especially when a committee includes several more or less competing interest groups, the minority may be almost obliged to support a policy that they have opposed in committee deliberations. For this reason the more aggressive groups are likely to prefer committees made up of relatively homogeneous elements in which they are less likely to find themselves in the awkward minority position. A unified committee can dissociate itself from an unwelcome agency decision and preserve the constituent groups' freedom to criticize.[41] Privileged access may then be preserved at a relatively low cost in maneuverability.

The significance of administration by interest groups as a channel of access is primarily a function of the number and conflicting character of the groups carrying on the particular activity. Where two or more conflicting groups share responsibility for decisions, the pattern differs only in degree from some of those occurring under the advisory committee device.

Outstanding instances of multiple-group administration are the tripartite industrial disputes boards that operated during World War II, the National Defense Mediation Board and the National War Labor Board. These were roughly identical in form, with equal representation from management groups, labor groups, and "the public." Their operations are a most instructive example of multiple memberships in more or less continual conflict. Only the "public" members were in a position to identify completely with the agency or to feel predominant attachment to the expectations concerning their role. The labor and management members experienced continual conflict between such loyalties and those to the interest groups from which they were

[40] U.S. Bureau of the Budget: *The United States at War*, pp. 187–9.
[41] Cf. Leiserson: *Administrative Regulation*, p. 158; Simon, Smithburg, and Thompson: *Public Administration*, pp. 464–5.

drawn. The strength of the latter in many cases stemmed from the representatives' connections with the internal politics of their groups as well as from the frames of reference they tended themselves to adopt in approaching labor disputes. The function of the "public" members was to strengthen the claims of membership in the agency upon the other two participant elements (more than two where the A.F. of L. and C.I.O. spokesmen were also in conflict). At the same time there had to emerge a settlement that would meet the issues at hand and be reconcilable with the participants' positions in their interest groups. When the National Defense Mediation Board failed to do this in 1941 and the C.I.O. members resigned, the board ceased to operate. Its successor, as we noted earlier in the chapter, had a more fortunate but no less precarious existence. One group representative or another had regularly to tolerate and defend a decision with which his group disagreed. It was always possible that someone would refuse to go along. The tripartite formula both reflected and perpetuated the unsettled, controversial issues that the agency was charged with handling.[42]

Where one homogeneous interest group is directly or indirectly charged with the administration of a function, we have the kind of situation that characterizes the occupational licensing boards and similar "independent" agencies that we discussed in Chapter 13. Arrangements of this sort have become increasingly familiar in regulatory statutes at all levels of government. At the national level these include not only the National Industrial Recovery Act and the Agricultural Adjustment Acts, but also the Bituminous Coal Acts of 1935 and 1937, the Taylor Grazing Act of 1934, and the Agricultural Marketing Agreement Act of 1937.[43]

The essential feature of all such arrangements for administration by a single group is the more or less complete control of administrative action through the delegation of governmental power, especially rule-making power, to the organized interest group. In most such cases the groups are enabled to do more effectively under legislative sanction what they would attempt to do directly without the aid of

[42] See U.S. Bureau of the Budget: *The United States at War*, pp. 190–202. Cf. Leiserson: *Administrative Regulation*, pp. 130–2; James M. Burns: "Maintenance of Membership: A Study in Administrative Statesmanship," *Journal of Politics*, Vol. 10, no. 1 (February, 1947), pp. 101–16.

[43] Leiserson: *Administrative Regulation*, chaps. 7–9, discusses a number of these cases. For a review of the legal aspects see Louis L. Jaffe: "Law-Making by Private Groups," *Harvard Law Review*, Vol. 51, no. 2 (December, 1937), pp. 210–53.

legal authority. Because the restrictions on such delegation are largely formal, the groups' access is complete so long as the administrative practices do not so violate the "rules of the game" or so activate competing interests of other sorts as to force a change in the arrangements or in the policies pursued. These alterations may occur, however, through the activities of interests and agencies charged with carrying on functions with which a group-administered agency conflicts.

The Petroleum Administration for War was a group-administered agency in World War II, as we have noted before. Despite formalities, its essential characteristic was that it governmentalized the petroleum industry, or one might say that it oiled one segment of the government, for the duration. Both the P.A.W.'s survival as an agency and the cohesion of the oil industry organization required that war policies should make as little change as possible in the *status quo ante bellum* of competitive relations in the petroleum industry. When this merely involved provision for each major refining company to come out of the war with a modern catalytic cracking plant partially subsidized by favorable war-time depreciation allowances, little difficulty occurred. When the protection of prewar distribution patterns conflicted with rationed demand for fuel oil and gasoline in various parts of the country, so that unnecessary shortages occurred on the East Coast, the P.A.W. ran into trouble. Prolonged conflicts between it and the Office of Price Administration and the Office of Defense Transportation, backed by consumers of petroleum products in the East, forced some modifications in P.A.W. policies.[44] To some extent the survival of even a group-administered function depends upon the stability of the political context and the group's sensitivity to claims stemming from other sources, including the overlapping affiliations of its own members.

When we speak of administrative propaganda as a third formal device for group adjustment we are using the term in the same neutral sense in which we employed it in Chapter 8: it signifies a process of communication and not the merits of the content. As a device for controlling access to administrative decisions it functions by enlarging the public for the policies favored by the agency and consolidating the segments of the public that will support those policies. Especially where there is at stake not only an administrative policy but even the survival of the particular administrative activity, administrative

[44] U.S. Bureau of the Budget: *The United States at War*, p. 392; Paul M. O'Leary: "Wartime Rationing and Governmental Organization," *American Political Science Review*, Vol. 39, no. 6 (December, 1945), pp. 1089–1106, esp. 1095–8.

propaganda aims at influencing access to the legislature as well. In effect it is a means of protecting the access of one set of interests and restricting that of others by altering their relative strengths. The interests represented in such propaganda may be unorganized, or potential, groups—those reflected in the "rules of the game" or in the widespread expectations concerning the role of public officials—or they may be organized interest groups whose claims are expressed in existing or proposed legislation. Finally, the propaganda may be designed to perpetuate the acceptance of the agency's operations as "routine," to include proposed legislative authorizations in that bland category, or to reduce the hazards involved in currently controversial functions.[45]

An administrative agency charged with a highly ambiguous mandate, especially a mandate that has been enacted under the "demagogic" leadership of largely unorganized interests, is almost forced to use propaganda in order to control access to its decisions. If a stable adjustment of interests has not been reached at the legislative stage, the administrator must attempt to establish one by such means as he can. The prime example of this kind of problem in recent years is the Office of Price Administration, concerning which "the most obvious fact" is that "very little was ever done by the office without controversy." [46] Organized group support for price-control legislation and for the agency's policies was slight and precarious. The necessity for propaganda activities is well described by Mansfield:

> The major obstacle from the beginning was that OPA sprang not from the grass roots but from Washington, and that in its immediate impacts on the influential segments of the population it brought restraints on natural impulses. The benefits it promised were not so directly visible. . . .
> The momentous statutes enacted in peacetime during the past two generations which impose restraints . . . had a different origin. Popular agitation ultimately brought governmental action, but only after years of activity and debate, after elections which tested the popular response to campaigning, after periods of reaction and renewed demands. On such foundations a broad

---

[45] On this whole subject see James L. McCamy: *Government Publicity: Its Practice in Federal Administration* (Chicago: University of Chicago Press, 1939). Cf. Harold W. Stoke: "Executive Leadership and the Growth of Propaganda," *American Political Science Review*, Vol. 35, no. 3 (June, 1941), pp. 490–500.

[46] Mansfield: *A Short History of O P A*, p. 8.

basis of consent and understanding is built even though the decisive legislative struggles are sharp; . . .

OPA was not born that way. Its statutes and its regulations on specific commodities were law, not in answer to popular insistence, but because economists—worse yet, Government economists primarily—saw grave trouble ahead for the Nation and convinced the President and Congress that swift action according to their prescription was needed to ward off that trouble. . . . The decision was taken in the main on the Government's initiative and responsibility, with the people in an acquiescent rather than a demanding mood. *To say that such an undertaking required the fullest practicable explanation as it proceeded was to state the case mildly.*[47] (Italics added.)

The O.P.A.'s problem was exceptional only in degree. Its propaganda activity on behalf of legislation and administrative policy is duplicated in kind by all but the most routinized administrative activities, and by many of those.

From time to time Congress has imposed statutory restrictions upon administrative propaganda. The first of these restrictions was enacted in 1913 as the result of a particularly candid announcement of the specifications for a position as "publicity expert" in the Office of Public Roads. The agency indicated that it wanted a man who was, among other things, someone "whose affiliations with newspaper publishers and writers is extensive enough to insure the publication of items prepared by him."[48] The subsequent statute prohibited the hiring of a "publicity expert" by any government agency without specific authorization.[49] A 1919 law forbade the use of appropriated funds, unless congressional authorization had been given, for any "personal service" or "device" to influence the votes of members of Congress.[50] Restrictions similar to these have been placed in various statutes of general and particular application. It need hardly be said that the spirit if not the letter of these restrictions has been observed largely in the breach—partly, it is true, because of technical problems of enforcement.

Debates on the floor of Congress and committee hearings frequently resound with charges of administrative propaganda and

[47] Ibid., pp. 298-9. Chapter 10 of this volume discusses the O.P.A.'s "public relations" problems in most effective terms.
[48] Quoted in Key: *Politics, Parties, and Pressure Groups*, p. 714. Chapter 23 of this volume discusses various aspects of the problem.
[49] 38 U.S. Stat. at L. (1913) 212; 5 U.S. Code 54.
[50] 41 U.S. Stat. at L. (1919) 68; 18 U.S. Code 1913.

"lobbying." Congressional investigations of various executive agencies have heard testimony on the charge, and some full-scale investigations have appeared to address themselves to the subject in general.[51]

The significance of congressional restrictions on administrative propaganda is the product of three more or less interdependent factors. In the first place, such limitations may partly reflect those unorganized interests that support the "rules of the game," which keep propaganda methods within tolerable limits. The legislation is directed against blatant activities going beyond the behaviors expected of executive agencies. In the second place, the restrictions may derive in part from the claims of the legislative group itself. These are often described as congressional "jealousy" of the executive or as a defense of the Constitution's grant of "the legislative power" to the Congress. While such motives may be verbally important, more fundamentally these restrictions upon administrators reflect the basic political position of senators and representatives, regardless of party or group affiliations. If, as we have had occasion to observe in several other connections, the legislator is obliged by the party and constitutional system to be, for the most part, an independent political entrepreneur, he is unlikely to look with complacency upon activities from other branches of the government that tend to alter political relationships within his constituency through channels that are not subject to his influence. The situation might be somewhat different if his reelection depended primarily upon a disciplined national party organization that also could control such propaganda. Under prevailing arrangements, however, legislators as a group are likely to be extremely sensitive about executive efforts that may affect the balance of power within their constituencies.

The third and probably most important aspect of legislative restrictions upon administrative propaganda is that these are a means of interest-group attack and defense. The usual demand for the enforcement or amendment of such legislation is aimed at particular administrative units, not at the entire executive branch. These demands, often duplicated by organized groups, have as their objective the restriction of the strength and access of groups supporting the particular executive activity and maximizing the advantages of those who oppose it. In this respect the insistent legislator is acting on the basis of

[51] For example, see U.S. House of Representatives, Committee on Expenditures in the Executive Departments, Subcommittee on Publicity and Propaganda: Hearings, 80th Cong., 1st and 2d Sess. (1947–1948); U.S. House of Representatives, Select Committee on Lobbying Activities: Hearings, 81st Cong., 2d Sess. (1950), esp. part 1, pp. 127–63.

his "membership" in the opposition interest group. Congressional investigations of propaganda and "lobbying" by administrative agencies are similar to general "lobby" investigations, for they have as their targets specific groups or functions and not a general phenomenon. Within the limits of the "rules of the game", administrative propaganda is objected to when it is carried on in support of interests and functions of which the critical legislators and associated groups disapprove. Otherwise it is "information" disseminated by "responsible administrators" for the "benefit of the people." It was no accident that in 1950 some members of the House Select Committee on Lobbying Activities criticized the speeches and pronouncements of the Federal Security Administrator on behalf of compulsory health insurance legislation.[52] Groups opposed to the project had accused him of improper "propaganda" for some time. Investigation by the committee was but an extension of that activity. The doubtful constitutionality of any legislative effort to restrict such activities by the President's immediate subordinates was beside the point. Such charges are a form of counterpropaganda.

The Inflexibility of the Established Web

As the result of a composite of the influences discussed in this and the preceding chapters, an administrative agency that survives the vicissitudes of the political process develops a set of relationships—among its own staff, within the executive branch, with the legislature, and with organized interest groups—that are in a state of fairly stable equilibrium. The existence of such a standardized pattern of interactions is a condition of the unit's survival and of its movement from the area of controversy to that of routine. Through such devices as they can command, administrators will, as we have seen, attempt to stabilize these relationships, including efforts to promote the strength and cohesiveness of supporting interest groups.[53] Its established and stabilized relationships are the distinguishing features of what the Washington jargon designates as the "old-line" agency, whether department, bureau, or division.

As with any institutionalized pattern, the stabilized relationships of

---

[52] The *New York Herald Tribune*, July 29, 1950.

[53] For illustrations of the situations produced by lack of cohesion among important supporting groups see John P. Comer: *Legislative Functions of National Administrative Authorities* (New York: Columbia University Press, 1927), chap. 8.

an administrative agency are highly resistant to disturbance. They are an adequate vehicle for change as long as the alterations follow the established lines. New and expanded functions are easily accommodated, provided they develop and operate through existing channels of influence and do not tend to alter the relative importance of those influences. Disturbing changes are those that modify either the content or the relative strength of the component forces operating through an administrative agency. In the face of such changes, or the threat of them, the "old-line" agency is highly inflexible. If attempts are made through the chief executive or the department head, or through any of the other lines of access, to alter policy in such a way as to reduce the effectiveness of the other claimant elements, the latter, including all or many of the agency's administrators, will resist such efforts either directly or by struggling to minimize their effects.

The inflexibility of established administrative relationships provides part of the rationale for the effort in war and depression to create new agencies to handle emergency functions. (They are "emergency" in the sense that critical circumstances called them into being, not necessarily in the sense of being temporary.) Attempts to establish and operate the new agency may also be resisted both by "old-line" agencies and by various interest groups. Once establishment is achieved, however, the resistance will be less crippling than that encountered within the old unit. The "emergency" agency is thus a more effective instrument for the new function unless the dominant forces in the existing agency have been a major vehicle for the change. It was appropriate and inevitable that the U.S. Department of Agriculture should administer the New Deal farm programs of the 1930's, for its officials had participated actively in their development. It was inevitable but not entirely appropriate for the war effort that the Department of Agriculture in World War II retained control over most of the government programs dealing with food and fiber. The administrative historians have suggested the elements of the situation:

> Traditional production patterns were reflected in "parity" legislation passed since 1933 and designed to bolster the prices of basic crops. . . . Officials of the Department of Agriculture who had helped formulate parity legislation and were responsible for its administration were accustomed to work within the parity framework. They were slow to see that 1933 techniques, developed to deal with surpluses and low prices, were not relevant in a war economy of scarcity and high prices. Finally, the parity structure

was guarded jealously by potent farm-pressure groups and by a block of Congressmen whose Democratic leaders, by reason of seniority, were chairmen of powerful House and Senate Committees.[54]

The abandonment of "parity" for the duration and the modification of traditional production patterns were called for by the War, but these were changes that could not be accommodated by the Department of Agriculture without disrupting established relationships. "Parity" emerged from the War unbattered, and production patterns were but slightly changed.

One of the most instructive sets of established and highly inflexible relationships in the Federal government is that involving the Department of Agriculture (particularly the extension work carried on in co-operation with the land-grant colleges of agriculture and private farm organizations), the State agricultural colleges, the Association of Land Grant Colleges and Universities, the Farm Bureau, and, of course, congressmen (especially committee chairmen) from important farm States. The relationships among these are especially revealing because of their strength and their complexity. At the risk of oversimplification we shall examine briefly some of the highlights of the complicated pattern.

The origins of these relationships have been sketched in another connection in Chapter 4. It is unnecessary to repeat them here, but we may recall that the Farm Bureau developed, with the active encouragement of Department of Agriculture officials, out of the extension work carried on through the colleges of agriculture. The Association of Land Grant Colleges and Universities grew up around the numerous Federal programs for grants in aid of agriculture dating back to 1862. In the educational extension work in agriculture, the official relations exist between the Department and the State agricultural colleges. The relations between the latter and the Farm Bureau are so intimate, partly in consequence of the financial participation of the State and county bureaus in the work in many States, that the actual relations closely involve the Farm Bureau. In a good many States the extension service of the agricultural colleges and the county agents of the system are virtually identical with the Farm Bureau.[55] Federalism was also an important influence in developing

---

[54] U.S. Bureau of the Budget: *The United States at War*, pp. 338–9.
[55] See Baker: *The County Agent, passim*; McCune: *The Farm Bloc*, chap. 10 and *passim*; "The Farm Bureau," *Fortune* (June, 1944), pp. 156 ff. Cf. the incident reported in Key: *Southern Politics*, pp. 55–7.

this arrangement, since the grant-in-aid pattern of extension work and the resulting relations with the Farm Bureau grew up at a time when the Supreme Court had not granted the Federal government the direct powers over agriculture that later Court opinions have approved. The department's functions, aside from a few duties of regulation, were largely confined to research and promotion until the 1930's.

With the establishment of the American Farm Bureau Federation in 1919 as a national organization and one deeply interested in promoting certain pieces of legislation, the relations between it and the department became a source of some embarrassment to the latter. This embarrassment was accentuated by the resentments of rival farm organizations, notably the Grange and the Farmers Union, at the common practice among the county agents of promoting Farm Bureau membership and giving special attention to Farm Bureau members, despite the fact that the agents were paid in part from public funds. In 1920 this criticism resulted in the so-called Howard-True Memorandum of Understanding between the president of the A.F.B.F. and the director of what was then known as the Agriculture Department's States Relations Service. In effect it provided that county agents should not perform Farm Bureau work and should be impartial in their help to all farmers and farm organizations. Concerning the State and national federations the memorandum noted that these did not enter into formal arrangements with the Department of Agriculture and the colleges, but the document recognized the existence of "much advisory consultation." [56]

The relations among the Department of Agriculture, the Farm Bureau, the county agents, and the State extension services were little affected by the Howard-True Memorandum. It is hardly likely that they should be in view of the admitted fact at the time that "the greatest source of strength possessed by the Farm Bureau . . . arises from the interrelation and interdependence of the county agricultural agent and the local county farm bureau." [57] Competing farm organizations, such as the Farmers Union and the Grange, have been constantly critical of the county agents' partiality to the Farm Bureaus and their members, even in States where many farmers belong to both the Farm Bureau and the Grange. The existence of and basis

[56] The text of the Howard-True memorandum is contained in A. C. True: *A History of Agricultural Extension Work in the United States, 1785–1923*, U.S. Department of Agriculture, Misc. Pub. 15 (Washington, D.C.: Government Printing Office, 1928), pp. 168–71.

[57] Kile: *The Farm Bureau Movement*, p. 194. Cf. pp. 211, 214, and 217–9.

for these criticisms are admitted with candor by Kile, historian and former employee of the Farm Bureau. Commenting on a statement in 1931 by the director of extension work in Alabama that "the major project and the one standing first in importance for the Extension Service, is to take whatever steps are necessary to help the farm people build and maintain" among farmers "a high class business organization," he says: "To Mr. O'Neal [president of the A.F.B.F.] this meant first and foremost to stimulate and promote the organization of strong county and state farm bureaus."[58]

Documents indicating the Farm Bureau's use of Extension Service backing to build its organization, especially in the South, were included in the record of a congressional investigating committee in 1942.[59] In the summer of 1943 the Grange joined the Farmers Union in an unsuccessful effort to restrict what Kile calls the "close cooperation" between the Farm Bureau and the Extension Service by legislation to withhold extension funds from States that allowed extension officials to do work for private farm organizations.[60] Relating the failure of a 1945 Farm Bureau program for government supply of fertilizers, which included appointment of assistant county agents to conduct fertilizer demonstrations, Kile comments:

> The Grange has long complained about the tie-up between the Farm Bureau and the county agricultural agents and other extension forces. The Grange is not happy at the prospect of another assistant county agent in each county working on a job created primarily by the Farm Bureau—*particularly not, when this new federal employee would have the power to allocate to individual farmers valuable supplies of fertilizers for demonstration purposes.*[61] (Italics added.)

Kile himself admits that the relations between the Farm Bureau and the county agents are still a "problem." He probably does not exaggerate, however, when he says: "Since the present relationship between the Extension Service and the Farm Bureau is mutually agreeable and since the Farm Bureau is the dominant farm force in nearly

---

[58] Kile: *The Farm Bureau Through Three Decades*, pp. 178–9. Copyright 1948 by and used with the permission of Orville M. Kile.
[59] U.S. Joint Committee on Reduction of Nonessential Federal Expenditures: *Hearings*, 77th Cong., 2d Sess. (1942), pp. 766–74, 903–5, and *passim*.
[60] Kile: *The Farm Bureau Through Three Decades*, pp. 298–9.
[61] Kile: *The Farm Bureau Through Three Decades*, p. 318. Copyright 1948 by and used with the permission of Orville M. Kile.

all States, the chances of legislation designed to destroy this relationship are not great, either at the state level or the national." [62]

The protests of competing organizations have resulted in severing the financial connections between local farm bureaus and county agents in some States, such as in Vermont. This severance is almost meaningless, however, so long as the Farm Bureau retains a controlling influence upon the land-grant agricultural colleges and the extension services, partly through its access to the State and national legislatures. It is fair to say that the Association of Land Grant Colleges and Universities is largely responsible for whatever control the Department of Agriculture has over the extension services and the related State experiment stations.[63] Nevertheless, both groups are heavily dependent on grants-in-aid from Federal sources. They stand together if the decentralized system of control is under attack.

Paradoxically enough, the principal disturbance to these relationships stemmed from the new Federal agricultural programs of production control, price supports, soil conservation, and the like. Although the Farm Bureau had a major role in developing most of this legislation, the new programs invited the creation of new and different patterns of interaction between Federal administrators and farmers. These so-called "action" programs were not devoted simply to research and information. They involved the allocation of sizable benefits and penalties directly to farmers on a scale and in a fashion not easily adaptable to the customary methods of the State extension services. Interests with access to parts of the Department in Washington and to the president were not necessarily identical with those influencing the colleges of agriculture and the State extension workers. Since the changes after 1936 in the Supreme Court's views of Federal powers over agriculture, moreover, it was not legally essential that the new activities be financed by grants-in-aid. Most of these agencies, therefore, tended from the first to operate with their own employees in the field, by-passing the State extension services on what Farm Bureau officials call a "straight-line" basis. The considerations involved are well stated by Paul Appleby, whose direct connection with these developments gives his measured words considerable weight.

State Departments of Agriculture and state Extension Services often seek to have delegated to them powers of the secretary in

[62] Kile: *The Farm Bureau Through Three Decades,* p. 394–6. Copyright 1948 by and used with the permission of Orville M. Kile.
[63] Key: *The Administration of Federal Grants to States,* pp. 184–5.

action programs. Their efforts frequently are supported by pressure groups whose members are dissatisfied with what they feel to be a lack of responsiveness on the part of the Federal Department and who believe they could exert greater influence on state agencies. *No Secretary of Agriculture will ever use, willingly and continuously in direct administration, organizations and personnel not really responsible to him.*[64] (Italics added.)

The formal organization of these newer activities was not just a technical, academic matter. They all required, for their operation in any form, extensive field activities in direct contact with farmers. If these by-passed the existing structure of State extension services and county agents, to which the Farm Bureau had privileged access, they threatened to diminish the farmers' dependence upon the A.F.B.F. For similar reasons most of the agricultural colleges preferred to have the new programs operated through the extension services, although some were reluctant to participate in a dilution of their traditional educational functions. Key congressmen from farm areas were equally sensitive as a result of their "membership" in the Farm Bureau and the operations it dominated. The strength of this combination in the Congress was demonstrated in 1934 in the passage of a law subjecting a number of permanent appropriations to annual scrutiny. This legislation excluded appropriations for extension work, for instruction in the land-grant colleges, and for vocational education, omissions that the House committee explained in the following terms: "The singling out of these three items for an exception to the general rule . . . is but a recognition, on the part of the committee, of the power of the propagandizing agencies interested in these appropriations to perhaps defeat the entire bill on the strength of the inclusion of these items therein." [65]

A more basic congressional objection to the possible by-passing of the extension-county-agent-Farm-Bureau system lay in its unpredictable effects upon political relationships within congressional constituencies. The existing system was in many States and districts a base of power with which many legislators had developed stable relationships. Any weakening in that base would introduce the means for alternative lines of influence on which competing electoral organizations might be built. Where the new activities were aimed at raising the lot of previously underprivileged segments of the rural popula-

---

[64] Paul H. Appleby: *Big Democracy* (New York: Alfred A. Knopf, Inc., 1945), p. 87.
[65] Quoted in Key: *The Administration of Federal Grants to States*, p. 182.

tion, as was the ill-fated Farm Security Administration, they threatened to bring into the electorate, or to shift the political attachments of, whole segments of farm citizens. Such activities were a hazard of unpredictable proportions unless their functions were subsumed under existing lines of supervision and control. Although this threat might be verbalized in terms of patronage and the like, it was rarely so simple. Insistence on patronage control was merely one aspect of the fear felt toward the possible unsettling effects of a series of consequences—new functions breeding new relationships and new obligations. This is the source of the conventional congressional hostility to the development of decentralized field organizations by agencies with controversial functions. Most legislators will resist any decentralization that brings an agency into contact with a considerable body of citizens, unless they can control its political effects. They will be wary of appointments to key field positions in the agencies which must decentralize. Once such operations are established and routinized, as for example the field stations of the Weather Bureau, legislators will resist changes in power or location which may affect political structure or community self-esteem.[66]

The Farm Bureau and its allies were sensitive to these possibilities from the beginning of the first Agricultural Adjustment Administration in 1933. A.F.B.F. officials insisted that the extension-service-county-agent system be used for administering the program in the field.[67] It was so administered in most areas at first, if only because there were no effective alternative arrangements which could be made quickly. As the county and township A.A.A. committees developed, however, their ties in many localities were to Washington officials outside the influence of the extension services and the Farm Bureau. The latter saw these changes with what Kile calls "growing dissatisfaction in farm bureau circles about what seemed to be a political machine Mr. Wallace was building up among the county and township AAA production or allotment control committees."[68] Undoubtedly this was true in some localities, but more commonly it was a subtler shift in relationships.

[66] For discussion of some of the problems of this sort met in the war agencies see Emmette S. Redford: *Field Administration of Wartime Rationing* (Washington, D.C.: Government Printing Office, 1947), *passim*; Carroll K. Shaw: *Field Organization and Administration of the War Production Board and Predecessor Agencies* (Washington, D.C.: Civilian Production Administration, Special Study no. 25, 1947), pp. 155–9 and *passim*.
[67] Kile: *The Farm Bureau Through Three Decades*, p. 203.
[68] Kile: *The Farm Bureau Through Three Decades*, p. 260. Copyright 1948 by and used with the permission of Orville M. Kile.

While the A.A.A. threat was largely taken care of by designation of the county agent as a member of the county committee under the 1938 Act and by related developments, the Farm Security Administration, with its expanded tenant-purchase programs, was a new threat. Particularly after transfer to the Department of Agriculture in 1937 and its subsequent expansion, it involved what Kile calls "complications and interference with local farming conditions." [69] The nature of this "interference" is indicated in Kile's summary:

> The AFBF received much credit for stepping out boldly and scotching this bureaucratic machine which in its post-depression years was apparently doing its best to give a government-controlled socialistic, if not collectivistic, trend to American agriculture. At its peak FSA had a *nation-wide organization of over 18,000 employees, with approximately 2,000 offices,* and an annual payroll and expense account totaling at least $44,500,000. As of January 1, 1941, 737,204 *farm families were in debt to FSA and operating under the direction and virtual control of its county supervisors.*[70] (Italics added.)

Such threats to established relationships were intolerable to the Farm Bureau, to many of the extension services, and to segments within the Department. "The political implications of a government organization actively organized in practically every agricultural county in the United States and controlling or materially influencing the economic futures of three-quarters of a million farm families, became more and more menacing." [71] The threat of the F.S.A. and its field force was eliminated in 1946, after a long and complicated struggle, by shifting F.S.A. functions to the established and reliable Farm Credit Administration.

A significant five weeks' interlude in the story of established relationships in agriculture and of efforts to alter them occurred in 1942 and 1943. It reflected one aspect of the effort to adjust the Agriculture Department's "old-line" methods and relationships to wartime conditions; it illustrated some of the competing interests having a measure of access to the Department and the president; and it demonstrated the inflexibility of dominant relationships. Dissatisfied

[69] Kile: *The Farm Bureau Through Three Decades,* p. 266. Copyright 1948 by and used with the permission of Orville M. Kile.

[70] Kile: *The Farm Bureau Through Three Decades,* p. 264. Copyright 1948 by and used with the permission of Orville M. Kile.

[71] Kile: *The Farm Bureau Through Three Decades,* p. 267. Copyright 1948 by and used with the permission of Orville M. Kile.

with the wartime inefficiency of the department, and wishing to bring it into more effective harmony with the production needs of war, the President, on December 5, 1942, announced a reorganization of the department under three major divisions: a Food Production Administration, a Food Distribution Administration, and an Agricultural Research Administration. The newly designated head of the first of these, Herbert W. Parisius, was given the task of creating an organizational scheme for consolidating and integrating all Department activities regarding production. His most significant proposal for present purposes was a consolidation of the field services of the Farm Credit Administration, the Farm Security Administration, the Soil Conservation Service, and the A.A.A. under nine regional offices supervising a field force at the State and county levels. Although this proposal was likely to prove abortive under any circumstances, this outcome was aided by maladroit leadership such as proposing the Administrator of F.S.A. to head the new field service. This action played right into the hands of the Farm Bureau and its allies in and outside the department. Not only was the F.S.A. under fire at the time, but the whole proposal frontally challenged the Farm Bureau's insistence, clearly stated since 1940, that all field activities of the Department should be coordinated through the State extension services and the county agents. Parisius' plan would have placed in continuing contact with farmers an administrative organization directly answerable to the Washington officials and separate from the system to which the Farm Bureau had privileged access. If successful, it would have placed the Farm Bureau's political position in jeopardy, with repercussions in congressional constituencies. Faced with overwhelming opposition, Parisius resigned after five weeks, and the war brought no other significant proposals to change the pattern of the department's relations with farmers.[72]

After the neutralization of the Farm Security Administration, the only Agriculture Department agency with a field force not fully accessible to the Farm Bureau was the Soil Conservation Service. Kile states the interest group's position toward the S.C.S. with his usual pious candor:

> Remembering the trouble they had experienced with the Farm Security Administration and the Farm Credit Administration some years earlier, AFBF heads had noted with disapproval the rapid growth of another "straight-line" government agency reach-

[72] A summary of the Parisius case is presented in U.S. Bureau of the Budget: *The United States at War*, pp. 342–6.

ing straight from Washington to the local farm areas. This fast-growing agency was the Soil Conservation Service.[73]

In line with its policy of confining Department field services to the extension-service pattern, the Farm Bureau opened up on the Soil Conservation Service after World War II. The obstacles were greater than in the case of the F.S.A. The S.C.S. was relatively old, dating back to 1935, its activities were highly approved even by the Farm Bureau, and it could hardly be called socialist. The only charges against it had to be "duplication," lack of "co-ordination," and "waste." In pushing this line of argument before the House Appropriations Subcommittee in 1946, Edward O'Neal, President of the Farm Bureau, showed the extent to which the S.C.S. had fallen heir to the hostilities that beset other "straight-line" agencies:

> Instead of using the agencies and instrumentalities which were already functioning and in contact with the great majority of farmers, the Soil Conservation Service built up its own organization and administrative machinery to reach out into the States and counties, and deal directly with individual farmers.

> One of the basic weaknesses of the Soil Conservation set-up is that these local Soil Conservation districts are too dependent upon the Soil Conservation organization. . . . This dependence tends to give an undue measure of control over the program by the Soil Conservation Service.[74]

The Farm Bureau's plan, of course, was to divide all S.C.S. field operations between the extension services and the experiment stations.

The Farm Bureau's proposals for the Soil Conservation Service have been resisted by the other major farm organizations and by many elements within the Department. The Hoover Commission offered some compromise proposals in 1949, which were met with something less than enthusiasm in most affected quarters.[75] The persistence of the Farm Bureau, the divisions within the department, and the con-

[73] Kile: *The Farm Bureau Through Three Decades*, p. 335. Copyright 1948 by and used with the permission of Orville M. Kile.

[74] U.S. House of Representatives, Subcommittee of the Committee on Appropriations: *Hearings on the Department of Agriculture Appropriation Bill for 1947*, 79th Cong., 2d Sess. (1946), pp. 1633, 1636.

[75] U.S. Commission on Organization of the Executive Branch of the Government: *Department of Agriculture*, pp. 13–16, and *Task Force Report on Agriculture Activities*, pp. 34–41 (Washington, D.C.: Government Printing Office, 1949).

troversies in congressional committees reveal the political flesh and blood of issues of administrative organization. Co-ordination and simplification are desirable objectives, but they are posterior to the determination of who shall do the co-ordinating and to what end.

In addition to the Department of Agriculture's Extension Service, other government functions that operate on a basis of grants-in-aid to the States find themselves in a web of relationships that resist change and disturbance. Because of the influence of federalism, these patterns are more complicated than those of activities directly administered by the Federal government. Once they are established, however, both the directly administered and the grant-in-aid types of relationship resist change; interest groups with privileged access and administrators and legislators whose attitudes and positions reflect the stability of the pattern combine to resist disturbance. The existence of such conflicts, however, and the terms in which they are frequently settled reveal the complexity of the factors affecting administrative behavior. Not one but many determinants of access are normally involved in the discretionary judgments of executive officials.

15

Interest Groups and the Judiciary

THE activities of the judicial officers of the United States are not exempt from the processes of group politics. Relations between interest groups and judges are not identical with those between groups and legislators or executive officials, but the difference is rather one of degree than of kind. For various reasons organized groups are not so continuously concerned with courts and court decisions as they are with the functions of the other branches of government, but the impact of diverse interests upon judicial behavior is no less marked. Though myth and legend may argue to the contrary, especially concerning our highest courts, the judiciary reflects the play of interests, and few organized groups can afford to be indifferent to its activities.

The reasons why interest groups are concerned with the judiciary are not obscure, although they may not be readily recognized. The courts, particularly in the American system, are endowed with power to make choices that are important in the lives and to the expectations of individuals and groups. The exercise of such power is significant, whether it involves the awarding of money damages for defaulting on a contract or permits the annulment of an act of Congress as exceeding the powers granted by the Constitution. In making such determinations judges exercise a discretion more or less wide, depending on the circumstances. To be sure, they are guided by the rules of the law and by the facts of the case before them. But the rules of the law are not unambiguous, and the power to find or, as Jerome Frank puts it, to "make" the facts permits a significant freedom of choice.[1] Around points in the governmental institution where discretion is exercised the claims of organized and unorganized interests

[1] Jerome Frank: *Courts on Trial: Myth and Reality in American Justice* (Princeton, N. J.: Princeton University Press, 1949), pp. 23-4.

inevitably are arrayed. Choices are no less important to interest groups when they are announced from the bench than when they are made in legislative halls and executive chambers.

In the American system the most significant discretionary judgments made by the courts are those interpreting statutes and particularly those deciding the constitutionality of acts of the national and State legislatures. The interpretation of statutes is as surely a source of judicial as of administrative discretion and for essentially the same reasons. Few statutes admit of only one interpretation. Although some legislation is ambiguous through carelessness and sloppy draftsmanship, two already familiar sources of ambiguity are probably of more importance. In the first place, when legislation delegates authority to the executive to deal flexibly with a changing and technical problem, the wording of the delegation is likely to be rather general, simply because the legislators cannot anticipate the detailed circumstances in which the law will be applied. The meaning of the statute in a particular situation is thus a matter of choice both for the administrator and for the judge. In the second place, ambiguity in legislative language often represents an unresolved conflict among competing claims upon the law makers. Where the legislators feel a need to reconcile a set of fairly explicit and contradictory demands, the accepted formula is almost certain to be phrased broadly and in general terms. Just as such formulations shift to the administrator the onus of developing specific and viable meanings in concrete cases, so they leave to the judiciary a broad freedom to interpret the statute in the light of detailed facts.

The remarkable power of American courts to rule on whether the actions of the legislative and executive branches of the State and national governments are constitutional and therefore enforceable is the source of a most extensive discretion. Judicial interpretations of statutes, of course, may also afford a wide scope for judicial discretion, but their finality is not assured: the Congress or a State legislature may legitimately overrule the interpretation that a court has placed upon a legislative act. When an act has been declared unconstitutional, however, almost the only recourse, unless the court reverses itself, is the long, slow, and seldom-traveled road of constitutional amendment.

The Constitution of the United States has lived to magnificent maturity largely because it has so readily admitted of discretionary interpretation by its guardians. It was well and wisely drawn, but the skillful statesmen of the eighteenth century had no prescience of the peculiar problems of the twentieth. The document would have been long since abandoned to the antiquarians had not its broad and ambiguous phrases adequately accommodated the new interpretations and new demands of succeeding generations.

Interpretation of the Constitution through judicial review imposes upon the judiciary, particularly the Supreme Court, a task of statesmanship no less political than that assumed at Philadelphia in 1787. To the Court's arbitrament are submitted sooner or later most of the important political issues of the day, questions freighted with significance for the stability and even the continued existence of the nation. Consider the situation facing the country in January and February of 1935. Nearly two years before, as a part of the Administration's program of recovery from the depression, the Congress had passed a resolution declaring clauses in all notes, bonds, and other obligations that called for payment in gold to be contrary to public policy. Through a suit against the Baltimore and Ohio Railroad for $38.10 the Supreme Court was called upon to determine whether this resolution was a legitimate exercise of the power "to coin money, regulate the value thereof, and of foreign coin." At stake were several billions of dollars and the stability of the national economy. So crucial was the decision that on two occasions the Court felt obliged to state that its judgment would not be forthcoming on the next decision day. Finally, on February 18, Chief Justice Hughes announced that the Court, by a vote of five to four, upheld the government's position.[2]

To assert that such decisions are not policy choices but rather the largely automatic result of technical legal procedures and constitutional knowledge is to perpetuate a myth that is highly inaccurate, however useful it may be in inducing acceptance of the Court's views. To accept Mr. Justice Roberts' view of the process of judicial review is to misconstrue the governing role of the judiciary. In his 1936 opinion announcing the majority's decision against the constitutionality of the Agricultural Adjustment Act he observed:

> When an act of Congress is appropriately challenged in the courts as not conforming to the constitutional mandate the judicial branch of the Government has only one duty,—to lay the article of the Constitution which is invoked beside the statute which is challenged and to decide whether the latter squares with the former.[3]

Skillful lawyers who know a square when they see one can come to opposing views on questions of constitutionality, as the long tradition

[2] Norman v. Baltimore and Ohio Railroad Company, 294 U.S. 240 (1935).
[3] U.S. v. Butler, 297 U.S. 1 (1936).

of Supreme Court dissents amply demonstrates. The minority are rarely less qualified as technicians; they differ from the majority largely in their views of public policy. As Felix Frankfurter declared many years before he was appointed to the Court: "The simple truth of the matter is that decisions of the Court denying or sanctioning the exercise of federal power . . . largely involve a judgment about practical matters, and not at all any esoteric knowledge of the Constitution."[4] From the beginning of our history the judiciary has been a party to the struggles over policy and power. Because its own powers are great and its discretion broad, it is as clearly a part of the stream of conflicting interests as any other segment of the institution of government.

Differences in the Means of Access

The degrees of difference between the role of interest groups in the judiciary and their functions in the other two branches of the government not only define the place of the courts in the governmental process but also highlight the significance of interest groups in the entire system. The elements of access to the judiciary are not unlike those that operate in the legislature and the executive, but the relative importance of the different factors is not the same. A brief examination of these variations, therefore, will contribute materially to our understanding of the total functioning of political interests, organized and potential.

Although the evidence is not abundant, it is more than likely that differences in the modes of access to the judiciary are not decisively affected by variations in the procedures through which it is chosen. The selection of judges through the ballot box in two thirds of the States has not made the occupants of the bench in those jurisdictions demonstrably different from their appointed brethren in the remaining States and in the Federal government. The probable reason for this is that regardless of the mode of selection there are certain protections that have characterized all our judicial systems: judges have been free of civil liability for their actions on the bench; a judge's pay cannot be withheld or reduced during the time he serves; judges have been free from arbitrary removal, and elected judges are protected by the presumption of re-election. It is likely, according to

[4] Felix Frankfurter: *Law and Politics*, edited by Archibald MacLeish and E. F. Prichard, Jr. (New York: Harcourt, Brace & Company, 1939), p. 12. Cf. Bentley: *The Process of Government*, p. 393.

Hurst, that these three protections "gave all our main judicial posts more in common than they had in difference due to variations in manner of selection or tenure." [5]

The protections that have surrounded judges in the Anglo-American systems are significant here as supplying evidence of widespread expectations concerning judicial behavior. These safeguards testify to the expectation that judges should not be subject to the influences that may be exercised through civil liability for their official acts, reduction of pay, and arbitrary removal. Even in States where judges are elected for a limited term, it is their role to stand apart from the rest of the community and to avoid becoming identified with any of the vulgar forces that contend in the market for place and power. When a man becomes a judge he is expected to stand somewhat above the contests in the community, and if he is appointed to the Supreme Court he is elevated so high that for most of the populace he is "at least brushed with divinity." [6] The strength of these expectations is suggested by the contempt with which a judge is viewed who is convicted of partiality or of abuse of his position. Judges are assumed not to have the human frailties that are known and tolerated in those who fill legislative halls and executive offices.

The expectations about judicial behavior are both strengthened by and reflected in notions about the law-making functions of the bench. It is often argued by both lawyers and laymen that judges do not make law but merely declare or apply the law to a particular set of circumstances. Yet it is an admitted fact that the whole structure of the common law is the creation of centuries of court decisions. Allegedly the courts merely apply the Constitution, and yet most of the substantive meaning of the phrase "due process of law," to mention only one example, has been given it through court decisions handed down since the closing decades of the nineteenth century. Courts are often assumed to follow faithfully the precedents laid down in previous cases, and yet yesterday's decision may be essential to knowing what a rule of the law is or what a constitutional phrase means.[7] The polite fictions surrounding "judicial legislation" reflect expectations about the freedom of judges from ordinary human frailties, and their continued acceptance testifies to the adequacy with which the judiciary has satisfied those demands.

[5] Hurst: *The Growth of American Law,* p. 138. Copyright 1950 by James Willard Hurst and used with the permission of Little, Brown & Company.

[6] Frank: *Courts on Trial,* p. 255.

[7] Ibid., chap. 19; cf. Jerome Frank: *Law and the Modern Mind* (New York: Brentano, 1930).

Long before a man dons the judicial robes he has accepted and identified himself with large components of the judge's role. Especially if he has aspired to a judge's status, he is likely to have conducted himself, more or less unconsciously, in the fashion of one who is said to have "the judicial temperament." He is likely to have displayed the kinds of behavior that the judge's role demands. A large proportion of his experiences on the bench develop and reinforce such conformity, moreover. The ritualistic elements of investiture and of court procedure, the honorific forms of address, and even the imposing appearance of some court buildings serve to emphasize the demands upon his behavior. Even the most unscrupulous former ambulance chaser who owes his judicial position to a thoroughly corrupt political organization must conform at least in part to the behaviors expected of him as a judge.

As is true of other roles in the community, the expectations concerning a judge's behavior are interests, some of them reflected in organized groups but most of them merely by potential groups. Marked deviation from the demands of the judge's role will result in the activation of interest groups aiming at the enforcement of expectations concerning proper judicial behavior. A "corrupt" local judge may make appointments to the clerical and custodial positions in the court purely on the basis of political obligation, he may dispense lucrative receiverships in a similar fashion, and he may "go easy on the boys" in passing sentence. He may do many such things with impunity, but he cannot indiscriminately ignore the demands of his role without activating bar associations and other organized and potential interest groups. The threats of denunciation, of ostracism, of jeopardy to reputation, and of impeachment or defeat at the polls are sufficient to impose at least minimum conformity to role requirements.

Nor can persons and groups outside the judiciary indiscriminately attempt to interfere with the judge's conduct, in defiance of the expectations concerning his role. This is clearly one of the many conclusions to be drawn from the controversy over Franklin Roosevelt's 1937 "court plan." The opposition to the plan was motley, but it included many individuals and groups who, though dissatisfied with the Supreme Court's decisions in New Deal cases, were seriously disturbed by what appeared to be an interference with the detachment of the Court. The somewhat devious nature of the proposal was, in fact, a clumsy tribute to the greater opposition that might have been aroused by a more direct attack upon the Supreme Court.

When a man becomes a judge, he not only assumes a new role but also enters a new group made up of others who occupy judicial positions. He begins to interact both informally and formally with those who occupy similar positions in the institution. Like other groups, this one demands a measure of conformity as the price of acceptance. Even the judge of a lower court who sits alone interacts with other judges at least through the hierarchy of the judicial system. Failure to accept the demands of this group, including those that define the role of the judge, will result informally in nonacceptance. Formally such failure will be reflected in frequent reversal of his decisions by courts with appellate jurisdiction. Reversals may be made on many grounds, of course, but among the most exacting are those regarding proper judicial conduct, often embodied in technical procedural requirements such as those applying to the admissibility of evidence, comments from the bench, and proper charges to the jury.

If the court to which a man is appointed or elected includes a number of judges, as the Supreme Court and most other appellate tribunals in the United States do, the new man finds himself a continuous working member of a face-to-face group. With more immediacy of interaction than that between courts on different levels of the structure, the collegial court rather directly imposes upon its members behaviors that have come to be expected of them. Its rituals and deliberations obviously do not require uniformity in the decisions of its members, but they do reinforce the taboos of the judicial role.

"It will be difficult," wrote Jefferson to President Madison in 1810, "to find a character of firmness enough to preserve his independence on the same bench with Marshall." [8] He was advising Madison concerning an appointment to the Supreme Court. In making this statement Jefferson was testifying to the tremendous personal influence of John Marshall upon his associate justices. In documenting Marshall's personal power Beveridge has implied something of the importance of the Supreme Court as a group.[9] The group character of the Court has been little studied,[10] partly owing to the secrecy with which its activities are surrounded. We have evidence of the molding influence of personalities like Marshall and Holmes upon the views of the other members of the Court. This influence the collegial existence of the

---

[8] Quoted in Albert J. Beveridge: *The Life of John Marshall* (Boston: Houghton Mifflin Company, 1919), Vol. IV, p. 59.

[9] Ibid., chap. 2.

[10] C. Herman Pritchett, in *The Roosevelt Court: A Study in Judicial Politics and Values, 1937–1947* (New York: The Macmillan Company, 1948), has developed an ingenious and suggestive approach to studying the group life of the Court.

justices has facilitated. The rarity of open, personal clashes between the strong personalities that have been on the Court throughout its history indicates further the demands of the group for behavior in keeping with expectations concerning the dignity of the judiciary. The demands involved in the role behaviors of judges are obviously parallel to those influences upon access to legislators and members of the executive branch that we have discussed under such headings as the influence of office and the group life of the agency. As in the other two branches of the government, these factors are not always dominant. There are cases in which judges have shown obvious partiality, have accepted bribes, and have otherwise acted in violation of the "rules of the game." A primary difference between the courts and the other branches is the greater vitality and rigor of these controls upon the access of interest groups. The expectations concerning judicial behavior are more exacting and their limitations upon access are more severe.

There are other parallels between the determinants of access to the judiciary and those affecting the other branches of the government. For example, we noted in Chapter 14 that the administrator who received from the legislature a statute that represented a fairly stable and accepted adjustment of interests tended so to operate as to maintain that adjustment. He tended to identify with the established formula to the extent of trying to keep the atmosphere bland and the operation routinized. Access was significantly affected by such considerations. In the case of the judiciary the same factor is operative, although it applies far more broadly than merely to any single statute involved in a given case. The set of adjustments of which the judiciary is custodian includes the whole fabric of relationships within the society insofar as they are embodied in the rules of law. If the court is primarily a public-law institution, like the Supreme Court, its custody extends to most of the complicated relationships involved in the federal system and in the relations among the various branches of the government.

More than any other segment of the governmental institution, the courts are looked upon as the guardians of the "rules of the game." Judges are expected to identify themselves with those "rules" and to afford privileged access to the interests reflecting them. To a greater degree than legislators or executives they are, in a sense, leaders of widely shared but unorganized interests, i.e., potential groups, which must be effectively represented in court decisions. One function of the respect for precedents and of the juristic talk of certainty, stability, and predictability in the law is to help maintain the routine in the relationships of which the courts have custody. Both the administrator and the judge, therefore, tend to identify themselves with the patterns of adjustment that are committed to them. In both cases the relative access of interest groups is fixed or controlled by such identification. The adjustment becomes an object in itself, reinforced by expectations concerning the official role, especially that of the judge. The dynamics are of the same kind in both cases; the differences are of degree.

The elements involved in the adjustments that the courts inherit are not necessarily stable. The equilibrium must be a dynamic one. The limited discretion of the judiciary must, especially in courts that decide constitutional questions, be used to adjust legal formulations to basic shifts in political power. To apply to workers' organizations indiscriminately in an age of mass production and division of labor the rule of conspiracy developed in a simpler period is not to prevent the formation of such associations. Such adjudication does not promote stability except in a purely verbal sense, and it invites solutions through more violent means. The significance of a court system in any society is its usefulness as a means of arriving at a viable regulation of human relationships. This is the most basic adjustment placed in the custody of the judiciary. It cannot be maintained if this function of the judiciary is not widely accepted.

The discretion of the courts is not unlimited, however. Part of the acceptance of the judicial process is dependent upon a measure of continuity and predictability in the role-defining rules of the courts, as we have already observed. This means that in periods of rapid change in technology and in similar human relationships, with attendant shifts in interests and their relative strength in the society as a whole, defensive groups will be likely to enjoy a privileged access to the courts.

No political phenomenon has been more common in recent decades than the ability of groups whose strength has diminished in other segments of the governing institution to use the rules, the high costs, and the technical procedures of the judiciary to perpetuate their power. When the Clayton Act was passed in 1914, labor groups assumed that the legislation provided relief from the use of the injunction in labor disputes and from the applications of the Sherman Antitrust Act that limited the freedom of workers to organize and to strike. Despite the legislative achievement, however, the courts' interpretations were that the essential substance of the earlier law had not been changed.[11] While a variety of factors help to account for these and similar decisions, one of them clearly is the almost inevitable slowness with which the courts abandon established rules and, consequently, established patterns of access.

The awkward political position of the courts, therefore, results from their frequently contradictory responsibilities for maintaining continuity in legal determinations and for assuring equilibrium among the dynamic elements in controversies coming before them. They have often failed to harmonize these conflicting demands. Incidents of American history from Shays's Rebellion of 1786 to Franklin Roosevelt's "court plan" of 1937 testify to the frequency with which such reconciliation has been faulty or inadequate. As a constitutional tribunal the Supreme Court has saved itself from a few acute embarrassments by refusing to take jurisdiction in cases where its decisions are particularly likely to be ignored by the parties, including the other branches of the government. These "political questions" include whether a particular regime is the lawful government of a State, whether an emergency exists justifying the president's use of the militia, whether or not a State has a "republican form of government" as guaranteed by the Constitution, and a number of other issues involving discretionary acts by the Congress or the president.[12]

No doctrine of "political questions" will ever be broad enough to remove the decisions of the judiciary from the arena of politics. The deprivations and indulgences that judicial actions bring about are rarely matters of superficial importance to the parties, who will use whatever means are available to them to influence these dispensations or to alter them. Any court system may find its position challenged in the larger political arena. A system of constitutional courts, exercising the power to review the acts of other governmental agencies to which the affected interests have previously achieved effective access, cannot ignore the possibility that its decisions may be defied. A judiciary with power will inevitably be an object of the struggle for control.

The American courts cannot avoid being involved in the political process. Yet, at the same time, the prevailing expectations concerning

[11] See, for example, such cases as Duplex Printing Co. v. Deering, 254 U.S. 443 (1921), and American Steel Foundries v. Tri-City Trade Council, 257 U.S. 184 (1921).

[12] See Luther v. Borden, 7 Howard 1 (1849); Martin v. Mott, 12 Wheaton 19 (1827); Pacific States Telephone and Telegraph Co. v. Oregon, 223 U.S. 118 (1912).

judicial behavior, the degree of adjustment that an established court system implies, the traditions and group life of the judiciary, and other forces of the sort considered in the preceding pages combine to restrict or to eliminate many of the kinds of direct access that are characteristic of other parts of the governmental mechanism. All the formalities of adjudication are in a sense additional means of such restriction: the practice whereby a judge will disqualify himself if he has some connection with one of the parties to a dispute; the right to challenge jurors; the rules of evidence; the right of the accused to confront witnesses against him and to summon favorable ones; the requirement that a verdict must rest upon the evidence presented in court; and many others. Aside from bribery and physical violence, the incidence of which is rare, privileged access to the courts must be achieved, if at all, largely through indirect and circuitous means. Circuitous lines of access are to be found in other branches of the government also, but the circuity is accentuated in the judiciary by the formalizing of direct lines of access.

Selection and Indirect Access

Much the most important indirect means of access to the judiciary is through influencing the selection of judges. This process is described as indirect because securing the appointment or election of a favored candidate for the bench does not ordinarily provide a group with the opportunity privately to consult with and advise him on his desisions. Such is the most obvious advantage to be derived from successful support of an aspirant to legislative or executive position. It is accepted practice in the "political" branches of the government and is rarely challenged. The strength of expectations concerning the judicial role, and the potentialities of the largely unorganized interests these represent, normally confine such direct influence upon judges to a few exceptional cases of deviant behavior. Sponsorship of candidates for the judiciary must rely for its effect primarily upon the judge's informal "membership" in the interest group.

Whether they are village magistrates or distinguished justices of the Supreme Court of the United States, judges have their interest group affiliations. These may not be formal; in fact, it is customary for judges upon assuming office to divest themselves of formal membership in groups that might be involved in litigation before them. But, as we have seen in other connections, memberships need not be formal to be effective. Nor does this mean that judges regularly and consciously consult their personal preferences in arriving at their decisions. The process in most cases is a good deal more subtle. Many of the so-called rules of the law and particularly many of the more sweeping provisions of the Constitution have no very precise meaning. Even more than statutory provisions, they permit an interpreter to exercise discretion. For judges as for other individuals, the frames of reference within which these provisions are understood and in which the facts of a case are "found," are a function of interest affiliations. The myth of depersonalized and machinelike adjudication upon which rests in part the continued popular acceptance of the judicial function assumes that all such attachments are left behind when a man ascends the bench. As we have seen, this assumption has some limited basis in fact. It is strengthened by the effect of membership in the judicial group. This effect is in the nature of a modification, however, not a transformation. Judges do not cease to be human when they don their robes. They do not derive all their premises from the court room. As Hurst says in concluding that particular methods of selection have had little to do with the "liberalism" or "conservatism" of the bench: "The ideas and feelings prevailing in any given generation in those levels of the community from which judges came offered far more convincing explanation of judicial policy." [18] Like Wordsworth's infants, judges come to their places "not in entire forgetfulness."

Executive and legislative officials responsible for selecting judges have recognized the importance of a candidate's interest affiliations by their actions even when they have not done so in words. Such was the case as early as 1801, when a lame-duck Federalist Congress passed the second Judiciary Act, making needed changes in the court system and incidentally providing John Adams with an opportunity to fill the new posts with reliable Federalists who would withstand the onslaughts of the Jeffersonian mob.[14] The importance of interest affiliations was equally well recognized when the Jeffersonians repealed the act in 1802. At times the admission of concern for a judicial candidate's "memberships" is quite explicit. In September, 1880, shortly before he was elected to the presidency, James A. Garfield wrote to Whitelaw Reid, editor of the New York *Tribune* and an

[18] Hurst: *The Growth of American Law*, p. 146. Copyright 1950 by James Willard Hurst and used with the permission of Little, Brown & Company.
[14] See Charles A. Beard: *Economic Origins of Jeffersonian Democracy* (New York: The Macmillan Company, 1915), chap. 3; Max Farrand: "The Judiciary Act of 1801," *American Historical Review*, Vol. 5, no. 4 (July, 1900), pp. 682–6.

important Republican leader, assuring him that vested rights would be observed in making appointments to the Supreme Court.[15] In September, 1906, Theodore Roosevelt discussed the qualifications of Judge Horace H. Lurton for a Supreme Court appointment. Writing to Senator Lodge, he said:

> He is right on the negro question; he is right on the power of the Federal Government; he is right on the insular business; he is right about corporations; he is right about labor. On every question that would come before the bench he has so far shown himself to be in much closer touch with the policies in which you and I believe than even White, because he has been right about corporations, where White has been wrong.[16]

In the campaign of 1920 Professor William Howard Taft of the Yale Law School, ex-President, and soon to be appointed Chief Justice by President Harding, frankly made the personnel of the Supreme Court an issue in the election. Writing in October, 1920, he argued:

> Mr. Wilson is in favor of a latitudinarian construction of the Constitution of the United States, to weaken the protection it should afford against Socialist raids upon property rights. . . . He has made three appointments to the Supreme Court. He is said to be greatly disappointed in the attitude of the first of these (Mr. Justice McReynolds) upon such questions. The other two (Mr. Justice Brandeis and Mr. Justice Clarke) represent a new school of constitutional construction, which, if allowed to prevail, will greatly impair our fundamental law. Four of the incumbent Justices are beyond the retiring age of seventy, and the next President will probably be called upon to appoint their successors. There is no greater domestic issue in this election than the maintenance of the Supreme Court as the bulwark to enforce the guarantee that no man shall be deprived of his property without due process of law. . . .[17]

As president, moreover, Taft had gone to considerable lengths to make sure that his appointees to the Supreme Court shared his views

[15] Cited in Homer Cummings and Carl McFarland: *Federal Justice* (New York: The Macmillan Company, 1937), p. 527.
[16] Ibid., p. 528.
[17] Quoted in Frankfurter: *Law and Politics*, p. 37.

on matters of public policy whether or not they were of his own political party.[18]

The constitutional requirement of Senatorial confirmation of nominees to the Federal judiciary and similar provisions in several of the States frequently bring the interest affiliations of judicial nominees into sharp focus and produce considerable activity by organized interest groups. Although the process may often reflect no more than the particularist demands of party factions, these frequently originate in interest groups, as we have seen elsewhere. The effect of senatorial confirmation on court appointments is much the same as upon administrative appointments. Through the practice of "senatorial courtesy" the power of confirmation virtually transfers the power of appointing lower court judges from the president to individual Senators. In the case of Supreme Court appointments custom gives significant leverage to groups having access to the Senate and to the Judiciary Committee, which acts on nominations to the courts.[19]

A dramatic but not exceptional example of the effects of a prospective judge's interest affiliations occurred in 1930. President Hoover nominated to a vacancy on the Supreme Court an incumbent circuit court judge, John J. Parker of North Carolina, who had earned the hostility of labor groups by a decision upholding "yellow dog" contracts and who was also opposed by the national Negro groups. The successful effort to prevent confirmation of Judge Parker, led by the A.F. of L. and the National Association for the Advancement of Colored People, exhibited overt group activity on as complete a scale as a conflict over major legislation would have. In the same year Hoover's proposal to return Charles Evans Hughes to the Court as Chief Justice ran into considerable opposition, led by Senators who alleged that the nominee's long and lucrative corporation practice would have a bearing upon his conduct on the Court. When Woodrow Wilson in 1916 nominated Louis D. Brandeis to the Supreme Court there ensued a contest among interest groups that has been colorfully described as "six months of hot blood, cold fury, and calculated pressure." [20]

Controversies over judicial appointments occasionally center on the

[18] Daniel S. McHargue: "President Taft's Appointments to the Supreme Court," *Journal of Politics*, Vol. 12, no. 3 (August, 1950), pp. 478–510.

[19] Cf. Cummings and McFarland: *Federal Justice*, pp. 531 ff.; Hurst: *The Growth of American Law*, p. 128.

[20] Hurst: *The Growth of American Law*, p. 371. Copyright 1950 by James Willard Hurst and used with the permission of Little, Brown & Company.

nominee's juridical competence. More commonly, however, especially when a Supreme Court position is at stake, they reflect the activity of groups that recognize the bearing that a judge's group "memberships" may have upon his decisions.

The indirect protection of interest group access to the judiciary is even more apparent in those States where all or most of the judges are elected. Group activity in judicial elections, as in selections for the appointed bench, tends to be defensive rather than promotional. The myth of judicial detachment is usually strong enough to prevent any group from openly supporting a judicial candidate frankly on the ground of his interest affiliations. One exception, however, is the organized bar, which in some urban jurisdictions has actively supported judicial candidates without arousing criticism. A bar association's claims to expert knowledge of the qualifications needed on the bench enables it to play such a role with relative impunity.[21] On the other hand, the expectation of impartiality sanctions group efforts in opposition to a candidate whose preferences have been sufficiently marked to raise doubts concerning his acceptability. The generality of this expectation, moreover, helps to account for the common practice of re-electing incumbent judges who have no significant group opposition. This practice has been so well established in many States that a man appointed to a court vacancy by the governor is likely to be returned to the bench in a subsequent election unless he is opposed by a significant interest group.[22] Excepting such differences, group activity in the election of judges corresponds to that in other campaigns for public office.

There seems to be little doubt that an elected judge is more exposed to the claims of organized interest groups than is an appointed one who holds office during good behavior. Especially in the lower State courts, the necessity for a judge to keep his eye on election prospects is likely to make him sensitive to the claims of various interest groups, including party factions. The decisions of appellate judges, moreover, have often become issues in subsequent judicial elections. Although the available evidence suggests that the deficiencies of elective judgeships are easily exaggerated,[23] group relations with an elected judiciary may be as direct as those with legislators and executives.

[21] Cf. Edward M. Martin: *The Role of the Bar in Electing the Bench in Chicago* (Chicago: University of Chicago Press, 1936).
[22] Hurst: *The Growth of American Law*, pp. 133–4.
[23] Ibid., pp. 138–46.

Litigation and Indirect Access

Group influence upon the decisions of the courts is indicated by a variety of significant activities. Variations in the tendencies of individual judges and differences in their interest affiliations are often suggested by the care with which litigants select the courts in which they choose to bring suit. Where the circumstances permit a choice of the district in which a case is to be tried, selection of a court whose judge can be expected to look indulgently on the claims of the plaintiff may be the most important aspect of the case. Labor unions, for example, have found that their suits under Federal laws protecting collective bargaining receive a kind of treatment in some courts in the South quite different from that experienced in many equivalent jurisdictions in the North and West. Employers have found considerable variation in the willingness of courts to issue injunctions in labor disputes. Similar considerations may dictate whether to start a suit in the State or the Federal courts, although differences in procedure and in the speed of court action may be more important in such decisions than the tendencies of individual judges.

A large proportion of the cases coming before any court, State or Federal, deals only with individuals. The interests of organized and unorganized groups are often directly involved in the process, however, whether or not they play an explicit role. These group interests are particularly close to the surface in suits challenging the constitutionality of legislation. The acts of national and State legislatures represent, as we have seen, tentative and more or less stable adjustments among interest groups, organized and potential. Challenges to the constitutionality of legislative measures indicate that the legislative adjustments have not effected a fully acceptable settlement. Conflicts begun in the legislative stages, therefore, are continued not only in the executive but also before the judiciary.

Whether or not the names of organized groups are attached to a particular litigation, they may in fact be closely associated with it. The Edison Electric Institute, the major trade association of the private utility companies, vigorously opposed the establishment of the Tennessee Valley Authority and fought the passage of the Public Utility Holding Company Act of 1935 with such an excess of zeal as to provide material for a spectacular Senate investigation. Once these and related statutes were adopted, the Institute took an active part in initiating court tests of their constitutionality, although it was not recorded as a party to the suits.[24] An indication of the close connection between group strategies and individual court cases is afforded by an Institute news release shortly after passage of the Holding Company Act. This statement said in part:

> Utility executives were uncertain . . . how soon the court action would be started or which particular section or sections of the law would be chosen to bear the brunt of the attack. Until the attorneys had an opportunity to decide which company would lend itself most readily as the complainant there would be no decision.[25]

In this and in comparable struggles the strategy of the judicial process is an outgrowth of the contest in the legislature.

The direct involvement of organized groups in litigation, especially cases raising constitutional issues, is sometimes more clearly indicated where such groups intervene as "friends of the court." This is a procedure by which a court permits an individual or group as *amicus curiae* to appear or file a brief in a case to which it is not a party but on which, in the court's judgment, it can provide legal advice useful in arriving at a decision. Government attorneys and those representing both groups and individuals may be allowed to use this device. A long list of *amici curiae* appeared, for example, in the case which resulted in the invalidation of the first Agricultural Adjustment Act in 1936.[26] Among those arguing against the constitutionality of the legislation were the National Association of Cotton Manufacturers, the Farmers' Independence Council of America (an affiliate of the American Liberty League), Hygrade Food Products Corporation, American Nut Company, Berks Packing Company, and General Mills. Included on the other side were the League for Economic Equality, the American Farm Bureau Federation, the National Beet Growers' Association, the Farmers' National Grain Corporation, and the Texas Agricultural Association.[27]

The continuity of the political process, including the judicial, is further revealed in the frequency with which court decisions may precipitate action at other points in the institution. The most ob-

[24] U. S. Temporary National Economic Committee: *Economic Power and Political Pressures*, p. 77.

[25] Quoted ibid., p. 159, from The *New York Times*, September 13, 1935.

[26] U.S. v. Butler, 297 U.S. 1 (1936).

[27] U.S. Temporary National Economic Committee: *Economic Power and Political Pressures*, p. 78.

vious reaction is the attempt to initiate a constitutional amendment when court decisions have invalidated a particular governmental activity. Amendment being a slow and difficult process, it is resorted to rather infrequently. More common is the kind of effort which is a consequence of court interpretations of statutes in a fashion unwelcome to certain organized groups, namely, a revision of the statute. When the Supreme Court threw out the first Agricultural Adjustment Act, the forces that had supported that legislation at once began to work for a new law that would accomplish the same ends through means to which the Court would not object. Similarly, when the Court interpreted the Sherman Antitrust Act so as to prohibit basing-point pricing systems, the Cement Institute and associated groups with access to the Congress took steps to secure a "clarifying" amendment to the Act which would overrule the Court's decision.[28]

The continuing history of court injunctions as instruments in labor disputes, beginning as far back as the 1890's, has regularly involved appeals from the judiciary to the "political" branches of the government. No area of controversy better illustrates the point that the interest adjustments arrived at through the courts may be no more stable than those effected by the legislature and the executive. Where the rules of the law and the predispositions of judges have provided privileged access for employers and have led to accusations of "government by injunction," labor groups have persistently sought readjustment through electoral and legislative activity. These efforts have been aimed either at the restriction or the elimination of the courts' injunctive powers in strike situations.[29] Much the same circumstances are involved in the area of employers' liability for workmen's accidents. The slowness with which the courts adjusted old rules to the conditions of the modern factory produced activity that either modified the existing rules of the law or largely removed from the judiciary its authority to determine whether an employee is entitled to compensation for an industrial accident.

Occasionally in the early history of the nation there were attempts to use impeachment to remove a judge from office because of his interpretations of the law or the Constitution. This has not occurred in the Federal courts since the impeachment and acquittal of Jus-

[28] Earl Latham: "Giantism and Basing-Points: A Political Analysis," *Yale Law Journal*, Vol. 58, no. 3 (February, 1949), pp. 397–8.
[29] Millis and Montgomery: *Organized Labor*, pp. 629–51; Felix Frankfurter and Nathan Greene: *The Labor Injunction* (New York: The Macmillan Company, 1930).

tice Samuel Chase in 1805, and in the States such actions have been rare since the 1850's, when the spread of the system of electing judges for limited terms made such efforts largely unnecessary.[80] A renewal of this sort of response to the obstacles presented by adverse judicial interpretations of the Constitution occurred in the early decades of the twentieth century in the movement for the "recall" of judges and judicial decisions by popular vote. This movement, which represented an alliance of agricultural, labor, and other groups, reached its climax in the presidential campaign of 1912, in which the recall of judicial decisions was actively endorsed by Theodore Roosevelt. The effort at judicial recall, like other political movements affecting the judiciary at the time, sprang from what has been called "the judicial zeal . . . for transmuting *laissez faire* into constitutional dogma."[81] The retaliatory movement was evidence that such "judicial zeal" produced an adjustment of interests so unstable as to permit a serious challenge to the expectation of judicial detachment.

The recall of judges and judicial decisions was adopted by less than a dozen States and has been little used in those. The significance of such a movement, like the importance of the Roosevelt "court plan" of 1937, is determined not only by its reaching its announced objectives but at least equally by its indirect effects upon the manner in which judicial discretion is exercised. The storm that developed around the 1937 proposal revealed the intensity of the interests affected by the New Deal program. The central feature of the proposal, to permit the president to appoint an additional judge in any Federal court where a judge failed to retire within six months after reaching the age of seventy, was not new. The identical suggestion had been made in 1913 by Wilson's Attorney General, James C. McReynolds, one of the "old men" at whom the Roosevelt attack was aimed.[82] The President's plan was not adopted by the Congress, but during the months when the debate was raging, the Supreme Court, as a result of Mr. Justice Roberts' famous "switch in time that saved nine," handed down a series of opinions that effectively repudiated the point of view of the earlier controversial decisions.[83]

[80] Hurst: *The Growth of American Law*, pp. 135–8.
[81] Hurst: *The Growth of American Law*, p. 139. Copyright 1950 by James Willard Hurst and used with the permission of Little, Brown & Company.
[82] Cummings and McFarland: *Federal Justice*, p. 531.
[83] Notably West Coast Hotel Co. v. Parrish, 300 U.S. 379 (1937); National Labor Relations Board v. Jones and Laughlin Steel Corp., 301 U.S. 1 (1937); Steward Machine Co. v. Davis, 301 U.S. 548 (1937); and Helvering v. Davis, 301 U.S. 619 (1937).

Conclusion

The judiciary is inevitably a part of the political process. It is the locus of significant power, especially under our system of judicial review of the acts of co-ordinate branches of the government. Inevitably, therefore, the judiciary is one of the points at which the claims of interest groups are aimed. Access to the courts is governed by essentially the same factors that operate in the other segments of the governmental institution, but the relative importance of these factors is somewhat different in the case of the judiciary. Established expectations concerning the detachment of the courts reduce the significance of the more restricted group "memberships" of judges. These expectations are reflected in interest groups that are largely potential, but that involve overlapping claims upon the behavior of judges, legislators, executives, and the members of organized interest groups throughout the society. These claims, plus the molding effects of the judicial group itself, tend to reinforce the isolation of judges from direct means of access. Like administrators, judges are charged with the management of a structure of relationships which involve the demands of interest groups. Because the structure dealt with by the courts is more extensive and more highly routinized in most respects, the strength of judicial identifications with the existing structure is a stronger and more pervasive control upon group access than are the equivalent factors in most administrative situations. Consequently the most significant means of access to the judiciary are indirect and, in many instances, highly unpredictable.

PART FOUR

Conclusion

16

Group Politics and Representative Democracy

"GROUP organization," said the late Robert Luce, momentarily dropping his usually cautious phrasing, "is one of the perils of the times."[1] The scholarly Yankee legislator's opinion has been echoed and re-echoed, sometimes in qualified and sometimes in categorical terms, by an impressive number of journalists, academicians, and politicians. The common themes running through most of these treatments are: alarm at the rapid multiplication of organized groups; an explicit or, more frequently, an implicit suggestion that the institutions of government have no alternative but passive submission to specialized group demands; and an admonition that the stability or continuance of democracy depends upon a spontaneous, self-imposed restraint in advancing group demands. Thus we are told that "there is no escape from the pressure of organized power . . . ," that the pitiful plight of American government is that "there is nothing it can do to protect itself from pressures . . . ," and that unless these groups "face the kind of world they are living in . . ." it will be only a matter of time "until somebody comes riding in on a white horse."[2]

[1] Luce: *Legislative Assemblies*, p. 421.
[2] These three quotations, taken somewhat unfairly from their contexts, are, respectively, from Harvey Fergusson: *People and Power* (New York: William Morrow & Company, 1947), p. 101; J. H. Spigelman: "The Protection of Society," *Harper's Magazine* (July, 1946), p. 6; and Stuart Chase: *Democracy Under Pressure: Special Interests vs. the Public Welfare* (New York: The Twentieth Century Fund, 1945), p. 8. Cf. Robert C. Angell: *The Integration of American Society* (New York: McGraw-Hill Book Company, 1941); Brady: *Business as a System of Power;* and John Maurice Clark: *Alternative to Serfdom* (New York: Alfred A. Knopf, Inc., 1948).

We have seen earlier that the vast multiplication of interests and organized groups in recent decades is not a peculiarly American phenomenon. The causes of this growth lie in the increased complexity of techniques for dealing with the environment, in the specializations that these involve, and in associated disturbances of the manifold expectations that guide individual behavior in a complex and interdependent society. Complexity of technique, broadly conceived, is inseparable from complexity of social structure. This linkage we observe in industrialized societies the world over. In the United States the multiplicity of interests and groups not only has been fostered by the extent of technical specialization but also has been stimulated by the diversity of the social patterns that these changes affect and by established political practices such as those that permit ease and freedom of association. Diversity of interests is a concomitant of specialized activity, and diversity of groups is a means of adjustment.

We have also seen that the institutions of government in the United States have reflected both the number and the variety of interests in the society and that this responsiveness is not essentially a modern feature of our politics. We have argued, in fact, that the behaviors that constitute the process of government cannot be adequately understood apart from the groups, especially the organized and potential interest groups, which are operative at any point in time. Whether we look at an individual citizen, at the executive secretary of a trade association, at a political party functionary, at a legislator, administrator, governor, or judge, we cannot describe his participation in the governmental institution, let alone account for it, except in terms of the interests with which he identifies himself and the groups with which he affiliates and with which he is confronted. These groups may or may not be interest groups, and all the interests he holds may not be represented at a given point in time by organized units. Organized interest groups, however, from their very nature bulk large in the political process. Collections of individuals interacting on the basis of shared attitudes and exerting claims upon other groups in the society usually find in the institutions of government an important means of achieving their objectives. That is, most interest groups become politicized on a continuing or intermittent basis. In this respect, therefore, such organized groups are as clearly a part of the governmental institution as are the political parties or the branches formally established by law or constitution.

The activities of political interest groups imply controversy and conflict, the essence of politics. For those who abhor conflict in any form, who long for some past or future golden age of perfect harmony, these consequences of group activity are alone sufficient to provoke denunciation. Such people look upon any groups or activities, except those to which they are accustomed, as signs of degeneration, and they view with alarm the appearance upon the political scene of new and insistent claimants. Objections from these sources are part of the peripheral data of politics, but they offer little to an understanding of the process. There are other people, however, who do not shrink from controversy and who are ready to assume that politics inevitably emerges out of men's specialized experiences and selective perceptions. For many of these observers the kinds of activity described in the preceding sections of this book are a source of concern. They listen receptively if not with pleasure to alarms like those quoted at the opening of this chapter. They see a possibility that the pursuits of organized interest groups may produce a situation of such chaos and indecision that representative government and its values may somehow be lost. With such concerns we may appropriately reckon.

Interest Groups and the Nature of the State

Predictions concerning the consequences of given political activities are based upon conceptions of the governmental process. Predictions of any sort, of course, are outgrowths of understandings concerning the process to which the anticipated events are related. When the physiologist predicts that the consumption of a quantity of alcohol will have certain effects upon an individual's reflexes, when the chemist predicts that the application of heat to a particular mixture of substances will produce an explosion, and when the astronomer predicts that on a certain date there will occur an eclipse of the sun that will be visible from particular points on the earth's surface, each is basing his anticipation on a conception or an understanding of the respective somatic, chemical, and astronomical processes. Political prediction is no different. When an observer of the governmental scene says that the activities of organized political interest groups will result in the eclipse of certain behaviors subsumed under the heading of representative government, his statement reflects a conception of the dynamics of human relationships. Other elements enter into his prediction, but some such conception is basic to it.

A major difficulty in political prediction is that, in part because the relevant processes are extremely complex, our understanding of them is often not adequate; that is, the conceptions do not always account for all the variables and specify their relative importance. Such conceptions being inadequate in these respects, predictions based upon them are not reliable. Their accuracy is in large measure a matter of chance.[3] There are many people, both laymen and professional students of government, who argue that the complexity and irregularity of the political process are such that the reliability of predictions in this area will always be of a low order. We need not enter this controversy in these pages; one's position on the issue is in any case largely a matter of faith. We cannot, however, escape the necessity to predict. Government officials and private citizens must anticipate as best they can the consequences of political actions with which they are involved, though such predictions may have to rely heavily upon hunch, intuition, or calculated risk. In a good many cases our largely unformulated conceptions of the political process in America are adequate for prediction. For example, in every presidential election except that of 1860 one could have predicted, and many people tacitly did predict, that, whichever candidate was successful, his opponents and their supporters would not appeal from the decision of the ballot box to that of open violence. In many controversial areas of political behavior, however, our conceptions are almost completely lacking in predictive value.

A second handicap in political prediction is that the underlying conceptions are often almost completely implicit. They involve an array of partial and mutually contradictory assumptions of which the prophet is only dimly aware and of which many are derived from uncritically accepted myths and folklore concerning the political process in America. Predictions that are based upon such ill-formed, incomplete, and inaccurate premises are bound to be highly unreliable. Except as these unarticulated conceptions by chance happen to conform adequately to reality, they are a treacherous foundation for predictive statements. Many, if not most, predictions about the significance and implications of organized interest groups on the American scene rest on unreliable, implicit conceptions. To the extent that such statements are intended merely as a means of increasing or reducing the relative strength of competing interest groups, they may be evaluated wholly in terms of their effectiveness for that purpose. If they are presented, however, as systematic and responsible

[3] Cf. David B. Truman: "Political Behavior and Voting," in Mosteller *et al.*: *The Pre-election Polls of 1948*, pp. 225–50.

prognostications, they must be examined as such. In a large proportion of cases they will be found to rely on a flimsy conceptual structure, on a hopelessly inadequate and unacknowledged theory of the political process.

The principal task of this book has been to examine interest groups and their role in the formal institutions of government in order to provide an adequate basis for evaluating their significance in the American political process. It cannot be asserted that this effort has taken more than a few steps toward overcoming the difficulties of prediction in the study of politics or that a finished conception of the political process has been developed. The preceding chapters have attempted to present some of the major variables affecting the activities of interest groups and to work out a conception of the dynamics of American government that may give reliable meaning to those behaviors. A brief summary of this conception and a somewhat closer examination of its crucial features will help us to arrive at some of the implications of group politics for representative democracy in the United States.

Men, wherever they are observed, are creatures participating in those established patterns of interaction that we call groups. Excepting perhaps the most casual and transitory, these continuing interactions, like all such interpersonal relationships, involve power. This power is exhibited in two closely interdependent ways. In the first place, the group exerts power over its members; an individual's group affiliations largely determine his attitudes, values, and the frames of reference in terms of which he interprets his experiences. For a measure of conformity to the norms of the group is the price of acceptance within it. Such power is exerted not only by an individual's present group relationships; it also may derive from past affiliations such as the childhood family as well as from groups to which the individual aspires to belong and whose characteristic shared attitudes he also holds. In the second place, the group, if it is or becomes an interest group, which any group in a society may be, exerts power over other groups in the society when it successfully imposes claims upon them.

Many interest groups, probably an increasing proportion in the United States, are politicized. That is, either from the outset or from time to time in the course of their development they make their claims through or upon the institutions of government. Both the forms and functions of government in turn are a reflection of the activities and claims of such groups. The constitution-writing proclivities of Americans clearly reveal the influence of demands from such sources, and the statutory creation of new functions reflects their continuing operation. Many of these forms and functions have received such widespread acceptance from the start or in the course of time that they appear to be independent of the overt activities of organized interest groups. The judiciary is such a form. The building of city streets and the control of vehicular traffic are examples of such a function. However, if the judiciary or a segment of it operates in a fashion sharply contrary to the expectations of an appreciable portion of the community or if its role is strongly attacked, the group basis of its structure and powers is likely to become apparent. Similarly, if street construction greatly increases tax rates or if the control of traffic unnecessarily inconveniences either pedestrians or motorists, the exposure of these functions to the demands of competing interests will not be obscure. Interests that are widely held in the society may be reflected in government without their being organized in groups. They are what we have called potential groups. If the claims implied by the interests of these potential groups are quickly and adequately represented, interaction among those people who share the underlying interests or attitudes is unnecessary. But the interest base of accepted governmental forms and functions and their potential involvement in overt group activities are ever present even when not patently operative.

The institutions of government are centers of interest-based power; their connections with interest groups may be latent or overt and their activities range in political character from the routinized and widely accepted to the unstable and highly controversial. In order to make claims, political interest groups will seek access to the key points of decision within these institutions. Such points are scattered throughout the structure, including not only the formally established branches of government but also the political parties in their various forms and the relationships between governmental units and other interest groups.

The extent to which a group achieves effective access to the institutions of government is the resultant of a complex of interdependent factors. For the sake of simplicity these may be classified in three somewhat overlapping categories: (1) factors relating to a group's strategic position in the society; (2) factors associated with the internal characteristics of the group; and (3) factors peculiar to the governmental institutions themselves. In the first category are: the group's status or prestige in the society, affecting the ease with which it commands deference from those outside its bounds; the standing it and its activities have when measured against the widely held but largely unorganized interests or "rules of the game;" the extent to which government officials are formally or informally "members" of the group; and the usefulness of the group as a source of technical and political knowledge. The second category includes: the degree and appropriateness of the group's organization; the degree of cohesion it can achieve in a given situation, especially in the light of competing group demands upon its membership; the skills of the leadership; and the group's resources in numbers and money. In the third category, are: the operating structure of the government institutions, since such established features involve relatively fixed advantages and handicaps; and the effects of the group life of particular units or branches of the government.

The product of effective access, of the claims of organized and unorganized interests that achieve access with varying degrees of effectiveness, is a governmental decision. Note that these interests that achieve effective access and guide decisions need not be "selfish," are not necessarily solidly unified, and may not be represented by organized groups. Governmental decisions are the resultant of effective access by various interests, of which organized groups may be only a segment. These decisions may be more or less stable depending on the strength of supporting interests and on the severity of disturbances in the society which affect that strength.

A characteristic feature of the governmental system in the United States is that it contains a multiplicity of points of access. The federal system establishes decentralized and more or less independent centers of power, vantage points from which to secure privileged access to the national government. Both a sign and a cause of the strength of the constituent units in the federal scheme is the peculiar character of our party system, which has strengthened parochial relationships, especially those of national legislators. National parties, and to a lesser degree those in the States, tend to be poorly cohesive leagues of locally based organizations rather than unified and inclusive structures. Staggered terms for executive officials and various types of legislators accentuate differences in the effective electorates that participate in choosing these officers. Each of these different, often opposite, localized patterns (constituencies) is a channel of independent access to the larger party aggregation and to the formal government. Thus, especially at the national level, the party is an electing-device and only in limited measure an integrated means of policy determination. Within the Congress, furthermore, controls are diffused among committee chairmen and other leaders in both chambers. The variety of these points of access is further supported by relationships stemming from the constitutional doctrine of the separation of powers, from related checks and balances, and at the State and local level from the common practice of choosing an array of executive officials by popular election. At the Federal level the formal simplicity of the executive branch has been complicated by a Supreme Court decision that has placed a number of administrative agencies beyond the removal power of the president. The position of these units, however, differs only in degree from that of many that are constitutionally within the executive branch. In consequence of alternative lines of access available through the legislature and the executive and of divided channels for the control of administrative policy, many nominally executive agencies are at various times virtually independent of the chief executive.

Although some of these lines of access may operate in series, they are not arranged in a stable and integrated hierarchy. Depending upon the whole political context in a given period and upon the relative strength of contending interests, one or another of the centers of power in the formal government or in the parties may become the apex of a hierarchy of controls. Only the highly routinized governmental activities show any stability in this respect, and these may as easily be subordinated to elements in the legislature as to the chief executive. Within limits, therefore, organized interest groups, gravitating toward responsive points of decision, may play one segment of the structure against another as circumstances and strategic considerations permit. The total pattern of government over a period of time thus presents a protean complex of crisscrossing relationships that change in strength and direction with alterations in the power and standing of interests, organized and unorganized.

There are two elements in this conception of the political process in the United States that are of crucial significance and that require special emphasis. These are, first, the notion of multiple or overlapping membership and, second, the function of unorganized interests, or potential interest groups.

The idea of overlapping membership stems from the conception of a group as a standardized pattern of interactions rather than as a collection of human units. Although the former may appear to be a rather misty abstraction, it is actually far closer to complex reality than the latter notion. The view of a group as an aggregation of individuals abstracts from the observable fact that in any society, and especially a complex one, no single group affiliation accounts for all of the attitudes or interests of any individual except a fanatic or a compulsive neurotic. No tolerably normal person is totally absorbed in any group in which he participates. The diversity of an individual's activities and his attendant interests involve him in a variety of actual and potential groups. Moreover, the fact that the genetic experiences of no two individuals are identical and the consequent fact that the spectra of their attitudes are in varying degrees dissimilar means that the members of a single group will perceive the group's claims in terms of a diversity of frames of reference. Such heterogeneity may be of little significance until such time as these multiple memberships conflict. Then the cohesion and influence of the affected group depend upon the incorporation or accommodation of the conflicting loyalties of any significant segment of the group, an accommodation that may result in altering the original claims. Thus the leaders of a Parent-Teacher Association must take some account of the fact that their proposals must be acceptable to members who also belong to the local taxpayers' league, to the local chamber of commerce, and to the Catholic Church.

The notion of overlapping membership bears directly upon the problems allegedly created by the appearance of a multiplicity of interest groups. Yet the fact of such overlapping is frequently overlooked or neglected in discussions of the political role of groups. James Madison, whose brilliant analysis in the tenth essay in *The Federalist* we have frequently quoted, relied primarily upon diversity of groups and difficulty of communication to protect the new government from the tyranny of a factious majority. He barely touched on the notion of multiple membership when he observed, almost parenthetically: "Besides other impediments, it may be remarked that, where there is a consciousness of unjust or dishonorable purposes, communication is always checked by distrust in proportion to the number whose concurrence is necessary." John C. Calhoun's idea of the concurrent majority, developed in his posthumously published work, *A Disquisition on Government* (1851), assumed the unified, monolithic character of the groups whose liberties he was so anxious to protect. When his present-day followers unearth his doctrines, moreover, they usually make the same assumption, although implicitly.[4] Others, seeking a satisfactory means of accounting for the continued existence of the political system, sometimes assume that it is the nonparticipant citizens, aroused to unwonted activity, who act as a kind of counterbalance to the solid masses that constitute organized interest groups.[5] Although this phenomenon may occur in

---

[4] Cf. John Fischer: "Unwritten Rules of American Politics," *Harper's Magazine* (November, 1948), pp. 27–36.

[5] Cf. Herring: *The Politics of Democracy*, p. 32.

times of crisis, reliance upon it reckons insufficiently with the established observation that citizens who are nonparticipant in one aspect of the governmental process, such as voting, rarely show much concern for any phase of political activity. Multiple membership is more important as a restraint upon the activities of organized groups than the rarely aroused protests of chronic nonparticipants.

Organized interest groups are never solid and monolithic, though the consequences of their overlapping memberships may be handled with sufficient skill to give the organizations a maximum of cohesion. It is the competing claims of other groups *within* a given interest group that threaten its cohesion and force it to reconcile its claims with those of other groups active on the political scene. The claims within the American Medical Association of specialists and teaching doctors who support group practice, compulsory health insurance, and preventive medicine offer an illustration. The presence within the American Legion of public-housing enthusiasts and labor unionists as well as private homebuilders and labor opponents provides another example. Potential conflicts within the Farm Bureau between farmers who must buy supplementary feed and those who produce excess feed grains for the market, between soybean growers and dairymen, even between traditional Republicans and loyal Democrats, create serious political problems for the interest group. Instances of the way in which such cleavages impose restraints upon an organized group's activities are infinitely numerous, almost as numerous as cases of multiple membership. Given the problems of cohesion and internal group politics that result from overlapping membership, the emergence of a multiplicity of interest groups in itself contains no dangers for the political system, especially since such overlapping affects not only private but also governmental "members" of the organized group.

But multiple membership in organized groups is not sufficiently extensive to obviate the possibility of irreconcilable conflict. There is little overlapping in the memberships of the National Association of Manufacturers and the United Steelworkers of America, or of the American Farm Bureau Federation and the United Automobile Workers. Overlapping membership among relatively cohesive organized interest groups provides an insufficient basis upon which to account for the relative stability of an operating political system. That system is a fact. An adequate conception of the group process must reckon with it. To paraphrase the famous words of John Marshall, we must never forget that it is a going polity we are explaining.

We cannot account for an established American political system without the second crucial element in our conception of the political process, the concept of the unorganized interest, or potential interest group. Despite the tremendous number of interest groups existing in the United States, not all interests are organized. If we recall the definition of an interest as a shared attitude, it becomes obvious that continuing interaction resulting in claims upon other groups does not take place on the basis of all such attitudes. One of the commonest interest group forms, the association, emerges out of severe or prolonged disturbances in the expected relationships of individuals in similar institutionalized groups. An association continues to function as long as it succeeds in ordering these disturbed relationships, as a labor union orders the relationships between management and workers. Not all such expected relationships are simultaneously or in a given short period sufficiently disturbed to produce organization. Therefore only a portion of the interests or attitudes involved in such expectations are represented by organized groups. Similarly, many organized groups—families, businesses, or churches, for example—do not operate continuously as interest groups or as political interest groups.

Any mutual interest, however, any shared attitude, is a potential group. A disturbance in established relationships and expectations anywhere in the society may produce new patterns of interaction aimed at restricting or eliminating the disturbance. Sometimes it may be this possibility of organization that alone gives the potential group a minimum of influence in the political process. Thus Key notes that the Delta planters in Mississippi "must speak for their Negroes in such programs as health and education," although the latter are virtually unorganized and are denied the means of active political participation.[6] It is in this sense that Bentley speaks of a difference in degree between the politics of despotism and that of other "forms" of government. He notes that there is "a process of representation in despotisms which is inevitable in all democracies, and which may be distinguished by quantities and by elaboration of technique, but not in any deeper 'qualititative' way." He speaks of the despot as "representative of his own class, and to a smaller, but none the less real, extent of the ruled class as well."[7] Obstacles to the development of organized groups from potential ones may be presented by inertia or by the activities of opposed groups, but the possibility that severe disturbances

---

[6] Key: *Southern Politics*, pp. 235 and *passim*.

[7] Bentley: *The Process of Government*, pp. 314–5. Copyright 1908 by and used with the permission of Arthur F. Bentley.

will be created if these submerged, potential interests should organize necessitates some recognition of the existence of these interests and gives them at least a minimum of influence.

More important for present purposes than the potential groups representing separate minority elements are those interests or expectations that are so widely held in the society and are so reflected in the behavior of almost all citizens that they are, so to speak, taken for granted. Such "majority" interests are significant not only because they may become the basis for organized interest groups but also because the "membership" of such potential groups overlaps extensively the memberships of the various organized interest groups.[8] The resolution of conflicts between the claims of such unorganized interests and those of organized interest groups must grant recognition to the former not only because affected individuals may feel strongly attached to them but even more certainly because these interests are widely shared and are a part of many established patterns of behavior the disturbance of which would be difficult and painful. They are likely to be highly valued.

These widely held but unorganized interests are what we have previously called the "rules of the game." Others have described these attitudes in such terms as "systems of belief," as a "general ideological consensus," and as "a broad body of attitudes and understandings regarding the nature and limits of authority."[9] Each of these interests (attitudes) may be wide or narrow, general or detailed. For the mass of the population they may be loose and ambiguous, though more precise and articulated at the leadership level. In any case the "rules of the game" are interests the serious disturbance of which will result in organized interaction and the assertion of fairly explicit claims for conformity. In the American system the "rules" would include the value generally attached to the dignity of the individual human being, loosely expressed in terms of "fair dealing" or more explicitly verbalized in formulations such as the Bill of Rights. They would embrace what in Chapter 5 we called "the democratic mold," that is, the approval of forms for broad mass participation in the designation

[8] See the suggestive discussion of this general subject in Robert Bierstedt: "The Sociology of Majorities," *American Sociological Review*, Vol. 13, no. 6 (December, 1948), pp. 700–10.

[9] Kluckhohn: *Mirror for Man*, pp. 248 and *passim*; Sebastian de Grazia: *The Political Community: A Study of Anomie* (Chicago: University of Chicago Press, 1948), pp. ix, 80, and *passim*; Almond: *The American People and Foreign Policy*, p. 158; Charles E. Merriam: *Systematic Politics* (Chicago: University of Chicago Press, 1945), p. 213.

of leaders and in the selection of policies in all social groups and institutions. They would also comprehend certain semi-egalitarian notions of material welfare. This is an illustrative, not an exhaustive, list of such interests.

The widely held, unorganized interests are reflected in the major institutions of the society, including the political. The political structure of the United States, as we have seen, has adopted characteristic legislative, executive, and judicial forms through the efforts of organized interest groups. Once these forms have been accepted and have been largely routinized, the supporting organized interest groups cease to operate as such and revert to the potential stage. As embodied in these institutional forms and in accepted verbal formulations, such as those of legal and constitutional theory, the interests of these potential groups are established expectations concerning not only *what* the governmental institutions shall do, but more particularly *how* they shall operate. To the extent that these established processes remain noncontroversial, they may appear to have no foundation in interests. Nevertheless, the widespread expectations will receive tacit or explicit deference from most organized interest groups in consequence of the overlapping of their memberships with these potential groups.[10] Violation of the "rules of the game" normally will weaken a group's cohesion, reduce its status in the community, and expose it to the claims of other groups. The latter may be competing organized groups that more adequately incorporate the "rules," or they may be groups organized on the basis of these broad interests and in response to the violations.

The pervasive and generally accepted character of these unorganized interests, or "rules," is such that they are acquired by most individuals in their early experiences in the family, in the public schools (probably less effectively in the private and parochial schools), and in similar institutionalized groups that are also expected to conform in some measure to the "democratic mold." The "rules" are likely to be reinforced by later events. Persons who aspire to, or occupy, public office of whatever sort are particularly likely to identify with these expected behaviors as part of their desired or existing roles. With varying degrees of effectiveness the group life of government agencies—legislative, executive, and judicial—reinforces the claims of these unorganized interests, which overlap those of the official group itself and those of "outside" political interest groups. Marked and prolonged deviation from these expected behaviors by public officials,

[10] Cf. Bentley: *The Process of Government*, p. 397, and MacIver: *The Web of Government*, p. 79.

who are expected to represent what Bentley calls the "'absent' or quiescent group interests," will normally produce restrictive action by other governmental functionaries, by existing organized interest groups, by ones newly organized in consequence of the deviations, or by all three.

It is thus multiple memberships in potential groups based on widely held and accepted interests that serve as a balance wheel in a going political system like that of the United States. To some people this observation may appear to be a truism and to others a somewhat mystical notion. It is neither. In the first place, neglect of this function of multiple memberships in most discussions of organized interest groups indicates that the observation is not altogether commonplace. Secondly, the statement has no mystical quality; the effective operation of these widely held interests is to be inferred directly from verbal and other behavior in the political sphere. Without the notion of multiple memberships in potential groups it is literally impossible to account for the existence of a viable polity such as that in the United States or to develop a coherent conception of the political process. The strength of these widely held but largely unorganized interests explains the vigor with which propagandists for organized groups attempt to change other attitudes by invoking such interests.[11] Their importance is further evidenced in the recognized function of the means of mass communication, notably the press, in reinforcing widely accepted norms of "public morality."[12]

The role of the widespread unorganized interests and potential groups does not imply that such interests are always and everywhere dominant. Nor does it mean that the slightest action in violation of any of them inevitably and instantly produces a restrictive response from another source. These interests are not unambiguous, as the long history of litigation concerning freedom of speech will demonstrate. Subjectively they are not all equally fundamental. Thus since the "rules" are interests competing with those of various organized groups, they are in any given set of circumstances more or less subject to attenuation through such psychological mechanisms as rationalization. Moreover, the means of communication, whether by word of mouth or through the mass media, may not adequately make known particular deviations from the behavior indicated by these broad interests.

[11] Cf. Lazarsfeld et al.: The People's Choice, preface to 2d edition, pp. xxi–xxii.
[12] Cf. Paul F. Lazarsfeld and Robert K. Merton: "Mass Communication, Popular Taste and Organized Social Act," in Lyman Bryson (ed.): The Communication of Ideas (New York: Harper and Brothers, 1948), pp. 102 ff.

In a relatively vigorous political system, however, these unorganized interests are dominant with sufficient frequency in the behavior of enough important segments of the society so that, despite ambiguity and other restrictions, both the activity and the methods of organized interest groups are kept within broad limits. This interpretation is not far from Lasswell's view of the state as a relational system defined by a certain frequency of subjective events.[18] According to his definition, "the state . . . is a time-space manifold of similar subjective events. . . .That subjective event which is the unique mark of the state is the recognition that one belongs to a community with a system of paramount claims and expectations."[14] All citizens of the state as thus conceived need not experience this "event" continuously or with equal intensity. Nor need the attitudes of all citizens be favorable toward these "claims and expectations." But the existence of the state, of the polity, depends on widespread, frequent recognition of and conformity to the claims of these unorganized interests and on activity condemning marked deviations from them. "All this," says Lasswell, "is frequently expressed as the 'sense of justice'. . . ."[15]

Thus it is only as the effects of overlapping memberships and the functions of unorganized interests and potential groups are included in the equation that it is accurate to speak of governmental activity as the product or resultant of interest group activity. As Bentley has put it:

> There are limits to the technique of the struggle, this involving also limits to the group demands, all of which is solely a matter of empirical observation. . . . Or, in other words, when the struggle proceeds too harshly at any point there will become insistent in the society a group more powerful than either of those involved which tends to suppress the extreme and annoying methods of the groups in the primary struggle. It is within the embrace of these great lines of activity that the smaller struggles proceed, and the very word struggle has meaning only with reference to its limitations.[16]

To assert that the organization and activity of powerful interest groups constitutes a threat to representative government without measuring

[18] Lasswell: *Psychopathology and Politics*, pp. 240–61.
[14] Ibid., p. 245.
[15] Ibid., p. 246.
[16] Bentley: *The Process of Government*, p. 372. Copyright 1908 by and used with the permission of Arthur F. Bentley.

their relation to and effects upon the widespread potential groups is to generalize from insufficient data and upon an incomplete conception of the political process. Such an analysis would be as faulty as one that, ignoring differences in national systems, predicted identical responses to a given technological change in the United States, Japan, and the Soviet Union.

Interest Groups and Morbific Politics

No conception of the political process is adequate that does not take into account the possibilities of revolution and decay. There is some danger that recognition of the censoring and restraining functions of the widespread but unorganized interests in a viable polity will lead to the comforting but unwarranted assumption of some immanent harmony in the body politic. The existence of a going polity testifies to the present effectiveness of these functions, but it does not justify the projection of a present equilibrium into the indefinite future. Predictions concerning future stability, if they can be made at all, must be based upon an accumulation of research and measurement, even the barest outlines of which we cannot undertake in these pages. We can indicate, however, some of the factors that might contribute to the growth of a morbific politics and that might justify the predictions of those who view with alarm the development of organized political interest groups.

Because the unorganized interests may not be a central concern of most individuals and because those interests may have to be activated in the face of insistent violations, there is no guarantee that they will become operative in time to avoid profound disturbance or collapse. In a domestic crisis the continued latency of these unorganized interests may prevent the development of a viable compromise and encourage resort to less orderly means of adjustment.[17] In an international crisis the ineffectiveness of these interests may permit diplomatic or military decisions to be so warped and may allow shifts in prevailing policy to be so delayed that the governmental system will not survive the supreme test of war. These are typical possibilities. The conflict between more restricted organized interests may at any time be carried beyond safe limits before the struggle is seen as one affecting the interests of extensive potential groups.

Group conflict and a certain inconsistency of governmental policy

[17] Cf. Williams: *The Reduction of Intergroup Tensions*, p. 75.

are not in themselves signs of the weakening of the widespread potential groups. A measure of conflict is an unavoidable consequence of the multiplication of groups and of specialized individual activities.[18] The process of accommodating group claims, moreover, does not necessarily produce a nice symmetry of public policy. As in the feverish activity of the early New Deal, the adoption of superficially contradictory policies may in a larger view be a means of assuring the strength of the system rather than a sign of its decomposition.[19] Nor is dollar economy an indication of the health of the process. Fiscal neatness may or may not be a symptom of political stability. There is evidence, moreover, that the American political system is inherently productive of fiscal confusion and is "not highly suited to a straightforward business-like management of finance." As Herring has further observed: "Government has matters other than finances to manage. Our present form of government is not to be judged simply in terms of its ineptness for fiscal control."[20] Except as fiscal confusion may frustrate the expressed objectives of political policy, matters of financial efficiency are not close to the foundations of the governmental system.

The effective activation of widespread unorganized interests depends upon the character of the society's means of communication, broadly conceived. We have previously seen that one of the elements in a president's ability to lead these interests is the ease with which he can gain for his statements ample space in the media of mass communication. Research evidence indicates that individuals who hold a broad interest of the type we are here concerned with may or may not see a given set of events as bearing upon that interest. How they will perceive such occurrences depends not only upon the importance they attach to the interest but also upon the adequacy of the information available to them concerning the events.[21] The quality and character of the mass media, therefore, and of the various means of interpersonal communication—rumors, letters, and conversations—are of fundamental importance in assuring the influence of unorganized interests. Not only censorship and distortion in the channels of communication but inadequate coverage may prevent the

---

[18] See ibid., p. 56 and *passim*.

[19] See O. H. Taylor: "Economics Versus Politics," in Douglass Brown *et al.*: *The Economics of the Recovery Program* (New York: McGraw-Hill Book Company, 1934), pp. 160–88.

[20] Pendleton Herring: "The Politics of Fiscal Policy," *Yale Law Journal*, Vol. 47, no. 5 (March, 1938), pp. 737–8.

[21] M. Brewster Smith: "Personal Values as Determinants of a Political Attitude," *The Journal of Psychology*, Vol. 28 (1949), pp. 477–86.

assertion of claims based upon the interests of potential groups. There are indications, for example, that one reason for the improvements in recent years in the treatment of Negroes in the United States is that most of them are likely to know when one of their number is dealt with in a manner seriously violating the "rules of the game" and that many will act on the basis of such information.[22] Successive claims of this sort in defense of the "rules of the game" not only may check the specific violations but also may strengthen the affected interests throughout the society. In the absence of adequate communication, restraints upon governmental acts that violate widespread unorganized interests must rely upon officials' "memberships" in the potential groups. While these "memberships" are not to be discounted, without the likelihood of additional support they may be too weak to effect significant restraints.

Broadly speaking, the communications channels include not only the media but also group organizations to facilitate the expression of claims. Not only freedom of speech and of the press, but also the third in the classic triumvirate, freedom of assembly, is essential to the activation of unorganized interests. These freedoms are parts of the "rules of the game" in a representative democracy and at the same time are essential elements in the continued vitality of the unorganized interests. Obstacles to organization not only may obstruct communication but, by frustrating expectations based on the "rules of the game," may even weaken attachment to segments of the governmental institution. One of the most serious consequences of the courts' restrictive interpretations of the law in cases dealing with the organization of labor, especially between the 1890's and the 1930's, was workers' loss of confidence in the judiciary, reflected in a very general and not wholly unwarranted assumption that judges would not deal "fairly" with workers' attempts to organize.[23]

Since the major target for the claims of extensive potential groups is the institution of government, the established governmental patterns may operate to weaken the effect of widespread interests. Peculiarities of structure may so restrict and dam up the channels of adjustment that the "justice" interest may conflict with the claim for nonviolent change. Such a situation in the society as a whole is not materially different from those we have discussed in connection with particular organized interest groups. Just as the structure of the American Federation of Labor in the 1920's and early 1930's was poorly

[22] See Arnold and Caroline Rose: *America Divided: Minority Group Relations in the United States* (New York: Alfred A. Knopf, Inc., 1948), p. 192.
[23] Millis and Montgomery: *Organized Labor*, pp. 669–70.

representative of the dynamic elements within the group and among workers generally, so conventional patterns within the institution of government may be so rigid that they undermine the acceptance of representative methods of peaceful change. Established patterns of access, defended and rationalized in terms of the ambiguous "rules of the game," may block the assertion of claims based on alternative interpretations of widely held interests.

Adequate research has never been done on the incidence of widespread unorganized interests and on the extent to which they are central in the attitude hierarchies of various segments of the population. Such research needs to be carried on not only in terms of demographic aggregates, but also on the basis of classifications that reflect the relative power of individuals and organized groups.[24] The methods for such research are not fully developed, but existing techniques could provide far more information than is presently available. Though adequate evidence of this sort is not at hand, however, it seems probable that the widespread unorganized interests are adequately strong within power centers in and outside the government in the United States. If this assumption is valid, dangers to the continuance of representative government derive less from lack of basic support for these interests than from other features of the political system.

Perhaps the outstanding characteristic of American politics, as we have noted earlier, is that it involves a multiplicity of co-ordinate or nearly co-ordinate points of access to governmental decisions. The significance of these many points of access and of the complicated texture of relationships among them is great. This diversity assures a variety of modes for the participation of interest groups in the formation of policy, a variety that is a flexible, stabilizing element. On the other hand, multiple and generally co-ordinate lines of access mean that the locus of initiative in the making of policy is not sharply defined and that the necessity for maintaining a certain comity among many of these points of control—especially in the legislature, the executive, and the political parties—may promote delay and inaction.[25] In times of undramatized crisis, as in the diplomatic maneuvers in the months prior to a war or in the early phases of a severe inflation, delay or stalemate may have consequences that will threaten,

[24] See Almond: *The American People and Foreign Policy*, chap. 6; Avery Leiserson: "Opinion Research and the Political Process," *Public Opinion Quarterly*, Vol. 13, no. 1 (Spring, 1949), pp. 31–8; Truman: "Political Behavior and Voting."

[25] Cf. Almond: *The American People and Foreign Policy*, pp. 144–5.

the stability of the system. The peculiarities of American government have not prevented it from dealing with admitted crises of war and depression, but they may keep it from preventing or avoiding such severe tests of its capacity to survive.

Overlapping membership among organized interest groups and among these and potential groups is, as we have seen, the principal balancing force in the politics of a multigroup society such as the United States. We have further observed that these unifying widespread interests are not always mutually consistent and unambiguous. Variations in group experiences and, consequently, in frames of reference invite differences in the importance attached to these partially inconsistent interests, and their ambiguity permits divergent rationalizations in terms of these diversified frames of reference. Thus if the society has developed great differences in personal wealth, egalitarian demands may be rated above the claims of peaceful change by those in less privileged positions; and orderly adjustment may be regarded as more important than freedom of speech or assembly by those whose economic status is high. Each segment, moreover, can rationalize its preferences in terms of its own view of "fairness" and "individual dignity."

It follows that the stabilizing effects of overlapping memberships may be limited or eliminated if they operate primarily or exclusively within sharply defined social strata or classes that are characterized in part by the specialized priorities and meanings they give the widespread and ambiguous interests. An extreme hypothetical example may clarify this point. Assume a situation in which virtually all interaction takes place within social strata and in which there are few or no organized groups whose membership is drawn from more than one class. Overlapping memberships then would tend to reconcile differences within rather than between social levels. Since individuals' group experiences would largely be confined to a single stratum of the society, definitions of potential group interests, such as the proper limits to freedom of speech, would vary sharply from one social level to another. Moreover, if experiences were confined within class lines in this fashion, freedom of speech, for example, might be valued highly in one class but be regarded as dispensable in another. In such a case overlapping memberships in a potential "free speech" group might not effectively moderate conflicts between organized interest groups whose members were drawn exclusively from different social classes.

Reference to such a state of affairs is often implied in banal political phrases about "human rights versus property rights." The appearance of such statements in political discourse does not necessarily mark the demise of effective overlapping and may signify the reverse. But genuine stratification of memberships and of the limiting "rules," combined with restricted movement from one stratum to another, might weaken a system like that in America long before, or even without, the emergence of class warfare in the crude Marxist sense. Widespread interests might then fail to restrict the activities of antagonistic organized groups belonging to different classes, and differing interpretations of these "rules" might instead become sources of conflict *between* strata of the society.

The problems presented by rigid stratification are somewhat akin to those implied in the frequently expressed concern over any weakening of civilian control over our growing military establishment. A group of professional military officers, recruited at an early age, trained outside of civilian institutions, and practising the profession of arms in comparative isolation from other segments of the society, easily may develop the characteristics of a caste. Such a group not only will generate its own peculiar interests but also may arrive at interpretations of the "rules of the game" that are at great variance with those held by most of the civilian population. In such a case multiple membership in other organized groups is slight and that in potential widespread groups is unlikely.

The dynamics and power implications of class stratification in the United States are largely unexplored territory.[26] Vagueness of class lines, however, and a concomitant mobility from class to class have been marked characteristics of American society almost from its beginnings. There is some evidence that ease of mobility may be less great now than in times past, and occasionally it is asserted that the society shows a trend toward division into two sharply separate classes. The criteria of social class are not sufficiently established to justify such assertions, and adequate data on such supposed trends have never been collected.[27]

The expectations implied by the widespread unorganized interests characteristic of the United States would seem to require the existence of a great many patterns of interaction that cut across, or are independent of, class lines. If this be true, then any tendency for organized interest groups of the association type to operate within class lines or to be much more numerous in some classes of the population than in others may be a source of political instability. Evidence on this

---

[26] Edward Shils: *The Present State of American Sociology* (Glencoe, Ill.: The Free Press, 1948), pp. 15–25.

[27] See, for example, the statement in Centers: *The Psychology of Social Classes*, p. 74.

score is not altogether satisfactory, partly owing to the wide variety of senses in which the word "class" is used. Several bodies of data, however, indicate: (1) that the frequency of membership in formal organizations of the association type increases from the lower to the upper reaches of the class structure, and (2) that the members of many, if not most, such groups are drawn from the same or closely similar status levels.[28] At the same time, the findings of Warner and his associates in Newburyport led them to conclude that the number of formal organizations that cut across several classes and that facilitated social mobility served as an important unifying influence in the community.[29]

The specialization of organized interest groups along class lines and the atrophy or deficiency of such groups in the less privileged classes may be a source of political instability for at least two reasons. In the first place, organized interest groups normally provide standardized procedures for asserting group claims and for settling conflicts. Established interest organizations, moreover, may be presumed to have conformed in some measure to the interests of potential groups in the community. Segments of the population that lack such organized means of participation in the political process may none the less experience drastic changes in expected relationships, changes that may result in their making increased demands upon the political institutions. In the absence of standardized means of participation they may more readily identify with movements that poorly reflect widespread unorganized interests or that explicitly repudiate portions of them. Extensive unemployment and severe inflation bring such drastic changes, and the history of movements of the fascist type illustrates the destructive forms that such situations can produce. In the second place, even where the widespread unorganized interests are strong enough to prevent the emergence of a movement of the sort just mentioned, specialization of organized groups in certain classes of the population may provide a pattern of governmental access in which only those groups reflecting a particular class interpretation of the broad interests can gain expression through the governmental institutions. The emergence in the disadvantaged classes of groups that reflect materially different interpretations of the widespread interests

[28] Warner and Lunt: *The Social Life of a Modern Community*, chap. 16; Lazarsfeld *et al.*: *The People's Choice*, pp. 145–7. For some suggestions on the reasons for less working-class participation in formal organizations see Seymour Bellin and Frank Riessman, Jr.: "Education, Culture, and the Anarchic Worker," *Journal of Social Issues*, Vol. 5, no. 1 (Winter, 1949), pp. 24–32.
[29] Warner and Lunt: *The Social Life of a Modern Community*, pp. 114 ff., 301 ff.

may encourage conflict and at the same time provide an inadequate basis for peaceful settlement. The appearance of groups representing Negroes, especially in the South, groups whose interpretations of the "rules of the game" are divergent from those of the previously organized and privileged segments of the community, are a case in point.[30] Caste and class interpretations of widespread unorganized interests may be at least as ready a source of instability as conflicts between more restricted organized groups.

This rather cursory examination suggests that a pathogenic politics in the United States is possible, though not necessarily imminent. The processes through which unorganized interests restrain the activities of organized groups may not become operative in time to avert serious crises. Potential groups may remain latent as a result of deficiencies in the means of communication. The claims of both organized and unorganized interests may assume an explosive character as a result of restraints upon the ability to organize, in consequence of rigidity in the established patterns of access, and as an outgrowth of delay and inaction made possible by the diffusion of lines of access to governmental decisions. The frustration of group claims may be dangerously prolonged and the bitterness of group conflict may be intensified through class interpretations of the "rules of the game." Similarly, the expectations of groups emerging out of the less privileged segments of the society may be poorly represented or dangerously frustrated in consequence of the concentration of, and privileged access of, organized groups among persons of higher status.

These factors are obviously not the only ones that might lead to a disruption of representative government in the United States. Others might be mentioned, but it is not the purpose of these pages to develop a complete theory of the process of revolution as it might operate in America.[31] We are here merely interested in pointing out that no political system is proof against such upheaval and concerned with noting what kinds of connections may exist between the development of a revolutionary crisis and the presence of a multiplicity of highly organized interest groups. None of the factors of instability discussed in the preceding paragraphs is inherently a consequence

[30] Cf. Myrdal: *An American Dilemma*, chap. 1 and *passim*; Williams: *The Reduction of Intergroup Tensions*, pp. 62–3.
[31] Among the most suggestive treatments of this subject are Crane Brinton: *The Anatomy of Revolution* (New York: W. W. Norton & Company, Inc., 1938); Lyford P. Edwards: *The Natural History of Revolution* (Chicago: University of Chicago Press, 1927); George S. Pettee: *The Process of Revolution* (New York: Harper and Brothers, 1938); and Pitrim Sorokin: *The Sociology of Revolution* (Philadelphia: J. B. Lippincott Company, 1925).

of the existence of such groups. The crucial element in all of them is the relationship of these groups and of the established patterns of access to the widespread potential groups in the society. This relationship in each instance may become morbid either because the unorganized interests are inadequately activated or because recurrent and prolonged frustration of more restricted claims leads to the rejection of a large segment of the "rules of the game." In a healthy political system there is a connection between some minimum recoᵣ tion of the claims of organized groups and the vitality of widespread unorganized interests. Without such recognition, the latter cease to be accepted as "rules of the game." As Hartz has observed in somewhat different terms: "Norms of policy that recognize nothing but the interplay of [organized] interest pressures are inadequate; but norms that scarcely recognize them at all lead directly to a disillusionment with the political process." [32] The continued strength of civil liberties, representative techniques, and other widespread interests requires that support of these "rules" not become identified with the prolonged frustration of organized group demands. [33]

The strength of the unorganized "rules of the game" in the United States has been remarked by foreign observers from De Tocqueville to Myrdal. The latter, for example, speaks of them as being more "explicitly expressed" and "more widely understood and appreciated" in America than in other Western nations. [34] The great political task now as in the past is to perpetuate a viable system by maintaining the conditions under which such widespread understanding and appreciation can exist. These conditions are not threatened by the existence of a multiplicity of organized groups so long as the "rules of the game" remain meaningful guides to action, meaningful in the sense that acceptance of them is associated with some minimal recognition of group claims. In the loss of such meanings lie the seeds of the whirlwind.

Nostrums and Palliatives

No political system is proof against decay and dissolution. Regardless of the flexibility of the structure, within any society changes of great

---

[32] Hartz: *Economic Policy and Democratic Thought*, p. 310.

[33] There is a resemblance between the position taken in these pages and the concept of *anomie*. For an acute analysis of the political implications of Durkheim's theory see deGrazia: *The Political Community*.

[34] Myrdal: *An American Dilemma*, p. 3. For similar comments see De Tocqueville: *Democracy in America*, Vol. I, pp. 196–8, 393.

severity and extent may occur that will rupture the established governmental process. At the same time governments vary in the ease with which they can adjust to changes, in the adequacy with which their procedures reflect the widespread unorganized interests in the society, and in the speed with which they can arrive at acceptable solutions for the problems which confront them. In the United States, as in other countries, proposals appear from time to time that promise to improve the capacities of the governmental system in these respects. Many reforms in particular propose to deal with the activities of organized interest groups. Some of these are programs that, though phrased in general terms, reflect the efforts of organized groups to achieve more effective access to the government; some represent efforts to strengthen unorganized interests in the face of practices that appear to endanger them; a few purport to do away with organized interest groups as a disease of the body politic. With the last named we need not concern ourselves further. Some examination of the other types is in order.

In the first two decades of this century there appeared numerous proposals for the direct representation of organized interest groups in the legislative body, the intellectual sponsors of which were a school of pluralists influenced by the English guild socialists.[85] Crudely stated, these proposals argued that the territorial system of representation was a sham and that it should be abolished in favor of a system that allotted legislative seats to interest groups. Little has been heard of such suggestions since the early 1930's, but occasionally they crop up in the writings of a commentator who wants to do away with the supposed evils of "pressure" groups by having these groups elect the members of Congress.[86]

These proposals are worth noting, not because they are likely to be adopted (except in the wake of an authoritarian revolution), but because their recurrence illustrates how easily the nature of the political process may be misunderstood. Typically such suggestions are made by persons who assume that political conflicts involve no fundamental cleavages and that, if the legislature can be made "truly representative," differences will be easily and peacefully resolved. Their proponents need to contemplate the wisdom of Mr. Dooley's trenchant observation that "politics ain't bean bag."

Most proposals for "functional" representation also grossly oversimplify the group structure of the society and neglect the phenomenon of overlapping membership. They usually assume, in fact, that occu-

[85] Kung Chuan Hsiao: *Political Pluralism*.
[86] See, for example, Fergusson: *People and Power*, pp. 110-1.

pational groups are the only ones requiring representation in such a legislature. Even in so restricted an arrangement the distribution of seats would have to be relatively arbitrary. If this difficulty were surmounted, the resulting scheme would freeze the patterns of access and confine them to groups recognized in the apportionment. The ambiguities of the territorial system permit a representative to shift with the changes in the group complexion of his constituency. No such flexibility would be likely under occupational representation. Occupational groups, moreover, would become parties, and to the extent that cohesive groupings actually followed occupational lines, the whole process of group adjustment and compromise would have to take place after, rather than during, elections. Any proposal that delays the beginnings of compromise and favors organized interest groups against the unorganized is highly explosive. It would be difficult to contrive a system more certain to create political apoplexy and paralysis.

The activities of organized interest groups have produced a long train of proposals for restricting their activities, and some of these proposals have been placed on the State and national statute books. Aside from general laws making bribery of any public official a crime, most of these suggestions deal with the relationships between interest groups and legislatures, relationships collectively designated in popular parlance and in many statutes by the term "lobbying." The legal history of lobbying legislation is a long one. The Alabama constitution of 1874 made "corrupt solicitation" of legislators a crime, and in 1877 the Georgia constitution outlawed "lobbying." In 1890 Massachusetts passed the first statute regulating "legislative agents," and by 1950 38 States and Alaska had similar laws on their books. At the Federal level such statutes are of later date, aside from a rule adopted by the House of Representatives in 1876 for the Forty-fourth Congress, requiring "persons or corporations" to register counsel or agents representing them in connection with pending legislation.[87] As early as 1907 bills were introduced in Congress to control "lobbying," and similar proposals have come up in most subsequent sessions. The first Federal enactment of this sort was a provision in the Public Utility Holding Company Act of 1935 requiring the representatives of such companies and their subsidiaries to register with the Securities and Exchange Commission in connection with dealings

[87] U.S. House of Representatives, Select Committee on Lobbying Activities: *Hearings*, 81st Cong., 2d Sess. (1950), part 1, p. 52. Belle Zeller's testimony in these hearings, pp. 58–97, contains an excellent summary of the State legislation on lobbying.

with Congress, with the S.E.C., or with the Federal Power Commission. A similar requirement concerning shipbuilders and ship operators dealing with the Congress or the Maritime Commission was passed in 1936. The Congress enacted the first general statute of this type in the Federal Regulation of Lobbying Act, a part of the Legislative Reorganization Act of 1946.[38]

Like the legislative investigations from which most proposals to regulate "lobbying" have sprung, these acts are attempts to inject more explicitly into the legislative process certain widespread expectations concerning access to and operation of the legislature. Both the proposals and the statutes have usually emerged from publicized allegations of privileged access or from charges of attempts to achieve such a favored position through covert means. This situation was beautifully illustrated in the 1949 California statute, which closely resembled the Federal law. This was passed at a special session of the legislature, following the publication of a series of articles in a national magazine in which "the secret boss of California" bragged of his control over the legislature.[39] In the words of the Governor's call, the revelations involved "the honor of our State." [40]

The proposals and enactments concerning "lobbying" usually provide for some form of registration or licensing of individuals and groups who have dealings with legislators. This registration often includes a requirement that the registrant not only indicate what legislation he is concerned with but also record his receipts and disbursements. These measures also usually establish penalties for failure to conform. That these provisions normally do not make illegal any group action other than unregistered "lobbying" and that they include highly ambiguous definitions of the groups and persons covered as well as of the "lobbying" activity, suggests that they are chiefly significant as declarations against privileged access of a covert nature or achieved by such means.

Measures purporting to regulate "lobbying" may not be completely without importance in reinforcing the "rules of the game" and the influence of office. They may have some competitive political value as well. Groups whose status in the community is such that announcement of their connection with a legislative measure would weaken

[38] Belle Zeller: "The Federal Regulation of Lobbying Act," *American Political Science Review*, Vol. 42, no. 2 (April, 1948), pp. 239–71.
[39] Lester Velie: "The Secret Boss of California," *Collier's Magazine*, August 13, 20, 1949, pp. 11 ff., pp. 12 ff.
[40] Quoted in U.S. House of Representatives, Select Committee on Lobbying Activities: *Hearings*, 81st Cong., 2d Sess. (1950), part 1, p. 76.

its chances may find themselves somewhat handicapped by a registration statute. Similarly, official reports of a group's sources of financial support and of unusually large expenditures in connection with legislation may be an advantage to those representing opposing interests. Like legislative investigations, these measures, whether proposals or statutes, may be a means of protecting the claims of the legislative group itself against overly insistent interest group demands. Lobbying, as a congressman has put it, becomes "dangerous" only "when it is perverted and takes on the sinister nature of unwarranted pressure" and involves an "attempt to turn the heat on."[41] A registration proposal, like a threat of investigation, may function as a political asbestos suit.

Privileged access has roots far deeper, as we have earlier seen, than those exposed by reports of face-to-face relations with legislators or by records of extensive propaganda activity. Groups able to achieve highly effective access are not likely to be bothered by these regulatory statutes, as an incident that occurred in Wisconsin in 1910 will show. The Anti-Saloon League in that year secured exemption from the provisions of the State "lobbying" statute, on the grounds that it was not concerned with legislation of financial benefit to the group.[42] The relative unimportance of registration statutes is further suggested by the ease with which their requirements are ignored, by the common failure to establish enforcing agencies, and by the fact that indictment under the laws is extremely rare. As minor weapons in group politics and as reaffirmations of the "rules of the game," the attempts to regulate "lobbying" have some importance. Their political significance, however, is probably far less than the investigations that usually father them. They operate well out on the periphery of the political process.

Over the past several decades and particularly in the years since the advent of the New Deal many and diverse proposals have been made for dealing with organized interest groups by changing the structure of American government. Almost all of these projects have in common the object of reducing the diversity of lines of access to governmental decisions. Though they have not stated their concern in these terms, the sponsors of these proposals view with alarm the threats to the international security and internal stability of the American system stemming from the shifting and complicated patterns of influence that characterize its present operation. They see the likelihood, if not the present existence, of contradictory and self-defeating policies, of

[41] Ibid., p. 11.
[42] Odegard: *Pressure Politics*, p. 105.

half measures, and of delay and inaction, all of which may invite military or diplomatic disaster and a weakening of the widespread unorganized interests supporting the system of representative government.[43] That there is some merit in such concerns need hardly be reargued here. It is entirely possible, as we have noted before, that associations that must operate through the governmental mechanism and whose functions of stabilizing relationships in a complex society require a measure of co-ordinated treatment of group demands will, in the absence of stable and integrated lines of access, disrupt the political system. There is little doubt that the American governmental process lends itself with peculiar facility to the purposes of obstruction and that skilled political leadership may not be able to surmount that tendency with sufficient vigor. Diffusion of leadership and disintegration of policy are not hallucinations.

A large number of proposals for structural reform are confined to changes in the formal institutions of the government. Almost invariably they concentrate upon the separation of powers, particularly the division between the Congress and the chief executive.[44] Some support the outright importation of the cabinet or parliamentary system as it allegedly operates in Great Britain, including a drastic reduction in the powers of the Senate.[45] Others would retain the popular election of the president, but would provide for presidential authority to dissolve the Congress and call for a general election and would make the terms of both president and Congress coincident.[46] The less ambitious suggestions would effect limited alterations in formal structure and in the allocation of powers. Some of these aim at increasing the power of the president. They include proposals to grant the president the authority to veto individual items in appropriation bills and to provide more effective means of presidential control over the executive branch through reorganization and through expansion of his general staff facilities. Also aimed at reducing conflict between executive and

[43] Representative of the most suggestive of these proposals are William Y. Elliott: *The Need for Constitutional Reform* (New York: Whittlesey House, McGraw-Hill Book Company, Inc., 1935); Henry Hazlitt: *A New Constitution Now* (New York: Whittlesey House, McGraw-Hill Book Company, Inc., 1942); Thomas K. Finletter: *Can Representative Government Do the Job?* (New York: Reynal and Hitchcock, 1945).

[44] Henry L. Stimson was among the distinguished and experienced advocates of abandoning the separation between executive and legislative. See Stimson and Bundy: *On Active Service*, pp. 61-2.

[45] For example, Hazlitt: *A New Constitution Now*.

[46] Elliott: *The Need for Constitutional Reform*; Finletter: *Can Representative Government Do the Job?*

legislature are proposals to make wider use of consultative arrangements between executive departments and joint congressional committees, such as those that have developed informally between the State Department and the two principal committees dealing with foreign policy. Other critics would work toward a similar objective by restricting the diffused leadership within the Congress. A leading example of this tack is the proposal to abandon the practice of selecting committee chairmen on the basis of seniority, a custom that has the doubtful virtue of avoiding controversy over the organization of a newly elected legislature at the expense of an integrated legislative program. A less drastic suggestion is that for reducing the tendency toward committee monopoly of information by providing for regular question periods before the Congress, in which members of the president's cabinet would use an entire chamber and not merely isolated committees as a forum in which to defend their policies.

As intellectual exercises the more sweeping reform designs are instructive. As symptoms of dissatisfaction with existing arrangements they are significant and may accelerate the possibility of change even when their specific suggestions are fruitless. As concrete programs of political development, however, they are visionary. Like all utopias, they sketch a most inviting destination, but they do not indicate how we can get from here to there. An examination of the route is at least as important as a tempting description of the journey's end.

The relevant features of the political terrain are many and need not be treated at length in these pages. We may note, however, that those who propose the more sweeping constitutional reforms are likely to suggest, by way of persuasive argument, that this is not the late eighteenth century. One may reply with the observation that in more than one sense we are not dealing with the conditions of 1787. We are not dealing with a system that has had a formal existence of only ten years. The crises now confronting the United States may be quite as serious as those fostered by the Articles of Confederation, and our constitutional structure may be as deeply involved in them. For better or for worse, however, the Constitution has acquired a quality of sacred writ that renders it immune to examination *de novo*. Nothing seems more certain than that peaceful constitutional change in the United States will take place only in such fashion as to permit the continued existence of the fiction that the system remains essentially as it came to us from the Founding Fathers. A crisis so severe as to permit a wholesale revamping would be revolutionary in the most complete sense.

The more restricted proposals for structural change do not have to reckon to the same extent with the obstacles that bar complete revision. Many of them, however, do not reach the heart of the problem of integrated access and co-ordinated policy because they are not based upon the concrete facts of political relationships in the United States. Take, for example, the proposal for the appearance of cabinet officers on the floor of the House or Senate. What would such appearance do to an executive branch already split by agency rivalries and by strong "horizontal" relationships between subordinate administrators and legislative committees? How would it operate in the context of diffused leadership, group "membership," and localism that characterizes legislative behavior? A significant lesson to be learned from the history of the electoral college is that bits of structure that do not conform to, or reckon adequately with, the existing and emergent facts of political behavior will be twisted from their purpose and will be made amenable to those facts or will be left as dry and hollow formalities. Changes must take off from the existing patterns of the political process and strengthen relationships that do not sharply diverge from them. The relationships essential to more effectively co-ordinated policy, as the discussion in earlier chapters should suggest, are present in the existing pattern. The task is less to contrive new ones than to alter relative weights and frequencies among those now operating. The separation between executive and legislature is partial, not total. Diffusion of leadership is not complete.

Recognizing, at least implicitly, the obstacles to complete constitutional revision and similarly accepting the necessity to work through existing relationships susceptible of development, many observers look to the political party as the significant vehicle for change.[47] Although it is hedged about with a variety of statutory arrangements that to some extent control its operations, the political party in its various forms is probably the most flexible and adaptable extraconstitutional element in the governmental institution. Its protean character, which is in part responsible for the fact that even today we know comparatively little about it, is evidence of its potentialities. It is as appropriate to observe today as it was at the turn of the century, however, when Henry Jones Ford was producing his studies of American politics, that the national political party is the "sole efficient means"

[47] Among the more useful critical discussions are those in Herring: *Presidential Leadership*, chap. 4 and *passim*, and his "Executive-Legislative Responsibilities," *American Political Science Review*, Vol. 38, no. 6 (December, 1944), pp. 1153–65; Don K. Price: "The Parliamentary and Presidential Systems," *Public Administration Review*, Vol. 3, no. 4 (Autumn, 1943), pp. 317–34; and Burns: *Congress on Trial*, chaps. 8–10.

of producing "union between the executive and legislative branches of the government." [48]

No responsible observer argues that the loose confederations we call national parties are now particularly efficient for the integrating functions the critics demand of them. We need not here restate their limitations except to recall that the federal system, elections set by the calendar, and overlapping terms of office are among the factors that have emphasized local considerations in the party, have made the quadrennial creation of presidential parties an exercise in improvisation, and have made of the congressional constituencies something resembling feudal baronies. These centrifugal tendencies have been reinforced in turn by statutes regulating party finance that restrict the financial sanctions that might provide the sinews of national party control; and by administrative arrangements that subordinate Federal powers to local demands. No single organization elects the president and a majority in the Congress, and party government in any meaningful sense is scarcely operative at the national level. What the critics seek is a set of relationships at the national level that will integrate the lines of access and provide the power to govern.

In dealing with changes in the national political party, as in examining potential developments elsewhere in the governmental system, it is misleading to sketch rootless structures and final blue prints. The essential problem in securing co-ordinated legislative-executive leadership is to shift the nature of the risks that beset the legislator and bring them into somewhat closer conformity with those confronting the president. Many a congressman is well aware of the likelihood that the seeds of inflation may lie in pork-barrel appropriations for local improvements, yet he works manfully to see that the local flood-control project is included. Many a legislator can see that a tariff increase for a local industry is a threat to the stability of the national and the international economies, yet he bends every effort toward getting a higher rate. Suppose he does not, in deference to the national party policy; he then runs the risk that rivals in or outside his district party will promise that they can and will get an appropriation for the flood wall or an increase in the tariff on enameled widgets. On the other hand, if he ignores the presidential policy, he almost certainly runs no risks at all. He supplies no ammunition to his opponents; he loses no campaign contributions; he alienates no workers who will help to mobilize his vote. Unless he can be insured against such risks or unless refusal to follow the party can be made

[48] Henry Jones Ford: *The Rise and Growth of American Politics* (New York: The Macmillan Company, 1898), p. 356.

a greater hazard, his course will be clear. The remarkable thing is not that so few legislators will risk their local positions, but that so many will. The first step toward party discipline is likely to be one that makes party solidarity more profitable for the incumbent legislator than an appearance of independence.

It should be obvious that any development in the direction of unified and disciplined national parties will take place in the context of organized and unorganized interest groups. It is inaccurate and misleading to view the organized interest group as a parasite whose power derives exclusively from the failure of the parties to mobilize governing majorities. The political interest group has had no such simple origins as this would suggest. The peculiarities of both party and interest group spring from the facts of a diversified and complex society of continental sweep. They are not likely to be eliminated by any trends now observable. It is not the malignant power of any organized group that prevents the imposition of party discipline upon Southern congressmen in connection with legislation guaranteeing equal rights to Negroes. The stubborn facts of diversity always constrict the sphere in which co-ordinated access and party discipline can operate.

No political party, regardless of its internal discipline, can be indifferent to the local impact of national decisions. That is, no elected official can ignore the possible reactions of voters, particularly groups of voters, in his constituency. Where these local reactions are certain to vary sharply from one constituency to another, to require uniform partisan voting in the legislature would be unthinkable, even if the power existed to compel it.

If something approaching party government is to develop, therefore, it seems likely that it must form around selected lines of policy on which variations in local reaction are largely within rather than between constituencies. Thus no sharp and formalized shift from present practices is imminent. Diffused access will certainly prevail except on issues whose impact is sufficiently generalized to divide most constituencies internally rather than one from another. Such generalized issues, moreover, will have to be so continuously at the focus of attention of voters and interest group members that party discipline can be enforced against elected officials at the polls regardless of their performance on matters of entirely localized concern.

What these integrating lines of policy might be is far from clear. The most likely ones would seem to be those emerging out of our growing urbanism and industrialization. Others might be those lying close to the heart of an international situation that seems certain to be characterized by prolonged high-tension diplomacy and the constant threat of war. With the continued weakening of independent local party organizations through national assumption of welfare responsibilities and the like, with increased and continuing concentration upon issues of high-level employment, inflation, and war, power may move to a significant degree into the hands of national leaders, both legislative and executive. From the continued exercise of such power may grow the sanctions for its continuance and extension.

In any such development interest groups organized on a national scale are likely to play a major role, as they have in the past. Increase in the political activity of the large labor unions and their federations is evidence of the tendency to undertake partisan political activity, a tendency that, if it is continued by labor groups, may appear in other groups as well. Such partisan activities may include more than efforts to organize and mobilize a segment of the electorate that has previously been relatively inactive; they may also, and sometimes do, consist of aid to candidates for Congress even in districts where the formal members of these groups are few. Such efforts may eventually create a situation in which legislators are responsible to more than a purely local constituency. They will not eliminate parochial demands, but they may increase the relative importance of issues that cut across such boundaries. Whether a definite trend in this direction is emerging, it is impossible to say.

Looking thus briefly at the roster of proposals for change in the political system as we have analyzed it in the foregoing chapters, we are forced to the conclusion that the prospects for marked and immediate alteration are slight. Diffusion of leadership and disintegrated patterns of access are likely to characterize American government in the predictable future, as they have over most of its past. Although many of the factors entering into the process are far from static, the data at present are insufficient to warrant a conclusion that the system will be materially less complicated, less contradictory, or less bewildering than it has been up to now.

We can be fairly certain that such changes as occur in the basic relationships that characterize the American governmental process will be gradual, slight, and almost imperceptible. Like the growth of universal suffrage, the development of the executive budget, and the assumption of governmental responsibility for individuals afflicted by disasters beyond their control, these changes may be cumulative. Their total, long-run impact upon the patterns of government may produce a series of adaptations and modifications that will amount to a complete reconstruction. Individually, however, they are not likely to be easily recognizable as steps toward constitutional reform.

Confidence in gradual adaptation assumes that the system will not so operate as to produce domestic or international disasters that will result in its being completely discredited. Of this there can be no certainty. On examining the country's stormy past one may in bewilderment conclude that "the Lord takes care of drunkards, little children, and the United States of America." For the future, however, we can feel no assurance that the peculiar arrangements that define the American system will hold some special place in the affections of an indulgent Providence.

To the extent that the kind of dynamic stability that permits gradual adaptation is a function of elements within the system itself, the key factors will not be new. The group process will proceed in the usual fashion. Whether it eventuates in disaster will depend in the future as in the past basically upon the effects of overlapping membership, particularly the vitality of membership in those potential groups based upon interests held widely throughout the society. These memberships are the means both of stability and of peaceful change. In the future as in the past, they will provide the answer to the ancient question: *quis custodiet ipsos custodes?* Guardianship will emerge out of the affiliations of the guardians.

Selected Bibliography

The literature relevant to the study of interest groups in American government is voluminous. In fact, few documents dealing in any way with public policy do not contain some materials bearing upon interest groups. A large number of useful references will be found in such bibliographies as BRUCE L. SMITH, HAROLD D. LASSWELL, AND RALPH D. CASEY: *Propaganda, Communication, and Public Opinion: A Comprehensive Reference Guide* (Princeton, N. J.: Princeton University Press, 1946). The following items, selected from among those which have been most useful in preparing this study, may be helpful for the reader who wishes to examine the subject further.

1. *References of a general character dealing with political interest groups or broadly with the role of various social groups.*

Among the social psychological discussions likely to prove most suggestive:

GORDON W. ALLPORT: "The Psychology of Participation," *Psychological Review*, Vol. 53, no. 3 (May, 1945), pp. 117–32;

HADLEY CANTRIL: *The Psychology of Social Movements* (New York: John Wiley & Sons, Inc., 1941);

P. F. LAZARSFELD, B. BERELSON, AND H. GAUDET: *The People's Choice: How the Voter Makes Up His Mind in a Presidential Campaign* (New York: Columbia University Press, 1948);

ALEXANDER H. LEIGHTON: *The Governing of Men* (Princeton, N. J.: Princeton University Press, 1945);

RALPH LINTON: *The Cultural Background of Personality* (New York: Appleton-Century-Crofts, Inc., 1945);

THEODORE M. NEWCOMB: *Personality and Social Change* (New York: The Dryden Press, 1943); *Social Psychology* (New York: The Dryden Press, 1950);

MUZAFER SHERIF: *The Psychology of Social Norms* (New York: Harper and Brothers, 1936); "An Experimental Approach to the Study of Attitudes," *Sociometry*, Vol. 1 (1937), pp. 90–8;

MUZAFER SHERIF AND HADLEY CANTRIL: *The Psychology of Ego-Involvements* (New York: John Wiley & Sons, Inc., 1947);

ROBIN M. WILLIAMS, JR.: *The Reduction of Intergroup Tensions: A Survey of Research on Problems of Ethnic, Racial, and Religious Group Relations* (New York: Social Science Research Council, Bulletin No. 57, 1947).

Among those books that focus generally upon political interest groups the most significant is ARTHUR F. BENTLEY: *The Process of Government* (Chicago: University of Chicago Press, 1908). Reprinted, 1935 and 1949, by the Principia Press, Bloomington, Indiana.

See also:

GRACE L. COYLE: *Social Process in Organized Groups* (New York: Richard R. Smith, Inc., 1930);

JOHN DEWEY: *The Public and Its Problems* (New York: Henry Holt & Company, Inc., 1927);

ROBERT M. MACIVER: *The Web of Government* (New York: The Macmillan Company, 1947).

A book that effectively discusses some of the circumstances that have led to the rapid development of associations peripheral to economic institutions is KARL POLANYI: *The Great Transformation* (New York: Farrar & Rinehart, Inc., 1944).

The recent efforts of a group of cultural anthropologists and associated social scientists to advance the methods of observing and measuring human relationships have a direct bearing upon the study of political behavior. Among these consult:

E. D. CHAPPLE AND C. ARENSBERG: "Measuring Human Relations," *Genetic Psychology Monographs*, Vol. 32 (August, 1940), pp. 3–147;

ELIOT D. CHAPPLE AND CARLTON S. COON: *Principles of Anthropology* (New York: Henry Holt & Company, Inc., 1942);

F. J. ROETHLISBERGER: *Management and Morale* (Cambridge, Mass.: Harvard University Press, 1941);

W. LLOYD WARNER AND J. O. LOW: *The Social System of the Modern Factory* (New Haven, Conn.: Yale University Press, 1947);

W. LLOYD WARNER AND PAUL S. LUNT: *The Social Life of a Modern Community* (New Haven, Conn.: Yale University Press, 1941); *The Status System of a Modern Community* (New Haven, Conn.: Yale University Press, 1942);

T. N. WHITEHEAD: *Leadership in a Free Society* (Cambridge, Mass.: Harvard University Press, 1936);

WILLIAM F. WHYTE: *Street Corner Society* (Chicago: University of Chicago Press, 1943).

2. *References bearing upon the origins and formal organization of political interest groups.*

GLADYS BAKER: *The County Agent* (Chicago: University of Chicago Press, 1939).

CLARENCE E. BONNETT: *Employers Associations in the United States* (New York: The Macmillan Company, 1922); "Employers Associations," *Encyclopaedia of the Social Sciences;* "The Evolution of Business Groupings," *The Annals,* Vol. 179 (May, 1935), pp. 1–8.

ROBERT A. BRADY: *Business as a System of Power* (New York: Columbia University Press, 1943). This study contains a useful body of data, but its conclusions are highly controversial.

ROBERT R. R. BROOKS: *When Labor Organizes* (New Haven, Conn.: Yale University Press, 1937).

HARWOOD L. CHILDS: *Labor and Capital in National Politics* (Columbus, Ohio: Ohio State University Press, 1930). This early study deals with the American Federation of Labor and the Chamber of Commerce of the United States.

ARTHUR S. CLEVELAND: "N. A. M.: Spokesman for Industry?" *Harvard Business Review,* Vol. 26, no. 3 (May, 1948), pp. 353–71.

MARCUS DUFFIELD: *King Legion* (New York: Cape & Smith, 1931).

OLIVER GARCEAU: *The Political Life of the American Medical Association* (Cambridge, Mass.: Harvard University Press, 1941).

E. PENDLETON HERRING: *Group Representation Before Congress* (Baltimore: The John Hopkins Press, 1929).

JAMES WILLARD HURST: *The Growth of American Law: The Law Makers* (Boston: Little, Brown & Company, 1950).

LOUIS C. KESSELMAN: *The Social Politics of FEPC: A Study in Reform Pressure Movements* (Chapel Hill, N. C.: University of North Carolina Press, 1948).

ORVILLE M. KILE: *The Farm Bureau Movement* (New York: The Macmillan Company, 1921).

LEWIS L. LORWIN: *The American Federation of Labor* (Washington, D.C.: The Brookings Institution, 1933).

WESLEY McCUNE: *The Farm Bloc* (Garden City, N. Y.: Doubleday, Doran & Company, 1943).

DAYTON D. McKEAN: *Pressures on the Legislature of New Jersey* (New York: Columbia University Press, 1938).

HARRY A. MILLIS AND ROYAL E. MONTGOMERY: *Organized Labor* (New York: McGraw-Hill Book Company, Inc., 1945).

PETER H. ODEGARD: *Pressure Politics: The Study of the Anti-Saloon League* (New York: Columbia University Press, 1928).

STUART A. RICE: *Farmers and Workers in American Politics* (New York: Columbia University Press, 1924).

M. LOUISE RUTHERFORD: *The Influence of the American Bar Association on Public Opinion and Legislation* (Philadelphia: The Foundation Press, Inc., 1937).

JOSEPH SHISTER: "Trade Union Government: A Formal Analysis," *Quarterly Journal of Economics,* Vol. 60, no. 1 (November, 1945), pp. 78–112.

PHILIP TAFT: "Labor's Changing Political Line," *Journal of Political Economy,* Vol. 45, no. 5 (October, 1937), pp. 634–50.

U. S. DEPARTMENT OF COMMERCE: *National Associations of the United States* (Washington, D.C.: Government Printing Office, 1949). This is the latest and most complete catalogue of groups in the United States. Most of those listed function as interest groups and as political interest groups.

U. S. HOUSE OF REPRESENTATIVES, COMMITTEE TO INVESTIGATE CAMPAIGN EXPENDITURES: *Hearings*, 78th Cong., 2d Sess. (1944).

U. S. SENATE, COMMITTEE ON EDUCATION AND LABOR: *Senate Report No. 6*, Part 6, 76th Cong., 1st Sess. (1939). The LaFollette committee on the rights of labor produced a wealth of material on the National Association of Manufacturers and other employer groups.

U. S. SENATE, COMMITTEE ON INTERSTATE COMMERCE: *Senate Report No. 26*, Part 2, 77th Cong., 1st Sess. (1941). This report of a committee chaired by Senator Burton K. Wheeler deals with the origins and activities of various railroad organizations.

U. S. TEMPORARY NATIONAL ECONOMIC COMMITTEE: *Trade Association Survey*, Monograph No. 18 (Washington: Government Printing Office, 1941).

WARNER AND LOW: *Social System of the Modern Factory*.

W. LLOYD WARNER AND LEO SROLE: *The Social Systems of American Ethnic Groups* (New Haven, Conn.: Yale University Press, 1948).

BELLE ZELLER: *Pressure Politics in New York* (New York: Prentice-Hall, Inc., 1937).

3. *References containing materials on the internal politics of political interest groups.*

GABRIEL A. ALMOND: *The American People and Foreign Policy* (New York: Harcourt, Brace & Company, 1950).

ZACHARIA CHAFFEE, JR.: "The Internal Affairs of Associations Not for Profit," *Harvard Law Review*, Vol. 43, no. 7 (May, 1930), pp. 993–1029.

CHILDS: *Labor and Capital in National Politics*.

"RENOVATION IN N. A. M.," *Fortune Magazine* (July, 1948), pp. 72 ff.

GARCEAU: *The Political Life of the A. M. A.*

ELI GINZBERG: *The Labor Leader* (New York: The Macmillan Company, 1948).

JUSTIN GRAY: *The Inside Story of the Legion* (New York: Boni & Gaer, 1948).

HERRING: *Group Representation Before Congress*.

KESSELMAN: *The Social Politics of FEPC*.

ORVILLE M. KILE: *The Farm Bureau Movement; The Farm Bureau Through Three Decades* (Baltimore: The Waverly Press, 1948).

MARTIN KRIESBERG: "Cross-Pressures and Attitudes: A Study of the Influence of Conflicting Propaganda on Opinions Regarding American-Soviet Relations," *Public Opinion Quarterly*, Vol. 13, no. 1 (Spring, 1949), pp. 5–16.

EARL LATHAM: "Giantism and Basing-Points: A Political Analysis," *Yale Law Journal*, Vol. 58, no. 3 (February, 1949), pp. 383–99.

AVERY LEISERSON: "Problems of Representation in the Government of Private Groups," *Journal of Politics*, Vol. 11, no. 3 (August, 1949), pp. 66–77.

ROBERT MICHELS: *Political Parties: A Sociological Study of the Oligarchical Tendencies of Modern Democracies*, translated from the Italian by Eden and Cedar Paul (London: Jarrold & Sons, 1915). Republished, 1949, by the Free Press, Glencoe, Illinois.

MILLIS AND MONTGOMERY: *Organized Labor.*

C. WRIGHT MILLS: *The New Men of Power: America's Labor Leaders* (New York: Harcourt, Brace & Company, 1948).

ARTHUR M. ROSS: *Trade Union Wage Policy* (Berkeley, Calif.: University of California Press, 1948).

RUTHERFORD: *The Influence of the American Bar Association.*

JOSEPH SHISTER: "The Locus of Union Control in Collective Bargaining," *Quarterly Journal of Economics*, Vol. 60, no. 4 (August, 1946), pp. 513–48.

PHILIP TAFT: "Democracy in Trade Unions," *American Economic Review*, Vol. 36, no. 2 (May, 1946), pp. 359–69; "Judicial Procedure in Labor Unions," *Quarterly Journal of Economics*, Vol. 59, no. 3 (May, 1948), pp. 370–85; "Opposition to Union Officers in Elections," *Quarterly Journal of Economics*, Vol. 58, no. 2 (February, 1944), pp. 246–64; "Understanding Union Administration," *Harvard Business Review*, Vol. 24, no. 2 (Winter, 1946), pp. 245–57.

WARNER AND LOW: *Social System of the Modern Factory.*

In addition to the social psychological literature already cited, suggestive studies dealing in general with the nature of leadership include:

CECIL A. GIBB: "The Principles and Traits of Leadership," *Journal of Abnormal and Social Psychology*, Vol. 42, no. 3 (July, 1947), pp. 267–84;

WILLIAM O. JENKINS: "A Review of Leadership Studies with Particular Reference to Military Problems," *Psychological Bulletin*, Vol. 44, no. 1 (January, 1947), pp. 54–79;

IRVING KNICKERBOCKER: "Leadership: A Conception and Some Implications," *Journal of Social Issues*, Vol. 4, no. 3 (Summer, 1948), pp. 23–40;

RALPH M. STOGDILL: "Personal Factors Associated with Leadership: A Survey of the Literature," *Journal of Social Psychology*, Vol. 25 (1948), pp. 35–71.

4. *References containing analyses of the involvement of interest groups in the formal institutions of government.*

ALMOND: *The American People and Foreign Policy.*

PAUL H. APPLEBY: *Policy and Administration* (University, Ala.: University of Alabama Press, 1949).

STEPHEN K. BAILEY: *Congress Makes a Law: The Story Behind the Employment Act of 1946* (New York: Columbia University Press, 1950).

BAKER: *The County Agent.*

JAMES M. BURNS: *Congress on Trial* (New York: Harper and Brothers, 1949).

ARTHUR CAPPER: *The Agricultural Bloc* (New York: Harcourt, Brace & Company, 1922).

CHILDS: *Labor and Capital in National Politics.*

KENNETH G. CRAWFORD: *The Pressure Boys: The Inside Story of Lobbying in America* (New York: Julius Messner, Inc., 1939). Although a journalistic account, this book contains a variety of useful information.

DOROTHY DETZER: *Appointment on the Hill* (New York: Henry Holt & Company, Inc., 1948), the reminiscences of a woman who was for many years an active representative in Washington for various women's organizations.

DUFFIELD: *King Legion.*

ALLAN S. EVEREST: *Morgenthau, the New Deal, and Silver: A Story of Pressure Politics* (New York: Kings Crown Press, 1950).

MERLE FAINSOD: "Some Reflections on the Nature of the Regulatory Process," in C. J. Friedrich and Edward S. Mason (eds.): *Public Policy* (Cambridge, Mass.: Harvard University Press, 1940), pp. 297–323.

GRAY: *The Inside Story of the Legion.*

JOHN M. GAUS AND LEON O. WOLCOTT: *Public Administration and the United States Department of Agriculture* (Chicago: Public Administration Service, 1940).

ERNEST GRUENING: *The Public Pays: A Study of Power Propaganda* (New York: The Vanguard Press, 1931).

CHARLES M. HARDIN: "The Bureau of Agricultural Economics Under Fire: A Study in Valuation Conflicts," *Journal of Farm Economics*, Vol. 28, no. 3 (August, 1946), pp. 635–68; "Political Influence and Agricultural Research," *American Political Science Review*, Vol. 41, no. 4 (August, 1947), pp. 668–86.

E. PENDLETON HERRING: *Group Representation Before Congress; Public Administration and the Public Interest* (New York: McGraw-Hill Book Company, Inc., 1936).

HURST: *The Growth of American Law.*

V. O. KEY, JR.: *The Administration of Federal Grants to States* (Chicago: Public Administration Service, 1937); *Politics, Parties, and Pressure Groups* (New York: Thomas Y. Crowell Company, 2d edition, 1947); *Southern Politics in State and Nation* (New York: Alfred A. Knopf, Inc., 1949); "The Veterans and the House of Representatives: A Study of a Pressure Group and Electoral Morality," *Journal of Politics*, Vol. 5, no. 1 (February, 1943), pp. 27–40.

KILE: *The Farm Bureau Movement; The Farm Bureau Through Three Decades.*

AVERY LEISERSON: *Administrative Regulation: A Study in Representation of Interests* (Chicago: University of Chicago Press, 1942); "Interest Groups in Administration," in Fritz Morstein Marx (ed.): *Elements of Public Administration* (New York: Prentice-Hall, Inc., 1946).

EDWARD B. LOGAN: "Lobbying," supplement to *The Annals*, Vol. 144 (July, 1929).

NORTON E. LONG: "Power and Administration," *Public Administration Review*, Vol. 9, no. 4 (Autumn, 1949), pp. 257–64.

ROBERT LUCE: *Legislative Assemblies* (Boston: Houghton Mifflin Company, 1924).

McCUNE: *The Farm Bloc.*

McKEAN: *Pressures on the Legislature of New Jersey.*

E. M. MARTIN: *The Role of the Bar in Electing the Bench in Chicago* (Chicago: The University of Chicago Press, 1936).

MILLIS AND MONTGOMERY: *Organized Labor.*

ODEGARD: *Pressure Politics.*

ROY V. PEEL: *The Political Clubs of New York City* (New York: G. P. Putnam's Sons, 1935).

P. S. REINSCH: *American Legislatures and Legislative Methods* (New York: The Century Company, 1907).

RICE: *Farmers and Workers in American Politics.*

FRED W. RIGGS: *Pressures on Congress: A Study of the Repeal of Chinese Exclusion* (New York: Kings Crown Press, 1950).

ROBERT DE ROOS AND ARTHUR MAASS: "The Lobby That Can't Be Licked," *Harper's Magazine*, August, 1949.

RUTHERFORD: *The Influence of the American Bar Association.*

E. E. SCHATTSCHNEIDER: *Politics, Pressures and the Tariff* (New York: Prentice-Hall, Inc., 1935).

PHILIP M. SELZNICK: *T. V. A. and the Grass Roots* (Berkeley, Calif.: University of California Press, 1949).

TAFT: "Labor's Changing Political Line."

U. S. BUREAU OF THE BUDGET: *The United States at War* (Washington, D.C.: Government Printing Office, 1946).

U. S. FEDERAL TRADE COMMISSION: *Report on Resale Price Maintenance* (Washington, D.C.: Government Printing Office, 1945).

U. S. SENATE, COMMITTEE ON EDUCATION AND LABOR: *Senate Report No. 6*, Part 6, 76th Cong., 1st Sess. (1939).

U. S. SENATE, COMMITTEE ON INTERSTATE COMMERCE: *Senate Report No. 26*, Part 2, 77th Cong., 1st Sess. (1941).

U. S. TEMPORARY NATIONAL ECONOMIC COMMITTEE: *Economic Power and Political Pressures*, Monograph No. 26 (Washington, D. C.: Government Printing Office, 1941). The data in this monograph are useful, although the thesis it argues is of dubious validity.

U. S. TEMPORARY NATIONAL ECONOMIC COMMITTEE: *Trade Association Survey.*

PAUL M. ZEIS: *American Shipping Policy* (Princeton, N. J.: Princeton University Press, 1938).

BELLE ZELLER: "The Federal Regulation of Lobbying Act," *American*

Political Science Review, Vol. 42, no. 2 (April, 1948), pp. 239–71; *Pressure Politics in New York.*

Investigations of "lobbying" have usually produced significant, if highly selective, material on the activities of political interest groups. The most important of these legislative hearings in the Congress are:

U. S. HOUSE OF REPRESENTATIVES, SELECT COMMITTEE ON LOBBY INVESTIGATION: *Hearings*, 63d Cong., 1st Sess., 4 vols. (1913);

U. S. SENATE, COMMITTEE ON JUDICIARY: *Hearings on Maintenance of a Lobby to Influence Legislation*, 63d Cong., 1st Sess. (1913);

U. S. HOUSE OF REPRESENTATIVES, JUDICIARY COMMITTEE: *Hearings*, 63d Cong., 2d Sess. (1914);

U. S. SENATE, SUBCOMMITTEE OF THE COMMITTEE ON THE JUDICIARY: *Lobby Investigation Hearings*, 71st Cong., 1st, 2d, 3d Sess., 72d Cong., 1st Sess. (1929–31);

U. S. HOUSE OF REPRESENTATIVES, COMMITTEE ON RULES: *Hearings on Investigation of Lobbying on Utility Holding Company Bills*, 74th Cong., 1st Sess. (1935);

U. S. SENATE, SPECIAL COMMITTEE TO INVESTIGATE LOBBYING ACTIVITIES: *Hearings*, 74th Cong., 1st and 2d Sess., 75th Cong., 3d Sess. (1935–38);

U. S. HOUSE OF REPRESENTATIVES, SELECT COMMITTEE TO INVESTIGATE LOBBYING ACTIVITIES: *Hearings*, 81st Cong., 2d Sess. (1950).

Index